THIRD EDITION

PEOPLE IN CRISIS

UNDERSTANDING AND HELPING

LEE ANN HOFF

Addison-Wesley Publishing Company, Inc.
HEALTH SCIENCES, REDWOOD CITY, CALIFORNIA
MENLO PARK, CALIFORNIA ▪ READING, MASSACHUSETTS ▪ NEW YORK
DON MILLS, ONTARIO ▪ WOKINGHAM, UK ▪ AMSTERDAM ▪ BONN
SYDNEY ▪ SINGAPORE ▪ TOKYO ▪ MADRID ▪ SAN JUAN

To Frans
Courageous and loving through crises
and beyond

Sponsoring Editor: Armando Parces Enriquez
Production Supervisor: Anne Friedman
Interior and Cover Designer: Irene Imfeld
Copyeditor: Jenny Hale Pulsipher
Compositor: Kachina Typesetting, Inc., Tempe, Arizona
Illustrator: Irene Imfeld

Library of Congress Cataloging-in-Publication Data
Hoff, Lee Ann.
People in crisis

Bibliography: p.
Includes index.
1. Crisis intervention (Psychiatry)
I. Title.
RC480.6.H64 1989 616.89'025 88–8057
ISBN 0–201–12927–2

ABCDEFGHIJ-AL-898

Addison-Wesley Publishing Company, Inc.
Health Sciences
390 Bridge Parkway
Redwood City, CA 94065

PREFACE

SUBJECT AND SCOPE

This book is about people in crisis and those who help them. As social beings, most of us need help to weather the storm of events such as sickness, divorce, or the death of a loved one. This book offers those who provide that help—health and social service professionals and others—a comprehensive yet concise view of how people feel, think, and behave during their periods of crisis, and of what strategies and resources can be used to help them.

Personal crises do not occur in a social or cultural vacuum. *People in Crisis: Understanding and Helping,* Third Edition is unique among contemporary texts in the extent to which it recognizes this fact. The inclusion of cultural and social content, the clearly drawn relationship between crisis theory and practice, the emphasis on human development, the blending of individual, family, and group approaches to intervention, and the humanistic thrust of the book all reflect the commitment to view crisis squarely in the context of a whole human life.

AUDIENCE

The comprehensiveness and interdisciplinary facets of this book also reflect the fact that helping people in crisis is everybody's business and not just the specialty of any one helping profession. All of us can grow in the knowledge and art of helping ourselves and others in crisis. *People in Crisis,* Third Edition was written to help readers in that learning process, in particular:

1. Front-line crisis workers: nurses, physicians, police, clergy, teachers, and welfare and rescue workers.
2. Therapists and specialized crisis workers, both volunteers and others.
3. Health and mental health educators who train physicians, nurses, social workers, psychologists, and counselors.
4. Human service administrators who must plan, develop, and supervise crisis services.
5. The general reader who seeks a better understanding of personal crises.

NEW IN THIRD EDITION

Since the first and second editions of *People in Crisis* were published in 1978 and 1984, new world developments have underscored two facts: crisis intervention is an integral aspect of human service delivery systems; crisis work should be sensitive to the relationship between personal, family, and socio-cultural issues. Some of these issues include the AIDS crisis and violence against gays; Surgeon General's workshops on violence and on AIDS; continuing escalation of health care costs and the lack of health insurance for millions; the growing epidemics of suicide and violence among youth; increasing numbers of homeless people, especially women and children; the farm crisis; infertility and reproductive technologies; the widening gap between rich and poor; health hazards in the natural and work environment.

To meet the challenges posed by these developments, this Third Edition presents updated information along with an expanded theory and research foundation for the book. The research-based crisis paradigm introduced in the Second Edition also forms this book's conceptual framework. The paradigm has been revised and its application extended through all chapters. An entirely new chapter, "People with AIDS: A Crisis Update" (Chapter 12) deals with the AIDS crisis and accompanying issues such as violence against gays, the nursing shortage, and potential burnout among family and other caretakers. Content has been expanded in the following areas:

- self-help groups (Chapter 5);
- youth suicide, ethical issues regarding suicide and AIDS (Chapter 6);
- date rape, victimization assessment (Chapter 8);
- technological disaster (Chapter 9);
- infertility and reproductive technologies, homelessness, farm crisis (Chapter 10).

As in previous editions, the examples were drawn from all major racial, ethnic, and socioeconomic groups in the United States, so that the variety of people seeking help in crisis would be accurately conveyed. In writing case examples, I have also used my experience and study in urban and rural settings, in this country and abroad, including volunteer work with battered women and AIDS projects. The cases are real but have been disguised to protect the identity of the people concerned.

While drawing on insights from several health and social sciences—among them nursing, medicine, social work, psychology, and the social sciences—I have tried to avoid technical jargon. The book should thus be understandable to student, professional, and lay reader alike, with additional references provided for those who wish to continue their study of a particular topic.

ORGANIZATION

The book consists of three parts. Part One presents the basic concepts and strategies necessary to understand, identify, and help people in crisis. Part

Two deals with violence, both as an origin of crisis (eg, victimization) and as a response to crisis (eg, suicide). The growing and fearful presence of violence not only in US society but throughout the world necessitated the expanded treatment of topics such as routine assessment for victimization, and crises originating from technological and human factors as in the Challenger disaster. Part Three discusses those crisis states traditionally defined as situational and transitional, with an emphasis on the theme of passage and the need for "contemporary rites of passage" to assist individuals through these normal life events. The new concluding chapter on AIDS illustrates the danger and opportunity presented by this unprecedented pandemic, and shows how this crisis is linked to other critical issues faced by people with AIDS, their families and friends, and all of society.

FINAL WORD

Crisis is intrinsic to life, but crisis intervention is not a panacea for all of life's problems. We can, however, determine for ourselves whether we come through a crisis enriched and stronger, or stagnating and hopeless; whether we gain new awareness and coping ability, or lose our emotional and physical health and the opportunity to die a peaceful death. It is my hope that this book will make a difference for all those who read it.

ACKNOWLEDGMENTS

As this third edition goes to press I thank all those who read and provided feedback to earlier editions of *People in Crisis.* The reviewers who provided detailed recommendations for revision—Margaret Edmands, EdD, RN, University of Massachusetts, Boston; Julia C. Tiffany, RN, MSN, University of Southern Main; Anne E. Durkin, BSN, MSN, St. Francis Hospital School of Nursing, Hartford, Connecticut; and Laura Aromando, RN, MSN, Seminole Community College, Sanford, Florida, were particularly helpful. Thanks also go to Marcia Lynch, DNSc, Kelly Mayo, MSN, and Linda Rosenbaum, RN, PhD, who provided feedback on certain chapters. The thousands of students, workshop participants, and other readers who have used the first and second editions and who have affirmed the need to produce this edition and to keep people current with a comprehensive book on life crises. I thank you all.

I am also especially grateful to those who made their time and experience available as I developed the new chapter on people with AIDS: Robert Cabaj, MD, Lee Ellenberg, MSW, and Rhonda Linde, PhD, of the Fenway Community Health Center in Boston; Betty Morgan, MSN, of the Lemuel Shattuck Hospital AIDS unit in Boston; Don Cooper, Dave Dumas, Rosa Matara, Michael Gross, Lori Novick, Lucy Sewall, David Smith, and other staff and buddies of the Boston AIDS Action Committee and the Worcester Area AIDS Project. Rhonda Linde also reviewed the manuscript and offered constructive suggestions.

At Addison-Wesley I especially thank Jenny Hale Pulsipher for her precise and sensitive copyediting of the manuscript, and Anne Friedman for her direction and supervision of the production process. I also thank Debra Hunter for her hours of time and most constructive editorial and marketing suggestions in developing and launching this third edition, and Armando Parces Enriquez for seeing the process through its final phases. Their support, encouragement, and patience were a major boon in completing the work. Last but not least I thank my family and friends who continued to understand and support me when manuscript preparation demanded time I would like to have spent with them.

LEE ANN HOFF
Boston, Massachusetts

Contents

Part One
THE UNDERSTANDING AND PRACTICE OF CRISIS INTERVENTION

Chapter One
Crisis Theory and Practice: Introduction and Overview

Chapter Two
Understanding People in Crisis

Chapter Three
Identifying People in Crisis

Chapter Four
Helping People in Crisis

Chapter Five
Family and Social Network Strategies During Crisis

PART TWO
VIOLENCE AS ORIGIN OF AND RESPONSE TO CRISIS

CHAPTER SIX
SUICIDE AND OTHER SELF-DESTRUCTIVE BEHAVIOR: UNDERSTANDING AND ASSESSMENT

CHAPTER SEVEN
HELPING SELF-DESTRUCTIVE PEOPLE AND SURVIVORS OF SUICIDE

Chapter Nine
Violence and Crisis from Disaster

Part Three
Crises Related to Situational and Transition States

Chapter Ten
Changes in Health, Occupational, and Residential Status

Chapter Eleven
Stress and Change During Life Passages

Part One

THE UNDERSTANDING AND PRACTICE OF CRISIS INTERVENTION

THE CONCEPTS AND strategies that form the nucleus of crisis theory and practice are fundamental to understanding and helping people in crisis. Chapter 1 sets the concepts in historical context, linking contemporary crisis intervention to the theories and practices that preceded it. A social-psychologic and cultural perspective is highlighted in a crisis paradigm that is introduced in Chapter 1, is discussed in detail in Chapter 2, and provides the theoretical framework for the entire book. In Chapter 3, the concepts are applied to the process of assessing individuals and families for crisis risk. Chapter 4 focuses on planning and implementing helping strategies, while Chapter 5 extends the helping process to family, group, and community crisis situations. The concepts and strategies discussed in Part One constitute the foundation for all remaining chapters.

CHAPTER ONE

Crisis Theory and Practice: Introduction and Overview

WHAT IS CRISIS AND CRISIS INTERVENTION?

Deborah, age 50, is married and the mother of two teenage children. One day at work she has a heart attack and is taken to the hospital by an ambulance. This is clearly a medical emergency and a source of stress for Deborah and her family. However, Deborah's heart attack may also precipitate an emotional crisis for her and her entire family. Chronic stress following Deborah's physical illness could lead to an emotionally troubled family or to mental breakdown of individual family members, depending on the various psychological, social, and cultural factors involved in the crisis.

Whether this crisis experience results in growth and enrichment for Deborah and her loved ones or in a lower level of functioning for one or all of them depends largely on their previous problem-solving abilities, cultural values regarding illness and health, and current levels of social and economic support (Robinson 1971). Deborah, it turns out, is a health care executive who has just received a promotion. She comes from a working class family. One of her major life ambitions is to achieve professional success while also maintaining the stability of her family life. Deborah's husband and children are devoted to her, but she feels constant pressure to set an example of strength and perform to an exacting standard. Being a responsible wife and mother and a successful professional are all-important to Deborah. These facts of Deborah's life and the lives of people like her suggest that the crisis experience is subjective. This subjectivity contributes to the difficulty of scientific research and theory building about crisis (Danish, Smyer, and Nowak 1980, Hoff 1984, Smith 1978, Taplin 1971).

There are meaningful differences and relationships between these key words: stress, predicament, emergency, crisis, and emotional or mental breakdown. Stress is not crisis; *stress* is tension, strain or pressure. Predicament is not crisis either; *predicament* is a condition or situation that is unpleasant, dangerous, or embarrassing. Emergency is not crisis; *emergency* is an unforseen combination of circumstances that calls for immediate action, often with life or death implications. Finally, crisis is not emotional or mental illness. Webster defines crisis as "a serious or decisive state of things, a turning point." (Chapter 2 elaborates on these distinctions.)

If Deborah or members of her family become extremely upset as a result of her heart attack and feel emotionally unable to handle the event, they are said to be in crisis. In this book, *crisis* refers to an acute emotional upset arising from situational, developmental, or social sources and resulting in a temporary inability to cope by means of one's usual problem-solving devices. A crisis does not last long and is self-limiting. *Crisis management* consists of the entire process of working through the crisis to its end point of crisis resolution. This process usually includes activities not only of the individual in crisis but also of various members of the person's natural and/or institutional social network. The positive or negative resolution of a crisis often depends on *crisis intervention,* that aspect of crisis management carried out by a crisis worker—nurse, police officer, physician, counselor, or minister. Crisis intervention is a short-term helping process. It focuses on resolution of the immediate problem through the use of personal, social, and environmental resources. Crisis intervention is related to but differs from psychotherapy. *Emergency psychiatry* is a branch of medicine that deals with acute behavioral disturbances related to severe mental or emotional instability. It may overlap with crisis intervention but it also implies the need for distinct medical intervention such as medication or admission to an inpatient psychiatric service. The paradigm for this helping process during crisis and the theory supporting it are sometimes referred to as the *crisis model.*

Predicaments, conflicts, and emergencies such as Deborah's lead to stress that can evolve into a crisis state. Stress is a common denominator as we move from infancy through childhood to adolescence, adulthood, and old age. Your son finds himself in turmoil during adolescence; your son's friend does not. You face mid-life as a normal part of your human development; your friend becomes depressed; my neighbor becomes suicidal. Part of the beauty of life is the rebirth of peace following turmoil and pain. Few of us escape the depth and height of living through stressful events, such as the death of a loved one or a serious illness. Throughout life, there are numerous ups and downs, and sometimes life-threatening situations.

Stressful events, emotional upsets, and emergency situations are part of life. Though they are potential crises, a crisis does not necessarily follow a traumatic event. Nor does crisis imply or inevitably lead to emotional or mental breakdown. Something that is a crisis for me may not be a crisis for you. As long as we are able to handle stressful life events, we will not experience a crisis. But if stress overwhelms us and we are unable to find a way out of our predicament, a crisis may result; if a crisis is not resolved constructively, emotional or mental illness, addictions, suicide, or violence against others can be the unfortunate outcome. Once emotional breakdown occurs, a person is more vulnerable to other stressful life events, beginning an interacting cycle between stress, crisis, and destructive crisis outcomes. Thus, crisis does not occur in isolation, but is usually experienced in dynamic interplay with stress and illness in particular cultural contexts.

Note that it is not the events of our lives that activate crisis. Crisis occurs when our interpretation of these events, our coping ability, and the limitations of our social resources lead to stress so severe that we cannot find relief. Accordingly, an understanding of people in crisis and how to help them involves attention not only to the emotional tension experienced, but also to the social, cultural, and material factors that influence how people respond to stressful life events.

These key words will be elaborated on in the remainder of this chapter and the entire book. The principles and strategies necessary to understand and effectively assist people in crisis form the core of this text. They can be summarized broadly in the following aspects of crisis theory and practice:

1. Nature of the person in crisis (Chapter 1).
2. The crisis experience (Chapter 2).
3. The environment and context of crisis management and resolution (Chapters 1 and 2).
4. The formal process of crisis intervention and management (all remaining chapters).

VIEWS AND MYTHS ABOUT PEOPLE IN CRISIS AND HOW TO HELP THEM

People have been experiencing stress, predicaments, and life crises from the beginning of time. They have also found a variety of ways to resolve predicaments and live through crises. Other people have always helped in this process. Hansell (1976, pp. 15–19) cites the biblical Noah as an example of how our ancestors handled crises. Noah was warned of the serious predicament he and his family would be facing shortly. They prepared for the event and, through various clever maneuvers, avoided being overwhelmed by the flood.

Insights developed through the psychological and social sciences help people understand themselves and others in crisis. The advent of a more enlightened view of people in crisis has helped put to rest some old myths about "upset people." It is not so easy anymore to write off as "crazy" and put away a person who is not his or her usual self in the face of a very upsetting event. Modern crisis theory has helped establish a new approach to people with problems.

Crisis theory and its emphasis on the growth potential of the crisis experience raises questions about several notions:

1. *Myth*: People in crisis are suffering from a form of mental illness. *Fact*: People who are acutely upset or in crisis may have had a chronic emotional or mental disturbance before the crisis. Or, a negative resolution of crisis may have resulted in emotional or mental breakdown. Both of these statements are different from asserting that a crisis state is essentially the same as emotional disturbance. It is therefore important to distinguish between crisis and various forms of emotional and mental illness. Though not everyone claims that people in crisis are "ill," the common reference to crisis "therapy" implies such a belief (see Myth 5 and "Interrelationships Between Crisis Origins and Development" in Chapter 2).

2. *Myth*: People in crisis cannot help themselves. *Fact*: Not only is this proposition untrue, but action on such a belief about individuals in crisis can be very damaging to prospects for positive crisis resolution. This fact is based on recognition of our basic human need for self-mastery. It also speaks to the resentment (usually repressed, with depression often resulting) most of us feel when denied the opportunity for self-determination even when we are in crisis. Conscious resistance to this myth is important to counteract the rescue tendencies and "savior" tactics of some human service workers responding to distressed people, tactics that often result in burnout for themselves. Persistence in this myth compromises the possibilities of a healthy crisis outcome, whereas active fostering of doing for oneself contributes to the sense of control needed for positive crisis resolution. This is true especially when a fear of losing control is a major part of the crisis experience (see Chapter 4).

3. *Myth*: Only psychiatrists or highly trained therapists can effectively help people in crisis. *Fact*: A great deal of crisis work has been done by lay volunteers, police officers, ministers, and other front-line workers (McGee 1974). In some communities today crisis intervention by these groups often occurs in the absence of psychiatric and mental health professionals (Taft 1980). To date, many mental health professionals (in contrast to lay and professional staff of certified crisis centers) still do not receive the minimum 40 hours of training in crisis theory and practice recommended by the American Association of Suicidology, the national standard-setting body for crisis services (see "National Standards for Crisis Services," later in this chapter). This fact is related to the next myth.

4. *Myth*: Crisis intervention is a mere Band-Aid, a necessary preliminary, but trivial in comparison to the real treatment carried out by professional psychotherapists. *Fact*: This myth is fading as growing numbers of health and mental health professionals recognize the effectiveness and economy of the crisis approach to helping distressed people. It is also giving way to acceptance of crisis intervention as the third of three revolutionary phases that have occurred since the turn of the century in the mental and public health fields: (1) Freud's discovery of the unconscious, (2) the

discovery of psychotropic drugs in the 1950s, and (3) crisis intervention in the 1960s and after. The persistence of this myth in some circles, however, may be related to a chicken and egg dilemma in the crisis field: Health and human service administrators often do not formally develop crisis services in their agencies because they have not been trained for this task, yet educators do not routinely include crisis theory and supervised field practice in their professional training programs because the need and demand for it have not yet been convincingly demonstrated. This dilemma can certainly be traced in part to the fact that the crisis field is quite new as an organized body of theory and practice. The Band-Aid myth about crisis intervention is curiously related to another misconception in the helping arena.

5. *Myth*: Crisis intervention is a form of psychotherapy. *Fact*: Crisis intervention is not merely a Band-Aid, but neither is it psychotherapy. This myth follows from the myth of "crisis as illness" (Myth 1). The fact that such techniques as listening are used by psychotherapists and crisis workers alike does not equate psychotherapy and crisis intervention any more than either can be equated with friendship or consultation, which also employ listening. The Oxford English Dictionary defines psychotherapy as follows: "The treatment of disease by psychic' methods." Psychotherapy is a helping process directed toward changing a person's feelings and patterns of thought and behavior. It involves uncovering unconscious conflict and relieving symptoms that cause distress to the person seeking treatment. In contrast, crisis intervention avoids probing into deep-seated psychological problems. It is ironic that as long as traditionally trained mental health professionals were not generally doing crisis intervention, it was popularly referred to as a Band-Aid approach to people in distress. But now that crisis intervention is more commonly incorporated into human services as an essential element, it is often defined as a form of psychotherapy. This definition of crisis work and its relationship to "medicalization"* (Freidson 1970, Illich 1976) have important implications for theory development and practice in the crisis field. For example, the fact that people in crisis need support from others for positive crisis resolution can be explained in terms of the social nature of human beings rather than in terms of illness. Thus, the person who helps someone in crisis does not need to be a psychotherapist, and the helping process need not be defined as crisis therapy. Even when therapy is defined more broadly to include the social, cultural, and environmental facets of life, the word itself implies illness, which in turn has historically implied individual rather than sociocultural considerations (see Chapter 5). Since those who define crisis intervention as psychotherapy (for example, Ewing 1978) stress the importance of approaches that are generally foreign to psychotherapists (such as active

---

*Medicalization refers to the tendency to interpret life's problems in a medical framework.

involvement with the client, focus on the present problem, and avoidance of historical probing), one might ask: Why call it psychotherapy?

The ramifications of these myths and the differences and interrelationships between crisis and illness are explored in greater depth in later sections of this book. We will also discuss the foundation of these myths in social and cultural theory and research.

Views about people in crisis and how to help them will vary according to our value systems and the philosophical assumptions guiding our practice. But whatever these values and assumptions are, it is important to make them explicit. People who are involved in crisis intervention—parents, spouses, nurses, social workers, counselors, teachers—can be most helpful if they recognize that everyone has vast potential for growth and that crisis is a point of **opportunity** as well as **danger.** For most of us, our healthiest human growth and greatest achievements can often be traced to the trust and hopeful expectations of significant others. Successful crisis intervention involves helping people take advantage of the opportunity and avoid the danger inherent in crisis. Our success in this goal may hinge on our values and beliefs about the nature of the person experiencing crisis. In this book the following values are assumed:

- People in crisis are basically normal from the standpoint of diagnosable illness, even though they are in a state of high tension and anxiety. However, the precrisis state for some persons in crisis may be that of emotional or mental disturbance. In these instances, the person can be viewed as ill while simultaneously experiencing a crisis.
- People in crisis are social by nature and live in specific cultural communities by necessity. Therefore, their psychological response to hazardous events cannot be properly understood apart from a social/cultural context.
- People in crisis generally have the desire and capability of helping themselves, though this capacity may be impaired to varying degrees. Their capacity for growth from the crisis experience is usually enhanced with timely help from friends, family, neighbors, and sometimes trained crisis workers. Conversely, failure to receive such help when needed can result in diminished growth and disastrous crisis resolution in the form of suicide or assault on others. The strength of a person's desire for self-determination and growth, along with available help from others, will usually influence the outcome of crisis in a favorable direction.

Growing numbers of counselors, family members, and others regard the stress and crises of human life as normal, as opportunities to advance from one level of maturity to another. Such was the case for the self-actualized individuals studied by Maslow (1970). His study, unique in its time for its focus on normal rather than disturbed people, revealed that people are capable of virtually limitless growth and development. Growth, rather than stagnation and emotional breakdown, occurred for these people in the midst of the pain and turmoil of events such as divorce and physical illness. This optimistic view of people and their problems is becoming a viable alternative to the popular view of life and human suffering in an illness paradigm. Interpreting crisis as illness implies treatment or tranquilization, whereas viewing it as opportunity invites a human, growth-promoting response to people in crisis.

THE EVOLUTION OF CRISIS THEORY AND INTERVENTION CONTEXTS

In the broadest sense, crisis and crisis intervention are as old as humankind. Helping other people in crisis is intrinsic to the nurturing side of human character. The capacity for creating a culture of caring and concern for others in distress is implicit in the social nature of humans. In a sense, then, crisis intervention is human action embedded in culture and in the process of learning how to live successfully through stressful life events among one's fellow human beings.

When considered in the context of professional human services, however, crisis intervention is very new—less than two decades old. As an organized body of knowledge and practice, crisis intervention is based on humanistic foundations. However, knowledge and experience from the social and health sciences can often enhance our ability to help others.

Another aspect of crisis intervention is its interdisciplinary roots, shown by the growing attention it is receiving from many health and human service practitioners. In discussing the multifaceted foundation of contemporary crisis theory and practice the focus will be on the distinctive contributions of each area or pioneer in the field, with critique focused on current issues and differences.

FREUD AND PSYCHOANALYTIC THEORY

Decades ago, Freud made pioneering contributions to the study of human behavior and the treatment of emotional conflict. He laid the foundation for a view of people as complex beings capable of self-discovery and change. Through extensive case studies he demonstrated the profound effect that early life experiences can have on later development and happiness. He also found that people can resolve conflicts stemming from traumatic events of childhood and thereby live fuller, happier lives. His conclusions, however, are based largely on the study of disturbed rather than normal individuals. Psychoanalysis, the treatment method he developed from his theory, is costly, lengthy, available to few, and generally not applicable to the person in crisis.

Another limitation of Freudian theory is its foundation in biology, resulting in a mechanistic model of personality. Freud's model states that the three-part system of personality—id, ego, superego—must be kept in balance (equilibrium) to avoid unhealthy defense mechanisms and psychopathology. There are widespread objections to the concept of determinism in classical psychoanalytic theory (Greenspan 1983, Rieker and Carmen 1984, Walsh 1987). This concept is based on the idea that our personalities and later life problems are "determined" by early childhood experiences. However, the concept of equilibrium is commonplace in the literature on crisis (eg, Aguilera and Messick 1986, Burgess and Baldwin 1981, Infante 1982, Janosik 1984). Besides the works of Freud, the concept of equilibrium can also be traced to the scientific method in the helping professions, and the search for laws (as in the natural sciences) to explain human behavior. (This issue is explored more fully in the section on preventive psychiatry and in "Stress, Crisis, and Illness" in Chapter 2.)

In spite of the limitations of Freudian theory, certain psychoanalytic techniques such as listening and catharsis (the expression of feelings about a traumatic event) are useful in human helping processes, including crisis intervention and brief psychotherapy (Small 1979).

EGO PSYCHOLOGY

Awareness of the static nature of Freudian theory led to the development of new, less deterministic views of human beings. In the last 50 years, ego psychologists such as Fromm (1941), Maslow (1970), and Erikson (1963) did much to lay the philosophical base for crisis theory. They stress the person's ability to learn and grow throughout life, a developmental concept used throughout this book. Their views about people and human problems are based on the study of normal rather than disturbed individuals. Recently, however, Erikson has come under critical scrutiny because his theory supports patriarchal family structures (Buss 1979, pp. 326–29). These traditional family structures produce increased stress for women, including the disproportionate burden of caretaking roles through the life cycle (Kessler and McLeod 1984, Turner and Avison 1987).

MILITARY PSYCHIATRY

During World War II and the Korean War, members of the military who felt distressed were treated at the front lines whenever possible, rather than being sent back home to psychiatric hospitals. Studies reveal that the majority of these men were able to return to combat duty rapidly as a result of receiving immediate help, that is, crisis intervention, individually or in a group (Glass 1957, Hansell 1976).

This approach to psychiatric practice in the military assumed that active combat was the normal place for a soldier, and that the soldier would return to duty in spite of temporary problems. Thus, while military psychiatrists used crisis intervention primarily to expedite institutional goals, they made a useful discovery for the crisis field as a whole.

PREVENTIVE PSYCHIATRY

In 1942, a terrible fire raged through the Cocoanut Grove Melody Lounge in Boston, killing 492 people. Lindemann's (1944) classical study of bereavement following this disaster defined the grieving process people went through after sudden death of a relative. Lindemann found that survivors of this disaster who developed serious psychopathologies had failed to go through the normal process of grieving. His findings can be applied in working with anyone suffering a serious, sudden loss. Since loss is a common theme in the crisis experience, Lindemann's work constitutes one of the most important foundations of contemporary crisis theory. Unfortunately, four decades later, many poeple still lack the assistance and social approval necessary for grief work following loss, and instead are offered tranquilizers (see Chapter 4, "Tranquilizers: What Place in Crisis Intervention?" and "Loss, Change, and Grief Work"). Grief work consists of the process of mourning one's loss, experiencing the pain of such loss, and eventually accepting the loss and adjusting to life without the loved person or object. Encouraging people to allow themselves to go through the normal process of grieving can prevent negative outcomes of crises due to loss.

Tyhurst (1957), another pioneer in preventive psychiatry, has helped us understand a person's response to community crises such as natural disasters. During the 1940s and 1950s Tyhurst studied transition states such as migration, parenthood, and retirement. His work examined many crisis states that occur as a result of social mobility or cultural change.

Among all the pioneers in the preventive psychiatry field, perhaps none is more outstanding or more frequently quoted than Gerald Caplan. In 1964 he developed a conceptual framework for understanding crisis including especially the process of crisis development (discussed in detail in Chapter 2). Caplan also emphasized a community-wide approach to crisis intervention. Public education programs and consultation with various caretakers such as teachers, police officers, and public health nurses were cited as important ways to prevent destructive outcomes of crises. Caplan's focus on prevention, mastery, and the importance of social, cultural, and material "supplies" necessary to avoid crisis seems highly suitable to explaining the development and resolution of crisis (1964, 1974, 1981). All community mental health professionals should be familiar with his classic work, *Principles of Preventive Psychiatry* (1964).

Caplan's contribution to the development of crisis theory and practice is so basic that virtually all writers in the field rely on or adapt his major concepts (for example, Aguilera and Messick 1986, Burgess and Baldwin 1981, Golan 1978, Hansell 1976, Infante 1982, Janosik 1984, Smith 1978). However, because of the seminal importance of Caplan's work in the entire crisis field, and the controversy surrounding his work and the medical model (for instance, Danish, Smyer, and Nowak 1980, Hoff 1984, Narayan and Joslin 1980, Taplin 1971), a brief examination of his work is in order.

Caplan's conceptual framework can be questioned for its reliance on disease rather than health concepts. This limitation is offset, however, by his emphasis on prevention rather than treatment of disease. In developing crisis theory from the foundations laid by Caplan, the useful concepts of his theory should not be rejected along with those that are controversial. Let us consider what should probably be preserved and what should be questioned. This critique lays the foundation for the next chapter, which relies heavily on Caplan in explaining the phases of crisis development, and will be supported by analysis and case examples throughout the text.

Caplan grounds his work in the mechanistic concepts set forth by Freud, and one of the most popular theories in the social and health sciences—general systems theory.* The concepts of "homeostasis" and "equilibrium" are central to general systems theory. They are more suited to explain physical disease processes than emotional crisis, yet they are pivotal in much of crisis theory. Systems authority Ludwig von Bertalanffy (1968), a biologist, cites several limitations to the systems concept of homeostasis as applied in psychology and psychiatry. For example, homeostasis does not apply to processes of growth, development, creation, and the like (p. 210). Bertalanffy also describes general systems theory as a "preeminently mathematical field" (p. vii). This mathematical base of systems theory as applied to the crisis field is illustrated by the modified square root symbol (√‾ √‾ √‾): the downward stroke represents the "loss of functioning" during crisis, while the varying positions of the horizontal line symbolize the return to higher, the same, or lower levels of equilibrium following a crisis (Jacobson 1980, p. 8; Smith 1978, p. 399).

This interpretation of the crisis experience views people in crisis as being unable to take charge of their lives. If people accept this view of themselves when in crisis, they will be less likely to participate actively in the resolution of their crisis and enhance the possibility of growth. General systems theory also highlights the concept of equilibrium as a static notion. This idea comes from consensus theory in the social sciences, which states that people in disequilibrium are out of kilter in respect to both their personality and the social system; they are unbalanced rather than in the

*Some advocates of general systems theory have declared it a "new humanistic philosophy of man" and a "new skeleton of science," while critics accuse it of being more "general" than "theory" (Broderick and Smith 1979, p. 112). Urban (1978, p. 62) cites this asset of systems theory: "The language of the systems view permits one to operate disencumbered by the heterogeneous meanings attached to our concepts arising from our everday language, our prior technical attempts, and our personal, private, and idiosyncratic experience." In my opinion, nothing could be more contrary to the subjective nature of the crisis experience and to the importance of communication and personal meaning in understanding and helping people in crisis.

ideal state of equilibrium. In a system in equilibrium, people and behavior fit according to established norms (consensus).* Systems theory appeals to our desire and need for precision and a sense of order in our lives. However, the *reality* of our lives and the world at large suggests that dynamic, interactional theories correspond more closely to the way people actually feel, think, behave, and make sense of the crises they experience.

Another major criticism of the concept of equilibrium in crisis theory is that it is reductionist. It attempts to explain a complex human phenomenon in the framework of a single discipline, psychology, whereas the explanation of human behavior demands more than psychological concepts. Furthermore, existential philosophy, learning, and other humanistic frameworks are ignored by this deterministic notion borrowed from mathematics, engineering, and the natural sciences (Taplin 1971). For example, how can the concept of equilibrium explain the different responses of people to the crises encountered in concentration camps and atomic bomb blasts? Or, after the death of a child, a parent's "equilibrium" may still waver at the thought of the tragic loss, yet she or he may have resolved this crisis within a religious framework (Frank 1978).

Still another problem with the concept of equilibrium in crisis theory is its implications for practice. For example, Bograd (1984) discusses the negative impact of a family systems approach in attempts to help battered women in crisis. A systems approach here implies the importance of keeping the family intact in spite of abuse and often with the aid of tranquilizers. Chemical restoration of homeostasis with tranquilizers is common (see Tranquilizers: What Place in Crisis Intervention? in Chapter 4). It might be argued that other rationales explain the pervasive use of tranquilizers in crisis situations. Yet conscious attention to the theory underlying this practice might reduce this prevalent but misguided approach to people in crisis. It is possible that chemical tranquilization practiced without humanistic crisis intervention is related to iatrogenesis (illness induced by physicians and other helpers) (Ehrenreich 1978, Fuchs 1974, McKinlay 1979). Indeed, general systems theory supports the notion that, within the complementary health delivery and economic systems, budgets can be balanced and higher profits secured if a sufficient number of tranquilizers (plus other drugs and technological devices) are sold,† regardless of clinical contraindications for their use on people in crisis. Other frameworks, such as conflict and change theory, are needed to support the awareness and social action necessary to address some of these damaging practices in the crisis field.

*Consensus theory is also associated with structural functionalism in social science, a theory largely discredited for its static, conservative bias (Bernstein 1978). Parsons's (1951) definition of the "sick role" as a state of "deviance" is one of the most classic and controversial examples of consensus theory (Levine and Kozloff 1978).

†Valium is still the most prescribed drug in the United States, even though the problem of prescription drug abuse is frequently noted in the general press and on television documentaries.

In summary, since human beings are more than their bodies, one might ask: Why rely so heavily on natural science models when philosophy, the humanities, and political science are also available to help explain human behavior?

COMMUNITY MENTAL HEALTH

Caplan's concepts about crisis emerged during the same period in which the community mental health movement was born. An important influence on crisis intervention during this era was the 1961 Report of the Joint Commission on Mental Illness and Health in the United States. This book, *Action for Mental Health* (1961), laid the foundation for the community mental health movement in the United States. It documented through five years of study the crucial fact that people were not getting the help they needed, when they needed it, and where they needed it—close to their natural social setting. The report revealed that: (a) people in crisis were tired of waiting lists, (b) professionals were tired of lengthy and expensive therapy that often did not help, (c) large numbers of people (42%) went initially to a physician or to clergy for any problem, (d) long years of training were not necessary to learn how to help distressed people, and (e) volunteers and community caretakers (such as police officers, teachers, and ministers) were a large untapped source for helping people in distress.

One of the numerous recommendations in this report was that every community should have a local emergency mental health program. In 1963 and 1965 legislation made federal funds available to provide comprehensive mental health services through community mental health centers. Some communities still do not have such programs. But even among those that do, emergency and other services are often far from ideal. A Ralph Nader research team responded to this problem with a consumers' manual entitled, *Through the Mental Health Maze* (1975).

Hansell (1976) has refined many of the findings of Caplan, Tyhurst, military psychiatry, and community mental health studies into an entire system of response to the person in distress. His work is especially important to crisis workers in community mental health agencies, where many high-risk groups of people come for help.

SUICIDE PREVENTION AND OTHER SPECIALIZED CRISIS SERVICES

Another influence to be noted is the suicide prevention movement.* McGee (1974) has documented in detail the work of the Los Angeles Suicide

*The first suicide prevention program, the National Save-A-Life League in New York City, was founded in 1906 and is still active today.

Prevention Center and other groups in launching the suicide prevention and crisis intervention movement in the United States. The Los Angeles Suicide Prevention Center was born out of the efforts of Norman Farberow and Edwin Shneidman. In the late 1950s these two psychologists led the movement by studying suicide notes. Through their many projects and those of numerous colleagues, suicide prevention and crisis centers were established throughout the country, numbering over 100 by 1969.

The suicide prevention and crisis movement came alive during the decade when professional mental health workers had a mandate (*Action for Mental Health*) and massive federal funding to provide emergency services along with other mental health care. Remarkably, however, most crisis centers were staffed by volunteers and often were started by volunteer citizen groups such as mental health or ministerial associations. It would seem that volunteers were often willing and able to respond to an unmet community need, whereas professionals in mental health either could not or would not respond. This situation is currently changing, but it is still noteworthy in terms of some of the myths discussed earlier (Kalafat 1984, Levine 1981).

In recent years a number of these crisis centers in the United States have shut down because of insufficient funds or inadequate leadership. Others have merged with community mental health programs. Still others have adapted and expanded their services, or have begun new programs to meet the special needs of rape victims, abused children, runaway youths, battered women, or people with AIDS.

Currently, suicide prevention and crisis services exist in a variety of organizational frameworks. For example, many shelters for battered women, offering 24-hour telephone response and physical refuge, avoid traditional hierarchies in favor of a collective structure. Regardless of the models, however, every community should have a comprehensive crisis program, including services for suicide emergencies, discharged mental patients, and victims of violence (Hoff and Miller 1987).

The increasing recognition of the need for comprehensive crisis services has resulted in some relief from the dichotomy in practice between traditional psychiatric emergency care and grass roots suicide prevention and other specialized crisis services. The separation and territorial conflicts between these two aspects of crisis service are at best artificial and at worst a disservice to people experiencing life crises or psychiatric emergencies, the boundaries of which often overlap.

Unfortunately, some staff of these specialized services are initially suspicious and disdainful of anything associated with traditional psychiatric care, only to find that some professional skills and services are needed in spite of objections to how these services are sometimes delivered. Conversely, traditional mental health professionals often assume that they are the only real professionals. They may regard alternative crisis service providers as naive do-gooders, usually without having observed firsthand the quality of their work or recognized the funding and other types of problems faced in responding to community needs—problems generally ignored by professionals such as themselves. For example, if a battered woman in a refuge run by women becomes suicidal or psychotic, staff without crisis intervention training will almost invariably need to call on psychiatric professionals for assistance. On the other hand, a health or mental health professional treating a battered woman in a hospital emergency facility may hinder resolution of the problem by attitudes and practices that assume the woman is responsible for her victimization (see Chapter 8).

Greater collaboration between psychiatric and indigenous specialized crisis services is needed as victims of violence and increasing numbers of crisis-prone patients discharged from mental institutions seek assistance from 24-hour community crisis programs.

SOCIOLOGICAL INFLUENCES

Discussion of the evolution of crisis theory and practice thus far suggests that the momentum has largely come from psychological and psychiatric sources. It is true that the strongest influences on crisis theory and practice have stressed individual rather than social aspects of crisis. Nevertheless, the relative neglect of social factors in crisis theory does not reflect their unimportance, but rather represents a serious omission. Caplan (1964, pp. 31–34) refers to the psychological, social, cultural, and material supplies necessary to maintain equilibrium and avoid crisis. Yet in practice, while acknowledging the place of social support in the crisis development and resolution process, most writers focus on reducing psychological tension and returning to precrisis equilibrium, without emphasizing how social factors influence these processes (see Chapter 5). Among all writers in the field, Hansell (1976) has done the most to stress social influences on the development and management of crisis. His concept of crisis and its constructive resolution, elaborating on Caplan's theory, has been developed further by socially focused crisis practitioners in mental health agencies in Erie County, Buffalo, New York (see Chapter 3). Hansell's social-psychological approach to crisis theory and practice will be explained further in Chapter 2, in concert with cross-cultural influences in the field.

CROSS-CULTURAL AND FEMINIST INFLUENCES

Political, social, and technological developments have contributed to more permeable national boundaries, and at the same time have sharpened cultural awareness, unique ethnic identities, and sensitivity to gender issues. For instance, international relations are becoming more critical; cross-continental travel and communication are more accessible; women increasingly reject theories and practices that damage them outright or prevent their human growth and development. These observations have implications for cross-cultural and gender differences in the experience of crisis, plus cultural and gender variance in response to people in crisis

(Turner and Avison 1987). Another significant contribution of cultural and social anthropology to the understanding of life crises is the rich data on rites of passage marking human transition states in traditional societies. These insights from other cultures are particularly relevant to crises around transition states (see Chapter 11).

In American society, distinct contributions to crisis theory from native and immigrant ethnic groups and from women have particularly illuminated their responses to crises arising out of the social structure, associated values, and various discriminatory practices (see Chapter 2). Thus, while cross-cultural, ethnic, and feminist experiences are the newest in the historical development of contemporary crisis theory and practice, in a real sense they are the oldest influences, as suggested earlier by the origins of crisis intervention, bringing us full circle in this historical review.

LIFE CRISES: A SOCIAL-PSYCHOLOGICAL AND CULTURAL PERSPECTIVE

Our review of the diverse sources of crisis theory and practice suggests that understanding and helping people in crisis is a complex, interdisciplinary endeavor. Since human beings encompass physical, emotional, social, and spiritual functions, no one theory is adequate to explain the crisis experience, its origins, or the most effective approach to helping people in crisis.

Accordingly, this book draws on insights, concepts, and strategies from psychology, nursing, sociology, psychiatry, anthropology, philosophy, and political science to propose a dynamic theory and practice with these emphases:*

- Individual, social, cultural, and material origins of crisis.
- Development of the psychological crisis state.
- Emotional, behavioral, and cognitive manifestations of crisis.
- Interactive relationships between stress, crisis, and illness.
- Particular issues involved and skills needed to deal with suicidal crises, violence against others, disaster, and transition states.
- Resolution of crises by use of psychological, social, material, and cultural resources.
- Collaboration between the person or family in crisis and various significant others in the effective management of crisis.
- The social-political task of reducing the crisis vulnerability of various disadvantaged groups in our society.

*Sol Levine, a medical sociologist, refers to this approach as "creative integrationism," not to be confused with superficial eclecticism (1983, personal communication). Integrationism is also apparent in the work of Jerome Frank (1978).

These elements of crisis theory and practice are illustrated relationally in the Crisis Paradigm as a preview of Chapter 2. The Crisis Paradigm illustrates the crisis process experienced by the distressed person as well as the place of formal crisis management in promoting growth and development through healthy crisis resolution. This paradigm draws on research and clinical experience with victims of violence (Hoff 1984), other life event literature (eg, Cloward and Piven 1979, Gerhardt 1979), and work with survivors of man-made disasters (see Chapter 9). The inclusion of social-cultural origins of crisis expands on the traditional focus of crisis intervention on situational and developmental life events. The paradigm suggests a tandem approach to the crisis management process, that is, attending to the immediate problem while not losing sight of the social change strategies needed to address the complex origins of certain crisis situations, such as violence and man-made disaster. This social-psychological and cultural perspective on life crises is examined in detail throughout the book.

APPROACHES TO HELPING PEOPLE IN CRISIS

The approaches to crisis intervention used by helpers will vary according to their exposure to historical influences, their values, and their professional training in various disciplines.

DIFFERENTIATING APPROACHES TO HELPING PEOPLE IN DISTRESS

There are several approaches to helping people in crisis. The following discussion illustrates the differences, overlap, and similarities between these approaches and suggests the relationship between crisis intervention and other ways of helping distressed people.

Certainly crisis intervention should not be regarded as a panacea for all social, emotional, and mental problems (LaVietes 1974). It is not synonymous with psychotherapy, even though some techniques, such as listening and catharsis, are used in both. Nor is crisis intervention a mode of helping only poor people while reserving psychotherapy for the financially secure (Hallowitz 1975). The occurrence of crisis is not dependent on a person's socioeconomic status, and crisis intervention can be helpful regardless of that status.

It is possibly just as damaging to use a crisis intervention approach when it does not apply as it is to fail to use the approach when it does apply. For example, when suicide and crisis hotlines are not effectively supervised and linked with other mental health services, there can be negative side effects, sometimes referred to as "systems problems" (Hoff 1983). Callers seeking help from crisis centers can perceive that they must at least act as though they are in crisis in order to get attention and help. Thus, some callers may appear to be in crisis when, in reality, they are not. For example,

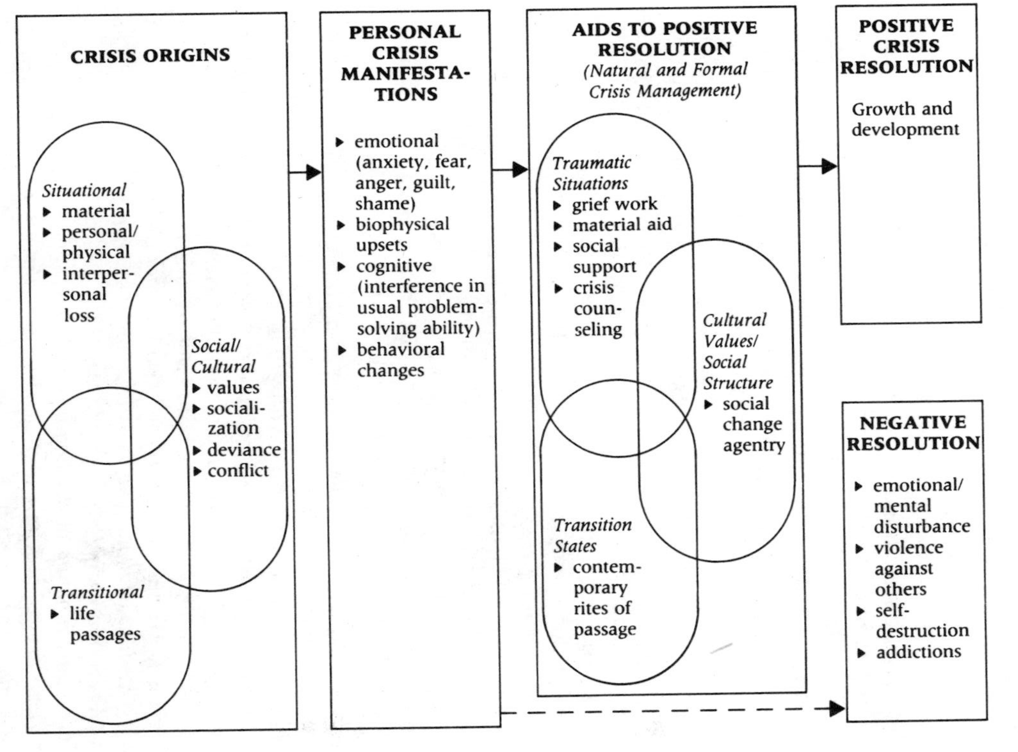

CRISIS PARADIGM

Crisis origins, manifestations, and outcomes, and the respective functions of crisis management have an interactional relationship. The intertwined circles represent the distinct yet interrelated origins of crisis and aids to positive resolution, even though personal manifestations are often similar. The solid line from origins to positive resolution illustrates the opportunity for growth and development through crisis; the broken line depicts the potential danger of crisis in the absence of appropriate aids.

a person who is crying may or may not be in crisis. Judgment of crisis should be based on assessment of the caller's total situation.

If workers are unskilled in crisis assessment, they may unwittingly encourage crisislike behavior, as exemplified in the "cry wolf" situation. Listeners assume that an individual is acting, fail to accurately assess through questioning, and therefore miss the underlying message of the distressed person. Suicide may be the eventual outcome of the cry wolf syndrome if no one responds with the appropriate mode of help.

Table 1-1 illustrates the range of services and differences among various services available to people with psychosocial problems. Crisis intervention is just one of the many services people need. Effective crisis intervention can be an important link to a mode of treatment such as psychotherapy (Perlmutter and Jones 1985). This is because during crisis people are more likely than at other times to consider getting help for chronic problems that made them crisis-prone in the first place. Crisis intervention is also a significant means of avoiding last resort measures such as institutional care. Evaluation of a regional mental health center's clinical services revealed that short-term community-oriented crisis approaches were not enough for people with serious mental and social disabilities (Smith 1975). Such individuals need long-term rehabilitation programs as well, including, for example, training for jobs and instruction in home management.

The limitations of crisis intervention and the need to see it in a larger sociocultural and political perspective are dramatically illustrated in the following vignette. McKinlay (1979, p. 9) discusses the "manufacture of illness" and the futility of tinkering with "downstream" versus "upstream" endeavors:

> *My friend, Irving Zola, relates the story of a physician trying to explain the dilemmas of the modern practice of medicine: "You know," he said, "sometimes it feels like this. There I am standing by the shore of a swiftly flowing river and I hear the cry of a drowning man. So, I jump into the river, put my arms around him, pull him to shore and apply artificial respiration. Just when he begins to breathe, another cry for help. So back in the river again, reaching, pulling, applying, breathing and then another yell. Again and again, without end, goes the sequence. You know, I am so busy jumping in, pulling them to shore, applying artificial respiration, that I have no time to see who the hell is upstream pushing them all in."*

This story underscores the need for crisis practitioners to take time to see their work in a broader perspective, not only for the sake of people in crisis, but in order to prevent burnout and a loss of meaning in their work.

Within the array of services available to people in crisis, the different helping modes obviously overlap (see Table 1-1). It should be remembered that charts and models are intended to clarify points and issues in theoretical

Table 1-1

Differential Aspects: Crisis, Mental Health, and Social Service Models

Psychotherapy	Medical-Institutional	Crisis Intervention	Social-Rehabilitation
	Type of People Served		
Those who wish to correct neurotic personality or behavior patterns	People with serious mental or emtional breakdowns	Individuals and families in crisis or precrisis states	Those who are chronically disabled
	Service Goals		
Work through unconscious conflicts	Control, adjust	Growth-promoting	Return to normal functioning in society as far as possible
Reconstruct behavior and personality patterns	Recover from acute disturbance	Personal and social integration	
Personal and social growth			
	Service Methods		
Introspection	Medication	Social and environmental manipulation	Work training
Catharsis	Behavior modification		Resocialization
Interpretation			Training in activities of daily living
Free association	Electric shock	Focus on feelings and problem solving	
	Group activities		
(Use of additional techniques depends on philosophy and training of therapist)	(Use of additional techniques depends on philosophy of institution)	May use medication to promote goals Decision counseling	
	Activity of Workers		
Exploratory	Direct, noninvolved or indirect	Active/direct (depends on functional level of client)	Structured by less than in crisis intervention
Nondirective			
Interpretive			

Table 1-1

Differential Aspects: Crisis, Mental Health, and Social Service Models

Psychotherapy	Medical-Institutional	Crisis Intervention	Social-Rehabilitation
Length of Service			
Usually long-term	Short or long (depends on degree of disability and approach of psychiatrist) High repeat rate	Short—usually 6 sessions or less	Long-term—a few months to 2–3 years
Beliefs about People			
Individualistic or social (depends on philosophy of therapist)	Individualistic—social aspect secondary	Social—people are capable of growth and self-control	People can change
	Institution and order often more important than people		Mental disability or a diagnosis should not spell hopelessness
Attitudes toward Service			
Emphasis on wisdom of therapist and 50-minute hour	Scheduled Staff attitudes may become rigid and institutionalized	Flexible, any hour	Willingness to stick with it and observe only slow change
Flexibility varies with individual therapist			Hopefulness and expectation of goal achievement

discussion, not to represent an exact picture of reality. Also, while the Crisis Paradigm presented in this book is strongly linked to public and community services, the intervention strategies outlined can be applied in various settings: homes in different cultural milieux, clinics, hospitals, and social agencies. In spite of hazy boundaries between crisis and other service models, there are fundamental differences between their purposes and assumptions about people needing help. For example, in the medical model, intervention consists of treatment or therapy directed toward cure or alleviation of symptoms of a person presumed ill or diseased. The focus is on the individual, who is generally assumed to harbor the source of difficulty within himself or herself. In contrast, the crisis model proposed in this book stresses:

- Social, cultural, and environmental factors in addition to personal origins of crisis.

- Prevention of destructive crisis outcomes such as suicide or mental breakdown (or, if psychopathology was present prior to the crisis, the prevention of further breakdown and chronic pathology).
- Psychosocial growth and development as the ideal outcome of crisis—a possibility greatly enhanced through social support and other crisis management strategies.

Prevention strategies are usually associated conceptually with the medical (disease) model. In growth and development theory the term "enhancement" is used to describe health and development-promoting activities (Danish, Smyer, and Nowak 1980, pp. 348–359). The theoretical distinction between prevention and enhancement has not been well documented in practice. Therefore, these concepts are considered together in the next section, on the assumption that crisis intervention is relevant for preventing disease (and other negative outcomes) as well as enhancing growth and development.

PREVENTING CRISIS AND PROMOTING GROWTH

Viewing crisis as both an opportunity and a danger allows for some kind of preknowledge about the event. Aided by that knowledge, we can prepare for normal life events and usually prevent development of crises. For many people, however, these normal events do lead to hazard rather than opportunity.

While we cannot predict events such as sudden death of a loved one, the birth of a premature child, or natural disaster, we can anticipate how people will react to them. In his study of survivors of the Cocoanut Grove fire, Lindemann (1944) demonstrated the importance of recognizing crisis responses and preventing negative outcomes of crisis. Once a population or individual is identified as being at risk of crisis, we can use a number of time-honored approaches to prevent crisis and enhance growth. Caplan and others (Caplan and Grunebaum 1967, Schulberg and Sheldon 1968) speak of primary, secondary, and tertiary prevention in the public health-mental health field.

Primary Prevention and Enhancement

Primary prevention, in the form of education, consultation, and crisis intervention, is designed to reduce the occurrence of mental disability and promote growth, development, and crisis resistance in a community. There are several means of doing this:

1. Eliminate or modify the hazardous situation. Everyone is familiar with the routine practice of immunizing children against smallpox and diphtheria. This practice is based on the knowledge that failure to immunize can expose large numbers of people to the hazards of disease.

Knowlege of social-psychological hazards should motivate us to make similar efforts to eliminate or modify these hazards. For example, alter hospital structures and practices to reduce the risk of crisis for the hospitalized child and the adult surgical patient; eliminate substandard housing for crisis-prone older people and others; educate people about the nature and effects of these risks.

2. Reduce the person's exposure to the hazardous situation. Public health measures help people avoid exposure to the risks of physical danger. For example, a flood warning allows people to escape from the disaster; a public health announcement of outbreak of infectious hepatitis at a restaurant warns people not to eat there and gives directions to persons exposed to the danger.

In the social-psychological sphere, crisis can be prevented by advising and screening people entering potentially stressful situations such as graduate school, an unsual occupation such as working in a foreign country, or a demanding occupation such as crisis counseling.

In respect to the AIDS pandemic, physical and psychosocial preventive practices must be combined. The current lack of a vaccine for immunization against AIDS underscores the importance of reducing people's exposure to the AIDS virus through education and the modification of sexual behavior.

3. Reduce the person's vulnerability by helping him or her increase coping ability. In the physical health sector people with certain diseases are directed to obtain extra rest, eat certain foods, and take prescribed medicines. In the psychosocial sphere, older people and the poor are most often exposed to the risk of urban dislocation. They can be provided with extra physical resources, social services, and social action skills to counter the negative social and emotional effects of a hazardous event. New parents will feel less vulnerable if they are prepared for the hazards and experiences of rearing their first child. Marriage and retirement are other important life events that we can consider in advance and prepare for so that they become occasions for continued growth rather than deterioration.

The success of anticipatory preventive measures depends largely on the person's openness to learning, cultural values, previous problem-solving success, and general social supports. Jacobson, Strickler, and Morley (1968) refer to anticipatory prevention as generic; that is, it is applicable to general target groups known to be at risk. Anticipatory prevention is similar to the developmental notion of using education to assist people at risk to better handle stressful life events (Danish, Smyer, and Nowak 1980, pp. 349–350).

When hazardous events or a person's vulnerability to events cannot be accurately predicted or people are unable to respond to generic, anticipatory prevention, participatory techniques are indicated for the person or family in crisis (Caplan 1964, 1974, Caplan and Grunebaum 1967). These involve a thorough psychosocial assessment and counseling of individuals or families by professional crisis workers. Participatory techniques correspond to Morley's concept of individually tailored intervention (1980, p. 16) and are discussed in detail in later chapters. In developmental frameworks, the individual and the family participate actively in resolving the crisis. If such participation is not actively encouraged, the style of service might more appropriately be identified with the medical model, in which there is often an assumption of illness and loss of normal functioning (Danish, Smyer, and Nowak 1980). (For a further discussion of primary prevention in relation to crisis see Hoff and Miller 1987, Chapter 8.)

Secondary Prevention

The term "secondary prevention" implies that some form of mental disability has already occurred because of the absence of primary activities or because of a person's inability to profit from those activities. The aim of secondary prevention is to shorten the length of time a person is mentally disabled. A major means of doing this is to provide easily accessible crisis intervention services. If such services—using social approaches (see Chapter 5)—are offered, emotionally and mentally disturbed people can be kept out of mental hospitals. The disabling effects of institutional life and increased cost are thereby avoided, as well as the destructive results of removal from one's natural community. Individuals who already respond to stress with mental or emotional disturbance are more crisis-prone than others. These people need more active help than might others in crisis. The thousands of homeless mentally ill persons illustrate this principle.

Tertiary Prevention

The goal of this level of prevention is to reduce long-term disabling effects for those who are recovering from a mental disorder. Social and rehabilitation programs are an important means of helping these people return to former social and occupational roles or learn new ones (Berger and Potter 1976). Crisis intervention is also important for the same reasons noted in the discussion of secondary prevention. The recovery process includes learning new ways of coping with stress through positive crisis resolution. Thus, even if the precrisis state is one of mental disability, it is never too late to learn new coping devices, as implied in a growth and development model.

CRISIS SERVICES IN A CONTINUUM PERSPECTIVE

Anticipatory and participatory techniques can be viewed as a continuum of services for people with different kinds of psychosocial problems (see Figure 1-1). The continuum suggests that people with problems vary in their dependency on other people and agencies for help. It also illustrates the economic implications of crisis intervention in addition to its clinical and

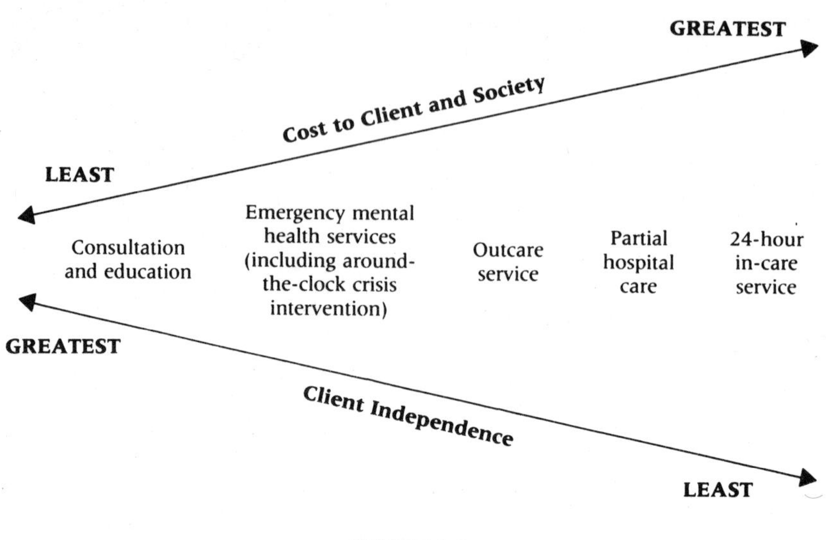

FIGURE 1-1

Continuum of mental health services: Cost and client independence. Assisting distressed people in their natural social roles (homemaker, paid worker, student) through consultation, education, and crisis services is the *least* costly means of service and allows the *greatest* client independence; institutional-based care is the *most* costly means and allows the *least* client independence.

humanistic benefits. However, health and human service workers trying to implement community-based crisis approaches in their individual practice are often frustrated by insurance policies that reimburse only for hospital-based care. Current activities to develop a national health plan suggest the possibility of change around this issue.

Services in the continuum include the basic elements of community mental health programs. These five essential services were originally mandated by the Community Mental Health Acts of 1963 and 1965. Recommendations by the US Joint Commission on Mental Illness and Health formed the basis of these mental health acts (1961). Recent federal guidelines for basic services include rehabilitation, addiction services, victim services, services for the elderly and children, and evaluation programs, though many of these programs have been placed in jeopardy recently by federal budget cuts. Crisis intervention is considered a part of these mental health and social services.

Among the crisis intervention approaches and settings encompassed in this continuum, consultation and education come under the general umbrella of primary prevention and enhancement. Twenty-four-hour crisis services can also be seen as primary prevention, depending on the precrisis state of the individual in crisis. Emergency mental health is most closely related to traditional psychiatry and the management of "behavioral emergencies" in hospital settings (Bellak and Siegel 1983, Kravis and Warner 1986). As noted earlier, some of these programs are linked to independent crisis and suicide prevention agencies. Outcare, partial hospital care, and 24-hour in-care (residential) services should include crisis intervention. These elements of care are primarily concerned with underlying emotional and mental problems and can be linked with secondary and tertiary prevention. The application of crisis intervention in these settings will be illustrated further in Chapters 8 and 10.

To underscore the social and cultural concepts central to the Crisis Paradigm (see p. 19) presented here, to redress the relative inattention to community-based crisis intervention, and to illustrate the economy of a comprehensive approach (in terms of family stability and prevention of costly institutionalization), we will now consider crisis intervention practice in homes, natural settings, and peer group situations.

NATURAL AND PEER GROUP SETTINGS

Once a health or other human service worker becomes enculturated into minisocieties such as hospitals and other bureaucratic agencies, he or she may easily forget that others experience "culture shock" when entering them—not unlike what some anthropologists and tourists feel in a foreign country. This point is illustrated by the comment of some visitors to modern hospitals: "I couldn't stand the smells." For a person in crisis, admission to a hospital for the purpose of receiving help during the crisis can itself be a hazardous event. Polak (1967) outlined this fact in his study of 104 men admitted to a psychiatric hospital in Scotland. Polak found that these men or their families had typically requested psychiatric hospital admission following previous unresolved crises around separation, physical illness, death, and migration. However, while offering temporary relief, admission also was frequently the occasion for another crisis because family patterns of interaction were disrupted, and the patient and his or her family often had disturbing and unrealistic fantasies and expectations about the purpose and meaning of hospitalization.

Hansell (1976) notes how inviting a hospital environment seems to a person deprived of normal community supports. Hospitalization can also be misused by families who lack personal and social resources for relating to disturbed members. Hansell suggests that crisis can just as well lead to improved friendships as to "asylum."

Research thus not only supports the hazards of being uprooted from natural social settings, but also provides a sober reminder of this social reality: Agencies are indeed subcultures of the larger society in which crisis intervention by family members, friends, and neighbors is an everyday occurrence. This does not preclude the need for formal crisis intervention by persons specially trained for this task. Rather, it highlights the fact that the prospects for positive crisis resolution by individuals, families, and peer groups is enhanced and negative complications are reduced when crisis management and intervention occur as close as possible to natural settings. These points are illustrated in the following account of a counselor doing crisis work in a home.

Case Example: Ray

Last week another counselor and I made a home visit to a family that was very upset because they reported that their 22-year-old son Ray had "flipped out" on drugs. They called with the express purpose of getting their son into a psychiatric hospital, even though he had refused to go before. I told the family when they called that we would not automatically put Ray in the hospital, but that we would come over to assess the situation and help the entire family through the crisis. We worked out a strategy for telling Ray directly and clearly the reasons for our visit. Ray refused to come to the phone, shouting, "They're the people who will take me to the hospital in an ambulance." When we got there, we had a family session, which showed Ray up as the scapegoat for many other family problems. We worked out a crisis service plan and Ray started to show some trust in us after about two hours with the whold family. He could see that we didn't just come to whisk him off to a mental hospital, which was what he had suspected we would do. In the end, even Ray's family was relieved that he didn't have to go to the hospital. Before our home visit, they just couldn't see any other way out. They had talked with several psychiatrists before, but no one had ever come to the house or worked with the whole family. Working with families is a great thing, especially when they are so upset and, with a little help, can come around as far as Ray's family did.

The diversity and merits of innovative approaches can be illustrated further by the following example of crisis intervention by a volunteer in a peer group setting.

Case Example: Ramona

Ramona was one of a group of eight battered women in a shelter. This shelter, like most, screens its residents for acute suicidal tendencies, addictions, and mental disturbance. Nevertheless, Ramona became suicidal and one night locked herself in the living room to protect herself from acting on her suicidal tendencies with kitchen knives. When she slept she did so on the office sofa so she would not have to ever be alone. Ramona had not told her fellow house members why she did these things, though the other women did know that she was suicidal. Tension among the residents grew because they did not understand Ramona's behavior. They were afraid that if they asked, she would become more suicidal (see Chapter 6 regarding this popular myth). One of the residents said she would leave the house if the staff "didn't get rid of Ramona."

Assessing the total situation, Diane, a volunteer staffer who was also a registered nurse trained in crisis intervention, called a meeting to discuss the problem. She explained to Ramona that other residents were worried about her and asked "Are you willing to meet with them and explain what's happening with you?" Ramona replied: "Sure," and eagerly jumped off the sofa. The volunteer added that she had experience with suicidal people and was not afraid to discuss suicide. This brought a sigh of relief and "Thank, God" from Ramona. (Ramona was on the waiting list for admission to a local hospital psychiatric unit.)

When asked, Ramona explained her behavior as self-protection, not hostility, as her fellow residents had perceived, and shared with the group that she felt the most protected and least suicidal when another resident had gone for a walk with her. Ramona also reassured everyone that in the event she hurt herself or died it was her responsibility, not theirs. All residents expressed relief at having the problem out in the open and agreed to keep open future communication with Ramona instead of trying to second-guess her.

These examples illustrate the need for more widespread attention to the basic principles of suicide prevention, crisis management, and standards for crisis service delivery. The benefits of using peer support and home settings for crisis intervention are illustrated further in later chapters.

BASIC STEPS OF CRISIS MANAGEMENT

As we have observed, crisis resolution will occur with or without the assistance of others, while crisis intervention can be carried out in a variety of settings, some natural, some institutional. Regardless of the context or variations in personal style, the probability of positive crisis outcomes is greatly enhanced by attention to the basic steps of crisis management. These steps include:

1. Psychosocial assessment of the individual or family crisis. This assessment always includes evaluation of the risk of suicide or assault on others.*
2. Development of a plan with the person or family in crisis.
3. Implementation of the plan, drawing on personal, social, and material resources.
4. Follow-up and evaluation of the crisis management process and resolution of the crisis.

Broadly, these steps correspond to those of the nursing process, medical practice, and other human service protocols. The basis steps can be observed in natural situations or as a formal, structured process. That is, people in natural settings are always making assessments of suicidal and assault risks. For example, everyone recognizes when someone is "crazy"—when a person is not acting according to commonly accepted social norms. For example, in the case discussed earlier, the family's assessment of their crisis was that their son Ray had "flipped out," he needed psychiatric hospitalization, and they were unable to handle the crisis alone. They managed the crisis by calling for and cooperating with professional help. Rather than discounting assessments by the people involved in the crisis, a focus on prevention would include public education to provide the average person with more skills in detecting high risk of suicide or assault and in assessing the advantages and limits of psychiatric hospitalization.† After all, professional assessments must in the end rely on data presented by the suicidal or disturbed person, his or her family, police, and other lay persons (Atkinson 1978). Figure 1-2 illustrates the link between natural and formal crisis management, as introduced in the Crisis Paradigm (p. 19). The details of formal crisis assessment and management strategies (as practiced by the counselor in Ray's case) are dealt with throughout the remainder of the book.

NATIONAL STANDARDS FOR CRISIS SERVICES

The importance of basic principles of crisis management was highlighted by the launching in 1976 of a program to certify comprehensive crisis services in the United States. This program was developed and is directed by

*Nurses and other health professionals may wish to include a diagnosis following this step.

†The American Association of Suicidology expresses the importance of public education with their motto, "Suicide prevention is everybody's business."

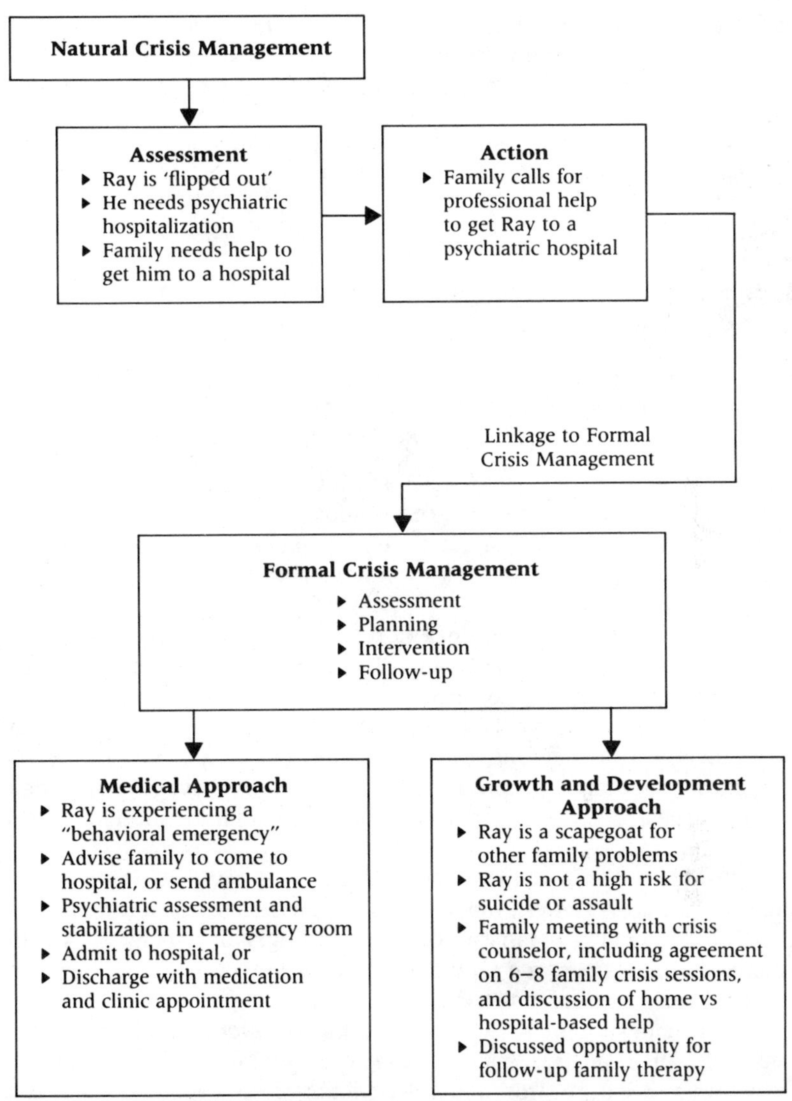

FIGURE 1-2

Natural and formal crisis management. The medical approach is compared to the growth and development approach to formal crisis management.

the American Association of Suicidology (AAS), the national standard-setting body for suicide prevention and crisis services. Certification is intended to assure people in crisis that the services provided by a certified crisis program meet at least the minimum standards of service performance and program administration recommended by the AAS. In an age when consumers are increasingly conscious of the quality of service they receive, certification is a step in the direction of assuring such quality (Hoff and Miller 1987).

Briefly, the AAS certification process includes evaluation of a crisis program in seven areas (Wells and Hoff 1984):

1. Administration.
2. Training procedures.
3. General delivery system of crisis services.
4. Suicide prevention services.
5. Ethical issues.
6. Community integration.
7. Program evaluation.

Programs are evaluated by examination of written materials describing the center's operation. Two regional certification committee members make a site visit. The evaluation team rates the program on a scoring sheet according to predefined standards. Data is gathered about the program and forms the basis for evaluation.

The certification process does more than give a "stamp of approval" to acceptable or high-quality programs. The process also helps agencies improve services if they do not meet minimum standards. Consultation for program upgrading is available through the certification committee and other members of the American Association of Suicidology. Further information regarding AAS certification and standards is available by inquiring at the nearest crisis center, which should have information on specific AAS resources.*

To date, over 50 crisis programs have been certified. These include independent crisis centers, branches of The Samaritans (a suicide prevention and befriending organization started in England), emergency mental health programs operating within community mental health centers, and various professional psychiatric agencies.

The relevance of these standards to the interagency coordination needed for high-quality comprehensive crisis programs is illustrated by the following case excerpt from the 1984 edition of the *Certification Standards Manual:*

> *At 11:00 PM a police officer calls the 24-hour telephone crisis service. A team of professional crisis workers (a psychiatric nurse with a master's degree, and a volunteer with a BA in psychology) makes an outreach visit to the home of David Jones, whom the police and the Jones family believe to be acutely suicidal, noncooperative, and in need of assessment for possible involuntary*

*Information is also available at the AAS Central Office: 2459 S. Ash, Denver, Colorado 80222. Telephone (303)692-0985.

hospitalization. Mr. Jones has refused police and family recommendations for treatment. The outreach team spend one and one-half hours interviewing Mr. Jones and his family in their home. Mr. Jones finally agrees to go to the emergency department of a community hospital, where he will be examined by psychiatric liaison staff for possible hospitalization. Following assessment of Mr. Jones and his family situation, he remains overnight in the emergency department holding bed. The following morning, outpatient therapy for Mr. Jones and his family takes place at the community mental health center, where the hospital has an interagency service contract for follow-up of such mental health emergency cases. The family is also given the telephone number of the 24-hour telephone and outreach crisis program where the police had originally called on behalf of the family. (Adapted from Wells and Hoff 1984, p. 2) This example highlights the comprehensive approach to crisis management that is elaborated in remaining chapters.

SUMMARY

The development of crisis theory and practice has sprung from diverse sources in the health field and social sciences. Approaches to crisis intervention vary with the needs of the person in crisis and the training and experience of helpers. Preventing crises, especially the negative outcomes of crises, is central to the approach of this book. Formal crisis management consists of four steps: assessment, planning, intervention, and follow-up, carried out in a social-psychological and cultural framework. The development of national standards for crisis services attests to the growing maturity of formal crisis intervention as a recognized field grounded in knowledge and practice.

REFERENCES

Action for Mental Health: Report of the Joint Commission on Mental Illness and Health. Basic Books, 1961.

Aguilera DC, Messick JM: *Crisis Intervention,* 5th ed. Mosby, 1986.

Atkinson JM. *Discovering Suicide: Studies in the Social Organization of Sudden Death.* University of Pittsburgh Press, 1978.

Bellak L, Siegel H. *Handbook of Brief and Intensive Emergency Psychotherapy.* Larchmont, NY: CPS, 1983.

Berger M, Potter K: The adjunct consumer group. *Comm Men Health J* 1976; 12:52–60.

Bernstein RJ: *The Restructuring of Social and Political Theory.* Philadelphia: University of Pennsylvania Press, 1978.

Bertalanffy L von: *General System Theory,* rev. ed. Braziller, 1968.

Bograd M: Family systems approaches to wife battering: A feminist critique. *A J Orthopsych* 1984; 54(4):558–568.

Broderick C, Smith J: The general systems approach to the family. In *Contemporary Theories about the Family.* Burr W et al (editors). Free Press, 1979.

Burgess AW, Baldwin BA: *Crisis Theory and Practice.* Prentice Hall, 1981.

Buss AR: Dialectics, history, and development: The historical roots of the individual-society dialectic. *Life-span Devel Behav* 1979; 2:313–333.

Caplan G: *Principles of Preventive Psychiatry.* Basis Books, 1964.

Caplan G: *Support Systems and Community Mental Health.* Behavioral Publications, 1974.

Caplan G: Mastery of stress: Psychological aspects. *A J Psych* 1981; 138(4):413–420.

Caplan G, Grunebaum H: Perspectives on primary prevention: A review. *Arch Gen Psych* 1967; 17:331–346.

Cloward RA Piven FF: Hidden protest: The channeling of female innovations and resistance. *Signs: J women culture soc* 1979; 4:651–669.

Danish SJ, Smyer MA, Nowak CA: Developmental intervention: Enhancing life-event processes. *Life-span Devel Behav* 1980; 3:339–366.

Ehrenreich J (editor): *The Cultural Crisis of Modern Medicine.* New York: Monthly Review Press, 1978.

Erickson E: *Childhood and Society,* 2nd ed. W.W. Norton, 1963.

Ewing CP: *Crisis Intervention as Psychotherapy.* Oxford University Press, 1978.

Frank J: In *Psychotherapy and the Human Predicament.* Dietz PE (editor). Schocken Books, 1978.

Friedson E: *Profession of Medicine.* Harper and Row, 1970.

Fromm E: *Escape from Freedom.* Holt, Rinehart and Winston, 1941.

Fuchs V: *Who Shall Live?* Basic Books, 1974.

Gerhardt U: Coping and social action: Theoretical reconstruction of the life-event approach. *Sociol Health Illness* 1979; 1:195–225.

Glass AT: Observations upon the epidemiology of mental illness in troops during warfare. In: *Symposium on Preventive and Social Psychiatry.* Washington, DC: Walter Reed Army Institute of Research and The National Research Council, 1957.

Golan N: *Treatment in Crisis Situations.* Free Press, 1978.

Greenspan M: *A New Approach to Women and Therapy.* McGraw-Hill, 1983.

Hallowitz D: Counseling and treatment of the poor black family. *Soc Casework* 1975; 56:451–459.

Hansell N: *The Person in Distress.* Human Sciences Press, 1976.

Hoff LA: *Violence Against Women: A Social-cultural Network Analysis.* (PhD dissertation.) Boston University. University Microfilms International. No. 8422380, 1984.

Hoff LA: Interagency coordination for people in crisis. *Information and Referral* 1983; 5(1):79–89.

Hoff LA, Miller N: *Programs for People in Crisis: A Guide for Educators, Administrators and Clinical Trainers.* Boston: Northeastern University Custom Book Program, 1987.

Illich I: *Limits to Medicine.* Penguin Books, 1976.

Infante MS (editor): *Crisis Theory: A Framework for Nursing Practice.* Reston, 1982.

Jacobson GF: Crisis theory. *New Dir Ment Health Serv* 1980; 6:1–10.

Jacobson GF, Strickler M, Morley W: Generic and individual approaches to crisis intervention. *Am J Public Health* 1968; 58:338–343.

Janosik EH: *Crisis Counseling.* Wadsworth, 1984.

Kalaft J: Training community psychologists for crisis intervention. *Am J Comm Psych* 1984; 12(2):241–251.

Kessler RC, McLeod JD: Sex differences in vulnerability to undesirable life events. *Am Sociol Rev* (Oct) 1983; 49:620–631.

Kravis TC, Warner CG (editors): *Emergency Medicine: A Comprehensive Review,* 2nd ed. Aspen, 1986.

LaVietes R: Crisis intervention for ghetto children: Contraindications and alternative considerations. *Am J Orthopsych* 1974; 44:720–727.

Levine M: *The History and Politics of Community Mental Health.* Oxford University Press, 1981.

Levine S, Kozloff MA: The sick role:

Assessment and overview. *Ann Rev Sociol* 1978; 4:317–343.

Lindemann E: Symptomatology and management of acute grief. *Am J Psych* 1944; 101:101–148. Also reprinted in *Crisis intervention: Selected Readings.* HJ (editor). Family Service Association of America, 1965.

Maslow A: *Motivation and Personality,* 2nd ed. Harper and Row, 1970.

McGee RK: *Crisis Intervention in the Community.* University Park Press, 1974.

McKinlay JB: A case for refocusing upstream: The political economy of illness. In *Patients, Physicians, and Illness,* 3rd ed. Jaco EG (editor). Free Press, 1979.

Morley WE: Crisis intervention with adults. *New Dir Ment Health Serv* 1980; 6:11–22.

Nader R: *Through the Mental Health Maze.* Washington, DC: Health Research Group, 1975.

Narayan SM, Joslin DJ: Crisis theory and intervention: A critique of the medical model and proposal of a holistic nursing model. *Adv Nurs Sci* 1980; 2:27–40.

Parsons T: Social structure and the dynamic process: The case of modern medical practice. Pages 428–479 in *The Social System.* Free Press, 1951.

Perlmutter RA, Jones JE: Assessment of families in psychiatric emergencies. *Am J Orthopsych* 1985; 55(1):130–139.

Polak P: The crisis of admission. *Soc Psych* 1967; 2:150–157.

Rieker PP, Carmen EH (editors): *The Gender Gap in Psychotherapy: Social Realities and Psychological Processes.* Plenum, 1984.

Robinson D: *The Process of Becoming Ill.* Routledge and Kegan Paul, 1971.

Schulberg HC, Sheldon A: The probability of crisis and strategies for preventive intervention. *Arch Gen Psych* 1968; 18:553–558.

Small L: *The Briefer Psychotherapies,* 2nd ed. Brunner/Mazel, 1979.

Smith LL: A review of crisis intervention theory. *Soc Casework* 1978; 59:396–405.

Smith WG: Evaluation of the clinical services of a regional mental health center. *Comm Ment Health J* 1975; 11:47–57.

Taft P: Dealing with mental patients. *Police Mag* (Jan) 1980; 20–47.

Taplin JR: Crisis theory: Critique and reformulation. *Comm Ment Health J* 1971; 7:13–23.

Turner RS, Avison WR: Gender and depression: Assessing exposure to life events in a chronically strained population. Paper presented at Annual Meeting of American Public Health Association, October 1978, New Orleans, LA.

Tyhurst JS: The role of transition states—including disasters—in mental illness. *Symposium on Preventive and Social Psychiatry.* Washington, DC: Walter Reed Army Institute of Research and the National Research Council, 1957.

Urban HB: The concept of development from a systems perspective. *Life-span Devel Behav* 1978; 1:45–83.

Walsh MR: *The Psychology of Women: Ongoing Debates.* Yale University Press, 1987.

Wells JO, Hoff LA (editors): *Certification Standards Manual.* Denver: American Association of Suicidology, 1984.

CHAPTER 2

UNDERSTANDING PEOPLE IN CRISIS

UNDERSTANDING: THE BASIS FOR ASSESSMENT AND INTERVENTION

Understanding people in crisis is the foundation for assessment, planning, intervention, and follow-up—steps intrinsic to the crisis management process. A recurring problem in the social sciences is that theories are often formulated without sufficient grounding in reality (Bernstein 1978). On the other hand, practitioners frequently do not study the values and theoretical assumptions implicit in research (Hoff 1984, Roberts 1981). For example, recent census figures reveal that mothers are awarded custody of their children in 90% of cases. If fathers are routinely denied custody without examining the comparative parenting abilities of mothers and fathers, a belief in biological determinism (eg, women are naturally better parents) is implied. In another example, the excessive use of tranquilizers in crisis intervention practice suggests theoretical assumptions about the nature of crisis and the people receiving the drugs, who are in this case predominantly women (BWHBC 1983, Corea 1985, Nellis 1980). Also, crisis theories may rely too exclusively on the experience of ill rather than healthy individuals. As Antonovsky (1980, pp. 35–37) suggests, the crucial question may be "Why do people stay healthy?" (salutogenesis) rather than "What makes them sick?" (pathogenesis).

Understanding requires an examination of the central concepts of crisis theory. These concepts provide the building blocks to understand the crisis experience and its resolution. They help answer the following questions about theory-based crisis management:

1. What are the origins of crisis?
2. How are the origins related to prediction and management of crisis?
3. How is crisis related to stress and illness?
4. How does the crisis state develop and how is it manifested?
5. How do different people resolve crises?

6. How does the interaction between natural and formal crisis management work to produce positive crisis outcomes?

In Chapter 1, crisis was broadly linked to stress, emergencies, and emotional and mental disturbance. This chapter shows how these human distress situations are related and addresses the questions just listed.

THE ORIGINS OF CRISIS

The importance of examining the origins of crisis is based on the assumption that insight into how a problem begins enhances our chances of dealing effectively with the problem. In this discussion the term origin is used in the sense of "that from which something is ultimately derived" (Webster's Dictionary). Considerations of origins may or may not include "causes." A causal framework is avoided because of its association with deterministic, cause-and-effect laws common to the natural sciences but questionable in a humanistic framework (Brim and Ryff 1980, pp. 383–387). This interpretation of origin also suggests that instead of asking "What causes crisis?" one would examine other matters: how some people respond to stressful events by crisis and others do not; the reasons why some people resolve crisis by problem solving and growth, some by suicide, and others by chronic emotional illness. The following discussion clarifies the relationship between crisis origins, risk factors, manifestations, and strategies for managing crises, depending on their origins and development. Broadly, crisis origins fall into three categories: Situational (traditional term: unanticipated), transitional state (traditional term: anticipated), and cultural/social-structural.

SITUATIONAL ORIGINS

Crises defined as situational originate from three sources: (1) material or environmental (such as fire or natural disaster), (2) personal or physical (heart attack, diagnosis of fatal illness, loss of limb or other bodily disfigurement from accidents or disease), and (3) interpersonal or social (death of a loved one or divorce) (see upper circle, first box in Crisis Paradigm). Such situations are usually unanticipated. Since the traumatic event leading to possible crisis is unforeseen, one generally can do nothing to prepare for it except in the indirect sense: careful driving habits can reduce auto accident risk; life-style factors such as smoking, diet, and exercise can reduce risk of heart attack or cancer; open communication may lessen the chance of divorce; a change in sexual behavior can reduce risk of AIDS. Crises arising from such cases would be viewed as originating at least indirectly from personal life choices. For example, keeping in good physical and psychological health, nurturing a social support system, and avoiding too many changes at one time prepares one indirectly to better handle these unforeseen events. In other cases, such as loss of a child by sudden infant death syndrome (SIDS), the origin is simple rather than multifaceted, so if there is inappropriate self-blame in the crisis response, crisis counseling and grief work will usually result in a positive outcome (unless psychopathology was present before the crisis). In crises originating from complex social/cultural or interrelated sources the implications for intervention are also more complex. At the other end of the spectrum, the stress and possible crisis originating from a natural event such as being struck and injured by lightening might be the easiest of all to handle, depending on the degree and type of physical injury.

TRANSITION STATE ORIGINS

The next broad category of crisis origins, transition states, consists of two types: (1) universal: life cycle or normal transitions consisting of human development phases from conception to death, and (2) nonuniversal: passages signalling a shift in social status (see lower circle, first box in Crisis Paradigm). The first type of transition state is universal in that no one escapes life passages, at least not the first and last phases. Erikson (1963) and other developmental psychologists have identified human transition states as follows:

- Prenatal to infancy
- Infancy to childhood
- Childhood to puberty and adolescence
- Adolescence to adulthood
- Maturity to middle age
- Middle age to old age
- Old age to death

During each phase a person is subject to unique stresses. He or she faces the challenge of specific developmental tasks. Failure in these tasks stunts human growth; the personality does not mature according to one's natural potential. Growth toward maturity is an exciting process, but it is also a challenging one. People generally experience a higher level of anxiety during developmental transition states than at other times. The natural change in roles, body image, and attitudes toward oneself and the world create internal turmoil and restlessness. Successful completion of developmental tasks requires energy. It also demands nurturance and social approval from others.

With appropriate support, a person normally is able to meet the challenge of growth from one stage of life to another. It is in this sense that developmental crises are considered normal. These developmental turning points are also anticipated. It is possible, therefore, to prepare for them.

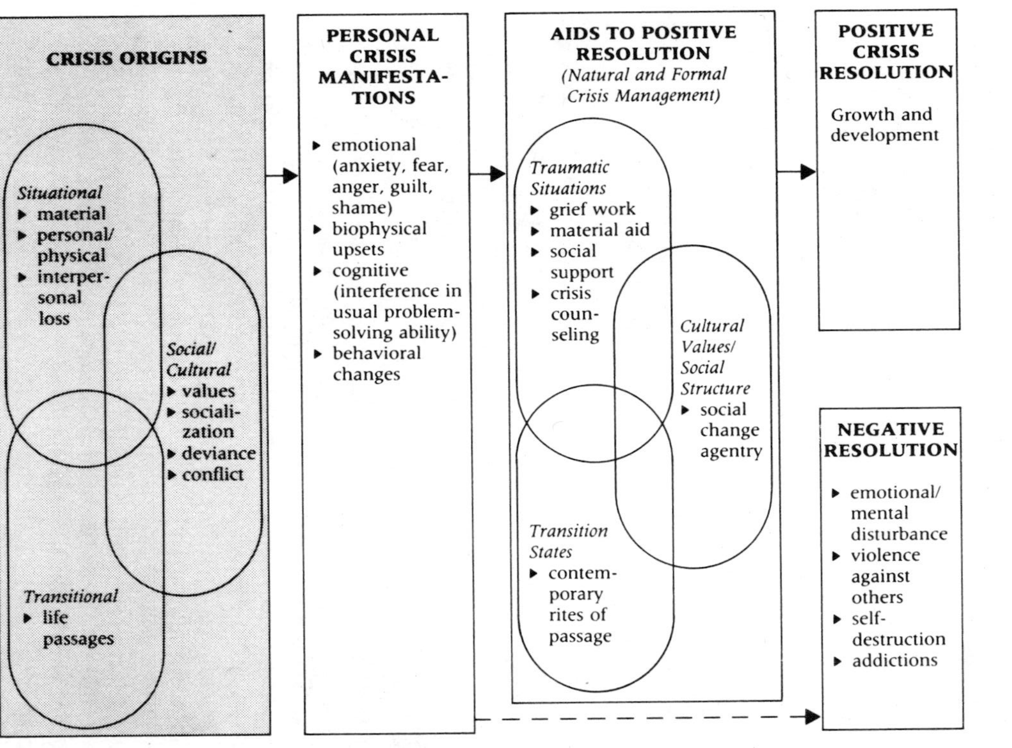

CRISIS PARADIGM

Crisis origins, manifestations, and outcomes, and the respective functions of crisis management have an interactional relationship. The intertwined circles represent the distinct yet interrelated origins of crisis and aids to positive resolution, even though personal manifestations are often similar. The solid line from origins to positive resolution illustrates the opportunity for growth and development through crisis; the broken line depicts the potential danger of crisis in the absence of appropriate aids.

Developmental transition states need not be nightmares; they can be happy times. People can enjoy a sense of self-mastery and achievement from successful completion of developmental tasks.

However, these turning points can become more than natural periods of turmoil and stress. This occurs when the individual does not receive the normal social supports needed for the process of maturation. Each successive stage of development is affected by what took place in the previous phase. For some, the challenge of human growth is indeed a nightmare; life's turning points become crises with destructive effects rather than normal periods of challenge and turmoil. Some people greet adolescence, middle age, and old age with suicide attempts, depression, or withdrawal to a closed, more secure, and familiar world. They approach life with a deep rejection of self and suspicion of the surrounding world.

The unique challenge in human life is to move forward, not to stagnate or regress. For some, however, various situational factors make this a seemingly impossible task.

The other category of transition states—nonuniversal—includes turning points such as the change from student to worker and worker (including homemaker) to student, migration, and retirement. Crises originating from such sources differ from situational crises. Like the developmental transition states, nonuniversal passages are usually anticipated and can therefore be prepared for. Unlike developmental transitions, however, everyone does not experience them. The transition states (universal and nonuniversal) from which some crises stem can be seen not only as markers along life's pathway, but also as processes that can develop in positive or negative directions (Danish, Smyer, and Nowak 1980, p. 342) (see Chapter 11).

Crises developing from situational and transitional states are the easiest to understand and to handle successfully. The personal values involved in resolving such crises generally do not clash with common interpretations of life's experiences. For example, if one loses precious possessions and is left homeless by a fire caused by arson, one's ability to handle the stress involved is generally assisted by knowledge of laws designed to bring the arsonist to justice, and insurance, which may partially compensate for the material loss. To summarize, situational crises and crises arising from transition states are distinct yet related. An individual in a major transition state is usually vulnerable. When the stress of an unanticipated traumatic event is added, however, the person is even more likely to experience a crisis since his or her coping capacity may be strained to the limit by these combined stressors.

Case Example: Sandra and Mark

Sandra, age 43, had an unhappy childhood. She worked successfully as a bookkeeper until her marriage at age 25. However,

she always felt a sense of failure as a woman before she became a wife and mother. Her husband Mark, on the other hand, feels trapped by marriage and resents the demands on him as a husband and father. Sandra definitely does not want a divorce; Mark does. Sandra wants the children but resents the role of single parent. She is also threatened by her anticipated menopause. For her, divorce is symbolic of her failure as a woman. She views career and work outside the home as a necessary evil at best and has placed almost exclusive value on her role as wife and mother. Mark is glad to be free of the daily demands of marriage and fatherhood. His sense of guilt and responsibility, however, makes him lavish his children with material gifts while visiting them as infrequently as possible. Under these circumstances, divorce would almost certainly be the occasion of a crisis, especially for Sandra and probably for Mark as well. Menopause for Sandra will be more than normally stressful, unless she has the advantage of counseling to help her change her views and goals regarding self. Adolescence for their son Steve will more than likely exceed the normal level of stress during this time of his life.

In contrast let us consider Carol and Jim, who had a more fortunate history of growth and development.

CASE EXAMPLE: CAROL AND JIM

Carol, age 38, and Jim, age 36, decide mutually to obtain a divorce. They have been married 13 years and have two children: Dean, age 12, and Cindy, age 9. Together they work out a custody and visiting agreement, satisfying their desires and taking the children's wishes into consideration. Carol and Jim had essentially untroubled childhoods and feel secure and confident as individuals. They can, therefore, avoid the common tactic of using their children as weapons against each other. The divorce is decidely a source of stress to Dean and Cindy; however, neither of the children experience it as a crisis. Both their parents are mature in their marital and parental roles. Thus Carol and Jim do not deny their children the nurturance they continue to need from their parents. The divorce also is not the occasion of a crisis for either spouse. In fact, they both saw their marriage as stagnating for their personal growth. Their decision to divorce is not a crisis, but, as Maslow (1970) shows, an occasion for further "self-actualization," or growth.

These cases, in their contrasting manifestations, illustrate: (a) the highly subjective nature of the crisis experience, (b) the various factors that influence the development of a crisis state, and (c) the intrinsic relationship between transitional and situational crisis states.

CULTURAL/SOCIAL-STRUCTURAL ORIGINS

Crises arising from cultural values and the social structure include job loss stemming from discrimination on the basis of age, race, sex, sexual preference, and class (as opposed to job loss from illness or poor personal performance, which can be viewed as a result of a prior crisis or illness) (see right circle, first box in Crisis Paradigm). Job loss occurring from discriminatory treatment in the work force is rooted in cultural values about race, age, sex, and sexual preference—values that are embedded in the social structure. Also in this category are crises resulting from deviant acts of others, behavior that violates accepted social norms: robbery, rape, incest, marital infidelity, physical abuse. Crises from these sources are never truly expected; there is something shocking and catastrophic about them. Yet in a sense they are predictable. An elderly infirm woman living in a high crime area is more likely to be attacked than a stronger and younger person. Other examples of cultural/social-structural crises include institutionalization of the elderly (related to values about old people and the nuclear family structure);* violence against children and women (related to values about discipline, women, and social-structural factors in the family), and residential dislocation (related to economic, class, and ethnic issues such as "gentrification"—the displacement of the poor by the "gentry" during the "upgrading" of urban centers).

In general, crises originating from sociocultural sources are less amenable to control by individuals than crises arising from personal action or neglect. Thus, a person of a racial minority group facing a housing crisis due to suspected discrimination and a woman in job crisis due to alleged sex discrimination must be prepared to confront the local and perhaps the federal justice system. Social factors should not be misconstrued as personal liabilities producing crises. Consider the challenge of resolving a crisis originating from the following twist in justice: a woman is brutally beaten and threatened with her life; she and her children are left homeless, while the man who has committed the crime enjoys the comfort and security of the marital dwelling. This example of battering also illustrates the interrelationship between crisis origins. That is, a battered woman may suffer physical injury and loss of home (situation events), and be forced into a

*If institutionalization is truly indicated but avoided out of misplaced guilt, failure to institutionalize can be the occasion of individual (often the caretaker) and/or family crisis.

status change from married to single (transitional), but the *primary* origin of her crisis can be traced to cultural values about women, the socialization of men toward aggression, and a widespread cultural climate approving of violence (eg, war, capital punishment, pornography) (Hoff 1989). Therefore, intervention strategies focused only on the upper and lower circles (see third box, Crisis Paradigm) without attention to social change strategies and public compensation for the woman's injuries usually will not be sufficient (see Chapter 8). Interrelated crisis origins are also apparent in people with AIDS, their families, and caretakers (see Chapter 12).

To illustrate further, note the difference in the element of control in the following crisis situations: (a) a heavy cigarette smoker with full knowledge of the evidence linking smoking to lung cancer receives a diagnosis of lung cancer; more than likely, insurance benefits will be available in spite of this self-chosen high-risk life-style; (b) a Japanese-American survivor of the nuclear bomb blast at Hiroshima receives a diagnosis of leukemia; the victim is refused insurance coverage for the required medical care by private insurers and the US government (*Survivors* 1982, pp. 17–18) (see Chapter 9).

A more complex example of crisis from these sociocultural sources involves the perpetrators of deviant acts. Here social and personal elements are intertwined. For example, the parents of an infant they have abused and brought to a hospital for treatment will probably be in crisis, as will a mother who loses custody of her children because of drug abuse (see Chapter 10). Such child abuse and neglect may be rooted in cultural values about physical discipline, mothers (as opposed to mothers and fathers together) as primary child rearers, and socioeconomic factors. Even though such deviance may be strongly influenced by social and cultural factors, individual perpetrators of violence against others need to be carefully considered for personal liability (see Chapter 8).

These illustrations provide a preview of the relationship between origins of crisis and strategies of intervention (to be discussed in detail later). For example, it seems ironic that tranquilizers, grief work, or psychotherapy might be considered "treatment of choice" for Hiroshima survivors in crisis over the news of their nuclear-induced cancers; as will be shown, political action is more appropriate since the *source* of the crisis is political (see Disasters from Human Origins in Chapter 9).

In short, whenever a crisis originates outside of the individual, it is usually beyond the individual alone to control and manage successfully (Cloward and Piven 1979, Gerhardt 1979). Thus, the person is usually more vulnerable and has greater difficulty making sense of the traumatic event and avoiding negative coping strategies (Perloff 1983; Sales, Baum, and Shore 1984; Silver, Boon, and Stones 1983; Thomas 1931). Therefore, public, social strategies need to accompany any individual interventions on behalf of people whose crises originate in the sociocultural milieu.

INTERRELATIONSHIPS BETWEEN CRISIS ORIGINS AND DEVELOPMENT

Identifying the origins of a crisis, important as it is, is only one step in the crisis management process. Various situational, developmental, and sociocultural factors do not in themselves constitute a crisis state. The factors placing people at risk vary and interact to produce a crisis that is manifested in emotional, cognitive, behavioral, and biophysical responses to traumatic life events (see second box, Crisis Paradigm).

Developmentalists Danish, Smyer, and Nowak (1980, pp. 342–345) cite several factors that affect how a person responds to events occuring during life:

- *The timing of the event:* For example, first marriage at age 16 or 40 may be more stressful than at other times.
- *Duration:* This factor highlights the process aspect of life events such as pregnancy or retirement.
- *Sequencing:* For example, birth of a child before marriage is usually more stressful than after.
- *Cohort specificity:* For example, a man becoming a house-husband and a woman a corporate executive.
- *Contextual purity:* How the event relates to other events and the lives of other people.
- *Probability of occurrence:* For example, the majority of married women will become widows.

The clinical relevance of these factors can be seen in Schulberg and Sheldon's (1968, pp. 553–558) "probability formulation" for assessing which persons are most crisis prone:

1. The probability that a disturbing and hazardous event will occur: Death of close family members is highly probable, whereas natural disasters are very improbable.
2. The probability that an individual will be exposed to the event: Every adolescent faces the challenge of adult responsibilities, whereas few people face the crisis of an unwanted move from their settled dwelling.
3. The vulnerability of the individual to the event: The mature adult can adapt more easily to the stress of moving than a child in his or her first year of school.

In assessing risk, then, one should consider (a) the degree of stress stemming from a hazardous event, (b) the risk of people being exposed to that event, and (c) the person's vulnerability or ability to adapt to the stress (Schulberg and Sheldon 1968). Such probability predictions are an important preliminary to the prevention and enhancement activities discussed in Chapter 1.

Case Example: Dorothy

Dorothy, age 38, has been in the hospital for depression three times during the past nine years. Before her marriage and the birth of her three children, Dorothy held a job as a secretary. Now she works full-time as a homemaker and often feels isolated. Dorothy's husband accepted a job transfer—his first—to a new location in another city. This city is known for its hostile attitudes toward black families like Dorothy's. Dorothy dreaded the move and considered joining her husband a few months later. She thought this might allow her some time to see whether the new job was going to be permanent. However, she abandoned the idea because she could not tolerate the thought of being away from her husband for that length of time. One month after the move, Dorothy made a suicide attempt and was taken to a psychiatric hospital by her husband.

In this case, the initial probability of the occurrence of the hazardous event, the move, was small. The probability of Dorothy's exposure to the event was high considering her marital status and her dependence on her husband. Her racial identity made her more vulnerable to stress from sociocultural sources such as housing discrimination. Her vulnerability in view of her past history was also very high. Taken together, these factors made Dorothy a high risk for crisis. Recent research on vulnerability to life events underscores the emotional cost of caring for women like Dorothy. That is, women are more exposed to acute life stresses because of nurturant role expectations and greater concern for events that happen to significant others in their social network, with consequent increased risk of depression (Kessler and McLeod 1984, Kessler, McLeod, and Wethington 1985, Turner and Avison 1987). For women like Dorothy, the risk further increases if they are faced with a hazardous event such as the death of a husband.

In the Schulberg and Sheldon formulation, the probability factors that contribute to a favorable outcome of crisis include the following:

1. If the person encounters and resolves a great number and variety of difficult situations, she or he is less likely to experience a crisis in future hazardous circumstances.
2. If the person has or perceives that he or she has the ability to resolve a problem, it is more likely that the individual will successfully resolve a given problem.
3. The person who has strong social supports is very likely to resolve life crises successfully and without destructive effects.

In another example, George (see Case Study: George Sloan, p. 58) is affected by the concurrence of crisis with his son's school problem and his wife's menopause. Also, if Deborah and her family, discussed in the first chapter (see p. 1), are black, the chance is increased that racially-related stress on the job contributed to her heart attack, while risk for future job-related crises is also increased due to her position in the social structure based on race.

The interactional nature of crisis origins is illustrated further by the case of Sandra (see Case Study: Sandra and Mark, p. 40): In the immediate sense Sandra's crisis originates in the unanticipated divorce she doesn't want and in her anticipated menopause. Her chances of resolving these crises positively, however, are related to her age and to the roots of her vulnerability as a woman in the social structure—a woman socialized to the cultural value of women as somehow incomplete without marriage and less womanly after menopause.

The case of a family in crisis as a result of a teenager's suicide attempt also suggests the interactional aspect of crisis origins. While the teenager's crisis may stem directly from personal feelings of failure and worthlessness and indirectly from family conflict, the family's crisis of dealing with a suicidal member is usually affected by the culturally situated stigma still attached to self-destructive behavior (see Chapter 6).

These illustrations link the origins of crisis to life events, sociocultural factors, and personal values that influence the development and subjective manifestations of crisis in different individuals. This discussion highlights the need to identify specific crisis origins during assessment and to tailor intervention strategies to distinctive or interrelated origins. Appropriate strategies will increase the probability of positive crisis resolution and growth (see third box, Crisis Paradigm). Details of such assessment and intervention strategies are presented in the remainder of the book.

STRESS, CRISIS, AND ILLNESS

Theories and research on stress and coping occupy a prominent position in the literature of psychology, sociology, nursing, medicine, and epidemiology (Brown 1974, Brown and Harris 1978, Dohrenwend and Dohrenwend 1974, Levine and Scotch 1970, Ramsey 1982, Selye 1956). The issue of coping with stressful life events often revolves around the relationship between stress and illness; virtually all authorities agree that stress and illness are related. The questions for this book are:

- Do stressful life events cause illness, and if so, what is the process involved?
- Do sick people experience more stressful life events than the healthy?

- To what extent do social and psychological resources buffer the impact of stressful life events?
- What effect, if any, do "resistance resources" (Antonovsky 1980) have on stress arising from the social structure, eg, race, class, sex, or age disparity?
- What is the relationship between stress and the concept and experience of crisis?

Imprecise definitions can create problems with these questions; sometimes the concepts of stress, crisis, and illness are used interchangeably. The following definitions may clarify the discussion:

STRESS Selye (1956, p. 15) describes stress as a specific syndrome that is nonspecifically induced. Stress can also be viewed as a relationship between the person and the environment (McElroy and Townsend 1985). Ramsey (1982, p. 30) notes that the word stress has an indefinite meaning and that it symbolizes different things to people of various disciplines. For this book, stress is defined as the discomfort, pain, or troubled feeling arising from emotional, social, or physical sources and resulting in the need to relax, be treated, or otherwise seek relief. Stress can be grouped into two categories: (1) *acute* stress is brief in duration and occurs with fairly predictable manifestations and results, one of which may be crisis; (2) *insidious* stress is longer in duration (weeks, months, or years) with less awareness by the person experiencing it, and with long-range cumulative but less clearly certain effects, which may include burnout and disease (Landy 1977, p. 311). Stress is inherent in the fact of living and may be experienced from any source: invasion of the body by organisms, internal psychological turmoil, cultural values, and social organization.

BURNOUT This is a fairly recent concept. Spaniol and Caputo (1979, p. 2) define burnout as "the inability to cope adequately with the stresses of our work or personal lives." Fruedenberger and Richelson (1980, p. 2) refer to burnout as a "malaise . . . a demon both of the society and times we live in and our ongoing struggle to invest our lives with meaning." It is manifested in physical signs and symptoms, feelings of cynicism, anger, and resentment, and poor social performance at home and work. Cherniss (1980) discusses the issue of burnout for staff in the human services. Burnout is distinguished from crisis by its chronic rather than acute character. Also, people suffering from burnout often are not aware of the connection between their feelings and behavior and the chronic stress they are under.

DISEASE Disease is a pathological concept describing a condition that can be objectively verified through clinical observation and various laboratory tests (Foster and Anderson 1978, p. 40). Such objective organic lesions or behavioral disturbances are observable by others regardless of the "diseased" person's awareness of them (Dubos 1977, p. 32).

ILLNESS Illness is related to disease but is distinguished by its subjective character. It is a cultural concept that implies the social recognition that one cannot carry out expected social roles (Foster and Anderson 1978, p. 40). For example, a person may have an early cancerous lesion, but not feel ill. Once the lesion is diagnosed as cancer, the person is considered ill and the social, psychological, and cultural dimensions of the disease surface (stigma, denial, fear of death). Illness may be claimed subjectively as a reason for inability to perform normally. For example, a person may say "I don't feel well . . . I have a backache" (a condition not easily diagnosed), although no objective indicators of disease may be present. Thus, illness can be seen as:

- Punishment, for example, "What did I do to deserve cancer?"
- Deviance, such as Parsons's (1951) concept of the "sick role."
- An indicator of social system performance, for example, absenteeism due to "illness," although the real reason is job dissatisfaction.
- A social control device, for example, attaching a psychiatric label to battered women.
- A response to stress from physical, environmental, social, psychologic, or cultural sources (Foster and Anderson 1978, pp. 145–153; Lieban 1977, pp. 24–27; McElroy and Townsend 1985, pp. 268–325).

EMOTIONAL BREAKDOWN An ability to manage one's feelings to the point of chronic interference in normal functioning. It is manifested in depression, anger, fear, and so on.

MENTAL BREAKDOWN A disturbance in cognitive functioning manifested in the general inability to think and act normally. It progresses to the point of interference in expression of feelings, everyday behavior, and interaction with others.

CRISIS An acute emotional upset affecting one's ability to cope emotionally, cognitively, or behaviorally and to solve problems by usual devices.

Research on stress, crisis, and emotional and mental breakdown reveals a lack of integration between clinical and social science insights (Pearlin and Schooler 1978). There is a need to correct the imbalance between clinical and developmental/social analysis of coping with stressful life events (Brim and Ryff 1980, p. 376–377; Gerhardt 1979, p. 196; Pearlin and Schooler 1978, p. 2). Researchers trained clinically and in social science may be able to bridge some of these gaps. However, the influence of medicalization and causal scientific models in all branches of human service practice have dominated the stress research field.

A noted example of stress research that excludes personal meaning is the Holmes and Rahe (1967) Social Readjustment Rating Scale, designed to predict one's risk of illness or accident based on a cumulative stress score from life events. The scale is useful in sensitizing people to the various events in their lives that might be sources of stress, potential crisis, illness, or accidents. The assumption here is that awareness of potentially hazardous events enhances the possibility of constructive preventive action by the individual (see Preventing Crisis and Promoting Growth in Chapter 1). However, the scale leaves out the individual's interpretation of events, which influences whether the experience of stress is positive or negative. Sarason, Johnson, and Siegel, in a revised scale (1978), have reduced the deficiency of the Holmes and Rahe scale by providing an opportunity to evaluate various events in positive or negative terms.

Conclusions from much of the research on stress point to the limitations of causal models in the analysis of stress (Brim and Ryff 1980, pp. 383–387). Increasing attention, however, is being directed to studying the process of stress and its relationship to hazardous events, illness, coping, and social support (Caplan 1981, Hoff 1984, Kessler and McLeod 1984, McElroy and Townsend 1985, Pearlin et al. 1981).

Oversimplistic psychological accounts of stress and illness are not the only problem in the crisis intervention field. Durkheim's (1951) notion that people's positions in the social structure are causes of anomic and egoistic suicides* is a prime example of sociological reductionism; it fails to account for differences in the way individuals interpret and cope with stressful life events from various sources. While cause-and-effect laws certainly operate in regard to the physical stressors of a gunshot wound to the heart or repeated inhalation of carcinogens (it is accurate to say that these stressors *cause* death or lung cancer, respectively), *social action* such as suicide or violence against others cannot be explained within the same causal framework (Cicourel 1964, Hoff 1984, Louch 1966). What is the relevance of this notion to crisis response and management?

Acute or chronic stress does not automatically lead to emotional imbalance or mental incompetence, abuse of alcohol and other drugs, suicide, or assault on others. If it did, humans, who by nature are rational, conscious, and responsible for their behavior, could routinely attribute their behavior to causes external to themselves and be excused from accountability. This, in fact, is the case in certain instances where various mitigating circumstances allow an excuse for some behaviors that might otherwise be punishable.† In general, however, responses to stress vary. Maslow's (1970)

---

*Lack of social integration and a sense of attachment to society are purported causes of suicide (see Chapter 6).

†The most noted recent example of this issue is the John W. Hinckley jury acquittal (on "grounds of insanity") for his attempt to assassinate President Reagan. As the Hinckley case attests, excuse on "grounds of insanity" has become a controversial issue in forensic psychiatry and among the general public.

research, for example, underscores the apparent growth-promoting function of high-stress situations for achieving self-actualization, not destruction of self and others. Antonovsky's (1980) cross-cultural research on concentration camp survivors and women in menopause suggests similar conclusions. He proposes the concept of "resistance resources" (pp. 99–100)—including social network support and a sense of "coherence"—as intervening variables in stressful situations. Such resources can make the difference between positive or negative responses to developmental transitions or to extreme stress (which a clinician might define as "crisis") such as that experienced by concentration camp survivors. Research on battered women (Hoff 1984) supports these views and the position taken in this book: Stress, crisis, and illness (physical, emotional, and mental) are *interactionally*, not causally, related.

Another argument about the relationship between stress, crisis, and illness concerns the popular belief that crises of violence against women are precipitated by a woman's provocative behavior. Such provocation is often presumed to result from the woman's own emotional or mental disturbance. This is one of the most pervasive "blaming the victim" interpretations accepted by professional and lay persons alike (Ryan 1971). Research reveals little to support such conclusions (Hilberman 1980, Hoff 1984). The belief that a battered woman's mental and emotional state is the *cause* of her battering implies that women themselves are responsible for the beatings they receive. On the contrary, research reveals that the emotional and mental symptoms identified in battered women almost invariably occur *after* being victimized both physically and psychologically.

One of the most popular notions surrounding women's crises stemming from violence is that the violent man was under high stress (or drunk, and suffering from a "disease"): for instance, "I was drunk and didn't know what I was doing." To the extent that this explanation is accepted, the person's violence is excused on the basis of presumed mental incompetence. While it is true that the extreme stress and anxiety associated with a crisis state can distort cognitive functions such as memory and decision making, mental incompetence would not be assumed if history revealed that mental faculties were intact *before* the crisis (see Chapter 3). Thus, a person's decision to hit or kill his or her spouse during the high tension of a marital fight is neither wise nor excusable. Most social research (such as Gelles 1974 and Pagelow 1981) supports the proposition that temporary insanity claims are really "excuses" used to evade responsibility for one's violent behavior. Another excusing claim is that the woman "asked for it." This does not negate recognition that some crimes are committed by people who are diagnosed as mentally ill according to commonly accepted criteria such as delusions, hallucinations, or bizarre behavior. Some recent jury acquittals of women who killed their husbands suggest that these women were not viewed as mentally ill; rather, the stress and danger of their circumstances after years of abuse were considered sufficient grounds for acquittal. Similarly, many men are excused from their battering, while some are convicted.*

There is a remarkable similarity between these findings and Erich Lindemann's classic study (1944): Survivors of the Cocoanut Grove disaster might have been spared the negative experience of serious psychopathology if they had had assistance, such as with grief work, at the time of the crisis; battered women without resources and assistance for constructive crisis resolution may become suicidal, homicidal, addicted, or emotionally disturbed, especially after repeated abuse (see Chapter 8). The reciprocal relationship between stress, crisis, and illness is observed further in the multifaceted stressors a battered woman must deal with while in crisis after a violent attack: physical injury, psychological upset, and change in social situation (eg, disrupted marriage, residential or economic loss). This relationship is illustrated in Figure 2-1.

In a scientific sense, then, concepts of crisis, stress, and illness are imprecise and complexly associated with the political economy, a medicalized approach to people in distress, and dominant values about people and illness in the social and cultural milieu. Research, however, supports the view of an interactional, rather than causal, relationship between stress, crisis, and illness. What simplistic models miss is the influence of an individual's experience of stress, crisis, and illness. Table 2-1 illustrates the distinctions and relationships between these concepts. It also links the concepts with their origins, providing a preview of the next section and remaining chapters.

DEVELOPMENT AND INDIVIDUAL MANIFESTATIONS OF CRISIS

We have seen how crisis originates from physical, material, personal, social and cultural sources, and how it fits into the larger picture of life's ups and downs. Let us now consider the experience of crisis at the individual, personal level.

WHY PEOPLE GO INTO CRISIS

People in crisis are, by definition, emotionally upset; they are unable to solve life's problems in their usual way. A happy, healthy life implies an

*One of the most striking findings of Hoff's (1984) research with battered women was their tendency to excuse their *husband's* violence but *not* their own retaliatory violence, even if wives were under the influence of drugs or alcohol. When women are convicted of murdering their husbands, however, research suggests gross discriminatory practices (Jones 1980, Browne 1987).

TABLE 2-1

Distress Differentiation

Type of Distress or Problem	Origins	Possible Manifestations
Stress (acute)	Hazardous life events (such as heart attack, accident, death of loved one, violent attack, sudden job loss, natural disaster)	Emotional crisis General Adaptation Syndrome
	Invation by microorganisms	General Adaptation Syndrome Disease process
	Man-made disaster	Annihilation of present civilization
Stress (chronic)	Strain in social relationships (such as marriage) Position in social structure age, sex, race, class) Socioeconomic problems (such as unemployment) Chronic ill health	Burnout Psychosomatic or "stressed-related" illness Emotional or mental breakdown
	Developmental transition states	Emotional, Behavioral, Cognitive, Biophysical } Changes
Crisis	Traumatic situations (material, personal/physical, interpersonal) Transition states (developmental and other) Cultural values, social structure	
Emotional or mental breakdown	Failure of positive response to acute stress and/or crisis Continuation of chronic stress from various sources	Neurotic and/or psychotic symptoms (such as learned helplessness or self-denigration of a battered woman)

ability to solve problems effectively. It also implies that basic human needs are fulfilled. Our basic needs include a sense of physical and psychological well being; a supportive network of friends, family, and associates; and a sense of identity and belonging to our society and cultural heritage.

Possible Responses		
Positive	**Negative**	**Duration**
Grief work Adaptation, emotional and social growth through healthy copint	Failure to ask for and accept help Suicide, assault, addiction, emotional/mental breakdown	Brief
Medical treatment, rest, exercise	Refusal of treatment, complications, possible death	
Prevention: Political action	Denial, possibity	
Life-style changes (such as diet, rest, exercise, leisure Social change strategies	Exacerbation of burnout All of the above, and mystification by and response to *symptoms vs. sources* of chronic stress	Weeks, months, years, or lifetime
Transition state preparation	Inability to accomplish new role tasks	
Grief work	Same as for acute stress	Few days to 6 weeks
Crisis coping and management by use of personal, social, and material resources **Prevention:** Education about sources of crisis and appropriate preventive action (such as comtemporary rites of passage, action to reduce social disparity)		
Reorganization or change of ineffective emotional, cognitive, and behavioral responses to stress and crisis (usually with help of therapy) Action to change social sources of chronic stress	Same as all of above, and increased vulnerability to crisis and inability to cope with acute and chronic stress	Weeks, months, years, or lifetime

Hansell (1976, pp. 31–49) describes our essential needs as the "seven basic attachments." All of us have a stable arrangement of transactions between ourselves and our environment. According to Hansell, we are essentially attached to:

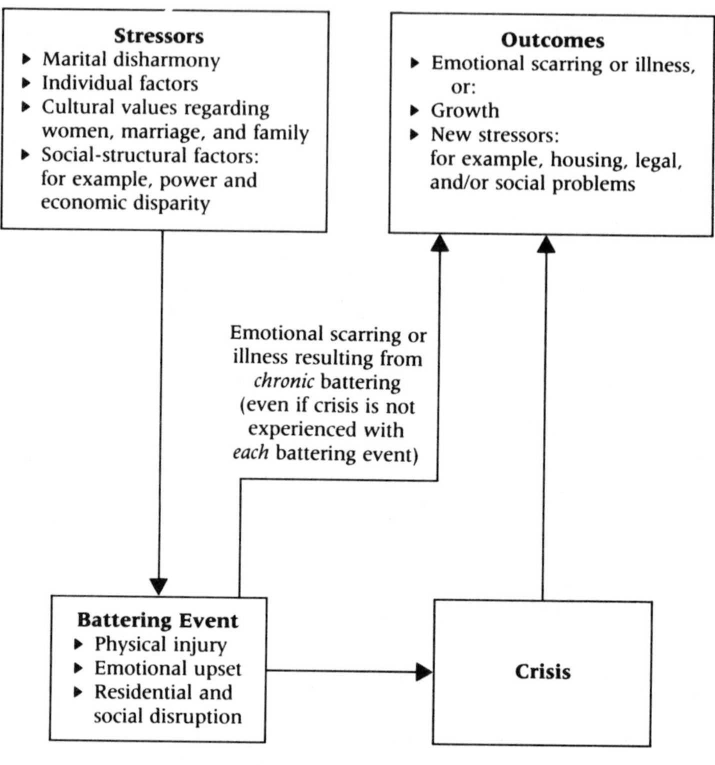

FIGURE 2-1

Interactive relationship between *stress* and *crisis* and possible *illness* in a battering situation. The arrows suggest the interactional relationship between stress, crisis and illness. Trouble and stressors in a marriage can lead to positive or negative outcomes through several different routes, depending on personal, social, and economic circumstances.

1. Food, oxygen, and other physical supplies necessary to life.
2. A strong sense of self-identity.
3. At least one other person in a close, mutually supportive relationship.
4. At least one group that accepts us as a member.
5. One or more roles in which we feel self-respect and can perform with dignity.
6. Financial security, or a means of participating in an exchange of the goods and services we need and value.

7. A comprehensive system of meaning, or a set of values that help us to set goals and to understand ourselves and the world around us.

People in crisis suffer a sudden loss of psychosocial and other supports. One or several of their basic attachments are severed or are at risk of being severed (Hansell 1976). For example, the shock of the unexpected death of a loved one by car accident or heart attack can leave a person feeling incomplete and at a loss about what to do, where to turn. The individual's familiar source of support and comfort disappears without warning, with no time to adjust to the change. Similar shock occurs in response to the suicide of a friend, diagnosis of a terminal illness such as AIDS, or an operation such as a mastectomy, which mutilates one's body. A person with AIDS, for example, not only loses health and faces the probability of a drastically shortened life cycle, but may be abandoned by friends and family and scorned by would-be helpers.

Shock and a resulting crisis state can also occur at the time of normal role transitions. For example, Mary, age 19, relied very heavily on her mother for advice and support in all aspects of her life. One month after her honeymoon and the move into an apartment with her husband, she became depressed and suicidal and was unable to function at home or at work. Mary was obviously not ready for the move from adolescence into the more independent role of a young adult.

A person can also go into crisis because of a threat of loss of anything considered essential and important. A common example of this crisis-provoking occasion is the man or woman whose spouse threatens divorce.

Caplan (1964) and Tyhurst (1957) note that for some people a crisis is triggered when they face a particularly challenging psychosocial event. A crisis for such individuals represents a call to new action that they cannot face with their present resources.

Case Example: Edward

Edward, age 45, has been an outstanding assistant director of his company. When he is promoted to the vacated position of executive director, he becomes depressed and virtually nonfunctional. Edward, in spite of external signs of success, lacks basic self-confidence; he cannot face the challenge of the new job. The possibility of failure in his new position is unbearable. His anxiety about success prevents him from achieving the success he desires. Edward is one of the many people who, with the help of family and friends, and perhaps a crisis counselor, can avoid possible failure and depression. He has his whole past career, including many successes, to draw on profitably in his present job.

With help, he might see that failure in his present position need not mean the end of a happy and productive life.

Case Example: Joan

Joan, age 19, is another person who cannot meet the challenge of increasing her personal and social resources; she cannot obtain a college credential for teaching and she worries about "coming out" as a lesbian. She is paralyzed by her fear of the responsibilities involved in a teaching career. At examination time, she is unable to study and fails over half of her courses. The challenge to increase her "supplies" in preparation for an adult teaching responsibility is more than she can face without additional resources.

HOW A CRISIS DEVELOPS

A crisis does not occur instantaneously. There are identifiable phases of development—psychosocial in character—that lead to an active crisis state. These phases were first described by Tyhurst (1957) in his study of individual responses to community disaster. Survivors experience three overlaping phases: (a) a period of impact, (b) a period of recoil, and (c) a posttraumatic period. This breakdown of phases applies most appropriately to crises originating from catastrophic, shocking events such as rape and other violent attacks, sudden infant death syndrome, or sometimes the news of a terminal disease. (See Individual Responses to Disaster in Chapter 9 for a detailed description of these phases.)

Caplan (1964) describes four phases in the development of extreme anxiety and crisis. His description of phases is applicable to crises occurring in a gradual process from less catastrophic stressors. Recognizing of these phases of crisis development aids us in preventing a stressful life event from becoming a crisis.

Phase 1 A traumatic event causes an initial rise in one's level of anxiety. The person is in a predicament and responds with familiar problem-solving mechanisms to reduce or eliminate the stress and discomfort stemming from excessive anxiety. For example, John, age 34, is striving toward a career as an executive in his company when he receives a diagnosis of multiple sclerosis. His wife Nancy is very supportive. He adjusts to this unexpected disturbing event by continuing to work as long as he can. John also has the advantage of the most advanced medical treatment available for multiple sclerosis. In addition, John's physician is skillful in applying his knowledge of the emotional impact of John's diagnosis. At this stage, John's traumatic event does not result in a crisis for him.

PHASE 2 In this phase the person's usual problem-solving ability fails, and the stimulus that caused the initial rise in tension continues. To continue with the illustration of John's case: The disease process is advancing despite excellent medical treatment. John's wife, Nancy, begins to participate less in some of her own interests so she can spend more time with her husband. The accumulating medical expenses and loss of work time strain the family's financial resources. John and Nancy receive a report from school that their son Larry, age 14, is having behavioral problems. At this stage, since there is greater stress, the possibility of a crisis state for John increases, but a crisis is not inevitable. It depends on what happens next in John's life.

PHASE 3 In this phase the individual's anxiety level rises further. The increased tension moves the person to use every resource available—including unusual or new means—to solve the problem and reduce the increasingly painful state of anxiety. In John's case, he fortunately has enough inner strength, confidence, and sensitivity to recognize the strain of his illness on his wife and child. He looks for new ways to cope with his increasing stress. First, he confides in his physician, who responds by taking time to listen and offer emotional support. His physician also arranges for home health services through a public health nursing agency. This outside health assistance frees Nancy from some of her steadily increasing responsibilities. The physician also encourges John and Nancy to seek help from the school guidance counselor regarding their son, Larry, which they do.

Another way to prevent a crisis state at this phase is to redefine or change one's goals. This means of avoiding crisis is not usually possible for someone who is emotionally isolated from others and feels locked into solving a problem alone. With the help of his physician, John could accept his illness as something that changed his capacity to function in predefined, expected ways. However, he does not have to alter his fundamental ability to live a meaningful, rewarding life because of illness. As John's illness progresses, it becomes necessary to change his role as the sole financial provider in the family. John and Nancy talk openly with each other about the situation. Together, they decide that Nancy will take a job to ease the financial strain. They also ask the public health agency to increase the home health services, as Nancy is beginning to resent her confinement to the house and the increasing demands of being nurse to her husband.

PHASE 4 This is the state of active crisis that results when:

- Internal strength and social support are lacking.

- ▶ The person's problem remains unresolved.
- ▶ Tension and anxiety rise to an unbearable degree.

An active crisis does not occur in John's case because he is able to respond constructively to his unanticipated illness. John has natural social supports and is able to use available help, so his stress does not become unbearable. The example of John illustrates how a full-blown crisis (phase 4) can be avoided by various decisions and actions taken during any one of the three preceding phases.

The following example of George Sloan is in sharp contrast to that of John above. George's case will be continued and discussed in subsequent chapters.

Case Example: George Sloan

George, age 48, works as a machinist with a construction company. Six evenings a week he works a second job as a cab driver in a large metropolitan area; his beat includes high crime sections of the city. He has just come home from the hospital after his third heart attack. The first occurred at age 44 and the second at age 47.

Phase 1: George is advised by his physician to cut down on his high number of work hours. Specifically, the doctor recommends that he give up his second job and spend more time relaxing with family and friends. George's physician recognizes his patient's vulnerability to heart attacks, especially in relation to his life-style (Friedman and Rosenman 1974). George rarely slows down. He is chronically angry about things going wrong and about not being able to get ahead financially. He receives his physician's advice with mixed feelings. On the one hand, he sees the relationship between his life-style and his heart attacks; on the other hand, he resents what he acknowledges as a necessary change to reduce further risk of death by heart attack.

In any case, his health and financial problems definitely increase his usual level of anxiety. George talks superficially to his wife Marie about his dilemma but receives little support or understanding from her; their marital relationship is already strained. Marie suggests that in place of George's second job, she increase her part-time job to full time. George cannot accept this because of what it implies about his image of himself as the chief provider.

George's discouragement and anger about not getting ahead are aggravated by Marie's complaints of never having enough money for the things she wants. George also resents what he perceives as the physician's judgment that he is not strong enough to do two jobs. At this stage, George is in a precrisis state, with a high degree of stress and anxiety.

Phase 2: George fails to obtain

relief from his anxiety by talking to his wife. He does not feel comfortable in talking with his physician about his reluctance to cut down the work stress as advised. When he attempts to do so, he senses that the physician is rushed. So he concludes that his doctor is only concerned about giving technical advice, not about how George handles the advice. The prospect of quitting his second job and bringing home less money leaves George feeling like a failure as supporter of his family (see Work Disruption in Chapter 10). His initial conflict and rise in tension continue. If he quits his second job, he cannot preserve his image as adequate family supporter; yet he cannot reduce the risk of death by heart disease if he continues his present pace. Help from other resources seems out of his reach.

Phase 3: George's increased anxiety moves him to try again talking with his wife. Ordinarily, he would have abandoned the idea based on the response he received earlier. Thus, this action constitutes an unusual effort for him, but he fails again in getting the help he needs. To make matters worse, George and Marie learn that their 16-year-old son, Arnold, has been suspended from school for a week due to suspected drug involvement. This makes George feel even more like a failure, as he is seldom home during normal family hours. Also, Marie nags him about not spending enough time with the kids. George's high level of anxiety becomes so obvious that Marie finally suggests "Why don't you talk to the doctor about whatever's bothering you or go see our pastor?" George knows that this is a good idea but cannot bring himself to do it. He had been brought up to believe that somehow it is unmanly to get outside help to solve one's problems. His image of himself as the strong masculine supporter of the family makes it impossible for him to give up the second job, although he knows the risks involved in continuing. For the same reason, he cannot bear the thought of his wife's working full time, though she herself has proposed the idea several times. Personality and social factors block him from redefining or changing his set goals as a means of problem resolution and prevention of crisis. Financial concerns along with the new problem of his son further increase his anxiety level. George is in a predicament he does not know how to resolve.

Phase 4: George is at a complete loss about how to deal with all the stress in his life—the threat to his health and life if he continues his present pace, the threat to his self-image if he quits the second job, the failure to communicate with his wife, and the sense of failure and guilt in his role as a parent. His anxiety increases to the breaking point:

- He feel hopeless.
- He does not know where to turn.
- He is in a state of active crisis.

George's case illustrates situational (heart disease), maturational (adolescent changes), and social-cultural (sex-role stereotyping) factors in the development of life crises. It also highlights the subjective elements that contribute to a crisis state at different points in people's lives. George's heart disease was clearly an unanticipated, stressful event. His son Arnold's threat of suspension was unanticipated and a source of added stress. Yet, Arnold's adolescence was anticipated as a normal phase of human development. If George's heart disease had developed at a time when his marriage was less strained, he might have received more help and support. Also, Arnold might have made it through adolescence without school suspension if there had been regular support from both parents. As it turned out, George and Marie had their first report of Arnold's behavior problems in school shortly after George's first heart attack four years earlier. They were advised at that time to seek family or marital counseling; they did, but only for a single session. Finally, socialization of George and Marie to stereotypical male and female roles was an added source of stress and a barrier to constructive crisis resolution.

For another person, such as John in the previous case, or for George at another time of life, the same medical diagnosis and the same advice could have had an altogether different effect. This is true also for Arnold. A different response from his parents when he gave his first signals of distress, or a more constructive approach from school officials and counselors might have prevented Arnold's crisis of school suspension. Or, different cultural expectations for husbands and wives could alter individual interpretations of the situation following stressful life events.

THE DURATION AND OUTCOMES OF CRISIS

People cannot stay in crisis forever. The state of crisis and the accompanying anxiety are too painful. There is a natural time limitation to the crisis experience. This is because the individual cannot survive indefinitely in such a state of psychological turmoil. The emotional discomfort stemming from the extreme anxiety moves the person toward action to reduce the anxiety to an endurable level as soon as possible. This aspect of the crisis experience underscores the danger and opportunity that crisis presents.

Experience with people in crisis has led to the observation that the acute emotional upset lasts from a few days to a few weeks. The person needs to move toward some sort of resolution and expresses that need in terms such as: "I can't go on like this anymore," "Something has got to give," "Please, tell me what to do to get out of this mess—I can't stand it," or "I feel like I'm losing my mind."

What, then, happens to the person in crisis? Several outcomes are possible:

1. The person can return to his or her precrisis state. This happens as a result of effective problem solving, made possible by internal strength,

values, and social supports. Such an outcome does not necessarily imply new psychological growth as a result of the experience; the person simply returns to his or her *usual* state of being.

2. The person may not only return to the precrisis state but can grow from the crisis experience through discovery of new resources and ways of solving problems. These discoveries result from the crisis experience itself. John's case is a good example of such growth. He took advantage of resources available to him and his family, such as his physician and the school guidance counselor. He found new ways of solving problems. The result for John was a process of growth: (a) His concept of himself as a worthwhile person was reinforced in spite of the loss of physical integrity from his illness. (b) He strengthened his marriage and ability to relate to his wife regarding a serious problem. This produced growth for both of them. (c) He developed in his role as a father by constructively handling the problem with his son in addition to his own personal stress.

3. The person responds to his or her problem by lapsing into neurotic or psychotic patterns of behavior. For example, the individual may become very withdrawn, suspicious, or depressed. His or her distorted perception of events may be exaggerated to the point of blaming others inappropriately for the misfortunes experienced. Others in crisis resolve their problems, at least temporarily, by excessive drinking or other drug abuse, or by impulsive disruptive behavior. Still others resort to more extreme measures by attempting or committing suicide or by abusing or killing others.

All these negative and destructive outcomes of the crisis experience occur when the individual lacks constructive ways of solving life's problems and relieving intolerable anxiety. George, for example, came to the conclusion in his despair that he was worth more dead than alive. Consequently, he was brought to the hospital emergency room after a car crash. George crashed his car deliberately, but did not die as he had planned. This was his chosen method of suicidal death which he thought would spare his family the stigma of suicide. He felt that he had already overburdened them. George's case will be continued in Chapters 3 and 4 in respect to his treatment in the emergency room and his follow-up care.

Considering all the possible outcomes of a crisis experience, it becomes obvious that helpers should have the following goals:

- To help people in crisis to at least return to their precrisis state.
- To do all that is possible to help people grow and become stronger as a result of the crisis and effective problem solving.
- To be alert to danger signals in order to prevent negative, destructive outcomes of a crisis experience.

The last goal is achieved by recognizing that negative results of crisis are often not necessary but occur because of insensitivity to another's problems and a lack of appropriate resources and crisis management skills in society's human service sector (see Crisis Paradigm, upper and lower boxes on far right).

INDIVIDUAL AND SOCIAL CHANGE AGENTRY APPROACHES TO LIFE CRISES

THE SOCIAL/CULTURAL CONTEXT OF PERSONAL CRISIS

The contrasting cases of John (with multiple sclerosis) and George (with a heart attack) illustrate both the success and limitations of individual approaches to life crises. Let us suppose that John and George each had identical help available from human service agencies. If George's crisis response is rooted partially in social and cultural sources—as seems to be the case—then intervention must consciously address these factors in order to be successful. Otherwise, unattended social and cultural issues can form a barrier to a strictly psychological crisis counseling approach. They also underscore McKinlay's (1979) argument about "downstream" versus "upstream" endeavors and link individual crisis management efforts to complimentary preventive strategies and social change action.

Preventive strategies were discussed in the previous chapter. Individual and social network crisis intervention approaches are considered in detail in the remaining chapters. Social action ideas are incorporated in relevant cases throughout the book. The social change aspects of comprehensive crisis work belong to the *follow-up* phase of the total process. In the Crisis Paradigm such crisis management strategies are illustrated in the right circle of the third box corresponding to sociocultural crisis origins in the first box. However, the foundation for such action is laid in one of the cognitive aspects of healthy crisis resolution—*understanding* the traumatic event, its sources, and how it affects the way one feels during crisis. For example, a rape victim can be helped to understand that she feels guilty and dirty about being raped not because she is in fact guilty and dirty, but because of the widely accepted social value that women are responsible if they are raped (because they dress femininely or hitchhike).

Because of the tradition of alleged "value-neutrality" among human service workers, some may object to including social change strategies as a formal part of service. Yet to offer only short-term crisis counseling or psychotherapy around problems stemming from cultural and social origins is value laden in itself;* that is, it suggests that the person adjust to a

*Consider the case of Freudian psychoanalytic therapy for women, implying woman's "innate" inferiority (Chesler 1972, Millet 1970). See also Halleck's (1971) discussion of the "ethics" of individual therapy for a suicidal prisoner as opposed to group consultation with the administrative staff regarding prison conditions.

disadvantaged position in society rather than develop and act on an awareness of the underlying factors contributing to depression or suicidal feelings, for example (Cloward and Piven 1979, Kessler and McLeod 1984). Thus, it is not a question of whether crisis workers are value free, since such work is almost inevitably affected by our values. Rather, values should be made explicit so that clients can make their own choices (such as accepting or acting on their disadvantaged position) from a more enlightened base.

SOCIAL CHANGE STRATEGIES IN COMPREHENSIVE CRISIS APPROACHES

Since readers are perhaps less familiar with social change strategies than with other aspects of crisis management follow-up (such as psychotherapy for underlying personality problems), the following summary is offered to highlight the principles of social change agentry as presented in the work of Chin and Benne (1976).

Stragegies Based on Reason and Research

Foremost among these strategies are research findings, new concepts, and the clarification of language to more closely represent reality as experienced by people, not as theorized by academics (see Stress, Crisis, and Illness in this chapter for the discussion of emotionally disturbed women assumed to be responsible for the violence they suffer). These strategies rest on the assumption that people are reasonable and that, when presented with evidence, they will take appropriate action to bring about needed change. However, this strategy alone is often not enough to move people toward change.

Strategies Based on Reeducation and Attitude Change

These approaches to change are based on the assumption that people are guided by internalized values and habits and that they act according to institutionalized roles and perceptions of self (for example, some parents remain in unhappy marriages "for the sake of the children"). This group of strategies includes an activity central to contemporary crisis theory: fostering learning and growth in the persons who make up the system to be changed. This includes people who are in crisis because of greater vulnerability stemming from a disadvantaged position in society. This change strategy is also relevant to people whose usual coping devices leave something to be desired, such as people with learned helplessness, excessive drinking, or abuse of others. Thus, the psychic pain of the crisis experience (in contrast to chronic unhealthy coping) often moves people to learn new ways of coping with life's problems.

Power-coercive Approaches

The emphasis in these strategies is on political and economic sanctions in the exercise of power, along with moral power moves of playing on sentiments of guilt, shame, and a sense of what is just and right. It is assumed that political action approaches will probably not succeed apart from reeducation and attitude changes; that is, new action (such as a strike by nurses who have been traditionally socialized to a subservient role in the health care system, by ethnic minorities demanding an end to housing discrimination, or gays protesting increased harassment and violence since the AIDS crisis) usually requires "new knowledge, new skills, new attitudes, and new value orientations" (Chin and Benne 1976, p. 42; Hoff 1984).

In a similar view, Marris (1987, pp. 156–164) proposes that new formulations of social meaning should accompany struggles to assert what the ideals of our societies should be and to implement social justice policies. This presumes collective planning by people concerned with those who are distressed or in crisis because of discrimination and repressive policies—feminists, racial equity groups, gay and lesbian activists and others.

The incorporation of these social change strategies into a comprehensive approach to crisis prevention and management underscores the suggestions of social analysts to consider intervention strategies that correspond to the origins of stress and crisis (Gerhardt 1979). Also, Cloward and Piven (1979), in their discussion of female deviance, claim that women's coping through depression, passive resistance, and lower rates of violence is related to the source of their stress. Many women have been socialized to accept the view that women's sress is determined biologically and from natural psychic weakness (Sayers 1982). Thus, women may expect that they are to *endure* what is from nature (not unlike survivors of natural disaster). However, social sources of stress can be *resisted,* not unlike the threat of man-made disaster (Lifton 1967). These ideas support the importance of consciousness-raising in the civil rights and women's movements.*

Table 2-2 illustrates how these ideas are encompassed in a comprehensive crisis management approach in respect to the various elements of the crisis experienced by George and his family and by Ramona, a battered woman (see Case Study: Ramona, p. 28). The different approaches can be grouped into: preventive/enhancement, immediate or short-term, and long-range (follow-up). This diagram suggests that primary prevention and enhancement activities can abort a destructive crisis outcome like suicide. It demonstrates, too, the interactions and relationship (not necessarily an orderly sequence) between strategies, and the fact that various

*It is becoming increasingly more common for health and mental health professionals to refer battered women or rape victims to women's support groups, which sensitize women to these kinds of social and political issues.

TABLE 2-2

Comprehensive Crisis Management

Crisis Element	Approaches to Crisis Management and Resolution: Preventive/ Enhancement	Immediate or Short-term	Long-range (Follow-up)
George			
Heart attack	Life-style factors (such as diet, exercise, relaxation)	Life support measures	Life-style factors
Marital strain	Marriage preparation Communication	Marriage counseling	Normative reeducative change
Mid-life change and marital strain	Rites of passage (such as a support group)*	Women's support group Men's support group	Normative reeducative change strategies
Arnold's school suspension	Rites of passage (such as adolescent support group)	Family and social network crisis counseling	Family counseling or therapy
George's suicide attempt	Family support and normative reeducative change following first heart attack	Individual and family crisis counseling	Family counseling Normative reeducative change Life-style factors
Ramona†			
Threat to life, homelessness	Women's support group Normative reeducative change	Physical refuge and peer support in shelter Crisis counseling (personal, legal, residential focus)	Political-coercive and normative reeducative change strategies
Self-blame, depression	Same as above	Counseling, peer support, or psychotherapy	Same as above, as well as possible psychotherapy

*Contemporary substitutes for traditional "Rites of Passage" will be duscussed in Chapter 11.
†See Chapter 1.

elements of comprehensive crisis management may be included in a single encounter with a person in crisis. The diagram reveals that it is never too late to consider preventive/enhancement approaches (such as at secondary and tertiary levels), even if a suicide attempt has been made, or in the broader sense, to learn from the experience on behalf of others (Hoff and Resing 1982).

The case of George suggests the intersection of responses relevant to crises originating from two sources: traumatic personal situations and transition states. Ramona's case reveals the interaction of crises from three sources: a traumatic event, life cycle development, and social and cultural factors. These illustrations also underscore the point made in the last chapter that people will resolve their crises with or without the help of significant others. People rich in personal, social, and material resources are often able to resolve crises positively in a natural (as opposed to institutional) context with the help of family, friends, and neighbors. Many, however, lack such resources, or for personal, cultural, and political reasons, the resources cannot be successfully mobilized during crisis. In these instances more formal help in the form of "crisis intervention" is needed to manage the crisis and promote positive crisis resolution (see Crisis Paradigm). The rest of this book is devoted to the principles and strategies necessary for effective crisis intervention—assessment, planning, implementaion of plan, follow-up—the formal aspect of crisis management in various life crisis situations.

SUMMARY

Success in crisis assessment and intervention is built on our understanding of the origins of crisis, how crisis differs from stress and illness, and the development and individual manifestations of crisis. Regardless of the origin of crisis, people in crisis have a number of characteristics in common. Preventing negative outcomes for these individuals is influenced by our sensitivity to the origins of crisis and application of appropriate intervention strategies in distinct sociocultural contexts. These concepts are illustrated in the Crisis Paradigm, which provides the theoretic framework of this book.

REFERENCES

Antonovsky A: *Health, Stress and Coping*. Jossey-Bass, 1980.

Bernstein RJ: *The Restructuring of Social and Political Theory*. Philadelphia: University of Pennsylvania Press, 1978.

BWHBC (Boston Women's Health Book Collective): *Our Bodies, Ourselves*, 3rd ed. Simon and Schuster, 1983.

Brim OG, Ryff CD: On the properties of life events. *Life-span Development Behavior* 1980; 3:367—388.

Brown GW: Meaning, measurement, and stress of life events. In: *Stressful Life Events: Their Nature and Effects*. Dohrenwend BS, Dohrenwend BP (editors). Wiley, 1974.

Brown GW, Harris T: *The Social Origins of Depression*. Tavistock, 1978.

Browne A: *When Battered Women Kill*. Free Press, 1987.

Caplan G: *Principles of Preventive Psychiatry*. Basic Books, 1964.

Caplan G: Mastery of stress: Psychosocial aspects. *Am J Psych* 1981; 138(4):413–420.

Cherniss C: *Staff Burnout*. Sage, 1980.

Chesler P: *Women and Madness.* Doubleday, 1972.

Chin R, Benne KD: General strategies for effecting change in human systems. In: *The Planning of Change,* 3rd ed. Bennis WD, Benne KD, Chin R et al. (editors). Holt, Rinehart and Winston, 1976.

Cicourel AV: *Method and Measurement in Sociology.* Free Press, 1964.

Cloward RA, Piven FF: Hidden protest: The channeling of female innovations and resistance. *Signs: J Women Culture Soc* 1979; 4:651–669.

Corea G: *The Hidden Malpractice: How American Medicine Treats Women,* updated ed. Harper Colophon Books, 1985.

Danish SJ, Smyer MA, Nowak CA, Developmental intervention: Enhancing life-event processes. *Life-span Devel Behav* 1980; 3:339–366.

Dohrenwend BS, Dohrenwend BP, (editors): *Stressful Life Events: Their Nature and Effects.* Wiley, 1974.

Dubos R: Determinants of health and disease. Pages 31–40 in: *Culture, Disease, and Healing: Studies in Medical Anthropology.* Landy D (editor). Macmillan, 1977.

Durkheim E: *Suicide.* Free Press, 1951 (1st ed. 1897).

Erickson E: *Childhood and Society,* 2nd ed. W. W. Norton, 1963.

Foster GM, Anderson, BG: *Medical Anthropology.* Wiley, 1978.

Freudenberger HJ, Richelson G: *Burnout.* Bantam Books, 1980.

Friedman M, Rosenman R: *Type A Behavior and Your Heart.* Knopf, 1974.

Gelles RA: *The Violent Home.* Sage, 1974.

Gerhardt U: Coping and social action: Theoretical reconstruction of the life-event approach. *Sociol Health Illness* 1979; 1:195–225.

Halleck S: *The Politics of Therapy.* Science House, 1971.

Hansell N: *The Person in Distress.* Human Sciences Press, 1976.

Hilberman E: The 'wife-beater's wife' reconsidered. *Am J Psych* 1980; 137:1336–1347.

Hoff LA: *Violence Against Women: A Social-Cultural Network Analysis.* (PhD dissertation.) Boston University. University Microfilms International, No. 8422380, 1984.

Hoff LA: Violence against women: Understanding assessment, intervention, prevention. *Issues Ment. Health Nurs.,* 1989.

Hoff LA, Resing M: Was this suicide preventable? *Am J Nurs* 1982; 82:1106–1111.

Holmes TH, Rahe RH: The social readjustment rating scale. *Psychosom Med* 1967; 11:213–218.

Jones A: *Women Who Kill.* Holt, Rinehart and Winston, 1980.

Kessler RC, McLeod JD: Sex differences in vulnerability to undesirable life events. *Am Sociol Rev* (Oct) 1984; 49:620–631.

Kessler RC, McLeod JD, Wethington E: Cost of caring: A perspective on the relationship between sex and psychological distress. In: *Social Support: Theory, Research and Application.* Sarason IG, Sarason RR (editors). The Hague: Martinus Nijhof, 1985.

Landy D (editor): *Culture, Disease, and Healing: Studies in Medical Anthropology.* Macmillan, 1977.

Levine S, Scotch, N: *Social Stress.* Aldine, 1970.

Lieban RW: The field of medical anthropology. Pages 13–31 in: *Culture, Disease and Healing: Studies in Medical Anthropology.* Landy D (editor). Macmillan, 1977.

Lifton RJ: *Death in Life.* Simon and Schuster, 1967.

Lindemann E: Symptomatology and management of acute grief. *Am J Psych* 1944; 101:101–148.

Louch AR: *Explanation and Human Action.* Berkeley: University of California Press, 1966.

Marris P: *Meaning and Action: Community Action and Conceptions of Change,* 2nd ed. Routledge and Kegan Paul, 1987.

Maslow A: *Motivation and Personality,* 2nd ed. Harper and Row, 1970.

McElroy A, Townsend PK: *Medical Anthropology in Eycological Perspective.* Boulder and London: West View Press, 1985.

McKinlay JB: A case for refocusing upstream: The political economy of illness. In: *Patients, Physicians, and Illness,* 3rd ed. Jaco EG (editor). Free Press, 1979.

Millet K: *Sexual Politics.* Doubleday, 1970.

Nellis M: *The Female Fix*. Houghton Mifflin, 1980.

Pagelow MD: *Woman-battering: Victims and Their Experiences*. Sage, 1981.

Parsons T: Social structure and dynamic process: The case of modern medical practice. Chapter 10 in: *The Social System*. Free Press, 1951.

Pearlin LE, Schooler C: The structure of coping. *J Health Soc Behav* 1978; 19:2–21.

Pearlin LE., et al.: The stress process. *Health Soc Behav* 1981; 22(4):337–356.

Perloff LS: Perceptions of vulnerability. *J Soc Issues* 1983; 39(2):41–61.

Ramsey JM: *Basic Pathophysiology: Modern Stress and the Disease Process*. Addison-Wesley, 1982.

Roberts H (editor): *Doing Feminist Research*. Routledge and Kegan Paul, 1981.

Ryan W: *Blaming the Victim*. Vintage Books, 1971.

Sales E, Baum M, Shore B: Victim readjustment following assault. *J Soc Issues* 1984; 40(1):117–136.

Sarason IG, Johnson, J.H. Siegel JM: Assessing the impact of life changes: Development of the life experiences survey. *J Consulting Psych* 1978; 46:932–946.

Sayers J: *Biological Politics*. Tavistock, 1982.

Schulberg HC, Sheldon A: The probability of crisis and strategies for preventive intervention. *Arch Gen Psych* 1968; 18:553–558.

Selye H: *The Stress of Life*. McGraw-Hill, 1956.

Silver RL, Boon C, Stones MH: Searching for meaning in misfortune: Making sense of incest. *J Soc Issues*. 1983; 39(2):81–102.

Spaniol L, Caputo JJ: *Professional Burnout*. Lexington, MA: Human Service Associates, 1979.

Survivors. A public television documentary. Boston: WGBH Educational Foundation, 1982.

Thomas WI: *The Unadjusted Girl*. Little Brown, 1931. Chapter 2 reprinted in: *Symbolic interaction*, 3rd ed. Manis JG, Meltzer BN (editors). Allyn and Bacon, 1978.

Turner RJ. Avison WR: Gender an depression: Assessing exposure and vulnerability to life events in a chronically strained population. Paper presented at annual meetings of American Public Health Association, October, 1987.

Tyhurst JS: The role of transition states—including disasters—in mental illness. *Symposium on Preventive and Social Psychiatry*. Washington, DC: Walter Reed Army Institute of Research and The National Research Council, 1957.

CHAPTER 3

IDENTIFYING PEOPLE IN CRISIS

PEOPLE AT RISK

We have observed the general origins of crisis and have formed a framework for predicting and preventing crisis or destructive crisis outcomes in large population groups. This *general* knowledge about people in crisis and how crises develop must be made accessible for use with *individuals* in actual or potential crisis. Crises from some sources are predictable and therefore more easily prepared for. Preparation reduces the risk of crisis and helps us avoid possible damaging outcomes. Common sources of predictable crises are developmental and other transition states and the role changes marking adolescence, adulthood, marriage, mid-life, retirement, and old age. Typically, a person may first be a student, then get a job, marry, become a parent, and reach the age of retirement. Since we usually anticipate these role changes we can take precautions to avoid a crisis. But some people do not, or cannot, prepare themselves for one or more of these events. The possibility of crisis for them is increased. For example, a youth whose parents have been overindulgent and inconsistent in their responses will find it difficult to move from adolescence into adulthood. Some parents are overprotective and stifle a child's normal development. Consequently, the move to adulthood becomes a risk and a hazard rather than an opportunity for further challenge and growth. Also, a person need not rush into marriage, but can thoughtfully consider the possibility and the related role changes. Yet many do rush, and crises result.

Another factor affecting these predictable role changes is the element of timing (see Chapter 2 and Chapter 11). For example, a man or woman marrying for the first time at age 40 may have planned very carefully for this life change. Nevertheless, one's pattern of living alone and need for independence could lead to unanticipated stress at an atypical marriage age. Also, parental and other social supports for newlyweds are less likely in later marriages. On the other hand, while a planned event such as a return to school at mid-life can be hazardous due to atypical timing, an older student may also be less vulnerable to crisis. That is, the more mature student or marriage partner often has the advantage of experience, financial security, and clear-cut goals—valuable resources that younger people may possess in lesser measure.

Another aspect of a potentially hazardous role transition, even if prepared for, is its timing with other life events—what Danish, Smyer, and Nowak (1980) call "contextual purity." By scanning the Holmes and Rahe (1967) Social Readjustment Rating Scale, we can see that some of the many life changes are within one's control (marriage or returning to school in mid-life), while others are not (menopause or death of an elderly parent). By careful planning and delay of certain life changes that are personally controllable, one can reduce one's cumulative stress score and the hazards of crisis, illness, and accidents.

Other life events are less predictable: sudden death of a loved one; serious physical illness; urban dislocation; personal and financial loss through flood, hurricane, or fire; birth of a premature infant. When these unanticipated events occur during transition states, or when the person experiencing them is socially disadvantaged, the probability of crisis is increased.

These examples and the interactive nature of crisis origins (see Crisis Paradigm in Chapters 1 and 2) underscore the subjective nature of the crisis experience and the need to identify *individuals* at risk. Regardless of how predictable crisis responses might be among groups, it is important to translate *general* risk factors into an assessment of the issues and problems faced by *this* person or family at *this* moment in history. Such an assessment, and assistance based on it, implies the need for precise information about individuals and families we think may be in crisis. For example:

1. In what developmental phase is the person or family?
2. What recent hazardous events have occurred in the life of this person or family?
3. How has this person or family interpreted these developmental and situational events?
4. Is there actual or potential threat to life? How urgent is the need for intervention?
5. What is the social/cultural milieu in which all of this is happening?

The ramifications of these and related questions are the basis of this discussion on identification and assessment of people in crisis.

THE IMPORTANCE OF CRISIS ASSESSMENT

For the crisis worker, consideration of various life events, transition states, and hazardous sociocultural factors is central to assessing whether a particular individual is in crisis. A person who is emotionally upset may be judged by observers as obviously being in a state of crisis. This is not necessarily so; accurate assessment should precede such a judgement. Still, an untrained observer may quickly dismiss the need for assessment with the conclusion that the more important task is to *help* the individual immediately. However, well intended "help" sometimes turns out to have the opposite effect for the individual concerned. One way to avoid misplaced helping is to identify people at risk through the process of assessment.

IMPEDIMENTS TO ADEQUATE ASSESSMENT

Assessment can be impeded by the very nature of the crisis intervention process. Crisis intervention work is a humane function that is growing in popularity. Helping people in crisis is immediate and often highly rewarding. However, those human service workers most inclined to action and involved in obtaining immediately observable results often do not take time to study and evaluate their own work (Hoff and Miller 1987, Schulberg and Sheldon 1968). When this lack of self-review is combined with the inherent difficulty of objectively evaluating any human helping process, it is easy to see how crisis intervention can flounder. Without a sound theory base and established techniques, there is little to distinguish it from intuitive first aid.

HAZARDS OF INADEQUATE ASSESSMENT AND PSYCHIATRIC LABELING

The failure to assess prior to helping is often responsible for the misapplication of the crisis model. In the human service field it is particularly unfortunate to misjudge a person in crisis by poor observation and inadequate assessment. Ultimately, these errors result in failure to help, which can have lifelong destructive effects. Crisis prediction and assessment is intricately tied to the possibility of preventive intervention and the avoidance of hospital admission and its accompanying potentially hazardous results (see Preventing Crisis and Promoting Growth in Chapter 1).

The importance of assessment and resolution of crisis as an alternative to psychiatric hospitalization is further highlighted by what happens after admission:

> *The admission itself tends to promote denial of the social forces in the family and community that have produced it [the admission]. The patient may then emerge as the scapegoat for these family and community problems, and psychiatric assessment [vs.* crisis assessment] *after admission tends to focus on the patient's symptomology [vs. strengths and problem-solving ability] as the major cause of admission. (Polak 1967, p. 153)*

People in distress and mental health workers helping them sometimes find it easier to use the temporary shelter of a hospital as a refuge than to face and seek to resolve a crisis. The upset person is diagnosed, takes on the identity of a patient, and falls into roles expected by the institution (Becker 1963, Goffman 1961, Lemett 1951). Essentially the same thing happens to an adolescent confined to a detention home, and to an old person placed in a nursing home. The strong inclination of some families to place disturbed people in institutions is a by-product of our society's low tolerance of behavior that falls outside "normal" limits.

Every society has social norms, that is, expectations of how people are to interact with others. When people deviate from these norms, sanctions are applied or stigmas attached to pressure the deviant member to return to acceptable norms of behavior, suffer the consequences of their deviance, or behave according to their stigmatized status. Thus, deviance can be considered from three perspectives as illustrated in the following examples:

1. In Western societies, a widow may be socially ostracized if she mourns the loss of her husband beyond what some think should be only a few weeks. Implicitly, she has deviated from the expected norm for grief and mourning in a death-denying society.
2. A person who is caught and convicted of stealing a car or molesting a child has engaged in behavior that is explicitly forbidden in most societies. While on the surface these are clear-cut examples of deviance, the results of such explicit violations vary.* For example, a black person is more likely to be apprehended and judged harshly for the car theft than is a white person. Within a family, incest may be overlooked in favor of keeping the family together.
3. Some people are considered deviant not for particular actions but for an aspect of their being. Thus, a gay person, a woman in menopause, an old person, or a handicapped individual carries a "mark" and is stigmatized as a result of a physical, social, or mental attribute. The physical or social mark or difference may become indistinguishable from the individual's identity. Goffman (1963) refers to this as "spoiled identity." Thus, a person does not *suffer* from paraplegia or schizophrenia but *is* a paraplegic or schizophrenic; the person who takes his or her own life does not just *commit* suicide but *is* a suicide. The person's identity becomes encompassed in a particular behavior or physical or mental characteristic.

"Labeling theory," a controversial topic in social science, has been the subject of lively debate for years (Gove 1975, Scheff 1975). Briefly, labeling

*One factor influencing such variance is "police discretion" (Bittner 1967), which in turn is influenced by racial climate. Another is the "social construction of reality" (Berger and Luckmann 1967, Daniels 1978).

theory proposes the concepts of primary and secondary deviance in an interactive relationship as illustrated in Figure 3-1. The argument between advocates and critics of labeling theory centers around this question: would secondary deviance occur without the changed self-concept and perception by others that occur after being labeled for deviant behavior? An extreme view is that primary deviance could virtually be dismissed if not for the detrimental effects of labeling and secondary deviance following it. In contrast, Gove (1978) suggests that the higher rates of depression among women have nothing to do with the labeling of mental illness. Rather, he says, depression among women is related to their disadvantaged position in society. This is so particularly if, as Cloward and Piven (1979) suggest, women are socialized to *endure* rather than *resist* oppression. There is probably some truth in each of these positions regarding labeling theory that has implications for crisis assessment. That is, certain personal attributes or behaviors do not fall into the range of behavior and conditions commonly accepted as normal and desirable. This is primary deviance, which exists whether or not it is identified with a label. For example, some people break social rules even though they are not always caught and identified as rule breakers.

Yet, there are distinct disadvantages to using labels, for example, gender and sexual preference bias (Holden 1986, Rabin, Keefe, and Barton 1986). People may try to "pass" or hide their identities because of the biases and prejudices of others. For example, gay and lesbian people are very careful about "coming out"; many women will not reveal their age, or they become avid consumers of beauty aids for keeping a youthful appearance; and people with a psychiatric problem may not wish to reveal the diagnosis, as they often experience prejudice in the job market. Alternatively, people may feel compelled to act as others expect. Convicted law breakers often repeat their offenses; a person with a diagnosis of schizophrenia may say, "How do you expect me to succeed in this job? I'm a schizophrenic." Diagnostic labeling has also been critiqued for its inappropriate application cross-culturally (Hagey 1984).

The relevance of labeling theory to crisis practice especially concerns assessment and the relationship of crisis to illness. If crisis is viewed as an opportunity for change and growth rather than as an illness or occasion for social or psychiatric labeling, the approach to assessment is an important step in that developmental process. Crisis assessment should not be confused with traditional psychiatric diagnosis, since psychiatry is not highly scientific and diagnoses can often be contradictory.* This does not mean that efforts to improve the objectivity of psychiatric diagnostic procedures should stop. Nor does it deny the fact that some people in crisis are also mentally

*The most noted example of this is the "evidence" presented by psychiatrists representing the defense and the prosecution in criminal cases with insanity pleas, such as during the trial of John W. Hinckley.

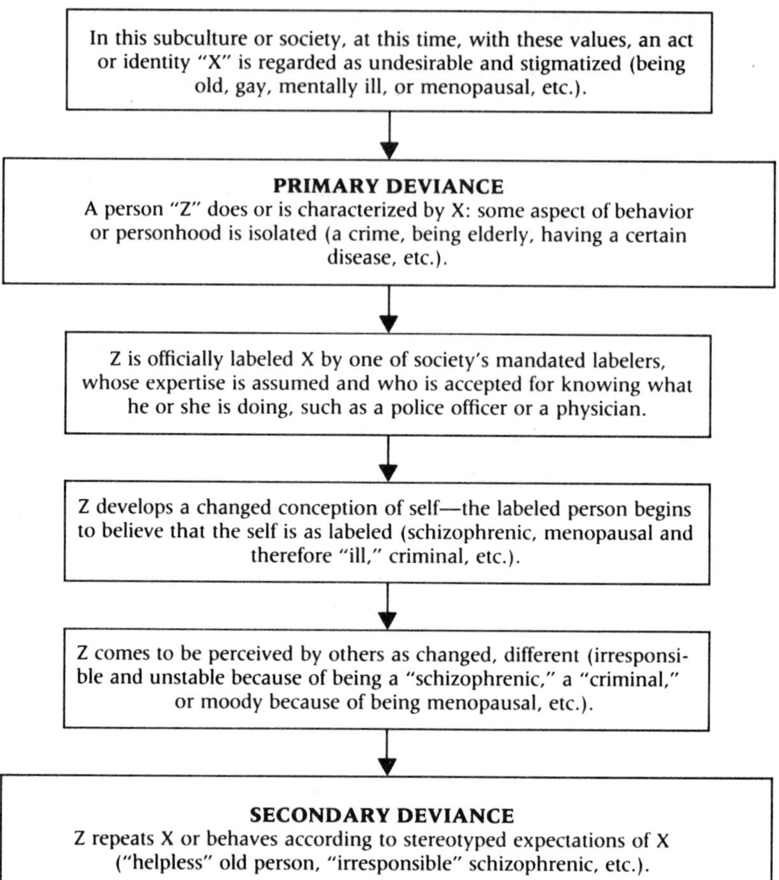

In this subculture or society, at this time, with these values, an act or identity "X" is regarded as undesirable and stigmatized (being old, gay, mentally ill, or menopausal, etc.).
PRIMARY DEVIANCE
A person "Z" does or is characterized by X: some aspect of behavior or personhood is isolated (a crime, being elderly, having a certain disease, etc.).
Z is officially labeled X by one of society's mandated labelers, whose expertise is assumed and who is accepted for knowing what he or she is doing, such as a police officer or a physician.
Z develops a changed conception of self—the labeled person begins to believe that the self is as labeled (schizophrenic, menopausal and therefore "ill," criminal, etc.).
Z comes to be perceived by others as changed, different (irresponsible and unstable because of being a "schizophrenic," a "criminal," or moody because of being menopausal, etc.).
SECONDARY DEVIANCE
Z repeats X or behaves according to stereotyped expectations of X ("helpless" old person, "irresponsible" schizophrenic, etc.).
X = A deviant act or identity
Z = A particular person labeled as deviant

FIGURE 3-1

Relationship between primary and secondary deviance. (Thanks to John McKinlay for his ideas about representing labeling theory in this format.)

disturbed and thus diagnosable in a psychiatric framework. It simply means that a crisis experience should be assessed and managed in a crisis rather than an illness framework, so that negative outcomes such as illness are avoided (or, if illness was present before, that chances of its repetition are reduced). Crisis assessment and intervention should not be cast in a medical framework because this currently accessible, humane approach to distressed people might then become bureaucratic and unapproachable like certain aspects of the traditional health care system. In short, one might ask: why give an illness label that is actually or potentially damaging, when illness may not be the central issue?

The negative results of inadequate assessment and psychiatric patient identity are dramatically revealed in a study by Rosenhan (1973). The study uncovered the destructive effects of placing disturbed people in psychiatric hospitals and labeling them with a psychiatric diagnosis such as "schizophrenia." Rosenhan demonstrated that the professional psychiatric helpers charged with admission and diagnosis of those regarded as insane could not distinguish between pseudopatients and the truly disturbed. This was so even when the professionals were forewarned by the researcher that certain people presenting themselves for hospital admission would be pseudopatients. Once the pseudopatients were hospitalized, their subsequent behavior was interpreted within the framework of their psychiatric label, although their behavior was normal. Consequently, they had a difficult time getting released from the hospital even though they had no "objective" signs of mental illness. The study supports Polak's (1967) observations that psychiatric hospitalization:

- Is a crisis in itself.
- Is the direct result of previously undetected and unresolved crisis.
- Should be avoided whenever possible.
- Should be used only as a last resort when all other efforts to help have failed.
- Should be substituted, whenever possible, with accurate crisis assessment and intervention in the person's natural social setting.

This discussion supports the earlier recommendations about assessment and intervention in natural settings (see Natural and Peer Group Settings in Chapter 1). It is not that psychiatrists and other mental health professionals do not understand the difference between crisis and mental illness; but once a patient is admitted to a medical or hospital establishment, it is difficult to avoid a "diagnosis," regardless of what individual crisis practitioners may think or do to the contrary. When diagnoses identify psychological and social states, values and therefore reduced objectivity are part of the process, with potentially damaging results, depending on a variety of factors. The person in crisis and his or her family should be advised, therefore, that there are many constructive ways of resolving life's crises (Hansell 1976, Polak 1976). Alternatives to hospitalization will be discussed in subsequent chapters.

The failure to adequately assess whether a person is in crisis has another negative result. It is ill advised to respond with a crisis approach when there is only the *appearance* of crisis. Such a response might reinforce crisislike behavior and the misperception some people have that the only way to get help is to convince the helpers that they are in crisis. The complexity and danger of such behavior is discussed further in Chapter 6.

THE DISTINCTIVENESS OF CRISIS ASSESSMENT

The ability to discriminate, then, between a crisis and a noncrisis state requires prediction and assessment skills. Good intentions are not enough.

The development of assessment skills does not take years of intensive study and training. It does require the ability to combine what we have learned from observing and helping people in crisis with the natural tendency of human beings to help one another when in trouble. Teachers, parents, nurses, police, physicians, and clergy are in the natural front lines where life crises occur. It is here that people can do the most to help others and prevent unnecessary life casualties. This is so especially when formal training is added to one's natural crisis management ability (Hoff and Miller 1987, McCarthy and Knapp 1984, Walfish 1983).

Ivan Illich (1975) claims that the bureaucratization of medicine has deprived the ordinary person of helping tools that he or she could readily use on behalf of others if allowed. This development may put in jeopardy the human aspect of the crisis intervention approach, which has made it an accessible, inoffensive way for distressed people to receive help. Similarly, the pervasiveness of the medical model presents a temptation to medicalize the crisis assessment and intervention process. As many tools as possible should be available for people who are willing and able to help others (Illich 1976). By sharpening the assessment and helping techniques that people have always used, front-line workers become particularly suited for prevention of acute crises, or what Jacobson, Strickler, and Morley (1968) call anticipatory intervention. When a full-blown crisis is in progress, front-line workers usually need to collaborate creatively with counselors and mental health professionals specially prepared to do a more comprehensive crisis assessment (Stein and Lambert 1984). The different levels of assessment are discussed in the next section. Thus, the crisis approach can be grounded in theory and sound principles of practice without taking on the disadvantages of elitism among human service workers.

The distinctiveness of crisis assessment can be summarized as follows:

1. The crisis assessment process, unlike traditional psychiatric diagnosis, is intricately tied to crisis resolution. Besides the issues already discussed, this is another compelling reason why assessment in comprehensive crisis management cannot be overstressed. For example, if an individual learns during assessment that the fear of "going crazy" is a typical crisis response, he or she is already helped along the path of positive crisis resolution.
2. Crisis assessment occurs immediately, rather than days or weeks later as in traditional psychiatric practice.
3. The focus in crisis assessment is on immediate, identifiable problems, rather than on personality dynamics or presumed coping deficits.
4. Historical material is dealt with in a special way in crisis assess-

ment. Probing into psychodynamic issues such as unresolved childhood conflicts and repressed emotions is inappropriate, whereas it is not only appropriate but *necessary* to obtain a person's history of problem solving and success or failure in constructively resolving past crises or dealing with stressful life events. Such historical material is vital for assessing and mobilizing an individual's personal and social resources toward positive crisis outcomes, and can be obtained by asking such questions as, "What have you done in the past that has worked for you when you're upset?"

5. Crisis assessment is not complete without an evaluation of risk to life (see Chapters 6 and 8).

6. Crisis assessment is not something done *to* a person, but a process carried out *with* a person and in active collaboration with significant others. Thus, a service contract is a logical outcome of appropriate crisis assessment.

7. Social and cultural factors and community resources are integral to a comprehensive crisis assessment since the origins and manifestations of crisis are social as often as they are individual.

THE ASSESSMENT PROCESS

Knowledge of probability factors about crisis guides us in assessing particular individuals in possible or actual crisis. However, a human service workers—including nurses, physicians, teachers, and police—encountering someone in distress still has many questions: What do I say? What questions should I ask the individual? How do I find out what's really happening with someone who seems so confused and upset? How do I recognize a person in crisis? If the person in crisis is not crazy, what distinguishes him or her from someone who is mentally disturbed but not in active crisis? What, if anything, does the family and community have to do with the person in crisis? In short, human service workers need a framework for the assessment process.

DISTINGUISHING LEVELS OF ASSESSMENT

There are two levels of crisis assessment that should be completed by the crisis worker. The human services person must ask the following questions at each level:

Level I Is there an obvious or potential threat to life, either the life of the individual in crisis or the lives of others? In other words, what are the risks of suicide, assault, and homicide?

Level II Is there evidence that the person is unable to function in his or her usual life role? Is the person in danger of being extruded from his or her natural social setting?

Level I assessment should be done by everyone. This includes people in their natural roles of friend, neighbor, parent, and spouse, as well as people in various professional positions: physicians, teachers, nurses, police, clergy, welfare workers, prison officials. This level of assessment is critical. It has life and death dimensions and forms the basis for mobilizing emergency services on behalf of the person, family, or community in crisis.

Every person in crisis should be assessed regarding danger to self and others. Techniques for assessment of suicidal danger are presented in detail in Chapter 6. Assessing risk of assault or homicide is discussed in Chapter 8.

If a lay person or a professional without special crisis training suspects that a person is a probable risk for suicide, assault, or homicide, he or she should always consult an experienced professional crisis worker. Some life-threatening situations should be approached collaboratively with the police and/or forensic psychiatry specialists (see Chapter 8).*

Level II assessment involves consideration of personal and social characteristics of the person or family. It is usually done by a trained crisis counselor or mental health professional. Level II assessment is comprehensive and corresponds to the elements of the total crisis experience:

1. Identification of the origins of the crisis. This includes the hazardous events, transition state turmoil, and social/cultural factors.
2. Development of the crisis: Is the person in the initial or acute phase of crisis? (See How a Crisis Develops in Chapter 2).
3. Individual manifestations of the crisis: How does the person interpret the hazardous events and what are the corresponding emotional, cognitive, behavioral, and biophysical responses to them? Are the events perceived as threat, loss, or challenge? Is the accompanying stress coped with effectively?
4. What personal, family, and interpersonal resources are relevant in this individual or family crisis?
5. What is the social/cultural milieu of the person or family in crisis?

All professional human service workers should acquire skill in this kind of assessment if they do not already have it. Close friends and family members are often able to make this kind of assessment as well. The chances for their success depend on their personal level of self-confidence, general experience, and previous success in helping others with problems. In gener-

*Crisis centers certified by the American Association of Suicidology have such collaborative relationships for handling high risk-crisis (see Wells and Hoff 1984).

al, however, if one is unaccustomed to dealing with people in crisis or has no special training in crisis intervention, one should consult with experienced professional crisis counselors. This is especially important in assessing people in complex, multicatastrophic, and problem situations. The different focuses and performances of Level I and II assessments are summarized in Table 3-1. Let us now consider the assessment process in detail.

IDENTIFYING ORIGINS AND PHASES OF CRISIS DEVELOPMENT

A basic step in crisis assessment is identification of the events or situations that led to the person's distress. Sifneos (1960, p. 177) and Golan (1969) elaborate Caplan's concept of crisis development in phases. They differentiate between the hazardous event and the precipitating factor, which along with the person's vulnerability constitute the components of the crisis state. As noted in Chapter 2, stressful and shocking events can arise from personal or material sources, transition states, or social/cultural situations.

The *hazardous event* is the initial shock that sets in motion a series of reactions culminating in a crisis (Golan 1969). In order to identify the hazardous event or situation, the helping person should ask directly, "What happened?" Sometimes people are so upset or overwhelmed by a series of things that they cannot clearly identify the sequence of events. In these instances, it is helpful to ask when the person began feeling so upset. Simple, direct questions should be asked about the time and circumstances

Table 3-1

Crisis Assessment Levels

	Focus of assessment	Assessment done by
Level I	Risk to life - Self (suicide) - Others (child, mate, parent, mental health worker)	Everyone (natural and formal crisis managers) - Family, friends, neighbors - Hotline workers - Front-line workers: clergy, police officers, nurses, physicians, teachers - Crisis and mental health professionals
Level II	Comprehensive psychosocial aspects of the person's life pertaining to the hazardous event, including differential assessment of chronic self-destructiveness	Counselor or mental health professional specially trained in crisis work (formal crisis managers)

of all upsetting events. Putting the events in order has a calming effect on the individual. The person experiences a certain sense of self-possession in being able to make some order out of confusion. This is particularly true for the person who is afraid of "losing control" or "going crazy."

The experience of stressful, hazardous events is not in itself a crisis. It is one of several components of the crisis state. After all, the process of living implies the everyday management of stressful life events. The question is: how is *this* particular event unusual in terms of its timing, severity, or the person's ability to handle it successfully? This component of crisis corresponds to Caplan's "first phase" of crisis development, which may or may not develop into a full-blown crisis, depending on personal and social circumstances (see the example of John, Chapter 2). People who seek help at the beginning stage of crisis development may avoid an acute crisis by early prevention and strategic intervention (Rapaport 1965, p. 30).

If hazardous events alone are insufficient to constitute a crisis state, we need to focus our assessment process further on the *immediacy* of the person's stress, the "precipitating factor." This is the proverbial "straw that broke the camel's back." It is the final, stressful event in a series of such events that pushes the person from a state of acute vulnerability into crisis. The precipitating event is not always easy to identify. This is particularly true when the presenting problem seems to have been present for a long time (Golan 1969).

The *precipitating factor* is often a minor accident. Nevertheless, it can take on crisis proportions in the context of other stressful events and the person's inability to use usual problem-solving devices. In this sense it resembles Caplan's third phase of crisis development, following the failure of ordinary problem solving (the second phase). It corresponds to what Polak (1967) calls the final event that moves a family to bring a member to a psychiatric hospital for admission after a series of "antecedent crises." In a series of crises experienced by the same person, the precipitating factor in one crisis episode may be the hazardous event in the next. Thus, in real life—as opposed to theoretic discussion and models—hazardous events and precipitating factors may be hard to distinguish. Yet, determining the mutual presence of these two components is useful in the assessment process, especially for distinguishing between *chronic* stress and an *acute* crisis state. For example, a chronic problem rather than a crisis is suggested in this interchange: Question: "What brought you here *today*? (since these problems have been with you for some time now)." Response: "I was watching a television program on depression and finally decided to get help for my problems."

ASSESSING INDIVIDUAL CRISIS MANIFESTATIONS

In crisis assessment the identification of hazardous events and the precipitating factor must be placed in meaningful context. This is done by ascertaining the subjective reaction of the person to stressful events. Sifneos

(1960) and Golan (1969) refer to this component of crisis assessment as the "vulnerable state." It corresponds to Caplan's second and fourth phases of crisis development. Its focus is on the emotional/biophysical, cognitive, and behavioral responses the person makes to recent stressful events. Information to determine the person's subjective response is elicited by questions such as those illustrated in Table 3-2. The answers to questions like these are important for several reasons:

- They provide essential information to determine whether a person is or is not in crisis.
- They suggest what the person's *usual* coping devices are, for example, healthy or unhealthy, and how these ways of coping are related to what Caplan calls the personal, material, and social/cultural "supplies" needed to avoid crisis.

Table 3-2

Assessing Personal Responses and Vulnerability to Hazardous Events

Sample Assessment Questions	Possible Verbal Responses	Interpretation in Terms of Personal Crisis Manifestations (Emotional, Cognitive, Behavioral)
How do you feel about what happened? (for example, divorce or rape)	*Divorce:* I don't want to live without her. . . . If I kill myself she'll be sorry.	Feelings of desperation, acute loss, revenge (emotional)
(Or, if the feelings have already been expressed spontaneously): I can see you're really upset.	*Rape:* I shouldn't have accepted his invitation to have a drink . . . I suppose it's my fault for being so stupid.	Guilt, self-blame (emotional, cognitive)
What did you do when she told you about wanting a divorce?	I figured, "good riddance," I only stayed for the kids' sake. But now that she's gone I'm really lonely and I hate the singles' bar scene.	Relief, ambivalence (emotional, cognitive)
	Or: I went down to the bar and got drunk, and have been drinking a lot ever since.	Unable to cope effectively, desire to escape loneliness (emotional, behavioral)
How do you usually handle problems that are upsetting to you?	I generally talk to my closest friend or just get away by myself for a while to think things through.	Generally effective coping ability (behavioral, cognitive)
Why didn't this work for you this time?	My closest friend moved away and I just haven't found anyone else to talk to that I really trust.	Realization of need for substitute support (cognitive, behavioral)

- They provide information about the meaning of stressful life events to various people and about the individual's particular "definition of the situation," which is essential to a personally tailored intervention plan.
- They link the assessment process to intervention strategies by providing baseline data for action and learning new ways of coping.

The relationship between hazardous events, how people respond to these events (their vulnerability), and the precipitating factor is illustrated in Figure 3-2.

The answers to our assessment questions provide a broad picture of what Hansell (1976) calls "crisis plumage," the distinguishing characteristics of a person in crisis compared to one who is not in crisis. This "plumage" consists of distress signals that people send to others when they experience a loss, a threat of loss, or a challenge to increase their life "supplies" (also referred to as basic needs or life attachments—see Chapter 2). Signals of distress to pay special attention to are:

1. Difficulty in managing one's feelings.
2. Suicidal or homicidal tendencies.
3. Alcohol or other drug abuse.
4. Trouble with the law.
5. Inability to effectively use available help.

These signals usually indicate that a person is coping ineffectively with a crisis and needs assistance to forestall negative crisis outcomes. In short, people proceed through life with material, personal, and social/cultural resources, and problem-solving devices for dealing with various stressors. When these problem-solving abilities and resources are intact, people generally avoid the possible negative outcomes of stressful life events. For example, in assessing the vulnerability of an assault victim, careful attention must be paid to the circumstances of victimization. In contrast, if the attack is linked to the victim's character traits, we are very close to "victim blaming," which will hamper the person's recovery (Sales, Baum and Shore 1984, pp. 132-133). When psychosocial resources are wanting, the person in crisis usually seeks help from others to compensate for a temporary inability to deal constructively with life's stressors. The help received is crisis intervention. If the help obtained is from human service institutions or professionals it is known as formal crisis management, as distinguished from natural crisis management (see Chapter 1). However, in order to be part of the crisis solution rather than part of the person's problem, crisis workers need to assess in greater detail the parameters of the individual's vulnerability. They must understand the emotional/biophysical, cognitive, and behavioral responses to hazardous events. Let us consider, then, the specific characteristics of "crisis plumage"—how people in crisis feel, think, and behave (see Crisis Paradigm, second box).

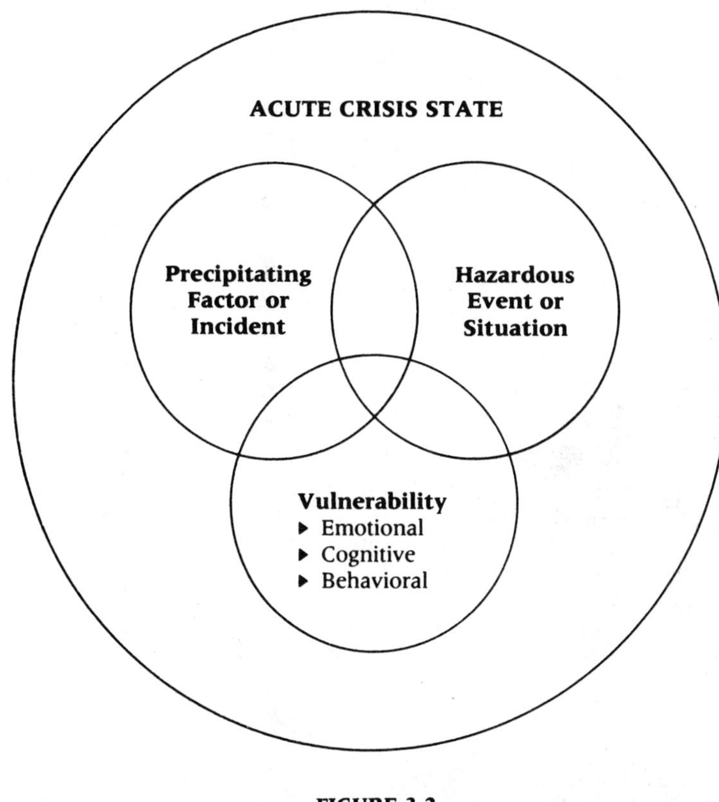

FIGURE 3-2

Components of the crisis state. The components in the intertwining circles represent the interactional process that characterizes the crisis experience.

Feelings and Biophysical Response

People in crisis experience a high degree of anxiety and tension. Another common theme is a sense of loss or emptiness. This feeling springs directly from an actual or threatened loss in self-esteem, material goods, social relationships, or a failure to meet a particular life challenge, such as a promotion or retirement. Other feelings frequently experienced are fear, shock, anger, guilt, embarrassment, or shame. Fear is often expressed in terms of losing control, or not understanding why one is responding in a certain way. Anger is directed inward for not being able to manage one's life, or at a significant other for leaving, dying, physical abuse, and so forth. Guilt and embarrassment often follow anger that does not seem justified. How can one be angry at a dead person when considering one's luck in being alive from an accident or disaster? People who are physically abused by someone they love often feel ashamed.

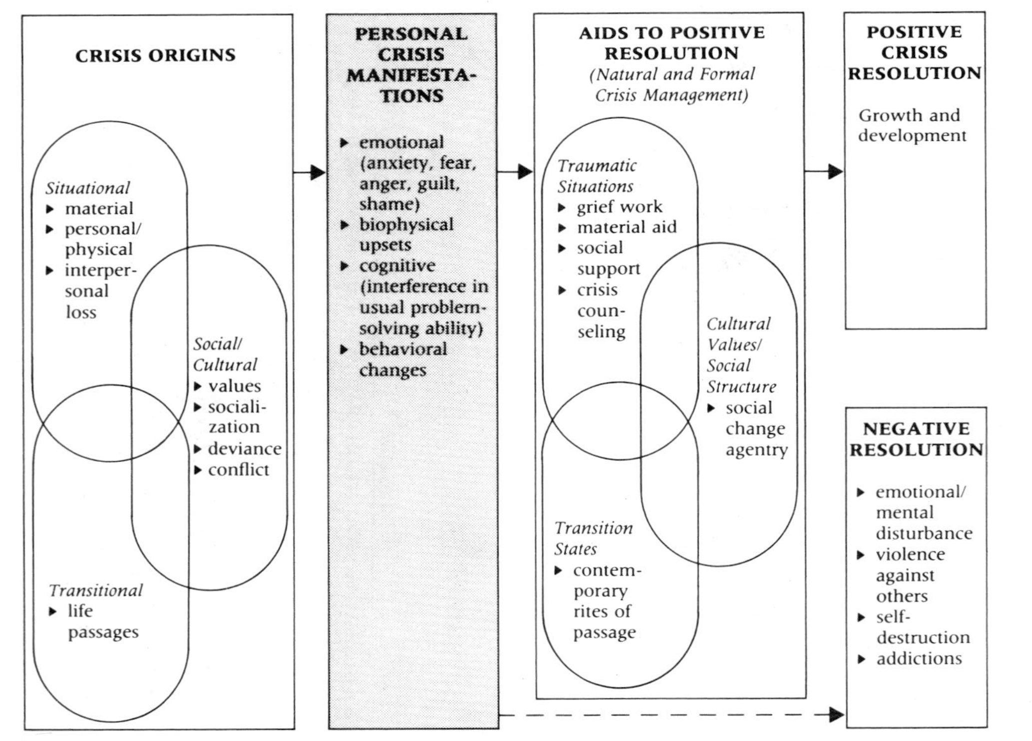

CRISIS PARADIGM

Crisis origins, manifestations, and outcomes, and the respective functions of crisis management have an interactional relationship. The intertwined circles represent the distinct yet interrelated origins of crisis and aids to positive resolution, even though personal manifestations are often similar. The solid line from origins to positive resolution illustrates the opportunity for growth and development through crisis; the broken line depicts the potential danger of crisis in the absence of appropriate aids.

Of all feelings common to the crisis experience, anxiety is probably the most familiar. A certain degree of tension is a normal part of life. It serves to move us to make appropriate plans to take productive action. For example, Terri, a student, has no anxiety about passing or failing a course. Therefore she does not exert the effort required to study and achieve a passing grade. When a person is excessively anxious, however, negative results usually occur. A state of great anxiety is one of the most painful experiences a human being can have.

Anxiety is manifested in a number of ways. Some characteristics will be peculiar to the particular person concerned. Commonly experienced signs of anxiety are:

- Sense of dread.
- Fear of losing control.
- Inability to focus on one thing.

Physical symptoms: sweating, frequent urination, diarrhea, nausea and vomiting, tachycardia (rapid heartbeat), headache, chest or abdominal pain, rash, menstrual irregularity, and sexual disinterest.

CASE EXAMPLE: DELAINE

Delaine, age 45, feels bereft after the recent death of her husband. Her friends have been supportive since his death from chronic heart disease. She chides herself and feels guilty about not being able to take the loss any better than she is. She knew that her husband's condition was precarious; nevertheless, she had depended on him as a readily available source of reassurance. Since she is basically a cheerful person, always on hand to support others in distress, she is embarrassed by what she perceives as weakness following her husband's death.

Because she cries more than usual, Delaine is afraid she may be losing control. At times she even wonders whether she is going crazy. It should be noted that Delaine is in major developmental transition to middle age. Also, the oldest of her three children was recently married, leaving her with a sense of loss in her usual mothering role. An additional anticipated loss is the recent news that one of her close friends will soon be leaving town. This threatens to erode further Delaine's base of support. Delaine feels angry about all the losses in her life, asking, "Why does all this have to happen to me all at once?" But she also feels guilty about her anger; after

all, her friend "deserves the opportunity that the move will afford her and her husband," and her daughter "has every right to get married and live her own life."

What Delaine doesn't acknowledge is that:

- She also has a right to whatever feelings she has about these disturbing events.
- She has a right and a need to express those feelings.
- Her feelings of loss and anger do not cancel the good feelings and support she can continue to have from her daughter and friend, though in an altered form.

Were it not for these developmental and situational factors, Delaine might not have experienced her husband's death as a crisis. The stability of Delaine's life transactions was disrupted on several counts:

- Her role as wife was changed to that of widow.
- Her role as mother of her oldest daughter was altered by her daughter's marriage.
- Her affectional attachment to her husband was completely severed.
- Affectional attachment to her friend will be altered in terms of physical distance and immediacy of anticipated support.
- Her notion of a full life includes marriage, so she must adjust—at least temporarily—to a change in that concept.

Thoughts, Perceptions, and Interpretations of Events

Feelings—especially high anxiety—have great impact on perceptions and thinking processes. In crisis, one's attention is focused on the acute shock and anguish being experienced and a few items concerning the crisis event. As a consequence, the person's usual memory and way of perceiving may be altered. He or she may have difficulty sorting things out. The relationship of events may not seem clear. People in crisis seem, by their own perception, caught in a maze of events that they cannot fit together. They often have trouble defining who they are and what their skills are. The state of anguish and resulting confusion can alter a person's ability to make decisions and solve problems—the very skills needed during a crisis. This disturbance in perceptual processes and problem-solving ability increases the individual's already heightened state of anxiety. Sometimes, the person fears that he or she is losing control.

The distorted perceptual process observed in crisis states should not be confused with mental illness, in which a person's *usual* pattern of thinking is disturbed. In a crisis state, the disturbance arises from and is part of the crisis experience. There is a rapid return to normal perception once the crisis is resolved.

Case Example: Joan

Joan, age 34, called a mental health center stating that her husband had just left the house with a shotgun and that she didn't know where he was going. She was afraid for her life as they had had an argument the night before during which she complained about his drinking and he had threatened her. On further questioning, it turned out that Joan's husband had left the house at his usual time for work in a neighboring town. He had left with the shotgun the previous evening after the argument. After three hours, he had returned and put away the gun. The gun was still in the house. There was nothing in the interaction to lead an outside observer to conclude that Joan's husband would not be home as usual after a day at work.

To be noted in this example is Joan's disturbed perceptual process. On questioning, she cannot recall certain details without help and cannot put all the facts into logical order. Joan is obviously very anxious about her personal safety. Complicating this feeling of anxiety is her sense of guilt about her role in precipitating the argument by mentioning her husband's drinking. Her anxiety is consistent with her *perception* of the threat to her safety. The determining factor is not the *fact* that she is not in any immediate danger, but how she perceives the event.

The feelings of people in crisis are usually consistent with their perception of the situation (Dressler 1973). Recognition of this fact should decrease the possibility of casting people with similar problems into a common mold. The perception of the event is one of the factors that makes an event a crisis for one person but not for another.

Joan's case illustrates how excessive anxiety interferes with effective problem solving. If Joan were not so anxious, she would probably have arrived at an obvious ways to ensure her immediate safety, that is, removing the gun or leaving the house herself and seeking help. Joan probably knows that the *use* of weapons is intrinsically connected with their availability, but her anxiety prevents her from using that knowledge.

Other aspects of cognitive functioning spring from different socialization processes and value systems that influence how particular events are interpreted. Illness, for example, has a different meaning and crisis potential for various ethnic and religious groups (see Chapter 10 and Zborowski 1952). A state legislator who was put in jail for a minor offense killed himself hours after being imprisoned. For this publicly elected figure, the transgression meant loss of reputation, whereas a person arrested for repeated drunken driving may interpret the event differently because he or she has less to lose. People socialized to feel incomplete without marriage will probably experience the loss of a spouse as an occasion of crisis, whereas others grow from the challenges of greater independence. These examples illustrate the importance of cultural sensitivity and not imposing our own values and behavior norms on others. No situation or disturbance affects two people alike, and the same person may respond differently to similar events at different times in life. Thus, varying, subjective interpretations of life events are integral aspects of a crisis response and must be assessed accordingly.

Behavior

Behavior usually follows from what people think and feel and from their interpretations of life events. If a person feels anxious and has a distorted perception of events, he or she is likely to behave in unusual ways. However, what may seem unusual, distorted, or "crazy" to an outsider may be considered normal behavior within certain cultural groups. In order to determine whether a person's behavior is normal or deviant, we need to start with *that* person's cultural definition of what is usual, not our own. This is particularly important if the crisis worker and person in distress are from different cultural, class, or ethnic groups. If the distressed person is too upset to provide this kind of information, it should be elicited from family or friends of the person whenever possible. Failing that, it is desirable to obtain a consultation from someone of the person's ethnic or cultural group.

A significant behavioral sign of crisis is the individual's inability to perform normal vocational functions in the usual manner, for example, when a person cannot satisfactorily accomplish required household chores, concentrate on studies, or do an outside job. Another sign is a change in the individual's social behavior. The person may withdraw from usual social contacts, or he or she may make unusual efforts to avoid being alone and become "clingy" or "demanding" (Hansell 1976). As social connections break down, the person may also feel detached or distant from others. Some people in crisis act on impulse; they may drive a car recklessly, make a suicide attempt, or attack others as a desperate means of solving a problem (see Chapters 6 and 8).

Some people will go out of their way to reject the assistance offered by friends. Often, this response rises out of the person's sense of helplessness and embarrassment at not being able to cope in the usual manner. The person fears that acceptance of help may be misinterpreted as a confirmation of one's perceived weakness. People in crisis are also observed to behave in ways that are inconsistent with their thoughts and feelings. For example, a young woman witnessed a shooting accident that caused the death of her boyfriend. Initially, she was visibly upset by the event. She was brought by her family to a mental health emergency clinic. During the interview with a counselor, she laughed inappropriately when talking about the shooting and death she had witnessed. Another behavioral signal of crisis is the observation of atypical behavior, such as driving while intoxicated by an individual with no previous record of such behavior.

In summary, when assessing vulnerability it is important to find out how *this* person is reacting *here and now* to whatever happened. The simplest way to assess a person's vulnerability is to ask, "How do you feel about what happened? What do you usually do when you're upset?" and similar questions suggested in Table 3-2.

FAMILY AND COMMUNITY ASSESSMENT

Our discussion of the assessment process thus far has focused primarily on techniques to determine the hazardous events precipitating the crisis and the individual's personal response to these events: emotional, cognitive, behavioral, and biophysical changes. Crisis assessment, however, is incomplete without evaluating the person's social resources and cultural milieu.* This includes the individual's estimate of his or her family and other social contacts as real or potential asset, or as liabilities: Are network members part of the problem or part of the solution? Unfortunately, this is often the full extent of social assessment in much of crisis practice, in spite of historic emphasis on sociocultural factors (Caplan 1964). In this book social assessment means that the person's social network members are *consciously* (not just incidentally) included in the assessment process. Technically, this is not as difficult as it appears. Often the rationalization of lack of time or inaccessibility of the family is used to justify an exclusively individual approach to assessment. This probably covers up the worker's lack of conviction or skills in the use of social approaches. In view of what is known about the social aspects of individual crisis responses, these issues need serious examination in order to refine crisis assessment and intervention strategies.

Including a social approach in crisis assessment reduces misidentification of the client in crisis. That is, sometimes the person appearing or brought for help may or may not be in crisis, but complete assessment reveals that an *entire family* is in crisis. For example, in the case of a suicide attempt by a teenager, the entire family, rather than only the teenager, is almost always in crisis.

Evaluation of the sociocultural context and community resources is related to family assessment; the context may figure in the origin and resolution of crises, as illustrated in the Crisis Paradigm discussed in Chapters 1 and 2. Evaluation should include questions about success or failure in receiving necessary help from community resources. It also involves cultural

*See Chapter 5 and Polak (1967), and Hansell (1976), Hoff (1984), Kaplan, Cassel, and Gove (1977), Polak (1967), and Stark, Flitcraft, and Frazier (1979).

Table 3-3

Differentiation: Effective and Ineffective Crisis Coping According to Crisis Episode

Crisis Episode			**Crisis Coping**	
Hazardous Event	**Origin**	**Personal Manifestations**	**Ineffective**	**Effective**
Loss of child by death	Situational: unexplained physical malfunctioning of child, for example, SIDS	Emotional	Depression	Grief work
		Biophysical	Stomach or other ailments	
		Cognitive	Conviction of having done something wrong to cause death of the child	Recognizing and accepting that there is nothing one could have done to prevent the death
		Behavioral	Inability to care for other children appropriately (for example, overprotective)	Attendance of peer support group
Physical battering by mate	*Sociocultural:* values and other factors affecting relationships	Emotional	Crying, depression, feelings of worthlessness, self-blame, and helplessness	Anger, shock ("How could he do this to me?"), outrage at the fact that it happened
		Cognitive	Assumption that the beating was justified; inability to decide what to do	Conviction of inappropriateness of violence between men and women; decision to leave and/or otherwise reorder one's life free of violence
		Behavior	Alcohol abuse, abuse of children, excusing of mate's violence	Seek refuge in nonviolent shelter; initiate steps toward economic independence; participate in peer group support and social change activities

and socioeconomic factors that may contribute to crisis vulnerability or personal ability to constructively resolve crises, such as racial unrest or opportunities for welfare mothers to become economically self-sufficient (see Why People Go Into Crises, Chapter 2). These aspects of comprehensive crisis assessment and their implications for intervention are elaborated further in Chapter 5.

The individual and sociocultural aspects of crisis assessment are summarized and illustrated with examples in Table 3-3. This diagram elaborates on the concept of healthy and unhealthy crisis coping (Caplan and Grunebaum 1967). It outlines the relationship between crisis origins and personal manifestations of crisis (see Crisis Paradigm, first two boxes p. 84). It also links the crisis assessment process to various intervention techniques: if assessment reveals that a person is coping inadequately in the broad aspects of human functioning—emotional, biophysical, cognitive, and behavioral—the groundwork has been laid in the information acquired to assist the person toward more effective crisis coping (see Comprehensive Crisis Assessment Framework and Tool in this chapter). On the other hand, careful assessment guides us in the decision of when *not* to intervene—in areas where the person's coping is adequate. A person who is acutely upset can be helped to realize that he or she is coping adequately in *some* aspects of life (for example, at work but not at home or vice versa). An old adage applies here: If it's not broken, don't fix it.

The next section describes a structured approach to carrying out the assessment process, using the concepts discussed in this and the previous two chapters.

AN ASSESSMENT INTERVIEW

The following interview with George Sloan, age 48, is conducted by an emergency room nurse. George is brought to the hospital by police following an attempt to commit suicide by crashing his car. (This case illustration is continued from Chapter 2.)

Case Example: George Sloan

Signals of Distress and Crisis to be Identified	Assessment Techniques Applied to Case of Mr. George Sloan
	Nurse: Hello, Mr. Sloan. Would you like to be called Mr. Sloan or George?
	George: George is fine.

Signals of Distress and Crisis to be Identified	Assessment Techniques Applied to Case of Mr. George Sloan
	Nurse: Will you tell me what happened, George?
	George: I had a car accident. Can't you see that without asking? (Slightly hostile and seemingly reluctant to talk.)
	Nurse: Yes, I know, George. But the police said you were going the wrong way on the expressway. How did that happen?
Active Crisis State: Extreme anxiety to the breaking point	*George:* Yes, that, right—(hesitates). Well, I just couldn't take it anymore—but I guess it didn't work.
	Nurse: Sounds like you've been having a rough time, George. Can you tell me what it is you can't take anymore?
Hazardous Event: Physical illness	*George:* Well, I've got heart trouble . . .
Vulnerable State: Loss of external social supports or inability to use them	It's gotten to be too much for my wife—I can't expect her to do much more. . . .
Loss of personal coping ability	We're having trouble with out 16-year-old son, Arnold. . . .
Inability to communicate stress to significant others	I just couldn't take it anymore. I figured I'd do everybody a favor and get rid of myself.
High lethal suicide attempt	*Nurse:* So your car accident was really an attempt to kill yourself?
	George: That's right—that way at least my wife wouldn't lose the insurance along with everything else she's had to put up with.
	Nurse: I can see that your heart trouble and all the other troubles have left you feeling pretty worthless.
Depression	*George:* That's about it—too bad I came out alive. I really feel I'm worth more dead than alive.
	Nurse: George, I can see that you're feeling desperate about your situation. How long have you felt this way?
	George: I've had heart trouble for about four years. After my last heart attack, the doctor told me I had to slow down or it would probably kill me. Well, there's no way I can change things that I can see.

Signals of Distress and Crisis to be Identified	Assessment Techniques Applied to Case of Mr. George Sloan
Precipitating Event: Inability to perform in expected role as father	*Nurse:* What happened this past week that made you decide to end it all? *George:* Well, our kid Arnold got suspended from school—that did it! I figured if a father can't do any better with his son than that, what's the use? *Nurse:* I gather from what you say and feel that you just couldn't see any other way out.
State of Active Crisis: Vulnerability: Fixated on role expectations; inability to use outside helping resources	*George:* That's right—money is really getting tight; my wife was talking about getting a full-time job and that really bothers me to think that I can't support my family anymore. And if she starts working more, things might get even worse with Arnold. There was no one to talk to. Suicide's the only thing left. *Nurse:* With all these problems, George, have you ever thought about suicide before?
History of poor coping ability	*George:* Yes, once, after my doctor told me to really watch it after my last heart attack. I felt pretty hopeless and thought of crashing my car then. But things weren't so bad then between me and my wife, and she talked me out of it and seemed willing to stick with me. *Nurse:* I see—but this time you felt there was nowhere else to turn. Anyway, George, I'm glad your suicide attempt didn't work. I'd really like to have you consider some other ways to deal with all these problems. *George:* I don't know what they could be. I really feel hopeless but I guess I could see what you've got to offer. *Nurse:* There are several things we can discuss. (To be continued in Chapter 4, "Helping People in Crisis")

Besides the technical aspects of asking clear, direct questions, this interview excerpt illustrates another important point. The nurse reveals an understanding of Mr. Sloan's problem and empathizes with the despair he must be feeling:

- "So your car accident was really an attempt to kill yourself?"
- "Sounds like you've been having a rough time, George."

- "I can see that your illness and all the other troubles have left you feeling pretty worthless."
- "George, I can see that you're feeling desperate about your situation."
- "I'm glad your suicide attempt didn't work."

The nurse clearly comes through as a human being with feelings and concern about a fellow human being who is in despair. Concern is conveyed by a gentle voice tone and unstylized manner. Furthermore, the nurse is able to express feelings without sounding sentimental and shocked and apparently is not afraid to be with a person in crisis.

As shown by this intervew, effective assessment techniques are not highly complicated or veiled in mystery. The techniques require:

- Straightforward approach with simple direct questions.
- Ability to empathize, or to "walk in another person's moccasins."
- Ability to grasp the depth of another's despair and share the feelings that this evokes.
- Courage not to run away from frightening experiences like suicide attempts.

The inverview also demonstrates that assessment for suicide risk is an integral part of thorough crisis assessment. Parents, teachers, friends, and police can add to their natural tendencies to help by learning these assessment techniques. Failure to use the techniques can mean the difference between life and death for someone like Mr. Sloan. It is not uncommon for people in George Sloan's condition to be treated medically or surgically in hospitals without anyone inquiring into underlying suicide intentions. If he receives only medical or surgical treatment and nothing else changes in his life, George Sloan will probably commit suicide within six to twelve months. He is already in a high-risk category for suicide (see Assessment of the Suicidal Person in Chapter 6).

Another objective that should be accomplished during the initial interview is to provide the person in crisis with some concrete help. Mr. Sloan feels the acceptance and concern of the nurse, or he would not have dropped his initial resistance to sharing his dilemma. The nurse has opened the discussion of alternatives to suicide.

Once an individual is identified as being in a state of crisis, the helping person proceeds to give or obtain whatever assistance is indicated. Strategies for carrying out this helping process are discussed in detail in Chapter 4. In complex situations or in circumstances involving life and death, the helper should engage the services of professional crisis workers (Hoff and Miller 1987, Wells and Hoff 1984).

Once the state of crisis is ascertained, the professional crisis worker will engage the person in full-scale assessment of his or her problems. Such an assessment will involve the person's family and other significant people. Assessment techniques of this nature are currently practiced in many crisis and counseling clinics and community mental health programs. A framework and tool for comprehensive assessment by professional crisis workers is discussed next.

COMPREHENSIVE CRISIS ASSESSMENT FRAMEWORK AND TOOL

A well-organized worker uses tools that aid in the assessment process. If a crisis worker lacks direction and a sense of order, this adds to the confusion felt by a person in crisis. While tools emphasize a structured approach to the assessment process, it should be remembered that no record system or mechanical tool such as computer analysis can ever substitute for the empathy, knowledge, and experience of a skilled clinician. Record systems are intended to *complement*, not displace, clinical judgment and expertise. Nor should records be allowed to depersonalize interaction with a distressed person.

PHILOSOPHY AND CONTEXT OF RECORD SYSTEM

The tool recommended to guide and record the crisis managment process as conceived in this book was selected for several reasons. This tool:

- Is based on the understanding of crisis in the social-psychologic and cultural perspective emphasized in this text.
- Is client-centered in that it includes the person's self-assessment as an integral aspect of the assessment process.
- Assumes that the client is a member of a social network (not simply an individual in psychological disequilibrium), and that disruption or threat of disruption from essential social attachments is often the occasion of crisis. The tool provides significant members of the person's social network an opportunity to participate actively in the assessment process.
- Provides a structured, standardized framework for gathering data while including subjective, narrative-style information from the client.
- Focuses on a view of the person in crisis as a human being functioning at varying degrees of adequacy or inadequacy, not merely as a diagnostic entity.
- Assists in fostering continuity between the various steps of the crisis management process (assessment, planning, intervention, follow-up) by providing relevant, organized information so that the client's level of functioning, goals, and methods for attaining these goals can be sharply defined and used as a guide in the course of service.

- Provides supervisory staff with information necessary to monitor service and assure quality care to clients on an ongoing basis.
- Provides administrative staff the data base necessary to monitor and evaluate service program outcomes in relation to stated objectives.

The record system of which this assessment tool is a part was developed by a special task force in the Erie County Mental Health System in metropolitan Buffalo, New York. It is unique in that it incorporates crisis management principles into the assessment and record-keeping requirements of a state and county mental health department, while retaining its client-centered focus. Clients at risk for crisis who were served in this mental health system included: (a) people experiencing various unanticipated hazardous life events and therefore at risk of extrusion from their natural social setting; (b) people vulnerable to crisis in relation to chronic mental or emotional distrubance, chemical dependence, or disadvantaged social circumstances. Many of the case examples cited in this book are drawn from people who requested service in this crisis-sensitive mental health system.

The record system was tested with crisis and mental health workers between 1974 and 1976 in the agencies that adopted the system. Included were the majority of publicly funded agencies serving urban, suburban, and rural communities in a metropolitan area with a population of l.25 million. Input was also obtained from people receiving service. Examples of client feedback were:

- "I'm not so bad off as I thought."
- "This takes some of the mystery out of mental health."
- "Getting help with a problem isn't so magical after all."
- "Now I have a diary of how I worked out my problems and got better."

Staff using the forms receive formal training in crisis intervention and in use of the record system according to written specifications. In 1982, the category of "Violence Experienced" was added to more appropriately assess the crises of child abuse, rape, and violence against one's mate as issues of growing public concern (Hoff 1984).

SERVICE FORMS

APPROACH TO USING FORMS

The following description for using the forms is excerpted from the complete specifications.* It illustrates assessment information as the foundation for

*For complete specifications for use of these forms, and information about reliability and validity studies, the reader is referred to the author who can be reached through Addison-Wesley.

coordinated service and follow-up (see Chapter 4). The forms are intended for use by crisis workers prepared to do Level II assessment. Sample forms appear at the end of this chapter.

INITIAL CONTACT SHEET

This form is intended to provide basic demographic and problem information at the time the client requests service or is presented for service by another person or agency. This information should provide the worker with sufficient data to make several key decisions early in the helping process:

- How urgent is the situation?
- Who is to be assigned responsibility for proceeding with the next step?
- What type of response is indicated as "the next step"?

This form is used chiefly by the worker designated to handle all incoming calls and requests for service during a specified period of time. The "Crisis Rating" section of the form should be completed according to the following guidelines.

Crisis Rating: How Urgent is Your Need for Help?

Very Urgent: Service request requires an immediate response within minutes; crisis outreach; medical emergency—requiring an ambulance to be called (overdoses); severe drug reaction; or police contacted if situation involves extreme danger or weapons.

Urgent: Response requires rapid but not necessarily immediate response, within a few hours. Example: low to moderate risk of suicide, mild drug reaction.

Somewhat Urgent: Response should be made within a day (approximately 24 hours). Example: planning conference in which key persons are not available until the following evening.

Slightly Urgent: A response is required within a few days. Example: client's funding runs out within a week and he or she needs public assistance.

Not Urgent: When a situation has existed for a long time and does not warrant immediate intervention, a week or two is unlikely to cause any significant difference. Examples: a child with learning disability; certain types of marital counseling.

CLIENT SELF-ASSESSMENT AND SIGNIFICANT OTHER WORKSHEETS

The Client Self-Assessment Worksheet can be used in two ways: (a) the form can serve as an interview guide in a face-to-face session with the client; (b) the client (if not acutely upset) can be given the form to complete, after which the items are discussed in a face-to-face interview. This assumes a literal interpretation of the traditional principle that "the record belongs to the client." It also reflects the view that clients are in charge of their lives and the value of demystifying the assessment and helping process. The worksheet is *never* to be used without a personal interview. The Significant Other Worksheet and the Child Screening Checklist can be used in a similar fashion.

COMPREHENSIVE MENTAL HEALTH ASSESSMENT FORMS

Completion of these forms follows the initial contact and provides more detailed demographic and client information. It may take anywhere from one to several contacts with the client to complete all relevant items on these forms. The crisis worker's assessment is based on information gathered from the client, significant others, from his or her own observations, and from clinical judgment. The rating scale descriptions and definitions found in the complete specifications (see footnote, p. 96) are intended to provide the worker with a more comprehensive understanding of the meaning of each assessment area. The examples cited in the definitions of each scale are just that, examples. The worker should recognize that there will be numerous other examples of real-life situations that are analogous to those provided. Also, while no rating of a person can be *completely* objective, the scale definitions provide a framework for eliminating subjective bias as much as possible. The "comment" space for each assessment area supports the subjective, unique response of each individual to various life crisis situations.

In keeping with the requirements of teamwork and immediacy of information access and action in the crisis model, the information on these forms is completed in handwriting, *not* stored in a dictaphone to be transcribed days or weeks later. One exception to this is the Termination Summary, because there is no longer a need for immediate access; also, the Summary may be used for interagency release of information, pending client consent. Another exception is for those who do routine writing with a typewriter or computer. The use of these forms is illustrated in part on the Initial Contact Sheet and Client Self-Assessment Worksheet in reference to the case example of George Sloan.*

---

*Samples from this record are reproduced in this chapter by permission of the Erie County Department of Mental Health, Buffalo, New York.

INITIAL CONTACT SHEET

Today's Date 1-15-89
Time 5:30 AM (PM)

Walk-in ____
Phone ____
Outreach Police
Written ____

ID # 101
SS # 123-98-456
Welfare/ Medicaid # ____

SERVICE REQUESTED FOR
Client's NAME George (First) O. (Middle) Sloan (Last)

Address 33 Random Avenue (Street) Middletown (City/Town) 01234 (Zip) Central (County)
Permanent ✓ Temporary ____ Catchment Area 3

Phone # 123-0987 Means of Transportation Ambulance
Directions to home (if outreach) ____
Sex Male ✓ Female ____ Date of Birth 1941 Age 48

SERVICE REQUESTED BY
☐ AGENCY Name ____
☐ OTHER Address ____
☐ SELF If Agency- Contact Person ____
Phone # ____
Time(s) seen by the agency ____

PRESENTING SITUATION/PROBLEM - What made you decide to seek help today?
(use other side if needed)

George Sloan, 48, was brought to E.R. by police following a suicide attempt by car crash. His intention was to die as he saw no way out of his personal and family problems. Has had heart trouble for 4 years. Was urged to quit second job and take office job in Police Dept. His 16-yr. old son's suspension from school adds to his sense of failure. Feels he has no one to talk to. Had considered suicide after last heart attack but support from his his wife prevented him then from crashing his car. While initially reluctant, Mr. Sloan now seems open to counseling assistance.

Have you talked with anyone about this? Yes ____ No ✓ Who? ____
Address ____ Phone # ____
Date of last contact- ____
Are you taking ANY medication now? Yes ✓ (If more than 3 begin list on MH-2) No ____
What? 1. nitroglycerine
2. ____
3. ____

CRISIS RATING How urgent is your need for help?
☒ Immediate (within minutes)
☐ Within a few hours
☐ Within 24 hours
☐ Within a few days
☐ Within a week or two

Comments
Recommend Mr. Sloan receive full assessment and crisis counseling while being treated for injuries from suicidal car accident, plus follow-up with entire family.

DISPOSITION (Check all that apply)
☒ Crisis
☒ Medical Emergency
☒ Assessment (specify)- Individual and Family
☐ Discharge Planning
☐ Expediting/Advocacy
☐ Other (explain)- ____
☒ Referral made to- Psychiatric Liason Service Confirmed—Yes ✓ No ____ Date 1-15-89
Date of Next Contract ____ Assigned to John Doe, MSW
Date of Assignment ____ Request taken by Jane Doe, RN

MH-1

COMPREHENSIVE MENTAL HEALTH ASSESSMENT

Client Self-Assessment Worksheet

Date 1-15-89 Name George Sloan

Circle one for each question.

1. **Physical Health**

   How is your health?

   Comments: No problems except for heart. Feel OK except for chest pain which is getting more frequent.

   Excellent / Good / **(Fair)** / Poor / Very Poor

2. **Self-Acceptance/Self-Esteem**

   How do you fell about yourself as a person?

   Comments: Not very good – especially when I think about my son's trouble that its probably my fault. Seems like I'm no good at anything lately.

   Excellent / Good / Fair / **(Poor)** / Very Poor

3. **Vocational/Occupational**

   (Includes student & homemaker)

   How would you judge your work/school situation?

   Comments: I can still do patrol work but the doctor says I should slow down.

   Excellent / Good / **(Fair)** / Poor / Very Poor

4. **Immediate Family**

   How are your relationships with your family and/or spouse?

   Comments: Ever since my first heart attack we seem to be going from bad to worse, especially with our son Arnold.

   Excellent / Good / Fair / **(Poor)** / Very Poor

5. **Intimate Relationship(s)**

   Is there anyone you feel really close to and can rely on?

   Comments: Not really. Things used to be better between my wife and me, but we seem to be drifting apart.

   Always / Usually / Sometimes / **(Rarely)** / Never

6. **Residential**

   How do you judge your housing situation?

   Comments:

   (Excellent) / Good / Fair / Poor / Very Poor

7. **Financial**

   How would you describe your financial situation?

   Comments: As long as I have my second job it's OK, but I don't like the idea of my wife working full time.

   Excellent / **(Good)** / Fair / Poor / Very Poor

8. **Decision Making ability**

   How satisfied are you with your ability to make life decisions?

   Comments: Mostly around the problems we have with Arnold.

   Always Very Satisfied / Almost Always Satisfied / **(Occasionally Dissatisfied)** / Almost Always Dissatisfied / Always Very Dissatisfied

Circle one for each question.

9. Life Philosophy/Goals

How satisfied are you with how your life goals are working for you?

Comments: I almost always felt satisfied before the heart trouble started 4 years ago.

- Always Very Satisfied
- Almost Always Satisfied
- Occasionally Dissatisfied
- (Almost Always Dissatisfied) [circled]
- Always Very Dissatisfied

10. Leisure Time/Community Involvement

How satisfied are you with your use of free time?

Comments: I don't have much free time, but I really like my work. I suppose our whole family could use more time together

- Always Very Satisfied
- Almost Always Satisfied
- (Occasionally Dissatisfied) [circled]
- Almost Always Dissatisfied
- Always Very Dissatisfied

11. Feeling Management

How comfortable are you with your fe. ings?

Comments: Just during the last few months I really started feeling depressed. My wife says I bottle everything up.

- Always Very Comfortable
- Almost Always Comfortable
- (Occasionally Uncomfortable) [circled]
- Almost Always Uncomfortable
- Always Very Uncomfortable

12. Violence Experienced

To what extent have you been troubled by physical violence against you?

Comments:

- (Never) [circled]
- Once only
- Several times within 6 months
- Once or twice a month
- Routinely (every day or so)

13. Lethality (self)

Is there any current risk of suicide for you?

Comments: I still can't see any way out except suicide, but right now I feel a little better from talking with you.

- No Predictable Risk of Suicide Now
- Low Risk of Suicide Now
- Moderate Risk of Suicide Now
- High Rsik of Suicide Now
- (Very High Risk of Suicide Now) [circled]

14. Lethality (other)

Is there any risk that you might physically harm someone?

Comments:

- (No Predictable Risk of Assault Now) [circled]
- Low Risk of Assault Now
- Moderate Risk of Assault Now
- High Risk of Assault Now
- Very High Risk of Assault Now

15. Substance Use (Drug and/or Alcohol)

Does use of drugs/alcohol interfere with performing your responsiblities?

Comments:

- (Never Interferes) [circled]
- Rarely Interferes
- Sometimes Interferes
- Frequently Intereferes
- Constantly Interferes

16. Legal

What is your tendency to get in trouble with the law?

Comments:

- (No Tendency) [circled]
- Slight Tendency
- Moderate Tendency
- Great Tendency
- Very Great Tendency

17. Agency Use

How successful are you with at getting help from agencies (or doctors) when you need it?

Comments: I don't like going to doctors and avoid it if at all possible.

- Always Successful
- (Usually Successful) [circled]
- Moderately Successful
- Seldom Successful
- Never Successful

Any additional comments?

MH-6A

COMPREHENSIVE MENTAL HEALTH ASSESSMENT
Client Assessment by Other Worksheet

Date ____________ Name ______________________ Circle one for each question.

1. Physical Health
   How is ____________'s physical health?
   Comments: ______________________
   Excellent
   Good
   Fair
   Poor
   Very Poor

2. Self-Acceptance/Self-Esteem
   How does ____________ feel about him/ herself as a person?
   Comments: ______________________
   Excellent
   Good
   Fair
   Poor
   Very Poor

3. Vocational/Occupational
   (Includes student & homemaker)
   How would you judge ____________'s work/school situation?
   Comments: ______________________
   Excellent
   Good
   Fair
   Poor
   Very Poor

4. Immediate Family
   How are ____________'s relationships with his/her family and/or spouse?
   Comments: ______________________
   Excellent
   Good
   Fair
   Poor
   Very Poor

5. Intimate Relationship(s)
   Is there anyone who ____________ feels really close to and can rely on?
   Comments: ______________________
   Always
   Usually
   Sometimes
   Rarely
   Never

6. Residential
   How do you judge ____________'s housing situation?
   Comments: ______________________
   Excellent
   Good
   Fair
   Poor
   Very Poor

7. Financial
   How would you describe ____________'s financial situation?
   Comments: ______________________
   Excellent
   Good
   Fair
   Poor
   Very Poor

8. Decision Making Ability
   How satisfied do you think ____________ is with his/her ability to make life decisions?
   Comments: ______________________
   Always Very Satisfied
   Almost Always Satisfied
   Occasionally Dissatisfied
   Almost Always Dissatisfied
   Always Very Dissatisfied

MH-5

Circle one for each question.

9. Life Philosophy/Goals
How satisfied is ________________ with how his/her life goals are working for him/her?
Comments: ________________

- Always Very Satisfied
- Almost Always Satisfied
- Occasionally Dissatisfied
- Almost Always Dissatisfied
- Always Very Dissatisfied

10. Leisure Time/Community Involvement
How satisfied is ________________ with his/her use of leisure time?
Comments: ________________

- Always Very Satisfied
- Almost Always Satisfied
- Occasionally Dissatisfied
- Almost Always Disatisfied
- Always Very Disatisfied

11. Feeling Management
How comfortable do you think ________________ is with his/her feelings?
Comments: ________________

- Always Very Comfortable
- Almost Always Comfortable
- Occasionally Uncomfortable
- Almost Always Uncomfortable
- Always Very Uncomfortable

12. Violence Experienced
To what extent is ________________ troubled by physical violence?
Comments ________________

- Never (so far as I know)
- Once only
- Several times within 6 months
- Once or twice a month
- Routinely (every day or so)

13. Lethality (self)
Is there any current risk of suicide for ________________?
Comments: ________________

- No Predictable Risk of Suicide Now
- Low Risk of Suicide Now
- Moderate Risk of Suicide Now
- High Risk of Suicide Now
- Very High Risk of Suicide Now

14. Lethality (other)
Is there any current risk that ________________ might physically harm someone?
Comments: ________________

- No Predictable Risk of Assault Now
- Low Risk of Assault Now
- Moderate Risk of Assault Now
- High Risk of Assault Now
- Very high Risk of Assualt Now

15. Substance Use (Drug and/or Alcohol)
Does use of drugs/alcohol interfere with ________________ performing his/her responsiblities?
Comments: ________________

- Never Interefere
- Rarely Interfere
- Sometimes Interfere
- Frequently Interferes
- Constantly Interferes

16. Legal
What is ________________'s tendency to get in trouble with the law?
Comments: ________________

- No Tendency
- Slight Tendency
- Moderate Tendency
- Great Tendency
- Very Great Tendency

17. Agency Use
How successful is ________________ at getting help from agencies/doctors when he/she needs it?
Comments: ________________

- Always Successful
- Usually Successful
- Moderately Successful
- Seldom Successful
- Never Successful

Any additional comments

Child Screening Checklist

Child Screening Checklist

ID#__________

Child's Full Name______________________________Sex____Birthdate__________

School Problems

a) poor grades___
b) does not get along with students___
c) does not get along with teachers___
d) suspended___
e) poor attendance___

Family Relationship Problems

does not get along with: father___ mother___ brothers___ sisters___
refuses to participate in family activities___
refuses to accept and perform family responsibilities___

Peer Relationship Problems

prefers to be alone___
does not associate with age mates___
prefers to be with adults___
not accepted by others___

Dyssocial Behavior

excessive lying___ hurts others___ hurts self___ destructive___ runaway___
substance use___ court involvement___ other___

Personal Adjustment Problems

temper tantrums___ easily upset___ speech problems___ sleep disturbances___
nervous mannerisms___ eating problems___ fearful___ lacks self-confidence___
clinging and dependent___ wetting, soiling, retention___ other___

Medical and Developmental Problems

chronic illness___ allergies___ physical handicaps___ accident prone___
seizures___ physical complaints___ lengthy or frequent hospitalizations___
medication___ surgery___ MR___ other___

Development Milestones (Administer to all pre-schoolers. Check behaviors present, up to and including present age.)

Age		Activity	Age		Activity
1	____	imitates speech sounds	2 1/2	____	climbs stairs, alternating feet
1	____	feeds self with fingers			
1	____	pulls self to feet	3	____	forms sentences
1 1/2	____	uses single words	3	____	dresses self--no fasteners
1 1/2	____	walks alone	4	____	recognizes three colors
2	____	understands simple directions	4	____	throws ball overhand
2	____	scribbles with pencil or crayon	5	____	speaks clearly
2 1/2	____	combines words into phrases	5	____	buttons clothing

In years or months, at what age do you think your child is functioning _____

Strengths and assets:

Comments:

Screened by ____________________________ Date ______________

COMPREHENSIVE MENTAL HEALTH ASSESSMENT

ID # ______________

Name ______________ First ______________ Middle ______________ Last ______________

Assessment Date ______________ Time ______ AM PM Place of Assessment ______________

RATING SCALE

1	2	3	4	5
High Functioning	High/Moderate Functioning	Moderate Functioning	Low/Moderate Functioning	Low Functioning

(W = Worker; C = Client; O = Other)

A. LIFE FUNCTIONS

1. Physical Health -Medical Information (Include relevant items; eg. illnesses, surgery, physical impairment, allergies, pregnancy, birth defects)

Current medical care Yes___ No___

Family Physician or Medical Clinic(s) NAME ______________

Address ______________ Last time seen ______________

Phone ______________

Medication Use	Name	Dosage	Duration	Physician/Clinic
1.				
2.				
3.				
4.				
5.				

Comments:

W ___ C ___ O ___

2. Self-Acceptance/Self-Esteem

Comments:

W ___ C ___ O ___

3. Vocational/Occupational ___Employed___Homemaker___Student___Other ___

Employer/School

Name ______________ Job Title (Functional) ______________

Address ______________ How long? ______________

Phone # ______________ Unemployed ______________ How long? ______________

(Optional) Education/Training ______________

Comments:

W ___ C ___ O ___

4. **Immediate Family** **Parental Status-**

Children? Yes____No____How many? ____________

Comments:

W C O

(Refer to Child Screening Checklist if appropriate)

5. **Intimate Relationships** Martial Status-

Never Married_____ Married_____ Widowed_____ Divorced_____ Separated____ Living Together_____ How Long _____

Comments:

W C O

6. Residential Living situation-

Lives alone____Lives with family____Other____(specify)______________________________

Comments:

W C O

SIGNIFICANT OTHER INFORMATION

Name	Nature of Relationship	Age	Grade *	Within Household	Outside Household Address	Phone

***Special Class Placement**

Name ______________________ ID# ______________

7. **Financial** Source of income ______________

Comments:

W C O

_ _ _

8. Decision Making/Cognitive Functions

Comments:

W C O

_ _ _

9. Life Philosophy/Goals

What are your life goals?

i. ______________
2. ______________
3. ______________

Comments:

W C O

_ _ _

10. Leisure Time/Community Involvement

Comments:

W C O

_ _ _

11. Feeling Management

Comments:

W C O

_ _ _

RATING SCALE

1	2	3	4	5
High Functioning	High/Moderate Functioning	Moderate Functioning	Low/Moderate Functioning	Low Functioning

B. SIGNALS OF DISTRESS

12. Violence Experienced History of Attacks and Injury

Date(s)________

____within last month
____within last 6 months
____within last year
____over 1 year

Outcomes

____Medical treatment only
____Shelter
____Referral (social service or marital counseling)
____Referral (psychiatry)
____ No medical or other service
____ Other

Describe attack (beating, rape, etc.):

Total number of attacks ______ Date of last attack ______________

Comments (include context, injury, aftermath):

W C O
— — —

13. Lethality-Self History of Self-Injury-

Date ________________Method______________________ Outcome__________________

_____ within last month
_____ within last 6 months
_____within last year
_____ over 1 year ago

____ Medical Treatment Only
____ Hosp. Intensive Care
____ Hosp. Psychiatric
____Out-pt. Follow-up
____No Treatment

Total number of suicide attempts________Date of last attempt ________________

Comments: (include ideation and threats)

W C O
— — —

14. Lethality-Other

History of Injury to Other

Date(s)________Method-

____within last month
____within last 6 months
____within last year
____over 1 year

Client	Outcome	Other
____	Medical Treatment Only	____
____	Hosp. Intensive Care	____
____	Hosp. Psychiatric	____
____	Out-pt. Follow-Up	____
____	No Treatment	____

Total number of assaults__________ Date of last assault__________

Comments: (include ideation and threats)

W C O
— — —

15. Substance Use-Drug and/or Alcohol

Other Drug Use (include alcohol use)

	Type	Present Use	Past Use	Duration
1.				
2.				
3.				
4.				
5.				
6.				

Comments:

W C O
— — —

Name ______________________________ **ID#** ______________

16. Legal

a. Pending Court Action Yes___ No ___ When ______________________
b. On Probation Yes___ No___ Probation Officer ______________________
c. On Parole Yes___ No___ Parole Officer ______________________
d. Conditional Discharge Yes___ No___

Comments:

W C O

_ _ _

17. **Agency Use**

Previous Mental Health Service Contacts

Outcare: **Name of Agency** ______________________ **Phone #** ______________
Contact Person ______________________ **Date of last Contact** ______________
Address ______________________

Incare: **Name of Agency** ______________________ **Phone #** ______________
Contact Person ______________________
Address ______________________ **Date of last Hosp.** ______________
Reason for Admission ______________________
How often ______________ **How long** ______________ **Avg. length of stay** ______________

Comments:

W C O

_ _ _

Optional Information

Religious Concerns ___ **Yes** ___ **No** ___ **What** ______________________
Ethnic Cultural Background Problems **Yes** ___ **No** ___ **What** ______________________

Narrative Summary of Assessment:

Assessed by ______________________ **Date** ______________ **MH-4**

SUMMARY

Some people are at greater risk of crisis than others. Identifying groups of people who are most likely to experience a crisis is helpful in recognizing individuals in crisis. People in crisis have typical patterns of thinking, feeling, and acting. There is no substitute for thorough assessment of whether a person is or is not in crisis. The assessment is the basis of the helping plan and can avoid many later problems, including unnecessary placement of people in institutions.

REFERENCES

Becker HS: *Outsider: Studies in the Sociology of Deviance*. Free Press, 1963.

Berger PL, Luckmann T: *The Social Construction of Reality*. Anchor-Doubleday, 1967.

Bittner E: Police discretion in the emergency apprehension of mentally ill persons. *Soc Problems*. 1967; 14(3):278–292.

Caplan G: *Principles of Preventive Psychiatry*. Basic Books, 1964.

Caplan G, Grunebaum H: Perspectives on primary prevention: A review. *Arch Gen Psych* 1967; 17:331–346.

Cloward RA, Piven FF. Hidden protest: The channeling of female innovation and protest. *Signs: J Women Culture Soc* 1979; 4:651–669.

Daniels AK: The social construction of military psychiatric diagnosis. In: *Symbolic Interaction*, 3rd ed. Manis JG, Meltzer BN(editors). Allyn Bacon, 1978.

Danish SJ, Smyer MA, Nowak CA: Developmental intervention: Enhancing life-event processes. *Life-span Devel Behav* 1980; 3:339–366.

Dressler DM: The management of emotional crises by medical practioners. *J Am Med Wom Assoc* 1973; 28(12):654–659.

Goffman E: *Asylums*. Doubleday, 1961.

Goffman E: *Stigma*. Prentice-Hall, 1963.

Golan N: When is a client in crisis? *Soc Casework* 1969; 50:389–394.

Gove W (editor): *The Labeling of Deviance*. Wiley, 1975.

Gove W: Sex differences in mental illness among adult men and women: An examination of four questions raised regarding whether or not women actually have higher rates. *Soc Sci Med* 1978; 12:187–198.

Hagey R, McDonough P: The problem of professional labeling. *Nurs Outlook*. 32(3):151–157, 1984.

Hansell N: *The Person in Distress*. Human Sciences Press, 1976.

Hoff LA: *Violence Against Women: A Social-cultural Network Analysis*. (PhD dissertation.) Boston University. University Microfilms International. No. 8422380, 1984.

Hoff LA, Miller N: *Programs for People in Crisis: A Guide for Educators, Administrators and Clinical Trainers*. Boston: Northeastern University Custom Book Program, 1987.

Holden C: Proposed new psychiatric diagnoses raise charges of gender bias. *Science* 1986; 231:327–328.

Holmes TH, Rahe RH: The social readjustment rating scale. *Psychosom Med* 1967; 11:213–218.

Illich I: *Tools for Conviviality*. Great Britain: Fontana/Collins, 1975.

Illich I: *Limits to Medicine*. Penguin Books, 1976.

Jacobson GF, Strickler M, Morley W: Generic and individual approaches to crisis intervention. *Am J Pub Health* 1968; 58:338–343.

Kaplan BH, Cassel J, Gove S: Social support. *Med Care* 1977; 15:47–58.

Lemert WM: *Soc Path* McGraw-Hill, 1951.

McCarthy PR, Knapp SL: Helping styles of crisis interveners, psychotherapists and untrained individuals. *Am J Comm Psych* 1984; 12(5):623–627.

Polak P: The crisis of admission. *Soc Psych* 1976; 2:150–157.

Polak P: A model to replace psychiatric hospitalization. *J Nerv Ment Dis* 1976; 162:13–22.

Rabin J, Keefe K, and Burton M: Enhancing services for sexual minority clients: A community mutual health approach. *Social Work*, July–August: 294:298, 1986.

Rapaport L: The state of crisis: Some theoretical considerations. In: *Crisis Intervention: Selected Readings*. Parad H (editor). New York: Family Service Association of America, 1965.

Rosenhan DL: On being sane in insane places. *Science* 1973; 179:250–258. Also reprinted in Schwartz HD, Kart CS: *Dominant Issues in Medical Sociology*. Addison-Wesley, 1978; and in: *Transcultural Nursing*. Brink PJ (editor). Prentice-Hall, 1976.

Sales E, Baum M, Shore B: Victim readjustment following assault. *J Soc Iss* 1984; 40(1):117–136.

Scheff TJ (editor): *Labelling Madness*. Prentice-Hall, 1975.

Schulberg HC, Sheldon A: The probability of crisis and strategies for preventive intervention. *Arch Gen Psych* 1968; 18:553–558.

Sifneos PE: A concept of "emotional crisis." *Ment Hyg* 1960; 44:169–179.

Stark E, Flitcraft A, Frazier W: Medicine and patriarchal violence: The social construction of a "private" event. *Int J Health Serv* 1979; 9:461–493.

Stein DM, Lambert MJ: Telephone counseling and crisis intervention: A review. *Am J Comm Psych* 1984; 12(1):101–126.

Wells JO, Hoff LA (editors): *Certification Standards Manual*, 3rd Ed Denver: American Association of Suicidology, 1984.

Walfish S: Crisis telephone counselors' views of clinical interaction situations. *Comm Ment Health J* 1983; 19(3):219–226.

Zborowski M: Cultural components in responses to pain. *J Soc Iss* 1952; 8:16–30. Also reprinted in: *The Sociology of Health and Illness: Critical Perspectives*, Conrad P, Kern R (editors), St. Martin's Press 1981.

CHAPTER 4

Helping People in Crisis

GENERAL HELPING CONTEXTS

In the first chapter we considered broad approaches to helping people in crisis and precrisis states, including preventive intervention. We also discussed differences and similarities between the crisis model and other modes of helping. In Chapter 2 we examined the origins, development, and individual manifestations of crisis. Generic, individual, and social approaches to helping were differentiated. In the third chapter we shifted the discussion from the general crisis experience to the assessment process with particular persons in crisis. The focus in this chapter is on the interpersonal context of crisis management and on specific strategies for assisting people who are acutely upset: communication and rapport, planning, contracting, and working through the crisis toward a positive outcome. The principles and techniques suggested can be applied in a wide variety of crisis intervention settings: homes, hospitals, clinics, hotlines, and alternative crisis services. While these principles and techniques can be varied and adapted according to professional training, personal preference, and setting, the fundamental ideas remain.

COMMUNICATION AND RAPPORT: THE IMMEDIATE CONTEXT OF CRISIS WORK

Crisis management strategies are not likely to work if we have failed to establish rapport with the person in crisis. Just as assessment is part of the helping process (King 1971), rapport and effective communication are integrated throughout all stages of crisis management: assessment, planning, intervention, and follow-up.

THE NATURE AND PURPOSE OF COMMUNICATION

Crisis intervention is not anything if it is not human. Humans are distinguished from the animal kingdom by our ability to produce and use symbols, to create meaning out of the events and circumstances of our lives. Through language and nonverbal communication we let our fellow humans know what we think and feel about life and each other, for example, "Life is not worth living without her" (a person contemplating suicide after divorce because life without one's cherished companion is perceived as meaningless), "What did I do to deserve this" (a rape victim or fatally ill person accounting for the event through self-blame). Communication is the medium through which:

- We struggle to survive (for example, giving away prized possessions or stating "I don't care anymore" conveys a "cry for help" following serious loss).
- Meaningful human communion is developed and maintained (such as giving and receiving support during stress and crisis).
- We bring stability and organization into our lives (such as sorting out the chaotic elements of a traumatic event with a caring person).
- Social and political struggles at the national and international level are negotiated.

When communication fails, a person may feel alone, abandoned, worthless, and unloved, or conflict and tension may be created in interpersonal relations. The most tragic result of failed communication is violence toward self and others; at the societal level this translates into war. Such destructive outcomes of failed communication are more probable in acute crisis situations. Given the importance of communication in the development and resolution of crisis, let us consider some of the factors that influence our interaction with people in crisis.

FACTORS INFLUENCING COMMUNICATION

Many sources provide theoretical knowledge about human communication: psychology, sociology, cultural anthropology, ecology, and linguistics (for example, Gerhardt 1979; Hall 1969; Leach 1976; Pluckhan 1978; Trudgill 1974; Vetterling-Braggin, Elliston, and English 1977, pp. 105–170). These sources provide important insights into communication as it applies to crisis work.

Psychology

As noted in the previous chapter, cognitive functions are a key aspect of crisis response and coping. The way one perceives stressful events influences one's feelings about these events and how these feelings are communicated to or withheld from others. Major incongruities between a life event and one's perception of the nature and meaning of the event, and the expression of feelings culturally inappropriate to the event may point to mental impairment and greater vulnerability to stressful events. A person who feels depressed and unworthy of help will usually have difficulty in expressing feelings such as anger, which might be appropriate to certain traumatic events (violent attacks by others). A worker who feels insecure with the crisis model of helping can have difficulty communicating effectively; the worker may talk too much, or may fail to be appropriately active when the situation calls for worker initiative.

Sociology

Sociological factors affecting communication in crisis situations spring from society at large as well as the subculture of various crisis service delivery systems. These include status, role, and gender factors, and political and economic factors (Campbell-Heider and Pollock 1987). For example, a nurse may not communicate concern to a person in the hospital suspected of being suicidal, assuming that "assessment for suicide risk is the physician's responsibility." Or, the policies and economics of insurance and hospital care may prevent many consumers from realizing that community-based help is often more appropriate than hospital care. Similarly, the predominance of individualistic approaches may obscure the highly effective group medium of helping people in crisis (see Chapter 5).

Cultural Anthropology

Insights from cultural anthropology are pivotal in communication with people in crisis. Our sensitivity to another person's values and beliefs is crucial to understanding what life events mean to different people—their personal definition of the situation. Members of particular cultural groups are almost invariably characterized by a certain degree of ethnocentrism—the conviction that one's own value and belief system is superior. At its best, ethnocentrism is a necessary ingredient of cultural identity and a person's sense of belonging to a social group. At its worst, ethnocentrism can become exaggerated and destructive, for example, in resolving community problems among different ethnic groups. Members of a cultural group may impose their values on others, assume an attitude of superiority about their own customs, or be disdainful toward people unlike themselves. Pluckhan (1978, p. 117) refers to this as "internal noise," which interferes with effective communication.

It is important to remember in crisis work that, for many people, certain values are worth dying for. Needless to say, if an *imposed* (rather than negotiated) crisis management plan contradicts one's dearly held values and threatens one's sense of self-mastery, the chances of success are minimal. Examples of values in common life crises include the meaning of death, illness, and health, the issue of seeking and accepting help, or the meaning of *how* help is offered; for example, a person contemplating suicide but seeking "one last chance" to get some help may interpret a prescription for sleeping pills as "an invitation to die" (Jourard 1970). Crisis workers should also be aware that most human service professionals in the United States hold values of the white middle class majority.

Ecology

Environmental factors are intricately tied to cultural values regarding privacy. Examples from the previous chapters suggest that the environment in which crisis service is offered influences the outcome of the crisis. If a person lacks privacy (such as in a busy hospital emergency room) the likelihood of successful communication during crisis is reduced. Thus, a serious commitment to crisis service delivery in emergency rooms would provide for separate rooms to facilitate the kind of communication necessary for people in crisis, such as rape victims and families of heart attack victims. The skills of an individual crisis worker are useless if staffing and material factors prevent the effective application of those skills (Hoff and Miller 1987).

Similarly, in crisis work done by police and outreach staff, such as mediating a marital fight, spatial factors can be critical in saving lives. As Hicks and Dolphin (1979, p. 53) state, to many Americans "a man's home is his castle," and thus is a personalized and defended territory. Inattention to these unstated but culturally shared experiences can result in violent *behavioral* (nonverbal) communication about this hidden dimension of public and private life (Hall 1969). Police officers often refer to the "sixth sense" they develop through street experience and sensitivity to environmental factors related to crisis. With crime on the increase, would-be victims should be advised to sensitize themselves to various aspects of their environment that may signal a crisis of violence, that is, develop "street smarts" to protect themselves. Police or neighborhood associations are good avenues for obtaining this kind of information.

Sociolinguistics

Sociolinguistics refers to social theories of language used in communication. It examines how social factors (race, sex, class, region, and religion) influence language and how language can condition thought and social action. Language is the common medium for verbal communication between particular linguistic communities. It is also the most observable avenue for ascertaining the ideas, beliefs, and attitudes of various cultural groups. Insensitivity to an individual's linguistic interpretation can reflect a lack of appreciation of cultural values. Crisis workers need to have something in common linguistically with various ethnic groups in order to serve them within the framework of their value system.

Language, then, serves as an important link between individual and social approaches to crisis. For example, an essential aspect of *individual* crisis work with a victim of rape or racially motivated violence is to talk about the event, work through feelings, and develop an action plan (such as reporting to the police). The *social* element affecting this kind of crisis concerns the cultural message to women and minorities that suggests to them that they are responsible for their victimization.* Such cultural messages are revealed in conversation and will influence how women and members of racial minorities respond emotionally, cognitively, and behaviorally to violent events.

The written word similarly conveys the beliefs and values of a cultural community. For example, many pages ago in this book the reader will have observed the nonmedical and nonsexist choice of language. This usage is based on the recognition that language is a powerful conveyor of social and cultural norms governing social status and behavior—in this case, relationships between women and men, and the contrast between medical and developmental approaches to crisis intervention.

Crisis workers will discover other examples in which sensitivity in communication affects interactions with people in crisis. Communication is not only a necessary medium for carrying out the crisis intervention process, it is also an integral aspect of the helping process itself.

RELATIONSHIPS, COMMUNICATION, AND RAPPORT

The most *technically* flawless communication skills are useless in the absence of rapport with the person in crisis. Conversely, if our values, attitudes, and feelings about a person are respectful, unprejudiced, and based on true concern, those values will almost always be conveyed to the person regardless of possible *technical* errors in communication. This point can hardly be overemphasized. For example, it is commonplace to hear the expression: "I thought he was suicidal but I didn't say anything because I was afraid I'd say the wrong thing." This argument represents a gross misconception of the nature of language. If we truly are concerned whether a person lives or dies, this concern will almost invariably be conveyed in what we say, unless we:

- Deliberately say the opposite of what we mean.
- Are mentally disturbed with an accompanying distortion and contradiction between thought and language.
- Lack knowledge about suicidal people, feel anxious about how the person will respond to our sincere message, and therefore fail to deliver the message (see Chapter 6).

Thus, crisis workers must learn the technical aspects of skillful communication with people who are upset; they must avoid asking "Why?"

*Consider, for example, the cultural double standard regarding male and female sexual behavior. Also, on a recent television documentary, a high school student stated in an interview that "Blacks wouldn't get hurt if they just stayed in their own section of town." See Ryan, *Blaming the Victim* (1971).

and questions leading to yes or no answers and must not make judgments or offer unrealistic reassurance.* But it is equally important to establish rapport with the person and foster the relationship necessary for the distressed individual to accept our help. Truax and Carkhuff (1967) make this point by demonstrating that, more than theoretical and technical knowledge, the *quality of the relationship* we establish affects the outcome of our work with people in crisis. In particular this includes the worker's ability to convey empathy, caring, and sincerity (McGee 1974, p. 274).†

In our efforts to establish rapport and use our relationshipwith people as a vehicle of help, we should strive for two objectives.

1. We should make the distressed person feel understood. We can convey understanding through our response by using reflective statements such as "You seem to be very hurt and upset by what has happened," and "Sounds like you're very angry." If our perception of what the person is feeling is incorrect, the words "seem to be" and "sounds like" provide an opening for the person to explain his or her perception of the traumatic event. The expression "I understand" should generally be avoided as it may be perceived as presumptuous; there is always the possibility that we do *not* truly understand. Parents who suffer the loss of a child say that *no* one but a similarly grieving parent can truly understand.

2. If we are unclear about the nature or extent of what the person feels or is troubled by, we need to ask questions or make a comment that will convey our desire and *attempt* to understand, for example, "Could you tell me more about that?" . . . "How do you feel about what has happened?" . . . "I'm not sure I understand—could you tell me what you mean by that?"

Besides these techniques for establishing rapport there are other means of removing barriers to effective communication (Pluckhan 1978, pp. 116–128):

1. Become aware of the internal and external noises that may inhibit our ability to communicate sincerely.
2. Avoid giving double messages. For example, we may convey concern at a verbal level but contradict our message by posture, facial gestures, or failure to give undivided attention. Traditionally, this is known as the "double bind" in communication (Bateson 1958).
3. Avoid unwarranted assumptions about other people's lives, feelings, and values.

*For further study of communication techniques, see some of the standard texts on this topic, such as Budd and Ruben (1972), Stewart and Cash (1974), and Brooks and Emmert (1976).

†Truax and Carkhuff (1967) also found that nonprofessional persons are highly capable of creating such relationships and that mental health professionals' demonstration of empathy *decreases* as the length of time from their original training *increases*.

4. Keep communication clear of unnecessary professional and technical jargon, and when technical terminology is unavoidable, translate it.
5. Be aware of the trust-risk factor in communication. We must periodically examine whether we are trustworthy and what kind of social, cultural, and personal situations warrant the trust needed to accept help from another (Pluckhan 1978, pp. 88–89). Also, keep in mind that some people are distrustful not because of us, but because they have been betrayed by others they trusted.
6. Take advantage of opportunities to improve self-awareness, self-confidence, and sensitivity to factors affecting communication (human relations courses, biofeedback training, assertiveness workshops).

These suggestions represent a small part of the field of communication as it pertains to crisis work. Since communication is inseparable from culture and human life, its importance in helping people in crisis can hardly be overestimated.* Keeping in mind these contextual aspects of crisis work, let us proceed to specific strategies of planning, intervention, and follow-up in the crisis management process. In the Crisis Paradigm these steps are illustrated in the intertwined circles in the third box.

PLANNING WITH A PERSON OR FAMILY IN CRISIS

IMPORTANCE OF PLANNING

There is no substitute for a good plan for crisis resolution. Without careful planning and direction, a helper can only add to the confusion already experienced by the person in crisis. Some may argue that in certain crisis situations there is no time to plan, as life and death issues may be at stake. This, rather than excusing the need for planning, only underscores its urgency. A good plan can be formulated in a few minutes by someone who knows the signs of crisis, is confident in his or her own ability to help, and is able to enlist additional, immediate assistance in cases of impasse or of life and death emergency.

*See Pluckhan (1978) and Haley (1963) for further theoretical discussion of this topic.

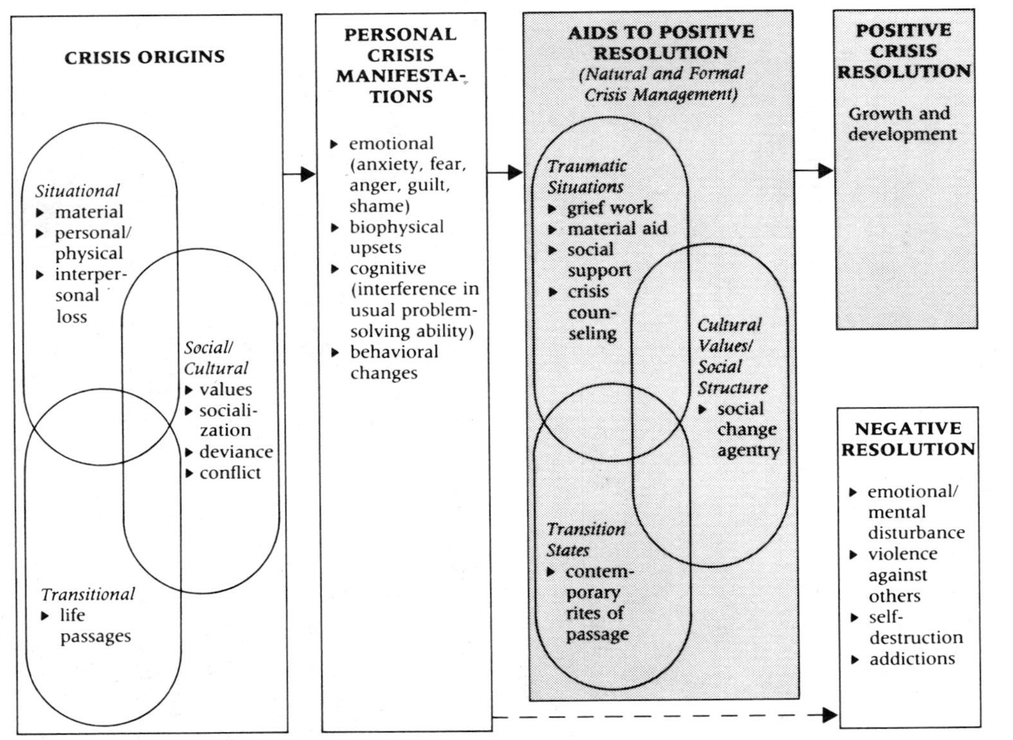

CRISIS PARADIGM

Crisis origins, manifestations, and outcomes, and the respective functions of crisis management have an interactional relationship. The intertwined circles represent the distinct yet interrelated origins of crisis and aids to positive resolution, even though personal manifestations are often similar. The solid line from origins to positive resolution illustrates the opportunity for growth and development through crisis; the broken line depicts the potential danger of crisis in the absence of appropriate aids.

Case Example: Robert

A police officer was called to the home of Robert (who had recently been discharged from a mental hospital) because he had angrily barricaded himself in the bathroom and was making threatening comments to his family. On arrival, the officer learned that a psychiatrist-social worker team was already at the home. They were frightened by Robert's threats and were unable to persuade him to unlock the door. The officer identified himself and asked Robert to open the door. He refused. The officer then forced the door open (there was no formal discussion between the officer and the mental health team). Robert became frightened and stabbed the officer in the shoulder with a kitchen knife.

This case illustrates several points:

1. Action occurred *before* planning. As a result, the combined resources of the professional mental health and police systems were not used to their fullest capacity.
2. When police officers and others are injured by mentally disturbed persons, the injury is often related to the worker's inadequate training in crisis intervention (see Violence Against Police Officers, Mental Health Workers, and Crisis Workers in Chapter 8). Bard (1972), in his action research in New York City, found that police deaths and injuries on the job were significantly reduced after officers received specific training in crisis intervention.
3. The time spent *planning*—even if it is only a few minutes—can prevent injuries and save lives (see Chapter 8 for a continuation of this case).

ASSESSMENT AND PLANNING LINKAGE

A useful plan consists of more than vague or haphazardly formulated intentions. Planning with a person for crisis resolution follows assessment that the person is in a crisis or precrisis state. The information needed for the plan is obtained from careful assessment (see Chapter 3). The following key questions represent a more general summary of the 17 items included in the assessment forms (see Service Forms in Chapter 3).

1. To what extent has the crisis disrupted the person's normal life pattern?

2. Is she or he able to go to school or hold a job?
3. Can the person handle the responsibilities involved in the activities of daily living, for example, eating and personal hygiene?
4. Has the crisis situation disrupted the lives of others?
5. Has the person been victimized by crime?
6. Is the person suicidal, homicidal, or both?
7. Does the person seem to be close to despair?
8. Has the high level of tension distorted the person's perception of reality?
9. Is the person's usual support system present, absent, or exhausted?
10. What are the resources of the individual helper or agency in relation to the person's assessed needs?

The answers to such questions provide the worker with essential data for the intervention plan, which involves: a thinking process; an ability to draw relationships between events and the way the person is thinking, feeling, and acting; and an ability to formulate some problem-solving mechanisms and solutions with the person and his or her family (McGee 1974).

To assure that the plan is specific to a particular person's crisis response and corresponding needs, a worker may set priorities by checking the assessment form for ratings of 3, 4, or 5 (the lower functional levels). The worker should then directly ask the person which problem or issue seems the most urgent, for example, "It seems there are a lot of things upsetting you right now. . . . Which of these is the most important for you to get immediate help with?"

DECISION COUNSELING

Skill in decision counseling (Hansell 1970) is intrinsic to the crisis assessment, planning, and intervention process. Decision counseling is cognitively oriented and allows the upset person to put distorted thoughts, chaotic feelings, and disturbed behavior into some kind of order. The person is encouraged to:

- Search for boundaries of the problem. For example: "How long has this been troubling you?" "In what kind of situation do you find yourself getting most upset?"
- Appraise the meaning of the problems and how they can be mastered. "How has your life changed since your wife's illness?"
- Make a decision about various solutions to the problem.

"What do you think you can do about this?" Or, "What have you done so far about this problem?"

- Test the solutions in a clear-cut action plan. (See "Developing a Service Contract" in this chapter.)

In decision counseling the crisis worker facilitates crisis resolution by helping the person decide:

- What problem is to be solved? "Of the things you are troubled by, what is it that you want help with now?"
- How is it to be solved? "What do you think would be most helpful?"
- When should it be solved? "How about coming in after school today with your husband and your son?"
- Where should it be solved? "Yes, we do make home visits. Tell me more about your situation so we can decide if a home or office visit is best."
- Who should be involved in solving it? "Who else have you talked to about this problem who could be helpful?"

Decision counseling also includes setting goals for the future and forming an alternative action plan to be used if the current plan fails or goals are not achieved.

In decision counseling the counselor must have thorough knowledge of the person's functional level and of his or her network of social attachments. Used effectively, this technique makes maximum use of the turmoil of crisis to: (a) assess current coping ability, (b) develop new problem-solving skills, (c) establish more stable emotional attachments, (d) improve the person's social skills, and (e) increase the person's competence and satisfaction with life patterns (Hansell 1970).

DEVELOPING A SERVICE CONTRACT

Once an action plan is agreed on by the person in crisis and the worker, it is important to confirm the plan in a service contract. The nature of the service contract is implied in the fact that the plan for crisis intervention is mutually arrived at by the helper and the person in crisis. If the person in crisis comes to the attention of professional crisis counselors or mental health professionals with training in crisis intervention, the service contract should be formalized in writing. It is implicit in the contract that:

- The person is essentially in charge of his or her own life.
- The person is able to make decisions.
- The crisis counseling relationship is one between partners.

- Both parties to the contract—the person in crisis and the crisis counselor—have rights and responsibilities, as spelled out in the contract.
- The relationship between the helper and person in crisis is a complementary one rather than a superior-subordinate one.

Institutional psychiatry and traditional mental health professions in the United States have come under serious attack in recent years for violating civil rights (Gotkin and Gotkin 1975, Kelly and Weston 1974, Szasz 1970). Individuals have been locked up, medicated, and "treated" with electric shock against their will in mental institutions. Many human rights and consumer groups have protested such treatment (Nader 1975). Currently, the Alliance for the Mentally Ill (AMI) does advocacy work around these issues. Protection of human rights has become an important public issue, making the idea of *contract* crucial.

The importance of making crisis services available to people who need them has been stressed. Equally important is the recognition that people have the right to either use or refuse these services. The formal service contract is one of the safeguards for protecting that right. In addition to protecting a person's basic right to voluntary service and treatment, the contract establishes the following:

1. What the client can expect from the counselor.
2. What the counselor can expect from the client.
3. How the two parties will achieve the goals on which they have agreed.
4. The target dates for achieving the goals defined in the contract.

Nothing goes into a contract that is not mutually developed by client and counselor through decision counseling. Both parties sign the contract and retain copies. Receiving help on a contractual basis has these effects: (a) reducing the possibility of the helping relationship degenerating into a master-slave or rescuer-victim stance, (b) enhancing the self-mastery and social skills of the client, (c) facilitating growth through a crisis experience, (d) reducing the incidence of failure in helping a person in crisis. The example of a service contract is from the record system described in Chapter 3.

EVALUATING THE CRISIS MANAGEMENT PLAN

If planning is indeed as important as has been suggested, it is useful to have some criteria by which to evaluate our plan (Caplan and Grunebaum 1967). The following characteristics of a crisis management plan can be used in several ways: (a) as a self-evaluation tool, (b) as a checklist for evaluating what might be missing or why progress seems to elude us as well as the

Service Contract

SERVICE CONTRACT

S=Satisfied U=Unsatisfied

Name________________ ID# ________

Significant Other ________________

Case Manager ________________

Back up________________

Code

1. Physical
2. Self-Acceptance
3. Vocational
4. Immediate Family
5. Intimate Relationship(s)
6. Residential
7. Financial
8. Decision Making
9. Life Philosophy
10. Leisure Time/ Community Involvement
11. Feeling Management
12. Lethality (self)
13. Lethality (other)
14. Substance Use
15. Legal
16. Agency Use
17. Violence Experienced

Code #	Date	Problem Statement	Method/Technique/Tasks for achieved goals (include review date)	Expected Outcome (include date)	Goal Achieved	
					S or U	Date

MH-7

person in crisis, (c) by supervisors responsible for monitoring client service, (d) by consultants who are brainstorming with workers about complex or difficult crisis situations.

1. *Developed with the person in crisis.* A good intervention plan is developed in active collaboration with the person in crisis and significant people in his or her life. Basically, the underlying philosophy is that people can help themselves with varying degrees of help from others. Doing things *to* a person in crisis without his or her active participation can lead to failure in crisis intervention. If the goals for crisis intervention and problem solving are formulated by the helper alone, then those goals are practically worthless—no matter how appropriate they appear. Inattention to this important element of the planning process is probably responsible for more failures in crisis resolution than any other single factor. Making decisions for the person in crisis violates the growth and development concept basic to crisis intervention. The person may feel devalued. If a worker takes over, it implies that the person cannot participate in matters of vital concern to him- or herself. When a counselor assumes control, other important characteristics of the plan are often overlooked, for example, attention to the person's cultural pattern.

2. *Problem oriented.* The plan focuses on immediate, concrete problems that directly contribute to the crisis, that is, the hazardous event and precipitating factor. For example, a teenage daughter has run away, a woman gets a diagnosis of breast cancer, a man learns he has AIDS. The plan should avoid probing into basic personality patterns or underlying psychological or marital problems contributing to the person's risk of crisis. These are properly the aim of psychotherapy or ongoing counseling, which the individual may choose *after* resolution of the immediate crisis. Exploration of previous successes and failures in problem solving *is* appropriate in the crisis model.

3. *Appropriate to person's functional level and dependency needs.* The helper assesses how the person is thinking, feeling, and acting. If the individual is so anxious that he or she cannot think straight and make decisions (as assessed through decision counseling), the helper takes a more active role than might otherwise be indicated. In general, a crisis worker should never make a decision for another unless thorough assessment reveals that the person is unable to make decisions independently. Put another way, the person in crisis is allowed to borrow some ego functions of the helper on a temporary basis.

If the person is feeling pent up with emotion, the plan should include adequate time to express suppressed feelings. It is legitimate to give specific directions for action if the person's behavior and thinking are chaotic. Success in this kind of action plan is based on the intrinsic belief in the person's ability to help him- or herself once the acute crisis phase is over. A firm, confident approach, based on accurate assessment and respect for the person, inspires confidence and restores a sense of order and independence to the individual in crisis.

Success in this aspect of planning implies an understanding of human interdependence. Obviously, it is necessary for the person in crisis to depend on others for help in resolving the crisis constructively. A healthy state of *inter*dependence is considered a good balance between the person's dependence and independence needs. Some individuals are too dependent most of the time; others are too independent most of the time. The excessively independent person will probably have a hard time accepting his or her own need for more dependence on others during a crisis. Asking for help is viewed as a loss of self-esteem. The very dependent person, on the other hand, will have the tendency to behave more dependently during a crisis than the situation warrants.

These dependency considerations underscore the need for thorough assessment of the person's strengths, resources, and usual coping abilities. A good rule of thumb is never to do something *for* a person until it is determined with a fair degree of certainty that the individual *cannot* do it alone. Basically, we all resent extreme dependence on others, as it keeps us from growing to our full potential. It is equally important that we, as helpers, do not fail to do for a person in crisis what assessment reveals he or she cannot do alone. The crisis intervention model calls for active participation by the worker. However, the crisis counselor needs to know when to let go, so the person can once again take charge of his or her life. This is more easily done by workers who are self-aware and self-confident.

4. *Consistent with person's culture and life-style.* Inattention to a person's life-style and cultural patterns can result in the failure of a seemingly perfect plan. We must be sensitive to the person's total situation and careful not to impose our own value system on a person whose life-style and values are different. Various cultural, ethnic, and religious groups have distinct patterns of response to events such as death, physical illness, divorce, and pregnancy out of wedlock. These differences merit respect by the helper (see Factors Influencing Communication in this chapter).

5. *Inclusive of significant other(s) and social network.* If people in crisis are viewed as social beings, then a plan that excludes their social network is incomplete. Since crises occur when there is a serious disruption in normal social transactions or in the way one perceives oneself in the social milieu, planning must attend to these important social factors. This is true even when the person's closest social contacts are hostile and contribute significantly to the crisis.

It is tempting for a crisis worker to avoid dealing with family members who appear to want the troubled person out of their lives. Still, significant others should be brought into the planning, at least to clarify whether or not they are a future resource for the person. In the event that the person is no longer really wanted (for example, by a divorcing spouse), the plan will include a means of helping the individual accept this reality and identify new social contacts. Put another way, our plan should include conscious consideration of the question: "Is the family (or other significant person) part of the problem or part of the solution?" (see Family and Community Assessment in Chapter 3, and Chapter 5).

Case Example: Jerry Bronson and Brenda

Jerry Bronson, a trainee in a crisis intervention group, played the role of counselor for Brenda, age 15. Brenda had run away from her mother's home where she fought constantly with her mother and her mother's second husband. She wanted to live with her father and his second wife. Brenda walked into a crisis center asking for help with the conflict she felt about her divorced parents. While she clearly wanted to live with her father, she also hoped to smooth things over with her mother.

After determining that Brenda was not suicidal and had a place to stay, Jerry's suggested approach was to exclude Brenda's mother from the helping process. His crisis trainer, however, demonstrated the importance of including Brenda's mother in the intervention plan even though Brenda chose not to live with her. Not to do so would ignore an important part of Brenda's conflict and hamper eventual resolution of her crisis.

6. *Realistic, time limited, and concrete.* A good crisis intervention plan is realistic regarding needs and resources. For example, a person too sick or without transportation or money should not be expected to come to an office for help. The plan should also have a clear time frame. The person or family in crisis needs to know that actions A, B, and C are planned to occur at points X, Y, and Z. This kind of structure is reassuring to someone in crisis. It provides concrete evidence that:

- Something definite will happen to change the present state of discomfort.
- The seemingly endless confusion and chaos of the crisis experience can be handled in terms familiar to the person.
- The entire plan has a clearly anticipated ending point.

For the person who fears he or she is "going crazy," or who finds it difficult to depend on others, it is reassuring to anticipate that within a certain period of time events will probably be under control again.

An effective plan is also concrete in terms of place and circumstances. For example: family crisis counseling sessions will be held at the crisis clinic at 7:00 PM twice a week; one session will be held at daughter Nancy's school and will include her guidance counselor, the school nurse, and the principal.

7. *Dynamic and renegotiable.* A dynamic plan is not carved in marble; it is alive, meaningful, and flexible. It is specific to *this person* with his or her unique problems and allows for ongoing changes in the person's life. It

should also include a mechanism for dealing with changes if the original plan no longer fits the person's needs, so that certain outcomes will not be perceived as failures.

CASE EXAMPLE: MARY

Mary calls a crisis hotline at 11:00 PM, very upset over the news of her husband's threat of divorce. After 45 minutes, she and the telephone counselor agree that she will call a local counseling center the next day for an appointment. She is given the name and phone number to aid in making the contact. The plan includes an agreement that Mary will call back to the hotline for renegotiation if for any reason she is unable to complete the planned contact.

A person who doubts whether anything can be done to help should be assured, "If this doesn't work, we'll examine why and try something else." This feature of a plan is particularly important for people who distrust service agencies or who have experienced repeated disappointment in their efforts to obtain help.

8. *Inclusive of follow-up.* Finally, a good plan includes an agreement for follow-up contact after apparent resolution of the crisis. This feature is too often neglected by crisis and mental health workers. If it is not initially placed in the plan and the service contract, it probably will not be done.

WORKING THROUGH A CRISIS: INTERVENTION STRATEGIES

Effective crisis management fosters growth and avoids negative, destructive outcomes of traumatic events. Helping a person through healthy crisis resolution means carrying out the plan that was developed after assessment. The worker's crisis intervention techniques should follow from the way the person in crisis is thinking, feeling, and acting and should be tailored to the distinct origins of the crisis (see Crisis Paradigm).

The specific manifestations of ineffective crisis coping are spelled out in the assessment form illustrated in Chapter 3. The 17 life areas and signals of distress represent a detailed picture of biophysical, emotional, cognitive, and behavioral functioning. Ineffective crisis coping in the emotional, cognitive, and/or behavioral realms can be thought of as a red flag signaling possible negative crisis outcomes. It is like a "go" sign for mobilizing aids to positive crisis resolution, that is, natural and formal crisis management strategies. Having assessed the person's coping ability in each of the functional areas, the crisis worker assists the person to avoid negative outcomes and move toward growth and development while resolving the crisis. The following crisis intervention strategies are suggested as ways to achieve this goal.*

LOSS, CHANGE, AND GRIEF WORK

No matter what the origin of one's distress, a common theme observed in people in crisis is that of loss, including loss of:

- Spouse, child, or other loved one.
- Health, property, and physical security.
- Job, home, and country.
- Familiar social role.
- Freedom and bodily integrity.
- The opportunity to live beyond one's youth.

From this it follows that a pivotal aspect of successful crisis resolution is grief work.

Bereavement is our response to any acute loss. Our rational, social nature implies attachment to other human beings and a view of ourselves and life in relationship to the rest of the world: our family, friends, pets, and home. Death and the changes following any loss are as inevitable as the ocean tide, but because loss is so painful emotionally, our natural tendency is to avoid coming to terms with it immediately and directly.

Grief work, therefore, takes time. Grief is not a set of symptoms to be treated, but rather, a process of suffering that a bereaved person goes through on the way to a new life without the lost person, status, or object of love. It includes numbness and somatic distress (tightness in the throat, need to sigh, shortness of breath, lack of muscular power), pining and searching, anger and depression, and finally a turning point toward recovery (Lindemann 1944, Parkes 1975). Care of the bereaved is a communal responsibility (Parkes 1975, p. 210). Traditional societies, however, have assisted the bereaved much more effectively than have industrialized ones. Material prosperity and the high value placed on individual strength and accomplishment tend to dull one's awareness of personal mortality and the need for social support. This issue will be discussed more fully in Chapter 11, Stress and Change During Life Passages, and in Chapter 12, People with

*The use of any psychosocial techniques of crisis intervention presumes assessment of medical emergency needs and appropriate linkage to medical resources. Common instances of such intervention are in the event of a suicide attempt, victimization by crime, or injury by accident. The integration of crisis intervention with medical emergency treatment is considered in detail in Chapters 7, 8, and 10.

AIDS: A Crisis Update. Because reconciliation with loss is so important in avoiding destructive outcomes of crises, the main features of bereavement reactions are included here:

1. A process of realization that eventually replaces denial and avoidance of the memory of the lost person, status, or object.
2. An alarm reaction, including restlessness, anxiety, and various somatic reactions. The person is painfully unable to initiate and maintain normal patterns of activity.
3. An urge to search for and find the lost person or object in some form. This is accompanied by painful pining and preoccupation with thoughts of the lost person or role, and events leading to the loss. The bereaved person is also inattentive to matters normally occupying attention.
4. Anger toward the one who has died, toward self, or toward others responsible for one's loss: "Oh John, why did you leave me?" "Why didn't I insist that he go to the hospital?" "If the doctor had come on time, he might not have died."
5. Following this is guilt—about perceived neglect by self or others, about one's protest to the person dead and gone, and about one's own survival. Lifton and Olson (1976) have called this "death guilt." There may also be outbursts against the people who press the bereaved person toward acceptance of the loss before he or she is psychologically ready.
6. Feelings of internal loss or mutilation: "He was a part of me," or, "Something of me ent when they tore down our homes and neighborhood." The "urban villagers" (Gans 1962) in Boston's West End are still mourning the loss of their community to an urban renewal project 25 years later.
7. Identification phenomena: By adopting the traits and mannerisms of the lost person, by trying to built another home of the same kind, the bereaved attempt to recreate and retain to some degree the world that has been lost.
8. The last feature of grief is a pathological variant of normal grief. That is, the above reactions may be excessive, prolonged, inhibited, or inclined to emerge in a distorted form. This is most apt to happen in the absence of social support.

These reactions have been observed in widows, among disaster survivors, in persons who lost a body part, in people who lost their homes in an urban relocation program, and among people who have lost a loved one to AIDS (Fried 1962, Lindemann 1944, Marris 1974, Moffatt 1986, Parkes 1975, and Silverman 1969).

Normal as well as pathological reactions are influenced by various factors existing before, during, and after the loss. These are similar to the personal, material, demographic, cultural, and social influences affecting the outcome of any other crisis, for instance, an inflexible approach to problem solving, poverty, the dependency of youth or old age, cultural inhibition of emotional expression, and the availability of social support. Assisting the bereaved in avoiding pathological outcomes of grief is an essential feature of a preventive and developmental approach to crisis work. Grief work, then, can be viewed as integral to any crisis resolution process in which loss figures as a major theme.

Normal grief work consists of (Johnson-Soderberg 1981, Lindermann 1944, Parkes 1975):*

1. Acceptance of the pain of loss. This means dealing with memories of the deceased.
2. Open expression of pain, sorrow, hostility, and guilt. The person must feel free to mourn his or her loss openly, usually by weeping, and to express feelings of guilt and hostility.
3. Understanding the intense feelings associated with the loss (for example, fear of going crazy) as a normal part of the grieving process. When these feelings of sorrow, fear, guilt, and hostility are worked through in the presence of a caring person, they gradually subside. The ritual expression of grief, as in funerals, greatly aids in this process.
4. Eventual resumption of normal activities and social relationships without the person lost. Having worked through the memories and feelings associated with one's loss, a person acquires new patterns of social interaction apart from the deceased.

When people do not do grief work following any profound loss, serious emotional, mental, and social problems can occur. All of us can help people grieve without shame over their losses. This is possible if we are sensitized to the importance of expressing feelings openly and to the various factors affecting the bereavement process.

OTHER INTERVENTION STRATEGIES

1. *Listen actively and with concern.* When a person is ashamed of his or her ability to cope with a problem or feels that the problem is too minor to be so upset about, a good listener can dispel some of these feelings. Listening helps a person feel important and deserving of help no matter how trivial the problem may appear. Effective listening demands attention to possible listening barriers such as internal and external noise and the other factors

*See contrasting case examples of Mona Anderson (Chapter 10) and Gerry Henderson (Chapter 11) in grieving for a child with a mental handicap or a stillborn birth.

influencing communication discussed earlier. Comments such as "hm hm," "I see," and "Go on," are useful in acknowledging to the person that we are listening. They also encourage more talking and build rapport and trust. The failure to listen forms a barrier to all other intervention strategies.

2. *Encourage the open expression of feelings.* Listening is a natural forerunner of this important crisis intervention technique. One reason some people are crisis prone is that they habitually bottle up feelings such as anger, grief, frustration, helplessness, and hopelessness. Negative associations with expressing feelings during childhood seem to put a permanent damper on such expression when traumatic events occur later in life. The crisis worker's acceptance of the person's feelings often helps him or her feel better immediately. It also can be the beginning of a healthier coping style in the future. This is one of the rewarding growth possibilities for people in crisis who are fortunate enough to get the help they need.

A useful technique for fostering emotional expression is role playing or role modeling. For example, the worker could say, "If that happened to me I think I'd be very angry," giving permission, in effect, for the person in crisis to express feelings that she or he may hesitate to share out of shame or for other reasons.

For extreme anxiety and accompanying changes in biophysical function, relaxation techniques and physical outlets can be encouraged. The high energy following a crisis experience can be channelled into constructive activity and socially approved outlets, such as assigning various tasks to disaster victims, or providing athletic facilities in acute service settings such as hospitals. The current popular emphasis on self-help techniques, such as physical exercise and leisure for stress reduction, should be encouraged as a wholesome substitute for chemical tranquilizers during crisis (see Tranquilizers: What Place in Crisis Intervention? in this chapter).

As important as listening and emotional/physical expression are, used alone they do not constitute crisis intervention. Without additional strategies these techniques may not necessarily result in positive crisis resolution. Listening and expression of feelings appeal to the emotional aspect of the crisis response, but cognitive and behavioral elements of the crisis are also important.

3. *Help the person gain an understanding of the crisis.* The individual may ask: "Why did this awful thing have to happen to me?" This perception of the traumatic event—threat of divorce, rape, diagnosis of AIDS, son or daughter in trouble—implies that the event occurred because the person in crisis was bad and deserving of punishment. The crisis worker can help the individual see the many factors that contribute to a crisis situation, and thereby curtail self-blaming. The individual is encouraged to examine the total problem, including his or her own behavior as it may be related to the crisis. Thoughtful reflection on oneself and one's behavior can lead to growth and change rather than self-deprecation and self-pity.

4. *Help the individual gradually accept reality.* Respond to the person's tendency to blame his or her problems on others. The person in crisis may be adopting the role of "victim." The counselor can help the individual gradually accept reality and escape from the victim position. A counselor may find it tempting to agree with the person in blaming others, especially when the person's story, as well as the reality, reveal especially cruel attacks, rejections, or other unfair treatment. Those whose crises stem primarily from social sources not only *feel* victimized, they *are* victimized. Such abused people though, are also survivors, and their survival skills can be tapped for constructive crisis resolution by encouraging them to channel their anger into action to change oppressive social arrangements and policies (see Crisis Paradigm).

The tendency to blame and scapegoat is especially strong in family and marital crises. The crisis counselor should help the person understand that victim-persecutor relationships are not one-sided. This can be done effectively when the counselor has established an appropriate relationship with the person. If the counselor has genuine concern, rather than inappropriate rescue attitudes, the individual can accept the counselor's interpretation of his or her own role in the crisis event. The victim-rescuer-persecutor syndrome occurs frequently in human relationships of all kinds, it is also common in many helping relationships. People viewed as victims are not rescued easily. Thus, crisis counselors who are bent on "rescuing" others usually are frustrated when their rescue efforts fail. Their disappointment may move them to "persecute" their "victim" for failure to respond. At this point the "victim: turns "persecutor" and punishes the counselor for the well-intended but inappropriate effort to help.*

In such "meta-complementary" relationships (Haley 1963), the egalitarian aspects of the service contract are sabotaged. That is, one person allows or pressures another to define a relationship in a certain way; for example, if A acts helpless and provokes B to take care of him or her, A is actually in control although A is manifestly dependent. Translated to the helping relationship, a counselor may not wish to be controlled any more than a client would, hence the initiation of the troublesome victim-rescuer-persecutor cycle that is so difficult to disrupt once started. (See Social Network Strategies in Chapter 5 for an effective means of interrupting the cycle.)

5. *Help the person explore new ways of coping with problems.* Instead of responding to crises as helpless victims, or with suicide and homicide attempts, people can learn new responses. Sometimes people have given up on problem-solving devices that used to work for them.

---

*The reader is referred to sources such as *Born to Win* (James and Jongeward 1971) for a fuller examination of this important phenomenon. Also, many of Haley's (1969) ideas in "The Art of Being a Failure as a Therapist" apply here.

Case Example: Jane

Jane, age 38, was able to weather a lot of storms until her best friend died. Somehow, after her friend's death, she could not find the energy necessary to establish new friendships. Exploration revealed that Jane had never worked through the grief she experienced over the death of her friend. The lack of healthy resolution of this crisis made Jane more vulnerable than she might otherwise have been when her daughter, age 18, left home and married. Jane had temporarily given up and stopped using her effective problem-solving devices.

In Jane's case one might ask about previous successful coping devices and whether she thinks any of these might work for her now. Jane could also be assisted with "delayed grief work" and exploring avenues for developing new friendships.

6. *Link the person to a social network.* The technique of exploring new coping devices leads naturally to this function. Just as disruption of social ties is an important precursor of crisis, so the restoration of those ties—or, if permanently lost, the formation of new ones—is one of the most powerful means of resolving a crisis. The crisis counselor takes an active role in reestablishing a person with his or her social network. This aspect of crisis management is also known as social network intervention, or the ecological approach to crisis intervention. This approach is discussed in detail in the next chapter.

Another way to enhance social network linkage is through "contemporary rites of passage" (see Crisis Paradigm). Such ritual support mechanisms are important in dealing with the common theme of loss during crisis, whether through unanticipated events or role changes. Chapter 11 discusses this strategy in detail.

7. *Reinforce the newly learned coping devices, and follow up resolution of the crisis.* The person is given time to try the proposed solutions to the problem. Successful problem-solving mechanisms are reinforced; unsuccessful solutions are discarded, and new ones are sought. In either case, the person is not cut off in an abrupt manner.

A follow-up contact is carried out as agreed in the initial plan. Some workers object that follow-up contact maintain people in an unnecessary state of dependency. It is also argued that contacting a person latter constitutes an invasion of privacy and an imposition of "therapy" on an unwilling client. Rarely does this argument hold when the person being helped has *initiated* the helping process and follow-up is included in a mutually negotiated service contract. There is no question about the ethical value of not imposing therapy or other services on people who do not want them. Yet we need to consider whether "invasion of privacy" and similar arguments may be covering the lack of sensitively designed follow-up programs (Hoff 1983).

Follow-up is more likely to be successful and less likely to be interpreted as an unwanted intrusion if:

- It is incorporated into the total service plan rather than added as an afterthought or an unexpected phone call.
- It is based on the principle of a person's self-determination (even if in crisis) and on avoidance of "savior" tactics and denigration of others' values and abilities.

When carefully designed, then, follow-up work can often be the occasion of reaching people who are unable to initiate help for themselves *before* an acute crisis occurs. This is especially true for suicidal and very depressed people. In such life-threatening situations, a person often feels worthless and is unable to reach out for help (see Chapters 6 and 7).

These crisis management techniques can be mastered by any helping person who chooses to learn them. Human service workers and community caretakers, volunteer counselors, welfare workers, nurses, physicians, police officers, teachers, and clergy should make it a part of their professional training to learn how to effectively help people in crisis. Effective helping techniques save time and effort spent on problems that can develop from ineffectively resolved crises (Hoff and Miller 1987). Primary prevention is much less costly in both human and economic terms. These basic strategies can be discussed in the remaining chapters. In highly charged and potentially violent crisis situations (both individual and group) additional techniques are indicated (see Part Two).

TRANQUILIZERS: WHAT PLACE IN CRISIS INTERVENTION?

We are bombarded with the idea that drugs are a solution for many problems. Advertisements constantly remind us: Feel upset? Can't sleep? Can't control your kids?—Take pills. Valium, a mild tranquilizer, seems to have become the all-American pill. It is currently prescribed more frequently than any other drug on the market. Statistics compiled by the National Institute on Drug Abuse (NIDA) shows that 120 million prescriptions of tranquilizers (an estimated 4 billion doses) are prescribed annually. Only 10% of these prescriptions were authorized by psychiatrists. Considering that the total US population is 240 million, these figures are staggering.

Women receive more than twice the amount of prescription drugs than men for the same psychologic symptoms (BWHBC 1984).

The press, television, and major newspapers are repeatedly drawing attention to this problem.* It is noteworthy that health and human service practitioners and institutions are quieter about prescription drug abuse (Rogers 1971). When confronted with the problems it is not uncommon to hear from practicioners: "But they want the pills. . . . They don't want to talk about or deal with what's troubling them. . . . What am I supposed to do?" Admittedly, when a person seeks a tranquilizer and refuses to talk, it may be futile to refuse a prescription, assuming that "If I don't provide it, someone else will" (Nellis 1980). Yet a more sophisticated example could hardly be found to illustrate "blaming the victim" (Ryan 1971) and the limitation of an *individual* approach to a problem with social, political, and economic origins. This is not to say that crisis practitioners should not try to alert people to the dangers and limitations of tranquilizers. Rather, it suggests the need to broaden our horizons, look "upstream" to the origins of this problem, and ask ourselves:

- What is the deeper significance of the widespread fact that "someone else will" give a prescription on request?
- How did so many people (professionals and the general public) come to believe that chemical tranquilization is a preferred way to deal with life's stresses and crises?
- What does the profit motive have to do with the overuse of tranquilizers? (See McKinlay, 1979, on "The Manufacture of Illness.")

The answers to these questions caution us about placing the blame for this serious problem on the victims. Certainly, individuals cannot evade *personal* responsibility because of the *social* roots of a problem; also, helpers have to acknowledge defeat in certain situations. But sensitivity to the complexity of the personal and social dimensions of the deadly habit of tranquilization will be valuable in our crisis practice with individuals. With this overview of the problem, let us consider the criteria for use of tranquilizers for people in crisis.

Tranquilizers taken during crisis temporarily relieve tension but do nothing about the problem causing the tension. At best, they are a crutch. At worst, they are addictive and can displace effective problem solving at the psychosocial level.

For the person in crisis, tranquilizing drugs should *never* be used as a substitute for crisis counseling and problem solving. However, there are times when a tranquilizer can be used in addition to the crisis intervention techniques outlined above. These instances are: (a) when a person is ex-

---

*See, for example, Gordon's *I'm Dancing as Fast as I Can* (1980), her autobiographical account of the "hell" of withdrawing from Valium.

periencing extreme anxiety and is fearful of losing control, (b) when the person is so distraught that it is impossible to engage him or her in the problem-solving process, (c) when extreme anxiety prevents sleep for a significant period of time. Sleeping pills should always be avoided. Exercise and nonchemical means of relaxation should be encouraged (see the second intervention strategy, p. 132, and Chapter 7).

Apart from these special circumstances, tranquilizing drugs should be avoided whenever possible. By relieving anxiety on a temporary basis, tranquilizers can have the effect of reducing the person's motivation to effectively solve a crisis. With chemical tranquilization, the person loses the advantages of his or her increased energy during a crisis state. The *opportunity* for psychosocial growth is often lost due to the temporary tranquility of a drugged psyche, while the *danger* is increased.

Caution is also suggested to crisis workers who have available to them physician or psychiatrist consultants. Sometimes crisis workers ask for psychiatric consultation simply because of their own lack of clinical experience, not because the service available only from a psychiatrist is needed. As long as the psychiatrist shares the worker's values regarding crisis work and has additional crisis intervention skills, there is no problem. However, this is not true of all psychiatrists (Wells and Hoff 1984); that is, some psychiatrists have little or no training or experience in crisis intervention but have the legal right to prescribe drugs.* The nonmedical crisis worker needs to remember that a consultation request may result in a drug prescription, when what is actually needed is the experience of highly skilled crisis specialists. Such specialists include, but are not limited to psychiatrists.

On the other hand, a comprehensive plan for certain individuals in crisis may include measures available only through the professions of medicine and psychiatry. A psychiatrist has a medical degree and has skills and legal powers unique to his or her training and position in the field of medicine. Unlike the nonmedical counselor or psychiatric practitioner, such as a social worker, a psychiatrist can prescribe medications, admit people to hospitals (Gotkin and Gotkin 1975), make differential diagnoses between psychologic/psychiatric and neurological disturbances; and diagnose and treat the symptoms of drug overdose.†

The appropriate use of psychiatrist's special skills may be aided by reflection on the following opinion of psychiatrist Halleck in his book, *The Politics of Therapy* (1971):

> *The focus of almost all psychiatric practice tends to be on the patient's internal system, that is, upon misery that the patient creates for himself. As a rule, the psychiatrist does not begin working*

---

*The traditional psychiatric management of behavioral emergencies has some aspects in common with crisis intervention, but it should not be equated with the crisis model if a strictly medical approach is used (see Gorton and Partridge 1982).

†In some states nurses and psychologists can also prescribe medication.

> *with emotionally disturbed people until he has had considerable experience working with the physically ill. Physical illness, for the most part, implies a defect in the individual, not in society. The psychiatrist's medical training and his constant work with individuals who seem handicapped subtly encourage him to view human unhappiness as a product of individual disorder. Even if he is exceptionally aware of social forces that contribute to his patient's unhappiness, the psychiatrist's orientation as a physician tends to distract him from dealing with such forces.*
>
> *Some psychiatrists focus almost entirely on the individual. They assume that the social institutions that regulate their patient's existence are more or less adequate. They recognize the social determinants of behavior, but they assume that each individual who requires psychiatric assistance is somehow defective; the patient has failed to adjust to a social order that his peers find acceptable. This concept of unhappiness ignores the factors in the patient's immediate environment that make him behave peculiarly; rather it directs the physician to search for the causes of emotional suffering in the anomalies of his patient's biological and psychological past.*

In short, steps taken by the crisis intervention movement to reduce the largescale dependence on drugs for problem solving during crisis and at other times will be steps forward.

CRISIS INTERVENTION INTERVIEW EXAMPLE

Some of the recommended planning characteristics and techniques of intervention are illustrated by George Sloan's case, continued from Chapters 2 and 3.

CASE EXAMPLE: GEORGE SLOAN

INTERVENTION TECHNIQUES	INTERVIEW BETWEEN MR. SLOAN AND EMERGENCY ROOM NURSE
Exploring resources	*Nurse:* You said you really can't talk to your wife about your problems. Is there anyone else you've ever thought about talking with?
	George: Well, I tried talking to my doctor once, but he didn't really have time. Then a few months ago my minister could see I was pretty down and he stopped by a couple of times, but that didn't help.

Facilitating client decision making	*Nurse:* Is there anyone else you think you could talk to?
	George: No, not really—nobody, anyway, that would understand.
Suggestion about new resources	*Nurse:* What about seeing a regular counselor, George? We have connections here in the emergency room with the psychiatric department of our hospital, where a program could be set up to help you work out some of your problems.
	George: What do you mean? You think I'm crazy or something? (defensively) I don't need to see a shrink.
Listening, accepting client's feelings	*Nurse:* No, George, of course I don't think you're crazy. But when you're down and out enough to see no other way to turn but suicide—well, I know things look pretty bleak now, but talking to a counselor usually leads to some other ways of dealing with problems if you're willing to give it a chance.
	George: Well, I could consider it. What would it cost? I sure can't afford any more medical bills.
Involving client in the plan *Facilitating client decision making* *Plan is concrete and specific*	*Nurse:* Here at our hospital clinic if you can't pay the regular fee you can apply for medical assistance. How would you like to arrange it? I could call someone now to come over and talk to you and set up a program, or you can call them yourself tomorrow and make the arrangements.
	George: Well, I feel better now, so I think I'd just as soon wait until tomorrow and call them—besides,
Involvement of significant other	I guess I should really tell my wife; I don't know how she'd feel about me seeing a counselor. But then I guess suicide really is kind of a coward's way out.
Reinforcing coping mechanism *Active encouragement* *Expression of empathy*	*Nurse:* George, you sound hesitant and I can understand what you must be feeling. Talking again with your wife sounds like a good idea. Or you and your wife might want to see the counselor together sometime. But I hope you do follow through on this, as I really believe you and your family could benefit from some help like this—after all, you've had a lot of things hit you at one time.
	George: Well, it's hard for me to imagine what

Intervention Techniques	Interview between Mr. Sloan and Emergency Room Nurse
	anyone could do—but maybe at least my wife and I could get along better and keep our kid out of trouble. I just wish she'd quit insisting on things I can't afford.
Conveying realistic hope that things might get better	*Nurse:* That's certainly a possibility, and that alone might improve things. How about this, George: I'll call you tomorrow afternoon to see how you are and whether you're having any trouble getting through to the counseling service?
Follow-up plan	*George:* That sounds fine. I guess I really should give it another chance. Thanks for everything.
	Nurse: I'm glad we were able to talk, George. I'll be in touch tomorrow.

SUMMARY

Without communication and rapport, the immediate context for crisis work, success will probably elude us. Resolution of crisis should occur in a person's or family's natural setting whenever possible. Effective planning and skills in crisis management are the best way to avoid extreme measures such as hospitalization and lengthy rehabilitation programs. Active involvement of the person in his or her plan for crisis resolution is a *must* for the success of crisis intervention as a way of helping people. The service contract symbolizes this active involvement. Use of tranquilizers decreases such involvement and sabotages the growth potential of the crisis experience.

REFERENCES

Bard M: *Police Family Crisis Intervention and Conflict Management: An Action Research Analysis.* US Department of Justice, 1972.

Bateson G: *Naven,* 2nd ed. Stanford University Press, 1958.

Brooks WD, Emmert P: *Interpersonal Communication.* Dubuque, IA: William C. Brown, 1976.

Budd RW, Ruben BD: *Approaches to Human Communication.* Spartan Books, 1972.

BWHBC (Boston Women's Health Book Collective): *The New Our Bodies Ourselves,* 3rd ed. Simon and Schuster, 1984.

Campbell-Heider N, Pollock D: Barriers to physician-nurse collegiality: An anthropolocial perspective. *Soc Sci Med* 1987; 25(5):421–425.

Caplan G, Grunebaum H: Perspectives on primary prevention: A review. *Arch Gen Psych* 1967; 17:331–346.

Fried M: Grieving for a lost home. In:

The Environment of the Metropolis. Duhl LJ (editor). Basic Bookc, 1962.

Gans H: *The Urban Villagers.* Free Press, 1962.

Gerhardt U: Coping and social action: Theoretical reconstruction of the life-event approach. *Sociol Health Ill* 1979; 1:195–225.

Gordon B: *I'm Dancing as Fast as I Can.* Bantam Books, 1980.

Gorton J, Partridge R (editors): *Practice and Management of Psychiatric Emergency Care.* Mosby, 1982.

Gotkin J, Gotkin P: *Too Much Anger, Too Many Tears: A Personal Triumph over Psychiatry.* Quadrangle/The New York Times Book Co, 1975.

Haley J: *Strategies of Psychotherapy.* Grune and Stratton, 1963.

Haley J: The art of being a failure as a therapist. *Am J Orthopsych* 1969; 39:(4):691–695.

Hall ET: *The Hidden Dimension.* Anchor Books, 1969.

Halleck S: *The Politics of Therapy.* Science House, 1971.

Hansell N: Decision counseling. *Arch Gen Psych* 1970; 22:462–467.

Hicks RD, Dolphin G: Avoiding family violence: The non-verbal communication of police intervention in family fights. *Police Chief* 1979; 50–55.

Hoff LA: Interagency coordination for people in crisis. *Inform Referral,* 1983; 5(1):79–89.

Wells JO, Hoff LA (editors): *Certification Standards Manual,* Denver: American Association of Suicidology, 1984.

Hoff LA, Miller N: *Programs for People in Crisis: A Guide for Educators, Administrators, and Clinical Trainers.* Boston: Northeastern University Custom Books Program, 1987.

James M, Jongeward D: *Born to Win.* Addison-Wesley, 1971.

Johnson-Soderberg S: Grief themes. *Adv Nurs Sci* 1981; 3(4):15–26.

Jourard S: Suicide: An invitation to die. *Am J Nurs* 1970; 70:49–55.

Kelley VR, Weston HB: Civil liberties in mental health facilities. *Soc Work* 1974; 19:48–54.

King JM: The initial interview: Basis for assessment in crisis. *Persp Psych Care* 1971; 9:247–256.

Leach E: *Culture and Communication.* Cambridge University Press, 1976.

Lifton RJ, Olson E: The human meaning of total disaster: The Buffalo Creek experience. *Psychiatry* 1976; 39:1–18.

Lindemann E: Symptomatology and management of acute grief. *Am. J Psych* 1944; 101:101–148. Also reprinted in: *Crisis Intervention: Selected Readings.* Parad HJ (editor). New York: Family Service Association of America, 1965.

Marris P: *Loss and Change.* Routledge and Kegan Paul, 1974.

McGee RK: *Crisis Intervention in the Community.* Baltimore: University Press, 1974.

McKinlay JB: A case for refocusing upstream: The political economy of illness. In: *Patients, Physicians and Illness,* 3rd ed. Jaco EG (editor). Free Press, 1979.

Moffat B: *When Someone You Love Has AIDS: A Book of Hope for Family and Friends.* Santa Monica, CA: IBS Press, in association with Love Heals, 1986.

Nader R: *Through the Mental Health Maze.* Washington, DC: Health Research Group, 1975.

Nellis M: *The Female Fix.* Houghton Mifflin, 1980.

Parad HJ, Resnik HLP, Parad LG (editors): *Emergency and Disaster Management: A Mental Health Source Book.* Bowie, MD: Charles Press, 1976.

Parkes CM: *Bereavement: Studies of Grief in Adult Life.* Penquin, 1975.

Pluckhan ML: *Human Communication.* McGraw-Hill, 1978.

Polak P: The crisis of admission. *Soc Psych* 1967; 2:150–157.

Rogers, MJ: Drug abuse: Just what the doctor ordered. *Psychol Today* (1971; 5:16–24.

Ryan W: *Blaming the Victim.* Vintage Books, 1971.

Silverman P: The widow-to-widow program: An experiment in preventive intervention. *Ment Hyg* 1969; 53:333–337.

Stewart CJ, Cash WB: *Interviewing: Principles and Practices.* Dubuque, IA: William C. Brown, 1974.

Szasz TS: *The Manufacture of Madness.* Harper and Row, 1970.

Truax CB, Carkhuff RR: *Toward Effective Counseling and Psychotherapy.* Aldine, 1967.

Trudgill P: *Sociolinguistics: An Introduction.* Penguin, 1974.

Vetterling-Braggin M, Elliston FA, English J (editors): *Feminism and Philosophy.* Part 33: Sexism in ordinary language, pp. 105–170. Totowa, NJ: Littlefield, Adams, 1977.

CHAPTER 5

FAMILY AND SOCIAL NETWORK STRATEGIES DURING CRISIS

SOCIAL ASPECTS OF CRISIS AND HUMAN GROWTH

We are conceived and born into a social context. We grow and develop among other people. We experience crises around events in our social milieu. People near us—friends, our family, the community—help or hinder us through crises. And finally, death, even for those of us who die in isolation and abandonment, demands some response from the society we leave behind.

The results of multidisciplinary research increasingly support a shifting emphasis from individual to social approaches to helping distressed people.* Despite the prevalence of individual intervention techniques, overwhelming evidence now shows that social networks and support are primary factors in one's susceptibility to disease, the process of becoming ill and seeking help, the treatment process, and the outcomes of illness—either rehabilitaiton and recovery or death.† The prolific social science literature supporting social approaches is complemented by the clinical impressions of practitioners (see Garrison 1974, Langsley and Kaplan 1968, Polak 1971). After using family and social network approaches, clinicians seldom return to predominantly individual practice (for example, Satir 1972, Satir, Stack-

*See, for example, the following sources: Epidemiology (Berkman and Syme 1979); Sociology (Granovetter 1973, Lopata 1973, Kaplan, Cassel, and Gore 1977); anthropology (Bott 1957, Mitchell 1969, Barnes 1972, Boissevain 1979, Hoff 1984); nursing (Norbeck, Lindsey, and Carrieri 1981, Maxwell 1982); medicine (Cobb 1976); social psychology (Antonovsky 1980, Sales, Baum, and Shore 1984).
†See, for example: Gottlieb 1981, Kaplan, Cassell, and Gore 1977, McKinlay 1973 and 1981, and Sarason and Sarason 1985.

owiak, and Taschman 1975, Speck and Attneare 1973). Hansell (1976) casts his entire description of persons in crisis in a social framework. Caplan (1964) laid the foundation for much of this work. The Crisis Paradigm in this book similarly stresses the pivotal role of sociocultural factors in the development, manifestation, and resolution of crises. This chapter presents an overview of social approaches to crisis intervention and suggests strategies for family and social network practice.

An interrelated assumption underlies this discussion: People often avoid social approaches because they have not been trained to use them; people are not trained in social strategies because of doubts about their usefulness. In addition, individual approaches are not evaluated for their effectiveness and underlying assumptions. Social strategies contrast strongly with approaches in which upsets are regarded primarily as results of personality dynamics and an individual's internal conflicts. Advocates of the latter view do not entirely disregard social factors, nor do advocates of social-interactional approaches ignore individual factors. Rather, the difference is a matter of emphasis and the influence of convictions about sources of problems on one's choice of a helping process.

One's social network may consist of family, friends, neighbors, relatives, bartender, employer, hairdresser, teacher, welfare worker, physician, lawyer—anyone with whom a person has regular social intercourse. It varies with different individuals. The following interview with a cocktail waitress illustrates the diversity of social network support and the *natural* crisis management process.

Case Example: The Cocktail Waitress

This is the dumpiest bar I've ever worked in but I really enjoy it. I like the people. When I quit my last job and came here, a lot of the old men followed me. There are all kinds of bars, but if it weren't for bars like this a lot of old people and "down and outers" wouldn't have any place to go. Our regulars don't have anything or anyone, and they admit it. I feel like a counselor a lot of times.

One of my customers, a pretty young woman, has had several children taken away. When her caseworker called me to ask if I thought she was ready to have her child back, I said *no*; and I told the woman too.

This bar is really the only social life that some people have. Take Montana. She's about 70 years old and used to be a popular dancer. Now she just goes from bar to bar and is taken care of . . . everybody loves her.

I think the people I feel closest to are the old men who are lonesome or widowed. I always talk to them when they come in. One old man does carving for a hobby, so he whittled out a little church and gave it to me.

One guy who shouldn't drink at all stayed on the wagon for quite a while, then went on a three-week binge. His girlfriend told him that she didn't want him anymore if he didn't stop drinking. So he came in here and got sick after two drinks. he fell on the floor and hurt himself. I called the police and asked them to take him to the hospital. I called the girlfriend, and she and I both convinced him to stay in the hospital for at least 30 days. When he got out, he came in and thanked me. This is really rewarding.

I work hard at helping people get on the right track, and I'm really tough on people who don't do anything with their lives, like these old guys. I know just how much they can drink. Take Ben, he can drink only three and I tell him, "O.K. . . . you can have them either all at once or you can stick around for awhile." I was brought up to respect my elders, and I don't want to see these guys go out and fall on their faces. A lot of people working in bars might not agree with me, because I think they're more interested in making money. But I don't want any part of helping guys mess themselves up by too much drinking.

I have a good friend who's a priest. We argued for years about my work in the bar. He told me for a long time that I shouldn't work here. Finally he agreed that it wasn't a bad thing to do. Someone has to do it.

The case example below highlights the individual versus social approach to *formal* crisis management.

Case Example: Ellen

Ellen, age 16, ran away from home. Shortly after police returned her to her home, she attempted suicide with approximately ten aspirin and five of her mother's tranquilizers. Ellen had exhibited many signs of depression. She was seen for individual counseling at a mental health clinic for a total of 12 sessions. Ellen's parents were seen initially for one session as part of the assessment process. The counselor learned that Ellen was always somewhat depressed and withdrawn at home, and that she was getting poor grades in school.

Counseling focused on Ellen's feelings of guilt, worthlessness, and anger centered around her relationship with her parents. She complained that her father was aloof and seldom available when there was a problem. She felt closer to her mother but said her mother was unreasonably strict about her friends and hours out. At the conclusion of the individual counseling sessions,

Ellen was less depressed and felt less worthless, though things were essentially the same at home and school. Two months after termination of counseling, Ellen made another suicide attempt, this time with double the amount of aspirin and tranquilizers.

This case reveals that involvement of Ellen's family and the school counselor—primary people in her social network—was not an integral part of the helping process.

By contrast, a social network approach to Ellen's problem would also have attended to her feelings of depression and worthlessness. But these feelings would be viewed not as a natural result of her withdrawn personality and internal psychologic processes, but as directly related to her interactions with the people closest to her. In other words, in crisis intervention, people and their problems are seen in a psychosocial rather than a psychoanalytic context.

Within the psychosocial framework, Ellen's counselor would have included at a minimum her family and the school counselor in the original assessment and counseling plan. This initial move might have revealed still other people important to Ellen and able to help. For example, when Ellen ran away, she went to her Aunt Dorothy's house; she felt closer to Dorothy than to her parents.

The social network is central to the process of human growth, development, and crisis intervention. Ellen is in a normal transition stage of human development. The way she handles the natural stress of adolescence depends on the people in her social network: her parents, brothers and sisters, friends, teacher, and relatives. Her relationship with these people sets the tone for the successful completion of developmental tasks. A counselor with a social view of the situation would say that necessary social supports were lacking at a point in Ellen's life when stress was already high. So instead of normal growth, Ellen experienced stress to the point of a destructive outcome: a suicide attempt—a clear message that support from members of her social network was weak.

Even if stress reaches the point where a suicide attempt seems the only alternative, it is not too late to mobilize a shaky social network on behalf of a person in crisis. Failure to do so can result in the kind of outcome that occurred for Ellen, that is, another crisis within two months. Individual crisis counseling was not necessarily bad for Ellen, it simply was not enough.

Before considering the specifics of how a person's social network is engaged or developed in crisis resolution, let us examine more closely two important facets of the social network: the family and the community in crisis.

FAMILIES IN CRISIS

Social relations are a key factor for an individual in crisis. Just as significant is the fact that members of a person's social network are themselves often in crisis. The family unit can experience crises just as individuals can.

Family researchers consider family troubles in terms of sources, effect on family structure, and type of event affecting the family (Hill 1965, Lynch 1987, Parad and Caplan 1965). If the source of trouble is from within the family, the event is more distressing than an external source of trouble such as flood or racial prejudice. Often, an individual in crisis may precipitate a family crisis. For example, if family members make suicide attempts or abuse alcohol, the family usually lacks basic harmony and internal adequacy—as suggested in the case of Ellen, discussed in the previous section.

Family troubles must be assessed according to their effect on the family configuration. Eliot (1955) and Hill (1965) suggest that families experience stress from dismemberment (loss of family member), accession (an unexpected addition of a member), demoralization (loss of morale and family unity), or a combination of all three. This classification of stressor events casts in a family context the numerous traumatic life events associated with crises. Death and hospitalization, crisis-precipitating events for individuals, are examples of dismemberment for families. Unwanted pregnancy, a source of crisis for the girl or woman, is also an example of accession to the family and, therefore, a possible precipitant of family crisis as well. A person in crisis because of trouble with the law for delinquency or drug addiction may trigger family demoralization and crisis. Divorce and acquisition by children of stepparents and stepfamilies (Stanton 1986) also constitutes dismemberment and accession. The Stepfamily Association of American estimates from divorce and remarriage figures that 1300 new stepfamiles (sometimes called "blended" families) are being formed each day, that there are some 35 million stepparents, and that 10% of children under 18 are living in a stepfamily (Jarmulowski 1985, p. 34). Ahrons (1982) found in her study of families after divorce that role and relationship loss were the sources of greatest stress. Suicide, homicide, illegitimacy, imprisonment, or institutionalization for mental illness are examples of demoralization and dismemberment or accession.

Communal or "New Age" families may provide more avenues of support for some people than do traditional nuclear families.* Lindsey

---

*The nuclear family (father, mother, and children) is the norm in most Western societies, whereas the extended family (including relatives) is the norm in most non-Western societies. The Western tradition in which only the father works outside the home is no longer the dominant pattern. Masnick and Bane (1980) predict that by 1990 only half of the nation's households will consist of husband, wife, and young children, while in 1960 three-fourths of all households fit the traditional ideal.

(1981) writes in her *Friends as Family* of a time when she, a single woman, became ill and called on her friends for essential material and social support. Masnick and Bane's (1980) work on the "peer network" supports the increasingly common experience of contemporary substitutes for traditional family support. However, these new family forms can also be the source of unanticipated conflict when lines of authority are unclear, when opinions differ about privacy and intimacy, and when the group cannot reach consensus about how to get necessary domestic work done.

Whether or not stressful events lead to crisis depends on a family's resources for handling such events. Hill (1965) gives a vivid description of the nuclear family and its burden as a social unit:

> *Compared with other associations in society, the family is badly handicapped organizationally. Its age composition is heavily weighted with dependents, and it cannot freely reject its weak members and recruit more competent teammates. Its members receive an unearned acceptance; there is no price for belonging. Because of its unusual age composition and its uncertain sex composition, it is intrinsically a puny work group and an awkward decision-making group. This group is not ideally manned to withstand stress, yet society has assigned to it the heaviest of responsibilities: the socialization and orientation of the young, and the meeting of the major emotional needs of all citizens, young and old.*

The family holds a unique position in our society. It is the most natural source of support and understanding, which many of us rely on when in trouble, but it is also the arena in which we may experience our most acute distress. All families have problems, and all families have ways of dealing with their problems. Some are very successful in problem solving; other are less successful. Much depends on the resources available to them in the normal course of family life.

Besides the ordinary stressors affecting families, in recent years US families face extraordinary stress stemming from a *laissez-faire* approach to public policy affecting families: around 40 million Americans have no health insurance coverage and many lack money for the most basic health care; because of the lack of affordable, quality child care millions of children are left alone; while 70% of adults in a national survey want employers to provide on-site child care, only 9% do so (Rubin 1987, p. 44); 58% of caretakers in the few day-care centers there are earn poverty-level wages or less, while 90% of women caring for children in the home earn at that level (Trotter 1987, p. 38). Millions of families cannot afford to buy a home and thousands of others are homeless due primarily to cuts in federal housing programs since 1981 (see Chapter 11). Of the 72% of mothers in the paid labor force, most are there not only for personal fulfillment but because they need the money (Trotter 1987, p. 34), yet as a group women earn only about 70% of what similarly qualified men earn in spite of civil rights legislation decades ago. Traditional caretaking patterns in the home are additional sources of stress for families, particularly for women (Goodrich et al. 1988, Reverby 1987, and Sommers and Shields 1987). This source of stress on families will only increase with the AIDS crisis, increasing numbers of elderly needing care, and the nursing shortage, unless we shift radically the prevailing attitude and practice regarding caretaking roles (see Chapters 11 and 12).

In addition to resources available to families in stress, a family's vulnerability to crisis is also determined by how it defines the traumatic event. For some families a divorce or a pregnancy without marriage are regarded as nearly catastrophic events; for others these are simply new situations to cope with. Much depends on religious and other values. Similarly, financial loss for an upper middle class family may not be a source of crisis if there are other reserves to draw up. On the other hand, financial loss for a family with very limited material resources can be the last straw, as such families are more vulnerable in general (Hollingshead and Redlich 1958). If the loss includes a loss of status, however, the middle class family that values external respectability will be more vulnerable to crisis than the family with little to lose in prestige.

As important as a family perspective is, one also needs to look beyond the family for influences on family disharmony and crisis. A well-known example of the failure to look further is Moynihan's report, "The Negro Family, the Case for National Action" (1967). Moynihan concluded that causal relationships existed between juvenile delinquency and black households headed by women, and between black women wage earners and "emasculated" black men. When these factors were examined in relation to poverty, however, there was no significant difference between black and white female-headed households. This study is now largely discredited for its race, class, and sex bias but it still represents a sophisticated example of "blaming the victim" (Ryan 1971) using scientific "evidence" that masks economic injustice.

Such blaming of families in crisis due to deeply rooted social problems becomes more significant when considering that the United States stands alone with South Africa as the only industrialized country without a national family policy to deal with issues such as maternity and paternity leaves, child care, and flexible work schedules when the two-income family is the norm rather than the exception (see Chapter 11). The question of whether day care is harmful or helpful for infants and toddlers is frequently debated in the popular press. However, in spite of passionate arguments about abortion, "collapse" of the family, and traditional versus alternative family structures, everyone agrees that human beings need other human beings for development and survival. In short, support from social network members—or the lack of it—influences the outcomes of everyday stress, crisis, and illness, including whether the resolution of crisis is human growth or death (Hoff 1984, Kaplan, Cassel, and Gore 1977, McKinlay 1981, Pearlin et al. 1981).* The probability, then, of people receiving support during crisis *includes* family issues, but is not limited to them. We must also consider community stability and resources and public policy issues that affect individuals and families (see also Chapter 11).

COMMUNITIES IN CRISIS

Just as individuals in crisis are entwined with their families, so are families bound up with their community. An entire neighborhood may feel the impact of an individual in crisis. In one small community a man shot himself in his front yard. The entire community, to say nothing of his wife and small children, was obviously affected by this man's crisis. Also, the murder or abduction of a child in a small community invariably incites community-wide fear on behalf of other children. A crisis response to the entire community, including special sessions for school children, is indicated in these situations (NOVA 1987).

Clearly then, communities ranging from small villages to sprawling metropolitan areas can go into crisis. In small communal or religious groups the deprivation of individual needs or rebellion against group norms can mushroom into a crisis for the entire membership. Some modern communal groups have dissolved because of such problems. Social and economic inequities among racial and ethnic groups can trigger a large-scale community crisis, for example, The Howard Beach incident in New York City and race riots in South Africa. The risk of crisis for these groups is influenced by:

- Social and economic stability of individual family units within a neighborhood.
- Level at which individual and family needs are met within the group or neighborhood.
- Adequacy of neighborhood resources to meet social, housing, economic, and recreational needs of individuals and families.
- Personality characteristics and personal strengths of the individuals within the group.

Psychosocial needs must be met if individuals are to survive and grow. Maslow (1970) has described a hierarchy of needs. As a person meets basic survival needs of hunger, thirst, and protection from the elements, other needs emerge, such as the need for social interaction and pleasant surroundings. We cannot actualize our potential for growth if we are barely

*See Stress, Crisis, and Illness in Chapter 2. For a fuller discussion of theory and research and the family, see Burr et al. 1979, and McCubbin and Figley 1983.

surviving and using all our energy just to keep alive. To the extent that people's basic needs are unmet, people are increasingly crisis prone.

This is the case, for example, of individuals and families living in large inner-city housing projects. Poverty is rampant. Slum landlords take advantage of people already disadvantaged; there is a constant threat of essential utilities being cut off for persons with inadequate resources to meet skyrocketing rates. An elderly couple in an eastern state, unable to pay their bills, died of exposure after a utility company cut off their heat. Emergency medical and social services are often lacking or inaccessible through the bureaucratic structure.

The social and economic problems of the urban poor have been complicated further by the recent trend toward "gentrification": in a partial reversal of "white flight" from inner-city neighborhoods, middle and upper-middle class professionals (mostly white) are returning to the city. Property values increase beyond the reach of the less affluent, displacing poor people. Housing crises or homelessness are the unfortunate outcome for many (see Chapter 10).

Similar deprivations exist on North American Indian reservations and among migrant farm groups. As a result of the personal, social, and economic deprivations in these communities, crime becomes widespread, adding another threat to basic survival. Another crisis-prone setting is the subculture of the average jail or prison. Physical survival is threatened by poor health service, and there is danger of suicide. Prisoners fear physical attack by fellow prisoners. Social needs of prisoners go unmet to the extent that the term "rehabilitation" does not apply to prisons. This situation, combined with community attitudes, unemployment, and poverty, makes ex-offenders highly crisis prone after release from prison (see Chapter 8).

Natural disasters such as floods, hurricanes, and severe snowstorms are another sources of community crisis (see Chapter 9). A community crisis can also be triggered by real or threatened acts of terrorism. This is true not only in such internationally publicized cases as Northern Ireland, but also in small communities. In one small town, families and individual children were threatened and virtually immobilized by an 18-year-old youth suspected but not proven to be a child molester. Another small community feared for everyone's safety when three teenagers threatened to bomb the local schools and police station in response to their individual crises of school expulsion and unemployment.

Communities in crisis have several common charateristics similar to those observed in individuals in crisis. First, within the group an atmosphere of tension and fear is widespread. In riot-torn US cities in the 1960s, for example, an atmosphere of suspicion prevailed. It was not uncommon for restaurant patrons to be questioned by police who were making routine rounds. Second, rumor runs rampant in a crisis community. Individuals in large groups color and distort facts out of fear and lack of knowledge. Third, as with individuals in crisis, normal functioning is inhibited or at a standstill.

Schools and businesses are often closed; health and emergency resources may be in short supply.

However, as is the case with families, traumatic events can also mobilize and strengthen a group or nation. Examples include racial prejudice, bombing by an enemy country, or Nazi persecution of the Jews in Europe.

INDIVIDUAL, FAMILY, AND COMMUNITY INTERACTION

Individuals, families, and communities in crisis must be considered in relation to each other. Basic human needs and the prevention of destructive outcomes of crises form an interdependent network.

PRIVACY, INTIMACY, COMMUNITY

Human needs in regard to the self and one's social network are threefold:

1. The need for privacy.
2. The need for intimacy.
3. The need for community.

To lead a reasonably happy life free of excessive strain, people should have a balanced fulfillment of needs in each of these three areas. With a suitable measure of privacy, intimate attachments, and a sense of belonging to a community, they can avoid the potentially destructive effects of the life crises they may encounter. Figure 5-1 illustrates these needs concentrically.

In the center of the interactional circle is the individual with his or her personality, set of attributes and liabilities, view of self, view of the world, and goals, ambitions, and values. The centered person who is self-accepting not only has a need but a definite capacity for privacy. Well-adjusted people can retreat to their private world as a means of rejuvenating and coming to terms with self and with the external world (Moustakas 1968).

We all have differing needs and capacities for privacy. However, equally vital intimacy and community affiliation needs should not be sacrificed to an excess of privacy. The need for privacy can be violated by (a) the consistent deprivation of normal privacy, and (b) retreat to an excess of privacy, that is, isolation. Examples of privacy deprivation are the child in a family with inadequate housing, or a marriage in which one or both partners are extremely clinging.

The excessively dependent and clinging person is too insecure to ever be alone in his or her private world. Such an individual usually assumes that

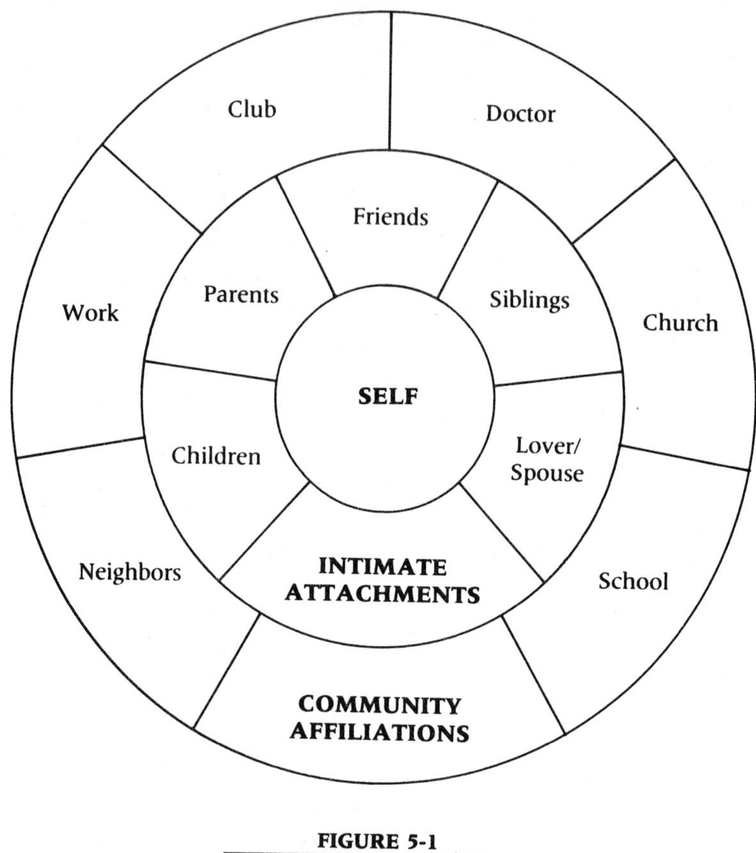

FIGURE 5-1

Privacy, intimacy, community.

there can be no happiness alone; the person's full psychosocial development has been stunted and her or his capacity for privacy is therefore unawakened. The person is unaware of the lack of fulfillment in an overly dependent relationship. Someone involved in this kind of relationship is a prime candidate for a suicide attempt when threatened, for example, by divorce. The person clung to is also deprived of essential privacy needs and feels exhausted by the demand to relate continually to another person.

The problem of an excess of privacy leads to consideration of the needs for intimacy and community. In one sense, an excess of privacy is the other side of the coin of lack of intimacy and community. A person can seldom have too much privacy if his or her social needs are also met. An extreme example of social need deprivation is the isolated person who eventually commits suicide. The concentric circle of needs illustrates the continuous interaction between privacy, intimacy, and community.

THE INDIVIDUAL'S EXTENSION BEYOND SELF

Individuals who feel in charge of themselves and capable of living in their private world are in an advantageous position to reach out and establish intimate attachments. Examples are a mature marital relationship or a small circle of intimate friends one can rely on (Figure 5-1). Need fulfillment in this second circle enables the individual to establish and enjoy additional relationships in the work world and in the larger community. The development of this interactional system can be halted in many situations—for example, if a person feels too insecure to establish intimate or communal attachments; if a couple establishes an intimate attachment that is essentially closed and turned in on itself, thus limiting need fulfillment from the larger community (O'Neill and O'Neill 1972); or if a small communal group turns in on itself and fails to relate to society outside of its confines, healthy interaction is halted.

SOCIAL NETWORK INFLUENCES ON THE INDIVIDUAL

The capacity of individuals to live comfortably with themselves and to move with ease in the world is influenced by families and communities. A child born into a chaotic, socially unstable family may find it difficult to settle into a hostile world. Such a child is more crisis prone at developmental turning points such as entering school, puberty, and adolescence. The child's family, in turn, is affected by the surrounding community. The child and the family's crisis proneness are influenced by factors such as economic and employment opportunities, racial or ethnic prejudice, the quality of available schools, family and social services, and recreational opportunities for youth. When a sufficient number of individuals and families are adversely affected by these factors, the whole community is more prone to crisis.

This concept of individuals, families, and communities interacting underscores the importance of assessing and managing human crises in a social framework. Certainly a person in crisis needs individual help. But this should always be offered in the context of the person's affectional and community needs. Halleck (1971) goes even further in urging a social approach to human problems and crises. He suggests that it may be unethical for a therapist to spend professional time focusing *only* on an individual in prison who has made a suicide attempt. Besides tending to the individual in crisis, a more responsible approach would be to use one's professional skills to influence the prison system that contributes to suicidal crises.

Gil (1987), discussing the social roots of violence, extends this argument. He suggests that emergency treatment of abused children and others must be combined with attention to social institutions such as schools and beliefs about parenting that perpetuate violent behavior. Research with battered women (Hoff 1984) and rape victims (Holstrom and Burgess 1978) supports similar conclusions: these individuals' crises originate from a society's values about women, marriage, the family, and violence (see Crisis Paradigm).

SOCIAL AND GROUP PROCESS IN CRISIS INTERVENTION

The foundations have been laid for a crisis paradigm that stresses the dynamic relationship between individual, family, and sociocultural factors. The task now is to consider the application of this perspective in actual work with people in crisis.

A SOCIAL NETWORK FRAMEWORK

Social approaches to crisis intervention never lose sight of the interactional network between individuals, families, and other social elements. Helping people resolve crises constructively involves helping them reestablish themselves in harmony with intimate associates and with the larger community. In practice this might mean:

- ▶ Relieving the extreme isolation that led to a suicide attempt.
- ▶ Developing a satisfying relationship to replace the loss of a close friend or spouse.
- ▶ Reestablishing ties in the work world and resolving job conflicts.
- ▶ Returning to normal school tasks after expulsion for truancy or drug abuse.
- ▶ Establishing stability and a means of family support after desertion by an alcoholic parent.
- ▶ Allaying community anxiety concerning bomb threats or child safety, such as in the recent murders of children in several cities.
- ▶ Identifying why an individual feels "no one is helping me" when five agencies are officially involved.

In each of these instances an individual psychotherapy approach is often used. However, a social strategy in these examples seems so appropriate that it suggests a question: considering evidence cited earlier about the role of social factors in the origin, response to, and resolution of crises, why do so many practioners persist in using predominantly *individual* approaches to intervention, including a reliance on drugs? The answer is complex and related to issues such as the medicalization of life problems and political-economic factors influencing illness, as discussed in Chapters 1 and 4.

Increasing numbers of practitioners, however, are choosing social strategies for helping distressed people. The experience of social psychiatrists (for example, Halleck 1971, Hansell 1976 and Polak 1971,) and nonmedical practitioners (such as Garrison 1974) suggests that social network techniques are among the most practical and effective available to crisis workers.* Their use in resolving highly complex crisis situations is unparalleled in mental health practice. The technique is effective because it is based on recognition and acceptance of the person's basic social nature. Social network techniques, therefore, are essential crisis worker skills.

An effective crisis worker has faith in members of a person's social network and in the techniques for mobilizing these peopleon behalf of a distressed person. A worker's lack of conviction translates into a negative self-fulfilling prophecy, that is, the response of social network members is highly dependent on the worker's *expectations* of response. A counselor skilled in social network techniques approaches people with a positive attitude and conveys an expectation that the person will respond positively, that he or she has something valuable or essential to offer the individual in crisis. Such an attitude eliminates the need to be excessively demanding, an approach that could alienate the prospective social resource. Workers confident in themselves and in the use of social network techniques can successfully use an assertive approach that yields voluntary participation by those whose help is needed.

SOCIAL NETWORK STRATEGIES

Besides confidence in the usefulness of social approaches, the crisis worker also needs practice skills. Social network strategies can be used at any time during the course of service: at the beginning when we feel at an impasse, when evaluation suggests the need for a new strategy, or at the termination of service (Hansell 1976, Garrison 1974, Polak 1971). The social network approach is particularly effective where chronic and crisis episodes intersect (see Figure 5-2). Putting social network strategies into operation involves several steps:

1. Clarify with the client (individual or family) the purpose of network approaches and his or her active involvement in the process. Because a person who seeks help usually expects an individual approach, he or she may be surprised at the social emphasis. Tradition, after all, dies hard. Therefore, education of clients, based on our own convictions, is an essential aspect of success with social network strategies. Similarly, clients

*Hansell (1976) refers to such network strategies as the Screening-Linking-Planning Conference Method. This method was developed and used extensively in community mental health systems in Chicago and Buffalo on behalf of high-risk former mental patients and others. Polak (1971) called this method "Social Systems Intervention" in his community mental health work in Colorado.

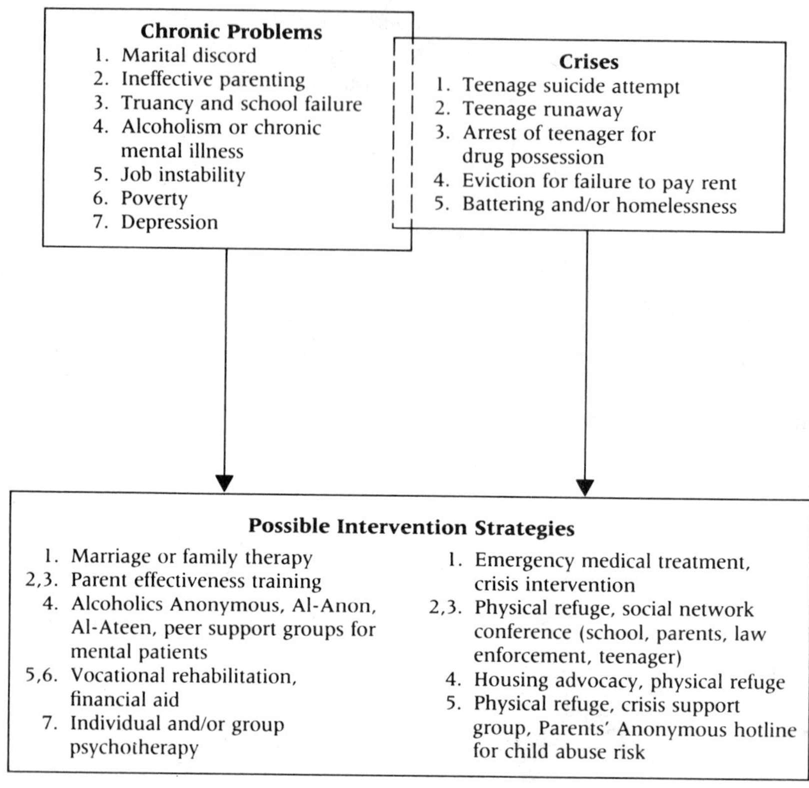

Chronic Problems
1. Marital discord
2. Ineffective parenting
3. Truancy and school failure
4. Alcoholism or chronic mental illness
5. Job instability
6. Poverty
7. Depression
Crises
1. Teenage suicide attempt
2. Teenage runaway
3. Arrest of teenager for drug possession
4. Eviction for failure to pay rent
5. Battering and/or homelessness
Possible Intervention Strategies
1. Marriage or family therapy
2,3. Parent effectiveness training
4. Alcoholics Anonymous, Al-Anon, Al-Ateen, peer support groups for mental patients
5,6. Vocational rehabilitation, financial aid
7. Individual and/or group psychotherapy
1. Emergency medical treatment, crisis intervention
2,3. Physical refuge, social network conference (school, parents, law enforcement, teenager)
4. Housing advocacy, physical refuge
5. Physical refuge, crisis support group, Parents' Anonymous hotline for child abuse risk

FIGURE 5-2

Differentiation between chronic problems and crises and respective intervention strategies. The permeable boundaries between the two types of distress suggest the mutual influence these situations have on each other.

may be surprised to learn that they not only have an *opportunity* but are *expected* to participate actively in the crisis management process. This is especially true for people who may have developed unhealthy dependencies on agencies: the "agency shopper," the "revolving door client," the multi-problem family, the repeat caller, the person with "chronic stress."

The purpose of a network conference can be clarified with a statement such as the following: "John, you've been coming here for some months now, each time with a new crisis around an old problem, it seems. . . . We don't seem to be helping you with what you need. And you say other agencies aren't helping you either. I think we should all get together and try to figure out what's going wrong. Whatever it is we're doing now doesn't seem to be working." A positive presentation like this usually elicits a positive response.

2. Identify all members of the social network, including everyone

involved with the person either before or because of the individual's crisis. In general, this step will be accomplished by the comprehensive assessment suggested in Chapter 3.

Identification includes brainstorming and creative thinking with the client about possible substitutes for missing elements of a support network. This includes social resources that are currently unused by the individual but that could lead to successful crisis resolution. People who lack a *natural* support network (such as discharged mental patients who have been institutionalized for many years) may rely extensively on institutional network support. When such support is suddenly withdrawn they are particularly vulnerable to "chronic crises" and need substitute sources of support. This problem has been particularly acute in communities where adequate community-based services were not developed in concert with the virtual emptying of state mental institutions (see Homelessness in Chapter 10). A network conference about such problems may also yield the necessary evidence for community political action to alleviate these problems.

3. Identify the "symptom bearer" for a family or social network. This is the person whose crisis state is most obvious. Sometimes this individual is labelled as "crazy." Mental health workers often refer to this person as the "identified client"—recognizing that the entire family or community is, in reality, the client, but they are unaware of their role in the individual's crisis. The symptom bearer is also commonly referred to as the "scapegoat" for a disturbed social system.

4. Establish contact with the identified social resources, and explain to them the purpose of the conference. Elicit the cooperation of these people in helping the person in crisis. Explain how you perceive the crisis situation and how you think someone can be of help to the person in crisis. Finally, arrange the conference at a mutually satisfactory time and place.

Case Example: Alice

Mr. Rothman (by telephone): "Mrs. Barrett, this is Mr. Rothman at the crisis clinic. Your daughter Alice is here and refuses to go home. . . . Alice and I would like to have you join us in a planning conference."

Mrs. Barrett: "So that's where she is. . . . I've done everything I know of to help that girl. There's nothing more I can do."

Mr. Rothman: "I know you must feel very frustrated, Mrs. Barrett, but it's important that you join us even if it's agreed that Alice doesn't go back home."

After a few more minutes, Mrs. Barrett agrees to come to the clinic with her husband. (Alice is age 34, has been in and out of mental hospitals, and cannot hold a job. She and her mother had a verbal battle about household chores. Mrs. Barrett threatened to call the police when Alice started throwing things. Alice left and went to the crisis clinic).

If our approach is positive, others involved with a multiagency client will usually express relief that someone is taking the initiative to coordinate services. Families of people with chronic crises often respond similarly.

When there are problems at this stage, it may be because of lack of conviction and persuasion about the need for the conference. Or people may raise the issue of confidentiality. This is actually not an issue, since the client has been actively involved in the process of planning the conference: "Why, of course John consents. . . . He's right here with me now." Consent forms should not be a problem in view of the client's active participation. An honest approach to this method is important to its success.

People may object that conference participants will work together against the client. This too is not an issue, as the purpose of the conference is problem solving for the client's benefit, not punishment. If intentions are sincere, if the purposes of the conference are adhered to, and if the leader is competent, the group process should yield constructive, not destructive results. People tend to surpass their own expectations in these kinds of situations—even the worker who is frustrated by dependent self-destructive persons. Often the conference represents hope of success. This hope in turn is conveyed to the client. Another recommended strategy to diffuse fears about "attacking" a client is to appoint a client advocate, someone who will assure that the interests of the client are not sacrificed in any way during the conference. Staff should thus work in teams of two in conducting these conferences.

5. Convene the client and network members. The network conference should be held in a place that is conducive to achieving the conference objectives. A conference might be held in the home, office, or hospital emergency room.

6. Conduct the network conference with the person in crisis and members of his or her social network. During this time, the problem is explored as it pertains to everyone involved. The complaints of all parties are aired, and possible solutions are proposed and considered in relation to available resources.

Case Example (continued): Alice

Conference leader to Alice: **"Alice, will you review for everyone here how you see your problem?"**

To Mr. Higgins, counselor from emergency hostel: **"Will you explain your emergency housing service, eligibility requirements, and other arrangements to Alice and her parents?"**

To Alice: **"How does this hous-**

ing arrangement sound to you, Alice?"

To Alice's parents: "What do you think about this proposal?"

---

7. Conclude the conference with a definite plan of action for resolution of the crisis. For example, the person in crisis is actively linked to a social resource such as welfare, emergency or transitional housing, emergency hospitalization, or job training.

The details of the action plan are clearly defined: *who* is going to do *what* and within *what time frame*. This includes a contingency plan that specifies what is to be done if the plan fails (see "Planning with a Person or Family in Crisis" in Chapter 4).

8. Establish a follow-up plan. That is, determine the time, place, circumstances, membership, and purpose of the next meeting.

9. Record in *writing* the results of the conference and distribute copies to *all* participants. This step is based on the principles of contracting discussed in Chapter 4. It also provides the basis for evaluating progress, or what went wrong in the event the action plan is unsuccessful.

Workers who have tried social network techniques seem completely confident in them, as the strategy usually yields highly successful results. Its success can be traced to the effective implementation of group process techniques combined with *active client involvement*. For example, how can a client continue to protest that no one is helping when confronted with six to eight representatives in the same room with no other purpose than brainstorming to help more effectively? How can agency representatives continue to "blame the victim" for repeated suicide attempts or lack of cooperation when confronted with evidence that *part* of the problem may be:

- Lack of interagency coordination.
- Cracks and deficits in the system that leave the clients' needs unmet.
- Lack of financial resources to pay rent and utility bills.
- Previous failure to confront the client in a united, constructive manner.

Social network strategies are also effective in avoiding unnecessary hospitalization. Certainly individual help and sometimes hospital treatment are indicated for a person in crisis. But once the person enters the subculture of a hospital, the functions of the natural family unit are disrupted. In the busy bureaucratic atmosphere of institutions it is all too easy to forget the family and community from which the individual came, although some hospital staffs do excellent work with families. Even when social network members (natural and institutional) contribute to the problem rather than offer a source of support, it is important to include them in crisis resolution to help the person in the crisis clarify more precisely the positive and negative aspects of social life. Steps of the social network intervention process are illustrated in Figure 5-3.

A final observation is offered for readers who are new to this approach or feel intimidated by it. Social network *principles* (if not all the steps outlined here) can be applied in varying degrees. In noninstitutional crisis settings, for example, some of the steps may be unnecessary. A very simple example of network intervention in a highly charged situation was described in Chapter 1 (Ramona, the suicidal woman in a shelter). Years of special training are not required for success in network techniques. On the other hand, professionals and others trained in the group process should be quite comfortable in applying this method in very complex situations.

CRISIS GROUPS

The idea of helping people in groups developed during and after World War II. Because of the large number of people needing help, it was impossible to serve all of them individually with limited resources. From the experience of working with people in groups, the group mode of helping was often found to be the method of choice rather than of expediency. The choice of group modes in crisis intervention is influenced by the worker's training and experience with group methods. Attitudes toward the use of groups have been strongly influenced by the psychiatric/psychoanalytic or medical model of practice, which emphasizes individual rather than social factors.

Traditional emphasis on individual rather than group approaches has contributed to the relative lack of study of group methods in crisis intervention (Allgeyer 1970, Strickler and Allgeyer 1967, Morley and Brown 1968, Walsh and Phelau 1974). As is true of social network techniques, the successful use of crisis groups depends on the worker's conviction of the group's usefulness and on appropriate application in the crisis intervention process.

Group work in crisis intervention is indicated in several instances:

1. As a means of assessing a person's coping mechanisms, which are revealed through interaction with a group. Direct observation of a person in a group setting can uncover behaviors that may have contributed to the crisis situation. Examination of how a crisis developed is part of the process of crisis resolution. The individual is helped to grasp the reality and impact of his or her behavior in relation to others (Walsh and Phelau 1974). Such understanding of the crisis situation can lead to discovery of more constructive coping mechanisms in interaction with others. The group is an ideal medium for such a process.

2. As a means of crisis resolution through the helping process inherent in a well-defined and appropriately led group. For the group members in crisis the number of helpers is extended from one counselor to the total number in the group. The process of helping others resolve crises

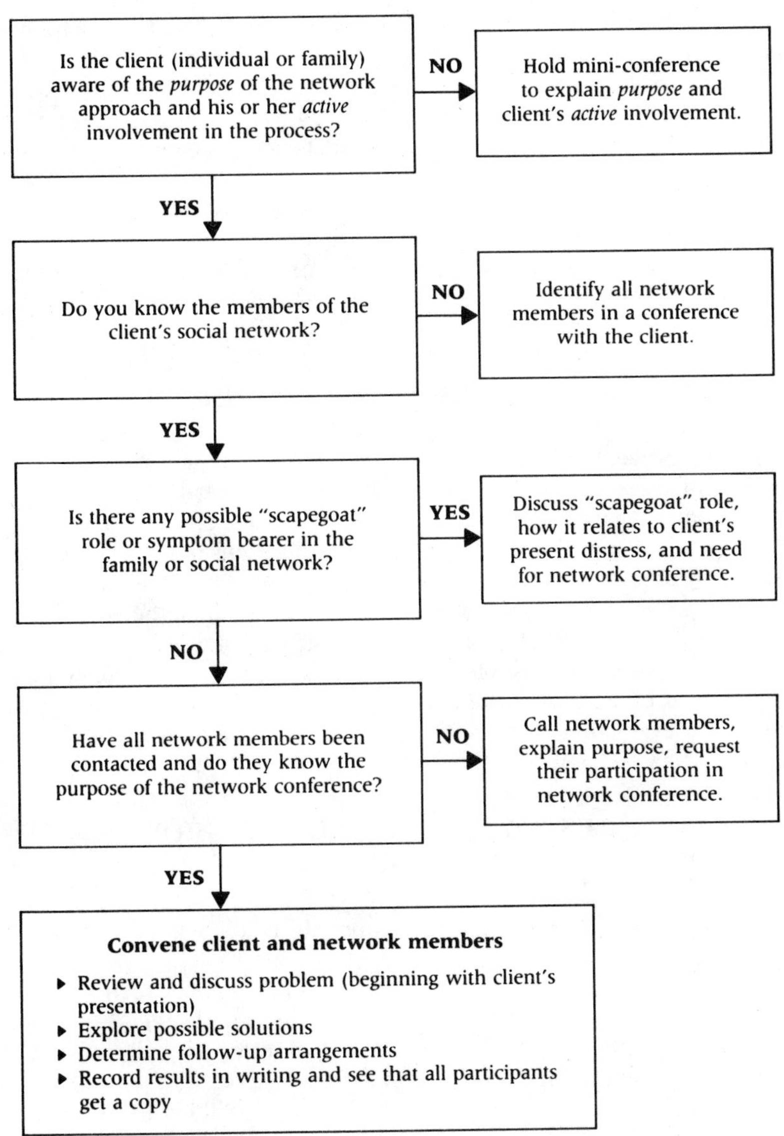

FIGURE 5-3

Steps in social network intervention strategies.

restores a person's confidence. It can also relieve a member's fear of going crazy or losing control.

3. As a means of relieving the extreme isolation of some individuals in crisis. For persons almost completely lacking in social resources or the ability to relate to others, the crisis group can be a first step in reestablishing a vital social network.

4. As a means of immediate screening and assessment in settings where large numbers of people come for help and the number of counselors is limited. This is the case in some metropolitan areas where the population is more crisis prone due to housing, financial, employment, and physical health problems.

CRISIS ASSESSMENT IN GROUPS

A crisis assessment group should be used only when counseling resources are so limited that the people asking for help would otherwise not be seen at all or would be placed on a waiting list. The chief value of a crisis assessment group is to screen out and assist people in most serious need of help before helping those in less critical need (triage). This kind of screening is often necessary in busy emergency mental health clinics. Not all the people who come to such clinics are in crisis. The crisis assessment group is a means of identifying, as soon as possible, those persons in need of immediate help. This method of assessment should not be used as a substitute for a comprehensive evaluation of individuals, including active involvement of the person's social network members.

SUGGESTED PROCEDURE FOR GROUP CRISIS ASSESSMENT

Ideally, crisis assessment group work proceeds as follows:

1. Several people appear for service in an emergency mental health clinic within one hour: Joe, age 28; Jenny, age 36; Charles, age 39; Louise, age 19. There are only two counselors available for assessment, one of whom is involved in an assessment interview.

2. Each person is asked whether he or she is willing to be seen for initial assessment with a group of people who also desire crisis counseling. During this initial presentation each person is also told that: (a) the reason for the group assessment is to give some immediate assistance and prevent a long period of waiting due to staff shortages; (b) the group assessment is not a substitute for individual assessment and counseling needs that are revealed in the group. If the person refuses, he or she is reassured of being seen individually as soon as a counselor is available.

3. The crisis counselor explores with each group member the nature of his or her problem. Each is asked to share the reason for coming to the

emergency mental health service. Members are specifically asked why they came *today.* This line of questioning will usually reveal the precipitating event as well as the person's current coping ability. Some responses might be:

> *Joe:* "I had another argument with my wife last night and I felt like killing her—I couldn't control myself and got scared. Today I couldn't face going to work, so I thought I'd come in."
>
> *Jenny:* "I've been feeling so depressed lately. . . . The only reason I happened to come in today is that I was talking with my best friend and she convinced me I should get some help."
>
> *Charles:* "I've been so nervous at work—I just can't concentrate. Today I finally walked off and didn't tell anyone—I'm afraid to face my wife when I get home because we really need the money, so I decided to come here instead."
>
> *Louise:* "I took an overdose of pills last night and they told me at the hospital emergency room to come in here today for some counseling."

4. Coping ability and resources are explored in detail. The counselor ascertains in each case the degree of danger to self or others. Members are asked how they have resolved problems in the past. Group members are invited to share and compare problem areas and ways of solving them:

> *Joe:* "Usually I go out drinking or something just to keep away from my wife. Maybe if I'd have done that last night, too, I wouldn't have felt like killing her. . . . No, I've never hit her, but I came pretty close to it last night."
>
> *Jenny:* "Usually it helps a lot to talk to my friend. We both think I should get a job so I can get out of the house, but my husband doesn't want me to. . . . No, I've never planned anything in particular to kill myself."
>
> *Charles:* "I find, too, that it helps to talk to someone. . . . My wife has been really great since I've had this trouble on the job. She convinced me to talk with the company doctor. Maybe I could do that tomorrow and get medical leave or something for a while."
>
> *Louise:* "My mother said I had to come in here. . . . They think I'm crazy for taking those pills last night. I feel like you, Joe. I can't stand going back home but I don't know where else to go. . . . Maybe if someone else could just talk to my folks."

5. Action plans are developed with the members. Again, members are invited to share ideas:

> *Joe's Plan:* An individual assessment is scheduled for later in the afternoon. A phone call to Joe's wife asking her to participate in the assessment is also planned. Joe is extremely tense and uses alcohol to calm his nerves. This, in turn, upsets his wife, so a referral to Alcoholics Anonymous will be considered after the full assessment.
>
> *Jenny's Plan:* An individual assessment interview is planned for Jenny three days later, as Jenny is depressed but not in crisis or in immediate danger of harming herself. She is also given the agency's emergency number should she become upset between now and her scheduled appointment (see "Assessment of the Suicidal Person" in Chapter 6). Jenny is also given the names and phone numbers of private psychotherapists accepting referrals.
>
> *Charles' Plan:* He agrees to talk with the company doctor tomorrow and request medical leave. He will call in the results and return for a detailed assessment and exploration of his problem the next day.
>
> *Louise's Plan:* A phone call is planned to Louise's parents to solicit their participation in working with the counselor on behalf of Louise. If they refuse to come in, a home visit will be planned within 24 hours.

This example illustrates the function of the crisis assessment group as a useful way to focus helping resources intensely on people whose problems are most critical, without neglecting others. The crisis assessment group rapidly reveals the degree of stress that people are feeling and their ability to cope with problems. It is apparent, for example, that Jenny has a problem with which she needs help, though she is not in crisis.

Mental health agencies with limited counseling resources need to develop techniques to assure that those in crisis or in life and death emergencies receive immediate attention (Hoff and Miller 1987). The assessment worker who uses social resources and network techniques also facilitates the use of resources outside the agency and the individual. Charles, for example, is supported in his self-preservation plans of seeing the company doctor for medical leave, with the intent of resolving his basic problem through counseling.

As is true with crisis groups generally, crisis assessment groups develop rapid cohesion. Members receive immediate help in a busy agency. Sharing their problems voluntarily with others and assisting fellow group members with similar or more difficult problems gives people a sense of self-mastery. It also strengthens their sense of community. An appropriately conducted crisis assessment group can lay the foundation for: (a) network techniques in each individual's particular social milieu, (b) later participation in a crisis counseling group that may be recommended as part of the total plan for crisis resolution, (c) participation in self-help groups such as Alcoholics Anonymous (AA), widows' clubs, Parents-in-Crisis, and others.

CRISIS COUNSELING IN GROUPS

An important facet of crisis intervention is determining when group work is indicated. Counselors need to guard against unnecessarily protecting people in crisis from groups. This attitude is often revealed in workers' statements such as: "I'll see her individually just for a few sessions"; or, "She's not ready for a group yet." These statements can be interpreted in several ways:

1. A person actually needs individual crisis counseling.
2. A person is so terrified of the prospect of a group experience that he or she is, in fact, not ready.
3. The counselor believes that counseling people individually is always better and that a group approach is indicated *only* when there is not enough time for individual work.

Consider the following responses to these interpretations:

1. The need for individual crisis counseling does not negate the need for group crisis counseling. If both are indicated, both should be offered simultaneously.
2. If a person is indeed terrified of a group experience, this may be an even greater indication of his or her need for the experience. In the individual sessions preparatory to the group experience, the counselor should convey the expectation that group work will be a helpful process. An overprotective attitude will confirm the person's fear that groups are basically destructive and should be avoided. The person's learning of coping skills will thus be limited to individual encounters.
3. If the counselor believes in group work only as an expedient measure, rather than the intervention of choice according to assessed needs, he or she will not use this effective method of crisis counseling in instances when it is indicated.

GROUP STRUCTURE

Another facet of crisis counseling in groups is the structure, content, and conduct of the group itself. Some crisis workers recommend structuring the group to a strict limit of six sessions. A more flexible approach takes into consideration the different coping abilities and external resources available to individuals. Therefore, while group members should be asked to attend sessions once or twice a week (average session length 1 ½ to 2 hours) for a minimum of six sessions, they might be permitted a maximum of ten sessions if a particular crisis situation warrants it. Group "crisis counseling" beyond ten sessions indicates that: (a) the counselor does not recognize the difference between crisis counseling and long-term therapy; (b) the person in crisis also has an underlying mental health problem of a chronic nature that should be dealt with in a traditional group therapy setting; (c) the person in crisis may be substituting the group for other, more regular social contacts, and the counselor is inadvertently fostering such restricted social engagement by failure to limit the number of group sessions.

The content and conduct of the crisis counseling group are determined by its purpose: resolution of crisis by means of a group process. Therefore, the group sessions focus on the crises identified by the group members. Individual historical information and feelings not associated with the crisis are restricted in group discussion. There is a continued focus on resolution of the crisis that brought the person to the group. All techniques employed in crisis management for individuals should be used: encouraging expression of feelings appropriate to the traumatic event, gaining an understanding of the crisis situation, exploring resources and possible solutions to the problem, and examining social change strategies that might reduce crisis risk in the future (see Chapter 4).

A major difference between group and individual work is that in group work the counselor facilitates the process of all group members helping one another in the resolution of crises. Another difference is that individuals in crisis inevitably feel less isolated socially as a result of the bonds created in the group problem-solving process. Such relief of isolation with an accompanying sense of group solidarity can be an important forerunner of social action designed to prevent future crises, for example, peer support groups for people with cancer, parents who have lost a child, battered women, or widowed people.

We also need to consider whether a crisis group should be open or closed. The size of the agency and the potential number of individuals can partially determine this. In an agency where many individuals in crisis are seen daily, closed groups are indicated. That is, six or eight people are assigned to a crisis counseling group with the understanding of the contracted six- to ten-session limit, and no new members are admitted to the group once it is formed.

In an agency with fewer clients, where it is difficult to form an initial group of even five people, the group might be structured in an "open" fashion. This means that new members can be admitted up to a maximum of eight or ten. To avoid constantly dealing with the initiation of new members, admissions are best limited to every second or third session. Even though the group is "open" to new members, each individual is expected to abide by the six- to ten-session contract. The nature and structure of the group are explained to prospective members in orientation sessions conducted by the group crisis counselor.

Admission to and termination of the group can serve as a medium for discussion about the events that are often an integral part of life crises: admission of a new family member by birth of a baby, revelation of minority sexual preference, a divorce, an unwanted pregnancy, a rape, death, or absence of a family member through illness. As individuals come and go to and from the group, members are provided an opportunity to work through possible feelings associated with familiar personal losses. Crisis groups can also be viewed as contemporary substitutes for traditional rites of passage. This idea is explored more fully in Chapter 11.

Group counseling is a valuable means of facilitating individual and social growth from a crisis experience. More counselors are now availing themselves of this method of helping people in crisis.

COUNSELING FAMILIES IN CRISIS

Social network techniques apply in general to the family. Group crisis work resembles family crisis work, but scapegoating and established family patterns and roles add complexity to helping families in crisis.

Assessing the "scapegoat" or identified symptom bearer in crisis, along with his or her social network, will reveal the purpose of this person's symptoms in maintaining a family's function, unhealthy and maladjusted as the family may appear at times. For example, Julie, age 15, is identified by the school as a "behavior problem." She violates all the family rules at home. John, age 17, is seen by contrast as a "good boy." Through this convenient labeling process, the mother and father can overlook the chronic discord in their marital relationship and childrearing practices. Julie's mother and father always seem to be fighting about disciplining Julie. It is, therefore, easy for them to conclude that they would not be fighting if it weren't for Julie's behavior problems. Julie becomes very withdrawn and threatens to kill herself, and finally runs away from home to her friend's house. A naive counselor could simply focus on Julie as the chief source of difficulty in the family. If, however, the counselor were attuned to the principles of human growth, development, and life crises in a social context, the analysis would be different. Julie would be viewed as the symptom bearer for a disturbed family. The entire family would be identified as the client.

Crisis intervention for a family such as Julie's includes the following elements:

1. Julie's mother brings her to the crisis clinic as recommended by the school guidance counselor.
2. Julie and her mother are seen in individual assessment interviews.
3. A brief joint interview is held in which the counselor points out the importance and necessity of a family approach if Julie is to get any real help with her problem. The mother is directed to talk with her husband and son about this

recommendation, with the understanding that the counselor will assist in this process as necessary.

4. Individual assessment interviews are arranged with the husband and son.

5. The entire family is seen together and a six- to eight-session family counseling contract is arranged.

6. Crisis counseling sessions are conducted. As in group crisis counseling, the counselor facilitates the participation of all family members in resolution of the crisis. The group process will inevitably reveal that Julie indeed has a problem, but that the entire family has contributed to and is an integral part of the problem. For example, Julie's mother and father give Julie conflicting messages regarding their expectations. John is an "ideal boy," and Julie "never does anything right." Julie feels her father ignores her. The guidance counselor had asked Julie's parents to come to the school for a conference, but they "never had time."

   The sessions will focus on helping Julie and her parents reach compromise solutions regarding discipline and expected task performance. Parents are helped to recognize and change their inconsistent patterns of discipline. All members are helped to discover ways to give and receive affection in needed doses. Parents and John are helped to see how John's favored position in the family has isolated Julie and contributed to her withdrawal and running away.

7. A conference is held after the second or third session with the entire family, school guidance counselor, and Julie's friend. This conference will assure proper linkage to and involvement of the important people in Julie's social network.

8. During the course of the family sessions, basic marital discord between Julie's mother and father becomes apparent. They are recommended to receive ongoing marital counseling from a family service agency.

9. Family sessions are terminated with satisfactory resolution of the crisis as manifested by the family symptom bearer, Julie.

10. A follow-up contact is agreed on by the family and the counselor.

In some families the underlying disturbance is so deep that the symptom bearer is forced to remain in his or her scapegoat position. For example, if Julie's mother and father refused to seek help for their marital problems, Julie would continue her role in the basic family disturbance. Unfortunately, these situations often get worse before they improve. For example, if in her desperation Julie becomes pregnant or carries out her suicide threat, the family might be jolted into doing something about the underlying problems leading to such extreme behavior.

For children and adolescents in crisis, family crisis counseling is recommended as the preferred helping mode in nearly all instances. Bypassing this intervention method for young people is a grave disservice and ignores the concepts of human growth and development and the key role of family in this process. Langsley and Kaplan (1968) have demonstrated the effectiveness of family crisis intervention in other instances as well.

When dealing with suicidal persons family approaches may be life saving (see Chapter 7, Hoff 1981, and Hoff and Resing 1982). Figure 5-2 highlights the relationship between crises and chronic problems. It also illustrates:

- The interface between crisis and longer-term help for families such as Julie's, Ellen's, and others.
- The greater crisis vulnerability of people with chronic problems.
- The inherent limitations of applying only a crisis approach to chronic problems.
- The possible threat to life when crisis assistance is unavailable to people with chronic problems.
- The consequent need to use a tandem approach to certain intertwined chronic/crisis situations.*

SELF-HELP GROUPS

While social network and family groups are typically led by trained mental health professionals, self-help groups emphasize the strengths of the group members themselves. With roots in the consumer movement, self-help groups play an important part in all phases of crisis management: during the acute phases, in preventive endeavors, and in follow-up support. Key factors in the success of such groups are the creation of a climate of empowerment of individuals, plus bonding with others. People in crisis who share with others an acute loss such as sudden infant death syndrome (SIDS) or the stress of a child with AIDS will feel less isolated. The group is also a source of affirmation and information. Victims of violence, for example, can encourage one another to externalize their misfortunes rather than blaming themselves (Perloff, 1983, p. 57). Self-help groups exist in most communities for practically every kind of problem or health issue (eg, parents of murdered children, incest survivors, families of people with

*For further discussion of family dynamics and intervention strategies see Getty and Humphreys 1981, Rodgers 1973, Satir 1967, 1972, and Satir, Stackowiak, and Taschman 1975.

AIDS, mastectomy patients). While professionals do not usually "lead" such groups, they can help as catalysts, as a resource for getting a self-help group started, and for referrals to groups. As a source of help for people in crisis and with chronic problems, self-help groups have assumed growing importance in an era of increased consumer awareness of responsibility for one's health. However, such groups should never become a substitute (because of fiscal constraints) for the comprehensive professional health services that every citizen is entitled to.

SUMMARY

Individuals, families, and communities interact with one another in inseparable ways. Crises arise out of this interaction network and are resolved by restoring people to their natural place. Attention to these principles can be the key to success in crisis intervention; inattention to the social network is often a source of destructive resolution of crises. In spite of the heavy influence of individualistic philosophies in all helping professions, a social network approach is being used effectively by increasing numbers of human service workers.

REFERENCES

Ahrons D: Sources of stress in family reorganization after divorce. Presented at the National Conference on Social Stress at the University of New Hampshire, Durham, NH, 1982.

Allgeyer L: The crisis group: Its unique usefulness to the disadvantaged. *Int J Group Psychother* 1970; 20:235–240.

Antonovsky A: *Health, Stress and Coping*. Jossey-Bass, 1980.

Barnes JA: *Social Networks*. Addison-Wesley, 1972.

Berkman LF, Syme SL: Social networks, host resistance, and mortality: A nine-year follow-up study of Alameda County residents. *Am J Epidem* 1979; 109:186–204.

Boissevain J: Network analysis: A reappraisal. *Curr Anthro* 1979; 20(2):392–394.

Bott E: *Family and Social Network*. Tavistock, 1957.

Burr W et al. (editors): *Contemporary Theories about the Family*, Vol 2. Free Press, 1979.

Caplan G: *Principles of Preventive Psychiatry*. Basic Books, 1964.

Cobb S: Social support as a moderator of life stress. *Psychosom Med* 1976; 38:300–314.

Eliot TD: Handling family strains and shocks. In: *Family, Marriage and Parenthood*. Backer H, Hill R (editors). Heath, 1955.

Garrison J: Network techniques: Case studies in the screening-linking-planning conference method. *Fam Proc* 1974; 13:337–353.

Getty C, Humphreys W (editors): *Understanding the Family: Stress and Change in American Family Life*. Appleton-Century-Crofts, 1981.

Gil D: Sociocultural aspects of domestic violence. In *Violence in the Home: Interdisciplinary Perspectives:* Edited by M. Lystad. Brunner/Mazel, 1987.

Goodrich TJ, Rampage, C. Ellman, B. and Halstead, K. *Feminist Family Therapy*. W. W. Norton, 1988.

Gottlieb BH (editor): *Social Networks*

and Social Support. Sage, 1981.

Granovetter MS: The strength of weak ties. *Am J Sociol* 1973; 78:1360–1380.

Halleck S: *The Politics of Therapy.* Science House, 1971.

Hansell N: *The Person in Distress.* Human Sciences Press, 1976.

Hill R: Generic features of families under stress. In: *Crisis Intervention: Selected Readings.* Parad H (editor). New York: Family Service Association of America, 1965.

Hoff LA: Families in crisis. In: *Understanding the Family: Stress and Change in American Family Life.* Getty C, Humphreys W (editors). Appleton-Century-Crofts, 1981.

Hoff LA: *Violence against Women: A Social-cultural Network Analysis.* (PhD dissertation.) Boston University. University Microfilms International. No 8422380, 1984.

Hoff LA, Miller N: *Programs for People in Crisis:* Boston: Northeastern University Custom Book Program, 1987. *A Guide for Educators, Administrators, and Clinical Trainers.*

Hoff LA, Resing M: Was this suicide preventable? *Am J Nurs* 1982; 82:1106–1111. Also reprinted in: Psychiatric/Mental Health Nursing: Contemporary Readings, 2nd ed. Backer BA, Dubbert PM, Eisenman EJP (editors). Wadswortts, 1985.

Hollingshead AB, Redlich FD: *Social Class and Mental Illness.* Wiley, 1958.

Holmstrom LL, Burgess AW: *The Victim of Rape: Institutional Reactions.* Wiley, 1978.

Jarmulowski V: The blended family: Who are they? *MS* 1985; 13(8):33–34.

Kaplan BH, Cassel J, Gore S: Social support. *Med Care* 1977; 15:47–58.

Langsley D, Kaplan D: *The Treatment of Families in Crisis.* Grune and Stratton, 1968.

Lindsey K: *Friends as Family.* Beacon Press, 1981.

Lopata HZ: *Widowhood in an American City.* Cambridge, MA: Schenkman, 1973.

Lynch MM: *Unplanned Hospitalization of a Child: Mother and Father Perceptions of Stress, Recent Family Life Events and Coping Resources.* (PhD dissertation.) Boston University. *Diss Abst Int* 1987; 48(4), 1005B, 1006B.

Maslow A: *Motivation and Personality,* 2nd ed. Harper and Row, 1970.

Masnick GS, Bane MJ: *The Nation's Families.* Auburn House, 1980.

Maxwell MB: The use of social networks to help cancer patients maximize support. *Cancer Nurs* 1982; 5:275–281.

McCubbin H, Figley C: Stress and the family. Vol. II: Coping with *Catastrophic Stress.* Brunner/Maze, 1983.

McKinlay JB: Social networks, lay consultation and help-seeking behavior. *Soc Forces* 1973; 51:275–292.

McKinlay JB: Social netowrk influences on morbid episodes and the career of help-seeking. In: *The Relevance of Social Science for Medicine.* Eisenberg I, Kleinman A (editors). The Hague: Reidel, 1981.

Mitchell JC (editor): *Social Networks in Urban Situations.* Manchester, England: Manchester University Press, 1969.

Morley WE, Brown VB: The crisis intervention group: A natural meeting or a marriage of convenience? *Psychother* 1968; 6:30–36.

Moustakas C: *Individuality and Encounter.* Doyle, 1968.

Moynihan DP: The Negro family, the case for national action. In: *The Moynihan Report and the Politics of Controversy.* Rainwater L, Yancey W (editors). MIT Press, 1967.

Norbeck JS, Lindsey AM, Carrieri VL: The development of an instrument to measure social support. *Nurs Res* 1981; 30(5):264–269.

NOVA: *Crisis Response.* Washington, DC: National Organization for Victim Assistance, 1987.

O'Neill N, O'Neill G: *Open Marriage.* New York: M. Evans, 1972.

Parad H, Caplan G: A framework for studying families in crisis. In: *Crisis Intervention: Selected Readings.* Parad H (editor). New York: Family Service Association of America, 1965.

Pearlin LE et al.: The stress process. *J Health Soc Behav* 1981; 22(4):337–356.

Perloff LS: Perceptions of vulnerability of victimization. *J Soc Issues,* 1983; 39(2):41–61.

Polak PR: Social systems intervention. *Arch Gen Psych* 1971; 25:110–117.

Reverby S: A caring dilemma: Woman-

hood and nursing in historical perspective. *Nurs Res* 1987; 36(1):5–11.
Robinson D: *The Process of Becoming Ill.* Routledge and Kegan Paul, 1971.
Rodgers RH: *Family Interaction and Transaction.* Prentice-Hall, 1973.
Rubin K: Whose job is child care: *MS* 1987; 15(9):32–44.
Ryan W: *Blaming the Victim.* Vintage Books, 1971.
Sarason AG, Sarason BR (editors): *Social Support: Theory, Research and Application.* The Hague: Martinus Nijhof, 1985.
Satir V: *Conjoint Family Therapy.* Science and Behavior Books, 1967.
Satir V: *People Making.* Science and Behavior Books, 1972.
Satir V, Stackowiak J, Taschman HA: *Helping Families to Change.* New York: Jason Aronson, 1975.
Sommers T, Shields L: *Women Take Care: The Consequences of Caregiving in Today's Society.* Gainsville, FL: Triad, 1987.
Speck R, Attneave C: *Family Networks.* Pantheon, 1973.
Stanton S: Preventive Intervention with Stepfamilies. *Social Work.* 1986; May–June: 201–206.
Strickler M, Allgeyer J: The crisis group: A new application of crisis theory. *Soc Work* 1967; 12:28–32.
Trotter RJ: Project Day-care. *Psychol Today.* 1987; 21(12):32–38.
Walsh JA, Phelau TW: People in crisis: An experimental group. *Comm Ment Health J* 1974; 10:3–8.

PART TWO

VIOLENCE AS ORIGIN OF AND RESPONSE TO CRISIS

THE CRISIS PARADIGM presented in Part One links the origins of crisis with their possible outcomes. In Part Two, violence is discussed both as an origin of and a response to crisis (see Crisis Paradigm). Violence toward oneself and others is a major, life-threatening factor for individuals, families, and whole communities in many crisis situations. Chapters 6 and 7 focus on assessing and helping people who respond to crisis by suicide or other forms of self-destructiveness. Chapter 8 deals with violence toward others, including the crises of both victims and perpetrators of violence. In Chapter 9, violence affecting entire communities—disaster—is traced to natural and human sources. Because the effects of violence are destructive and often irreversible, the theme of prevention is reemphasized in discussing crisis and violence.

CHAPTER 6

Suicide and Other Self-destructive Behavior: Understanding and Assessment

A FRAMEWORK FOR UNDERSTANDING SELF-DESTRUCTIVE BEHAVIOR

THE PROBLEM

Some people respond to life crises with suicide or other self-destructive acts. George Sloan, whose case was noted in previous chapters, tried to kill himself in a car crash when he saw no other way out of his crisis (see Crisis Paradigm, lower right box).

Suicide is viewed as a major public health problem in many countries (Linden and Breed 1976, McGinnis 1987). In the United States, it is the eighth leading cause of death generally (McGinnis 1987, p. 20), the third leading cause among adolescents and young adults (Mercy et al. 1984) and the second leading cause of death among college students (Silver, Goldstein, and Silver 1984). The suicide rate among males ages 15–24 increased 50%, from 13.5 to 20.2 per 100,000, between 1970 and 1980 (US Department of Health and Human Services 1985), while the rate for women of all ages remained stable, around 4.3 per 100,000 (McGinnis 1987, pp. 23–24). While white males constituted 70% of all suicides in the United States in 1980 (McGinnis 1987, p. 21), Hendin (1987, pp. 152–153) found that in New York City the suicide rate among urban blacks of both sexes ages 15 to 30 was consistently higher than for whites of the same age for the first 70 years of this century, suggesting their continuing struggle with devastating social and individual circumstances. Similar factors place many American Indian adolescents at risk (Berlin 1987). The rate of suicide for all ages and groups in the US is about 12 per 100,000 and has remained relatively constant over several decades (National Center for Health Statistics

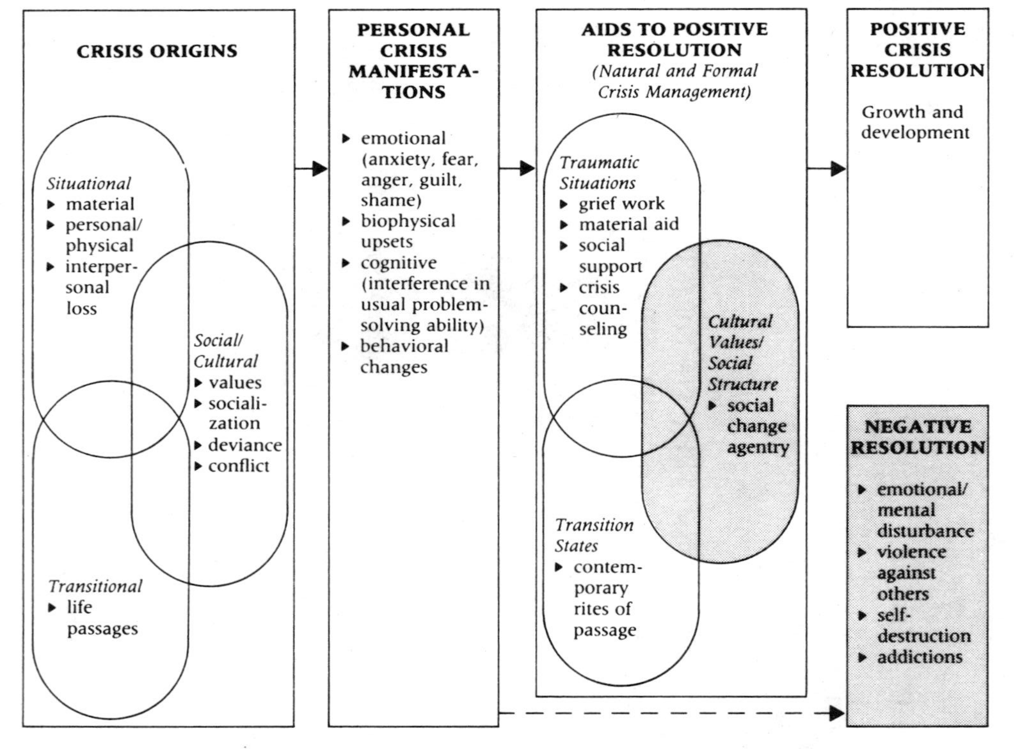

CRISIS PARADIGM

Crisis origins, manifestations, and outcomes, and the respective functions of crisis management have an interactional relationship. The intertwined circles represent the distinct yet interrelated origins of crisis and aids to positive resolution, even though personal manifestations are often similar. The solid line from origins to positive resolution illustrates the opportunity for growth and development through crisis; the broken line depicts the potential danger of crisis in the absence of appropriate aids.

1986). Contrary to popular belief, suicide rates drop around the holidays, except for a slight fluctuation among white teenagers (Phillips and Wills 1987).

The suicide rate among those under 40 has risen over the past 25 years; however, this rise can be attributed solely to suicide by firearms, particularly handguns (Boyd 1983, pp. 872–874). Among young males, around 60% of suicides are by firearms, and these occur at the top as well as the bottom of the socioeconomic scale (Hendin 1987, p. 155). Suicide rates among adolescents also reveal clusters, suggesting the controversial phenomenon of "suicide contagion" (Phillips 1985, Phillips and Carstensen 1986), a phenomenon contested by others (eg, Littman 1985). In spite of increased attention to adolescent suicide, the suicide rate among older white males is at least twice that of younger men (Maris 1985, McGinnis 1987, p. 21). Since white males in general enjoy greater socioeconomic status than all other groups, they appear to suffer more from the fall in social status in old age (Seiden 1981).

Suicide attempts occur at least ten times more frequently than suicides, with a total of approximately 300,000 annually. Among adolescents, particularly females, the attempt rate may be 20 to 50 times higher. Smith and Crawford (1986, p. 323) estimate that the suicide attempt rate among high school students ranges from 8.4% in Kansas to 13% in California.

Stephens's (1985) research on suicidal women suggests strong links to conflict and abuse in intimate relationships. She suggests that women with histories of exaggerated passivity may be at greater risk of future suicide than the rebellious (Stephens 1987). Women in general have higher rates of depression, commonly associated with socioeconomic disparities (Brown and Harris 1978, Kessler and McLeod 1984). However, research on why greater numbers of women who are abused or otherwise disadvantaged do not kill themselves is yet to be done.

Internationally, the wide range of suicide rates reveals further the complexity of the suicide problem. In Canada the age-adjusted suicide rate is 13.6.* In England, France, Italy, Denmark, and Japan the rates for men are consistently higher than for women. England has the lowest rate for old people and Italy the lowest rate for the young. In Japan the rate for women between 15 and 24 is half that for men (McGinnis 1987, p. 25), while in India for every 100 suicides, 70 are women (Menon 1988).

Because reporting systems differ widely, there are probably more

---

*For current comprehensive information on suicide, contact the Suicide Information and Education Centre, 1650 10th Ave. S.W., Calgary, Alberta, Canada T2N 2A4. Telephone 403-245–3900. The S.I.E.C., administered by the Canadian Mental Health Association of Alberta, contains a reference library that is kept current through international computer networking. Material is available to agency staff, educators, students, and researchers.

suicides than are reported. Cultural taboos, insurance policies, and other factors strongly influence the reporting of suicide. Some coroners, for example, will not certify a death as suicide unless there is a suicide note. However, everyone who commits suicide doesn't leave a suicide note. Research supports the claim that the compilation of suicide statistics, like suicide itself, is a social—not strictly scientific—process affected by cultural, social, and economic considerations (Atkinson 1978, Douglas 1967). Because of all these factors, we lack accurate and comprehensive statistics. Statistics about suicide, therefore, should be used primarily as an indicator of trends, not as a substitute for sensitive interpersonal work with particular suicidal people. For example, since suicide rates among adolescents and ethnic minority groups have increased the most dramatically in recent years, greater public attention is warranted than earlier lower rates seemed to indicate.

Suicide as a response to crisis is used by all classes and kinds of people with social, mental, emotional, and physical problems—including our relatives and neighbors. In short, people of every age, sex, religion, race, and social or economic class commit suicide. Perhaps most important of all, in a Judeo-Christian ethic, suicide is generally considered the most stigmatizing sort of death.

In this and the following chapter, suicide and self-destructive behavior are discussed from the perspective of the Judeo-Christian value system and the development of social science and crisis intervention in industrialized societies. Suicide conveys universally the value "death is preferred over life," making this discussion relevant in cross-cultural terms as well. However, particular belief systems will influence how and why suicide occurs and is interpreted in various non-Western societies. For a fuller cross-cultural discussion of suicide, see Bohannan 1960, Counts 1987, Edgerton 1976, and Farberow 1975.

PERSPECTIVES, MYTHS, AND FEELINGS ABOUT SELF-DESTRUCTIVE PEOPLE

Nearly everyone has had contact with self-destructive people. Some of us have relatives and friends who have committed suicide or made suicide attempts. We know others who slowly destroy themselves by excessive drinking or abuse of other drugs.

Among the readers of this book, a certain percentage will have responded to a life crisis by some kind of self-destructive act. For example, the suicide rate among physicians is one of the highest of any occupational group. Also, narcotic addiction, as a way of coping with stress, is prevalent among physicians and nurses. It is a tragedy that those whose main work is service to others often find it difficult to ask for help for themselves when in crisis. Perhaps more than any other group, physicians and nurses, particularly in hospital emergency rooms, come in direct contact with self-destructive people—individuals who have cut their wrists, attempted to kill themselves in a car crash, overdosed on pills, or attempted to drown their troubles in alcohol. These are only a few of the many consequences of self-destructive incidents that emergency service personnel have to deal with.

Volunteers and other workers in suicide and crisis centers are another group that has frequent contact with self-destructive people. About 20% of callers to these centers are in suicidal crisis. Counselors and psychotherapists also work with self-destructive people.

All of these workers and people in general have varying degrees of knowledge about suicide and self-destructive people. Unfortunately, myths and false beliefs about suicidal people are widespread. Some of the most common myths are (Pokorny 1968, Shneidman 1981, pp. 213–214):

> *Myth:* People who commit suicide are mentally ill. *Fact:* People who commit suicide are usually in emotional turmoil, but this is not the same as being "crazy" or mentally ill.
>
> *Myth:* Good circumstances–a comfortable home or a good job—prevent suicide. *Fact:* Suicide cuts across class, race, age, and sex differences, though its frequency varies among different groups in society.
>
> *Myth:* People who talk about suicide won't commit suicide. *Fact:* People who die by suicide almost invariably talk about suicide or give clues and warnings about their intention through their behavior, even though the clues may not be recognized at the time.
>
> *Myth:* People who threaten suicide, cut their wrists, or don't succeed with other attempts are not at risk for suicide. *Fact:* The majority of people who succeed in killing themselves have a history of previous suicide attempts. All threats and self-injury should be taken seriously. Not to do so may precipitate another attempt.
>
> *Myth:* Talking about suicide to people who are upset will put the idea in their heads. *Fact:* Suicide is much too complex a process to occur as a result of a caring person asking a question about suicidal intent.
>
> *Myth:* People who are deeply depressed don't have the energy to commit suicide. *Fact:* The "energy level" of another person is subjective and difficult to assess. People may kill themselves when depressed or following improvement. Frequent and repeated assessment is therefore indicated.

Some of these myths can probably be recognized among ourselves, family, friends, and associates. Even among professional mental health workers, these myths are more common than one would expect.

Professional suicidologists (those trained in the study of suicide and suicide prevention) believe that "suicide prevention is everybody's business." This is a difficult order, however, considering how many false beliefs about suicide still persist. It is not uncommon for nurses and physicians to resist dealing with self-destructive people with the mental excuse, "That's sombody else's job." People can hardly deal with something they know little about. We face a number of difficulties in trying to learn more about self-destructive people:

- Cultural taboos against suicide
- Strong feelings that people have about suicide and other self-destructive acts.
- Limitations of doing research on human beings.
- Intrinsic difficulty of examining the self-destructive process in those who commit suicide; such study is limited to determining the probable causes of suicide from survivors closely associated with the person.

In spite of these limitations, research and direct work with self-destructive persons have yielded promising results. Suicidology (the study of suicide and suicide prevention) is by no means an exact science. Yet the scientific knowledge and practices developed in the last few decades are a considerable advancement over responses based on myths and taboos.

Knowledge alone, however, is no guarantee of use of that knowledge. Many false beliefs about self-destructive people and responses to them persist because of intense feelings about suicide, death, and dying. What are some of the most common feelings people have about a self-destructive person? And why are these feeings particularly intense in the helper-client interaction?

As we try to help self-destructive people, we may feel sadness, pity, helplessness, desire to rescue, anger, or frustration. Some of these feelings are mirrored in the following comments:

- *Curious bystander:* "Oh, the poor thing."
- *Friendly Neighbor:* "What can I possibly do?"
- *Family:* "Why did she have to disgrace us this way?"
- *Nurse:* "I can't stand wasting my time on these people who are just looking for attention."

Feelings that follow suicide may include: disgust—especially if we hold strong beliefs about the "sinfulness" of suicide; relief—not uncommon among family members or therapists who have exhausted themselves trying to help the suicidal person; and guilt—which often follows feelings of disgust or relief.

Understanding these feelings and their sources is crucial if we are to prevent them from interfering with helping distressed people find alternatives to suicide. Our feelings about suicide and responses to self-destructive persons can be clarified from three perspectives: social, psychological, and cultural.

Social Perspective

Physicians, nurses, and other helpers are often frustrated in working with self-destructive people. This can be traced in part to the socialization these professionals receive in their role of helping the sick person return to health. Success in this role depends partly on whether patients behave according to expectations of people in the "sick role." Parsons (1951, pp. 436–437) identified the following exemptions and responsibilities associated with the sick role:

1. The person is exempt from normal social responsibility, depending on the nature and severity of the illness. This implies that the illness has been legitimized by a "mandated labeler," usually a physician (Becker 1963; see also Chapter 3). Such legitimation gives moral approval to being sick and also prevents people from using sickness inappropriately for seconday gains (Ehrenreich and Ehrenreich 1978, Zola 1978).
2. The sick person is expected to accept help and depend as necessary on the caregiver; it is understood that the person cannot improve merely by an act of will.
3. The person is obligated to want to get well as expeditiously as possible.
4. The person must seek technically competent help and cooperate with the helper.

This concept of the sick role is unproblematic if applied to acute illness such as appendicitis or kidney stones. In fact, it was the study of persons with precisely such acute physical illnesses that resulted in Parsons' "sick role" formulation. However, the concept is inadequate if it is applied to chronic illnesses or any condition with significant social, psychological, or cultural components—in short, any condition in which life-style or a willful act of the individual is directly related to the malady, such as smoking, drinking, or sexual contact (Levine and Kozloff 1978).

If so-called "social" illnesses do not fit the traditional sick role/helper model, think of the model's limitations when applied to a person who is self-destructive. Not only do suicidal people defeat the medical role of fostering and maintaining life, but self-injury appears as a deliberate flaunting of the natural instinct to live. The self-destructive person is requesting, directly or indirectly, a departure from the usual roles of patient and helper. If helpers deal with suicidal people according to rigid role expectations, the helper-patient relationship can lead to conflict. And if helping is limited to a medical approach when the problem is as philosophical, religious, and social as it is medical, the trouble of health professionals working with suicidal persons becomes more understandable.

Psychological Perspective

Role conflicts are complicated further if helpers have an unrecognized or excessive need to be needed or to rescue the self-destructive person. Not only is the helper denied fulfillment of traditional role expectations, but the suicidal person says in effect, "I don't need you. How can you save me when I don't even want to save myself?" This question is very much on target considering what we know about the failure of therapy without the client's voluntary collaboration.

The most complex manifestation of the social-psychological roots of conflict with suicidal people is in the victim-rescuer-persecutor triangle discussed in Chapter 4. In no aspect of crisis work is it more important than here that we be sensitive to a person's need for self-mastery, as well as our own need to control our rescue fantasies. Not to do so could result in a vicious cycle of exactly the opposite of our intentions:

1. Rejection of our misguided rescue attempts.
2. Frustration in our helper role.
3. Persecution of the suicidal person for failure to cooperate.
4. Suicidal person feeling rejected.
5. Suicidal person repeating self-injury.
6. Helper feeling like a victim.

Preventing and interrupting the victim-rescuer-persecutor cycle is one of the most challenging tasks facing the crisis worker, especially in dealing with self-destructive people. The social network strategies discussed in Chapter 5 are particularly helpful in this task.

Cultural Perspective

Self-destructive behavior takes on added meaning in cultural-historical perspective. Suicide and self-destructive behavior have been part of the human condition from the beginning of time; views about suicide, its honorability or shamefulness, have always varied (Rosen 1975). In the Judeo-Christian tradition, neither the Hebrew Bible nor the New Testament prohibits suicide. Jews (defenders of Masada) and Christians (martyrs) alike justified suicide in the face of military defeat or personal attack by pagans. Later, however, suicide took on the character of a sinful act.

Over the centuries we have seen transitions in considering suicide from a religious, legal, and finally medical perspective. Today these three major social institutions overlap in their interpretations of suicide (as will be discussed further in the next section). In spite of professionals' and civil libertarians' sophistication about the topic, the taboo on suicide persists.

Now, it is seen less as a moral offense than as a socially disgraceful act.

When thus viewed in social, psychological, and cultural perspective, our beliefs and feelings about suicide are not surprising. We are, after all, members of a cultural community with distinct values about life, ourselves, and other people and how we all ought to behave. These cultural facts of life are even more complex when considering the multiethnicity of American society and the current emphasis on preserving one's unique cultural heritage. It is impossible for us to know in detail the beliefs and customs of cultures to which we have had little direct exposure. What we can do, however, is educate ourselves about ethnocentrism (see Factors Influencing Communications in Chapter 4) and sensitize ourselves to not imposing our values on others. For example, in some belief systems the idea of an afterlife is meaningless, while for others, suicide might be precisely the avenue toward a better life after reincarnation.

It is easier to accept and deal with our feelings if we remember that these feelings and attitudes have historical roots and are complicated by contemporary socialization to professional roles. Failure to remember this can prevent us from being helpful to self-destructive people. This fact places a heavy burden on emergency and rescue personnel, who need an opportunity to express and work through their feelings about self-destructive behavior. Dealing with feelings and their origins, then, is a basic step in a worker's acquiring the knowledge and skills necessary to help people in suicidal crisis. Team relationships, peer support groups, and readily accessible consultation are some of the avenues that should be available to people working with suicidal persons.

ETHICAL ISSUES REGARDING SUICIDE

Closely related to our coping with feelings about self-destructive behavior are our positions on the issues of the right to die and responsibility for the lives of others. Within circles of suicidology, philosophy, psychiatry, and the general public the following are hotly debated topics:

- The right to die by suicide.
- The right and/or responsibility to prevent suicide.
- Related topics of euthanasia and abortion.*

There are several ethical and legal questions with implications for the crisis worker:

- How do we respond to a person's declaration: "I have the right to commit suicide and you don't have the right to stop me"?

*For a full discussion of these ethical issues, see Battin and Maris 1983; Battin and Mayo 1980; Brandt 1975; Humphrey 1987; Maris 1986; McGuire 1974; Richman 1988, and related works cited by these authors.

- If our own belief system forbids suicide, how might this belief influence our response to such a person?
- If a person commits suicide, whose responsibility is it?
- If we happen to believe that it is the suicidal person's own responsibility, why do we often feel guilty?
- What is the ethical basis of depriving the person of normal, individual rights through commitment to a mental health facility to prevent suicide?

In considering these questions, the intent is not to persuade the reader to give up cherished beliefs or to impose a libertarian view about suicide. Rather, it is to provide an ethical and clinical basis for dealing with the issues without either abandoning our own beliefs or imposing them on others.

Some workers may confuse suicide prevention efforts with a distorted sense of obligation to prevent any and all suicides whenever physically possible and by whatever means possible. The term "distorted" is used to emphasize the fact that:

1. It is physically impossible to prevent suicide in some instances unless we place a person in a padded cell and strip him or her of all clothing. This does not mean that suicide is inevitable; it means that if social-psychological aid is lacking, *physical* protection alone is inadequate.
2. *Forced* physical protection attacks a person's basic need for mastery and self–determination; therefore, it may result in the opposite of what is intended in the long run, even though suicide may be physically prevented in the short run. Such suicide prevention efforts may (a) impose on others the belief that people do not have the right to commit suicide, (b) result in the worker's unresolved "savior complex."

These beliefs and unconsious conflicts often exist along with lack of scientific knowledge about self-destructive behavior and inability to assess suicidal risk. The results may promote rather than prevent suicide:

1. Placing a hospitalized suicidal person in isolation. This is done for closer observation, but it increases the person's sense of abandonment, which, for someone suicidal, is already acute.
2. Involuntary commitment of a suicidal person to a mental hospital, in the belief that others know what is best for a suicidal person. This can be an attack on the person's sense of dignity and self-worth, yet mental health laws in many states encourage the practice among those working in public agencies or mental health professions. There is often little awareness that restricting individual freedoms can give the suicidal person one more reason to choose death over life.

3. Punitive medical practices, for example, using a larger tube than necessary to remove the stomach contents of the person who has taken an overdose of pills. Such a practice is based on the belief that physical discomfort will discourage future suicide attempts. In fact, the self-destructive person feels attacked and more worthless than ever.

The hidden function of these practices among workers is probably the expression of anger against the self-destructive person for violating the suicide taboo and for frustrating their helper roles. The suicidal person has little or no ability to understand such messages. He or she already has an overdose of self-hatred. Rejection by helpers as they carry out their service responsibilities can only increase a person's self-destructiveness.

Ethical and other opinions differ regarding the issue of responsibility to save others and the right of people to determine their own deaths.* Crisis workers need to consider the relevance of theoretical debates to their everyday interaction with suicidal people. The following case analyses illustrate some of the ethical questions.

Case Example: Rachel
The "Right" to Commit Suicide

Rachel, age 69, lived with her daughter and son-in-law and was dying of cancer. The community health nurse learned that she was entertaining suicidal ideas. In fact, Rachel spoke openly of her "right" to kill herself, though she had no immediate plan. After the nurse worked with the daughter and explored her feelings regarding her dying mother, the relationship between the daughter and mother improved. The daughter was put in touch with a respite service for families of cancer patients. Rachel was no longer suicidal and decided not to exercise her "right" to kill herself.

This case demonstrates the philosophical dilemma posed by rational versus "manipulated" suicide (Battin 1980). Among the rank and file of health and social service workers the word manipulation is commonplace, especially in respect to suicidal people. Several things are noteworthy about this usage: When a person is unsuccessful with a suicide attempt, the assumption is that he or she is inappropriately trying to manipulate a staff

*We need to distinguish between *ethical* and *legal* aspects of certain issues. For example, many people believe that suicide is ethically acceptable in certain circumstances, but regardless of personal beliefs, it is illegal in the US and most other countries to assist another in the act of suicide. Conversely, abortion is *legal* in the US, though people differ about whether it is ethically or morally acceptable.

person, family, or others. Thus, there is a moral connotation to the term. Yet crisis workers often do not acknowledge that manipulation is common in all social life; for example, the average person manipulates for a larger salary, different work shift, or better housing. When considering the right to commit suicide, we need to examine whether we, the members of a suicidal person's social world, have manipulated a person into "choosing" suicide. A person can be manipulated into suicide through material and social circumstances and through ideology.

Rachel's case illustrates: (a) her social circumstances, highlighted by the relationship with her daughter and changed through home health care given to the daughter; thus Rachel is no longer suicidal; (b) her ideology (belief about her value as an older person dying of cancer) about herself changes from nonproductive and worthless to valuable in the eyes of her daughter and herself, and she stops arguing her right to commit suicide. Thus, the argument of Rachel and others regarding their right to kill themselves becomes a moot point if the reasons for choosing suicide are the failure to: (a) relieve intolerable pain (Fagerhaugh and Strauss 1977), (b) provide relief to family caretakers (Skorupka and Bohnet 1982), and (c) examine critically a value system that holds no place for the "nonproductive" old, ill, or disabled. Jourard (1970) underscores this point in defining suicide as "an invitation [from social network members] to die." Rachel's case suggests that the "right to commit suicide" argument can cloak hidden social processes and values at work. Ironically, acknowledging a person's right to commit suicide can have a curious suicide prevention effect. Even if our own belief system disallows such a right, it is empowering (and therefore life-promoting) to respect and acknowledge our respect for others' beliefs. (See next chapter, p. 229, for conversation example and intervention plan for Rachel.)

At the other end of the age spectrum, let us consider the alarming increase in adolescent suicides:

- What are our children telling us about the life and the world we have created for them if they choose death over life at a time when life has just begun?
- Have we perhaps "manipulated" our children into suicide by creating a material and social world and value system that they feel are not worth staying alive for?
- If we acknowledge the "right" of an adolescent to commit suicide, do we ignore a larger question about reasons for hope or despair among young people?

Case Example: Diane—Adolescent Suicide

Diane, a high school senior, age 18, resisted all alternatives to suicide as proposed by a crisis counselor. She learned she was

pregnant, was rejected by her lover, and could not share her distress with her parents or friends. Abortion was not an acceptable alternative to her. She feared that continuing the pregnancy would mean failure to graduate. The counselor agreed with Diane's assertion of her basic right to commit suicide, but expressed regret if she followed through on that decision during the peak of her crisis. This acknowledgment seemed to give Diane a sense of dignity and control over her life and a new will to live, even though the only resource she perceived at the moment was the counselor.

Case Example: John—Mental Health Commitment

John, age 48, was placed in a state mental hospital against his will when he became highly suicidal after his wife divorced him. He also had a serious drinking problem. John had two very close friends and a small business of his own. The main reason for hospitalizing John was to prevent him from committing suicide. John found the hospital worse than anything he had experienced. He had no contact with his friends while in the hospital. After two weeks, John begged to be discharged. He was no longer highly suicidal but was still depressed. John was discharged with antidepressant medicine and instructed to return for a follow-up appointment in one week. He killed himself with sleeping pills (obtained from a private physician) and alcohol two days after discharge. The staff of the mental hospital did not understand how they had failed John.

John's case represents the complexity of the debate between commitment to protect against suicide and infringement on the right to self-determination. As the paralyzed hero of a movie put it regarding his resistance to treatment to keep him alive: "Whose life is it, anyway?" (also the the movie title). Even though suicide can be seen as rational in certain circumstances, John's decision could be seen as "not in his own best interest" (Brandt 1975). As such it comprises the ethical basis for depriving a person of personal freedom in the name of suicide prevention and treatment. That is, John had friends, and by objective standards something to live for, even though he could not see that at the time he killed himself. It could be argued, therefore, that the extreme saving action of the helpers is thereby justified.

John's eventual suicide, though, illustrates the care that must be taken in implementing mental health laws on behalf of suicidal people. First of all, the decision to commit a person must be based on thorough assessment. Second, even if he were found to be a serious risk for suicide, involuntary hospitalization seemed to contribute to rather than prevent John's suicide. Hospitalization is indicated for suicidal people only when natural social network resources are not present. This case is analyzed further in Team Analysis Following a Suicide in the next chapter.

Some people choose suicide even after considering the alternatives with caring people. The most public and controversial example was the planned suicide of artist Jo Roman several years ago. Her suicide plans and discussion with her family and friends were aired on national public television, followed by an interdisciplinary panel discussion of the issues by authorities on the topic.

Case Example: Paul—Rational Suicide?

Paul, age 64, had chronic heart disease. He had been depressed since his wife's death three months earlier. When he was laid off from his job, he became suicidal and talked with his doctor. Paul's doctor referred him to a community mental health center for therapy. He received individual and group psychotherapy and antidepressant drugs. After three months, Paul's depression lifted somewhat, but he was still unconvinced that there was anything left to live for. He had been very dependent on his wife and seemed unable to develop other satisfying relationships, even through the support group he joined with other widowed people. Paul killed himself by carbon monoxide poisoning after terminating therapy at the mental health center.

Paul's situation does not imply that suicide is inevitable. Rather, it suggests that it seemed rational for Paul to commit suicide rather than live in circumstances to which he apparently could not adjust. However, Paul's case also shows us what can be done to help people find alternatives to suicide, even though these alternatives may be rejected. The people who tried to help Paul can take comfort in the fact that they acted humanely on his behalf, though they may still feel regret. But we need to recognize our limitations in influencing the lives of other people (see Survivors in Crisis in the next chapter).

Currently, rational suicide is being discussed with respect to people with AIDS.

Case Example: Dennis—Rational Suicide?

Dennis, age 33, held a good job as a university professor when he was diagnosed with AIDS. Initially, Dennis was overwhelmed with shock, rage, and despair. He had been successful in his career, enjoyed a supportive circle of friends, and was comfortable with his gay identity. He decided to kill himself, but after surviving an anti-gay physical attack and helping two of his friends cope with a similar episode of violence, he became involved in a local activist group and no longer felt suicidal. Dennis reserves for himself, though, the possibility of suicide at a future time if AIDS progresses to the point of dementia for him.

Dennis' case illustrates the importance of control and self-determination for anyone in crisis. While we need to respect the decisions of people like Dennis, we must be particularly careful in reference to AIDS not to proffer rational suicide as a substitute for our humane response to this worldwide crisis (see Chapter 12).

The following is offered as a practical guideline to helpers in respect to the rights and responsibility issue regarding suicide: each person has the final responsibility for his or her own life. This includes the way one chooses to live it or end it. We have a communal responsibility to do what we reasonably can to help others live as happy lives as possible. This includes the prevention of suicide when it appears to be against a person's own best interests. It also involves examination of values and social practices that inadvertently lead people to "choose" suicide only because they are socially disadvantaged and see no other way out. Choice in these instances is not truly free. Our social responsibility does not require that we prevent a suicide at all costs. We need to recognize that misguided "savior" tactics can result in suicide if overbearing help is interpreted as control. Workers in human service professions such as nursing, medicine, mental health, and law enforcement have an additional responsibility: they should learn as much as they can about self-destructive people and how to help them find alternatives to suicide.

CHARACTERISTICS OF SELF-DESTRUCTIVE PEOPLE

To be understood is basic to the feeling that someone cares, that life is worth living. When someone responds to stress with a deliberate suicide attempt, those around the person are usually dismayed and ask "Why?" The wide range of self-destructive acts adds to the observer's confusion. There are many overlapping features of self-destructive behavior. For example, Mary, age 50, has been chronically destroying herself through alcohol abuse for 15 years, but she also takes an overdose of sleeping pills during an acute crisis.

Volumes have been written about suicide—by philosophers, the clergy, psychiatrists and psychologists, nurses, and crisis specialists. Academics and researchers have profound discussions and varied opinions regarding the process, meanings, morality, and reasons involved in the act of self-destruction. Precise definitions and a clear understanding of such behavior, therefore, are complex and difficult to achieve. However, in spite of academic differences, most people agree that self-destructive behavior signals that a person is in turmoil, or "perturbation" (Shneidman 1976, p. 53). We can enhance our effectiveness in working with suicidal people by becoming familiar with several aspects of self-destructive behavior and intervention practices widely accepted by experts:

- The range and complexity of self-destructive behavior.
- Communication and the meaning of self-destructive behavior.
- Ambivalence and its relevance to suicide prevention.
- The importance of assessing for suicidal risk.
- Sensitivity to ethical issues as an aid to understanding, assessment, and appropriate intervention.

SELF-DESTRUCTIVENESS: WHAT DOES IT INCLUDE?

Self-destructive behavior includes any action by which a person emotionally, socially, and physically damages or ends his or her life. Broadly, the spectrum of self-destructiveness includes biting nails, pulling hair, scratching, cutting one's wrist, swallowing toxic substances or harmful objects, cigarette smoking, banging one's head, alcohol and other drug abuse, reckless driving, neglect of life-preserving measures such as taking insulin, direct suicide attempts, and outright suicide (Farberow 1980, Menninger 1938).

At one end of the spectrum of self-destructiveness is Jane, who smokes but is in essentially good emotional and physical health. She knows the long-range effects of smoking and chooses to live her life in such a way that it may in fact be shortened. However, Jane would hardly be regarded as suicidal on a lethality assessment scale. Smoking by Arthur, who has severe emphysema (a lung disease), is another matter. His behavior could be considered a slow form of deliberate self-destruction. At the other end of the spectrum is James, who plans to hang himself. Unless saved accidentally, James will most certainly die by his own hand.

There are four broad groups of self-destructive people:

1. *Those who complete suicide:* Suicide is defined as a fatal act that is self-inflicted, consciously intended, and carried out with the knowledge that

death is irreversible. This definition of suicide generally excludes young children, since a child's conception of death as final develops around age 10 (Nagey 1965, Pfeffer 1986). Self-destructive deaths in young children are usually explained in terms of learning theory; the child learns—often by observing parents—that physical and emotional pain can be relieved by ingesting pills or banging one's head.

Classically defined, suicide is one of four modes of death, the others being natural, accidental, and homicidal. Shneidman (1973 p. 384) emphasizes the role of intention in an individual's death and proposes a reclassification of death as: (1) intentioned, (2) subintentioned, (3) unintentioned. If full information is not available about the person's intentions, it is difficult to determine whether the act is suicidal or accidental. Suicide is not an illness or an inherited disease, as popular opinion and some professional practice seem to imply.

2. *Those who threaten suicide:* This group includes those who talk about suicide and whose plans for suicide may be either very vague or highly specific. Some in this group have made suicide attempts in the past; others have not. To be noted here is that only suicidal people threaten suicide, and all suicide threats should be taken seriously and examined in relation to the person's intention and social circumstances.

3. *Those who make suicide attempts:* Stengel (1968) defines *suicide attempt* as any nonfatal act of self-inflicted damage with self-destructive intention, however vague and ambiguous. Sometimes the individual's intention must be inferred from behavior. Technically, "suicide attempt" should be reserved for those actions in which one *attempts* to carry out one's *intention* to die, but for reasons unanticipated (such as lack of knowledge of lethality of the means, or unplanned rescue) one *fails* in that attempt. Other self-destructive behavior can more accurately be defined as "self-injury" (McGee 1979). The neutral term "self-injury" should be substituted for the term "suicide gesture" since the latter suggests that the behavior need not be taken seriously, or that the person is "just seeking attention."

Some suicidal persons are in a state of acute crisis—in contrast to some who are chronically self-destructive—and therefore experience a high degree of emotional turmoil. As noted in Chapter 3, people in crisis may experience a temporary upset in cognitive functioning. This upset can make it difficult for a person to clarify his or her intentions or may interfere in making wise decisions. This feature of the crisis state is the basis for the general wisdom of delaying serious decisions such as getting married, selling one's house, or moving to a foreign country while in crisis. Certainly, then, it is similarly unwise to make an irrevocable decision such as suicide when in a state of emotional turmoil and crisis.

The ambiguity arising out of the crisis state should not be confused with a psychotic process, which may or may not be present. Nor should one go along with the prevalent myth that "only a crazy person could seriously consider, attempt, or commit suicide." Loss of impulse control influences some suicide attempts and completed suicides. In the large majority of instances, however, self-destructive behavior is something that people consciously and deliberately plan and execute.

4. *Those who are chronically self-destructive:* People in this group may habitually abuse alcohol and/or other drugs and are often diagnosed with personality disorders. A recent study of self-harm patients revealed that 65.8% had a previous history of self-harm (Barnes 1986). The complex relationship between multiple self-harm episodes and suicide risk is discussed further in Assessment of the Suicidal Person later in this chapter. Other people may destroy themselves by the deliberate refusal to follow life-sustaining medical programs for heart disease or diabetes. Still others engage in high-risk life-styles or activities that bring them constantly into the face of potential death. Such individuals seem to need the stimulation of their risky life-styles to make life seem worth living (Weisman 1973). These behaviors are not, of course, explicitly suicidal. However, individuals who engage in them may, like others, become overtly suicidal. This complicates whatever problems already exist.

When considering chronic self-destructiveness, Maris' (1981, pp. 62–69) concept of *suicidal careers* is relevant. In this framework suicide can be seen as "one product of a gradual loss of hope and the will and resources to live, a kind of running down and out of life energies, a bankruptcy of psychic defenses against death and decay" (p. 69).* Or as Shneidman (1987, 1985) puts it: "people reach 'the point of no return' in response to unendurable psychological pain"

THE PATH TO SUICIDE

Suicidal behavior can be viewed on a continuum, or as a "highway leading to suicide." The highway begins with the first suicide threat or attempt and ends in suicide. As in the case of any trip destined for a certain endpoint, one can always change one's mind, take a different road to another destination, or turn around and come back. The highway to suicide can be conceived either as a short trip (as in acute crisis states) or a long trip (chronic self-destructiveness extending for years or over a lifetime). But in either case, it suggests that suicide is a *process* involving:

- One's perception of the meaning of life and death.
- The availability of psychological and social resources.

---

*For an extensive analysis of suicide types see Baechler 1979.

- Material and physical circumstances making self-destruction possible (for example, a bedridden, helpless person may be capable of self-destruction only through starvation).

The continuum concept is also useful in understanding suicides that *appear* to result from impulsive action, as in adolescents. Even with adolescent suicides, though, examination and hindsight usually reveal a *process* including, for example, alienation, family conflict, depression, self-doubt, and cynicism about life.

A destiny of suicide is not inevitable. Whether one continues down the highway to suicide depends on a variety of circumstances. People traveling down the suicide highway give clues to their distress. The suicide continuum, therefore, can be interrupted at any point: after a first attempt, fifth attempt, or as soon as clues are recognized. Much depends on the help available and the ability of the suicidal person to accept and use help. It is never too late to help a despairing person or to change one's mind about suicide.

Lacking help, some suicidal persons try to relieve their pain by repeated self-injury. Their gamble with death becomes more dangerous. As they move along the suicide highway repeating their cries for help, they are often labeled and written off as manipulators or attention seekers. This usually means that professional helpers and others regard them as devious and insincere in their "demands" for attention. Some conclude that if a person were serious about suicide he or she would try something that "really did the job." Such a judgment implies a gross misunderstanding of the meaning of a suicidal person's behavior and ignores his or her real needs.

Individuals who are thus labeled and ignored will probably continue to injure themselves. The suicidal episodes typically become progressively more serious in the medical sense, signaling increasing desperation for someone to hear and understand their cries for help. They may also engage in the "no lose game" as they plan the next suicide attempt (Baechler 1979). The "no lose game" goes something like this:

"If they (spouse, friend, family) find me, they care enough and therefore life is worth living." (I win by living.)

"If they don't find me, life isn't worth living." (I win by dying.)

The suicide method chosen is usually fatal, but with the possibility of rescue, such as swallowing pills. "No-lose" reasoning is ineffective in instances when one could not reasonably expect rescue (for example, a family member rarely checks a person at 2:00 AM). It is nevertheless an indication of the person's extreme distress and illustrates the logic of the "no lose game."

THE MESSAGES OF SELF-DESTRUCTIVE PEOPLE

Despite differing explanations for suicide, most people agree that self-destructive acts are a powerful means of communicating; suicidal people are trying to tell us something by their behavior. Interrupting the suicide continuum depends on understanding and responding appropriately to messages of pain, distress, or despair.

Most individuals get what they need or want by simply asking for it. Or friends and family are sensitive and caring enough to pick up the clues to distress before the person becomes desperate. Some people, however, spend a lifetime trying to obtain, without success, what they need for basic survival and happiness. This may be because they cannot directly express their needs, because their needs are insatiable and therefore unobtainable, or because others don't listen and try to meet their needs. Finally, these people give up and attempt suicide as a last effort to let someone know that they are hurting and desperate.

Typically, then, suicidal people have a history of unsuccessful communication. Their problems with communication follow two general patterns:

1. Some people habitually refrain from expressing feelings and sharing their concerns with significant others. People in this group use the "stiff upper lip" approach to life's problems. Men socialized to be "cool" and rational in the face of adversity, and women to be social and emotional experts for everyone but themselves, contribute to the withholding of feelings. This kind of failure in communication is typified by:

a. A successful businessman who obtains a promotion, is threatened by his fear of not being able to handle his new responsibilities, and kills himself.

b. A mother of five children who works devotedly and without complaint for her children and husband, is considered an ideal mother, but one day kills two of her children and then herself.

c. A boy, age 17, who is an honor student, plans to go to law school, is the pride of his parents and the school, but one day is found dead of carbon monoxide poisoning in the family car.

In each of these cases, the response is great shock and consternation: "He seemed to have everything. . . . I wonder why? . . .There doesn't seem to be any reason." Yet hindsight usually reveals that there *were* clues (Shneidman and Farberow 1957), subtle changes in behavior that, along with a general tendency to repress feelings, should be regarded as quiet cries for help. The messages of these suicidal people are less explicit and there often is no history of suicidal behavior. Caring others, therefore, need great sensitivity; they need to encourage the suicidal person to share life's joys, troubles, and suicidal fantasies without feeling like an "unmanly" man, a "failure" as a wife and mother, or a "sissy" as an adolescent. Lacking invitations to share and live instead of to die, these people's despair may be forever unexpressed in the eternity of death.

2. The second pattern of communication problems is less subtle than the first. People in this group typically include those who threaten suicide or have actually injured themselves. Their suicidal messages are quite direct and are often preceded by other cries for help (Farberow and Shneidman 1961). Consider, for example, an adolescent girl's signals that something is wrong:

- At age 11: Sullenness and truancy from school.
- Age 12: Experimentation with drugs.
- Age 13: Running away from home.
- Age 14: Pregnancy and abortion.
- Age 15: First suicide attempt.

After a person's first suicide attempt, family and other significant people in the individual's life are usually shocked. They are more disturbed by a suicide attempt than by anything else the person might have done. Typically, a parent, spouse, or friend will say, "I knew she was upset and not exactly happy, but I didn't know she was *that* unhappy." In other words, the first suicide attempt is the most powerful of a series of behavioral messages or clues given over a period of time.

We should all be familiar with suicidal clues or cries for help such as: "You won't be seeing me around much anymore." "I've about had it with this job." "I can't take it anymore."

- "I'm angry at my mother. She'll really be sorry when when I'm dead."
- "I can't take any more problems (such as financial, alcoholic husband, housing) without some relief."
- "I can't live without my boyfirend," that is, "I don't really want to die, I just want him back or somebody in his place."
- "I can't take the pain and humiliation [for example, from AIDS] anymore."
- "There's nothing else left since my wife left me. I really want to die."

Behavioral clues may include making out a will, taking out a large life insurance policy, giving away precious belongings, despondency after a financial setback, distress from a critical life event, or engaging in behavior unusual for the individual.

Studies reveal that a majority of persons who commit suicide have made previous attempts. In the absence of attempts, 80% have given other significant clues of their suicidal intent (Barnes 1986, Brown and Sheran

1972). These behavioral, verbal, and affective clues can be interpreted in two general ways: (1) "I want to die", (2) "I don't want to die, but I want something to change in order to go on living" or "If things don't change, life isn't worth living. I want to die. . . . Help me find something to live for—please save me from myself."

It is up to the interested helping person to determine the meaning of suicidal behavior and identify clues from words and attitudes of the self-destructive person. This is done not by inferring the person's meaning, but by *asking*. For example:

- "What do you mean when you say you can't take your problems anymore? Are you thinking of suicide?"
- "What did you hope would happen when you took the pills (or cut your wrists)? Did you intend to die?"

There is no substitute for simple direct communication by a person who cares. Besides providing the information we need in order to help, it is helpful to the suicidal person. It tells the person directly that we are interested and concerned about motives for the contemplated suicide. Often self-destructive people have lacked the advantages of direct communication all their lives.

Unfortunately, many people lack the knowledge or resources to respond helpfully to a suicidal person. The self-destructive person is often surrounded by others who potentially could help, but whose own troubles prevent them from providing what the self-destructive person needs. Some families are so needy that the most they can do is obtain medical treatment for the suicidal person. This situtation is not helped by the fact that 24-hour crisis services are absent in some communities.

Some would-be helpers fail to communicate directly about suicide in the false belief that talking to the person about possible suicide intentions may trigger the person into the idea, if he or she doesn't already have it. The process of deciding to commit suicide is much more complicated than such reasoning implies. A person who is not suicidal will not become so by a direct question from someone intending to help. In fact, experience reveals that suicidal people are relieved when someone is sensitive enough to respond to their despair and thus help protect them from themselves.

For three reasons, then, communication is crucial in our work with people who respond to crisis by self-destructive behavior:

1. It is a key element in discerning the *process* of self-destruction (understanding).
2. It is the most effective means of ascertaining the person's intention regarding death (assessment of risk).
3. It is an essential avenue for helping the person feel reconnected to other human beings and finding a reason to live (crisis intervention).

AMBIVALENCE: WEIGHING LIFE AND DEATH

Suicidal people usually struggle with two irreconcilable wishes: the desire to live and, at the same time, the desire to die. Simultaneously, they consider the advantages of life and death. This state of mind is known as *ambivalence.* As long as the person has ambivalent feelings about life and death, it is possible to help the individual consider choices on the side of life. Suicide is not inevitable. People can change their minds if they find realistic alternatives to suicide. The concept of ambivalence is basic to the purpose of suicide prevention and crisis work; those who are no longer ambivalent do not usually come to emergency rooms or call police and suicide hotlines.

CASE EXAMPLE: SALLY

Sally, age 16, made a suicide attempt by swallowing six sleeping pills, which, medically, is a nonserious attempt. Though she contemplated death, she also wanted to live. She hoped that the suicide attempt would bring about some change in her miserable family life so that she could avoid the last resort of suicide itself. Before her suicide attempt, Sally was having trouble in school, ran away from home once, experimented with drugs, and in general engaged in behavior that brought disapproval from her parents.

All these behaviors were Sally's way of saying "Listen to me! Can't you see that I'm miserable . . . that I can't control myself . . . that I can't go on like this anymore?" Sally had been upset for several years by her parents' constant fighting and playing favorites with the children. Her father drank heavily and frequently was away from home. When Sally's school counselor recommended family counseling, her family refused out of shame. Her acting out was really a cry for help. After her suicide attempt, her parents accepted counseling, Sally's behavior improved generally, and she made no further suicide attempts.

If Sally had not obtained the help she needed, it is probable that she would have continued down the highway to suicide. The usual pattern in such a case is that the attempts become more serious in the medical sense, the person becomes more desperate and finally commits suicide. Helping the ambivalent person move in the direction of life is done by understanding and responding to the meaning of the *message* of his or her behavior.

ASSESSMENT OF THE SUICIDAL PERSON

Communication leads to understanding, which is the foundation for decision and action. Helping suicidal people without understanding the meaning of their behavior and the degree of suicide risk is difficult. *Suicide risk assessment* is the process of determining the likelihood of suicide for a particular person.* The assessment tries to answer the question: What is the risk of death by suicide for this individual?

Some workers use lethality assessment scales to predict suicidal risk. Most of these scales are not very effective (Brown and Sheran 1972). Motto et al. (1985, p. 139) state: "The use of a scale has never been intended to predict suicide, but simply to supplement clinical judgement at the time an evaluation is done." The problem with most scales is that they do not exclude the nonsuicidal population. For example, let's consider depression as a predictive sign. A large number of people who commit suicide (approximately 70%) have been diagnosed as depressed; however, the majority of depressed people do not commit suicide. Similarly, the majority of people who commit suicide have made previous suicide attempts; yet 8 out of 10 people who attempt suicide never go on to commit suicide. These statistics do not invite complacency; they simply indicate that something changed—a cry for help was heard. Standard psychological tests such as the Minnesota Multiphasic Personality Inventory (MMPI) are also not very helpful in assessing suicide risk.

THE IMPORTANCE OF ASSESSING SUICIDE RISK

The importance of suicide risk assessment can be compared to the importance of diagnosing a cough before beginning treatment. Effective assessment of suicide risk should accomplish the following:

- Cut down on guesswork approaches in working with self-destructive people.
- Reduce the confusion and disagreement that often occur among those trying to help suicidal people.
- Provide a scientific base for service plans for self-destructive people.
- Assure that hospitalization of suicidal persons is used appropriately.
- Decrease a worker's level of anxiety in working with suicidal persons.

*Lethality assessment refers to the degree of physical injury incurred by a particular self-destructive act. Sometimes "lethality assessment" and "suicide risk assessment" are used interchangeably.

Failure to assess the degree of suicide risk results in unnecessary problems. For example, Linda, age 22, who lives alone and feels alienated from her family, was treated medically for her cut wrist and discharged without follow-up counseling. The emergency room staff assumed that she was "just seeking attention." Since the message and long-range risk of Linda's suicide attempt were missed, we can predict that she will very probably make another attempt in the future.

Another problem arising out of guesswork about suicide risk is unnecessary hospitalization. It is inappropriate to hospitalize a suicidal person when the degree of suicide risk is very low and other sources of protection are available. A person who hopes, by a suicide attempt, to relieve his or her isolation from family may feel even more isolated in a psychiatric hospital. This is especially true when community and family intervention are indicated instead.

Sometimes community and hospital workers hospitalize suicidal people out of their own anxiety about suicide. Unresolved feelings of guilt and responsibility regarding suicide usually precipitate such action. On the other hand, as we assess highly suicidal persons we should recognize the hospital as a resource to relieve isolation and prevent suicide when social supports in the community are lacking. As with personal factors, assumptions about the presence or absence of social supports should not be made if a systematic social assessment has not been done (see Chapters 3 and 5).

SIGNS THAT HELP ASSESS SUICIDE RISK

Lethality assessment techniques are based on knowledge obtained from the study of completed suicides. Suicide research is one of the most difficult among human scientific studies (Smith and Maris 1986). Nevertheless, the study of completed suicides has explained much about the problem of predicting suicide. Brown and Sheran (1972), Beck, Resnink, and Lettieri (1974), Motto (1977), and others have identified signs that help us predict the degree of risk for suicide. The most reliable predictors help us distinguish people who commit suicide from the population at large and also from those who only attempt suicide. These signs, however, have their limitations. For instance, there is not enough research on suicide to warrant general conclusions abut suicide for different population groups (Smith and Maris 1986). One should not be overconfident in applying signs to a suicidal person. It is impossible to predict suicide in any absolute sense. However, attention to the signs of suicide risk that we know about is a considerable improvement over an approach based on myth, taboo, and unresearched guesswork. The chaos of a crisis situation and anxiety about suicide can be reduced by thoughtful attention to general principles based on research.

The following material regarding signs that help us predict suicide is summarized from the works of Alvarez (1971); Beck, Resnik, and Lettieri (1974); Brown and Sheran (1972); Dublin (1963); Durkheim (1951); Farberow (1975); Hatton, Valente, and Rink (1984); Hendin (1982, 1987);

Jacobs (1971); Litman (1987); Maris (1981, 1985); Shneidman (1985); and Wandrei (1985). These principles for assessing suicide risk apply to *any* person in *any* setting contacted through *any* helping situation: telephone, office, hospital, home, jail, nursing home, school, or pastoral care. The following discussion is based on research in Western societies. It is recognized that suicide signs and methods will vary in other cultural settings (see Farberow 1975). Sensitivity to these differences, however, is also important in helping various immigrant and ethnic groups in distress in North America.

Suicide Plan

Studies reveal that the majority of persons who die by suicide planned deliberately to do so. This is in contrast to the myth that people who commit suicide do not know what they are doing, or are crazy. In respect to the plan, people suspected of being suicidal should be asked several direct questions concerning the following subjects:

1. *Suicidal ideas:* "Are you so upset that you're thinking of suicide?" or "Are you thinking about hurting yourself?"

2. *Lethality of method:* The interviewer should ask: "What are you thinking of doing?"

▶ *High lethal methods*:

Gun

Jumping

Hanging

Drowning

Carbon monoxide poisoning

Barbiturates and prescribed sleeping pills

Aspirin (high dose) and acetaminophen (Tylenol)

Car crash

Exposure to extreme cold

Antidepressants (such as Elavil)

▶ *Low lethal methods:*

Wrist cutting

Nonprescription drugs (excluding aspirin and Tylenol)

Tranquilizers (such as Valium and Dalmane)

The helper should also determine the person's knowledge about the lethality of the chosen method. For example, a person who takes ten tranquilizers with the mistaken belief that the dose is fatal is alive more accidentally than by intent.

3. *Availability of means.* "Do you have a gun? Do you know how to use it? Do you have ammunition?" "Do you have pills?" Lives have often been saved by removal of very lethal methods such as guns and sleeping pills. A highly suicidal person who calls a crisis center is often making a final effort to get some help, even though he or she may be sitting next to a loaded gun or bottle of pills. Such an individual will welcome a direct, protective gesture from a telephone counselor such as: "Why don't you put the gun away?" or, "Why don't you throw the pills out . . . and then let's talk about what's troubling you." When friends and family are involved, they too should be directed to get rid of the suicide means. In disposing of lethal weapons it is important to engage the suicidal person actively in the process, keeping in mind that power ploys can trigger rather than prevent suicide. If trust and rapport have been established, engaging the suicidal person is generally not difficult to do.

4. *Specificity of plan:* "Do you have a plan worked out for killing yourself? How do you plan to get the pills (the gun)?" A person who has a well-thought-out plan—including time, place, and circumstances—with an available high lethal method is an immediate high risk for suicide. We should also determine whether any rescue possibilities are included in the plan: "What time of day (or night) do you plan to do this?" "Is there anyone else around at that time?" We should also find out about the person's intent. Some people really intend to die; others intend to bring about some change that will help them avoid death and make life more liveable.

It is important to remember that we can seldom discover a person's suicide plan except through direct questioning. An individual who believes in the myth that talking about suicide may suggest the idea to the person will hesitate to ask direct questions.

The suicide plan is a less important sign of risk in the case of people with a history of impulsive behavior. This is true for some adults and for adolescents in general, who are inclined to be impulsive as a characteristic of their stage of development.

History of Suicide Attempts

In the US adult population, suicide attempts occur eight to ten times more often than actual suicide. Among adolescents there are about 50 attempts to every completed suicide. Most people who attempt suicide do not go on to commit suicide. Usually some change occurrs in their psychosocial world that makes life more desirable than death. On the other hand, the majority of people who kill themselves have made previous suicide attempts. A history of suicide attempts (65% of completed suicides) is especialy prominent among suicidal people who find that self-destructive behavior is the most powerful means they have of communicating their distress to others. Those who have made previous high lethal attempts are at greater risk for suicide than those who made low lethal attempts.

Another historical indicator is a change in method of suicide attempt.

A person who makes a high lethal attempt after several less lethal attempts that elicited increasingly indifferent responses from significant others is a higher risk for suicide than a person with a consistent pattern of low lethal attempts. This is particularly true in the case of suicidal adolescents.

We should also determine the outcome of previous suicide attempts. For example: "What happened after your last attempt?" "Did you plan any possibility of rescue, or were you rescued accidentally?" A person living alone who overdoses with sleeping pills, has unexpected company, and is rescued, is alive more by accident than by intent. He or she falls into a high risk category for future suicide if there are other high risk indicators as well. Suicide risk is also increased if the person has a negative perception of a psychiatric hospital or counseling experience. This finding underscores the importance of extreme caution in employing mental health laws to hospitalize suicidal people against their will for self-protection.

Resources and Communication with Significant Others

Internal resources consist of one's strengths, problem-solving ability, and personality factors that help in coping with stress. External resources include a network of persons on whom one can rely routinely as well as during a crisis. Communication as a suicide sign includes: (a) the statement to others of intent to commit suicide, and (b) the quality of the bond that exists between the suicidal person and significant others. A large number of people who finally commit suicide feel ignored or cut off from significant people around them, some to the point of feeling there are no significant people in their lives. This is extremely important in the case of adolescents, especially regarding their attempts to communicate with their parents. Research suggests that most adolescents who kill themselves are at odds with their families and feel very misunderstood (Jacobs 1971).

Institutionalized racism and the unequal distribution of material resources in the United States appear to contribute to the rapidly increasing rate of suicide among minority groups. This is especially true among the young (under 30) who realize early in life that many doors are closed to them. Their rage and frustration eventually lead to despair, suicide, and other violent behavior. An example of violence that is closely linked to suicide is *victim-precipitated homicide.* In this form of homicide, the person killed is suicidal, but instead of committing suicide, the victim incites someone else to kill, thus precipitating the homicide.

Others may have observable resources such as a supportive, caring spouse, but the conviction of their worthlessness prevents them from accepting and using such support. This is especially true for suicidal people who are also extremely depressed. Adequate personality resources include the ability to be flexible and to accept mistakes and imperfections in oneself. Some people who kill themselves seem to have happy families, good jobs, and good health. Observers therefore assume that these people have no reason to kill themselves. Research by Breed (1972) reveals that this kind of person perceives him- or herself in very rigid roles imposed by culture, sex identity, or socioeconomic status. A typical example is the middle-aged male executive who rigidly commits himself to success by climbing up the career ladder in his company. A threatened or actual failure in this self-imposed rigid role performance can precipitate suicide for such a person.

Such perceived failure is usually sex specific: work failure for men and family or mate failure for women (Stephens 1985). Other research, however, suggests that women may be committing suicide in response to "superwoman demands" to be the perfect unpaid domestic worker *and* paid public worker (Neuringer 1982). Investigation of completed suicides reveals that a person with rigid role perceptions commits suicide *after* receiving, for example, a long anticipated promotion, an event that leads the person to doubt his or her ability to fulfill higher expectations (Perrah and Wichman 1987). Such rigidity in personality type is also revealed in the person's approach to problem solving. The individual sees narrowly, perceiving only one course of action or one solution to a problem: suicide. This has sometimes been described as telescopic or "tunnel vision" (Hatton, Valente, and Rink 1984, p. 29, Shneidman 1987, p. 57). Such people typically are candidates for psychotherapy to help them develop more flexible approaches to problem solving. We should recognize this rigidity as a possible barrier in our efforts to help suicidal people consider alternatives. Thus, a person of this type whose personal and social resources are exhausted and whose only remaining communication link is to a counselor or helping agency is a high risk for suicide.

Research and clinical experience suggest that workers should look not only at the predictive signs but also at the complex *patterning* of signs (Brown and Sheran 1972, Farberow 1975). Let us apply this evidence to the pattern of the signs considered above. If the person (a) has a history of high lethal attempts, (b) has a specific, high lethal plan for suicide with available means, and (c) lacks both personality and social resources, his or her immediate and long-range risk for probable suicide is very high, regardless of other factors. The risk increases, however, if other factors are also present. These are discussed next.

Sex, Age, Race, Marital Status, and Sexual Orientation

The ratio of suicide among American men and women is approximately 3(male):1(female), although female suicides are increasing at a faster rate than male suicides. Among children between the ages of 10 and 14, the suicide rate is 0.3 to 0.6 per 100,000. Among children below the age of 10, suicide is almost nonexistent—less than one annually in the United States. Suicide risk increases with age only for white males. Among blacks, Chicanos, and Native Americans, the suicide rate reaches its peak under the age of 30.

The overall suicide rate among white persons is three times that among black persons. However, among young urban black men between 20 and 35 years of age, the rate is twice that of white men the same age. In Native American communities the suicide rate varies from group to group. In general, suicide rates are increasing among adolescents and racial minority groups.

If a person is separated, widowed, or divorced, the risk of suicide increases. Those who are married or who have never been married are at less risk (Smith, Mercy, and Conn 1988). This seems related to the loss factor among suicidal people, but does not seem to apply to two specific groups: older married white men who are simply "tired of living," and married black people who have lost a love relationship. While sexual orientation has been omitted in previous studies of suicide, Rich et al. (1986) found little difference in suicide rates between homosexual and heterosexual men. See Maltsbergser 1986 regarding limitations of statistical data to predict suicide in particular individuals.

Recent Loss

Personal loss or threat of loss of a spouse, parent, status, money, or job increases a person's suicide risk. Loss is a very significant suicide indicator among adolescents. Loss should also be kept in mind as a common theme in most people's experience of crisis in general (see Loss, Change, and Grief Work in Chapter 4).

Physical Illness

Studies reveal that many people who kill themselves are physically ill. Also, three out of four suicide victims have been under medical care or have visited their physician within four to six months of their death. The visit to a physician does not necessarily imply that the person is physically ill. But it highlights the fact that a large number of people with any problem seek out either physicians or the clergy. In the case of suicidal people, the visit may be their last attempt to find relief from distress. Of 12 men with AIDS who committed suicide, five had seen a psychiatrist within four days before suicide and two had seen psychiatric consultants within 24 hours of suicide (Marzuk et al. 1988, p. 1336)

These facts suggest the influential role physicians can have in preventing suicide if they are attentive to clues. The physician's failure to ascertain the suicide plan or to examine the depression disguised by a complaint with no physical basis often leads to the common practice of prescribing a mild tranquilizer without listening to the person and making a referral for counseling. Such a response by a physician can be interpreted by the individual as an invitation to commit suicide.

The possibility of suicide is even greater if a person receives a diagnosis that affects his or her self-image and value system or demands a major switch in life-style, for example, AIDS, heart disease, breast cancer, amputation of a limb, or cancer of sex organs.

Drinking and Other Drug Abuse

Drinking increases impulsive behavior and loss of control and therefore increases suicide risk, especially if the person has a high lethal means available. Alcohol also reduces the number of sleeping pills needed for a lethal overdose. Alcohol is involved in many deaths by suicide (Motto 1980). Many adolescents who die by suicide were involved in drug or alcohol abuse before their death.

Physical Isolation

If a person is isolated both emotionally and physically, risk of suicide is greater than if he or she lives with close significant others. According to Durkheim (1951), "egoistic" suicide occurs when people feel they do not belong to society; "anomic" suicide occurs among people who cannot adjust to change and social demands. One of the basic human needs is approval by others of our performance in expected roles. The lack of such approval leads to social isolation.

Negative reactions from significant people are incorporated into the sense of self. Rejection from significant others can lead to a conviction of worthlessness. When this happens, the person believes that others also see him or her as worthless. People who suffer from discrimination are at risk for "egoistic" suicide. However, once minority groups and women achieve equality and better conditions, studies indicate that their risk for "anomic" suicide will increase. If white society or male dominance can no longer be blamed, the person may internalize failure. This process can lead to suicide. As one black person put it: "Being on the ground floor left no room to jump." Thus, upward mobility may increase suicide risk.

A person who is physically alone and socially isolated is often a candidate for hospitalization or other extraordinary means to relieve isolation. In such cases hospitalization can be a life-saving measure.

Unexplained Change in Behavior

Changes in behavior, such as reckless driving and drinking by a previously careful, sober driver, can be an indicator of suicide risk. It is particularly important to observe behavior changes in adolescents since these changes are often clues to inner turmoil. Again, direct communication about observed behavior changes can be a life-saving measure, signaling that someone cares and is sensitive to another's distress, even though talking about it initially may seem impossible.

Depression

Depressed people may experience sleeplessness, early wakening, slowed down functioning, weight loss, menstrual irregularity, loss of appetite, inability to work normally, disinterest in sex, crying, restlessness, and feelings of hopelessness. Depressed adolescents are often overactive, may fail in school, or withdraw from usual social contacts. Not all people who kill themselves show signs of depression. However, a sufficient number of suicide victims are depressed to make this an important indicator for suicide. This is particularly true for the depressed person who is convinced of his or her worthlessness and is unable to reach out to others for help. Depression is a significant avenue for opening direct discussion of possible suicide plans: "You seem really down. . . . Are you so depressed that perhaps you've considered suicide?"

Social Factors

Social problems such as family disorganization, a broken home, and a record of delinquency, truancy, and violence against others increase a person's risk of suicide. Many adolescents who kill themselves had prior physical fights with their families. A person with a chaotic social background is also likely to follow the suicide attempt pattern of significant others. Suicide risk also increases for people who are unemployed or are forced to retire or move, especially when these upsets occur during a developmental transition stage.

Mental Illness

Some people falsely believe that only a mentally ill person could commit suicide. If an individual hears voices directing him or her to commit suicide, the risk of suicide is obviously increased. However, the number of individuals who fall into this category is extremely small. People who are diagnosed as psychotic should also be assessed for suicide risk according to the criteria outlined in this section.

Table 6-1 illustrates how signs of suicide risk help distinguish people who kill themselves from those who injure themselves nonlethally and from the general population. In the next section the pattern of these signs is described in a typology of suicide risk.

TYPOLOGY OF SUICIDAL BEHAVIOR: ASSESSING IMMEDIATE AND LONG-RANGE RISK

People tend to classify the seriousness of self-destructive behavior according to whether there is immediate danger of death. A person might engage in several kinds of self-destructive behavior at the same time. For example, an individual who chronically abuses alcohol may threaten, attempt, or commit suicide—all in one day. We should view these behaviors on the continuum noted earlier; all are serious and important in terms of life and death. The difference is that for some the danger of death is immediate, whereas for others it is long range. Still others are at risk because of a high-risk life-style, chronic substance abuse, and neglect of medical care.

Table 6-1

Signs That Help Predict Suicide Risk: Comparing People Who Complete or Attempt Suicide with the General Population

Signs	Suicide	Suicide Attempt	General Population
Suicide plan*	Specific, with available, high lethal method; does not include rescue	Less lethal method, including plan for rescue; risk increases if lethality of method increases	None, or vague ideas only
History of suicide attempts*	65% have history of high lethal attempts; if rescued, it was probably accidental	Previous attempts are usually low lethal; rescue plan included; risk increases if there is a change from many low lethal attempts to a high lethal one	None or low lethal with definite rescue plan
Resources* **• psychologic** **• social**	Very limited or nonexistent; or, person *perceives* self with no resources	Moderate, or in psychologic and/ or social turmoil	Either intact or able to restore them through nonsuicidal means
Communication*	Feels cut off from resources and unable to communicate effectively	Ambiguously attached to resources; may use self-injury as a method of communicating with significant others when other methods fail	Able to communicate directly and nondestructively for need fulfillment
Recent loss	Increases risk	May increase risk	Is widespread but is resolved nonsuicidally through grief work, etc.
Physical illness	Increases risk	May increase risk	Is common but responded to through effective crisis management (natural and/or formal)
Drinking and other drug abuse	Increases risk	May increase risk	Is widespread but does not lead to suicide of itself
Isolation	Increases risk	May increase risk	Many well-adjusted people live alone; they handle physical isolation through satisfactory social contacts

Table 6-1

Signs That Help Predict Suicide Risk: Comparing People Who Complete or Attempt Suicide with the General Population *(continued)*

Signs	Suicide	Suicide Attempt	General Population
Unexplained change in behavior	A possible clue to suicidal intent, especially in teenagers	A cry for help and possible clue to suicidal ideas	Does not apply in absence of other predictive signs
Depression	65% have a history of depression	A large percentage are depressed	A large percentage are depressed
Social factors or problems	May be present	Often are present	Widespread but do not of themselves lead to suicide
Mental illness	May be present	May be present	May be present
Age, sex, race, marital status	These are statistical predictors that are most useful for identifying whether an individual belongs to a high risk group, not for clinical assessment of individuals	May be present	May be present

*If all four of these signs exist in a particular person, the risk for suicide is very high regardless of all other factors. If other signs also apply, the risk is further increased.

Distinguishing between immediate and long-range risk for suicide is not only a potential life-saving measure, it is also important for preventing or interrupting a vicious cycle of repeated self-injury. If immediate risk is high and we do not uncover it in assessment, a suicide can result (see Hoff and Resing 1982). On the other hand, if immediate risk is low (as in medically nonserious cases of wrist slashing or swallowing a few sleeping pills) but we respond as though life were at stake medically while remaining indifferent to the *meaning* of this physical act, we run the risk of *reinforcing* self-destructive behavior. The person, in effect, is told by our behavior: "Do something more serious (medically, that is) and I'll pay attention to you." The reality is that in the long-range sense, medically nonserious self-injury is a life and death issue. That is, if the person's cries for help are repeatedly ignored there is high probability that eventually the person will accept our invitation to do something more serious—commit suicide.

The following schema assists in assessing suicide risk by means of a structured guide (see Table 6-2). Examples illustrate the application of risk criteria to people at low risk, moderate risk, and high risk. This assessment guide highlights the importance of the patterns of signs and the use of *clinical judgment* along with a data base—not simply mechanical rating—in evaluating suicidal risk.

Low-Risk Suicidal Behavior

This includes verbal threats of suicide with no specific plan or means of carrying out a plan. Also defined in this behavior is an attempt that, with knowledge of the effects of the method, involves no physical danger to life or clearly provides for rescue. Ambivalence in low-risk behavior tends more in the direction of life than death.

Table 6-2

Lethality Assessment Scales*

Key to Scale	Danger to Self	Typical Indicators
1	No predictable risk of immediate suicide	Has no notion of suicide or history of attempts, has satisfactory social support network, and is in close contact with significant others
2	Low risk of immediate suicide	Person has considered suicide with low lethal method; no history of attempts or recent serious loss; has satisfactory support network; no alcohol problems; basically wants to live
3	Moderate risk of immediate suicide	Has considered suicide with high lethal method but no specific plan or threats; or, has plan with low lethal method, history of low lethal attempts, with tumultuous family history and reliance on Valium or other drugs for stress relief; is weighing the odds between life and death
4	High risk of immediate suicide	Has current high lethal plan, obtainable means, history of previous attempts, has a close friend but is unable to communicate with him or her; has a drinking problem; is depressed and wants to die
5	Very high risk of immediate suicide	Has current high lethal plan with available means, history of high lethal suicide attempts, is cut off from resources; is depressed and uses alcohol to excess, and is threatened with a serious loss, such as unemployment or divorce or failure in school

*Adapted from specifications for use of forms discussed in Chapter 3.

The immediate risk of suicide is low, but the risk of an attempt, a repeat attempt, and eventual suicide is high, depending on what happens after the threat or attempt. The risk is increased if the person abuses alcohol and other drugs. Social and personal resources are present but troubled for people in this behavior group.

Case Example: Sarah

Sarah, age 42, took five sleeping pills at 5:00 PM with full knowledge that the drug would not kill her, and obtained the temporary relief she wanted in sleep. When her husband found her sleeping at 6:00 PM, he had at least some message of her distress. Sarah is troubled by her marriage. She really wants a divorce but is afraid she can't make it on her own. Sarah also takes an average of six to eight Valium per day. She has not made any other suicide attempts.

Suicide Risk for Sarah: The immediate risk of suicide is low (rating scale: 2). The risk of repeat suicide attempts is moderate to high, depending on what Sarah is able to do about her problem.

Moderate-Risk Suicidal Behavior

This includes verbal threats with a plan and available means more specific and potentially more lethal than those involved in low-risk behavior. Also included are attempts in which the possibility of rescue is more precarious. The chosen method, though it may result in temporary physical disability, is not fatal, regardless of whether there is rescue or not. Ambivalence is strong; life and death are seen more and more in an equally favorable light.

The immediate risk for suicide is moderate. The risk for a repeat suicide attempt and eventual suicide is higher than for low-risk behavior if no important life changes occur after the attempt or revelation of the suicide plan. The risk is significantly increased in the presence of chronic alcohol and drug abuse.

Case Example: Susan

Susan, age 19, came alone in a taxi to a local hospital emergency room. She had taken ten 5 mg tablets of Valium a half hour ear-

lier. Susan and her three-year-old child, Debbie, live with her parents. She has never gotten along well with her parents, especially her mother. Before the birth of her child, Susan had a couple of short-lived jobs as a waitress. She dropped out of high school at age 16 and has experimented off and on with drugs. Since the age of 15, Susan had made four suicide attempts. She took overdoses of nonprescription drugs three times and cut her wrists once. These attempts were assessed as being of low lethality.

At the emergency room, Susan had her stomach pumped and was kept for observation for one hour. She was discharged without a referral for follow-up counseling. While in the emergency room, Susan could sense the impatience and disgust of the staff. A man with a heart attack had come in around the same time. Susan felt that no one had the time or interest to talk to her. She and the nurses knew each other from emergency room visits after her other suicide attempts. Twice before Susan had refused referrals for counseling, so the nurses assumed that she was hopeless and didn't want any help.

Suicide risk for Susan: Susan is not in immediate danger of suicide (rating scale: 3). She does not have a high lethal plan and has no history of high lethal attempts. Her personal coping ability is poor (for example, her drug use and school failure), but she is not cut off from her family, though her relationship with them is disturbed. She has not suffered a serious personal loss. However, because there is no follow-up counseling or evidence of any changes in her disturbed social situation, she is at risk of making more suicide attempts in the future. If such attempts increase in their medical seriousness, Susan's risk of eventual suicide also increases significantly. On the ambivalence scale, life and death may begin to look the same for Susan if her circumstances do not change.

High-Risk Suicidal Behavior

This includes a threat or attempt with an anticipated fatal outcome unless accidental rescue occurs. Such behavior also includes instances when the method fails to end in death for an unplanned reason, such as in a suicide attempt by car crash. Another example is a threat that will be carried out unless a potential rescuer (such as friend, family member, or crisis worker) can convince the person that there are good reasons to go on living. Ambivalence in high-risk behavior tends more in the direction of death than life.

The present and long-range risk of suicide is very high unless immediate help is available and accepted. Chronic self-destructive behavior increases the risk even further.

Case Example: Edward

Edward, age 41, had just learned that his wife Jane had decided to get a divorce. He threatened to kill himself with a gun or carbon monoxide on the day she filed for the divorce. Jane's divorce lawyer proposed that their country home and the twenty adjoining acres be turned over completely to Jane. Edward told his wife, neighbors, and a crisis counselor that his family and home were all he had to live for. He and Jane have four children. Edward also has several concerned friends but doesn't feel he can turn to them. Jane's decision to divorce Edward has left him feeling like a complete failure. He has several guns and is a skilled hunter. A major factor in Jane's decision to divorce Edward was his chronic drinking problem. He had threatened to shoot himself eight months earlier after a violent argument with Jane when he was drinking.

Several strong signs of high risk can be identified in Edward's case:

1. He has a specific plan with an available high lethal means: the gun.
2. He threatened suicide with a high lethal method eight months previously and is currently communicating his suicide plan.
3. He is threatened with a serious interpersonal loss and feels cut off from what he regards as his most important social resources—his family and home.
4. Edward has a rigid expectation of himself in his role as husband and provider for his family. He sees himself as a failure in that role and has a deep sense of shame about his perceived failure.
5. His coping ability is apparently poor, as he resorts to the use of alcohol and is reluctant to use his friends for support during a crisis.
6. Edward is also a high risk in terms of his age, sex, race, marital status, and history of alcohol abuse.

Suicide risk for Edward: Edward is in immediate danger of committing suicide (rating scale: 5). Even if he makes it through his present crisis, he is also a long-range risk for suicide because of his chronic self-destructive behavior—abuse of alcohol and threats of suicide by available high lethal means.

CASE EXAMPLE: BARBARA

Barbara, age 77, is noted in the nursing care facility for her disagreeable personality and suspiciousness of staff and other residents. She has diabetes, heart disease, and asthma, the symptoms of which are exacerbated when she has an unpleasant encounter with others. Barbara has been moved to several different wings of the institution because staff "can take only so much of her." After her last move Barbara refused to eat or receive visits from other residents, resisted taking her medication, and said she just wanted to die. Barbara has a daughter and son-in-law who see her every few months. She also attends religious services routinely, the only usual activity she has continued.

Suicide risk for Barbara: Barbara is a high risk for suicide in both immediate and long-range terms (rating scale: 4). The outcome of her self-destructive behavior will depend on how staff and her family understand and respond to her distress. On the ambivalence scale, unless her circumstances change, Barbara will probably continue to see death as more desirable than life.

CASE EXAMPLE: SHIRLEY

A woman went to visit her mother, Shirley, at a mental hospital. She was not allowed to see her mother; Shirley was hearing voices telling her to kill herself, and was therefore placed in a special room with restraints. Her treatment consisted of psychotropic drugs and staff members periodically checking on her. After the psychiatrist convinced the daughter that a visit was not to Shirley's benefit, the daughter asked to be allowed to see her mother through the peek hole, unobserved by her mother. The daughter had had a dream about her mother dying and told the psychiatrist she would not be able to forgive herself if her mother did die and she hadn't seen her. The psychiatrist refused, then switched his argument and claimed to be protecting the daughter.

Suicide risk for Shirley: Shirley is an immediate and long-range risk for suicide (rating scale: 5). The physical restraint of Shirley decreased her immediate risk; however, it is now known that social isolation only pro-

Table 6-3
Suicide Risk Differentiation

Suicidal Behavior	Ambivalence Scale		Rescue Plan	Immediate Risk	Long-Range Risk	
Low Risk	Life ↓	Desires life more than death	Present	Low	High	Depending on immediate response, treatment, and follow-up
Moderate Risk		Life and death seem equally desirable	Ambiguous	Moderate	High	
High Risk	Death	Desires death more than life	Absent, or rescue after past attempts was accidental	Very high	High	

motes suicidal tendencies. Therefore, the long-range probability of suicide by Shirley is increased by the coercive measures used and by the psychiatrist's refusal to allow a caring daughter to visit.

The immediate and long-range risks of these suicidal behaviors are summarized in Table 6-3.

UNDERSTANDING AND ASSESSING RISK IN SPECIAL POPULATIONS

This entire chapter documents the wide range of people who are self-destructive and need help. The general principles of assessment apply to all people actually or potentially suicidal—the old, the young, different ethnic groups, institutionalized people, the unemployed, the educated, patients in medical/surgical wards, and psychotic and nonpsychotic persons in psychiatric settings. Still, trends and issues in the suicidology field suggest the need to highlight the special needs of adolescents, distinct ethnic groups, and suicidal people in hospitals and other institutions.

YOUNG PEOPLE

As we have seen, suicidal behavior is a cry for help, a way to stop the pain when nothing else works. Unnecessary death by suicide is a tragedy regardless of age, gender, class, race, or sexual preference, and regardless of variations in suicide rates among these different groups. But suicidal death by those who have barely begun life's journey is particularly poignant—for the victims themselves, their families, and all of society. The tragedy of youth suicide must not be lost sight of in statistical comparisons to other at-risk groups. Rather, it seems important to note that young people who kill themselves not only prefer death over life, but they are telling us in powerful behavioral language that they do not even want to try out the society we have created for them. The question is: Why? And what can we do to prevent these premature deaths? And how is youth suicide related to other problems such as substance abuse, violence against others, and entrenched social problems?

Increased public attention to these questions has resulted in a recent surge in literature on the topic (eg, Klerman 1986; Kraft 1980; Pfeffer 1986; Smith and Crawford 1986; and Sudak, Ford, and Rushforth 1984). The general criteria for assessing risk of suicide, as already discussed, are similar for adolescents and adults, except for adolescents' greater tendency toward imitation and impulsivity as seen in cluster suicides (Coleman 1987; Maris 1985; Smith and Crawford 1986). However, the issues are complex and the answers are not always clear. Recognition of the individual developmental, familial, and societal factors that interact in self-destructive youth will enhance the understanding and empathic communication necessary for risk assessment and suicide prevention among young people.

Teens in the US today feel great pressure to avoid failure in a society that is very achievement oriented. Yet as Maris (1985, p. 100) notes, citing Paul Goodman's *Growing Up Absurd* (1960), "the greatest problem that young people have today is their *uselessness*." As a distinct and increasingly prolonged phase in the life cycle, adolescence exaggerates this sense of uselessness while cultural messages emphasize that anything can be had in modern society if one only works hard and takes advantage of opportunities. This means that traumatic life events such as failure of an exam or breakup of a relationship are perceived as disasters by at-risk teens. Furthermore, the brutal reality for many is that individual efforts are not enough to overcome obstacles such as race and class divisions that are deeply embedded in the social structure and cultural values. This is particularly true for black urban males who face unemployment rates as high as 50% (Hendin 1987, Maris 1985, p. 100).

Complicating the increased hassles teenagers face today is the flux and change occurring throughout society, particularly in traditional roles for women and men. All adolescents face normal confusion and sexual identity issues, but family instability and the frequency of divorce create additional stresses for children. Thousands of teens also encounter problems with alcoholism, violence, and incest. Many suicidal runaway teens are victims of these family problems. Add to this the threat of nuclear disaster, and a teenager's hopelessness and disillusionment with planning a career and entering adult life are understandable (Bonner and Rich 1987, Hoff 1986, Joan 1986).

This is not to suggest that living in the nuclear age causes teen suicide. Rather, an attitude of societal fatalism regarding nuclear disaster combines with individual stressors, family and other social issues to create a climate from which many teens today will want to escape (see Chapters 1 and 2 on crisis origins). These issues are elaborated further in Chapters 8 and 11.

DISTINCT ETHNIC AND SEXUAL PREFERENCE GROUPS

The tragedy of suicide among ethnic minority groups in this society is often hidden behind the predominant presence of the white majority. Similarly, research about suicide among gay men and women has been neglected in favor of the heterosexual majority. Social and cultural factors have been cited as the origin of many crises, especially for those disadvantaged by the economic, political, and social factors stemming from personal and institutionalized racism and homophobia (Hendin 1987, Rofes 1983) (see Chapters 10 and 12). Understanding and assessment of individual pain and suicide risk in these instances is incomplete without particular attention to the cultural context of this pain. It is ironic to speak of the right of disadvantaged people to commit suicide when the basic rights of life are enjoyed on an unequal basis. Our common humanity demands a renewed effort to combine understanding of individuals in crisis with keen sensitivity to the social and political origins and ramifications of these crises (see Crisis Paradigm, right circle in first and third boxes, p. 176).

PEOPLE IN HOSPITALS AND OTHER INSTITUTIONS

Finally, a number of people are in institutions because they are suicidal or for other reasons: illness, infirmity, crime, or behavioral problems. Admission to an institution is often a crisis in itself. Not infrequently the "culture shock" experienced in this process is so extreme that suicide seems the only way out. This is one of the reasons suicides are more frequent in temporary holding centers than in prisons. Often, a person already suicidal feels so disempowered by the experience of institutionalization that suicide is the single action that says, "I am in charge of my life (and death)."

Preventing suicide, self-injury, and indirect self-destruction in institutions demands that:

- We do not use hospitals as a "catch-all" to prevent suicide.
- We abandon the notion that when a patient is under a physician's care, responsibility for intelligent assessment and intervention by others ceases.
- We recognize that the general principles of suicidology and risk assessment apply equally to hospitalized and other people: If physical and social isolation and powerlessness in-

crease suicidal risk, people in hospitals and other institutions who are isolated and powerless are at increased suicide risk (Farberow 1981).

This discussion of special population groups and the previous case examples is continued in the next chapter.

There are two final points about assessment of suicide risk to be noted:

1. Suicide risk assessment is an ongoing process. A person at risk should be reassessed continually. If important social and attitudinal changes occur as a result of a suicide attempt, the person who is suicidal today may not be suicidal tomorrow or ever again. The opposite is also true: a crucial life event or other circumstance can drastically affect a person's view of life and death. Someone who has never been suicidal may become so.

2. Suicide risk assessment is an integral aspect of the crisis assessment process. No assessment of a person who is upset or in crisis can be considered complete if evaluation of suicide risk is not included. See Chapter 3 for interview examples of how to incorporate these suicide risk assessment principles and techniques into routine crisis and mental health practice in emergency rooms and elsewhere (see also Hoff and Resing 1982).

SUMMARY

Suicide and self-destructive behavior are extreme ways in which some people respond to crisis. The pain and turmoil felt by a self-destructive person can be compared to the confusion and mixed feelings of those trying to help. People destroy themselves for complex reasons. Understanding what a self-destructive person is trying to communicate is basic to helping that individual find alternatives to suicide. Assessment of suicide risk is a difficult task. It is made possible by recognition of signs that portend the likelihood of suicide for particular individuals. Assessment of suicide risk is an important basis for appropriate response to self-destructive people.

REFERENCES

Alvarez A: *The Savage God.* London: Weidenfield and Nicolson, 1971.

Atkinson JM: *Discovering Suicide: Studies in the Social Organization of Death.* University of Pittsburg Press, 1978.

Baechler J: *Suicide.* Basic Books, 1979.

Barnes RA: The recurrent self-harm patient. *Suicide Life-threat Behavior.* 1986; 16(4):399–408.

Battin MP: Manipulated suicide. In:

Suicide: The Philosophical Issues. Battin MP, Mayo DJ (editors). St. Martin's Press, 1980.

Battin MP, Maris RW (editors): Special Issue: Suicide and ethics. *Suicide Life-threat Behav* (winter) 1983; 13(4).

Battin MP, Mayo DJ (editors): *Suicide: The Philosophical Issues.* St. Martin's Press, 1980.

Beck AT, Resnik HLP, Lettieri DJ (editors). *The Prediction of Suicide.* The Charles Press, 1974.

Becker H: *Outsiders: Studies in the Sociology of Deviance.* Free Press, 1963.

Berlin IN: Suicide among American Indian adolescents: An overview. *Suicide Life-threat Behav* 1987; 17(3):218–232.

Bohannan P (editor): *African Homicide and Suicide.* Princeton University Press, 1960.

Bonner RL, Rich AR: Toward a predictive model of suicidal ideation and behavior: Some preliminary data in college students. *Suicide Life-threat Behav* 1987; 17(l):50–63.

Boyd JH: The increasing rate of suicide by firearms. *N Engl J Med* 1983; 308(15):872–874.

Brandt RB: The morality and rationality of suicide. In: *A Handbook for the Study of Suicide.* Perlin S (editor). Oxford University Press, 1975.

Breed W: 1972 Five components of a basic suicide syndrome. Life Threatening Behavior, 2:3–18, 1972.

Brown GW, Harris T: *The Social Origins of Depression.* Tavistock, 1978.

Brown TR, Sheran TJ: Suicide prediction: A review. *Suicide Life-threat behav* 1972; 2:67–97.

Coleman L: *Suicide Clusters.* Faber and Faber 1987.

Counts DA: Female suicide and wife abuse: A cross-cultural perspective. *Suicide Life-threat Behav* 1987; 17(3):194–204.

Douglas JD: *The Social Meanings of Suicide.* Princeton University Press, 1967.

Dublin LI: *Suicide: A Sociological and Statistical Study.* New York: Ronald Press, *1963.*

Durkheim E: *Suicide,* 2nd ed. Spaulding JA, Simpson G (translators). Free Press, 1951 (first ed. 1897).

Edgerton RB: *Deviance: A Cross-cultural Perspective.* Benjamin/Cummings, 1976.

Ehrenreich B, Ehrenreich J: Medicine and social control. In: *The Cultural Crisis of Modern Medicine.* Ehrenreich J (editor). Monthly Review Press, 1978.

Fagerhaugh S, Strauss A: *The Politics of Pain Management.* Addison-Wesley, 1977.

Farberow NL (editor): *Suicide in Different Cultures.* University Park Press, 1975.

Farberow NL: Indirect self-destructive behavior: Classification and characteristics. In: *The Many Faces of Death,* Farberow NL (editor). McGraw-Hill, 1980.

Farberow NL: Suicide prevention in hospitals. *Hosp Comm Psych* 1981; 32(2):99–104.

Farberow NL, Shneidman ES (editors: *The Cry for Help.* McGraw-Hill, 1961.

Goodman P: *Growing up Absurd.* Random House, 1960.

Hatton C, Valente S, Rink A: *Suicide: Assessment and Intervention,* 2nd ed. Appleton-Century-Crofts,

Hendin H: *Suicide in America.* W. W. Norton, 1982.

Hendin H: Youth suicide: A psychosocial perspective. *Suicide Life-threat Behav* 1987; 17(2):151–165.

Hoff LA: Suicidal adolescents in the U.S.A.: A sociocultural psychological approach to assessment and treatment. Paper presented at Psychiatry in Africa and the Americas today, Nairobi, Kenya, African Psychiatric Association and American Psychiatric Association, 1986.

Hoff LA, Resing M: Was this suicide preventable? *Am J Nurs* 1982; 80:1106–1111.

Humphrey D: Letter to the editor: The case for rational suicide. *Suicide Life-threat Behav* 1987; 17(4):335–338.

Jacobs J: *Adolescent Suicide.* Wiley, 1971.

Joan P: 1986 Preventing Teenage Suicide: *The Living Alternative Handbook.* Human Sciences Press, 1986.

Jourard SM: Suicide: An invitation to die. *Am J Nurs* 1970; 70:273–275.

Kessler RC, McLeod JD: Sex differences in vulnerability to life events. *Am Sociol Rev.* 1984; 49:620–631.

Klerman GL (editor): *Suicide and Depression in Young Adults.* Washington, DC: American Psychiatric Press, 1986.

Kraft DP: Student suicides during a twenty-year period at a state university campus. *College Health* 1980; 28:258–262.

Levine S, Kozloff MA: The sick role: Assessment and overview. *Ann Rev Sociol* 1978; 4:317–343.

Linden LL, Breed W: The demographic epidemiology of suicide. In: *Suicidology: Contemporary Developments.* Shneidman ES (editor). Grune and Stratton, 1976.

Litman RE: Mental disorders and suicidal intention. *Suicide Life-threat Behav* 1987; 17(2):85–92.

Littman SK: Suicide epidemics and newspaper reporting. *Suicide Life-threat Behav* 1985; 15:43–50.

Maltsberger JT: *Suicide Risk: The Formulation of Clinical Judgement.* New York: New York University Press, 1986.

Maris R: *Pathways to Suicide.* Johns Hopkins University Press, 1981.

Maris RW: The adolescent suicide problem. *Suicide Life-threat Behav* 1985; 15(2):91–109.

Maris RW Basic issues in suicide prevention: Resolutions of liberty and love (the Dublin lecture). *Suicide Life-threat Behav* 1986; 16(3):326–334.

Marzuk PM et al.: Increased risk of suicide in persons with AIDS. *J Am Med Assoc,* 259(9):1333–1337, 1988.

McGee RK: Crisis intervention workshop. Nurenberg, Germany: Boston University School of Nursing, 1979.

McGinnis JM: Suicide in America—Moving up the public health agenda. *Suicide Life-threat Behav* 1987; 17(1):18–32.

McGuire D 1974. Death by chance death by choice. *The Atlantic,* 233: 56–65

Menningker K: *Man against Himself.* Harcourt Brace Jovanovich, 1938.

Menon R: Personal Communication. June 26, 1988. Publisher: Kali for Women, New Delhi, India.

Mercy JA et al.: 1984. Patterns of youth suicide in the United States. *Ed Horizons* 1984; 62:124–127.

Motto J: Estimation of suicide risk by the use of clinical models. *Suicide Life-threat Behav* 1977; 7:236–245.

Motto J: Suicide risk factors in alcohol abuse. *Suicide Life-threat Behav* 1980; 10:230–238.

Motto J et al.: Preliminary field testing of a risk estimator for suicide. *Suicide Life-threat Behav* 1985; 15(3):139–150.

Nagey MI: The child's view of death. In: *The Meaning of Death.* Feifel H (editor). McGraw-Hill, 1965.

National Center for Health Statistics. Births, marriages, divorces, and deaths for January 1986 (provisional data). *Monthly Vital Statistics Report,* 35:1–12, 1986.

Neuringer C: Suicidal behavior in women. *Crisis* 1982; 3:41–49.

Parsons T: *The Social System.* Chapter 10: The case of modern medical practice. Free Press, 1951.

Perrah M, Wichman H: Cognitive rigidity in suicide attempters. *Suicide Life-threat Behav* 1987; 17(3):251–255.

Pfeffer CR: *The Suicidal Child.* Guilford, 1986.

Phillips DP: The Werther effect: Suicide and other forms of violence are contagious. *Sciences* 1985; 25:32–39.

Phillips DP, Carstensen LL: Clustering of teenage suicides after television news stories about suicide. *N Engl J Med* 1986; 315:658–689.

Phillips DP, Wills JS: A drop in suicides around major national holidays. *Suicide Life-threat Behav* 1987; 17(1):1–12.

Pokorny AD: Myths about suicide. In: *Suicidal Behaviors: Diagnosis and Management.* Resnik HLP (editor). Little, Brown, 1968.

Rich CL et al.: San Diego suicide study: Comparison of gay to straight males. *Suicide Life-threat Behav* 1986; 16(4):448–457.

Richman J: The case against rational suicide. *Suicide Life-threat Behav* 1988; 18(3): 285–289.

Rofes EE: *"I Thought People Like That Killed Themselves": Lesbians, Gay Men and Suicide.* San Francisco: Grey Fox Press, 1983.

Rosen G: History. In: *A Handbook for the Study of Suicide.* Perlin S (editor). Oxford University Press, 1975.

Seiden RH: Mellowing with age: Factors influencing the nonwhite suicide rate. *Int J Aging Devel* 1981; 13(4):265–284.

Shneidman ES: *Definition of Suicide.* Wiley, 1985.

Shneidman ES: At the point of no return. *Psychol Today.* 1987; 21(3):54–58.

Shneidman ES: Suicide. *Encyclopaedia*

Britannica. Reprinted in: *Suicide Life-threat Behav* 1973; 11:198–220, 1981.

Shneidman ES (editor): *Suicidology: Contemporary Developments*. Grune and Stratton, 1976.

Shneidman ES: Suicide. *Suicide Life-threat Behav* 1981; 11:198–220.

Shneidman ES, Farberow NL (editors): *Clues to Suicide*. McGraw-Hill, 1957.

Silver BJ, Goldstein SE, Silver LB: The 1990 objectives for the nation for control of stress and violent behavior: Progress report. *Public Health Reports, 1984*. 99:374–384.

Skorupka P, Bohnet N: Primary caregivers' perceptions that met their needs in a home care hospice setting. *Cancer Nurs* 1982; 5:371–374.

Smith JD, Mercy JA, Conn JM: Marital status and the risk of suicide. *Am J Pub Health* 1988; 78(1):78–80.

Smith K, Crawford S: Suicidal behavior among "normal" high school students. *Suicide Life-threat Behav* 1986; 16(3):313–325.

Smith K, Maris R: Suggested recommendations for the study of suicide and other life-threatening behaviors. *Suicide Life-threat Behav* 1986; 16(1):67–69.

Stengel E: Attempted suicides. In: *Suicidal Behaviors: Diagnosis and Management*. Resnik HLP (editor). Little, Brown, 1968.

Stephens BJ: Suicidal women and their relationships with husbands, boyfriends, and lovers. *Suicide Life-threat Behav* 1985; 15(2):77–90.

Stephens BJ: Cheap thrills and humble pie: The adolescence of female suicide attempters. *Suicide Life-threat Behav* 1987; 17(2):107–118.

Sudak HS, Ford AB, Rushforth NB (editors): *Suicide in the Young*. Boston: John Wright, 1984.

US Department of Health and Human Services: Suicide surveillance summary: 1970–1980. Atlanta: Centers for Disease Control, 1985.

Wandrei KE: Identifying potential suicides among high-risk women. *Soc Work*. (Nov/Dec) 1985:511–517.

Weisman A: Death and Self-destruction Behaviors. In *Suicide Prevention in the 1970s*. Washington, D.C. U.S. Government Printing Office, Pub. No (HSM), 72-9054.

Zola IK: Medicine as an institution of social control. In: *The Cultural Crisis of Modern Medicine*. Ehrenreich J (editor). Monthly Review Press, 1978.

CHAPTER 7

Helping Self-destructive People and Survivors of Suicide

COMPREHENSIVE SERVICE FOR SELF-DESTRUCTIVE PEOPLE

Everyone who threatens or attempts suicide should have access to all the services the crisis calls for. Three kinds of service should be available for suicidal and self-destructive people:

1. Emergency medical treatment.
2. Crisis intervention.
3. Follow-up counseling or therapy.

EMERGENCY MEDICAL TREATMENT

Emergency medical treatment is indicated for anyone who has already made a suicide attempt. Unfortunately, this is still all that is received by a large number of people who attempt suicide. Everyone—friend, neighbor, family member, passer-by—is obligated by simple humanity to help a suicidal person obtain medical treatment. The first-aid aspects of such treatment can be performed by police, volunteer fireworkers, rescue squads, or anyone familiar with first-aid procedures.

In any situation where there is immediate danger of death, the police should be called, because police and rescue squads have the greatest possibility of assuring rapid transportation to a hospital. If there is any question about the medical seriousness of the suicide attempt, a physician should be called. The best way to obtain a medical opinion in such cases is to call a local hospital emergency room. In large communities, there is always a physician there; in small ones, a physician is on call.

Most communities also have poison control centers, usually attached to a hospital. In cases of drug overdose, when the lethality level of the drug is not certain, a poison control center should be called. The amount of a drug necessary to cause death depends on the kind of drug, the size of the person, and the person's tolerance for the drug in cases of addiction. Sleeping pills are the most dangerous.

In general, *a lethal dose is ten times the normal dose.* In combination with alcohol, only *half* the amount is necessary to cause death. Aspirin is also much more dangerous than is commonly believed. One hundred five-grain tablets can cause death; less is needed if other drugs are also taken. Tylenol (acetaminophen), an aspirin substitute, is even more dangerous, as it cannot be removed from body tissue by dialysis. Tranquilizers are less dangerous; however, antidepressant drugs can be used as a suicide weapon.

Some suicidal people have gone through hospital emergency rooms, intensive care, surgical units, and on to discharge with no explicit attention paid to the primary problem that triggered the suicide attempt. The urgency of medical treatment for a suicidal person can be so engrossing that other aspects of crisis intervention are omitted. For example, if a person is in a coma from an overdose, or is being treated for injuries from a car crash, a careful suicide risk assessment may be forgotten after the person is out of physical danger. Great care should be taken to assure that this does not happen.

If a person whose suicide attempt is medically serious does not receive follow-up counseling, the risk of suicide within a few months is very high. Medical treatment, of course, is of primary importance when there is danger of death; still, we should remember that the person's physical injuries are a *result* of the suicide attempt. Dealing with those injuries is only a first step. The attitude of hospital emergency room staff can be the forerunner of more serious suicide attempts or the foundation for crisis intervention and acceptance of a referral for follow-up counseling. Emergency personnel also need to consider carefully the appropriate use of drugs for suicidal people in crisis, as discussed in Chapter 4, since prescribed drugs are one of the weapons used most frequently for suicide.

CRISIS INTERVENTION

People who threaten or attempt suicide as a way of coping with a crisis usually lack more constructive ways of handling stress. The crisis intervention principles outlined in Chapters 4 and 5 should be used on behalf of self-destructive persons. Several additional techniques are important for a person in suicidal crisis:

1. *Relieve isolation.* If the suicidal person is living alone, physical isolation must be relieved. If there is no friend or supportive relative with whom the person can stay temporarily, and if the person is highly suicidal, he or she should probably be hospitalized until the active crisis is over.
2. *Remove lethal weapons.* Lethal weapons and pills should be removed either by the counselor, a relative, or friend, keeping in mind the active

collaboration of the suicidal person in this process. If caring and concern are expressed and the person's sense of self-mastery and control are respected, he or she will usually surrender a weapon voluntarily so that it is safe from easy or impulsive access during the acute crisis.

3. *Encourage alternate expression of anger.* If the person is planning suicide as a way of expressing anger at someone, we should actively explore with the individual other ways of expressing anger short of the price of his or her life. For example: "I can see that you're very angry with her for leaving you. Can you think of a way to express your anger that would not cost you your life?" Or, "Yes, of course she'll probably feel bad if you kill yourself after the divorce. . . . But she most likely would talk with someone about it, and go on with her life. Meanwhile, you've had your revenge, but you can't get your life back."

4. *Avoid final decision of suicide during crisis.* We should actively assure the suicidal person that the suicidal crisis, that is, seeing suicide as the only option, is a temporary state. Also, we should try to persuade the person to avoid a decision about suicide until he or she has considered all other alternatives during a noncrisis state of mind, just as other serious decisions should be postponed until the crisis is over.

5. *Reestablish social ties.* We should make every effort to help the suicidal person reestablish social bonds if they are broken. This can be done through family crisis counseling sessions, or finding satisfying substitutes for lost relationships. Active links to self-help groups such as Widow-to-Widow or Parents Without Partners clubs can be life-saving (see Chapter 5).

6. *Relieve extreme anxiety and sleep loss.* If a suicidal person is extremely anxious and also has been unable to sleep for several days, he or she may become even more suicidal as a result. To a suicidal person, the world looks more bleak and death seems more desirable at 4:00 A.M. after endless nights of sleeplessness. A good night's sleep can temporarily reduce suicide risk and put the person in a better frame of mind to consider other ways of solving life's problems.

In such cases, it is appropriate to consider medication on an emergency basis. This should *never* be done for a highly suicidal person without daily crisis counseling sessions. Without effective counseling, the extremely suicidal person may interpret such an approach as an invitation to commit suicide. A tranquilizer will usually take care of both the anxiety and the sleeping problem, since anxiety is the major cause of sleeplessness. If medication is needed, the person should be given a *one- to three-day supply at most, always* with a specific return appointment for crisis counseling.

Sometimes nonmedical crisis counselors need to seek medical consultation and emergency medicine for a suicidal person. In such cases, the counselor must clearly advise the consulting physician of the person's suicidal state and of the recommended limited dose of drugs. This is particularly important when dealing with physicians who lack training in suicide prevention or who seem hurried and disinterested. Some practitioners accustomed to using medication in treatment programs may recommend tranquilization during crisis; however, tranquilizers are indicated only if a person is so upset that he or she cannot be engaged in the process of problem solving. Nonchemical means of inducing sleep should be encouraged (see Chapter 4). This assumes a thorough assessment and attempt to apply various psychosocial strategies of intervention *before* prescribing drugs. Crisis workers should never forget that many suicide deaths in the United States are by *prescribed* drugs.

Crisis assessment is never more important than when working with a self-destructive person. It determines our immediate and long-range response to the individual. A person who is threatening or has attempted suicide is either in active crisis or is already beyond the crisis and at a loss to resolve the crisis in any other way.

Everyone who engages in self-destructive acts is not in a life-and-death emergency. Anyone distressed enough to be self-destructive at any level should be listened to and helped; however, if the suicide attempt is medically nonserious, the counselor's response should not convey a sense of life-and-death urgency. This does not mean that the person's action is dismissed as nonserious. Rather, the underlying message of the behavior—its social-psychological dynamics—should receive the greatest part of our attention. To do otherwise may inadvertently lead to further suicide attempts. A helper reinforces self-destructive behavior by a dramatic and misplaced medical response while ignoring the problems signaled by the self-destructive act. For example, while suturing a slashed wrist, the physician and nurse should regard the physical injury neutrally, with a certain sense of detachment, while focusing on the *meaning* of self-injury: "You must have been pretty upset to do this to yourself. What did you hope would happen when you cut your wrists?" (see Chapter 10).

Thus, persons at all levels of risk should be responded to. The helper must differentiate between the *types* of response. Emergency measures are used when there is immediate danger of death from a medically serious failed suicide attempt. For the person whose suicide risk is long range, the approach should also be precisely that: long range, If the attempt is medically nonserious, we should avoid using only medical treatment or a life-and-death approach. We should help the person bring about needed psychosocial changes through aids to constructive crisis management rather than self-destructive acts.

FOLLOW-UP SERVICE FOR SUICIDAL PEOPLE

Counseling and Psychotherapy

Beyond crisis counseling, all self-destructive persons should have the opportunity to receive counseling or psychotherapy as an aid in solving the problems that led them to self-destructive behavior (Welu 1977). People who respond to life crises with self-destructive behavior often have a long-standing pattern of inadequate psychological and social coping (McLeavey et al. 1987, Snyder, Pitts, and Pokorny 1986). Individual and/or group psychotherapy, therefore, is frequently indicated (Farberow 1968, Frederick and Farberow 1970). Such therapy is the proper work of specially trained people. Usually these are clinical psychologists, psychiatric nurses, psychiatrists, and psychiatric social workers. Others qualified to counsel may be clergy, lay volunteers, and counselors in community mental health settings. The main concern is that the counselor or psychotherapist be properly trained and supervised (Hoff and Miller 1987).

Counseling should focus on resolving situational problems and expressing feelings appropriately. The person is helped to change various behaviors that are causing discomfort and that he or she is usually consciously aware of. Psychotherapy involves uncovering feeings that have been denied expression for a long time. It may also involve changing aspects of one's personality and deep-rooted patterns of behavior, such as an inability to communicate feelings or inflexible approaches to problem solving. People usually engage in psychotherapy because they are troubled or unhappy about certain features of their personality or behavior.

In most instances, counseling or psychotherapy should be made available to the suicidal person. It is particularly recommended for crisis-prone people who approach everyday problems with drug and alcohol abuse and other self-destructive behaviors. Such people have difficulty expressing feelings verbally, and self-destructive acts become an easier way to communicate. People who are extremely dependent, or who have rigid expectations for themselves combined with inflexible behavior patterns, are also good candidates for psychotherapy (Barnes 1986). A severely depressed, suicidal person should always have follow-up counseling or psychotherapy (Klerman et al. 1984, Williams 1984).

Counseling and psychotherapy can take place on an individual or group basis. A group experience is valuable for nearly everyone, but it is particularly recommended for the suicidal person who has underlying problems with social interaction and communication of feelings. For adolescents who have made suicide attempts, family therapy should frequently follow family crisis counseling (Richman 1986). Marital counseling should be offered whenever a disturbed marriage has contributed to the person's suicidal crisis. These therapies can be used in various combinations, depending on the needs of the individual and family.

Whether in a group or individually, counseling and psychotherapy goals should be directed toward:

- Correcting psychological and social disturbances in the person's life.
- Improving the person's self-image.
- Finding satisfactory social resources.
- Developing approaches to problems other than self-destructive behavior.

▶ Discovering a satisfying life plan.

Crisis counselors should keep in mind that a satisfying and constructive resolution of a crisis is an excellent foundation for persuading people to seek follow-up counseling or psychotherapy for the problems that made them crisis-prone in the first place. On the other hand, if people in crisis are placed on waiting lists they will of necessity find other means to resolve their crises. If such people are suicidal, the chances of a tragic crisis outcome are greatly increased (Hoff and Resing 1982). This is because, with or without our help, the pain of the crisis state compels one to move toward resolution—positive or negative. If waiting lists prevent people from getting help at the time they need it and later appointments are not kept, we should examine the adequacy of our service arrangements rather than conclude that the client was not motivated for therapy (Hoff and Miller, 1987).

Drug Treatment for Depression

Antidepressants are not emergency drugs. However, these drugs may be used successfully for some suicidal persons who experience severe recurring depression. Classic drugs for treating depression include tricyclic antidepressants (TCAs) and monoamine-oxidase inhibitors (MAOIs). A "second generation" of antidepressant drugs are no more effective than the classic types, but may be preferred because of a different profile of side effects (Prien, Blaine, and Levine 1985). Successful response to antidepressant therapy is highly variable. This may be due in part to the unclear demarcation between reactive depression and major depressive episodes, sometimes called "endogenous" depression. Thus, while some people respond favorably to antidepressant treatment, there are high rates of spontaneous remission as well as favorable response to placebos (Extein, Gold, and Pottash 1984, pp. 504–507).

Antidepressants should not be used for a person who is going through normal grief and mourning. Nor should they be used when the person is suffering from a reactive depression (Gilman, Goodman, and Gilman 1980, Levine 1983). A reactive depression occurs when a person in crisis surrounding a loss does not express normal feelings of sadness and anger *during* the crisis, and later reacts with depression. Sometimes this is referred to as a delayed grief reaction. Psychotherapy—not an antidepressant drug—is indicated for such persons.

Classic symptoms of a major depressive episode (endogenous depression) include weight loss, early morning wakening, loss of appetite, slowed down body functions, sexual and menstrual abnormality, and extreme feelings of worthlessness. The symptoms usually cannot be related to a conscious loss, specific life event, or situation. The assumption, therefore, is that the depression arises from sources within the person, whereas in reactive depression one is aware of the loss or depressing situation (see Loss, Change, and Grief Work in Chapter 4). Even in cases of endogenous depression, however, research suggests that the sources are social rather than physiologic; repression of painful situations clouds them from current awareness (Brown and Harris 1978, Cloward and Piven 1979, Gordon and Ledray 1985). For example, depression in the women studied by Brown and Harris was significantly associated with their economic circumstances and large numbers of children: less money and more children meant greater depression (see also Kessler and McLeod 1984).

Antidepressant drugs are dangerous and should be prescribed with extreme caution for suicidal persons. When taken with alcohol, an overdose of drugs can easily cause death. People using these drugs can experience side effects such as feelings of confusion, restlessness, or loss of control. Persons with a past history of psychosis or with symptoms of "borderline psychosis" can have serious side effects from antidepressants (Gilman, Goodman, and Gilman 1980).

Another problem with antidepressant drugs is that 10 to 14 days lapse before there is any noticeable lifting of the depression, even though the person sleeps better as a result of a sedative side effect. This delayed drug action should be explained carefully, because most people expect to feel better immediately after taking a drug. During the pretherapeutic phase, a suicide could occur as a result of drug side effects of confusion and agitation.

Case Example: Marilyn

Marilyn, age 42, was suffering from a delayed grief reaction a year after the death of her husband. She was also distressed about handling her adolescent daughter, Roseann, age 13. Marilyn had no history of suicide attempts. She had a close relationship with a brother and sister who lived nearby, and in general had a stable uvdisturbed life until the loss of her husband. Marilyn had seen a physician, who gave her a prescription for Tofranil and referred her to a counseling center. After four days of taking the antidepressant drug, Marilyn killed herself by extensive and bizarre body mutilation, even though she had seen a counselor twice during the past four days. (The counselor was highly trained and experienced and had done a careful suicide risk assessment.) Evaluation of this case led to the conclusion that Marilyn probably had a side reaction to the antidepressant drug, which should not have been prescribed in the first place since she was suffering from a reactive depression.

Another danger of suicide occurs after the depression lifts during drug treatment. This is especially true for the person who is so depressed and physically slowed down that he or she did not previously have the energy to carry out a suicide plan. Because of all these factors, it is preferable to use antidepressant drugs in combination with psychiatric hospitalization for a depressed person who is highly suicidal, especially if he or she is also socially and physically isolated.

Case Example: Jack

Jack, age 69, had seen his physician for bowel problems. He was also quite depressed. Even after complete examination and extensive tests, he was obsessed with the idea of cancer and was afraid that he would die. Jack also had high blood pressure and emphysema. Months earlier he had had prostate surgery. His family described him as a chronic complainer. Jack's doctor gave him a prescription for an antidepressant drug and referred him to a local mental health clinic for counseling. Jack admitted to the crisis counselor that he had ideas of suicide, but he had no specific plan or history of attempts. After two counseling sessions, Jack killed himself by carbon monoxide poisoning. This suicide might have been prevented if Jack had been hospitalized and if the delayed reaction of the drug had been properly explained. He lived alone and probably expected to feel better immediately after taking the antidepressant. An alternative might have been prescribing a drug to relieve his acute anxiety in combination with a plan to live with relatives for a couple of weeks.

Crisis counselors should always remember that antidepressants are *not* emergency drugs. These drugs should usually not be prescribed for a highly suicidal person during the acute crisis state—unless the individual is hospitalized. The crisis counselor should routinely ask a person in crisis what drugs he or she is taking or possesses. The prescription of *any* drug as a substitute for effective counseling is irresponsible. Not only can drug use precipitate a suicide, but the unwarranted prescription of drugs can also lead to serious drug abuse problems (Rogers 1971, see also Tranquilizers: What Place in Crisis Intervention? in Chapter 4).

INTERVENTION WITH SELF-DESTRUCTIVE PEOPLE: CASE EXAMPLES

The following cases are continued from Chapter 6. They illustrate the resolution of ethical dilemmas regarding suicide, as well as planning for emergency, crisis, and follow-up services for self-destructive people.

THE "RIGHT TO DIE": CONVERSATION EXAMPLE

CASE EXAMPLE: RACHEL (AGE 69, DYING OF CANCER AND FEELING SUICIDAL; SEE P. 185, CHAPTER 6)

Rachel: This cancer is killing me. I have nothing to live for.

Nurse: You sound really depressed, Rachel.

Rachel: I am. I'm a burden to my daughter. . . . I don't want to live like this anymore.

Nurse: You mean you're thinking of suicide, Dorothy?

Rachel: Yes, I guess you could say that—at least I don't want to go on living like this. . . . Yes, I want to die, and no one can stop me. I'm old and I'm sick. If there is a God, I'm sure I wouldn't be punished. How could any God expect me to go on living with this? Yes, I want to die. It's my right.

Nurse: I know you feel old and I know you're sick, and I agree, Rachel, that you have the right to determine your own life. But I'd feel bad if you acted on that now, Rachel, when you're feeling so depressed and like such a burden to your daughter. I'd really like to help you find some other way . . . (Rachel interrupts).

Rachel: There's no other way that I can see. I've thought about it a lot. I don't know exactly what I'd do, but I'd figure something out. I just don't know how things could change for me. . . . After all, my daughter's got her own life.

Nurse: Rachel, I'd like to go back to something you said earlier. You seem to feel you're a burden to your daughter. Can you tell me some more about that? (Conversation continues.)

OTHER POSSIBLE ELEMENTS OF SERVICE PLAN FOR RACHEL:

1. Continue problem exploration on a one-to-one basis.
2. Talk with daughter (with Rachel's consent) after exploring the "burden" issue further with Rachel.

3. Have a joint session with Rachel and her daughter (see Chapter 5).
4. Continue weekly visits.
5. Explore home health respite service for daughter (see Skorupka and Bohnet 1982).

LOW-RISK SUICIDAL BEHAVIOR

Case Example: Sarah (age 42, troubled by her marriage; see p. 210, Chapter 6)

Emergency medical: Medical treatment for Sarah is not indicated because pills are absorbed from the stomach into the bloodstream within a half hour. The dose of five sleeping pills is not lethal or extremely toxic. Therefore, other medical measures such as dialysis are not indicated.

Crisis intervention: Crisis counseling should focus on the immediate situation related to Sarah's suicide attempt and decision-making about her marriage.

Follow-up service: In follow-up counseling Sarah can examine her extreme dependency on her marriage, her personal insecurity, and her dependency on Valium as a means of problem solving. Sarah might also be linked to a women's support group that focuses on career counseling and the mid-life transition faced by women (see Chapter 11).

MODERATE-RISK SUICIDAL BEHAVIOR

Case Example: Susan (age 19, with a history of repeat suicide attempts; see p. 210, Chapter 6)

Emergency medical: Treatment for the overdose is stomach lavage (washing out the stomach contents).

Crisis intervention: Crisis counseling for Susan should include contacts with her parents and should focus on situational problems she faces: unemployment, upsets with her parents, and dependence on her parents.

Follow-up service: Since Susan

has had a chaotic life for a number of years, she could benefit from ongoing counseling or psychotherapy, if she so chooses. Family therapy may be indicated if she decides to remain in her parents' household. Group therapy is strongly recommended for Susan.

HIGH-RISK SUICIDAL BEHAVIOR

CASE EXAMPLE: EDWARD (AGE 41, JUST DIVORCED, AND THREATENING TO SHOOT HIMSELF; SEE P. 212, CHAPTER 6)

Emergency medical: No treatment is indicated as no suicide attempt has been made.

Crisis intervention: Remove guns (and alcohol, if possible) or have wife or friend remove them. Arrange to have Edward stay with a friend on the day his wife files for divorce. Try to get Edward to attend a self-help group, such as Alcoholics Anonymous (AA), and to rely on an individual AA member for support during his crisis. Arrange daily crisis counseling sessions for Edward.

Follow up service: Edward should have on-going therapy—both individually and in a group—focusing on his alcohol dependency problem, his rigid expectations of himself, and ways of finding other satisfying relationships after the loss of his wife by divorce.

CASE EXAMPLE: BARBARA (AGE 77, IN A NURSING HOME AND REFUSING TO EAT; SEE P. 213, CHAPTER 6)

Emergency medical and crisis intervention: Barbara should be assigned to a nurse or other staff person she trusts who can persuade her noncoercively to take her medication. Her daughter and son-in-law should be called and urged to visit immediately so Barbara has some evidence that someone cares whether she lives or dies. A stable staffing arrangement should be instituted and further moves of Barbara to different wings of the nursing facility should be avoided. Thus a trusting, caring relationship can be established with at least one or two staff members, which is necessary for understanding what makes Barbara upset and suspicious.

Follow up service: Organize problem-solving and service-planning meetings with Barbara, her daughter and son-in-law, the chaplain, and the nursing staff who have worked with Barbara the most closely—her social network (see Chapter 5). Examine the rotation practices and support system for staff, which gives temporary "relief" from troublesome residents like Barbara. Frequent rotations exacerbate the underlying insecurity of an older person who has decreased ability to adjust to environmental changes and disruptions in staff-resident relationships.

Case Example: Shirley (Age 55, Acutely Suicidal and Psychotic in a Psychiatric Hospital; See P. 213, Chapter 6)

Emergency medical and crisis intervention: Institute routine precautions with sharp objects, belts, etc. (see Farberow 1981). Assign a staff member for one-to-one care of Shirley. Place Shirley in a bedroom arrangement with at least one other patient and close to the nurses' station. Engage patients or other volunteers to assist in offering support and protection to Shirley during her acute psychotic episodes. Contact relatives and encourage frequent visits.

Follow-up service: Family meetings are recommended to encourage on-going support and help prevent future psychotic and suicidal episodes; drug therapy can help alleviate thought disorder and depression. Institute daily ward meetings in which acute suicidal episodes of patients can be discussed openly and dealt with cooperatively among all residents. Develop staff in-service training programs on suicide prevention as a means of critically examining and eliminating destructive and inhumane measures such as isolation and physical restraint of suicidal people.

SUICIDE PREVENTION AND INTERVENTION WITH SPECIAL POPULATIONS

YOUNG PEOPLE

The tragedy of youth suicide has commanded national attention at several levels recently. The National Institute of Mental Health has convened a Task Force on Youth Suicide in several locations to address the problem. Since the occurrence of cluster suicides in recent years, a National Committee on Youth Suicide has been formed, with a focus on suicide education in the schools. The American Association of Suicidology has information about model school suicide prevention programs. Current information about these activities is available from: AAS Central Office, 2459 South Ash, Denver, CO 80222; telephone 303-692-0985.

In general, suicide prevention programs for young people focus on educational and support activities for the young themselves, their parents, and teachers. Pastors, recreation workers, school nurses, physicians, and police officers should also receive such education. Intervention in community settings should include drop-in services, where troubled youth can receive individual help without being stigmatized and can be referred to peer support groups or family counseling services. School health programs, counseling agencies, and local suicide prevention centers usually collaborate on such programs.

If suicidal young people are referred to mental health and psychiatric agencies, the treatment of choice should include the family in an active way (Richman 1986). This is particularly true for an adolescent still living with parents. The adolescent's cry for help might otherwise be misunderstood; often the problem is related to family issues, or the adolescent depends on the family for necessary support during this hazardous transition state (see Chapters 5 and 11).

Suicide prevention for young people is illustrated in a special program developed by the Tompkins County Suicide Prevention and Crisis Service in Ithaca, New York.* Among the elements of this countywide service are:

- A suicide prevention information program each semester for students in junior and senior high schools and colleges. This includes cards with "Warning Signs," "Myths and Facts" about suicide, and emergency telephone numbers.
- Training of students in communication skills, including role playing and "modeling" of reaching out to others.

*Further information about this program can be obtained from: Suicide Prevention and Crisis Service of Tompkins County, Ithaca, NY 14850; telephone 607-272-1505 (see also Joan 1986).

- Development of suicide prevention curriculum packets to be used by faculty.
- Special information programs for parents.
- Provision of drop-in centers staffed by trained persons sensitive to the special needs of adolescents.

Similar programs exist in other cities (Webb 1986), particularly in response to the national efforts noted above (contact AAS Central Office for further information). Students are trained to become peer counselors for classmates who feel left out, lonely, and depressed. Such programs include role playing real-life crises and exploring dramatically how to avert tragedy.

DISTINCT ETHNIC AND SEXUAL PREFERENCE GROUPS

Besides the general principles of helping suicidal people, some other points should be kept in mind with respect to individuals in these groups.

1. In agencies routinely serving people with language, cultural, and other differences, staff should be recruited from the distinct communities served. This does not mean that a distressed person can only be helped by someone from his or her own ethnic or sexual identity group. Rather, it provides a resource for special problems related to different belief systems and life-styles. It also helps to avoid the appearance of discriminatory practices, which can be a barrier to accepting help. In instances of rare language immigrants, International Institute staff can be called on to assist (see Residential Changes in Chapter 10). Communication in respect to *process, intention,* and helping is pivotal during suicidal crises; thus, human bonds formed through language, culture, life-style, and sexual preference are crucial.

2. The suicidal crises of people in these groups may be strongly linked to their disadvantaged social position. When this appears to be the case, the social change strategies discussed in Chapter 2 are a particularly important aspect of follow-up after crisis intervention. For example, a black woman with three small children became suicidal each time she was threatened with cutting off the heat because she could not pay the bill. To offer this woman only crisis counseling without linking her to social support or social action groups would not approach the social roots of the problem. In Boston, for example, there is an organization called the Coalition for Basic Human Needs, a welfare rights group. Gay rights organizations are also becoming increasingly visible in their advocacy work for civil rights. People in crisis because of discriminatory treatment should be linked to such groups or at least be informed that they exist on their behalf (see Crisis Paradigm, third box, right circle, p. 176).

PEOPLE IN HOSPITALS AND OTHER INSTITUTIONS

People in crisis, like other human beings, have a need for self-mastery and control of their lives. Sensitivity to this need is an important element of positive crisis resolution. People in crisis who are suicidal not only do not lose their need for self-determination, but frequently feel powerless to solve their problem except by suicide, an act of self-determination. As noted in Shirley's case earlier, staff in institutions should examine various approaches to suicidal people; many approaches used to protect people from suicide may result in exactly the opposite of what is intended. While physical restraint and isolation measures may prevent self-injury in the short run, in the long run they will probably increase suicide risk. Such results are especially probable if the physical measures are carried out with authoritarian attitudes and an absence of communication, warmth, and genuine concern. People who already feel powerless may interpret such harsh, outmoded practices as another attack on their self-esteem and ability to control their lives. As Farberow (1981) states, people in hospitals (and other institutions) "are continually impressed with a sense of powerlessness; their lives must conform to a schedule designed essentially for the convenience of the staff. Most things happen *to* them, not because of or *for* them; other people continually make the most important decisions about their lives" (Farberow 1981, p. 101; see also Berman 1983, Berman and Cohen-Sandler 1982, and Wells 1976).

Many people commonly expect institutionalized people to conform to the sick role. But it is unrealistic to conduct our practice within this framework for suicidal people. The problem of expecting suicidal people to fit the traditional sick role is exacerbated if there is no systematic effort to include family or other social contacts in hospital treatment programs. Once institutionalization has taken place, it is often forgotten that a person belongs to a natural social community (Polak 1967). Or, if the person is suicidal because of *lack* of such supports, it takes special effort for hospital staffs to help develop substitute support systems (such as transitional housing services) prior to discharge. Also, admission to institutions is frequently the occasion of suicidal impulses based on "culture shock" for people not acculturated to institutions through routine work or residence.

Attention to these points can help prevent self-injury and suicides in hospitals *and* reduce the high rate of suicde after discharge from mental hospitals. See Farberow's work (1981) for additional ideas and recommendations for suicide prevention in hospitals.

Suicide prevention in holding centers and correctional institutions presents similar but even more complex problems. In one sense, the isolation cell is like an instrument of death. Yet relieving the physical isolation of a suicidal inmate may expose the person to possible abuse or attack by fellow inmates.

The crisis of suicide behind bars is gaining attention. In Boston, an Episcopal deacon, David Hogarth, directs a unique program, Lifeline, in cooperation with The Samaritans, a worldwide suicide prevention organization. Inmates—including murderers, arsonists, and rapists—receive special training to work as befrienders of the lonely and depressed. Besides reducing the number of suicides from seven to less than one per year over a three-year period, the program is noted for its benefits to the befriending inmates: they have the satisfaction of saving others' lives and of feeling useful and appreciated for their caring (Hogarth 1982). Says Hogarth, who works 60 hours a week at this program: "It's a bizarre ministry, but this is my life."*

Another authority on suicide behind bars is psychiatrist Bruce Danto, who has also worked as an officer in the Wayne County Sheriff's Department in Detroit (Danto 1981, 1973). Danto has also trained police to detect risk of suicide among citizens who are arrested and locked up.

Halleck (1971) addresses chronic self-destructiveness among inmates. He suggests that the repeated suicide attempts of prisoners are a symptom of conditions in the institution that bear examination and probable reform. Halleck questions whether it is ethical for a psychotherapist to use his or her time in such institutions primarily for treating individual suicide attempters apart from also consulting with prison authorities regarding the meaning of these attempts in relation to prison conditions (see Chapter 8).

HELPING SURVIVORS OF SUICIDE

SURVIVORS IN CRISIS

When a suicide occurs, it is almost always the occasion of a crisis for survivors: children, spouse, parents, other relatives, friends, crisis counselor, therapist—anyone closely associated with the person. The usual feelings associated with any serious loss are felt by most survivors of a suicide: sadness that the person ended life so tragically, and anger that the person is no longer a part of one's life.

In addition, however, survivors often feel enormous guilt. This arises usually from two main sources:

1. The sense of responsibility that somehow one should have prevented the suicide. This is especially true when the survivors were very close to the person.
2. The sense of relief that some survivors feel after a suicide. This happens when relationships were very strained or when

*Further information about this program can be obtained from: David Hogarth, The Samaritans, 500 Commonwealth Avenue, Boston, MA 02215; telephone 617-247-0220.

the person attempted suicide many times and either could not or would not use available help.

A common tendency among survivors of suicide is to blame or "scapegoat" someone for the suicide. This reaction often arises from a survivor's sense of helplessness and guilt about not preventing the suicide. Deeply held beliefs about suicide also contribute to this response.

Some survivors deny that the suicide ever took place. This seems to be the only way they can handle the crisis. Often, this takes the form of insisting that the death was an accident.

Case Example: Denial of Suicide

One couple instructed their nine-year-old daughter, who was a patient in the pediatric ward, to tell the hospital supervisor that her older brother died of an accident. (The supervisor knew the family through the hospital psychiatric unit.) The parents had insisted that he be discharged from psychiatric care, even though he was highly suicidal and the physician advised against it. A few days later, the boy shot himself at home with a hunting rifle. These parents were apparently very guilt ridden and went to great lengths to deny the suicide.

Cain (1972) and others have documented many problems that can occur throughout survivors' lives if they do not have help at the time of the crisis of suicide. Problems for survivors include depression, serious personality disturbances, and obsession with suicide as the predestined fate for oneself, especially on the anniversary of the suicide or when the person reaches the same age. A mother of 35 became very depressed and suicidal on the second anniversary of her 15-year-old son's death by suicide. Counseling at a community mental health clinic helped this woman eventually accept and live with the reality of her son's suicide.

The tragic effect of suicide is particularly striking in the case of children after a parent's suicide. In studies of child survivors, some of the symptoms found were learning disabilities, sleep walking, delinquency, and fire setting (Cain and Fast 1972). Crisis counseling should therefore be available for all survivors of suicide. Shneidman (1972) calls this "postvention," an effort to reduce some of the possible harmful effects of suicide on the survivors. Making such support available, however, presents a special challenge.

TEAM ANALYSIS FOLLOWING A SUICIDE

Some people commit suicide while receiving therapy or counseling through a crisis center, mental health agency, or private practitioner, or while receiving hospital or medical care. In these cases, the counselor, nurse, and/or physician is in a natural, strategic position to help survivors. Unfortunately, what often happens is that workers miss the opportunity for postvention because they may be struggling with the same feelings that beset the family. It is more effective to deal with the family immediately than to wait for an impasse to develop, but if staff have not dealt with their own feelings, they may avoid approaching family survivors of suicide.

The most useful preventive measure is for helpers to learn as much as they can about suicide and constructive ways of handling feelings one can have in working with self-destructive people. There will always be strong feelings following a suicide. However, a worker with a realistic concept of the limits of responsibility for another's suicide can help other survivors work through their feelings and reduce the scapegoating that often occurs.

In counseling and health care settings, a counselor or nurse should immediately seek consultation with a supervisor after a suicide occurs. Team meetings are another important step. They provide staff with an opportunity to air feelings and evaluate the total situation. For example, team analysis of John's case (Chapter 6, p. 187) illustrates how easy it is to forget a person's natural place in the world and to fail to draw on social resources once the patient is in an institutional subculture; John's friends were never contacted, nor was a peer support source like Alcoholics Anonymous considered. Involuntary commitment for self-protection, although well intentioned, was not enough. Analysis of this case sharpened the staff's awareness that the sense of isolation and powerlessness often experienced in mental hospitals may increase rather than decrease suicide risk. Through open discussion the staff was able to acknowledge that John's suicide might have been prevented with a different approach to intervention, including helping him to reestablish himself socially after serious interpersonal loss (see Chapter 5). If suicide prevention efforts are based on current standards in suicidology, the staff is less likely to feel guilty, and malpractice suits are less likely (Berman and Cohen-Sandler 1982). In addition, self-examination and hindsight after a suicide usually yield knowledge that can be applied on behalf of others (Hoff and Resing 1982).

Team meetings also provide a forum to determine who is best able to make postvention contact with the family. If the counselor who has worked most closely with the victim is too upset to deal with the family, a supervisory person should handle the matter, at least initially. In hospitals or mental health agencies where no one has had training in basic suicide prevention and crisis counseling, outside consultation with suicidologists or crisis counselors should be obtained whenever possible.

SUPPORT AND CRISIS INTERVENTION FOR SURVIVORS

Most suicides do not occur among people receiving help from a health or counseling agency. This is one reason why many survivors of suicide get so little help. In some communities there are special bereavement counseling programs or self-help groups, such as widow-to-widow clubs, to help survivors of suicides. Ideally, every community should have an active outreach program for suicide survivors as a basic part of comprehensive crisis services (Hoff and Miller 1987). Survivors are free to refuse an offer of support, but such support should be available.

A parent survivor, Adina Wrobleski (1982), has developed Suicide Survivors' Grief Groups in the metropolitan Minneapolis area since the suicide of her teenage daughter. National efforts are now underway to establish similar groups elsewhere.* Wrobleski's work is significant in two respects: (1) Following the suicide of her daughter, there were no peer support groups available to her and her husband. (2) Survivors of suicide do not necessarily need professional therapy as much as they need support from people who have experienced the same kind of loss. This point has been illustrated by groups such as the Sudden Infant Death Syndrome Foundation and self-help groups for health and social problems, such as Alcoholics Anonymous and groups for mastectomy patients (see Chapters 4, 5, 10, 11, and 12).

In the absence of these avenues of help, survivors of suicides can still be reached by police, clergy, and funeral directors, if such caretakes are sensitive to survivors' needs (see, for example, Grollman 1977). These key people should take care not to increase guilt and denial, recognizing how strong the suicide taboo and scapegoating tendency can be. The least one can do is offer an understanding word and suggest where people might find an agency or person to help them through the crisis.

Techniques in helping survivors of suicide are essentially the same as those used in dealing with other crises. A survivor should be helped to:

1. Express feelings appropriate to the event.
2. Grasp the reality of the suicide.
3. Obtain and use the help necessary to work through the crisis (including sometimes his or her own suicide crisis).

If a survivor depended on the suicide victim for financial support, he or she may also need help in managing money and housing, for example.

HELPING CHILD SURVIVORS OF PARENT SUICIDE

A surviving spouse with young children, including preschoolers as young as 3 or 4, usually needs special help in explaining to the children the death by suicide of their parent. The tendency is to hide the facts from children in the mistaken belief that they will thus be spared unnecessary pain. What adults often fail to realize is that children know a great deal more than adults often

*Information about such groups and how to start them can be obtained for $5.00 from a quarterly newsletter entitled *Afterwards,* edited by: Adina Wrobleski, 5124 Grove Street, Minneapolis, MN 55436; telephone 612-929-6448.

think they know. Even if children do not know the full facts, they do know that something much more terrible than an accident has occurred. If the suicide is not discussed, the child is left to fill in the facts alone; usually a child's fantasies are much more frightening than the actual facts. For example, a child may fear that the surviving parent killed the dead parent or that the child's own misbehavior may have caused the parent's death. The child may have unrealistic expectations that the dead parent will return: "Maybe if I'm extra good, Daddy will come back."

What children do not create in their fantasy lives will often be filled in by information from neighborhood and school companions. Some child survivors also suffer from jeers and teasing by other children about the parent's suicide.

Survivors should explain the death by suicide clearly, simply, and in a manner consistent with the child's level of development and understanding. The child should have an opportunity to ask questions and express feelings. He or she needs to know that the surviving parent is also willing to answer questions in the future, as the child's understanding of death and suicide grows. A child should never be left with the impression that the issue is closed and is never to be discussed again.

Examples of Discussions with Children:

> "Yes, Daddy shot himself. . . . No, it wasn't an accident; he did it because he wanted to."
>
> "Mommy will not be coming back anymore. . . . No, Mommy didn't do it because you misbehaved last night."
>
> "No one knows exactly why Daddy did it. . . . Yes, he had a lot of things that bothered him."

Surviving parents who cannot deal directly with their children about the other parent's suicide have usually not worked through their own feelings of guilt and responsibility regarding the suicide. In these cases, parents need the support and help of a counselor for themselves as well as for their children. Parents often do not understand that serious consequences can arise from hiding the facts from children. Counseling should include an explanation of the advantages of talking openly with children about the suicide.

In some cases, a child is completely aware that the parent committed suicide, especially if there were many open threats or attempts of suicide. Sometimes a child finds the dead parent or has been given directions by the other parent to "call if anything happens to Mommy" (Cain 1972). If the suicidal person was very disturbed or abusive prior to committing suicide, the child may feel relief. In all of these cases, surviving children may feel guilt and misplaced responsibility for the death of their parent.

Parents will usually need the assistance of a crisis worker or a child guidance counselor to help a child through this crisis. Jarmusz (1976) reported the successful use of a natural play group for four young boys who had found a man hanging. All four boys became restless and fearful and refused to sleep in their own beds. Crisis intervention programs for such children are far too uncommon.

ADDITIONAL OUTREACH TO SURVIVORS

Help for survivors of suicides has always been one of the goals of the suicide prevention movement. Such work is important but difficult to carry out. Many people, including those in some coroners' offices, tend to cover up the reality of a suicide. The suicide taboo in modern times continues, despite a growing acceptance of the morality of suicide in certain instances (Battin and Mayo 1980, Hall and Cameron 1976; see also Ethical Issues Regarding Suicide in Chapter 6).

One means of reaching a large number of survivors is through coroners' offices. It is there that every death is eventually reported and recorded. In Los Angeles County, all suicide deaths as well as equivocal deaths (those in which suicide is suspected but not certain) are followed up by staff from the Los Angeles Suicide Prevention Center. Suicidologists do a "psychological autopsy" (Litman 1987). This is an intensive examination to determine whether the death was by suicide, and if it was, to define the probable causes of the suicide. Information for the psychological autopsy is obtained from survivors and from medical and psychiatric records.

Research is the primary purpose of the psychological autopsy; however, it is an excellent means of contacting the large number of survivors who are not in contact with a crisis center, physician, or mental health agency (Sanborn and Sanborn 1976). Survivors are, of course, free to refuse participation in such postmortem examinations. Experience reveals, however, that the majority of survivors do not refuse to be interviewed and welcome the opportunity to talk about the suicide. This is especially true if they are contacted within a few days of the suicide, when they are most troubled with their feelings. Many survivors use this occasion to obtain some help in answering their own questions and dealing with suicidal inclinations following a suicide. The "official" interview situation is somehow a more acceptable circumstance for some people to open up about an otherwise taboo subject, and thus provides an ideal opportunity for the interviewer to suggest follow-up counseling resources to the survivor. If weeks or months pass, survivors may resent the postmortem interview. By that time, they have had to settle their feelings and questions on their own and in their own way, which may include denial and resentment. A delayed interview may seem like unnecessary opening of an old wound.

McGee (1974) has documented the excellent postvention work done by the Death Investigation Team in Gainesville, Florida. Various other suicide prevention centers, certified by the American Association of Suicidology, also conduct survivor counseling programs (Wells and Hoff 1984). Many communities, however, still do not have formal programs available to survivors of suicides. Obviously, a great deal of work remains to be done in this important area.

SUMMARY

People who get help after a suicide attempt or other self-destructive behavior may never commit suicide. Much depends on what happens in the form of emergency, crisis, and follow-up intervention. However, when suicide does occur, survivors of suicides usually are in crisis and are often neglected because of cultural taboos and the lack of aggressive outreach programs for them. Children, spouses, and parents who lose a loved one by suicide are especially vulnerable if they do not receive support during this crisis. This is an area of great challenge for crisis centers.

REFERENCES

Barnes RA: The recurrent self-harm patient. *Suicide Life-threat Behav* 1986; 16(2):399–408.

Battin MP, Mayo DJ (editors): *Suicide: The Philosophical Issues.* St. Martin's Press, 1980.

Berman AL, Cohen-Sandler R: Suicide and the standards of care: Optimal vs. acceptable. *Suicide Life-threat Behav* 1982; 12(2):114–122.

Berman AL, Cohen-Sandler R: Suicide and malpractice: Expert testimony and the "standards of care." *Prof Psychol* 1983.

Brown GW, Harris T: *The Social Origins of Depression.* Tavistock, 1978.

Cain AC (editor): *Survivors of Suicide.* Charles C. Thomas, 1972.

Cain AC, Fast R: Children's disturbed reactions to parent suicide: Distortions of guilt, communication and identification. In: *Survivors of Suicide.* Cain AC (editor). Charles C. Thomas, 1972.

Cloward RA, Piven FF: Hidden protest: The channeling of female innovation and resistance signs. *J Wom Culture Soc* 1979; 4:651–669.

Danto B: *Jail House Blues.* Orchard Lake, MI: Epic Publications, 1973.

Danto B: *Crisis Behind Bars: The Suicidal Inmate.* Warren, MI: Dale Corporation, 1981.

Drummond H: Of medicine and melancholy. *Mother Jones* (Jan) 1987; 10–14.

Extein I, Gold MS, Pottash ALC: Psychopharmacologic treatment of depression. *Psych Clin North Am* 1984; 7(3):503–517.

Farberow NL: Group psychotherapy with suicidal persons. In: *Suicidal Behaviors: Diagnosis and Management.* Little, Brown, 1968.

Farberow NL: Suicide prevention in the hospital. *Hosp Comm Psych* 1981; 32(2):99–104.

Frederick CJ, Farberow NL: Group psychotherapy with suicidal persons: A comparison with standard group methods. *Int J Soc Psych* 1970; 16:103–111.

Gilman AG, Goodman LS, Gilman A (editors): *The Pharmacological Basis of Therapeutics,* 6th ed. Macmillan, 1980.

Gordon VC, Ledray LE: Depression in women: The challenge of treatment and prevention. *J Psychol Nurs Ment Health Serv* 1985; 23(1):26–34.

Grollman E: *Living—When a Loved One Has Died.* Beacon Press, 1977.

Hall E, with Cameron P: Our failing reverence for life. *Psychol Today* 1976; 9:104–113.

Halleck S: *The Politics of Therapy.* Science House, 1971.

Hoff LA, Miller N: *Programs for People in Crisis: A Guide for Educators, Administrators, and Clinical Trainers.* Boston: Northeastern University Custom Book Program, 1987.

Hoff LA, Resing M: Was this suicide preventable? *Am J Nurs* 1982: 82:1106–1111.

Hogarth DJ: *Lifeline: Manual of Suicide Prevention.* Boston: Suffolk County Jail, 1982.

Jarmusz RT: Crisis intervention with four boys, members of a natural play group. *Vita* (Official newsletter of the International Association for Suicide Prevention), 1976.

Joan P: *Preventing Teenage Suicide: The Living Alternative Handbook.* Human Sciences Press, 1987.

Kessler RC, McLeod JD: Sex differences in vulnerability to undesirable life events. *Am Sociol Rev* (Oct) 1984; 49:620–631.

Klerman GL et al.: *Interpersonal Psychotherapy of Depression.* Basic Books, 1984.

Levine R: *Pharmacology: Drug Actions and Reactions,* 3rd ed. Little, Brown, 1983.

Litman RE: Mental disorders and suicidal intervention. *Suicide Life-threat Behav* 1987; 17(2):85–92.

McGee RK: *Crisis Intervention in the Community.* University Park Press, 1974.

McLeavey BC et al.: Interpersonal problem solving deficits in self-poisoning patients. *Suicide Life-threat Behav* 1987; 17(1):33–49.

Polak P: The crisis of admission. *Soc Psych* 1967; 2:150–157.

Prien RF, Blaine JD, Levine J: Antidepressant drug therapy: The role of the new antidepressants. *Hosp Comm Psych* 1985; 36(5):513–516.

Richman J: *Family Therapy of Suicidal Individuals.* Springfield, 1986.

Rogers MJ: Drug abuse: Just what the doctor ordered. *Psychol Today* 1971; 5:16–24.

Sanborn DE, Sanborn CJ: The psychological autopsy as a therapeutic tool. *Dis Nerv Syst* 1976; 37:4–8.

Shneidman ES: Forward. In: *Survivors of Suicide.* Cain AC (editor). Charles C. Thomas, 1972.

Skorupka P, Bohnet N: Primary caregivers' perceptions that met their needs in a home care hospice setting. *Cancer Nurs* 1982; 5:371–374.

Snyder S, Pitts WM, Pokorny AD: Selected behavioral features of patients with borderline personality traits. *Suicide Life-threat Behav* 1986; 16(1):28–39.

Webb ND: Before and after suicide: A preventive outreach program for colleges. *Suicide Life-threat Behav* 1986; 16(4):469–480.

Wells JO: The development of suicide precautions in a general hospital. Paper presented at the American Association of Suicidology Ninth Annual Meeting, Los Angeles, 1976.

Wells JO, Hoff LA (editors): *Certification Standards Manual,* 3rd ed. Denver: American Association of Suicidology, 1984.

Welu TC: A follow-up program for suicide attempters: Evaluation of effectiveness. *Suicide Life-threat Behav* 1977; 7(1):17–30.

Williams JMG: *The Psychological Treatment of Depression: A Guide to the Theory and Practice of Cognitive Behavior Therapy.* Free Press, 1984.

CHAPTER 8

Crises Stemming from Violence by Others

A FRAMEWORK FOR UNDERSTANDING VIOLENCE

THE PROBLEM

The United States has been called the most violent society in the Western world. In the US in 1980, homicide was the 11th leading cause of death, with 24,000 lives lost through violence; among black males aged 15 to 24, homicide is now the most likely cause of death (Wolfgang 1986, p. 11). Firearms accounted for 10,715 criminal homicides in the United States in 1980, compared with only 48 in Japan. While figures vary, about 20% of spouses are enmeshed in abuse. The majority of victims in such violence are women (between 1.5 and 2 million per year), while 5% are abused husbands. Of intrafamilial homicides, about half are between partners: two-thirds are wives killed by their husbands and one-third are husbands killed by their wives (Browne 1987, p. 10). Nearly 50% of husbands who batter their wives do so three or more times per year (Wolfgang 1986, p. 12). Wife abuse is probably the most unreported crime in the country. While rape in marriage is legally recognized in only 26 states, in a random sample of 920 women, 14% had been raped by their husband or ex-husband (Russell 1982, p. 2).

Acquaintance and date rape studies reveal wide disparity between women and men on what constitutes rape, the majority of men defining sexual violence as "normal" (Donnerstein and Linz 1986). Even though rape victims know their attackers in the majority of cases, acquaintance rapes are reported least because of the legacy of "blaming the victim." Among children and adolescents, nearly 1.5 million are physically or sexually abused each year (Gelles and Cornell 1985). Surveys of women reveal that 25% to 50% report some kind of sexual encounter with an adult male before the age of 16 (Herman 1981, p. 12, Wolfgang 1986, p. 12) and that abuse by stepfathers is seven times more common than by biological fathers (Russell 1986).

Although national data on elder abuse are not yet available, the House Select Committee on Aging estimates that one million or 4% of the elder population are abused by relatives each year, while only one in six cases are reported (Hudson 1986, p. 152). A random survey in metropolitan Boston (about 4 million population) revealed between 8,646 and 13,487 abused and neglected elders (Pillemer and Finkelhor 1987). In spite of civil rights legislation, violence originating from bias based on race, religion, and sexual preference continues. In fact, violence against gays is on the increase because of homophobia and mistaken perceptions of AIDS as a "gay disease."

Internationally, victimization is also receiving greater attention, although most research on the topic has been conducted in North America and Europe. For example, the UN has convened international meetings on the topic, and the UN-sponsored Forum '85, an international women's conference in Nairobi, featured numerous workshops on the worldwide problem of violence against women.*

The Surgeon General's Workshop on Violence and Public Health (1986) was convened in 1985 to emphasize the fact that victims' needs, treatment of assailants, and the prevention of violence should command much greater attention of health and social service professionals than it has until recently. The historical neglect of victimization, especially in the domestic arena, underscores the value placed on family privacy and the myth of the family as only a haven of love and security. Neglect of victimization also points to several related issues:

- Social values regarding children, how they should be disciplined, and who should care for them.
- Social and cultural devaluation of women and their problems.
- A social and economic system in which elderly citizens often have no worthwhile place.
- A social climate with little tolerance for minority sexual preference.
- A legal system in which it is difficult to consider the rights of victims without compromising the rights of the accused.
- A knowledge system that historically has interpreted these problems in private, individual terms rather than public, social ones (Mills 1959).

*Readers interested in violence in cross-cultural perspective are referred to Edgerton 1976 and Borkowski, Murch, and Walker 1983.

THEORIES ON VIOLENCE

Theories to explain violence and its prevalence fall into three categories: (1) psychobiological (2) social-psychological; and (3) sociocultural (Gelles and Straus 1979). Until recently, explanations of family violence were largely based on general violence and aggression theories in nonfamily settings (see Wolfgang 1958 and Goode 1971). Both professionals and laypersons have generally accepted psychological or medical explanations of family and other violence (see The Medicalization of Crime later in this chapter). Common sentiments include: "Only a sick man could beat his wife"; child abuse is a "syndrome" calling for "treatment" of disturbed parents; John W. Hinckley was acquitted and "treated" for his violent attack on President Reagan, not punished; a "crazed madman" is deemed responsible (and by implication, not held accountable) for the series of fatal Tylenol poisonings that became an issue of national concern.

Public debate is increasing regarding medical approaches to social problems. There is growing acceptance of the view that attention to violent persons and their victims in predominantly individual terms is incomplete at best and at worst does little to address the roots of violence. This view is in accord with the crisis paradigm of this book: crises stemming from violence should be treated with a tandem approach, with both individual and sociocultural factors taken into account. That is, a person in crisis because of violence will experience many of the same individual responses to this traumatic event as persons in crisis from other sources (Sales, Baum, and Shore 1984, p. 131; Silver and Wortman 1980). Similar intervention strategies are called for during the acute crisis phase; for example, listening and decision counseling. However, attention to the social and cultural *origins* of crises stemming from violence is important in prevention and follow-up strategies in order to avoid a circular approach that blames the victim (Ryan 1971). Indeed, the implications of the social/cultural framework of crisis intervention proposed here are even more critical when considering crises originating from violence than when dealing with crises from other sources. For victims of violence, a strictly individual approach can compound the problem rather than contribute to the solution (Baum, Stark, Flitcraft, and Frazier 1979; Sales, and Shore 1984).

There is no single "cause" of violence. Rather, there are complex, interrelated *reasons* that some individuals are violent and others are not. In cases of violence against children, wives, and elders, for example, physical, psychological, and socioeconomic factors are often present together. Children and elders and often wives are economically dependent on their caretakers and in most cases are physically weaker than their abusers. Caretakers of children and elders are often stressed psychologically by difficult behaviors and socioeconomically by lack of social and financial resources to ease the burdens of caretaking (Korbin et al. 1987). In cases of wife-battering and sex-role stereotyping, psychological and economic factors intersect at both ends of the social class continuum: poor women are less able to survive on their own, while women who earn more than their husbands are more vulnerable to attack than those who earn less (Rubenstein 1982). Violence toward others, then, is one way a person can respond to stress and resolve a personal crisis, such as low self-esteem or threat of loss due to suspected infidelity of a spouse. A violent response is not inevitable; it is chosen. The choice of violent behavior is influenced by the social, political-legal, and belief and knowledge systems of the violent person's cultural community. The element of choice implies an interpretation of violence as a moral act. That is, violence is social action engaged in by human beings who by nature are rational and conscious. Through socialization, humans become responsible for the actions they choose in various situations.

However, consciousness may be clouded and responsibility mitigated by social and cultural factors rooted in the history of human society. Under certain circumstances a person may be "excused" from paying the social consequences of his or her behavior, as in cases of self-defense, or in an irrational conception of the nature of the act. This does *not* mean that every violent act is a consequence of illness and is therefore to be "treated," as the popular conception of violence suggests.

Another troubling aspect of a simplistic interpretation of the nature of violence is the tendency toward "solutions" in the form of revenge, as suggested by voter choice of capital punishment. To describe violence as a moral act rather than a disease does not imply support of revenge as an appropriate response. As responses to the complex problem of violence, treatment and revenge represent opposite extremes. Excusing violent acts on the basis of psychiatric illness suggests that violent human beings are somewhat less than human, generally incapable of judging and acting according to the consequences of their behavior, and driven by aggressive impulses they are unable to control. Revenge, on the other hand—in the form of capital punishment, inhumane prison conditions, or a failure to provide true opportunities for learning to change one's violent life-style—implies a departure from the moral foundations of society.

Violence and our response to its victims and perpetrators can be interpretated in a multifaceted perspective: moral, social-psychological, legal, and medical. Violence can be defined as an infraction of society's rules regarding people, their relationships, and their property. It is a complex phenomenon in which social, political, medical, and psychological factors touch both its immediate and chronic aspects. Functioning members of a particular society normally know a group's cultural rules and the consequences for violating them. Those lacking such knowledge generally are excused, and instead of punishment receive treatment. Others are excused on the basis of self-defense or the circumstances that alter one's normal liability for rule infractions. A moral society would require restitution to individual victims from those not excused, and would design a criminal justice system to prevent rather than promote future crime. A truly moral approach to violence would also avoid or reform practices that discriminate

Table 8-1

Victimization Assessment Scale

Key to Scale	Victimization	Typical Indicators
1	No experience of physical violence or abuse	No memory of violence either recently or in the past. Very stable support network
2	Experience of abuse/violence with minor physical and/or emotional trauma	Currently, verbal arguments with family or intimates that occasionally escalate to pushing and shoving, or mild slapping. Stable support network. History *may* include: mild physical discipline as a child occasionally; one past incident of sexual abuse (eg, fondling) by a nonfamily member when under age 5; physical struggle with a stranger during purse snatching.
3	Experience of abuse/violence with moderate physical and/or emotional trauma	Physically abused by family member or intimate several times a month during past 2 years, resulting in mild physical injury, eg, bruises; no threat to life; no guns available. Unresponsive support network. History *may* include: one incident of sexual abuse (eg, fondling) by a parent or stepparent over 2 years ago; moderate physical injury during purse snatching; informal counseling for past victimization
4	Experience of abuse/violence with severe physical and/or emotional trauma	Physically abused by family member or intimate several times a month during past 2 years, resulting in serious physical injury, ie, requiring medical treatment. Threats to kill; no guns available. History *may* include: frequent sexual abuse (eg, including intercourse) by a parent or stepparent, stranger, acquaintance, or intimate within past 6 months; other physical attack by a stranger requiring medical treatment but no permanent scars; no counseling for past victimization

Table 8-1

Victimization Assessment Scale

Key to Scale	Victimization	Typical Indicators
5	Life-threatening or prolonged violence/abuse with very severe physical and/or emotional trauma	Recent (past 3 months) or current life-threatening physical abuse; guns available. History *may* include: severe abuse requiring medical treatment in past 2 years; routine sexual abuse (including intercourse) by a parent or stepparent now and in the past; recent rape at gun or knifepoint; other physical attack by a stranger requiring extensive medical treatment and leaving permanent physical scars. Real or perceived social isolation. No counseling or support around past or present abuse and victimization

on the basis of race, sex, class, or sexual preference—practices that create a climate in which crime flourishes with the implicit support of society (Dillon 1972, Sanford 1972, Surgeon General's Workshop 1986).

Decisions about crisis and follow-up approaches to victims and perpetrators of violence demand a critical examination of the theories and research supporting such practice, an examination not undertaken until recently. In the following discussion social-psychological and sociocultural theories will be examined as they apply to crises stemming from violence in repect to:

- Prevention.
- Intervention during crisis.
- Follow-up service.

Each of these topics is important, but the discussion in this chapter will focus on intervention, with general reference to the preventive and follow-up strategies necessary for a long-range political and social approach that will reduce crises stemming from violence (See Crisis Paradigm, third box).

Crisis workers in various entry-point settings should incorporate questions to ascertain possible victimization into their routine assessments. Table 8-1 presents an instrument for use by entry-point workers adapted from the Comprehensive Mental Health Assessment Guide discussed in Chapter 3. Once victimization status is identified, it should be followed by in-depth assessment (preferably by mental health professionals with victimology background) to ascertain the extent of trauma and the victim's response. (See also Campbell and Humphreys 1984, van der Kolk 1987.)

CHILD ABUSE

THE PROBLEM

Case Example: Richard

A young mother with four children felt overwhelmed trying to care for her 5-year-old hyperactive child, Richard. The woman's husband was employed as a hospital maintenance worker but found it difficult to support the family. The family could not obtain public assistance because the father lived at home and their income was just above the level to qualify even for food stamps.

The mother routinely spanked Richard with a strap several times during the day. By evening the child was even more hyperactive, so periodically the mother put him to bed without feeding him. The father and mother mutually approved of this form of disciplining Richard. A neighbor reported the parents of suspected abuse after observing the mother chase and verbally abuse Richard on the street, with a strap poised for spanking.

Case Example: Linda

Linda, age 15, had never told anyone about her father's repeated visits to her room where he sexually abused her over a 4-year period. Linda did not tell her mother because she thought her mother already knew and approved of what was happening. Linda looked forward to leaving home and marrying her boyfriend, age 19. One night her boyfriend raped her; she went to the bathroom and took 20 of her mother's sleeping pills. If her mother had not heard her crying and taken her to the hospital for emergency treatment, Linda would have died.

Child abuse can be physical, emotional, verbal, or sexual—any acts of commission or omission that harm or threaten to harm a child (Cook and Bowles 1980). The biblical expression "spare the rod and spoil the child" suggests a long history of child abuse. DeMause (1975) has written that the "helping mode" in caring for children is of very recent origin, and was preceded historically by infanticide and rampant cruelty toward children. The rejection of such practices has resulted in the "Good Samaritan" laws. Though the natural helplessness of children inspires most adults to aid and protect them, humane societies have found it necessary to have explicit laws protecting children. These laws protect physicians, nurses, and social workers from prosecution for slander when they report suspected child abuse to authorities.

Child abuse happens in families who are well-to-do and in poor families, in cities, suburbs, and rural areas. No one knows exactly how many children are abused each year since many cases are not reported. Besides the estimated 2,000,000 to 4,000,000 abused and neglected children, 2000 to 5000 deaths occur annually at the hands of parents and caretakers. One or both parents as well as siblings may be involved. In her study of women who killed their children, Korbin (1987) uncovered a dynamic similar to the "cry for help" noted in suicidal people. Had the women's networks of kin and professionals responded to their behavioral pleas for help they would have been "secretly relieved" and perhaps fatal abuse would have been avoided. There is disagreement on just what child abuse is. Most people agree that some kind of discipline is necessary and that a swat or controlled spanking for playing with fire or running in front of cars is not the same as child abuse. Yet it is difficult to persuade the average American that a child can be brought up without physical punishment, in spite of research supporting the negative effects of physical punishment (Straus, Gelles, and Steinmetz 1980; Victimology 1977).

The tragic reality of child abuse gained national attention with the works of Kempe and Helfer (1980) in pediatrics and Gil (1970) in social science. More recent work (for example, Finkelhor 1984) exposes the extent of sexual abuse, while Newberger and Newberger (1981) challenge single-factor approaches to the issue. They suggest instead an "ecologic" interactive theory and preventive practice in response to the problem.

A tragedy related to child abuse is that of runaway children; 35% of these children leave because of incest, and 53% because of physical neglect. The majority of runaway children are never reported missing by their parents; 80% are from white middle class families; 150,000 disappear each year, many dying of disease, exploitation, and malnutrition (Rader 1982 and Russell 1986).

When dealing with individual cases of child abuse or neglect, especially if the parents were abused themselves or problems of alcohol are involved, it is easy to lose sight of the evidence that child abuse is rooted in the fabric of our society:

1. Violence as an appropriate solution to problem solving is a culturally embedded value of American society. There is widespread evidence that the use of violence (such as in disciplining a child) trains a person for violence (Gil 1970, Straus, Gelles, and Steinmetz 1980). Thus, when a parent uses violent forms of discipline while interpreting it as an act of "love and

concern" for the child, the child is likely to absorb the value that violence is a socially approved form of problem solving.

2. Economic hardships and stress can often be traced to unequal social opportunities in the United States. The national survey on domestic violence (Straus, Gelles, and Steinmetz 1980) suggests a definite association between economic disadvantage and child abuse. This includes the difficulty of providing for survival necessities as well as special medical and social services for handicapped or sick children, a source of extraordinary parental stress. Such stress is exacerbated by the homelessness now suffered by millions of women and children (see Chapter 10).

3. Child care, though necessary for the continuation of society, is socially devalued, as revealed in several practices and institutional arrangements:

a. the failure to provide adequate child care services for working mothers,

b. the low pay scales for those who do provide child care,

c. the continuing acceptance of child rearing as a predominant responsibility of mothers.

As Miller (1976) suggests: If men and women wish to have children, let them also figure out how to take care of them so that the children have the benefit of paternal as well as maternal upbringing (see Birth and Parenthood in Chapter 11).

PREVENTIVE INTERVENTION

Preventive strategies are always important in crisis intervention, but they are particularly urgent concerning the tragedy of child abuse. A focus on the social origins of this problem is critical. Preventive intervention includes:

1. Critical examination of our child-rearing practices and incorporation of nonviolent approaches to discipline into high school curriculum courses for boys and girls (see Crary 1979, Judson 1984).

2. Social and political action to relieve the economic hardship and poverty of many families.

3. Social and political action to address the substandard child care programs in the United States and develop family policies appropriate to the resources and ideals of the nation.

4. Consciousness raising and education stressing the advantages to individuals and to society of having children reared in an egalitarian fashion by mothers and fathers. The involvement of extended family, foster grandparents, and other resources should also be encouraged.

5. Systematic examination of government departments of child welfare to assure that the problems of children are adequately attended to before abuse occurs.

6. Instituting public education programs on child abuse and providing in-service training programs for school nurses, teachers, and others working with children.
7. Developing hotlines and drop-in centers for children and adolescents as additional supports and outlets for troubled youth.
8. Instructing children that they own the private parts of their bodies and reassuring them that they have no obligation to satisfy the sexual desires of parents, relatives, or others (Conte, Wolf, and Smith 1987).
9. A renewed committment to improving the mental health of children as an aid to resisting seduction (Conte, Wolf, and Smith 1987).
10. Examining the values and social and economic arrangements that support the idea that many teenage mothers have absorbed: their most important contribution to society and means of feeling valuable is to produce a baby, irrespective of their emotional, social, and economic ability to care for a child. The congressional Select Panel for the Promotion of Child Health (1980) reported that 11,000 15-year-old girls give birth each year, incurring significant medical, psychological, and economical risks (Select Panel, pp. 45–46).

All these preventive strategies demand that we take the time to discover why so many of our children are being abused and neglected. A shift "from care to prevention" was highlighted in the Surgeon General's Workshop on Violence (1986) and in Newberger's (1980) testimony before the US House of Representatives:

> *A concentration on prevention will oblige our looking squarely at our promotion and acceptance of violence and exploitive sex in our culture and its impact on the care of children. It will force us to address how isolation, poverty, and lack of access to basic life supports are implicated in child abuse and neglect.*

LEGAL AND CRISIS INTERVENTION

Everyone should be aware of the signs of possible child abuse:

- Repeated injury of a child with unconcern on the part of the parent(s) or with unlikely explanations.
- Aggressive behavior by the child that implies a cry for help.

- Neglected appearance.
- Overcritical parental attitude.
- Withdrawal, depression, and self-injury (especially with incest).

Serious effects of child abuse include physical handicaps, emotional crippling (an abused child may never be able to love others), homelessness, psychiatric illness, antisocial or violent behavior later in life, and death (Carmen, Rieker, and Mills 1984).

Suspicions of child abuse must be reported to child protection authorities, although we need to be cautious and not make unthoughtful false accusations. All parents make mistakes; it is the crisis of child abuse and the *pattern* of abuse that must be reported. In cases of incest, it is important to note that the crisis for the child as well as the entire family occurs when "the secret" is revealed (Herman 1981). We can assume that most parents have the welfare of their children at heart. When parents do not appear to be concerned for the welfare of their children, they must be confronted with the reality that children as well as parents have rights. When abuse is suspected, then all who know the child must realize that a parent's rights are not absolute. The rationalization of "minding one's own business" makes neighbors and friends hesitant to report what they know about child abuse. Teachers especially are in strategic positions to assist the abused child; the school is often the only recourse open to the child (Manley-Casiner and Newman 1976). Although teachers are not trained to deal with disturbed parents, they are responsible for reporting suspected child abuse to child welfare authorities. Parents who think they are abusive or who are afraid of losing control should be encouraged to seek help on their own by contacting Parents Anonymous, a nationwide self-help organization in the United States and England. Hotlines for parents, children, and others concerned about child abuse can be contacted through any crisis or mental health agency, or by simply dialing the operator. In mental health and social service settings, early signs of child abuse can often be uncovered through family-focused assessment as discussed in Chapter 3. The Child Screening Checklist in Chapter 5 is part of this comprehensive record system.

Child abuse is a crisis for the parent as well as the child. It is often forgotten that the abused child is one whose behavior and problems sometimes cause extreme stress for the most forbearing parent. Parents in crisis are, unfortunately, sometimes overlooked by health personnel attending the battered child. The tragic situation of the helpless beaten child makes it very difficult for nurses and physicians to recognize the equally great need of the battered child's parents. Whether parents bring the abused child to the hospital themselves, or whether they are reported by nurses, teachers, or neighbors, they are usually guilt-ridden and shaken by the experience. In most cases, they are fearful for the child's life, remorseful about their uncontrolled rage, fearful of treatment at the hands of the law, and fearful of future outbursts of uncontrollable anger displaced to the child (Korbin 1987).

If nurses, physicians, and social workers can overcome their own aversion and feelings of rejection for these parents, the crisis can become a turning point in the adults' lives. Understanding the emotional needs of abusive or neglectful parents is important for doing crisis intervention with them. Work with parents of battered and neglected children reveals the following characteristics:

- Inability to understand and communicate with children.
- Emotional immaturity.
- Generally disturbed lives.
- Unhappy marriage.
- Stress related to economic, unemployment, and housing problems.
- Feelings of inadequacy in their role as parents.
- Frequent life crises as well as drug and alcohol problems.
- Deprived or abused childhood.
- Unrealistic and rigid expectations of their children.
- Minimal or inadequate parenting skills.

Crisis intervention in instances of child abuse includes:

1. Encouraging the parent to express feelings appropriate to the event.
2. Actively engaging the parent in planning medical care for the child. This is a corrective emotional experience, moving the parent in the direction of doing something constructive for the child, and would be appropriate in the case example of Richard.
3. Enlisting the parents' cooperation with child welfare authorities who have been appropriately informed by the nurse or physician. This includes correcting the parents' probable perception of child welfare authorities as punitive. In reality, the people representing such authorities generally are concerned and will help parents carry out their parental responsibilities. This point is important for preventing further tragedies such as murder of the children by a father accused of incest, as is possible in the case example of Linda.
4. Avoiding the removal of an incest victim instead of her assailant from the home. Removal of the victim perpetuates the notion that she is responsible for the abuse and the breakup of the family. It also further alienates her from her mother (see Herman 1981).
5. Referring the parent to self-help groups such as Parents Anonymous or Parents in Crisis. In these groups, they can

share their feelings and get help for their problem from other parents in similar situations. This would be helpful for the parents of both Richard and Linda (see Chapter 5).

6. Instituting job training and day-care services in cases of economic strain and where a mother is overwhelmed with the care of several children at home by herself, as is Richard's mother.
7. Providing concrete suggestions of nonviolent alternatives to discipline, such as isolation or thinking time for the child, and nonviolent stress management techniques for parents. There are excellent books on this topic written specifically for parents (for example, Crary 1979 and Judson 1984).

FOLLOW-UP SERVICE

Follow-up of child-abusing parents should include referral to a counseling agency where they can receive more extensive help concerning the underlying emotional problems leading to the crisis. Child welfare departments can facilitate parent counseling if they do not offer it themselves. Role modeling, home supervision, and parent-effectiveness training are other services that should be available to these parents.

The suggestions for prevention should be considered even if abuse has already occurred. It is never too late to consider ways to eliminate pain and unnecessary death of our children and to reduce this tragic waste of our nation's most precious resource.

RAPE

THE PROBLEM

Rape is a violent crime, not a sexual act. Because of people's attitudes toward the crime of rape, the crisis of rape victims has not received appropriate attention until recently. Feminists and others who have become sensitized to the horrors of this crime against women are slowly bringing about necessary changes in a legal system that often causes double victimization of the woman or girl who has been attacked.*

In a widely publicized rape conviction, the rapist's defense attorney

*Though most rape victims are female, male rape also occurs, leaving its victims with similar crisis manifestations, and in some instances, even greater reluctance to report the rape and seek help.

outraged public opinion by declaring on national television that the convictions would never have occurred if he had been allowed to enter into testimony the history of the victim's sex life. Similarly, there was public outcry against a judge who let an admitted rapist off with a light sentence for raping a 5-year-old girl because of the girl's "precocious sexual behavior." If a woman is sexually abused or raped by her physician, the chances of successful prosecution are reduced further because: (a) the social and political influence of the medical profession is enormous, (b) the average woman thus abused has been seduced into believing the action is part of medical practice, (c) the woman is often afraid to report the incident and cannot imagine that this could happen to anyone but herself, (d) she may have absorbed the message that she invited the rape or did something wrong.

Many states still do not recognize rape in marriage as an offense, due to the cultural notion of woman as the property and appropriate object of man's violence and pleasure (Russell 1982). Rape as a common crime of war also still goes unpunished.

The criminal justice system is not the only arena in which rape victims are blamed. Holmstrom and Burgess (1978) found that attitudes of hospital personnel (physicians and nurses) were the same as those of the police: there was considerable sympathy for the victim with obvious physical injuries, but general blaming and skepticism regarding the victim's "victimization" in less brutal rapes. This is significant when considering the threat to life accompanying many rapes and the great number of "acquaintance" rapes (47% of all rapes). In date rape, it is often assumed that if a woman says no she doesn't mean it and that in some way she invited the attack. This issue is complicated in instances where women have drunk too much and are victimized by a "gang" of rapists. The woman's intoxication is used as an excuse to exploit her. College women are particularly vulnerable to such attacks, which are the least often reported because of the continued attitude of excusing rapists on grounds of the *victims'* behavior. The *MS* magazine Campus Project on Sexual Assault revealed that one quarter of college women today have been victims of rape or attempted rape and almost 90% of the women knew their assailants (Sweet 1985). In two recent campus "gang rapes" even women made public "victim blaming" statements. One study of college students revealed that 50% of the men had forced sex on women but did not define it as rape, while only 33% said that under *no* circumstances could they rape a woman (Sweet 1985).

We should not, however, be surprised at these responses to rape victims in a culture in which women in general are often considered "fair game." Recently, psychiatric and general health personnel have responded to the research regarding attitudes of health professionals toward rape victims. These workers are developing rape crisis intervention programs in hospital settings based on principles of equality and a rejection of popular myths about rape (McCombie 1980).

The fallacy of blaming a woman for her attack because she was "dressed too provocatively" or "out on the street alone" becomes clear in the analogy of a well-dressed man who is robbed of his wallet; no one would justify the crime of robbery (the act of the attacker) on the basis of what the victim was wearing (an assumed freedom of the individual). Regarding women who are raped while out at night, we might attend to Golda Meir's response to the curfew proposal for Israeli women at risk of attack: let the men who are raping be curfewed instead.

Another popular myth about rape is that the victim "enjoys it" and that the average woman entertains fantasies of being raped. This notion is reinforced by popular movies such as "Last Tango in Paris," hard- and soft-core pornography, and advertising images in which women are depicted as appropriate objects of male violence (Langelan 1981). These myths about rape stem from the persistent interpretation of rape as a sexual event rather than as an act of violence.

Societal attitudes, then, play a major part in the outcome of a rape crisis experience. When rape victims are blamed rather than assisted through this crisis, it is not surprising that they blame themselves and fail to express feelings appropriate to the event, such as anger. Such attitudes also impede the process of long-term recovery (Sales, Baum, and Shore 1984).

There is still much to be done to change public attitudes, reform institutional responses to rape victims, and dismantle the widespread belief that women and girls who are raped are "asking for it." It is instructive to note that many victims fail to report rape because of fear and perceived ineffectiveness of police, plus the threat of further victimization by authorities (Kidd and Chayet 1984). Another study revealed that those victims who sought compensation were even more dissatisfied than those who did not, because payment was either inadequate or denied altogether (Elias 1984, p. 113).

PREVENTING RAPE

Long-range strategies to prevent rape include dismantling the myths discussed earlier that promote double victimization of women. Such a campaign should cover education, health, social service, and criminal justice systems as well as the public at large.

At the individual level a woman whose life is threatened can do little or nothing to prevent the attack. In some cases, however, women can lessen their chances of attack by training themselves to be "street wise" and alert at all times to their surroundings when outside. Potential victims should remember that even though crime may *appear* to be random, the would-be criminal has a plan. That plan includes attacking a person who *appears* to present the greatest chance of success at the crime with the least amount of trouble. Therefore, women on the street who are alert and have a plan in the event of attack have to some extent equalized the criminal/victim relationship. Such a plan may be as simple as looking around frequently or carrying a pencil flashlight—cues that alert the would-be attacker that you are not an easy target. Also, the attacker does not know what *else* you may possess (for example, mace or karate expertise) and generally will not take unnecessary chances with people who appear prepared to resist. Alertness in one's home is also important; for example, a 56-year-old woman was raped in her home by a man posing as a delivery man in spite of a highly organized neighborhood patrol on her street.

Self-defense training is also useful as an immediate prevention strategy (Kidder, Boell, and Moyer 1983). It provides physical resistance ability and the psychological protection of greater self-confidence and less vulnerability. However, women should not rely on self-defense excessively because: (a) it may lead to a false sense of security and neglect of planning and alertness; (b) some attackers are so fast and overpower the victim so completely that there may be no opportunity to put self-defense strategies to work.

Preventing rape of children includes not leaving children unattended, instruction about not accepting favors from strangers, and keeping communication open so that a child will feel free to confide in parents about a threat or attack.

CRISIS INTERVENTION

There is no question that girls and women who have been raped are in crisis (Burgess and Holstrom 1979). They are in shock, fear for their lives, and feel dirty and physically violated. Sometimes they feel shame and blame themselves for being attacked. They may or may not feel angry, depending on how much they feel responsible for their victimization. These feelings all lead to a temporary halting of their usual problem-solving ability and often delay reporting of the crime. Rape is sometimes accompanied by robbery and abandonment at the location where the victim was taken by the rapist. Such a series of events further reduces the victim's normal problem-solving ability.

Holmstrom and Burgess (1978), in their extensive research, have described the crisis and treatment of rape victims. Brownmiller (1975) deals with the historical and anthropological aspects of rape. Emergency and police personnel are referred to these works for more information about rape—that it is a serious crime and that the *victims* of this crime should not also be the defendants. McCombie et al. (1980) describe medical center protocols based on the works of these authors.

If a rape has occurred, friends, family, strangers, the police, and agency staff may be in a position to offer immediate crisis assistance to the victim. The rape victim is sometimes hesitant to ask for the help she needs from family and friends, especially in cases of date or acquaintance rape. Helpers should actively reach out in the form of crisis intervention in *every* case of rape. The chances of being asked for such help and our success in offering it during this crisis depends on our basic attitudes regarding rape and our technical knowledge of what to do. The following is quoted from the public information card of the Manchester, New Hampshire Women's Crisis Line. It contains essential information that anyone (including victims themselves) can use if someone has been raped. (Similar information cards are available at hospital rape crisis intervention programs and in police departments:)

What to Do if You Have Been Raped

Emotional considerations: A rape is usually traumatic. Call a friend and/or Manchester Women Against Rape (MWAR) for support. A trained MWAR volunteer can provide information, support, and referral, and is willing to accompany you to the hospital, police, and court.

Medical considerations: Get immediate medical attention. Take a change of clothing along to the emergency room of a hospital, or to a private physician (the police will provide transportation if you need it). The exam should focus on two concerns: medical care and the gathering of evidence for possible prosecution. You will have a pelvic examination and be checked for injuries, pregnancy, and VD. Be prepared to give enough details of the attack for the exam to be thorough. Follow-up tests for venereal disease (about six weeks later) and pregnancy are also important.

Legal considerations: Do not bathe, douche, or change clothes until after the medical exam; that would destroy evidence you will need if you should later choose to prosecute. Try to recall as many details as possible. Call the police to report the crime. Be prepared to answer questions intended to help your case, such as: Where were you raped? What happened? Can you identify the man?

If the victim does come to an emergency medical facility, emergency personnel should listen to the victim and support her emotionally while carrying out necessary medical and legal procedures. Victims should be advised that there are standard protocols for these procedures that are legally required if charges are filed. The victim should be actively linked with crisis counseling services. Some hospital emergency rooms are staffed with such counselors, and many cities have rape crisis services with crisis hotlines or women's centers. Where specialized services do not exist, rape victims should be offered the emergency services of local mental health agencies, which exist in nearly every community.

Crisis counseling by telephone for the rape victim is illustrated in the following interview example:

TELEPHONE CRISIS COUNSELING FOR THE RAPE VICTIM

CASE EXAMPLE: ELAINE

CHARACTERISTICS OF CRISIS AND INTERVENTION TECHNIQUES	TELEPHONE INTERVIEW BETWEEN VICTIM AND CRISIS COUNSELOR
	Counselor: Crisis Center, May I help you?
	Elaine: I just have to talk to somebody.
Establishing personal human contact	*Counselor:* Yes—my name is Sandra. I'd like to hear what's troubling you. Will you tell me your name?
Upset, vulnerable, trouble with problem solving	*Elaine:* I'm Elaine. . . . I'm just so upset I don't know what to do.
Identifying hazardous event	*Counselor:* Can you tell me what happened? *Elaine:* Well, I was coming home alone last night from a party. . . . It was late (chokes up, starts to cry).
	Counselor: Whatever it is that happened has really upset you.
	Elaine: (Continues to cry.)
Empathy, encouraging expression of feeling	*Counselor:* (Waits, listens—Elaine's crying subsides.) It must be really hard for you to talk about.
Self-blaming	*Elaine:* I guess it was really crazy for me to go to that party alone. . . . I should never have done it . . . on my way into my apartment this man grabbed me (starts to cry again).
Indentifying hazardous event	*Counselor:* I gather he must have attacked you.
Self-blame and distorted perception of reality	*Elaine:* Yes! He raped me! I could kill him! But at the same time, I keep thinking it must be my own fault.
Encouraging appropriate expression of anger instead of self-blame	*Counselor:* Elaine, I can see that you're really angry at the guy, and you should be. Any woman would feel the same, but Elaine, you're blaming yourself for this terrible thing instead of him.

Characteristics of Crisis and Intervention Techniques	Telephone Interview Between Victim and Crisis Counselor
Self-doubt, unable to use usual social support	*Elaine:* Well, deep down I really know it's not my fault, but I think my parents and boyfriend might think so.
Obtaining factual information, exploring resources	*Counselor:* In other words, you haven't told them about this yet, is that right? Is there anyone you've been able to talk to?
	Elaine: No, not anyone. I'm too ashamed (starts crying again).
Empathy	*Counselor:* (Listens, waits a few seconds.) I can tell that you're really upset.
Failure in problem solving	*Elaine:* (Continues crying.) I just don't know what to do—I feel like maybe I'll never feel like myself again.
Empathy Suicide risk assessment Feels isolated from social supports	*Counselor:* This is a serious thing that's happened to you, Elaine. I really want to help you. Considering how upset you are, and not being able to talk with your family and your boyfriend, is there a possibility that you've thought of hurting yourself?
Suicidal ideas only, is reaching out for help	*Elaine:* Well, the thought has crossed my mind, but no, I really don't think I'd do that—that's why I called here. I just feel so dirty and unwanted—and alone—I know I'm not really a bad person but you just can't believe how awful I feel (starts crying again).
Empathy Involving Elaine in the planning	*Counselor:* Elaine, I can understand why you must feel that way. Rape is one of the most terrible things that can happen to a woman (waits a few seconds). Elaine, I'd really like to help you through this thing—can we talk about some things that you might do to feel better?
Feels distant from social resources	*Elaine:* Well, yes—I know I should see a doctor, and I'd really like to talk to my boyfriend and my parents, but I just can't bring myself to do it right now.
Supporting Elaine's decision, direct involvement of counselor, exploring resources	*Counselor:* I'd recommend, Elaine, that you see a doctor as soon as possible. Do you have a private doctor?

CHARACTERISTICS OF CRISIS AND INTERVENTION TECHNIQUES	TELEPHONE INTERVIEW BETWEEN VICTIM AND CRISIS COUNSELOR
Decision	*Elaine:* Yes. I'll call and see if I can get in.
	Counselor: And if you can't get in right away, how about going to a hospital emergency room as soon as possible?
	Elaine: OK—I'll do that.
Obtaining factual information	*Counselor:* Elaine, I gather you didn't report this to the police. Is that right?
Helplessness, feeling isolated	*Elaine:* I didn't think it would do any good, and besides, just like with my boyfriend, I was too ashamed.
Obtaining factual information	*Counselor:* Were your clothes torn and do you have any bruises from the rape?
	Elaine: No, not that I'm aware of. I just feel sore all over, so maybe I do have some bruises I can't see. I probably shouldn't have taken a bath before going to the doctor, but, I felt so dirty, I just couldn't stand it.
Reinforcing decision, suggestion to reconsider reporting	*Counselor:* It's really important, Elaine, that you see your doctor soon. You may also want to reconsider reporting the rape to the police.
	Elaine: I guess maybe you're right.
Exploring continued crisis counseling possibility	*Counselor:* Elaine, considering how badly you feel about this and that you don't feel up to talking with your parents and your boyfriend yet, would you like to come in to see a counselor and talk some more about the whole thing?
Needs help in reestablishing contact with significant people in her life	*Elaine:* Not really . . . anyway, I, really feel better now that I've talked with you. But, I still can't really face my parents and boyfriend.
Encouraging further expression of feeling with significant others; paving way for this through crisis counseling	*Counselor:* This is a lot to handle all at one time. I'm sure you're going to be more upset about it, especially until you're able to talk with your boyfriend and parents about it. That's one of the things a counselor can help you with. . . . A counselor can also help you take a second look at the pros and cons of reporting or not reporting the rape to the police.

Characteristics of Crisis and Intervention Techniques	Telephone Interview between Victim and Crisis Counselor
Mutually agreed-on plan	*Elaine:* I guess maybe it's a good idea. I do feel better now, but I've been crying off and on since last night—and maybe I'll start crying all over again after I hang up. Besides, I called in sick today because I couldn't face going to work. So I guess I'll stay home tomorrow too and come in and talk to somebody. What time?
Concrete plan mutually arrived at by Elaine and counselor	*Counselor:* How about 10 o'clock? *Elaine:* That's OK, I guess. *Counselor:* How are you feeling right now, Elaine? *Elaine:* Like I said before, quite a bit better.
Reinforcement of plan	*Counselor:* Elaine, I'm really glad you called and that you're going to see a doctor and come here to see someone too. Meanwhile, if you get upset and feel you want to talk to someone again, please call, as there's always someone here, OK? *Elaine:* OK, I will—thanks so much for listening.

FOLLOW-UP SERVICE

Women who have been raped usually describe it as the most traumatic experience of their life. It should not be assumed, however, that the experience necessarily will damage the woman for life. Whether or not permanent damage occurs depends on two factors: (1) the resources available to the woman for working through the crisis and not blaming herself for the crime, (2) the woman's precrisis coping ability. If the woman has a supportive social network and a healthy self-concept, she will probably work through the crisis successfully. For women in such circumstances, crisis counseling will usually suffice and long-term therapy is not indicated. Without such support and precrisis coping, there is a danger of lasting psychological scars, such as paranoia about all men or inability to relate sexually to husband or boyfriend. This danger is increased by a rape trial in which the defense lawyer succeeds in making the victim rather than the rapist appear as the criminal or by her husband and others joining the defense in blaming her for the attack. In these cases, rape victims will probably need longer-term therapy.

In an era of social service cutbacks in funding, vigilance and advocacy are indicated to assure the continuation of special services to rape victims. In fact, with the current AIDS crisis, additional services are needed to assist the victim not only through the trauma of rape, but the additional crisis of the threat of infection by the HIV virus (see Chapter 12). Peer support groups of other abused women are also helpful. The difficulty of undoing the damage of sexual assault highlights the importance of preventing rape in the first place.

Finally, in regard to child victims, it is important not to project our own shock and horror about the crime onto the child. The child should be treated and supported in proportion to her or his actual trauma and perception of the event—physical and psychological—not in proportion to our adult view of the attack. Protection, sympathy, and anger are in order, but not in a way that might cripple a child's future development and normal interaction with others.

WOMAN BATTERING

THE PROBLEM

Vignettes from the Lives of Battered Women

> *One time when he beat me I started to fight back. . . . He threw kerosene around me and threatened to put a match to it. . . . I never fought back again . . . just kept trying to figure out what I was doing wrong that he would beat me that way. There were some good times together, like when we talked about going to college, and somehow I just kept hoping and believing he would change.*
>
> *Before I came to this shelter, I had no idea so many other women were going through the same thing I was. . . . I used to think the only way out of my situation would be a tragic one—to kill either myself or him.*
>
> *I'd go to my friends' and mother's house, but I just couldn't make ends meet. I didn't have a baby sitter, money, or the physical and mental strenth. . . . I was depressed about everything. My mother stuck it out for 40 years. I didn't believe in divorce, I believed in marriage. Basically, it was my religion and for financial support [that she didn't leave earlier]. (Hoff 1984)*

Until recently, it was widely assumed that women were beaten because the man was drinking, unemployed, or otherwise under stress, or the woman provoked his behavior by saying the wrong thing or failing to meet whimsical demands. If, for example, a man beat his wife while she was pregnant, it was because "women are so emotional during pregnancy." It was also claimed that women did not leave violent relationships because they were not sufficiently motivated and ignored the resources they possessed. Such conclusions were drawn in spite of the fact that when the same women sought help from the police, family, friends, or health or social service professionals they received little assistance or were blamed by their confidantes. A "resource" is hardly a resource if it provides a negative response to a woman in crisis.

More recent research (for example, Dobash and Dobash 1979, Hoff 1984, Martin 1976, Pagelow 1981, Schechter 1982, and Stark 1984) provides overwhelming evidence that legal, health care, and religious institutions support and approve wife battering by such actions as:

1. Defining assault on one's wife as a misdemeanor while the same assault on a stranger is a felony, and then failing to hold violent men accountable even at this level. This situation is changing with police training. Several class action suits brought against large police jurisdictions for failure to arrest and act on abuse prevention laws have also helped to effect change (Gee 1983).
2. Diagnosing a battered woman as mentally ill and psychiatrically excusing a violent man. This practice was uncovered in 1979 by Stark, Flitcraft, and Frazier in a study of 481 battered women using the emergency service of a metropolitan hospital. In this study, "medicine's collective response" to abuse was found to contribute to a "pathological battering syndrome," actually a socially constructed product in the guise of treatment (pp. 462–463). In the intervention strategy revealed in this research, problems such as alcoholism and depression were treated medically, masking the political aspects of violence. Thus, the abused woman was psychiatrically labeled, suggesting that she was personally responsible for her problems, and violent families were treated to maintain family stability. Stark, Flitcraft, and Frazier state that medical and psychiatric agencies play a major role in the violence related to the political and economic constraints of a patriarchal authority structure.* Battered women can relate numerous instances of efforts by professional counselors to uncover "what the woman is doing to provoke her husband to beat her" (Hoff 1984).

*See also Hilberman 1980, Lovell 1981, and Wardell, Gillespie, and Leffler 1981.

3. Counseling a woman to stay in a violent relationship "for the sake of the children' instead of examining the damaging effects of the violence on the children as well (see Bograd 1984).
4. Failing to enforce laws for equal pay and job opportunities, thus making it very difficult for women to support themselves and their children alone.
5. Failing to provide enough refuge facilities and emotional support to a battered woman in crisis, claiming that battering is a private matter between the woman and her husband.
6. Assuming that in spite of all these social, cultural, political, and economic roadblocks placed before a woman by others, a battered woman stays in a violent relationship because "she must enjoy being beaten"—a classical example of blaming the victim that ignores the public aspect of the problem.

While traditional responses to wife battering are damaging enough to women, they also are not complimentary to men. Maintaining simplistic explanations of this complex problem implies that men are less than human, moral beings. It suggests that they are essentially infants, driven largely by impulse and not to be held responsible for their actions. A recent study (Hoff 1984) supports earlier research (Dobash and Dobash 1979, and Stark, Flitcraft, and Frazier 1979) and provides new insights into the *process* of violence between spouses. It suggests that violence occurs not merely as a stress response, but as a complex interplay between conditions of biologic reproduction and economic, political-legal, belief and knowledge systems of particular historical communities. These interacting systems seem to produce a context in which cultural values, the division of labor, power allocation, and beliefs operate to sustain a climate of oppression and conflict. In such a climate, violence againts women flourishes, suggesting a link between the personal trouble of individual battered women and the public issue of women's status.

PREVENTION

This sociocultural interpretation of why men are violent with their mates and why battered women stay in abusive relationships aids our understanding of the problem. How, though, can this understanding help us deal constructively with the woman who repeatedly calls police and repeatedly receives emergency medical treatment but does not leave the relationship? This cyclic aspect of violence is one of the most complex issues facing police, nurses, physicians, and others trying to help battered women. There is probably nothing more frustrating for a concerned helper than the situation illustrated in the following case example.

Case Example: Staying in an Abusive Relationship

A woman calls a hotline, crying, afraid for her own life and worried that she might kill her husband if he returns. She says she wants to come to the shelter and wants to know how she can get there as she has no money. She agrees to a plan to have the police come and bring her to a designated place to meet the shelter staff member. The woman never shows up. On follow-up, the shelter volunteer learns that when the police arrived, the woman had changed her mind.

Even people who are sympathetic to the plight of women and eager to help are ready to give up in the face of such apparent "resistance." These kinds of situations make it tempting to blame the victim and assume that if a woman did not like to be beaten she would take advantage of available help. What prevents a helper from falling into this trap are: (1) remembering that the issue is much larger than the immediate crisis of a particular woman, and (2) realizing that though we may not understand or agree with the woman's decision to stay, she has *reasons* for her decision. Some of these might be: (a) fear of the unknown and how she can manage without her husband's financial support, (b) continued hope and belief that the man will act on his frequent promises and stop beating her, and (c) fear of retaliation, or even murder, after she leaves the shelter unless she leaves the geographic area permanently. The experience of women in shelters reveals that some men employ elaborate detective strategies to find a woman who has left. Some who find a woman in a shelter threaten to harm all the shelter residents unless the woman returns. This is why many shelters maintain a secret location.

The complexity of the problem is further illustrated by an analysis of what happens after the *first* time a woman is beaten. A woman faces a difficult situation: The first violent incident usually is very shocking to her ("How could he do this to me?") and is followed by the man's elaborate promises never to do it again. The woman believes her mate and decides not to leave. This apparently rational decision is reinforced by positive, valued aspects of the relationship that the woman wishes to salvage. When the man beats her a second time, he not only has broken his promise, but has distorted her trust and belief in his word into justification for beating her again ("If she didn't think it was all right for me to beat her, she'd leave"). The cycle is reinforced by the man's blaming his behavior on the woman (she doesn't cook right, dress right, or respect him), which she increasingly absorbs and believes. This complex interactional process underscores the importance of *preventing* violence in the first place. Once this cycle begins, it is very difficult to interrupt. Thus our prevention efforts should focus on the following:

1. Reinforcing and educating police, health, and social service workers about the Abuse Protection Acts, which define wife abuse as a crime punishable by law. Through the battered women's movement, these laws have been updated in most of the 50 states.*
2. Examining educational, social, and religious programs for their implicit support of violence through socialization of boys and men to aggressive behavior and girls and women to passive, dependent behavior (Broverman 1970)—a process that reinforces the view of wives as appropriate objects of violence.
3. Instituting campaigns to end the marketing of pornography and other products of popular culture that portray women as objects and glorify violence against them (Langelan 1981).
4. Enforcing the Equal Pay Act passed in 1967, and improving child care, and economic and educational services for women so that financial and educational disadvantages do not prevent them from leaving violent relationships.
5. Instituting community-wide consciousness raising groups for men and women and focusing on ways to promote egalitarian marriage and break out of dominant or excessively dependent behavior patterns.

These and other "upstream" preventive strategies should be carried out in tandem with immediate intervention for women in acute crisis (see Crisis Paradigm, third box).

CRISIS INTERVENTION

Vignette from the Life of a Battered Woman

Until I found out about and came to the shelter, I kept thinking I was the only one. I didn't have any idea so many other women were in the same boat. I was so ashamed and kept thinking that

---

*Legal information about battering can be obtained from local shelters, police, and the following resources: *Aegis: Magazine on Ending Violence against Women,* Box 21033, Washington, DC 20009; telephone 202-659-5983. National Woman Abuse Prevention Project, 2000 P Street, NW, Suite 508, Washington, DC 20036; telephone 202-857-0216. National Clearinghouse on Family Violence: Social Service Programs Branch, Health and Welfare, Ottawa, Ontario KlA lB5; telephone 603-957-2938.

> *it somehow must have been my fault. He told me it was my fault and I believed him—though I still don't know what I did wrong because I was always trying to second-guess and please him so I wouldn't get beaten. (Hoff 1984)*

Assistance during crisis should be available to women from family and friends. However, relatives and friends often view marital violence as a private issue and are reluctant to get involved. They may also be afraid of getting hurt themselves or making things worse. The least a relative or friend can do, though, is to put a woman in touch with local crisis hotlines, which have staff prepared to deal with the problem. Since many battered women call the police and contact emergency medical resources, putting these women in touch with crisis workers is the first and most important thing emergency workers can do after providing medical treatment.

Two factors, however, may impede the accomplishment of this task: some women do not acknowledge the cause of their physical injuries or provide a cover-up story. There are several reasons for this: (a) the woman may have been threatened by her mate with a more severe beating if she reveals the beating; (b) she may simply not be ready to leave for her own reasons; (c) she may sense the judgmental and unsympathetic attitude of a physician or nurse and therefore not confide the truth.

VIGNETTE FROM THE LIFE OF A BATTERED WOMAN

> *I used to come in [to my hospital job] with bruises and they [the nurses] would talk about it—"How can a woman be so stupid and stay with a guy like that?" The nurses were so unsympathetic. . . . I couldn't help seeing how the doctors would put them down and they stood there and took it. Women are too competitive with each other. They get that from men. They [the nurses] would complain about how they were treated by doctors and the hospital, but in their relationships you'd have thought they were perfect the way they acted and talked. (Hoff 1984)*

Such attitudes are related to the second factor impeding successful crisis intervention: our inability to control our frustration and disappointment in the woman for not leaving the violent relationship (see Other Intervention Strategies in Chapter 4). Sensitivity to these factors will help us interpret a woman's evasiveness about her injuries and recognize the implausibility of a cover-up story. Besides the physical injuries, a battered woman will show other signals of distress or emotional crisis (Hollen, Kamp, and Attala 1986). Medical and nursing staff who use a crisis assessment tool such as discussed earlier in this book can more accurately identify and appropriately respond to a battered woman in crisis. As is true in dealing with a person at risk of being suicidal, it is appropriate to question a woman directly, with the probable result that she will be relieved to know that someone is caring and sensitive enough to discern her distress. And, like suicidal people, if a woman refuses to acknowledge the battering, her refusal may have something to do with our attitude, not her willingness to disclose.

The important techniques to remember in these situations are: (1) withhold judgement, and (2) provide the woman at least with written information (a card or brochure with the numbers of hotlines and women's support groups), confident that this seemingly small act is central to the process of the woman's eventual decision to leave the violent relationship. The reason for confidence is that a woman feels empowered if she believes others *respect* her decision (even if it is to stay in the violent relationship for the time being). She also needs explicit recognition that it is ultimately *her* decision that makes the difference, and that she can also take credit for the decision. Since battered women often feel powerless and unrespected, we should convey to them that *they* are in charge of their lives. When a woman *believes* this, it becomes a premise for her eventual action. Thus, while a woman may not be ready for more than emergency medical treatment, she at least has the necessary information if she decides to use it in the future. These principles apply to police officers as well as medical workers.

It is also important to assure battered women that they are not responsible for their victimization, no matter what the person who battered them says to the contrary. In order to do this, we must be convinced that, except in self-defense, violence is not justified no matter what happens in the interaction or the relationship. Even when used in self-defense, a return of violence often escalates rather than decreases the violence (see Assessing Risk of Assault and Homicide in this chapter). In addition, we should not assume that battered women are routinely in need of therapy; this could add a psychiatric label to an already heavy burden (Stark, Flitcraft, and Frazier 1979). If a woman is suicidal, the principles and techniques discussed in Chapters 6 and 7 apply.

Once a woman is treated for physical trauma and resolves the dilemma of deciding what to do, she may be faced with the crises of emergency housing, care of her children, and money. If a community does not have a safe home network or emergency shelter, and a woman cannot stay with relatives and has no money, then she may have little choice but to return to the violent situation. When a woman decides to leave, up-to-date abuse prevention acts require police to accompany her to her home to get her children, legal documents, and whatever possessions she can bring to an emergency housing situation. Once the woman is in a shelter or linked to a support group network, further assistance is available to deal with legal, housing, and other aspects of the crisis (Germain 1984).

One aspect of the crisis is the effect of the battering situation on children. Often the children have either observed the abuse or been abused themselves. An important element of help for the mother in crisis, as well as the children, is the availability of child care services. The mother needs time away from children to deal with housing and other issues. The children, on the other hand, are often highly anxious and in need of a stable, calming influence, as well as appropriate physical outlets and nonviolent disciplining (Straus et al. 1987).

FOLLOW-UP SERVICE

When a battered woman has successfully dealt with the crisis aspect of her situation, the biggest decision she faces—if she has not already decided through the process of seeking refuge in a shelter—is whether to leave permanently and seek a divorce if married. Some women take months to make this decision even after living in a safe environment for some time. Peer support groups of other women who have been battered and have broken out of violent relationships are probably the most valuable resource for a woman at this time. Such groups are important for several reasons:

1. If a woman decides to return to her mate with hoping for a change and the battering continues, it is important for her to know that there are people who will not judge her for her decisions.

2. Many women come to shelters convinced that they are psychologically disturbed and in need of a therapist. They have absorbed the message that the battering occurred because of something wrong with them. When they begin to feel strong and in charge of their lives, they may discover that a therapist is not needed after all and that other women can help them in ways they had not imagined. This discovery by a battered woman is a significant contrast to her traditional to view of other women as her "competition" in what many perceive as the all-important life task of catching and holding a man. Finding alternatives to therapy occurs most often in shelters that actively encourage women to assume charge of their lives. It also happens through the process of decision making and taking action to obtain housing, money, and legal services. Observing women in responsible, independent, and caring roles in the shelter staffing arrangements also seems to help. After feeling powerless for so long, a woman does not need a program that dictates every hour and detail of her life.

3. These support experiences may provide the basis for battered women to join, if they wish, a wider network of women working on the larger social, political, and economic aspects of stopping violence against women. A woman's positive experience of support while in crisis is the best preparation for such possible involvement.

If women request therapy, referrals should be made to therapists working from a woman's perspective. Therapy may be indicated if, after crisis intervention and social network support, a woman continues to be depressed and suicidal or finds herself unable to make decisions and break out of patterns of dependency and self-blame. When the violent marriage and abuse of the children have left damaging scars, family therapy is indicated.

Other aspects of follow-up include:

- An opportunity for the woman to grieve and mourn the loss of a relationship if she finally decides to leave (see Loss, Change, and Grief Work in Chapter 4).

- For women who wish to marry again, a group to examine and share with others the complex aspects of avoiding relationships that may lead to a repeat of excessive dependency and violence (Campbell 1986).
- Parent effectiveness groups to explore nonviolent ways of dealing with children.

The preventive, crisis, and follow-up aspects of helping battered women should be practiced with a view to their vital connectedness. This triple approach to the problem may not only help to end the pain and terror of individual women who are attacked, but may also remove the negative consequences of violence for children, men, and the entire society (Hoff 1989).

MEN WHO BATTER

Earlier work in the violence literature often depicted batterers as incorrigible persons with character disorders or claimed that alcohol abuse excused them from accountability for their behavior. Gondolf's (1985, 1987) recent research with violent men reveals four types of batterers: sociopathic, antisocial, chronic, and sporadic. Gondolf suggests that sociopathic batterers need continual restraint to stem their violence, while those with antisocial behaviors need a variety of coordinated interventions. In a controversial experimental study, Sherman and Berk (1984) found that arrest had the greatest impact on reducing recidivism (repeat battering) compared with mediation and crisis intervention. One reason for this finding is that arrest may equalize the power relationship between the couple. In general, men who batter can be referred to therapy programs such as *Emerge* in Boston.* In this program, men receive individual and group counseling from male mental health professionals and from peers, that is, men who have been violent in the past but are no longer violent. The emphasis of the program is on consciousness-raising about the roots of their violence and on learning nonviolent ways of responding to stress and frustration in their relationships with women. Adams (1988a, 1988b), a counselor at Emerge, emphasizes that effective counseling of men who batter assumes that they take responsibility for their violence, in contrast to excusing it on grounds of insecurity and other problems. Unfortunately, only a few violent men have taken advantage of such services. Gondolf (1987, p. 5) proposes that this may occur in part because batterers have been typecast in a single mold. In general, instead of abused women and their children having

*More information is available from: Emerge, A Men's Counseling Service on Domestic Violence, 280 Green Street, Cambridge, MA 02139; telephone (617) 547-9870.

to leave home and seek refuge, violent men should be required to leave and receive counseling in alternative housing as an incentive to stop their violent behavior. This idea is akin to the curfew suggested by Golda Meir for rapists. Clearly, shelters are necessary life-saving measures for women and children, but more permanent solutions should eventually replace them.

HUSBAND BEATING

This discussion is incomplete without some attention to the controversial issue of husband beating. Women as well as men can be violent; not to acknowledge this fact is equivalent to viewing women as less than moral beings, in the same way that excusing male violence implies that men are less than moral beings. Women, like men, should be held accountable for their behavior.

Yet it has been suggested that the "real" domestic problem is husband battering, and that the reason it is still hidden is because it is too much of an assault on the male ego to acknowledge the shame of having been beaten by a woman. A national survey on domestic violence revealed that in numbers of violent acts, not quality or context, women and men were approximately equal (Straus, Gelles, and Steinmetz 1980). This statistical finding, however, needs to be drastically qualified: When women are violent it is primarily in self-defense, and their attacks are not as dangerous or physically injurious as are those of men. Also, when women kill their mates, it is usually after years of abuse, and they do so less frequently than men kill their wives (Browne, 1987, Jones 1980). Considering also the fact that 25% of pregnant women have a current or past history of being battered, the contrast is even more dramatic (Stark 1984).

The pattern of injustice and violence used primarily in self-defense should be kept in mind in trials of women who kill abusive husbands. Rather than medicalizing the woman's case by a contrived "insanity plea," women should have a fair trial on self-defense grounds when all evidence points in that direction.

The suggestion that husband beating is more rampant than wife-battering covers up the roots of violence against women in patriarchal structures and the low socioeconomic status of women that allows violence to flourish. To claim an equal problem of husband battering belies reality, especially as it is revealed in emergency settings and in the physical strength differential between most men and women. The majority of men are physically more capable of inflicting injury than are women. In addition, men who are beaten have much more freedom to leave if they wish because of their socioeconomic advantage in society and relative freedom from child care.

ABUSE OF ELDERS

THE PROBLEM

Attention to abuse of elders (age 60 and over) is so new that we do not have national survey data documenting its incidence, though estimates are in the 1,000,000 range. Elder abuse is defined as "the willful infliction of physical pain, injury or debilitating mental anguish, unreasonable confinement or willful deprivation by a caretaker of services which are necessary to maintain mental and physical health" (O'Malley et al. 1979, p. 2) Earlier, public attention was focused on abuse and substandard care in nursing homes. In spite of the prevalence of institutional care of the elderly in American society, the majority of elders (95%) live alone or with family or other caretakers. Though abuse and neglect may occur in institutions, legal protections limit such abuse. In private settings, legal protections are more difficult to enforce because of civil rights and family privacy issues (Tamme 1985). This discussion is particularly relevant to community health nurses, home health aides, pastors, and other professionals offering consultation and supervision on behalf of elders cared for at home.

Why are elders abused? As already noted, there are parallels between battered children and elders: (1) they are in a dependent position for survival; (2) they are presumed to be protected by love, gentleness, and caring; (3) they are a source of emotional, physical, and financial stress for the caretaker, particularly if the elder is also physically or mentally impaired (Sommers and Shields 1987, Steinmetz 1978, Tamme 1985).

Several other factors can be identified in tracing the roots of elder abuse. Inattention to these factors can form obstacles to prevention, crisis intervention, and follow-up service for elders at risk.

1. *Social:* In the nuclear family structure there is often no social, physical, and economic *room* for elders.* This is complicated by the trend of women working outside of the home (by necessity and choice) while maintaining their traditional responsibility for work at home as well.

2. *Cultural:* Our society is noted for idolizing youth and devaluing the elderly. The cultural emphasis on economic productivity tends to eclipse elders' contributions of wisdom, life experience, and often, continued work. Consequently, elders often lack status, respect, and similar rewards that are

---

*Goody's (1962) classic ethnographic study on death rituals in traditional African societies suggests that one of the reasons there are so few death rituals in developed societies is because "social death" occurs well before physical death for many elders; in traditional societies death includes transfer of social responsibility held by the deceased, not merely disposition of his or her body (see Chapter 11).

taken for granted in other societies. The culture of violence as it affects children and women flows over to the elderly as well. In spite of elders' increasing political influence, ageism is still rampant, particularly in respect to older women (Doress and Siegal 1987).

3. *Economic:* The poverty of many old people is an almost inevitable result of the social and cultural factors noted above. Strong economic motives for protecting children do not extend to the elderly. In addition, spiraling inflation for caretakers and a health care system that is inadequate in home care services increase further the risk of elder abuse (Estes 1986).

4. *Psychological:* One of the normal features of growing old is a decreased capacity to control impulses and adjust to change. A lifelong pattern of inflexibility can result in a demanding, unpleasant personality in old age. Considering also the interaction between physical dependence and fear of retaliation, elder abuse can remain hidden for some time. Elders abused by adult children—not unlike battered women—will feel deep shame and try to account for the abuse in terms of their own failure as parents. They say, in effect, "What kind of a parent am I that my own child would turn on me in my helplessness and old age?"

5. *Legal:* Civil liberties in democratic societies protect one's right to privacy, self-determination, and the refusal of services. Although most states now have Adult Protective Service authorities, all do not require mandatory reporting of suspected elder abuse cases, as in the case of child abuse (Tamme; 1985, p. 59). These factors, combined with an abused elder's shame and fear of retaliation, comprise formidable barriers to dealing effectively with elder abuse.

PREVENTION, CRISIS INTERVENTION, AND FOLLOW-UP SERVICE

As with crises discussed earlier, prevention, crisis intervention, and follow-up are interrelated and demand awareness of the origins of the crisis. Preventive measures related to the sociocultural and economic aspects of elder abuse suggest an examination of our values regarding old people. Social and political changes affecting the elderly are also needed, such as provision of tax and insurance benefits for families who would care for an older person at home if they could add a room to their house and obtain home health care assistance without serious financial hardship. Psychologically, we can reduce the risk of elder abuse by preparing for the social, economic, and physical realities of later life (see Chapter 11 for a detailed discussion). As we prepare for old age, it is wise to remember that old people with unpleasant personalities are the same as young people with unpleasant personalities, only in exaggerated form.

Crisis intervention for elders at risk of abuse demands careful application of the assessment, planning, and intervention strategies discussed in Chapters 3, 4, and 5, with particular attention to social network approaches. Emergency medical care and crisis intervention for abused elders are complicated for two reasons:

1. Mental incapacity or confusion on the part of the elder: State and county departments of mental health and elder affairs have standard protocols for these cases. Involuntary commitment or appointment of a legal guardian require clear and convincing evidence that the adult in question is incapacitated mentally and that an emergency exists. When these legal actions are taken they should be based on the principle of "least restrictive alternative" and the guarantee of civil liberties.

2. Carelessness in this area of care or "savior tactics" can contribute to the second complication: Misplaced emergency care or crisis intervention can alienate family members who may be needed in the long term. Considering shame, possibile retaliation, and the dynamic of family loyalty, follow-up after the emergency as well as future crisis intervention will be very difficult if family members are alienated. Unless foster care is readily available, great care must be taken to prevent complicating further an already difficult situation. Thus, while laws now exist for reporting elder abuse (similar to the "Good Samaritan" laws protecting children), overzealous action on these laws should not become the occasion for precipitating more trouble.

APPLICATION OF INTERVENTION AND FOLLOW-UP PRINCIPLES

Case Example: Martha

Martha, age 82, suffered crippling arthritis and heart disease. She was visited regularly in her daughter's home by a home health aide who bathed her three times a week. The rest of the time her daughter Jane, age 55, gave her medicine and helped Martha out of bed into the chair whenever she had time. Jane worked fulltime as a legal secretary. Jane's husband Robert, age 63, was home most of the day. He had been on disability support for 10 years after seriously injuring his back doing construction work. For the most part Robert felt useless, though he did help with shopping and laundry. The disabilities of both her mother and husband left Jane feeling very stressed.

The home health aide discovered black and blue marks on Martha's chest and back and suspected that abuse was occurring. Her attempts to talk to Martha about this were met by silence. The aide reported her observation to the community health nurse,

who in turn consulted a social worker. (The nurse had known this family for over a year and visited the home approximately once a month in a supervisory, coordinating, and teaching capacity). The nurse then called Jane and suggested she be seen by the social worker to discuss the problems of taking care of her mother. The nurse did not directly mention the suspicion of abuse. Jane felt threatened, refused to act on the suggestion, dismissed the nurse and home health aide, and hired a private nurse to care for Martha around the clock to "prove" she was not neglectful of her mother. This move was a great financial burden for the family. Three months later Jane again requested service for her mother from the home health agency.

Several things seem very clear in this example: (1) Everyone concerned appeared to be well-intentioned. (2) Jane was alienated by the approach used by the nurse. (3) The problem was complicated by an inappropriate intervention strategy. The nurse seemed to lack confidence in her ability to take on a key role in intervention; she assumed that a social worker was the more appropriate person to act on the suspected abuse in spite of her year-long relationship with the family.

Our success in dealing with sensitive issues like these depends very much on the quality of the relationship between the caregiver and receiver. Had the nursed recognized this, she would not have suggested what to Jane was perceived as implying she neglected her mother. Instead, the nurse might have used other intervention and follow-up strategies:

1. After hearing the aide's report, the nurse should have planned an extra visit to the home, spending some time with Martha and Jane individually to further assess the situation. To reinforce use of her communication skills, the nurse might bathe Martha herself once as an avenue to gain Martha's confidence. A concerned rather than accusatory approach to Jane might result in Jane confiding voluntarily the stress and apparent exasperation she experienced in carrying out her multiple responsibilities. A conversation might proceed as follows:

Nurse:	How are things going, Jane, with all the things you have to juggle these days? Terri, the aide, you know, has been coming in three times a week. Do you think you're getting all the help you need?
Jane:	Well, its hard, but somehow I'm managing. On the days I have to get Mother out of bed myself I sometimes feel like a nervous wreck—she screams with pain when I touch her. I can't stand the thought of putting mother in a home, but sometimes I don't know.

Nurse: So things are pretty rough. Jane, I was in to see your mother this week while Terri was bathing and dressing her. I noticed several black and blue marks on your mother. (Nurse tries to keep the aide's relationship with the family intact.) She wouldn't talk about it though, so I'm wondering whether things are getting too difficult for you, and if maybe we could be of more help to you.

Jane: If you're thinking I hit my mother, well, I didn't. A couple of times I might have handled her kind of roughly; she's really frail and thin, you know. But I certainly never hit her—after all, she's my mother.

Nurse: This is a really touchy thing to talk about, Jane, and I don't mean to make unfounded accusations. I know it must be very difficult at times. What I'm suggesting is that we work on this together to be sure both you and your mother get what you need. I know that you want the best possible care for your mother, and it seems like Robert's disability might wear on you, too. Can you tell me more about the problems you have in taking care of you mother?

(Problem exploration continues. Session ends with agreement to talk next week again to work on the problem uncovered. It never becomes explicit whether Jane did or did not abuse her mother. It is not a good strategy to try to prove that abuse occurred when Martha is refusing to talk and Jane is denying it. It is more important to focus on the underlying issues related to abuse.)

---

2. If, after this, the nurse still does not feel confident about proceeding, she might consult the social worker, but *not* to turn the problem over to her.

3. The nurse might also talk with Jane's husband Robert to explore his possible further extended involvement with household tasks.

4. After exploring the problem with all the individuals concerned, a social network conference might be indicated (see Chapter 5). This would include Martha, Jane and Robert, Terri, and possibly a social worker consultant and a representative from Respite Services (which should be discussed as one avenue of relief for Jane).

As the proportion of elders in the population increases, there is hope for favorable political change for elder affairs. With increasing public sensitivity to the problems of elders, we may devise more creative ways to foster the conditions for peace, safety, and health and social services during the later years. Changes are already occurring with "New Age" families, the Foster Grandparent Program, and intergenerational housing experiments. The latter include, for example, around 10 people of various ages, with 60% over 60, living in a large, ordinary family home. Each person has a separate room; other areas and general tasks are shared communally. Elders who participate in these programs feel socially useful, with beneficial effects for physical and mental health and less chance of violence directed against them.

BATTERING OF PARENTS AND TEACHERS BY CHILDREN

The abuse of infirm and dependent elders by adult children differs from another aspect of violence in families: the physical abuse of parents by their children. The national survey by Straus, Gelles, and Steinmetz (1980) revealed that almost 10% of children aged 3 to 18 attacked their parents. A pilot psychiatric study by Harbin and Madden (1979, p. 1288) uncovered repeated attacks on or threats against parents by more than half the adolescents in 15 families. Parricide, the most extreme form of parental assault, is usually associated with severe parental sexual and physical abuse of the child. Research suggests that in less lethal assaults, the teenagers may "want to punish their parents for having exploited them through permissiveness and lack of leadership" (Harbin and Madden 1979, p. 1290). The adolescent feels insecure and entrapped when forced, through lack of parental authority, to assume an independent role before feeling developmentally ready.

Parents experiencing abuse by their children are in a "Catch-22" situation: like their elder counterparts, confronting the situation implies an admission of failure in effective parenting; not confronting it reinforces the child's misplaced sense of omnipotence and need to control others (Harbin and Madden 1979, p. 1290).

Preventive strategies for this problem are similar to those discussed for child and elder abuse: At the societal level, fostering nonviolent solutions to child rearing and greater respect for the elderly can reinforce parental authority. Crisis and follow-up strategies include parent effectiveness training or, if necessary, family therapy. In addition, parents need channels through which they can get help during crisis without shame or denial of the problem. Crisis intervention planning with such families should highlight specific nonviolent tactics that can be used by a child when angry at a parent. Parents need alternatives to giving in to children who behave like dictators (see Crary 1979 and Judson 1984).

Parents, however, are not the only ones abused by violent children. For years now teachers have been terrorized, raped, knifed, and attacked in other ways. The same issues are at stake here; social and cultural approval of violence, poverty, racism, loss of respect for parental and other authority, and the need to listen to children. The widespread neglect of inner-city public schools and the disadvantages to students who attend them must also be remedied if we wish to stem the large-scale loss of disaffected, traumatized, and burned-out teachers. Poorly supported schools cannot be responsible alone for the intellectual and moral training of children.

In several Boston communities, a violence-prevention curriculum has been developed by Dr. Deborah Prothrow-Stith (1986). Teens are taught nonviolent approaches to conflict resolution, and troubled teens and their families are referred to hotlines and other crisis intervention services.

VICTIMS OF OTHER VIOLENT CRIMES

THE PROBLEM

Besides abuse from one's own family or spouse, there are many other sources of violent crime. A woman speaks of living with crime in a fashionable urban neighborhood:

> *My husband walks the dog, and he won't allow our daughter to go out alone at all. We keep the gate closed until the mailman arrives in the morning. When I shop I avoid rush hour, and I'm always very watchful, turning my head to see who's around me and behind. I'm continuously alert. I sweep the sidewalk and work in the garden every day just to be present and visible.*
>
> *The way you walk is important, too. (She makes military arm gestures like she's marching in Prague.) You walk with a stable pace, like you're going somewhere, like you know where you're going . . . no I won't move away, whatever happens. That's what you do in a war. You move away. You run. My husband and I moved away from Rome to flee the Nazis. We're not going to do that again. I love cities. I've lived in Paris and Rome. For me, to go to the suburbs is to die. (Muro 1982)*

Public opinion polls reveal continued concern about crime, even though the US Justice Department crime statistics show declining rates. At least one member of every 5 million households, or 6% of all American households, was raped, robbed, or assaulted in 1980. The FBI Uniform Crime Report shows a rate of 5900 major crimes per year per 100,000 citizens (FBI 1982).

People are angry and afraid. They blame it on the media, the courts, television, pornography, the economy, drugs, poor housing conditions, indifference to the poor, racial tension and discrimination, poverty, youth gangs, the police, handguns, and the disintegration of the American family. No doubt each of these factors plays some part in this complex problem.

Fear of crime seems to generate chronic stress, worry, paranoia, and a sense of helplessness. If no arrests are made and criminals receive light sentences or acquittals, victims and the general public often feel that no one cares, or that there is no justice. These feelings can lead to alienation, revenge, and a sense of callousness and insensitivity to others. This may account for the returning popularity of the death penalty and for the widespread public support of Bernhard Goetz, who felt entitled to take the law into his own hands on the New York subway system.

OUR RESPONSE: CRIME PREVENTION

What can we do to stem the growing fear and reality of crime? A brief discussion of this problem is relevant to people in crisis because of crime. Many of the social change strategies already cited apply to the complex task of preventing crime and its damaging effects. Experts on crime prevention call for a calm reassertion of communal values (Muro 1982). Residents of crime-ridden communities can mobilize neighborhood patrols and plan systematic ways of watching out for each other. This touches on the controversial issue of the ordinary citizen's role in assisting victims of crime. In France, such assistance is mandated by law; in the US it is not. Should we intervene on the victim's behalf or ignore a crime?

These two conflicting responses are dramatically illustrated in the following two stories, the first frequently quoted as a stereotype of the dangers of New York City.

> *Kitty Genovese was attacked over 20 years ago late one night while at least a dozen households heard her screaming. Nobody went to help or even bothered to call the police from within the safety of their own homes.*
>
> *Manhattan residents were awakened at about 3 AM by the cries of a woman who was being attacked. A witness said "Her cries woke me from a deep sleep. Then I heard the voice of a neighbor shouting from her window: 'I see you. I'm calling the police.' Then another voice and another. The guy who was beating up the girl in the street was completely unnerved by all this and he ran off, leaving her more or less unhurt." (Bierman 1982)*

These incidents suggest a solution to the dilemma of whether and how to intervene in a crime. A basic principle of crisis intervention is to protect ourselves from getting hurt while assisting others. While some people voluntarily sacrifice their lives for others, such a sacrifice is neither expected nor demanded. Frequently, it is heard that people do not intervene out of fear for their own safety, which is fair enough. But not to mobilize police on behalf of a victim seems to be a failure in the obligations stemming from our common humanity.

VICTIM ASSISTANCE AFTER A CRIME

There is now a specialty field called "Victimology," complete with an international journal and professional conferences. Yet at the practical level, victims of crime seem cruelly shortchanged in the criminal justice, emergency medical, and crisis service systems (Surgeon General's Workshop 1986). Consider this story of how it feels to be a victim, as told to a Presidential Task Force (1982) panel. The mother of a 17-year-old boy who was stabbed through the heart during a fracas at a friend's graduation party stated:

> *"A young doctor matter of factly said to me, 'your son has expired' and just walked away. I didn't even know he was badly hurt. They wouldn't let me see him because they wanted my financial history. I couldn't believe what he said; I just ran outside and screamed as hard as I could." She recalled for the panel a ride to the hospital with policemen who talked among themselves but never spoke to her; of not being told what progress was being made in the case by the district attorney's office; of not being able to recover her son's clothes or personal effects after the stabbing. (Mahoney 1982)*

Through federal task forces (President's 1982, Attorney General's 1984) and the advocacy and lobbying of the National Organization for Victim Assistance (NOVA), most county governments now have victim assistance programs, as do some crisis centers. In general, however, there are no constitutional protections for victims, nor is there much special training for police and emergency medical personnel in meeting the special needs of victims. NOVA has been instrumental in improving this situation, particularly through its Crisis Response Team, which offers service in instances of community-wide trauma, such as the massacre of 14 postal employees in Edmond, Oklahoma.* Funding of victim assistance programs is a continuing struggle, even when intentions are good. Instead, funding has been focused on programs that try to understand and reform the criminal. This is not to say that criminals' needs should be ignored, but, as stated in the Presidential Task Force hearing on Victims of Crime: "Taking justice out of the criminal justice system leaves behind a system which serves only the criminal" (Mahoney 1982). Indeed, the visibility of victims and their needs should benefit even the criminal.

Since the Presidential Task Force and Attorney General's federal legislation has supported the development of victim witness and assistance programs in the states. These include the development of self-help groups, training of victim advocates, and a plan for financial assistance to victims.

*For further information, contact NOVA, 717 D Street, NW, Washington, DC 20004; telephone (202) 393-NOVA.

Meanwhile, greater attention should be focused on the needs of victims in emergency medical, police, and criminal justice systems. Victims are people in crisis who should have the advantage of being listened to and helped by workers who are sensitive, knowledgeable, and skilled in crisis intervention. The report of the Surgeon General's Workshop on Violence and Public Health (1986) recommends that content in the care of victims be included in the curricula preparing *all* health and social service professionals, that board examinations of those practicing with a license (eg, nurses, physicians, social workers, psychologists) include questions on such content, and that practicing professionals who did not have preparation in the care of victims be offered appropriate inservice education programs. However, emphasizing crisis service does not mean we should neglect life-saving physical treatment in a hospital trauma unit. Even the victims' relatives expect appropriate priorities. But while doing what needs to be done medically and legally, psychosocial needs can be attended to as well. Thus, victims need a "bill of rights," for example, the right to:

- Be informed of the release of a prisoner who previously harmed them.*
- Receive information about protection services.
- A secure court waiting room separate from defendants.
- Receive restitution of stolen property.
- Social-psychological support in working through the crisis.

Perhaps the national attention currently focused on this problem will help to remedy this neglected area of crisis intervention.

VIOLENCE AGAINST POLICE OFFICERS, MENTAL HEALTH WORKERS, AND CRISIS WORKERS

Besides the general victims of crime, police officers, health, mental health, and crisis workers comprise another category of victims. The complex issue in these cases is that these workers are victims of violence, but without the certainty that a crime has been committed. This potentially dangerous situation in crisis work embroils us in the controversy introduced at the beginning of the chapter: the relationship and distinctions between crime

*California law obliges psychotherapists, for example, to inform potential murder victims of a person's murder plans. Other states act on the spirit of this law (see *Tarasoff* v. *The Regents of the University of California* 1976).

and mental illness.* Despite numerous debates on this topic, the distinctions between crime and mental illness overlap with relevance to life crises and our response to them; police and mental health professionals are often caught in the middle and become victims of violence. In many cases, their victimization could have been avoided (see Case Example: Robert, Chapter 4).

Why, then, is there an apparent increase in crisis workers who are injured, killed, or threatened on the job? In considering this question, the focus is not on what to do if attacked, but on why known crisis intervention strategies are not used, or why they are ineffective. Research (Bard 1972, Melick, Steadman, and Cocozza 1979) suggests that three factors are related to this issue: (1) the lack of crisis intervention training, (2) the widespread absence of appropriate collaboration between police and mental health professionals, and (3) the social trend toward medicalization of life.

CRISIS INTERVENTION TRAINING

Traditionally, nurses and psychiatric professionals have been taught that if and when they get hurt by mentally disturbed people it usually is because they missed cues to rising anxiety levels or antagonized or otherwise dealt inappropriately with the disturbed person. Over the years, mental health professionals have worked to dispel the myth that all mental patients are dangerous; only a small percentage are. Psychiatric facilities usually have precise protocols for preventing and responding to violence among mental patients (see Anders 1977, Engel and Marsh 1986, and Morton 1986). Police procedures are likewise precise and comprehensive. A basic principle in both disciplines is to avoid force and physical restraint except for protecting oneself and others. This interpretation is strongly supported by the research of Bard (1972) and his precedent-setting training for New York City police officers: The number of police injuries and deaths on the job were significantly reduced as a result of application of crisis intervention techniques, especially in "family trouble" calls. These techniques have been expanded to deal with terrorists through hostage negotiation strategies.

Details of hostage negotiation are beyond the scope of this book or the expected skills of an ordinary crisis worker. The highly sophisticated developments in this field, however, point to the importance of collaborative use of knowledge between police and behavioral science fields in responding to certain crises. Everyone who is even remotely involved with hostage situations (such as a mentally ill relative holding a child hostage and

---

*Interested readers are referred to Daniels (1978), Gove (1975), Price and Denner (1973), Scheff (1975), and Szasz (1970, 1974). One of the most thorough critical reviews of the issue, including a comprehensive bibliography, is Monahan's *The Clinical Prediction of Violent Behavior* (1981).

threatening to commit murder and then suicide if a rescue is attempted) needs to recognize that offers by civilians to "handle him . . . because I know him better than anyone" can backfire and need thorough investigation. Even police chosen for hostage negotiation are carefully screened on several counts, including their professional success in handling general crisis situations. Everyone should also be familiar with how to reduce the chances of injury or murder in the event of being taken hostage. The next section addresses this issue.

ASSESSING THE RISK OF ASSAULT AND HOMICIDE

Crisis intervention training should include principles of assessment for risk of assault and homicide. As in the case of suicide risk assessment, there is no absolute prediction of homicide risk. The topic itself is highly controversial; Monahan (1981, p. 6), for example, cites three criticisms regarding prediction:

1. It is empirically impossible to predict violent behavior.
2. If such activity could be forecast and averted, it would, as a matter of policy, violate the civil liberties of those whose activity is predicted.
3. Even if accurate prediction were possible without violating civil liberties, psychiatrists and psychologists should decline to do it, since it is a social control activity at variance with their professional helping role.

Nevertheless, assessment of risk for assault and homicide is an inherent aspect of a crisis worker's or police officer's job, while the average citizen is always calculating safety maneuvers when in known risk areas. As discussed here, it is distinguished from official predictions of risk that are part of psychiatric or psychological examinations requested by law of persons detained for crimes based on pleas of insanity (Halleck 1987). While assessment of dangerousness by crisis workers is far from an exact science, it can be based on principles and data, not merely guesswork. Based on Monahan's (1981) research, these principles include:

1. Statistics: For example, men between the ages of 18 and 34 commit a much higher percentage of violent crimes than older men or women of any age. Statistical indicators, however, should be viewed with the same caution as in the case of suicide risk assessment (see Chapter 6).
2. Personality factors, including motivation, aggression, inhibition, and habit.
3. Situational factors, such as availability of a weapon or behavior of the potential victim.
4. The interaction between these variables.

Toch (1969) claims that the interaction factor is a crucial one influencing violence. There are several stages in the interactional process.The potential victim is classified as an object or potential threat. Based on this classification, some action follows, after which the "object" of attack may make a self-protective move. Whether or not violence occurs depends on the interaction of variables, such as effectiveness of the victim's self-protection, or interpretation of resistance as a further "ego" threat demanding retaliation. This point is supported by Cooper (1976, p. 237), who states that the greatest threat to a potential victim is dehumanization of the victim. Establishing a bond, therefore, between victim and terrorist is a persuasive argument for prevention, though it should not be relied on in all cases. This is the basis for a widely-held principle in crisis intervention and hostage negotiation: *time* and keeping *communication* channels open—*not* precipitous action, taunts, or threats—are on the side of the negotiator and can save the lives of victims, terrorists, and suicidal persons.

Clearly, assessment of dangerousness is no simple matter, but lives can be saved by taking seriously the fact that only potentially dangerous people make threats of assault or homicide. Thorough training in crisis assessment and intervention is paramount, therefore, for professionals and others working with disturbed or potentially violent people.

POLICE-MENTAL HEALTH COLLABORATION

Crisis intervention alone is not enough to prevent violence. Another critical aspect of preventing victimization concerns collaboration between police and mental health professionals, especially when the boundaries of each institution overlap (Baracos 1974). The following case example illustrates the tragic results of failure in such collaboration.

CASE EXAMPLE: ARTHUR

A mentally disturbed man, Arthur, age 61, was brought to a hospital emergency room by two police officers for psychiatric examination on the request of his wife. Arthur had a history of paranoid delusions and at this time was accusing his wife of infidelity, though he threatened no harm to her. Arthur's wife had committed him three times before when he refused to seek treatment. On the way out of the car, Arthur grabbed the gun of one of the officers and shot him. The other officer in turn shot Arthur, who died instantly. The police officer died a few hours later. While Arthur had a history of mental distubance, he had no lethal weapons at the time of the police investigation. It was also learned after the deaths that in this man's history of mental disturbance he had never been violent, though he did get very angry each time his wife had him hospitalized.

This case suggests that if police had not been asked to perform the tasks of mental health professionals (such as assessment and crisis intervention with an acutely disturbed mental patient), two deaths might have been avoided. As it was, though, the community in which this double tragedy occurred had no mobile crisis outreach capacity. The same situation prevails in other communities to the point that "police are rapidly becoming the front line mental health workers" (Taft 1980). Many officers resent their mental health roles—with justification, since mental health professionals are often unavailable to police in consulting and collaborative roles. If mobile crisis outreach teams are not available, police officers should have 24-hour access to telephone consultation regarding mental patients. Such arrangements between police and mental health professionals skilled in crisis intervention should exist in every community.* The need has become more urgent since the trend toward deinstitutionalization of mental patients, often with inadequate community support. Mental patients are a high risk for all sorts of crises, often with no one available to help but police officers.

On the other hand, crisis intervention training for police should be routine. Some officers may resist such training, claiming that a police officer should spend time in more dramatic crime prevention activities. However, 80% of an average officer's time is spent in various service or domestic calls. Ignoring this reality is foolhardy and can cost officers' lives.

Even if officers are not physically injured in hostage or other crisis situations, they and their families invariably suffer psychological trauma that may require weeks or months for recovery. Reactions similar to those of disaster victims are common (see Chapter 9). Recognizing these reactions, and the need for support, the FBI and police departments are making special services available to officers involved in shooting and other highly traumatic incidents.

APPLICATION OF ASSAULT AND HOMICIDE RISK-ASSESSMENT CRITERIA

Translated into everday practice, the following criteria are helpful as guidelines to assess risk of assault of homicide:

- History of homicidal threats.
- History of assault.
- Current homicidal threats and plan.
- Possession of lethal weapons.
- Use or abuse of alcohol or other drugs.
- Conflict in significant social relationships, such as infidelity or threat of divorce.

---

*See the AAS Certification Standards Manual (Wells and Hoff 1984) for criteria regarding such programs.

- Threats of suicide following homicide.

An assault and homicide risk assessment is illustrated in a variation of the case cited earlier. This assessment is based on the risk criteria cited in the Comprehensive Mental Health Assessment presented in Chapter 3 (see Table 8-2). Suppose that Arthur was seen at home by two crisis outreach specialists and no guns were available. According to the criteria cited, Arthur was a low risk for assault or homicide, with a rating of 2 at most. The increased anxiety level in being forcefully taken to a hospital, plus availability of guns, seems to have dramatically increased the risk of homicide. It seems reasonable to suggest that both Arthur and the officer might be alive today had Arthur and his wife had the advantage of skilled crisis assessment and intervention from mental health professionals.

Table 8-2

Lethality Assessment Scales

Key to Scale	Immediate Dangerousness to Others	Typical Indicators
1	No predictable risk of assault or homicide	No homicidal ideation, urges, or history of same; basically satisfactory support system, social drinker only
2	Low risk of assault or homicide	Has occasional assault or homicidal ideation (including paranoid ideas) with some urges to kill; no history of impulsive acts or homicidal attempts; occasional drinking bouts and angry verbal outbursts; basically satisfactory support system
3	Moderate risk of assault or homicide	Has frequent homicidal ideation and urges to kill, but no specific plan; history of impulsive acting out and verbal outbursts while drinking and otherwise; stormy relationship with significant others with periodic high-tension arguments
4	High risk of homicide	Has homicidal plan; obtainable means; drinking history; frequent acting out against others, but no homicide attempts; stormy relationships and much verbal fighting with significant others, with occasional assaults
5	Very high risk of homicide	Has current high lethal plan; available means; history of homicide attempts or impulsive acting out, plus feels a strong urge to control and "get even" with a significant other; history of drinking, also with possible high lethal suicide risk

THE MEDICALIZATION OF CRIME

It is true that the standards of crisis intervention training among health and mental health workers are far from being met.* Still, the level of practice is probably not lower than it was 10 or 15 years ago, and in many instances workers have had some training in crisis intervention. Yet health and mental health professionals and others seem to be victims of violence during their work more often than in the past. Why?

A health or mental health professional could be a paragon of perfection in crisis intervention practice and might still be injured or killed on the job. Mental patients are probably no more violent than they were in the past; instead, nurses and others may be getting hurt more often by patients who should never had been admitted to a mental health facility in the first place. This assertion is based on the overwhelming evidence we have for the "medicalization" of life. Nowhere are the consequences of medicalization potentially more dangerous than when this social trend is applied to violent behavior, for example, when a violent criminal is classified as mentally ill and assigned to medical rather than penal supervision. As Melick, Steadman, and Cocozza (1979, p. 235) state in their research in the state of New York: "The reason that a case does not reach trial [for criminal justice versus mental health disposition] probably has as much to do with the strength of the prosecutor's case as it does with the mental state of the defendant." The medicalization of crime may also be related to overcrowded prisons and empty mental hospitals, created through the process of deinstitutionalization. The availability of state-owned space in mental hospitals provides a coincidental but convenient *material* argument for medicalizing criminal behavior. Aside from the public debate on this topic, practitioners in the crisis and mental health professions also need to critically examine the trend to interpret life's problems in an "illness" framework.

It is certainly true that some people who commit crimes are mentally deranged, thus entitling them to leniency before the law. Many insanity pleas, however, leave much room for doubt; "insanity" is a legal, not a mental health concept. Our difficulties in dealing with these issues are complicated by a criminal justice system that often denies a decent standard of treatment to criminals. The humanitarian impulse of most people is to spare even a violent person an experience that seems beyond the deserts of the crime. It is ironic, then, that the tendency to "treat" a person, rather than hold him or her responsible for violent behavior, exists in concert with the movement to assert the rights of mental patients (Gotkin and Gotkin 1975, Szasz 1974). It seems logical that we cannot have it both ways: on the one

*A minimum of 40 hours of training for all front-line and speciality crisis workers (such as nurses, physicians, police, and mental health professionals) is recommended by the American Association of Suicidology, the national standard-setting body for comprehensive crisis services (Hoff and Miller 1987; Wells and Hoff 1984).

hand, exercise one's freedom to reject treatment and hospitalization for behavioral disorders, and on the other hand plead "temporary insanity" if one then fails to control impulses and commits a crime. The following cases illustrate this point, as well as the need for mental health professionals to examine their misplaced guilt responses when they hold clients accountable for their behavior.

Case Example: Connie

Connie, age 51, was being treated in a private psychiatric facility for a drinking problem and depression following a divorce. Mental status examination revealed that Connie was mentally competent and not suffering from delusions or other thought disorders, though she was very angry about her husband's decision to divorce her because of her drinking problem. When Connie, therefore, decided to check out of the residential treatment facility "against medical advice" there was no basis for confining her according to any interpretation of the state's mental health laws for involuntary commitment. A discharge planning conference was held at which follow-up therapy sessions were arranged through a special program for alcoholic women. Connie failed to keep her counseling appointments. One week after leaving the psychiatric unit, Connie attempted to demolish her former husband's car by crashing her own car into it. She endangered the lives of other people by driving on sidewalks, where pedestrians successfully managed to escape her fury. Connie was arrested and taken to jail. Two mental health professionals involved with her case were called to testify. The defense attorney was incredulous that the mental health professionals did not plead with the judge to commit Connie to a mental health facility rather than to jail. The judge clearly seemed to prefer committing Connie to the psychiatric unit where she had been treated, but was assured (against the protests of the defense attorney) that there was no mental status basis nor physical capacity to keep her from being a further menace to society.

Case Example: Eric

Eric, age 28, was employed but distressed over interpersonal relationships on the job. He came to the group therapy session and, shortly after the session began, got up and swung his clenched fists first at one of the therapists, then at other clients, while making threatening statements. Eric had apparently had something to drink as the smell of alcohol was on his breath. But as he swung his fists at people, he seemed very controlled in coming just an inch or so from their noses. The therapists and other clients were unable to persuade Eric to stop his violent, threatening behavior, and therefore called the police. Eric was taken to the nearby jail. Meanwhile, the senior therapist—feeling overwhelmed with guilt about her client being in jail—reviewed the mental health laws to ascertain grounds for having Eric transferred from jail to a mental health facility. She reported the incident to the executive director (a psychiatrist) and explored with him the idea of having Eric committed for "treatment." The psychiatrist replied: "Treated for what? Threatening you and the other clients?" The therapist revised some of her traditional ideas about "treating" people for violent behavior rather than holding them accountable for it.

These cases suggest that our response to crises of violence directed at helpers, like other crises of social origin, may help perpetuate the problem if larger social ramifications of the issue remain unaddressed. Obviously, this takes us well beyond the individual crisis worker's responsibility. Yet our safety in the work setting and our common humanity in a very violent society demand such a two-pronged approach to this serious issue.

CRISES OF PERPETRATORS OF VIOLENCE

Many people believe that the perpetrators of crime have a clear advantage over their victims. While keeping in mind the issue of accountability for violent behavior, we need to remember that violent people (and those apprehended for nonviolent crimes), especially if they go to jail, are also in crisis—the parents who have beaten their child to death, the rapist, a woman-batterer, an 18-year-old who goes to jail after his first B and E (breaking and entering with intent to rob), the middle-class man who has sexually abused a child, the mother who loses custody of her children when she goes to prison for shoplifting and prostitution, and the murderer. In addition to the trauma of being arrested and incarcerated, the prisoner may experience extreme shame, desertion by family, or panic over homosexual advances. Or the prisoner may suffer from chronic mental illness. For mothers of young children, imprisonment may also result in permanent loss of custody of their children. With the increase in women prisoners, space and other conditions are often more deplorable than they are in overcrowded men's prisons. Suicides are more likely in brief detention facilities during the height of crisis, when there is great uncertainty about one's fate. Suicide attempts occur more frequently in long-term holding centers and often are related to prison conditions.

CRISIS INTERVENTION

All of the principles of crisis intervention apply to the violent person or someone in prison for other reasons. The application of these principles to violent people can be summarized as follows:

1. *Keep communication lines open.* As long as a person is communicating with us, he or she is usually not being violent.
2. Communicate by telephone or behind closed doors whenever possible when dealing with armed persons, especially until rapport is established and the person's anxiety subsides.
3. Always work in teams; not to do so can be life-threatening.
4. Insist on administrative support and emergency back-up help.
5. If dangerous weapons are involved, collaborate with police for their removal whenever possible; in inpatient settings, implement emergency procedures for appropriate application of force (see Anders 1977).
6. Develop *with* the dangerous person *specific* plans for nonviolent expression of anger, such as jogging, punching a pillow, or calling a hotline.
7. Make hotline numbers readily available, for example, Parents' Anonymous.
8. Examine social/institutional sources of violent behavior, for example, by geriatric and psychiatric patients.
9. Warn potential victims of homicide, based on risk assessment and principles of the Tarasoff case.
10. Follow-up: Engage in social/political activity to prevent violence.

Several factors, however, may become obstacles to providing aid to these people in crisis: (1) the sense of contempt or loathing one may feel toward a criminal, (2) fear of the prisoner, and (3) the need to work within the physical and social contraints of the detention setting. People working in these settings, therefore, need to assess and deal with crises according to the circumstances of their particular situations. The works of Danto (1973, 1981), Groth and Birnbaum (1979), Halleck (1971), Hogarth (1982), and Tavris (1983) are particularly recommended (see also Chapters 6 and 7).

FOLLOW-UP SERVICE

Specialists in criminal justice cite the problem of recidivism among people convicted of crimes. The ex-offender is stripped of status and community respect and often has been exposed to conditions that harden and embitter rather than rehabilitate. Considering the dire financial straits of the ex-prisoner (a situation that frequently was present before incarceration), lack of job skills, discrimination in employment, and the absence of follow-up programs, it is not difficult to understand why crime becomes a career for some.

Advocates of prison reform and various church groups are working to bring about long-term change in the conditions that seem to breed rather than prevent crime. For the nonviolent offender (more than half the American prison population), alternatives to jail sentencing are being tried in many states, a penalty system used in Europe for years already. These less costly and more effective options include: (1) community service, such as working in parks and public buildings; (2) restitution, a sanction that is particularly appealing because it takes into account the person most directly affected by the crime—the victim; (3) intermittent confinement, a strategy that spares total disruption of work and family; and (4) intensive probation, that is, no more than 25 persons per officer. These humane approaches need to be seriously weighed against the thousands of dollars spent each year to keep a person in prison.

THE FAMILIES OF PRISONERS

Dr. Alvin Poussaint (1980) of the Harvard Medical School has cited the neglect of families of prisoners, especially children. While there are generally fewer women than men in prison, at least 250,000 children have mothers who are incarcerated. Families not only lose a spouse, parent, or child to prison, but may also lose a source of income and status in the community. Poverty, loneliness, and boredom are just a few of the problems faced by these families. Those who attempt to sustain relationships find that prison regulations (such as body searches of visitors and lack of privacy) or societal pressure and personal circumstances thwart their efforts. Children of imprisoned parents feel sadness, anxiety, guilt, and anger. If a divorce occurs during or following imprisonment, the postrelease problems of the ex-offender are increased.

To address the crises of prisoners' families, more self-help groups such as "Families and Friends of Prisoners" in Dorchester, Massachusetts are needed. This group provides moral support, counseling, information, and inexpensive transportation to state and federal prisons. A similar group, Aid to Incarcerated Mothers (AIM), focuses on the special needs of mothers and children. A mother speaking about the services of this group wrote:

> *When I first came to prison I didn't want my children to have to see their mother in such a place. I didn't want them to have to go*

through the search, and transporation was a problem. I wanted desperately to see my children but was afraid of the impression the prison might have on them. After talking with AIM a lot of my fears were put to rest. . . . I can't explain the feeling I had when I went to the visiting room and saw my son and daughter, after not seeing them for two months. Seeing my children has put my mind at ease and made my time a little easier to deal with. . . . Ladies, your children love and care about you as much as you love and care about them. They want to know that you are OK just as much as you want to know they are OK. AIM is people who care about you and want to help you keep that bond between mother and children. So, let them help you as they have helped me. (AIM 1982)

SUMMARY

People in crisis because of the violence of others suffer emotional and physical injury and have their place in society disrupted if the violence is from a family member. In addition to assistance for individual victims of violence, social change strategies are paramount in addressing the culturally embedded values and social practices from which so much violence in American society originates. Such a tandem approach may eventually reduce the tragic effects of violence for individuals and society as a whole.

REFERENCES

Aid to Incarcerated Mothers (AIM): Newsletter. 2. Boston: AIM, 1982.

Adams D: Counseling men who batter: A profeminist analysis of five treatment models. In: *Feminist Perspectives on Wife Abuse*. Bograd M, and Yllo K (editors). Sage, 1988a.

Adams D: Feminist-based intervention for battering men. In: *Therapeutic Interventions with Batterers: Theory and Practice*. Caesar L, Hamberger K (editors). Springer, 1988b.

Anders RL: When a patient becomes violent. *Am J Nurs* 1977; 77:1144–1148.

Attorney General's Task Force on Family Violence: Final Report. US Department of Justice, 1984.

Baracos HA: Iatrogenic and preventive intervention in police-family crisis situations. *Int J Soc Psych* 1974; 20:113–121.

Bard M: Police family crisis intervention and conflict management: An action research analysis. US Department of Justice, 1972.

Bierman J: Intervene or look away? *Boston Globe*.

Bograd M: Family systems approaches to wife battering: A feminist critique. *Am J Psych* 1984; 54(4):558–568.

Borkowski M, Murch M, Walker V: *Marital Violence: The Community Response*. Tavistock, 1983.

Broverman IK et al.: Sex-role stereotypes and clinical judgements of mental health. *J Consult Clin Psychol* 1970; 34:1–7.

Browne A: *When Battered Women Kill*. Free Press, 1987.

Brownmiller S: *Against Our Will.* Simon and Schuster, 1975.

Burgess A W, Holstrom LL: *Rape: Crisis and Recovery.* Brady, 1979.

Campbell JD: A support group for battered women. *Adv Nurs Sci* 1986, 8(2):13–20.

Campbell JC, Humphreys JH: *Nursing Care of Victims of Family Violence.* Reston/Appleton-Century-Crofts, 1984.

Carmen E (Hilberman), Rieker PP, Mills T: Victims of violence and psychiatric illness. *Am J Psych* 1984; 141(3):378–383.

Child abuse and neglect—Special Issue. *Victomology* 1977; 2(2).

Conte JR, Wolf S, Smith T: What sexual offenders tell us about prevention: Preliminary findings. Paper presented at the Third National Family Violence Conference, Durhan, NH, 1987.

Cook JV, Bowles RT, (editors): *Child Abuse.* Scarborough, Ontario: Butterworths, 1980.

Cooper HHA: The terrorist and the victim. *Victimology* 1976; 1:229–239.

Crary E: *Without Spanking or Spoiling.* Seattle: Parenting Press, 1979.

Daniels AK: The social construction of military psychiatric diagnosis. In: *Symbolic Interaction,* 3rd ed, Manis JG, Meltzer BN (editors). Allyn and Bacon, 1978.

Danto B: *Jail House Blues.* Orchard Lake, MI: Epic Publications, 1973.

Danto B: *Crisis behind Bars: The Suicidal Inmate.* Warren, MI: Dale Corporation, 1981.

DeMause L: Our forbears made childhood a nightmare. *Psychol Today* 1975; 8:85–88.

Dillon WS: Anthropological perspectives on violence. In: *Perspective on Violence.* Usdin G (editor). Brunner/Mazel, 1972.

Dobash RP, Dobash RE: *Violence against Wives: A Case against the Patriarchy.* Free Press, 1979.

Donnerstein EI, Linz DG: The question of pornography. *Psychol Today* 1986; 20(12):56–69.

Doress PB, Siegal DL, and the Midlife and Older Women Book Project: *Ourselves, Growing Older.* Simon and Schuster, 1987.

Edgerton RB: *Deviance: A Cross-cultural Perspective.* Benjamin/Cummings, 1976.

Elias R: Alienating the victim: Compensation and victim attitudes. *J Soc Iss* 1984; 40(1):103–116.

Engel F, Marsh S: Helping the employee victim of violence in hospitals. *Hosp Comm Psych* 1986; 37(2):159–162.

Estes CL: Older women and health policy. Paper presented at the Women, Health and Healing Summer Institute. Berkeley: University of California, 1986.

Federal Bureau of Investigation: *Crime in the United States.* US Department of Justice, 1982.

Finkelhor D: *Child Sexual Abuse: New Theory and Research.* Free Press, 1984.

Gee PW: Ensuring police protection for battered women: The *Scott* v. *Hart* suit. *Signs: J Wom Culture Soc* 1983; 8:554–567.

Gelles RA: *The Violent Home.* Sage, 1974.

Gelles RJ, Cornell CP: *Intimate Violence in Families.* Sage, 1985.

Gelles RA, Straus MA: Determinants of violence in the family: Toward a theoretical integration. In: *Contemporary Theories about the Family.* Vol. 2. Burr WR et al. (editors). Free Press, 1979.

Germain CP: *J Psychosoc Nurs* 1984; 22(9):24–31.

Gil DG: *Violence against Children.* Harvard University Press, 1970.

Gondolf EW: *Men Who Batter: An Integrated Approach to Stopping Wife Abuse.* Holmes Beach, FL: Learning Publications, 1985.

Gondolf EW: Who are those guys? A typology of batterers based on shelter interviews. Paper presented at the Third National Conference on Family Violence, Durham, NH, 1987.

Goode W: Force and violence in the family. *J Marr Fam* 1971; 33:624–636.

Goody J: *Death, Property and the Ancestors.* Tavistock, 1962.

Gotkin J, Gotkin P: *Too Much Anger, Too Many Tears: A Personal Triumph over Psychiatry.* Quadrangle/The New York Times Book Company, 1975.

Gove W: *The Labeling of Deviance.* Wiley, 1975.

Groth AN, Birnbaum HJ: *Men Who Rape: Psychology of the Offender.* Plenum, 1979.

Halleck SL: *The Politics of Therapy*. Science House, 1971.

Halleck SL: *The Mentally Disordered Offender*. Washington, DC: American Psychiatric Press, 1987.

Harbin HT, Madden DJ: Battered parents: A new syndrome. *Am J Psych* 1979; 136:1288–1291.

Herman JL: *Father-Daughter Incest*. Harvard University Press, 1981.

Hilberman E: Overview: The 'wife-beater's wife' reconsidered. *Am J Psych* 1980; 137:1336–1347.

Hoff LA: *Violence against Women: A Social-cultural Network Analysis*. (PhD dissertation.) Boston University, 1984.

Hoff LA: Violence against women: Understanding, assessment, intervention, prevention (*in press*).

Hoff LA, Miller N: *Programs for People in Crisis: A Guide for Educators, Administrators, and Clinical Trainers*. Boston: Northeastern University Custom Book Program, 1987.

Hogarth DJ: *Lifeline: Manual of Suicide Prevention*. Boston: Suffolk County Jail, 1982.

Hollenkamp M, Attala J: Meeting health needs in a crisis shelter: A challenge to nurses in the community. *J. Comm Health Nurs* 1986; 3(4):201–209.

Holstrom LL, Burgess AW: *The Victim of Rape: Institutional Reactions*, Wiley, 1978.

Hudson MF: Elder mistreatment: Current research: In: *Elder Abuse: Conflict in the Family*. Pillemer KA, Wolf RS (editors). Auburn House, 1986.

Jones A: *Women Who Kill*. Holt, Rinehart and Winston, 1980.

Judson S (editor): *A Manual on Nonviolence and Children*. Philadelphia: New Society Publishers, 1984.

Kempe H, Helfer RE (editors): *The Battered Child*, 3rd ed. University of Chicago Press, 1980.

Kidd RF, Chayet EF: Why do victims fail to report? The psychology of criminal victimization. *J Soc Iss* 1984; 40(1):39–50.

Kidder LH, Boell JL, Moyer MM: Rights consciousness and victimization prevention: Personal defense and assertiveness training. *J Soc Iss* 1983; 39(2):155–170.

Korbin JE: Fatal child maltreatment. Paper presented at the Third National Conference on Family Violence, Durham, NH, 1987.

Korbin JE: Fatal child maltreatment. Paper presented at the Third National Conference on Family Violence, Durham, NH, 1987.

Korbin JE et al.: Elder abuse and child abuse: Commonalities and differences. Paper presented at the Third National Conference on Family Violence, Durham, NH, 1987.

Langelan M: The political economy of pornography. *Aegis* 1981; 32:5–17.

Lovell MC: Silent but perfect 'partners': Medicine's use and abuse of women. *Adv Nurs Sci* 1981; 3(2):25–40.

Mahoney F: Mother tells a tearful story at hearing on crime victims. *Boston Globe*, 1982.

Manley-Casiner ME, Newman B: Child abuse and the school. *Canad Welf* 1976; 52:17–19.

Martin D: *Battered Wives*. San Francisco: Glide Publications, 1976.

McCombie SL: *The Rape Crisis Intervention Handbook*. Plenum, 1980.

Melick ME, Steadman HJ, Cocozza JJ: The medicalization of criminal behavior among mental patients. *J Health Soc Behav* 1979; 20:228–237.

Miller JB: *Toward a New Psychology of Women*. Beacon Press, 1976.

Mills CW: *The Sociological Imagination*. Oxford University Press, 1959.

Monahan J: *The Clinical Prediction of Violent Behavior*. Rockville, MD: National Institute of Mental Health, 1981.

Morton PG: Managing assaultive patients. *Am J Nurs* 1986; 86(10): 114–116.

Muro M: The fear of crime. *Boston Globe*, 1982.

Newberger E: New approaches needed to control child abuse. Presented before the Subcommittee on Select Education of the Committee on Education and Labor. US House of Representatives, 1980.

Newberger CM and Newberger EH: 1981. Prevention of Child Abuse: Theory, Myth, Preactice. Presented at the Meeting of the Society for Research in Child Development. Boston, 1981.

O'Malley H: *Elder Abuse: A Review of Recent Literature*. Boston: Legal Research and Services for the Elderly, 1979.

Pagelow MD: *Woman-battering: Victims and Their Experiences.* Sage, 1981.

Pillemer K, Finkelhor D: *The Prevalence of Elder Abuse: A Random Sample Survey.* Durham, NH: Family Violence Research Program, 1987.

Poussaint A: Quoted by Matchan L in: *The Agony of Families with a Relative in Prison.* Boston Globe, 1980.

President's Task Force on Victims of Crime: Final Report. US Government Printing Office, 1982.

Price RH, Denner B (editors): *The Making of a Mental Patient.* Holt, Rinehart and Winston, 1973.

Prowthrow-Stith D: Interdisciplinary interventions applicable to prevention of interpersonal violence and homicide in Black youth. In: *Surgeon Generals Workshop on Violence and Public Health: Report.* Health Resources and Services Administration, 1986.

Rader D: Who will help the children? *Parade* 1982; 4–7.

Rafter NH, Stanko EA (editors): *Judge Lawyer Victim Thief.* Boston: Northeastern University Press, 1982.

Rubenstein C: Real men don't earn less than their wives. *Psychol Today* 1982; 16:36–41.

Russell DEH: *Rape in Marriage.* Collier Books, 1982.

Russell DEH: *The Secret Trauma: Incest in the Lives of Girls and Women.* Basic Books, 1986.

Ryan W: *Blaming the Victim.* Vintage Press, 1971.

Sales E, Baum M, Shore B: Victim readjustment following assault. *J Soc Iss* 1984; 40(1):117–136.

Sanford N: Collective destructiveness: Sources and remedies. In: *Perspectives on Violence.* Usdin G (editor). Brunner/Mazel, 1972.

Schechter S: *Women and Male Violence.* South End Press, 1982.

Scheff TJ (editor): *Labelling Madness.* Prentice-Hall, 1975.

Select Panel for the promotion of child health. Vol. 1. US Congress, 1980.

Sherman LW, Berk RA: The specific deterrent effects of arrest for domestic assault. *Am Sociol Rev* 1984; 49(4): 261–272.

Silver RL and Wortman CB: 1980 Coping with undesirable life events. In: J Garber and MEP Silgman, eds. *Human Helplessness.* Academic Press.

Sommers T, Shields, L: *Women Take Care.* Gainsville, FL: Triad, 1987.

Stark E: *The Battering Syndrome: Social Knowledge, Social Therapy and the Abuse of Women.* (PhD dissertation.) Binghamton: State University of New York, 1984.

Stark E, Flitcraft A, Frazier W: Medicine and patriarchal violence: The social construction of a "private" event. *Int J Health Serv* 1979; 9:461–493.

Steinmetz S: Battered parents. *Society* 1978; 15:54–55.

Straus MA, Gelles RJ, Steinmetz SK: *Behind Closed Doors: Violence in the American Family.* Anchor Books, 1980.

Straus MB et al.: Advocacy for battered women with abused children in a pediatric hospital. Paper presented at the Third National Conference on Family Violence, Durham, NH, 1987.

Surgeon General's Workshop on Violence and Public Health: Report. Washington, DC: Health Resources and Services Administration, 1986.

Sweet E: Date rape: The story of an epidemic and those who deny it. *MS/Campus Times* 1985; 14(4):56–59.

Szasz TS: *The Manufacture of Madness.* Harper and Row, 1970.

Szasz TS: *The Myth of Mental Illness,* rev. ed. Harper and Row, Perennial Library, 1974.

Taft PB: Dealing with mental patients. *Police Mag* 1980; 20–27.

Tamme P: Abuse of the adult client in home care. *Fam Comm Health* (Aug) 1986; 54–65.

Tarasoff v. *The Regents of the University of California.* 551 P. 2d 334. 1976. (Also in: 131 California Reporter 14. Supreme Court of California.)

Tavris C: *Anatomy of Anger.* Simon and Schuster, 1983.

Toch H: *Violent Men.* Aldine, 1969.

van der Kolk BA: *Psychological Trauma.* Washington, DC: American Psychiatric Press, 1987.

Wardell L, Gillespie DL, Leffler A: Science and violence against wives. Paper presented at National Conference for Family Violence Researchers. Durham, NH: University of New Hampshire, 1981.

Wells JO, Hoff LA (editors): *Certification Standards Manual,* 3rd ed. Denver:

American Association of Suicidology, 1984.

Wolfgang ME: Interpersonal violence and public health care: New directions, new challenges. In: *Surgeon General's Workshop on Violence and Public Health: Report.* Washington, DC: Health Resources and Services Administration, 1986.

Wolfgang M: *Patterns in Criminal Homicide.* Philadelphia: University of Pennsylvania Press, 1958.

CHAPTER 9

VIOLENCE AND CRISIS FROM DISASTER

NATURAL AND HUMAN POTENTIAL FOR CATASTROPHIC VIOLENCE

The natural world is both a nurturing home and a source of potential destruction. The sun warms us. The beauty of foliage, sea coasts, forests, plains, and mountains satisfy our aesthetic needs and inspire us to write, sing, and love one another. Yet these same elements have the capacity to destroy us—first, if we do not protect ourselves from the violent forces of nature, for example, by building shelters to prevent freezing in a snowstorm; and second, if we misuse or destroy nature's resources, for example, by the uncontrolled burning of coal that causes acid rain and destroys lakes and the creatures that live in them.

As human beings, we can see and respond to the differences and connections between natural elements and ourselves. Our ability to rationally construct our social and material world forms the basis of efforts to contain the forces of nature to protect ourselves. The natural world yields much of what we need for survival; yet the victims of fires, floods, tornados, tidal waves, earthquakes, and snowstorms provide ample evidence of nature's destructive potential, in spite of great technological feats in deciphering nature's mysteries and directing them for human ends.

> "My wife has never gotten over the shock of the flood. . . . For a while I thought I'd lose her."
>
> "We will bury our dead with sadness, but at the same time we will renew our will to live and to cure our wounds."
>
> "You'd think I'd be able to talk about it without crying."
>
> "I thought I was dying. . . . I felt the mud rising up, covering me over."
>
> "Where Armero was, you can hardly recognize anything. . . . The tragedy is too great for us to measure."
>
> "This is a village of people buried alive."

> "I'd never seen the ocean look like that. It was an angry, angry sea out there."
>
> "The teremoto [earthquake] came all of a sudden. There was a pushing up from the floor that lifted us up, and then this swaying of the whole house from side to side. Then the lights went out and everything came crashing down. I had the impression of hearing 100 tanks, all at the moment in the same place, rolling, rolling, rolling. It lasted one minute, the longest minute of our lives."
>
> "The setting seemed emerald green except for unburied livestock bloating on the hills."

These are a few of the reactions of disaster victims and survivors of floods in Rapid City, South Dakota; Buffalo Creek, West Virginia; and Wilkes Barre, Pennsylvania in 1972; the Morvi, India flood in 1979; the 1980 earthquake in southern Italy; the 1985 volcanic eruption in Armero, Colombia; and the 1986 freak gas leak in Camaroon.

Other disasters occurring throughout the world arouse similar reactions. Jetliner crashes have resulted in hundreds of deaths. The 1980 earthquake in Italy was the worst in several decades, with thousands dead or missing, nearly 200,000 homeless, and over 100 communities affected in all. In 1978, 14 states in India were flooded, leaving several thousand dead; 80,000 people were trapped for days clinging to embankments as cholera spread, and 1.5 million cattle were lost in the flood. In the worst natural disaster in Colombia's history, the 1985 eruption of a volcano in Armero killed more than 22,000 people, with another 20,000 injured or homeless and 200,000 evacuated. The 1985 earthquake and its afterquake in Mexico City left 10,000 dead, more thousands homeless, and millions in damage.

However, nature's potential for violence seems small next to the destructive possibilities of disaster caused by human beings. In Bhopal, India, a gas leak at a chemical plant killed 2,000 and disabled tens of thousands. The 1986 Chernobyl nuclear accident in the Soviet Union left at least 300 dead and 10,000 evacuated, with radioactive fallout affecting people and animals thousands of miles away. Future illness and death from this accident remain to be seen. The 1986 space shuttle disaster left a nation of mourning with many questions. Also, the famines in Ethiopia and Mozambique, though apparently "natural", can be traced to human origins (Wijkman and Timberlake 1984).

Human potential for both good and evil seems limited only by the technology we create. For example, a child can be saved through a liver transplant, amputated hands can be relaced, and energy from the sun can be collected and stored. Also through technology, however, inhuman experiments were performed by the Nazis on Jews and others in concentration camps, and the entire population of Hiroshima and Nagasaki were virtually

---

*Chernobyl has since been razed as it is totally unfit for human habitation.

destroyed. While many enjoy the benefits of scientific knowledge, others suffer. For example:

> *ASK THOSE WHO REALLY KNOW!*
>
> *Ask the Victims of Love Canal why they need immediate permanent relocation, and why some will refuse to leave their motel rooms once funds are cut off. Ask the innocent victims of corporate profits.*
>
> *The reasons are simple. We cannot lead a normal life, we:*
>
> *Cannot go in our basements because of contamination from Love Canal.*
>
> *Cannot eat anything from our gardens because of soil contamination.*
>
> *Cannot allow our children to play in our yards because of contaminated soils.*
>
> *Cannot have our children attend school in the area—two have been closed due to Love Canal contamination.*
>
> *Cannot breathe the outside air—because of air contamination we are now in hotels.*
>
> *Cannot become pregnant—miscarriage rate is state defined: 45%. Homeowners' survey: 75%.*
>
> *Cannot have normal children—because of 56% risk of birth defects.*
>
> *Cannot sell our homes. Love Canal was not mentioned in our deeds; who wants a contaminated house?*
>
> *Cannot get a VA or FHA loan in Love Canal; even the government is reluctant.*
>
> *Cannot have friends or relatives visit us on holidays; they're scared it's unsafe.*
>
> *Cannot have our pregnant daughters, or our grandchildren visit; it's unsafe for them.*
>
> *We need your support and your help to end the suffering of men, women, and especially children of Love Canal. We have lost our constitutional rights of life, liberty and the pursuit of happiness. Justice for all but not Love Canal Victims.*
> *We cannot live at Love Canal—We cannot leave Love Canal.*
> *(Gibbs 1982)*

The disastrous effects of violence from natural and human sources can be described in both personal and social terms. How do individuals and groups respond to disasters of natural origin compared with those of human origin? Why are disasters of human origin, such as Love Canal and Hiroshima, not usually viewed as a form of violence? What can individuals and groups do to reduce our vulnerability to disasters from natural and human sources? Our answers to these questions could affect:

- What happens to disaster victims.
- The quality of our everyday lives.
- What kind of life on earth can be realistically anticipated.
- Whether or not we ultimately destroy ourselves and our planet.

NATURAL AND ACCIDENTAL DISASTER: PREVENTION AND AID

One can only guess at the extent to which a disaster such as a flood, fire, or earthquake affects the people who experience it. The depth of the tragedy is private and hardly measurable. Though the negative consequences of disaster are not clear, some research suggests long-term stress responses (Baum, Fleming, and Singer 1983, p. 119). Preventive measures and help for survivors are therefore of great importance. What do we need to know about disaster and its victims in order to help? The nature of a disaster affects the victims' response. A disaster usually occurs rapidly and is therefore completely unexpected and shocking. The following account by Kizzier (1972) portrays vividly the depth of terror and destruction of life and property that resulted from the Rapid City flood.

> *And then it happened. The raging, silt-filled water burst through Clerghorn Canyon, loosening everthing in its way and pushing it miles downstream, sucking human lives into its muck with no more respect than it had for cars and houses and bridges. The entire canyon had become its creek bed.*
>
> *When the people of the upper canyon heard this news, they were afraid and many of them left their homes to move to higher ground, but still some stayed, clinging to the protective knowledge that it could not happen to them. They sat by their radios and waited and listened, unable to see any distance because of the darkness. They could only hear the noise, roaring constant noise as if a huge train was rumbling through their valley. By seconds, the water was rising and then it battered against doors and windows. Fear rose as panes of glass shattered, followed by the rushing water, and then the people raced to second floors, attics and rooftops. It was too late to get out, they had to stay together and remain calm. Surely the house would not break away from its foundation. And then they saw a house, an entire house, bobbing past them. They heard pleading voices and turned their flashlights toward the sound. People, people they knew, were clinging to the roof, panic stricken and screaming, wasting the little strength they*

> *had left. "Don't you know no one can get to you, my God, don't you know?"*
>
> *And then there were screaming voices all around them, young voices and old voices and the brief, chilling howl of a baby. They saw friends and neighbors struggling against this overpowering force; grabbing onto anything that could steady them long enough to gasp for air.*
>
> *And then they heard it, cracking noise of the timbers tearing loose with the growing force and weight of the water. They saw their car smash through the garage wall and spin out of sight. With a sucking noise, the garage followed and the house rocked back and forth on its foundation before it finally broke loose, pitching on it side and dumping its riders into the greedy river.*
>
> *Some survived. It was probably fate that saved them, or sheer super human strength, or anger, or revenge, or the gut determination to live—but some did survive . . . somehow, some way, they lived to tell about Rapid City's cold chilling night of terror . . . a memory that will plague them for the rest of their lives, a lesson that taught them how precious and fragile life itself is, a constant fear of the seemingly harmless stream where fishermen wade and children splash and ducks paddle about contentedly.*

Fortunately, tragedies like this happen rarely—or perhaps not at all—in the lives of most people. Most of us are therefore unfamiliar with disaster. Our expectations are usually of an intellectual nature. Moreover, the speed and unexpectedness of and the lack of experience with disaster greatly reduce a person's opportunity for escape and effective problem solving.

TECHNOLOGICAL AND POLITICAL FACTORS AFFECTING AID TO VICTIMS

Rescue operations and assistance with physical necessities occur in disaster-stricken communities throughout the world. Foreign countries and the International Red Cross assist in this aspect of disaster work. For example, millions of dollars in aid were sent to Italy, Colombia, and Mexico following their devastating disasters. In examining responses to worldwide disasters, it is apparent that an association exists between a country's ability to respond and its resources, technological developments, and the bureaucratic functioning of its government.

The uncontrolled forces of nature may not seem to differentiate between rich and poor, east and west, or white and those of color. Yet while widespread flooding in the United States is less frequent and results in fewer lives lost than it did years ago, in part because of the resources and technology available for flood prevention programs (such as building dams), a poor country like India still has difficulty preventing massive floods that take thousands of lives. In addition, a poor nation has fewer government resources for assisting survivors. Similarly, fires of the proportion of the Cocoanut Grove disaster, which claimed 492 lives in Boston in 1942, are rare today because political action enforced building safety regulations. Federal aviation policy likewise has been tightened to prevent jetliner crashes when crashes have resulted from faulty technology or nonenforcement of safety codes. However, news accounts of disaster worldwide repeatedly emphasize the difference between rich and poor countries' access to resources for preventing, or at least warning of, impending disaster. Camaroon's President Biija, for example, pleaded for "scientific assistance which would help us put up a mechanism [to] warn the people if such a thing is about to happen so that they can take measures to avoid injury" (Fisher 1986).

Material, financial, and human resources, then, play an important part in preventing disasters from natural or accidental causes. These economic, political, and technological conditions highlight the continued need for international programs of aid and cooperation in the distribution and use of natural and human resources. Bureaucratic and political rivalries can result in further tragedy and loss of life. Technology and effective political organizations are central to controlling nature and aiding disaster victims. Social and behavioral sciences also figure in the attempt to reduce human error and accidental sources of disaster, for example, research on pilots and air traffic controllers.

PSYCHOLOGICAL AND OTHER FACTORS

In the psychological realm, confronting the unhealthy mechanism of denial is central to preventing victimization by natural disaster. Because a natural disaster is a dreaded experience, most people deny that it could happen to them, even when they live in high-risk areas for floods, tornados, or earthquakes. People employ denial as a means to go on living normal lives while under more or less constant threat of disaster. Escape and problem solving are also affected by the extent of a person's denial. Jerry Jefferson in Wilkes-Barre ignored the flood warnings and convinced his wife that they should go to bed as usual because "it will never get so high that we'll have to move." His wife Ann was unconvinced and kept watch on the rising water during the night. Each new warning from Ann left Jerry unconvinced that the flood could really hit them. When the water reached the second floor of their house, Jerry finally gave up his denial. Fortunately, this couple was rescued and did not lose their lives. Francis King in Wilkes-Barre absolutely refused to leave his home despite all warnings. Eventually he clung to a telephone pole and was rescued by helicopter.

In Rapid City, Davis Heraty said:

> *"When we heard the warning we thought he (the mayor) was kidding. We just sat there, and pretty soon this big bunch of*

> *water came down the creek. We ran next door and suddenly the water was up to my neck. The top of a house came floating by and we grabbed on to that. A little way downstream we got off and climbed on the roof of a neighbor's house. We stayed there until the flood began to fall on Saturday" (The Rapid City Journal 1972).*

This family was lucky to come out alive in spite of their denial.

Others may be in special circumstances that prevent them from hearing the warnings.

Case Example: Martin and Evelyn Schoner

Martin Schoner, age 69, and his wife Evelyn, age 68, had lived all their lives in an intimate "valley" neighborhood. The Schoners had both been retired for several years, Martin as a men's clothing merchant, Evelyn as a nurse. They enjoyed the activities of their retirement years, including occasional babysitting of their five grandchildren in two neighboring towns. They and their two children exchanged visits frequently.

The evening before the flood Martin was admitted to the hospital for chest and stomach discomfort. There was some suspicion and fear that his symptoms signaled a problem with his heart. When Evelyn left her husband at the hospital that evening, they still did not know his diagnosis, nor did they have any suspicion of an imminent disaster.

Meanwhile, numerous flood warnings were being broadcast by radio and TV. Evelyn, however, heard none of these. She went to bed as usual, only to be awakened at 5:00 AM by a telephone call from a friend advising her of the flood and the need to leave her house quickly. She immediately packed a bag and drove to her friend's house. A few hours later, she learned on the radio that houses in her neighborhood were filled with water up to the second floor. She was unable to reach her husband; the hospital was also flooded and the patients were evacuated. Both Martin and Evelyn were beside themselves with fear and worry, for each had no idea of the whereabouts of the other.

One of Evelyn's special concerns was Martin's medical condition. She still did not know if his symptoms signaled heart trouble. As it turned out, Martin's symptoms were from food poisoning. He had been moved to a local college that was converted into a temporary shelter. Seriously ill patients were moved to another hospital. Martin, however was so upset and worried about his wife, Evelyn, that rescue workers finally sent a hospital chaplain to talk with him. Martin stated afterwards that he found it a tremendous relief to pour out his worry to a sympathetic listener. The chaplain helped him through a "good cry" without embarrassment or shame.

Evelyn had no way of knowing these facts because public communication networks were not operating. Her main support at this time was the friend she was staying with.

Two days later, Evelyn finally learned from a friend that Martin was at the college emergency shelter. Evelyn went to pick up Martin. They stayed for a few days together at their friend's house before returning to their neighborhood to assess the damage.

When they returned, they were grief-stricken over the loss of their possessions and destruction of the home they had treasured. Evelyn was particularly upset. She kept repeating, "If only I had known that this was going to happen, I would have moved at least some of our precious things upstairs or packed them up to take with me."

Martin and Evelyn, with the help of their friend, decided to stay in the neighborhood and rebuild their home with federal aid. In the aftermath of the crisis, Martin, despite the tragedy, gained a new lease on life. He no longer had any empty hours in his days; he single-handedly took the job of repairing the flood damage and refinishing the house. He became a source of support and encouragement for others in the neighborhood. Evelyn felt the flood left an indelible mark on her. She seemed unable to stop grieving over the loss they suffered. Evelyn also stated, "If only our minister hadn't been out of town at the time, I would have had someone to talk to when it happened."

Martin and Evelyn did not know that specially trained crisis counselors were available to survivors of the disaster. This highlights the fact that communication in a disaster-stricken community is often inadequate.

Martin, Evelyn, and their neighbors live in fear of another flood; they have no assurance that adequate precautionary measures have been taken to prevent a recurrence. They decided, however, to take a chance and live their last years in the neighborhood they love, with the resolution that, should another flood occur, they will move away once and for all.

It is difficult for anyone who has not experienced a flood to imagine that heavy rain alone can produce enough water to break a dam and flood a whole city. People are used to associating certain results with certain causes. When cause and effect are not familiar, it is easy to deny. For example, in the Rapid City flood people were suddenly surrounded by huge amounts of water that could not be accounted for by the heavy rain alone. The broken dam plus the spring thaw from the nearby Black Hills produced such sudden torrents that many people were unable to escape. As least 227 people died in the Rapid City flood; it was one of the worst natural disasters in US history.

PREVENTIVE INTERVENTION

It is impossible to prepare for the crisis of disaster the way one can prepare for transition states such as parenthood, retirement, or death. However, we can act on a communitywide basis before a disaster strikes. This is particularly important in communities at high risk for natural disasters. Such preparation is a form of psychological immunization.

There are several things a community can do to prepare for possible disaster:

1. Make public service announcements during spring rains or tornado seasons urging people not to ignore disaster warnings.
2. Broadcast educational programs on TV dramatizing crowd control techniques and what to do for a person who is panic stricken or in shock.
3. Review public safety codes to assure adequate protection against fire in public gathering places such as restaurants, theaters, and hospitals.
4. Make public service announcements urging people to take first-aid courses with local Red Cross and fire departments.
5. Broadcast educational programs on radio and TV to acquaint people with social agencies and crisis services available to them in the event of disaster.
6. Initiate a program of crisis intervention training for mental health and social service workers as an addition to their traditional skills.
7. Institute an upgraded program of disaster preparation by medical, health, and welfare facilities, including mechanisms for community coordination of disaster rescue services. It was apparent after the Rapid City flood that the community had an excellent medical disaster plan. As a result, survivors had adequate medical and health care during and after the flood. This is remarkable, since medical disaster plans sometimes are not well enough organized to be practical during an actual disaster.

These preparations will not prevent the devastating effects of a disaster, but they may reduce the impact of the trauma and equip people with personal tools for living through the experience with less physical, social, and emotional damage then they might otherwise suffer.

INDIVIDUAL RESPONSES TO DISASTER

Reactions to the stress and trauma of a disaster are not unlike reactions to transition states such as migration or loss of a loved one through death.

They also resemble responses to victimization by crime (see Chapter 8). Tyhurst (1951, 1957a, 1957b) has identified three overlapping phases in disaster reaction. These are similar to the four phases noted by Caplan (see Chapter 2) in the development of a crisis state:

1. *Impact:* In this period the person is hit with the reality of what is happening to him or her. In catastrophic events, the impact period lasts from a few minutes up to one or two hours.

The concern of disaster victims during the impact phase is with the immediate present. An automatic stimulus-response reaction occurs, with the catastrophe as stimulus. Victims are struck later with wonder that they were able to carry on as well as they did, especially if they break down under the full emotional impact of the experience. During the impact phase, individual reactions to the disaster fall into three main groups:

a. Ten to twenty-five percent of the victims remain calm and do not fall apart. Instead, they assess the situation, develop a plan of action, and carry it through.

b. Seventy-five percent of the victims are shocked and confused. They are unable to express any particular feeling or emotion. The usual physical signs of fear are present: sweating, rapid heart beat, upset stomach, and trembling. This is considered the "normal" reaction to a disaster.

c. Another ten to twenty-five percent become hysterical or confused, or are paralyzed with fear. These victims may sit and stare into space or may rum around wildly. The behavior of this group has the greatest implications for rescue workers and crisis counselors who may be on the scene during emergency operations.

Evelyn Schoner, caught in the Wilkes-Barre flood because she did not hear the warnings, fell into the first group of victim reactions during the impact phase. When she finally received the warning telephone call, she packed her bag and drove to safety. She had no difficulty doing this, even though she ordinarily depended heavily on her husband when in distress. (Her husband, as noted, was in the hospital.) Evelyn stated: "It really only hit me afterward . . . that everything I treasured was lost. I just had to drive away and leave everything behind. You don't know what that's like—saving precious things all your life, then all of a sudden they're gone—even the photographs of our family." There is no research to identify or predict which people will fall into the last group of reactors to disaster. However, prediction criteria (see The Assessment Process in Chapter 3) indicate that the following types of people are particularly vulnerable to crisis or emotional disturbance following acute stress from a disaster:

- The elderly who have few physical resources and a reduced capacity to adapt to rapid change.

- Those who already are coping with stress in self-destructive or unhealthy ways. Some people in disaster-struck communities take solace in alcohol in an effort to escape the reality they cannot face.
- Those who are alone and friendless and who lack physical and social resources they can rely on in an emergency.

During the San Fernando Valley earthquake, mental health staff at the Los Angeles County-Olive View Medical Center observed that some acutely distured mental patients reacted more rationally than usual during the acute phase of the quake. For example, they helped to rescue fellow patients (Koegler and Hicks 1972). In Rapid City, Gertrude Lux, 71, stood for five hours in shoulder-deep water balancing her disabled grandaughter Vicki on a foam mattress floating in the room where they were trapped. In Armero, Colombia, rescue workers dug with their bare hands and bailed out water with tin cans to save a 13-year-old girl trapped beneath a cement slab. These incidents speak to the commonly observed heroism and humanity of disaster victims despite personal pain and loss. People rise dramtically to the occasion and mobilize resources to help themselves and others.

2. *Recoil:* During this phase there is at least a temporary suspension of the initial stresses of the disaster. Lives are no longer in immediate danger though other stresses may continue, such as cold or pain from injury. In Rapid City there was the threat of another flood a day later. In Mexico City there was a second quake. During the recoil phase, survivors are typically enroute to friend's homes or have found shelter in community facilities set up for the emergency. They may look around for someone to be with. They want to be taken care of—to receive a cup of coffee or a blanket. Chilled survivors of the Italian earthquake, for example, huddled in makeshift camps and tent cities, lighting fires to keep warm. The disaster experience leaves some survivors with a childlike dependency and need to be with others. At this phase, survivors gradually become aware of the full impact of what they have been through. Both women and men may break down and weep. Survivors have their first chance to share the experience with others. Their attention is focused on the immediate past and how they managed to survive. This phase has the greatest implication for crisis workers helping the survivors.

3. *Posttrauma:* During this period, survivors become fully aware of what occurred during the impact phase: loss of home, financial security, personal belongings, and particularly, loved ones who may have died in the disaster. This is the phase during which much depends on one's age and general condition. As Jane Cantor, a Wilkes-Barre survivor put it, "A disaster can bring out the best and the worst in a person." Those who are too old to start over again find their loss of home and possessions particularly devastating. Older people who prize the reminders of their children and earlier life feel robbed of what they have worked for all their lives. Anger and frustration follow.

If loved ones have died in the disaster, grief and mourning predominate. Murphy (1986, p. 339) cites studies of bereavement suggesting that the "recovery period varies from several months to several years and is subjectively defined." Murphy found that among survivors who lost a loved one in a close relationship to the Mt. St. Helen's volcanic eruption, bereavement was intense and prolonged, especially if they perceived the disaster as preventable. Some survivors of the Rapid City flood had overwhelming guilt reactions to the death of loved ones: "Why me . . . why was I spared and not she?" Many survivors describe the horror of listening to screams, of watching people being swept past them to their deaths, and of being helpless to save them. Lifton and Olson (1976) have described this reaction as "death guilt." Survivors somehow feel responsible for the death of their relatives or others they were unable to save. They can't quite forgive themselves for living, for having been spared. At the same time, they may feel relief at not being among the dead. This, in turn, leaves them feeling guiltier.

During this third phase survivors may have psychotic episodes, reactive depressions, anxiety reactions, and dreams in which they relive the catastrophic experience. Some agencies report increased hospital admissions for emotional disturbances following disaster. Staff of the Child Guidance Center in San Fernando Valley counseled hundreds of parents and children following the earthquake. Children typically were afraid to be alone and afraid to go to sleep in their own beds. Bennet (1970), in his study of survivors of the 1968 floods in Bristol, England, found that twelve months after the disaster the health of flooded people was worse than the general health of those not in the flood and that the likelihood of older people dying within twelve months was increased. Lifton and Olson (1976) report that when survivors perceive the disaster as a reflection of human callousness—rather than an act of God or nature—the psychologic effects are more severe and long lasting. Effects of disasters from human origins are discussed later in this chapter.

This post-traumatic phase may last for the rest of a person's life, depending on his or her predisaster state, the help available during the disaster, and whether the disaster was natural or from human origins. Evelyn Schoner said: "I don't think I'll ever be the same. . . . I just can't get over it. . . . I live in constant fear that there might be another flood. . . . There's just no guarantee that there won't be another one."

A small group of disaster survivors gives up. These people remain despondent and hopeless for the rest of their lives (Farberow 1967). Most survivors, however, gather together and reconstruct their lives, their homes, and their community. While a number of people in Wilkes-Barre moved to higher elevations, many others rebuilt their homes on the same location, even though there was no guarantee against further flooding. This was particularly true for older people who found it too costly to start over and who wanted to keep the comfort of a familiar neighborhood, even though they had lost everything else.

Rescue and crisis workers have the most influence during the impact and recoil phases, while mental health workers play a key role during the posttraumatic phase. As noted thoughout this book, crisis intervention—available at the right time and in the right place—is the most effective means of preventing later psychiatric disturbances. As Evelyn Schoner said: "If only I would have had someone to talk to when it happened." The availability of crisis assistance to individuals, however, is intricately tied to the community response to disaster.

COMMUNITY RESPONSES TO DISASTER

IMPACT ON COMMUNITY

The most immediate social consequences of a disaster is the disruption of normal social patterns on which all community members depend (Tyhurst 1957a). The community suffers a social paralysis. People are separated from family and friends and spontaneously form other groups out of the need to be with others.

When disaster strikes, large numbers of people are cut off from public services and resources that they count on for survival. These can include water (one of the first resources to go in the event of a flood), electricity, and heat. People scamble for shelter, food, and water. Traffic controls are out, so accidents increase. In Wilkes-Barre, many people fell in the slippery mud and broke limbs, thus placing more demands on hospital staff. In Rapid City, one of the city's two hospitals was flooded out, and all patients had to be transferrred to other facilities. Schools and many businesses close, creating further strain and chaos in homes and emergency shelters.

As noted, a disaster can bring out the best and the worst kinds of human behavior. Some people take advantage of the disorder to loot and steal. Citizens in disaster-struck communities note that some businesses take advantage of the occasion to profit from others' misfortune by inflating prices of needed supplies.

Normal communication networks are either destroyed or are very limited in scope. Rumors grow, increasing panic and chaos. Communication problems and physical distance also result in uneven distribution of information about relief benefits available from the federal government or other sources. This causes resentment among those who feel they did not receive a fair share of the benefits. Residents not even on the scene of the disaster can be affected because of media generalizations and sensationalistic reports.

The Schoners in Wilkes-Barre observed that the flood was instrumental in bringing the people of their neighborhood closer together.

Professional evaluators observed the same phenemenon (Zusman, Joss, and Newman 1973). During the impact period of a disaster, there is greater cohesion among community members; later, people focus again on their individual concerns. People have to rely on one another for help and support during a disaster in a way that was not necessary before. This was illustrated in Rapid City. During the flood a group of professionals were attending a conference on death and dying. A call was put out to the conference participants to assist families in identifying members who had died. The helpers reported that many friends had already turned out to help the bereaved families.

During the impact and recoil stages of a disaster, community control usually passes from elected government officials to professionals who direct health, welfare, mental health, and public order agencies. This occurs out of necessity, because of the reactions cited above. Elected officials have the important function of soliciting assistance for the community from state, federal, and sometimes international resources. The community's priorities are rapidly redefined by professional leaders, and an emergency health and social system is quickly established. This emergency network focuses on:

- Preservation of life and health: rescue activities, inoculations, treatment of the injured.
- Conservation and distribution of resources: organization of emergency shelters, distribution of supplies such as water, food, and blankets.
- Conservation of public order: police surveillance to prevent looting and accidents rising out of the chaos and scramble for remaining resources.
- Maintenance of morale: dispatching mental health, welfare, and pastoral counselors to assist the panic-stricken and bereaved during the acute crisis phase.

Material, social, and psychological services should be available for as long as they are needed.

In summary, a community's response to disaster is poignantly revealed in the following description by Kizzier (1972) of Rapid City.

> *With all of this help from private, city, county, state and federal funds and with the compassion and support offered from an entire nation, Rapid City is restoring and rebuilding with a new appreciation for life. It has pulled together for a purpose before, but never before has it become a pulsating, throbbing being as it is now, in the aftermath of a flood.*
>
> *Not one person has been untouched by the drama of recovery. Through the silent heartache and compassion, we again remember what it is like to be patient with each other. There is a need for*

the comfort of physical contact as we greet each survivor with a thankful hug.

We are more aware of the things we take for granted, like the utility companies, bridges and the National Guard. We now look at the police with new respect, feel thankful for the closeness of the air force base and vow never again to pass the ringing Christmas bells of the Salvation Army without dropping in a coin.

We empty our food closets and our clothes closets in an attempt to lend a hand to someone who was left with nothing. We shake our heads in dismay as the big scoops move in on the destruction to clear away the mess.

We go to the city-wide memorial service on Sunday, feeling sad and empty and discouraged after being threatened by another torrent of rain the night before. We see people there who have lost far more than we have, bearing their burden with surprising spirit. We want to cry with all the pent up emotion, but we are being told that we must overcome our grief, rejoice and sing and carry on with life. And so we will, just like everyone around us will, because people need to laugh or they will break. We come from the memorial service feeling renewed and we try laughing and it makes us feel warm inside and a little lightheaded.

FACTORS AFFECTING RECOVERY OF SURVIVORS

Tyhurst (1957a) notes that the nature and severity of reactions to disaster and the process of recovery are influenced by several factors:

1. *The element of surprise.* If and when warnings are given they should be followed by instructions of *what to do.* Warnings followed by long silences and no action plan can heighten anxiety and lead to the commonly observed denial of some residents that a disaster is imminent.
2. *Separation of family members.* Children are particularly vulnerable to damaging psychological effects if separated from their family during the acute period of a disaster (Blanford and Levine 1972). Therefore, families should be evacuated as a unit whenever possible.
3. *Outside help.* Reasonable recovery from a disaster demands that aid be provided from areas not affected by the disaster. Since military forces possess the organization, discipline, and equipment necessary for dealing with a disaster, their instruction should include assisting civilians during disaster.
4. *Leadership.* As in any crisis situation, a disaster demands that someone have the ability to make decisions and give direction. The police, the military, and physicians have leadership

potential during a disaster. Their training should include preparation to exercise this potential appropriately.

5. *Communication.* Since failures in communication give rise to rumors, it is essential that a communication network and public information centers be established and maintained as a high priority in disaster work. Much impulsive and irrational behavior can be prevented by the reassurance and direction that a good communication network provides.
6. *Measures directed toward reorientation.* Communication lays the foundation for the reidentification of individuals in family and social groups. A basic step of reorientation is the registration of survivors, so that they can once again feel like members of society. This is also critical as a means of relatives and friends finding each other.
7. *Evacuation and populations.* In any disaster there is a spontaneous mass movement to leave the stricken area. Planned evacuation will prevent panic, especially if escape is blocked and delayed. Failure to attend to the psychological and social problems of evacuation can result in serious social and interpersonal problems.

RESOURCES FOR PSYCHOLOGICAL ASSISTANCE

Although federal aid to disaster-stricken communities for material reconstruction has been available for years, this has not been the case for meeting the psychological needs of victims. It was not until 1972 that the National Institute of Mental Health (NIMH) was prepared organizationally to provide disaster victims with emotional first-aid services, that is, crisis intervention (McGee and Heffron 1976). As a result of this change, the community of Wilkes-Barre, through its Luzerne-Wyoming County Mental Health-Mental Retardation agency, received financial aid to assist in offering crisis services to flood disaster victims through Project Outreach (Okura 1975, Zusman, Joss, and Newman 1973). The significance of this project is twofold:

1. It demonstrated the need for outside mental health assistance in times of disaster to supplement local resources. Local mental health workers may be disaster victims themselves and usually are temporarily unable to help others in distress.
2. It confirmed that the ability of people to help others in crisis was strongly influenced by their prior skill or training in crisis intervention.

In the Wilkes-Barre community the special federal aid for crisis intervention was a supplement to crisis services offered by other groups. For example, Jewish Social Services from New York deployed social workers to

Wilkes-Barre to assist disaster victims (Birnbaum, Coplon, and Scharff 1973). Other religious groups as well—Amish, Catholic, the Salvation Army, Protestant, Mennonite—traditionally offer help to disaster-stricken communities.

It is probably impossible to have an oversupply of crisis intervention services for people struck by a disaster. Gordon (1976) notes that community mental health agencies must have prior crisis intervention skills in order to mobilize the resources necessary when a disaster occurs. Health and mental health workers, along with other community caretakers, must know how to put these crisis intervention skills to use when a disaster strikes. Since there is little or no time to prepare for the disaster, there is no time to prepare as a crisis worker once a disaster is imminent. Workers must be ready to apply their knowledge, attitudes, and skills in crisis intervention.

In spite of much progress in this area, more long-term planning is still needed to better meet the psychological needs of disaster victims. Dr. Vincenzo Rizzo, an army surgeon in Italy, underscored this point regarding the earthquake survivors: "I wish we had counselors and psychiatrists to take care of some of these people . . . so many are suffering from a severe state of shock (Rizzo 1985). The National Organization for Victim Assistance (NOVA) recognizes this need through services offered by its Crisis Response Team.

DIFFERENTIAL HELP DURING IMPACT, RECOIL, AND POSTTRAUMA PHASES

The helping process during disaster takes on distinctive characteristics during the disaster's impact, recoil, and posttrauma phases. Table 9-1 illustrates the kind of help needed and who is best suited to offer it during the three phases of a disaster. The table also suggests the possible outcomes for disaster victims if help is not available in each of the three phases.

Table 9-1

Assistance during Three Phases of Natural Disaster

	Help Needed	Help Provided by	Possible Outcomes if Help Unavailable
Phase I: Impact	Information on source and degree of danger	Communication network: radio, TV, public address system	Physical injury or death
	Escape and rescue from immediate source of danger	Community rescue resources: police and fire departments, Red Cross, National Guard	

Table 9-1

Assistance during Three Phases of Natural Disaster

	Help Needed	Help Provided by	Possible Outcomes if Help Unavailable
Phase II: Recoil	Shelter, food, drink, clothing, medical care	Red Cross Salvation Army Voluntary agencies such as colleges to be converted to mass shelters Local health and welfare agencies Mental health and social service agencies skilled in crisis intervention Pastoral counselors State and federal assistance for all of the above services	Physical injury Delayed grief reactions Later emotional or mental disturbance
Phase III: Post Trauma	Physical reconstruction Social reestablishment Psychologic support concerning aftereffects of the event itself; bereavement counseling concerning loss of loved ones, home, and personal property	State and federal resources for physical reconstruction Social welfare agencies Crisis and mental health services Pastoral counselors	Financial hardship Social instability Long-lasting mental, emotional, or physical health problems

CRISIS INTERVENTION AND FOLLOW-UP SERVICES

The basic principles of crisis management should be applied on behalf of disaster victims. During and following a disaster, people need an opportunity to:

- Talk out the experience and express their feelings of fear, panic, loss, and grief.
- Become fully aware and accepting of what has happened to them.

- Resume concrete activity and reconstruct their lives with the social, physical, and emotional resources available.

To assist victims through the crisis, the crisis worker should:

- Listen with concern and sympathy and ease the way for the victims to tell their tragic story, weep, and express feelings of anger, loss, frustration, and despair.
- Help the victims of disaster accept the tragic reality of what has happened a little bit at a time. This means staying with them during the initial stages of shock and denial. It also may mean accompanying them back to the scene of the tragedy and being available for support when they are faced with the full impact of their loss.
- Assist victims in making contact with relatives, friends, and other resources needed to begin the process of social and physical reconstruction. This could mean making telephone calls to locate relatives, accompanying someone to apply for financial aid, and giving information about social and mental health agencies for follow-up services.

In the group setting where large numbers are housed and offered emergency care, the panic-stricken should be separated and given individual attention to avoid the contagion of panic reactions. Assignment of simple physical tasks will move the panic-sticken in the direction of constructive action. Any action that helps victims feel valued as individuals is important at this time. In spite of massive efforts to help survivors of disaster, it seems almost impossible to prevent life-long emotional scars among the people who live through the experience. It is important to make crisis and bereavement counseling services available to all disaster survivors so that the damaging effects of the experience can be reduced.

One lesson learned in Wilkes-Barre's Project Outreach was the necessity of actively seeking out those in need of crisis counseling (Zusman, Joss, and Newman 1973). Crisis workers became acquainted with residents on a block-by-block basis and were thereby able to assess needs and make crisis services available to people who otherwise might not have used them.

No local community can possibly meet all of the physical, social, and emotional needs of its residents who are disaster victims. The Wilkes-Barre experiment of providing federal funds for crisis services as well as for physical reconstruction sets a precedent for assisting communities that are struck by disaster in the future. This will be necessary even when local mental health, welfare, and health workers are better trained in crisis intervention. In most disasters the need is too great for the local community to act alone, especially since some of its own human service workers (police officers, nurses, clergy, and counselors) will themselves be among the disaster victims (Laube 1973).

In summary, individual responses and the needs of natural disaster victims—as in other crisis situations—varies according to psychological, economic, and social circumstances. Natural disaster victims seem to have something in common for coping with this kind of crisis: their interpretation of these tragedies as "acts of God," fate, bad luck—in general, an occurrence beyond their own or anyone else's control. Accounting for the event from a common viewpoint is an important aspect of constructive crisis coping at the cognitive level. Emotional coping can then occur through grief work and can be followed by behavioral responses to rebuild their lives. The victims' interpretation of these crises as "natural" is the basis for the hope felt by natural disaster survivors in spite of enormous suffering. It is the reason they are generally able to rise from the rubble and begin a new life—to move beyond the emotional pain and gain new strength from the experience. This element of disaster response and recovery constitutes the greatest distinction between natural disasters and those occurring from human indifference, neglect, or design.

DISASTERS FROM HUMAN ORIGINS

NATURE, EXTENT, AND RESPONSE

The world at large knows about the two atomic bombs dropped in Japan, the Nazi holocaust, and the destruction of Love Canal. War and environmental pollution are planned disasters that bring about physical, social, and emotional destruction of immeasurable proportions. Some survivors of Hiroshima describe the horror:

> *People who were laying there and dying and screaming and yelling for help and the people who were burned were hollering, "I'm so hot, please help me, please kill me" and things like that and I . . . it was terrible (Mary).*
>
> *We had a hospital near our place and many, many hundreds of injured people came to the hospital and there weren't too many adequate medical supplies and there were some doctors there, some nurses there, but they didn't have enough medicine to take care of all the people. And these people were thirsty and hurt and dying and all night long I could hear them calling, "mother, mother," and it sounded to me like ghosts calling out in the middle of the night (Mitsuo).*
>
> *In the Japanese tradition, you're supposed to look for your family. I walked for three weeks, every single day, looking for my*

> *grandparents and my brother. It was a feeling of real loneliness and looking at the devastation of the whole city wondering why God left me here alone. You know, why didn't he take me too. At the time, yeah, I did want to go too, I felt they should have . . . I should have gone too instead of being left alone (Florence). (Survivors* 1982, pp. 4, 5, and 6)

On August 6, 1945 the first atomic bomb was dropped on Hiroshima. Three days later Nagasaki was bombed. Six days later, World War II was over. Over 80% of the people within one kilometer of the explosion died instantly or soon afterwards. By December 1945 the number of dead in Hiroshima and Nagasaki was over 200,000. By 1950 another 140,000 people died from the continuing effects of radiation exposure. Since then there have been another 100,000 radiation-related cancer deaths. Before and during the same world war millions of Jews, Gypsies, homosexuals, mentally retarded people, and others viewed as "undesirable" by the Nazi were systematically exterminated in what many consider the most horrible crime in the history of the world.

When Japanese-American victims of the atomic bomb declared themselves as survivors, insurance companies withdrew their health and life insurance policies and employers discriminated against them. Nightmares, flashbacks, and fear for themselves and their children are common today among these survivors. Over ten years ago they formed the Committee of Atomic Bomb Survivors in the United States to gain medical benefits from the US government—to no avail, as several bills introduced to Congress have failed. Similarly, Vietnam veterans have tried to gain veterans' benefits for health damage they claim resulted from exposure to the defoliant Agent Orange.* For Vietnam veterans in general, America's most unpopular war rages on years later. Until Vietnam, veterans and their families typically had felt that the loss of life and limb were justified if the war itself was justified.

In Buffalo Creek, West Virginia, a mining corporation carelessly dumped coal waste, which formed artificial dams that eventually broke and caused dozens of deaths. Buffalo Creek residents knew that the dam was considered dangerous and that the mining corporation neglected to correct the danger (Lifton and Olson 1976). When loved ones, homes, and the natural environment were destroyed, survivors concluded that the mining company regarded them as less than human. One of the excuses offered by the company for not correcting the dangerous waste disposal method was that fish would be harmed by alternative methods. The survivors' feelings of devaluation were confirmed by their knowledge of the coal company's proposal of hasty and inadequate financial settlements. The physical dam-

*Recently, the US Supreme Court ruled in favor of compensation in cases of 100% disability from Agent Orange. A total of 250,000 families are affected (NBC News, June 30, 1988).

age to the community was never repaired by the company or through outside assistance. Thus, residents are constantly reminded of the disaster.

Unlike the Rapid City community described earlier, Buffalo Creek survivors did not respond to the disaster with community rejuvenation born out of the tragedy. Lifton and Olson (1976) attribute this tremendously different response to the disaster's human (rather than natural) origin. Even though the mining company was forced to pay 13.5 million dollars in a psychic damage suit, Buffalo Creek residents seem to feel that they and their community will never be healed. Considering genetic, health, and material damage, such as that suffered by Love Canal residents, monetary compensation becomes practically meaningless. Money cannot repair such losses. *Prevention* and *learning* from such tragic error and neglect seem the only reasonable responses.

Reactions of Buffalo Creek and Love Canal survivors are similar to those observed among survivors of Hiroshima and the Nazi holocaust (Lifton 1967). Lifton and Olson (1976) state: "As the source of stress shifts from indiscriminate violence by nature to the discriminate oppression by man, the damage to human personality become less remediable." Survivors of planned disaster—including war—feel that their humanity has been violated. Their psyches are bombarded to such a degree that their capacity for recovery is often permanently damaged. Rakoff et al. (1966), and others note similar long-lasting effects of destructiveness toward fellow human beings among the children and families of concentration camp survivors.

> *Steve, 35, is a grandchild of Holocaust victims. While his maternal grandparents fled after Hitler's election, their siblings stayed behind and were killed. Steve's mother refused to let him have Christian friends, citing her family's wartime experience as proof that non-Jews should not be trusted. She also banned him from playing baseball, riding a bike or learning how to swim. Although he realized that her fears stemmed from the legacy of the Holocaust, he has remained aloof and resentful toward his mother and her siblings since leaving home 15 years ago. (Matchan 1981)*

In a related category are victims and survivors of technological disaster, an increasing occurrence worldwide as people demand more goods and energy, technical errors occur, and more toxic wastes are produced (Baum, Fleming, and Singer 1983). The most outstanding international examples are the Bhopal and Chernobyl, and shuttle disasters already cited. On a less dramatic scale are the increasing numbers of people exposed to occupational hazards, as evidenced by increasing rates of infertility, especially among low-paid workers (predominately women of color) in the least protected environments. For example, two women in Silicon Valley, California developed an immune deficiency syndrome traced to their exposure to toxic chemicals in the so-called "clean" computer chip industry (Spake 1986). Central to the emotional recovery of persons exposed to such events are the concepts of "control" and "meaning." As discussed in Chapter 2, emotional recovery seems to demand that traumatized people be able to incorporate the event into their meaning system and to maintain at least some perception of control. If a situation seems beyond one's control, self-blame may be used as a way to cope with the event (Baum, Fleming, and Singer 1983, p. 134).

Thus, if the origin of trauma and/or prolonged distress is from external causes (as in the case of Three Mile Island residents studied by these researchers, people exposed to occupational hazards, or any disasters traced to negligence), it is important for victims to attribute responsibility for their trauma to its true sources rather than to themselves. Interpreting a person's anger and demand for compensation as a dependency conflict or in other psychopathology terms is a form of blaming the victim (Schottenfeld and Cullen 1985, p. 1126). Instead, such traumatized people should be linked to self-help and advocacy groups through which they might channel their anger into constructive action for necessary change—in this case, improved safety standards on the job (Chavkin 1984) (see Crisis Paradigm, third box, right circle.) This is not to say that prior psychopathologies do not play a role in some injury claims, but these should not be used to obscure the fact that injurious exposure reduces some people to joblessness, ill health, and poverty (Schottenfeld and Cullen, 1985, p. 1126) (see Chapters 3, 4, and 5).

Many of these ideas are now being examined in studies of "posttraumatic stress disorder" (PTSD), a controversial concept describing a chronic condition that may occur years after an original trauma experienced outside the normal range of life events (war, concentration camps) (Boehnlein et al. 1985, Davidson et al. 1985, Williams 1980). Though PTSD has some features common to depression, panic disorder, and alcoholism, its increasing prevalence underscores the importance of crisis intervention for all traumatized people, plus renewed efforts to prevent these traumas in the first place.

FOLLOW-UP AND PREVENTION

Vietnam veterans are still trying to rebuild their lives after a generation of being scapegoated for a nation's guilt and shame about the war they were not personally responsible for starting. Holocaust survivors have formed awareness groups as resources for support and preservation of history. Atomic bomb survivors say their sacrifice was worthwhile if only the bomb is never used again. Native Americans are fighting for their cultural survival as well as against the destruction of the environment, which they view as a crime against the harmony that should exist between nature and human beings. Lois Gibbs (1982) has told about the Love Canal tragedy; her story moved a nation to awareness of similar hazards in numerous other communities. Not unlike the parent survivors of teenage suicide, these survivors are trying to find meaning in their suffering by sharing the pain and tragedy of their lives for the sake of others. The survivors of human malice, greed, and prejudice tell us something about ourselves, our world, and the way we relate to each other and the environment.

Yet, over 100 years after the American Civil War, nearly 50 years after the Holocaust, and 20 years after the Vietnam war, we still have:

- Racially motivated violence and institutionalized racism across the US, which seems to be increasing in recent years.
- Crimes with apparent anti-Semitic and other racial, religious, and political motives from Boston to Ireland, Paris, South Africa, Latin America, and the Middle East.
- A systematic attempt to declare the Holocaust a "myth" that never happened.
- Repeated famines in Ethiopia and Mozambique that can be traced to war and to the widening gap between haves and have-nots of the world (Wijkman and Timberlake 1984).
- Responses by some Americans to the atomic bombs' effects on people: "Yes, but they bombed Pearl Harbor, so therefore they deserve it" (Lifton 1982, p. 17).
- An international nuclear capacity for destruction more than one million times the power of the atomic bomb dropped on Hiroshima.

To meet the challenges of these destructive symptoms there are now national and international debates on the nuclear arms race and defense strategies unparalleled in the history of the human race both for their passion and their importance to our ultimate survival.

The social, political, religious, and psychological ramifications of national and international crises and chronic problems are complex, controversial, and passionately debated. People are deeply divided, for example, in their views about:

- Whether we would be "better off dead than Red."
- What the division of government spending should be between "guns and butter."
- Whether the use of nuclear weapons is ever justified.

These issues will probably be argued for a long time. Nevertheless, the following facts remain:

- Many crises can be traced to social, economic, and political factors of local and global origins.
- Grade school children are pressing their teachers for answers about nuclear war.
- Stress levels of Three Mile Island, Pennsylvania residents can be traced to their fears about the nuclear power accident.
- Fear and controversy about nuclear power have increased since the Chernobyl disaster.

▶ Effective crisis intervention cannot be practiced without considering the cultural context of the crisis.

It is imperative that individual crises be understood in terms of their public meaning (Mills 1959). Public issues should be debated and acted on, not abstractly, but in terms of their impact on you, me, our families, friends, and others. We individuals are, after all, the public. Not only is there a dynamic interplay between public and private life, but in both realms our sensitivity to others' perceptions and value systems regarding controversial issues can foster cooperation and prevent conflict.

Each individual's unique perception of traumatic events is central to understanding and resolving a crisis. Without communication we cannot understand another's interpretation of an event or issue, and we may become a hindrance to constructive crisis resolution. In fact, one of the most compelling reasons to practice crisis intervention is the reward and stimulation of discovering the uniqueness of others, or of helping people in crisis discover their own capacities and talents for solving a problem. Communication is central to such discovery. The differences in interpretations of personal, social, and political problems are as diverse as community members themselves. Unquestionably, communication is the key to uncovering these interpretations and thus understanding and helping people in crisis. A person tells his or her traumatic experience through emotional display, behavior, and verbal communication; Hansell (1976) called this "crisis plumage." If we do not listen and respond with caring and support, or if there is no one to tell the story to, the chances of a constructive crisis outcome are diminished.

It is the same at the social and political level, or when large groups of people are in crisis—a situation we commonly refer to as disaster or calamity. What seems to be different, though, is that victims of disasters of human origin, like victims of crime, have a hard time finding people to listen to them. Friends or a crisis counselor may listen, but as noted in earlier chapters, these individual responses are not enough if the crisis did not originate from individual circumstances or if the whole community is affected. Social and political action are pivotal to a positive crisis outcome if the *origin* of a personal crisis is social and political (see Chapters 1 and 2).

No matter how public and widespread the calamity, we should remember that society is made up of individuals with particular interpretations of events—with distinct shades in their "crisis plumage." These individual people are more concrete than the casualty figures one hears on the evening news:

▶ Richard, a Vietnam veteran with recurrent nightmares, is someone's husband, father, son, and/or brother. He is 38 years old and lives on Locust Street in a town of 45,000.

▶ Shigeko is an atomic bomb survivor who had 26 operations on her face and lips and is glad that she is alive and that her 8-year-old son is not ashamed of her appearance.

- Diane is a woman from Love Canal who has had multiple miscarriages.
- Bobby is a little boy from Love Canal with nightmares about what "chemicals" look like. . . . He imagines a "thing" attacking him.
- Jane is a Love Canal resident, age 5, with toxic hepatitis.

These and many persons like them tend to get lost in statements of "statistically significant" incidences (of cancer, deformed children, or other medical problems), scientific jargon, and investigative "procedures" (to determine whether corrective action is in order). This process of generalizing from the particular people involved, and the grossness of the figures (such as 10,000,000 victims of the Holocaust; nearly 500,000 dead from two atomic bombs) contribute to denial and psychic numbing for the average person. The numbers, the destruction, and the sheer horror are unimaginable for most of us—too much to absorb. To defend ourselves against the terror, we deny and try to convince ourselves that it just could not happen.

Yet these figures pale at even a conservative estimate of the millions of deaths that would occur in this country alone with a nuclear exchange. The works of Kubler-Ross (1969) and others have documented the death-denying aspect of American life (see Chapter 11). Moreover, the denial of death itself indicates that we will not "win the race with death" (Goodman 1981). Unlike our personal mortality, however, the death of civilization is not inevitable; if it happens it will be through human decision and action. Denying our personal mortality, then, can result in agony and despair during our final phase of life (Tolstoy 1960). Denial of nuclear peril, with resulting failure to communicate our concerns and develop nonviolent solutions to political and ideological conflicts, can result in the final world disaster. This fact is increasingly recognized in the many peace and conflict courses being developed in high schools and colleges across the country (Wallis 1982).

Denial and scientific objectification of actual and potential disaster victims are similar to the process discussed in the last chapter:

- Dehumanization of victims and the enemy.
- Maintaining distance from the object of criminal terrorism so that ordinary human compassion and other feelings do not interfere with the ultimate control purposes of terrorism.

From a safe distance it is relatively easy to think of our enemies as less than human and therefore worthy of destruction. Like the "homeless," the deinstitutionalized "mental patients," and "unwed mothers," they are distant, thought of as groups and as the responsibility of the state or church. When they are thus objectified, we don't have to think of them as someone's sister, father, mother, or friend.

Our worst enemies are people like ourselves. They eat, sleep, make love, bear children, feel pain, fear, and anger, communicate with one another, bury their dead, and eventually die themselves. Statistics and machines will never be a substitute for human interaction, just as rating scales can aid but *not displace* clinical judgment in evaluating individual suicide risk. As Albert Einstein said: "Peace cannot be kept by force. It can only be achieved by understanding."

In the individual crisis situation, if we do not *communicate,* for example, with a suicidal person, we will not understand why death is preferable to life for that individual, and therefore may be ineffective in preventing suicide. If we take the time to *talk* with and *listen* to a person in crisis, we are less likely to suggest or prescribe a drug as a crisis response. Similarly, at the national and international levels, if we keep communication open and foster political strategies to handle crises, there is less likelihood of resorting to mechanical and chemical approaches to problem solving. Human communication, then, not only distinguishes us from the animal kingdom, it is central to our survival—as individuals and as a world community (see Chapter 4).

Nevertheless, our ethnocentrism is often so strong, and greed and power motives often so disguised, that the average person may find it difficult to think of disasters occurring from human design as a form of violence. Victims of disasters and trauma of human origin, however, feel violated. They have experienced directly the destruction of their health, their children, their homes, their sense of security, their hopes for the future, and their sense of wholeness and worth in the human community.

In many ways, the poignant testimonies and tragic lives of the victims of ethnic, class, and political conflicts speak for themselves. Still, two of the most painful aspects of their crises are that they feel ignored and they often cannot even receive material compensation for their enormous losses. They feel denied. If we have not listened, or if we have been silent when we should have spoken, convinced that we have nothing to say about public issues, perhaps we should reexamine what Nobel Peace Prize recipient Albert Schweitzer said in 1954: "Whether we secure a lasting peace will depend upon the direction taken by individuals—and, therefore, by the nations whom those individuals collectively compose." Survival matters are too serious to be confinmed to partisan politics, the government, or liberal/conservative debates. Every citizen—and certainly crisis workers—should be informed on what many think is the most critical issue ever to confront the human race.* If the arms race and threat of nuclear holocaust are important enough for the American Academy of Arts and Sciences, the National Conference of Catholic Bishops, and various consumer and pro-

*See, for example, Frank (1982), Foell and Henneman (1986), Powers (1982), and Schell (1982). Also, many professional groups have organized around this issue: scientists, physicians, nurses, women's groups, lawyers, and the clergy.

fessional groups to consider formally and in the ballot box, it is time for the crisis worker to confront denial and to understand its implications for prevention and for the response to victims. The traditional position of "therapist neutrality" will not do in cases of crisis originating in sociocultural and political sources.

When confronted with the enormity and horror of disaster from human sources, denial is understandable. Most of us feel helpless and powerless, but we are not. The opinions of officials and professionals are not necessarily wiser or more life-saving than those of ordinary citizens. Lois Gibbs (1982), in describing why she wrote *Love Canal—My Story*, documents this point and illustrates the urgency of our attention to the threat of disaster from human sources:

> *I wrote the book with two purposes in mind. The first is to show that the average citizen with limited education and almost no funds can fight city hall and the White House and win! The second is to tell the real story of Love Canal. A small glimpse of the tragedy, death, and human suffering that occurred in our community will expose the way officials and experts reacted to our situation, making many mistakes that can be avoided in the future. This is a quick course in the life-threatening problems posed by improper disposal of hazardous wastes.*

Murray Levine, a community psychologist (Gibbs 1982, pp. xiii–xviii), in his introduction to Gibbs's story, elaborates on why it should be told, at the same time illustrating crisis and preventive responses to a disaster of human origins. Gibbs' inspiring story should be told because:

1. Lois Gibbs is in many respects a typical American woman: a mother of two children and a housewife. In response to crisis and challenge she courageously "transcended herself and became far more than she had been."
2. Her story informs us of the relationship between citizens and their government, and shows that the government's decisions about a problem are not necessarily in the interests of ordinary people whose lives are threatened by these decisions.
3. Lois Gibbs' story is one of "inner meanings and feelings of humans," a story that "provides a necessary and powerful antidote to the moral illness of those cynics and their professional robots who speak the inhuman language of benefit-cost ratios, who speak of the threat of congenital deformities or cancers as acceptable risks."

In conclusion, the differences between disasters of natural and human origin are striking: The uncontrolled, violent forces of nature (fire, water, wind, and cold)—destructive as they are—are miniscule next to disasters from human sources (greed, indifference, and racial and religious hatred). The possible crisis outcomes for the victims are also markedly different, with enormous implications for prevention. Ironically, through technology and public health planning, much has been done to harness some of the destructive potential of nature. Natural disaster control technology and resources for aid to victims should now be shared more widely in disaster-prone areas of the world. Concerning disaster from human sources, however, we have been much less successful in directing and controlling conflict and indifference toward the health and welfare of others. This is unfortunate but not hopeless. Violence is not inevitable; it results from our choices, action, and inaction.

In the discussion of understanding people in crisis (Chapter 2), emphasis was placed on the examination of crisis origins. In the case of disasters of human origin, such an examination inevitably leads us into the most pressing social, political, and economic questions facing humankind. After hearing the voices of survivors of nuclear bombs, of the "downwind" fallout in Utah, of Love Canal, of the concentration camps, or of war, the crisis worker may well begin to question the social and political choices that led to these disasters. The broad view suggested by these questions is important for the crisis worker to develop, in tandem with individualized crisis intervention strategies. Without it, he or she may begin to perceive the task of helping victims of manmade disasters as an exercise in futility. Frustration, loss of effectiveness, and burnout may replace the understanding, sensitivity, and problem-solving ability that the crisis worker should bring to this task.

SUMMARY

Disaster is experienced as a crisis unlike any other a person will ever live through. Victims may experience a threat to their lives, may lose loved ones, homes, and personal belongings. Many spend the rest of their lives mourning these tragic losses and trying to rebuilt their homes and lives. Rescue services, crisis intervention, and follow-up care for physical, emotional, and social rehabilitation are necessary for all survivors. While financial aid for physical restoration and rehabilitation has been available for years, crisis counseling services are a newer phenomenon on the disaster scene. Communities will be better equipped to handle the emotional crisis related to the disaster experience when mental health and social service workers, as well as other caretakers, are prepared in advance with skills in crisis management. The urgency of preventing disasters of human origin is self-evident.

REFERENCES

Baum A, Fleming R, Singer JE: Coping with victimization by technological disaster. *J Soc Iss* 1983; 39(2): 117–138.

Bennet G: Bristol floods. Controlled survey of effects on health of local community disaster. *B Med J* 1970; 3:454–458.

Birnbaum F, Coplon J, Scharff R: Crisis intervention after a natural disaster. *Soc Casework* 1973; 54:545–551.

Blanford H, Levine J: Crisis intervention in an earthquake. *Soc Work* 1972; 17:16–19.

Boehnlein JK et al.: One year follow-up study of post traumatic stress disorder among survivors of Cambodian concentration camps. *Am J Psych* 1985; 142(8):956–959.

Chavkin W (editor): *Double Exposure: Women's Health Hazards on the Job and at Home.* Monthly Review Press, 1984.

Davidson J et al.: A diagnostic and family study of post traumatic stress disorder. *Am J Psych* 1985; 142(1):90–93.

Farberow NL: Crisis disaster and suicide: Theory and therapy. In: *Essays in Self-destruction.* Shneidman ES (editor). Science House, 1967.

Fisher D: Camaroon says 1,200 dead from volcanic gas. *Boston Globe,* August 26, 1986.

Foell E, Henneman R: *How Peace Came to the World.* MIT Press, 1986.

Frank J: *Sanity and Survival in the Nuclear Age,* 2nd ed. Random House, 1982.

Gibbs L: *Love Canal—My Story.* Albany: State University of New York Press, 1982.

Goodman LM: *Death and the Creative Life.* Springer, 1981.

Gordon N: Disaster, research, training, service. Workshop presented at the American Association of Suicidology Ninth Annual Meeting, Los Angeles, 1976.

Hansell N: *The Person in Distress.* Human Sciences Press, 1976.

Hilgartner S, Bell RC, O'Connor R: *Nukespeak.* San Francisco: Sierra Club Books, 1982.

Kizzier D: A chilling night of terror. In: *The Rapid City Flood.* Lubbock, Texas: C. F. Boone, 1972.

Koegler RR, Hicks SM: The destruction of a medical center by earthquake. *Cal Med* 1972; 116:63–67.

Kubler-Ross E: *On Death and Dying.* Macmillan, 1969.

Laube J: Psychological reactions of nurses in disaster. *Nurs Res* 1973; 22:343–347.

Lifton RJ: *Life in Death.* Simon and Schuster, 1967.

Lifton RJ: Interview for national public television documentary, *Survivors.* Boston: WGBH Educational Foundation, 1982.

Lifton RJ, Olson E: The human meaning of total disaster: The Buffalo Creek experience. *Psychiatry* 1976; 39:1–18.

Matchan L: A generation later. *Boston Globe,* 1981.

McGee RK, Heffron EF: The role of crisis intervention services in disaster recovery. In: *Emergency and Disaster Management: A Mental Health Source Book.* Parad HJ, Resnik HLP, Parad LG (editors): Charles Press, 1976.

Mills CW: *The Sociological Imagination.* Oxford University Press, 1959.

Murphy SA: Status of natural disaster victims' health and recovery 1 and 3 years later. *Res Nurs Health* 1986; 9:331–340.

Okura KP: Mobilizing in response to a major disaster. *Comm Ment Health J* 1975; 11:136–144.

Powers T: *Thinking about the Next War.* Knopf, 1982.

Rakoff V et al.: Children and families of concentration camp survivors. *Canad Ment Health* 1966; 14:24–26.

Rapid City Journal. Rapid City, SD,

Rizzo V: As quoted in the *Boston Globe,*

Schell J: *The Fate of the Earth.* Knopf, 1982.

Schottenfeld, RS, Cullen MR: Occupation-induced post-traumatic stress disorders. *Am J Psych* 1985; 142(2):198–202. See also "Reply" in Letters to the Editor, 142(9):1125.

Spake A: A new American nightmare? *MS* 1986; 14(9):35–42, 93–95.

Survivors. Boston: WGBH Educational Foundation, 1982.

Tolstoy, L: *The Death of Ivan Illyich.* New American Library, 1960 (first published 1886).

Tyhurst JS: Individual reactions to community disaster. *Am J Psych* 1951; 107:764–769.

Tyhurst JS: Psychological and social aspects of civilian disaster. *Canad Med Assoc J* 1957a; 76:335–393.

Tyhurst JS: The role of transition states—including disaster—in mental illness. Symposium on preventive and social psychiatry. Washington, DC: Walter Reed Army Institite of Research and The National Research Council, 1957b.

Wallis J (editor): *Waging Peace.* Harper and Row, 1982.

Wijkman A, Timberlake L: *Natural Disaster: Acts of God or Acts of Man?* London and Washington, DC: International Institute for Environment and Development, 1984.

Williams T: *Post-traumatic Stress Disorders of the Vietnam Veteran.* Cincinnati: Disabled American Veterans, 1980.

Zusman J, Joss RH, Newman PJ: *Final Report: Project Outreach.* Buffalo, NY: Community Mental Health Research and Development Corporation, 1973.

CRISES RELATED TO SITUATIONAL AND TRANSITION STATES

Hazardous life events—both anticipated and unanticipated—are traditionally defined as transitional and situational state crises (see Crisis Pardigm). In presenting these crises, the first two chapters of Part Three address the theme of passage: from health to illness, from employed to unemployed status, from one residence to another, from adolescence to adulthood, and other changes in status and role. Chapter 11 highlights rites of passage during life crises, including the final crisis for all—passage from life to death—and how we can help ourselves and others through this last developmental task. The concluding chapter illustrates situational, transitional, and sociocultural aspects of AIDS, one of the most devastating crises of the 20th century.

CHAPTER 10

Changes in Health, Occupational, and Residential Status

THREATS TO HEALTH, SELF-IMAGE, AND SOCIAL SECURITY

The unique hazard of some life events is that our health, image of self, material security, or life itself is threatened. To avoid a crisis state, all of us need to have:

- A sense of physical well-being.
- Some control in everyday life functions.
- Ability to be creative and productive in a way that is meaningful to us and accepted by others.
- Membership in a supportive community.
- Material supplies and protection from the elements.

These aspects of life are acutely threatened by illness, accidents, surgery, physical handicap, uncontrolled use of alcohol and other drugs, and loss of job or home. Several of our basic needs are in jeopardy when hazardous events like these occur. A full crisis experience can be avoided only if the threatened person is supported by family, friends, community caretakers, or health workers. Self-defeating outcomes such as suicide, homicide, mental illness, and depression can also be avoided if immediate help is available when such threats occur (see Crisis Paradigm, lower right box).

People in such crisis situations rarely come to the attention of mental health or crisis specialists at the high point of their crises. It is not uncommon, however, for mental health workers to see many of these people *after* the crisis, when they have become dependent on alcohol or drugs, have lapsed into depression, or have experienced other emotional disturbance. This fact highlights the important role of front-line workers, who are the most likely to see people at risk for crisis in the early stages of stress. Front-line helpers during crisis include people at the scene of an accident; in

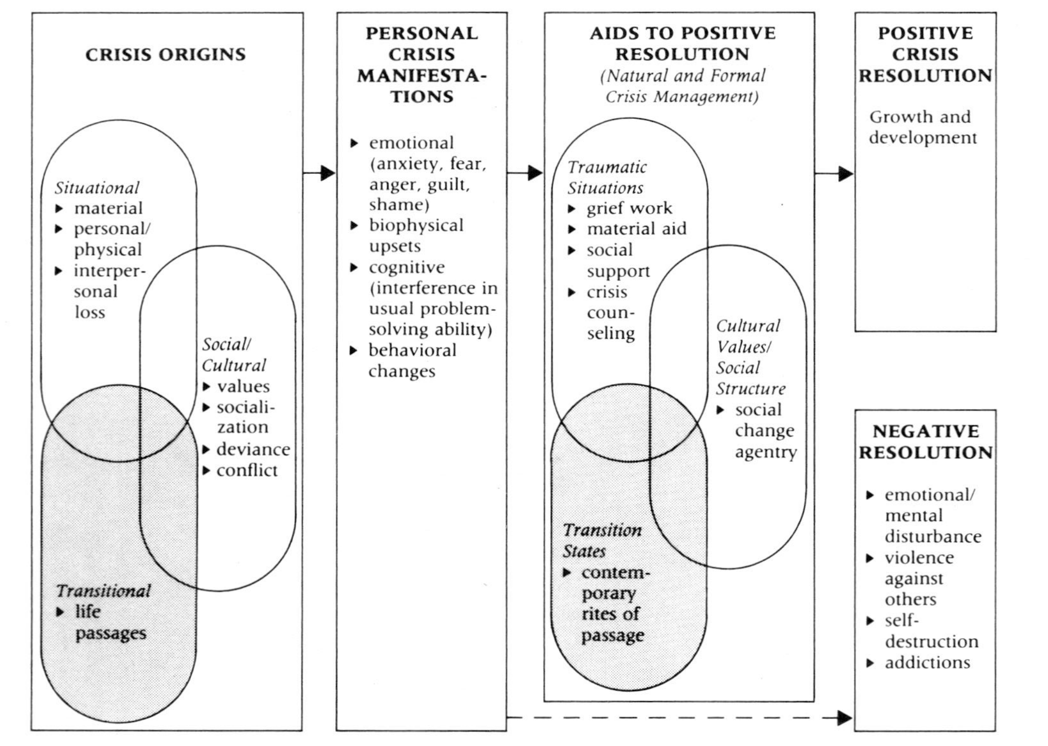

CRISIS PARADIGM

Crisis origins, manifestations, and outcomes, and the respective functions of crisis management have an interactional relationship. The intertwined circles represent the distinct yet interrelated origins of crisis and aids to positive resolution, even though personal manifestations are often similar. The solid line from origins to positive resolution illustrates the opportunity for growth and development through crisis; the broken line depicts the potential danger of crisis in the absence of appropriate aids.

police departments; in doctors' offices; in lawyers' offices; in emergency, intensive care, and other general hospital units (Bartolucci and Drayer 1973); in welfare departments; in public health offices; in shelters; and in residential settings for those who need supervision of daily living activities. They also include: caseworkers in the Travelers' Aid Association who help travelers in distress, employers and industrial nurses who notice the depression and poor performance of a newly promoted or transferred worker, indigenous community residents, and people in agencies who routinely or occasionally encounter refugees, immigrants, and homeless people in crisis.

Workers in these health and community settings are not expected to function as counselors or psychotherapists. The failure to distinguish between psychotherapy and crisis intervention may account, in part, for the reluctance of some workers to engage in crisis intervention as needed in these situations. Many front-line people are already doing crisis intervention but may lack self-confidence because they have no formal training. They often need reinforcement and confirmation from crisis specialists for work they are doing for people in distress.

In the following pages the principles and techniques of crisis intervention are applied on behalf of people in crisis by front-line workers. Case examples illustrate how health, welfare, and rescue workers can collaborate with mental health and crisis specialists to avoid destructive outcomes of events threatening security in health, occupational, and residential status. The discussions on Loss, Change, and Grief Work in Chapter 4 and Rites of Passage in Chapter 11 are particularly relevant when health, occupational, and residential status are threatened, such as when a person's status is changing from:

- Health to illness.
- Physical intactness to handicap.
- Home to streets.
- Having a job to the unemployment lines or poverty.

People need to mourn the losses that characterize these transitions. And they need the hope that comes from advocacy and social change to alleviate the conditions that threaten health and/or deprive people of jobs and home.

HAZARDS TO PHYSICAL AND EMOTIONAL HEALTH

ILLNESS, ACCIDENTS, SURGERY, AND HOSPITALIZATION

Physical illnesses or accidents are often the beginning of a series of problems for the individual as well as for his or her family (Lindemann 1979, Werner-

Beland 1980). If struck by a potentially fatal illness such as cancer, the person may experience the same sense of dread and loss that death itself implies. A person's self-image is also threatened by physical deformity resulting from a mastectomy, amputation of an arm or leg, scars from an accident or extensive burns, AIDS (see Chapter 12), or genital herpes (Hamilton 1980, McCloskey 1976, Murray 1972, Penman et al. 1987). People with sexually transmitted diseases such as herpes II are also particularly crisis prone. For example, shame, revulsion, ignorance, and fear about herpes have precipitated marriage breakups, suicidal tendencies, social isolation, self-loathing, and depression (Fiumara 1980).

In addition to facing the illness or accident itself, the person acutely or chronically ill often faces another crisis: institutionalization in a hospital or nursing home. Crisis intervention should be viewed as a routine part of comprehensive health care in community and institutional settings. When nurses and physicians do not communicate openly and are insensitive to the crisis aspects of illness, surgery, and hospitalization, they can become part of the person's problems rather than a source of help.

In some instances, people's illnesses and the crisis of hospitalization are complicated further by negligence, mishandling, or unethical medical practice. Millman (1978) discusses the systematic cover-up of iatrogenic illness and death (caused by physician or other practioner). In addition to the original illness, the patient (or survivor) must contend with personal damage or death inflicted by the people he or she trusted.

Patients and families, however, are not the only ones in crisis around these issues. Nursing and medical colleagues face the moral dilemma of collusion in cover-up of negligence. If lawsuits occur, a new series of crises may unfold: joblessness, financial loss, and damage to professional status.

A related issue concerns unnecessary surgery. An 8-year study at Cornell Medical School suggested that one in ten elective operations are unnecessary (Knox 1981). Among those surgeries with the highest nonconfirmed rates (in which the second opinion did not support the initial recommendation) are breast surgery, hysterectomy (removal of the uterus), and removal of the prostate gland in men. Women have the majority of unnecessary operations and also receive 50% more prescription drugs than men (BWHBC 1984). This practice is especially significant in terms of women's emotional and physical assets: on the average, women live seven years longer than men and are assumed to be the emotional and social caretakers of society. These facts are linked to the political economy of medicine and cultural values about women that portray women as sick and in need of medical intervention and control (Ehrenreich 1978, Ehrenreich and English 1979).

The issue of unnecessary surgery is particularly poignant in the case of breast surgery. Randomized control trials now reveal that radical mastectomy for breast cancer is no more effective than other forms of treatment. The first experimental research supporting this finding was carried out in England and Scandinavia, where surgeons' fees are significantly lower than they are in the US (Frankfort 1972). Considering the cultural symbolism of the female breast, it is not difficult to imagine the loss of a breast as the occasion for acute crisis in addition to crisis over the threat to life from cancer. Preparing a woman for a mastectomy and explaining alternative treatments can help her live through this crisis (Jamison, Wellisch, and Pasnaw 1978). Offering support through self-help referrals after surgery is equally important. Yet in one New England state, the legislature had to pass a law requiring physicians to make nonsurgical options known to women with breast cancer. In some hospitals women with mastectomies are not referred to self-help groups because the physician did not order it and no one else is permitted to make the referral. This kind of practice directly contributes to the emotional and physical damage of someone already in crisis.

Men having surgery on sex organs also need communication and accurate information. Nurses are in especially strategic positions to encourage male patients to communicate their feelings regarding this sensitive issue. The crisis for men having such surgery is heavily tinged by the cultural significance of the threat to male potency and self-image signaled by cancer or surgery affecting sex organs. The hazards of such a diagnosis are complicated by male socialization to refrain from crying and expressing feelings appropriate to the event. Education as well as communication with the man's sex partner are important here (Goldberg 1976, Shipes and Lehr 1982).

The physician plays a pivotal role in such crisis situations. Alex, for example, was upset with the news of his wife's intention to divorce him. When his physician diagnosed cancer of the testicle, he was even more distressed. The physician simply told him to check into the county hospital psychiatric unit 30 miles away if he continued to feel upset. Instead, Alex went home, told his wife what the physician had said, and shot himself in his front yard. Alex had been discussing the impending divorce with a crisis counselor who lived in the same community where Alex lived and the physician practiced. Even if the physician had no time to listen to Alex, he should have made a local referral. This case illustrates that local crisis specialty services may go unused if effective linkages with health and other front-line professionals are lacking (Hoff 1983, Hoff and Miller 1987).

If illness, surgery, and hospitalization are occasions of crisis for most adults, they are even more so for children and their parents. Research has revealed the traumatic effects of hospitalization on children, and a new organization has emerged: Association for the Care of Children in Hospitals.* Professionals with special training in child development now work in Child Life Departments of 240 US hospitals. They arrange preadmission tours, listen to children's questions, and offer explanations. For example:

▶ Sam, age 4, has been told by his doctor that a hole will have to be made in his stomach to make him well again. Because the doctor neglected to mention that the hole will also be

---

*Information can be obtained from 3615 Wisconsin Avenue, Washington, DC 20016.

stitched up again, Sam worries that "the things inside of me will fall out."

- Cindy, age 9, sees an intravenous bottle and tubes being wheeled to her bedside. She had once seen the same apparatus attached to her cousin Jeffrey, who later died. As the needle is being inserted, she wonders if she is as sick as Jeffrey was.
- Ken, a junior-high-school football player, is confined to a traction frame. Unable to dress or wash himself each morning, he suffers acute embarrassment in front of the nurses (Weisel 1979).

If a child is going to the hospital, Child Life workers offer the following advice to parents:

1. Accept the fact of the hospitalization.
2. Be honest with your child.
3. Prepare yourself; for example, find out about procedures.
4. Prepare your child, as through preadmission "get-acquainted" tours.
5. Whenever possible, stay with your child.

In addition to these general health care situations, front-line health workers need to increase their vigilance on behalf of victims whose *first* contact after injury is a health care professional or emergency medical technician (Surgeon General's Report 1986) (see Chapter 8).

Crisis Response

More specific consideration of assessment and management of crises around illness and hospitalization deals with the crisis response. How do sick and hospitalized people feel? What is their perception of the illness and its relationship to their beliefs and life-style? How do they behave in the "sick role" (Brody 1988)? The person whose physical integrity, self-image, and social freedom are threatened or actually damaged by these hazards to health shows many of the usual signs of a crisis state (see second box of Crisis Paradigm and Chapter 3.)

1. *Biophysical response:* Besides the pain and discomfort from the disease or injury itself, the person losing health and body integrity suffers many of the biophysical symptoms experienced after the loss of a loved one (see Loss, Change, and Grief Work in Chapter 4). For example, Parkes (1975) compares the "phantom limb" experience to the "phantom husband" of widows, noting the influence of psychological factors and nervous system connection.

2. *Feelings:* After an amputation or a diagnosis such as heart disease,

AIDS, herpes II, diabetes, or cancer, people respond with a variety of feelings:

- Shock and anger: "Why me?"
- Helplessness and hopelessness in regard to future normal functioning: "What's left for me now?"
- Shame of the obvious scar, handicap or reduced physical ability, and of dependence on others: "What will my husband think?"
- Anxiety about the welfare of spouse or children who depend on them: "How will they manage at home without me?"
- Sense of loss of body integrity and loss of goals the person hoped to achieve before the illness or accident: "I don't think I'll ever feel right again."
- Doubt of acceptance by others: "No one will want to be around me this way."
- Fear of death, which may have been narrowly escaped in an accident or which now must be faced in the case of cancer: "It was almost the end," or "This is the end."
- Fear that one's sex life is over: "Am I condemned to lead a celibate life now?"

3. *Thoughts and perceptions:* The fears raised by a serious illness, accident, or operation usually color the person's perception of the event itself—the understanding of the event, and how it will affect the future. For example, a young woman with diabetes assumed that her cocktail party circuit, which she felt was necessary in her high executive position, would be completely cut off. She obviously lacked knowledge about what social limitations might be imposed by diabetes.

A person with heart disease may foresee spending the future as an invalid; the reality is that he or she must only change the manner and range of performance. The woman with a mastectomy may perceive that all men will reject her because of the deformity; in reality only some men would do so. A woman who does not have a secure relationship with a man before a mastectomy may experience rejection. We can help such a woman consider the value of a relationship with a man who accepts her only for her body. In fact, women with stable relationships are seldom rejected by their husbands or lovers following a mastectomy.

4. *Behavior:* The behavior of people who are ill or suffering from the physical effects of an accident or surgery is altered by several factors. Hospitalization forces on people a routine of dependency, which is often necessary because of their physical condition. However, the enforced dependency role of the patient also keeps the hospital running according to established rules of hierarchy. This hierarchy has little or nothing to do with patient welfare. In fact, rigidity in the hierarchy often defeats the purpose for which hospitals exist: quality care of patients (Schain 1980).

The environment of an intensive care unit—the tubes, lights, and electrical gadgets—is a constant reminder to the conscious patient of his or her proximity to death (Kuenzi and Fenton 1975). Furthermore, a patient's fears, anger, and lack of knowledge about illness, hospital routines, and expectations can elicit the worst behavior from a person who is otherwise cooperative and likable. The rules and regulations governing visitors to these settings present a further hazard to people already in a difficult situation (Fuller and Foster 1982).

To understand and respond appropriately to the emotional, perceptual, and behavioral responses of people to illness, pain, and hospitalization, we must be sensitive to cultural differences. The role of culture and value systems in the development of and response to crisis was discussed in Chapters 1–4. Considering the addition of the elements of illness, pain, and hospitalization, the cultural component becomes more important. For example, Zborowski's (1952) classical study of Jewish, Italian, Irish, and other Americans revealed that: (1) similar reactions to pain by different ethnocultural groups do not necessarily reflect similar attitudes to pain; (2) similar reactive patterns may have different functions in various cultures. For instance, Jews' responses to pain elicit worry and concern, whereas Italians' elicit sympathy. Standard texts on health, illness, and healing in cross-cultural perspective offer further discussion of this topic (for example, Brink 1976, Conrad and Kern 1981, Foster and Anderson 1978, James, Stall and Gifford 1986, Landy 1977, McElroy and Townsend 1985, Moore et al. 1980).

Nurses, physicians, chaplains, and others familiar with common signs of patients in crisis can do much to relieve unnecessary stress and harmful outcomes of the hospital experience. The patient in crisis needs an opportunity to:

- Express the feelings related to his or her condition.
- Gain an understanding of the illness, what it means in terms of one's values, what limitations it imposes, and what to expect in the future.
- Have the staff understand his or her behavior, how it relates to the person's feelings and perception of the illness, and how the behavior is related to the attitudes and behavior of the entire staff.

Crisis Management

Case Example: Michael and Maria French

Michael French, age 55, suffered from cancer of the prostrate gland for several years. During the past year he was forced to retire from

his supervisory job in a factory. The cancer spread to his bladder and colon, causing continuous pain as well as urinary control problems. Michael became very depressed and highly dependent on his wife, Maria, age 51. Michael and Maria grew further apart in their marriage as stress for both of them increased. Michael began to suspect Maria of infidelity.

Maria was scheduled to go to the hospital for a hysterectomy for fibroids of the uterus, but repeatedly cancelled the surgery. Her husband always protested her leaving and, at the last minute, she would cancel. Finally, her doctor pressed her to go through with the operation. Since she was not visibly sick, according to his observations, Michael felt Maria was abandoning him unnecessarily. Along with the ordinary fears of anyone facing a major operation, Maria was very worried about her husband's condition when she went to the hospital. However, she was too embarrassed by Michael's accusations of infidelity to discuss her fears with the nurses or with her doctor.

After going to the hospital, Maria received a message from her friend that her husband threatened to kill her when she came home. He dismissed their tenants without notice and changed the locks on the doors. The friend, who was afraid of Michael in this state, also called a local community health nurse who, in turn, called a nearby crisis clinic. The nurse had been making biweekly visits to supervise Michael's medication.

Crisis management took the following form:

1. The crisis counselor called Maria in the hospital to talk about her concerns and to determine whether Michael had any history of violence, or whether guns were available. Michael's accusations of infidelity—which, according to Maria, were unfounded—may have been related to concern about his forced dependency on his wife and feelings of inadequacy as a man with cancer of the sex gland (Shipes and Lehr 1982).

2. The crisis counselor called Michael and let him know that he (the counselor), Maria, and the neighbor were all concerned about him. Michael accepted an appointment for a home visit by the counselor within the next few hours. He expressed his fears that people were trying to take advantage of him during his wife's absence. This was his stated reason for dismissing the tenants and changing the locks. Further exploration revealed that he felt inadequate to handle household matters and everyday requests of the tenants that his wife usually managed (Maxwell 1982).

3. Michael agreed to the counselor's recommendation for a medical-psychiatric-neurological check-up to determine whether metastasis (spreading of the cancer) to the brain had occurred. The counselor explained that brain tumors can contribute to acute emotional upsets such as Michael was experiencing.

4. Since Michael had no independent means of visiting Maria in the hospital, the counselor arranged for such a visit. The counselor also scheduled a joint counseling session between Michael and Maria after they had had a chance to visit. This session revealed that Michael and Maria each had serious concerns about the welfare of the other. In their two telephone conversations during Maria's stay in the hospital, Michael and Maria had been unable to express their fears and concern. As it turned out, the joint counseling session was the highlight in successful resolution of their crisis. Michael's threats to kill Maria were a once-in-a-lifetime occurrence triggered by his unexpressed anger at Maria for leaving him and the troubles he experienced during her absence.

5. When Maria returned from the hospital, a joint session was held at the French's home including the two of them, the community health nurse, and the friend who made the original calls (see Social and Group Process in Crisis Intervention in Chapter 5). This conference had several positive results: (a) It calmed the neighbor's fears for Michael. (b) It broadened everyone's understanding of the reactions people can have to the stress of illness and hospitalization. (c) The community health nurse agreed to enlist further home health services for the Frenches to relieve Maria's increasingly demanding role of nurse to her husband (Skorupka and Bohnet 1982). (d) Michael and Maria agreed to several additional counseling sessions to explore ways in which Michael's excessive dependency on his wife could be reduced. Michael and Maria had never before discussed openly the feelings they both had about Michael's progressive cancer (Sontag 1978). Future sessions were to deal with ways that the Frenches could resume social contacts with their children and friends, whom they had cut off almost completely.

Preventive Intervention

This case history reveals at least three earlier points at which crisis intervention should have been available to the Frenches:

1. At the time Michael received his diagnosis of cancer.
2. When Michael was forced to retire.
3. Each time Maria delayed her operation as well as at the point of Maria's actual hospitalization.

In each of these instances, nurses and physicians were in key positions to help the Frenches through the hazardous events of Michael's illness and Maria's operation. Sessions with the crisis counselor confirmed the fact that the Frenches, like many other people facing illness, received little or no attention regarding the fears and social ramifications of their illnesses and hospitalization.

When Maria expressed to the community nurse her original concern about Michael's early retirement, the nurse might have extended her ten-minute visits to a half hour, thus allowing time for communication of concerns. For example, the nurse might have said, "Maria, you seem really concerned about your husband being home all the time. Can we talk about what's bothering you?" Or the nurse might have made a mental health referral after observing Michael's increasing depression.

The gynecologist attending to Maria's health problems might have explored the reason for her repeated cancellations of the scheduled surgery, saying, "Mrs. French, you've cancelled the surgery appointment three times now. There must be some serious reason for this, as you know that the operation is necessary. Let's talk about what's at the bottom of this." Such a conversation might have led to a social service referral.

The nurse attending Maria prior to her operation—as well as the community health nurse visiting the home—might have picked up on Maria's concerns about the effect of her absence on Michael. Such a response requires listening skills and awareness of psychological cuses given by people in distress.

Case Example: Interview with Maria

Hospital nurse: Mrs. French, you've been terribly quiet, and you seem tense. You said before that you're not particularly worried about the operation, but I wonder if something else is bothering you.

Maria: Well, I wish my husband were here, but I know he can't be.

Nurse: Can you tell me more about that?

Maria: He's got cancer and isn't supposed to drive. . . . I hated leaving him by himself.

Nurse: How about talking with him by phone?

Maria: I've done that, but all we talk about is the weather and things that don't matter. . . . I'm afraid if I tell him how worried I am about him, he'll think I'm putting him down.

Nurse: Mrs. French, I understand what you're saying. A lot of people feel that way. But you know there's really no substitute for telling people honestly how we feel, especially those close to us.

Maria: Maybe you're right. . . . I could try but I'd want to be really careful about what I say. There's been a lot of tension between us lately.

Nurse: Why don't you start by letting him know that you wish he could be here with you and that you hope things are OK with him at home. (Pause) You said there's been a lot of tension—do you have anyone you can talk to routinely about the things that are bothering you?

Maria: No, not really.

The nurse might then explain the hospital resources, such as social services or pastoral care—ways of helping Maria explore the problem further.

In this brief interaction about a hazardous event such as surgery, the nurse has: (a) helped Maria express her fears openly, (b) conveyed her own understanding of Maria's fears, (c) helped Maria put her fears (of not communicating with her husband) in a more realistic perspective, (d) offered direct assistance in putting Maria in touch with the person most important to her at this time, and (e) made available the resources for obtaining counseling service if Maria so desires.

This type of intervention should be made available to everyone with a serious illness or who experiences the traumatic effects of an operation, burns, or an accident. Putting people in touch with self-help groups, as discussed in Chapter 5, is another important means of reducing the hazards of illness and hospitalization. Such groups exist for nearly every kind of illness or operation a person can have: heart disease, leukemia, diabetes, mastectomy, amputation, and others. Many hospitals also hold teaching and discussion groups among patients while still in the hospital. This is an excellent forum for people to air their feelings with others who have similar problems, gain a better understanding of the illness or operation and how it will affect their lives, and establish contacts with people who may provide lasting social support in the future.

CRISIS INTERVENTION IN MENTAL INSTITUTIONS AND HOSTELS

As noted in Chapters 2 and 3, admission to a mental hospital is a sign that crises have not been constructively resolved at various points along the way (Polak 1967). Whenever possible, crisis hostels and other alternatives to psychiatric hospitals should be used if a person cannot be helped in the home environment (Polak 1976). Although mental hospitals are intended to relieve acute breakdowns or stress situations, they—like general hospitals—create another kind of crisis.

Case Example: Angela

Angela, age 18, highly suicidal, upset, and dependent on her family, was brought to a private mental hospital by her mother on

the advice of a psychiatrist whom the mother had called a few hours earlier. Angela and her mother arrived at the hospital at 3:00 PM. The admitting nurse stayed with them until 3:30 PM when she was scheduled to go off duty. Angela was just beginning to calm down but became very upset again when the nurse left. The nurses were attempting to obtain an order from the psychiatrist for tranquilizing medication, but could not reach the physician. Meanwhile, visiting hours ended at 4:00 PM, and Angela's mother was asked to leave. At this point, Angela became even more upset. The nurse on the evening shift was unable to quiet or console her. By 6:00 PM there was still no medical order for tranquilizing medication. Angela's behavior now became uncontrollable, and she was placed in a high-security room as she became more suicidal.

In this case the rules and regulations of the hospital and the absence of a call system to obtain doctor's orders for emergency medication clearly contributed to Angela's crisis state, which reached the point of panic. Richardson's (1987) study of inpatients' perceptions of the seclusion-room experience revealed that in 58% of the cases patients experienced negative interaction with the staff before being secluded, 50% said that seclusion protected them, 58% perceived seclusion as a form of punishment, and 50% said that a different approach would have averted the need for seclusion.

In general, the same principles of crisis management discussed in earlier chapters apply in mental hospitals and residential settings: (a) help people to express their feelings; (b) help them understand their situation and develop new ways of problem solving; and (c) help them to reestablish themselves with family and community resources. The staff in residential facilities should examine their programs and routines to determine whether people become *more* upset than they were originally as a result of the rules, thus defeating the purpose of the residential program (Kavanagh 1988).

For example most psychiatric facilities routinely search patients on entrance for dangerous articles, contraband, and anything that might be used as a weapon against self or others. Considering the number of dangerous people now admitted to psychiatric centers instead of prisons, and the frequency of attacks on staff (see Chapter 8), such searches seem reasonable. They should not, however, be done without a full explanation to the patient as to the reasons. A person's psychotic condition provides no exception to the need for respect and personal integrity, even for those committed involuntarily to a mental institution (Anders 1977, Farberow 1981). The earlier discussion about "culture shock" experienced by most people admitted to a hospital is also useful in these instances (see Approaches to Helping People in Crisis in Chapter 1).

PHYSICAL AND MENTAL HANDICAP

Parenthood can be a crisis point even if everything occurs as expected. The type of crisis associated with role change will be dealt with in the next chapter on life passages. The birth of a handicapped child, however, presents a serious threat to the parents' image of themselves as successful parents. Frequently the parent asks: "What did I do wrong?" "What have I done to deserve this?" Parents conclude mistakenly that something they did or did not do is responsible for their child's handicapped condition.

Because of the strength of the parent-child bond, the child's physical or mental handicap is, in a sense, the parent's handicap as well (Childs 1985). The intergenerational and family aspects of handicap suggest that initial and successive crisis points related to birth and continued care of a handicapped person extend well beyond childhood. The degree of handicap and the level of parental expectation of a normal child are key factors influencing the likelihood of crisis for concerned parents. Handicaps vary greatly. Down's syndrome is a mental deficiency with distinctive physical signs: slanting, close-set, deep eyes that are often crossed; flattened nose; loose muscles; thick stubby hands; and short stature. Hydrocephalus is characterized by an enlarged head containing excessive fluid. In addition to Down's syndrome and hydrocephalus, the range of handicaps varies, from gross deformity to minor physical deformity, such as a sixth toe, to developmental disabilities that surface later, for example, a learning disability or hypothyroidism (Hutt and Gibby 1976).

Initial Crisis Point

In many cases birth defects are obvious immediately after birth. Sometimes, however, the handicap is not noticed until the child is obviously lagging in normal development. Whenever the handicap becomes known to the parents, the usual response includes anger, disbelief, a sense of failure, numbness, fear for the child's welfare, guilt, and an acute sense of loss—loss of a normal child, loss of a sense of success as parents. The parents' initial reactions of disbelief and denial are sometimes compounded unnecessarily by medical personnel who withhold the truth from them. Seventy to eighty percent of mentally retarded children also have physical disabilities, but parents should not be encouraged to believe that when these physical conditions are remedied, the mental condition will be cured as well.

Case Example: Anna

Edward and Jane took their six-year-old girl, Anna, for kindergarten evaluation. They were told bluntly that she required special education. They were shocked by the news. No psychological or so-

cial services had been made available to these parents. Edward and Jane had tried to ignore their daughter's obvious differences and had not questioned their physician, who was noncommittal. Finally, the grandparents and a sister convinced them to seek guidance from the local Association for Retarded Children.

The physical or mental handicap of a child can be a source of crisis for a parent even before birth. When parents learn through sophisticated medical technology about fetal handicap, they face the decision of whether or not to abort the fetus. An infant born with devastating brain damage can now be kept alive through advanced medical technology. Like spouses and children of the dying elderly parents are caught in the middle of passionate public debates on life and death issues: Is it morally justifiable to sustain physical life by extraordinary means when brain death is certain? Parents of unborn children who are certain to die now face another moral dilemma: whether to carry the infant to term in order to donate healthy organs to other infants. Sensitive health care workers will make themselves available to parents who need to work through these dilemmas.

Successive Crisis Points

Parents of children who are developmentally disabled or otherwise handicapped can experience crisis at many different times, the most common of which are:

- When the child is born.
- When the child enters and does not succeed in a normal classroom.
- When the child develops behavior problems peculiar to his or her handicap.
- When the child becomes an adult and requires the same care as a child.
- When the child becomes an intolerable burden and parents lack the resources to care for him or her.
- When it is necessary to institutionalize the child.
- When institutionalization is indicated and parents cannot go through with it out of misplaced guilt and a sense of total responsibility.
- When the child is rejected by society and parents are reminded once again of their failure to perform as expected.

The classic signs of crisis are easily identified in most parents of handicapped children:

1. *Feelings:* They deny their feelings and may displace their anger onto doctors, nurses, or each other. They feel helpless about what to do. Essentially, they feel they have lost a child as well as their role as successful parents.
2. *Thoughts:* Expectations for the child are often distorted. The parents' problem-solving ability is weakened; they lack a realistic perception of themselves as parents and sometimes expect the impossible. In short, they deny reality.
3. *Behavior:* Sometimes parental denial takes the form of refusing help. Sometimes help is not readily available, or parents are unable to seek out and use available help without active intervention from others.

The following case illustrates these signs of crisis and the manner in which a maternal health nurse successfully intervened.

Case Example: Mona Anderson

Mona Anderson, age 31, had been married for 10 years when she finally became pregnant after many years of wanting a child. Her baby girl was born with Down's syndrome. When Mona was tactfully informed of this by the physician and nurse in the presence of her husband, she became hysterical. For four days she refused to look at the baby. Whenever the nurse attempted to talk with her about the baby's condition, she denied that she could give birth to a "defective child." The nurse allowed her this period of denial, but gradually and consistently informed her of the reality of her child's condition. During this time, her husband was also very supportive. Neither he nor the nurse insisted that she see the baby before she was ready.

Four days after the delivery, she asked to see the baby. When the nurse brought the baby in, she broke down, crying, "All I wanted was a normal baby—I didn't expect a genius." Mona continued to grieve over her loss of a normal child. Gradually she was able to talk with the nurse about her hopes for her child, her sense of loss, and what she could and could not expect of her baby girl. While the nurse could not answer all of Mona's or her husband's questions, she referred them to a children's institute for genetic counseling. They were also given the name and number of a self-help group of parents of children with Down's syndrome.

The nurse was also helpful to other members of Mona's family who were drawn into the crisis. Mona's sister had had a baby two months previously. She concluded, wrongly, that she could not come to visit Mona with her normal baby because such a visit would only remind Mona again of her "abnormal" baby. The

nurse counseled the family members against staying away, as it would only support Mona's denial of the reality of her child's condition.

The nurse, in the course of her ordinary work in a maternity ward, practiced successful crisis intervention by supporting Mona through her denial and mourning periods, offering factual information about the reality of Down's syndrome, and actively linking Mona to her family as well as outside resources who could continue to help in the future. An important source of continued help for these families is the availability of respite care (Ptacek 1982).

Other crises associated with birth and parenthood are discussed in the next chapter.

SUBSTANCE ABUSE AND OTHER CHRONIC PROBLEMS

Alcoholism and drug and food abuse are not crises in themselves. A common view of these problems is that they are diseases; another view is that they are possible outcomes of crisis. In either case, the person who abuses alcohol, other drugs, or food is engaging in a chronic form of self-destructive behavior (see lower right box of Crisis Paradigm, and Chapter 6). The abuse of food by excess eating is sometimes accompanied by bulimia: compulsive gorging of followed by self-induced vomiting to avoid weight gain. This is related to excess dieting, which may result in anorexia nervosa, a life-threatening condition of severe weight loss. Since eating disorders are most common among young women, they are increasingly linked to female identity issues and the pressure on young women to conform to traditional images of women's roles (Chernin 1985).* Crises arising from these chronic problems can bring about lasting change in the tendency to abuse food. It can be assumed that when people were in crisis at earlier points in their lives, they lacked the social support and personal strength to resolve the crises in a more constructive manner. People abusing food, drugs, and alcohol commonly avoid getting help for their problem until another crisis occurs as a result of the addiction itself. Frequently, a crisis takes the form of a family fight, eviction from an appartment, loss of a job, or trouble with the law. Depending on the attitude and skill of helpers as such times, later crises can be the occasion of a turning point.

*For detailed information on eating disorders, contact: Patricia Rosalind Warner, Founder and Director, Anorexia Bulimia Care, Inc., Box 2123, Lincoln Center, MA 02073; telephone (617) 259-9767.

Case Example: Anita

Anita was abused physically and verbally by her husband for years. Her way of coping with the abuse was by overeating to the point of gaining over 100 pounds. When her husband threatened her life she finally left the violent marriage and sought refuge in a shelter for battered women. This crisis was a turning point, leading Anita to seek help for her compulsive overeating in Overeaters Anonymous, a peer support group similar to Alcoholics Anonymous.

Chronic Self-Destructive Behavior and Crisis Intervention

The opportunity to change a self-destructive life-style is often missed. This is due, in part, to the lack of appropriate long-term treatment facilities, and in part to the attitude of hospital and clinic staffs who hold negative attitudes toward self-destructive people. Careful application of crisis intervention techniques can greatly reduce the sense of defeat experienced by client and staff alike.

Crisis principles that especially apply to the drug-, alcohol-, or food-dependent person include:

1. Crisis represents a turning point, in this case away from drugs or food as a means of coping with stress. For example, intravenous drug users are at high risk for AIDS and therefore are offered clean needles, in a nonjudgemental manner, to reduce risk of transmission. They might thereby reach a "turning point" in their drug use life-style through this constructive interaction with health and social service workers.

2. In crisis intervention we avoid doing things *for* rather than *with* people. Proposed solutions to problems are mutually agreed on by client and staff person. The substance-dependent person will often act helpless and try to get staff to do things for him or her unnecessarily, thus increasing dependency even more. While expressing concern, staff should avoid falling into this rescue trap.

3. Basic social attachments that have been disrupted must be reinstated or a substitute found to help avoid further crises and more self-destructive behavior. Usually, people who abuse drugs, alcohol, and food are more isolated than most.

4. For all of these reasons, the principles and techniques of social network intervention (see Chapter 5) are particularly helpful in assisting the person in repeated crisis because of chronic underlying problems. While other approaches often yield little progress, clinicians skilled in network techniques point to impressive results (Garrison 1974, Hansell 1976, and Polak 1971).

Failure to observe these points leads to greater dependency of the client and increasing frustration of the staff.

These crisis management techniques should be practiced in hospitals, in doctors' offices, and by police and rescue services—wherever the food-or chemical-dependent person is in crisis. The use of these techniques would be a first step for many persons toward a life free of these harmful addictions.

CASE EXAMPLE: EMMA JEFFERSON

Mrs. Emma Jefferson, age 42, had been drinking heavily for about 15 years. When she was 35 her husband divorced her after repeated pleading that she do something about her drinking problem. He also obtained custody of their two children. Emma was sufficiently shocked by this turn of events that she gave up drinking, joined Alcoholics Anonymous (AA), remarried at age 37, and had another child at age 38. She had hurried into her second marriage, the chief motive being that she wanted another child.

A year later Emma began drinking again and was threatened with divorce by her second husband. Emma made superficial attempts to stop drinking and began substituting Valium when she had episodes of anxiety and depression. Her second husband divorced her six months later. This time Emma retained custody of her child, though it was a close fight.

Emma took a job, was fired, went on welfare assistance, and began spending a lot of time in bars. On the urging of a friend, Emma finally decided to seek help for her alcohol and Valium dependency. She gave up drinking but continued a heavy use of Valium, sometimes taking as many as six 5 mg tablets a day. Emma was inconsistent in carrying out plans to reorganize her life to include less dependence on drugs and more constructive social outlets.

One day a neighbor reported to the Child Protection Agency that she believed Emma was neglecting her child and should be investigated. The child welfare worker learned that Emma indeed had few social contacts outside the bars and occasionally left her two-year-old child unattended. Emma was allowed to maintain temporary custody of her child with regular home visits by a welfare worker to su-

pervise her parenting activity. The threat of loss of her third child was apparently a sufficient crisis to act as a turning point for Emma. The welfare worker urged Emma to seek continued help with her problems from her counselor. Emma finally gave up her dependency on Valium, developed a more satisfying social life, and returned to work. She also made plans for another marriage, this time being more selective in her choice of a mate and less desperately dependent on a man for security.

The crisis of losing her children, resulting from chronic dependence on alcohol and drugs, led Emma to give up her self-destructive life-style. Two divorces resulting from her drug dependency were *not* crisis occasions impelling her to make a change. In fact, Emma did not seek available counseling on either of these occasions. She stated that she was ashamed to ask for help, and in any case did not think she could afford it.

Other people abusing drugs and alcohol seek help and make changes after serious financial or job failures, threats or actual experiences of imprisonment, or brushes with death such as DTs (delirium tremens, a sign of advanced alcoholism), bleeding ulcers, liver damage, or near-fatal suicide attempts.

Emma's case illustrates the damaging effects of alcoholism on children. According to the National Institute on Alcoholism and Alcohol Abuse, an estimated 26,000,000 American minors living at home have at least one alcoholic parent. Whereas 11% of American children have divorced parents, 41% of children from alcoholic families have lived through divorce before the age of 10. Besides the daily stresses and crises experienced by these children, many become alcohol-dependent themselves. The increasing availability of crisis services and follow-up treatment programs should result in earlier choices toward growth rather than self-destruction for substance-dependent people. Also, there are increasing numbers of self-help groups for adult children of alcoholics that can be contacted through local AA branches.

Influence of Societal Attitudes

The values of a given society naturally affect the use of drugs in that society. In the US, many attitudes toward drug use are contradictory. For example, a drug such as marijuana is often regarded as "dangerous," while the excessive use of alcohol is considered by many as acceptable. A stable, law-abiding citizen can be censored or convicted for the use of marijuana, yet if the same person chose to use alcohol instead there would be no legal restrictions.

If alcohol is consumed privately with no damage to others, there are no sanctions against even its excessive use. Yet those who use alcohol chronically often suffer eventual liver or brain damage (Shannon 1976). A legal crisis can occur for the user of alcohol only if he or she excessively indulges in public and then damages others or others' property, as in the case of reckless driving.

For the drunken person's innocent victims, however, it is different. Society's implicit support of alcohol abuse is illustrated by the looseness of laws punishing drunken drivers. For the most part, alcoholism has been decriminalized and the concept of alcoholism as a disease is now widely accepted. However, whether or not alcoholism is a disease, the combination of drinking and driving has an enormous social toll. The loss and crises of drunk driving victims and their families are the focus of a concerted effort to stop what has been called a national slaughter on US highways resulting from the abuse of alcohol.

The user of other drugs can experience a crisis simply by the purchase or possession of a substance like marijuana. In the US, a few states have changed the drug possession laws in this regard, but the use of drugs other than alcohol is still predominately a political issue. Little effort is made to distinguish between the *user* and the *abuser* of drugs (Yankelovich 1975). Many crises, such as arrest and imprisonment of people using illegal drugs, occur by design of the social system. The most serious drug abuse problems receive the least attention. The most widespread and dangerous abuse problems today are alcoholism and the overuse or misuse of prescribed drugs, both of which are legal.

The story of Ruth below illustrates further the complex interplay between chronic problems and acute crises: beatings as a child, feelings of rejection, a troubled marriage, suicide attempts, depression, death of husband by suicide, and alcohol dependence (see Stress, Crisis, and Illness in Chapter 2). It also highlights how crisis intervention (in contrast to something like electric shock "treatment") can be the occasion for a turning point in a chronically troubled life.

Case Example: Ruth

I called the Crisis Center because I was afraid I'd attempt to take my life again. All my suicide attempts stemmed from feeling rejected. As a child I always felt my father rejected me. Now I think this was just his way of punishing me. He picked on me and favored my older sister. I couldn't do anything right. Once I stole some money from my mother's purse so I could buy a gift for my friend (now I think I was trying to buy friendship). My father beat me so that my hands were bleeding; then he made me show my hands to my mother. My mother cried when

he beat me, but I guess she was afraid to stop him. When my father was dying, he asked me to forgive him.

I dropped out of school after tenth grade and got a job in a stockroom and later worked as a bookkeeper. I got married when I was 19. Our first five years were beautiful. We had three boys. I loved my husband very much and waited on him hand and foot. We bought a home, and he helped finish it. During the second five years, he started changing and got involved with another woman. My family and everyone knew, but I kept denying it. Then he left for about four months. I made a suicide attempt by turning on all the gas. I didn't really want to die, I just wanted him to stop seeing the other woman and come back to me. He came to pick me up at the hospital, and two weeks later I went over to his girlfriend's house and beat her up. I could have gotten in trouble with the law for that, but she didn't press charges.

After that, we tried to patch things up for about four months, but it didn't work. Then I started seeing other men. We had lots of arguments. I threatened divorce and he threatened to kill himself, but I didn't believe him.

One night he sat in his car and wouldn't come in to go to bed when I asked him. At 7:00 AM my oldest son reported finding Dad dead in his car. I thought it was my fault. Even today I still tend to blame myself. His parents also blamed me. My father was still alive then, and he and my mother stood by me. After my husband's death, I made another suicide attempt. I was in and out of the hospital several times and received a lot of shock treatment. Nothing seemed to help in those days.

Three years after my first husband's death, I remarried. We argued and fought and again I felt rejected. When I was afraid of taking an overdose of aspirin, I called the Crisis Center and was referred to the local crisis and counseling center near my home. I can't say enough good things about how my counselor, Jim, helped me. After all those years of being in and out of hospitals, having shock treatments, and making several suicide attempts, I'm so glad I finally found the help I needed long ago.

I don't think I'd ever attempt suicide again. I still struggle with the problem of feeling rejected, which I think is the worst thing in the world to go through. But I can cope a lot better now and am not half as bad about condemning myself as I used to be. My counselor has really helped me to get to the place I am now. He keeps reminding me that I've done these things for myself, but I have a hard time giving myself credit for anything.

Even though I feel I'm on the horizon of something much better, I still have my down days and have to watch that I don't drink too much. But I don't think I'd ever let myself get as down and out as I've been in the past. I've seen that real help is available when I need it.

RESCUE WORKERS, NURSES, AND PHYSICIANS IN ACUTE SETTINGS

Crisis situations demanding response are as diverse as the people experiencing them. Health practitioners have numerous opportunities to assist people in crisis because of threats to health, life, and self-image from illness, accidents, and related problems. All human service workers have a responsibility to assist people in crisis, but health care personnel in emergency and acute care settings are in a particularly strategic position to influence the outcome of high-risk crisis situations. The nature of emergency and acute care settings, with a focus on life-saving procedures, precludes the opportunity to assist a person to complete resolution of an emotional crisis originating from threats to health and life. If life is at stake, there is no one who would place expression of feelings (however intense these may be while worrying about whether one's child or spouse is dead or alive after an accident) ahead of life-saving measures for a loved one.

Yet, because of the tense atmosphere of emergency medical scenes, it is important to remember that emotional needs do not disappear when physical needs take on life and death importance. It is not a question of meeting *either* physical *or* emotional needs of people in emergency and acute care situations. The issue is one of appropriate *attitude* and sensitivity to emotional needs of victims and survivors *while* carrying out necessary life-saving procedures. A team approach, therefore, is needed to meet people's needs in these high-risk medical and potential crisis situations. The strain on individual nurses, physicians, and emergency medical technicians would be enormous without teamwork. Staff burnout in these setting is often very high. Lack of teamwork and staff support, inappropriate placement of personnel in such high-risk work, or lack of training in crisis intervention frequently contribute to such burnout (Hoff and Miller 1987). Not everyone is suited for crisis work. But those who are need not feel burned out or develop callous attitudes toward people encountered in life-threatening situations. Acute care nurses, for example, need the time and opportunity to air their feeling about the person who is comatose for days from an overdose. When the patient comes through the critical stage and survival seems certain, many nurses find it difficult to communicate empathetically with such a person (see A Framework for Understanding Self-destructive Behavior in Chapter 6, and Caring for People with AIDS in Chapter 12).

In cases of cardiac arrest at hospitals, teamwork combines emergency medical work with crisis intervention. Without effective teamwork emergency medical intervention might fail. Nurses have observed that the emergency code system is so effective that it often brings more staff to the scene than are needed; however, no provision is routinely made for attending to the emotional needs of anxious family members. In one hospital the psychiatric nurses ("surplus" personnel) routinely designate themselves to attend to family members, who are usually ignored. Nurses and physicians can be routinely trained to assist in emotional crises as well as medical emergencies.

In general, health care practitioners in emergency and acute care settings need to focus on two key aspects of the crisis management process: (1) the initial contact, and (2) referral and follow-up. These two aspects are interrelated: the likelihood of a person accepting a referral for crisis counseling, physical refuge, Alcoholics Anonymous, or other service following emergency medical treatment (such as after a suicide attempt, rape, battering, or crisis related to drinking) will often be influenced by the health care worker's attitude and recognition of the many facets of the situation. In short, health practitioners in emergency settings are not usually expected to assist people through *all* phases of crisis resolution. Effective crisis management, however, does require assessment of the emotional aspects of events threatening health and life, and referral for further assistance. Besides clinical skills in crisis management, workers in emergency settings also need an up-to-date resource file with procedures to assure follow-up when referrals are made (Hoff 1983).

Case Example: Rescue Team

No matter how long we work in the rescue business, there are still scenes we never get used to. One of the hardest things is the death of children. Lately it seems we've had so many calls for children—an eight-year-old killed on the expressway, a ten-year-old hit by a car. My heart really goes out to the parents. I'm a parent too, and it hurts to witness these tragedies.

One of the saddest things happened last night. We were called to the foster home of a child who had originally been abandoned. She dies of liver cirrhosis in spite of the foster mother's efforts to make up for years of neglect. It's very sad to watch a child die; I thought about it all day.

Another scene that haunts me is the man we found yesterday in the driveway of the hospital when we pulled in with our ambulance. He was just standing there with tears rolling down his cheeks. We asked the hospital guards and EMTs (emergency medical technicians) what was wrong. They said they didn't know and just laughed. We had to go out on another call right away. It's hard to believe that our fellow EMTs and the guards wouldn't help the man. I probably should have called the hospital, but I got busy and didn't. Now I can't get the man out of my mind; maybe I'll still call the hospital.

There seem to be a lot of overdose cases at our local college dormitory. For this kind of call we need to know how to handle crowds. If there is an illegal drug involved, it's sometimes hard for us to carry out our life-saving procedures. Sometimes the other students interfere and even the residence counselor won't give us the information we need because of fear of getting someone in trouble. If residence counselors were trained better, they could help us a lot in this kind of emergency.

Another frequent call is to the scene where a death has already taken place. One call that I remember well was for an elderly woman who died of cancer. She had taken a bath and told her daughter to leave her alone, that she wanted to go to sleep. The daughter thought her mother was still alive when she called. From what the daughter said, it seems this lady knew her time was up and prepared herself to die. Often, the dying seem to be thinking more of those left than of themselves.

One of the hardest things to deal with is a call for person with a chronic drinking problem. We take some people into the hospital a dozen times or more, and nothing seems to change. It's really discouraging, especially when we see so many accident victims of drunken driving. Usually it's the sober person who is hurt. There ought to be more treatment centers, but I also think that some drunk drivers ought to be locked up. There's just not enough attention paid to our country's alcohol and drug problem. Some parents simply deny that their child is drinking. One of the saddest cases was of a 14-year-old girl who died of alcohol poisoning.

Rescue work is exciting. But there's only so much we can do. In most cases it's up to the hospital emergency room staff to pick up where we leave off. Sometimes that doesn't happen, I'm afraid, and that's really sad.

Case Example: Hospital Emergency Room Nurse

What I like about emergency nursing is the chance to follow the patient and develop a relationship. Many people who come to the emergency room don't have a private doctor; they use the hospital emergency room as a family physician.

Any number of people come to the emergency room for social or psychological problems, which are covered over with complaints of abdominal pain, back trouble, or other aches and pains. We examine them and reassure them that nothing is wrong physically. Sometimes the reason for the complaint is to get a statement from the doctor as an excuse for missing work. Even though there's nothing wrong physically, we never take anyone's problem lightly. We have developed a referral system to a primary care clinic for minor medical complaints, so we can concentrate more on the *emergency* function of the emergency room.

In cases of true medical emergency, such as an accident, many people come in extremely upset. For example, if a child has been hurt, the parents need reassurance that everything possible is being done. I wish we had a private room for talking with people; usually we just have to hunt around for an empty office or treatment room. It's also important to let parents stay with an injured or sick child as much as possible.

In cases of serious injury or accident it's hard to keep in mind the family's state of emotional upset because we're so busy doing all the necessary procedures to keep the person alive. I think everyone understands and wants us to focus our effprts on necessary life-saving procedures, but at the same time it's important to keep the family posted on the progress being made. I have to keep reminding myself of people's psychological needs in a busy place like this.

One of the hardest problems to deal with in the emergency room is the case of battered children. I remember a father who brought in his 4-year-old child. He had pushed her down the stairs when she wouldn't eat the steak he brought home. I have a hard time being helpful to parents like this, but I did make a social service referral.

Even though this is an emergency room, you'd be surprised how many teenagers we see with venereal disease, pregnancy, or both. I know this is a sign that kids must really be troubled, and that social and other circumstances have to change. It's really too bad that a 16-year-old boy feels that he doesn't belong if he hasn't fathered a child.

Case Example: Family Physician

I spend only one day a week working in the emergency room. Once in a while things are quiet, but most of the time I run into all kinds of crisis situations. Whenever there is a true emergency, there is almost always a crisis as well, because the person's body image is altered in a lot of cases. For example, if someone comes in with the symptoms of a heart attack, I tell the person the facts as gently as I can and try to minimize the negatives: "You may be having a heart attack; you have to be treated in the intensive care unit for a while."

Some people come to the emergency room because they *think* they have an emergency or are in crisis. One young man came in with a very unusual story regarding his operations and medicine. He thought he had appendicitis. We examined him and did various diagnostic tests. I assured him that he did not have appendicitis and referred him to his regular doctor. This young man was grossly overweight; it occured to me that he was probably destroying himself by overeating. I think that we should make a mental health as well as medical referral for people like this.

Most of the people who make suicide attempts are not at high risk medically. But I carefully examine what led to the suicide attempt in each case; I assume it must be pressure of some kind. A sympathetic, supportive approach is really important. If the family is involved, I often get caught in between. Sometimes they get angry and ask, "Why are you keeping her here? She'll never do it again!" I make a mental health referral in spite of the family's objections. Besides believing the referral is best for the patient and family, I could get into medical-legal trouble if I didn't follow through.

A fairly typical crisis in the emergency room is the case of an accident victim. The magnitude of the crisis usually depends on the degree of injury. The family always needs help. In our hospital we take them to as private a place as we can find with out crowded conditions so that we can talk with them freely. Again, it's important to give them straight facts along with sympathy and support.

Another typical situation happened last night. The volunteer fire department sent an ambulance to a home where someone was having a cardiac arrest. They also alerted the hospital emergency room. The man was dead on arrival and his wife was very upset. Besides her normal grief, she blamed herself for her husband's death because she didn't force him to follow his doctor's advice and go to the hospital when he first had symptoms. I asked the nurse to put the woman in a nearby room so I could talk with her. This kind of situation is never easy. . . . Words seem so hollow when one is confronted with the death of a loved one. I sensed disbelief and denial in this woman. One way I've found to approach this sad situation is with the opener: "I have some very bad news to tell you." She cried. I stayed with her and listened to her story. At first she demanded that I bring her husband back to life. I told her that we couldn't bring him back, and gradually she accepted that. In a case like this, when the woman is blaming herself for her husband's death, I find it helpful to use my medical authority to assure the person that she and the rescue team did everything they could to save her husband. I also try to capitalize on the positive things people did do to help. During the ten minutes I spent with this woman, I learned that her daughter was at home. This was fortunate, because the woman seemed helpless to make arrangements by herself. Another thing I learned was that religion was important to her and her husband. Her involvement in the final anointing helped her accept the reality of her husband's death.

Another thing that's hard for me to deal with is the parents of child abuse victims. I try to control my revulsion and talk with them about what I've found in examining the child, and my obligation to report the facts. At first they deny, then they usually cooperate, maybe because I try to be supportive in spite of my feelings about this kind of thing.

There's a lot that can be done in the emergency room, if we only take the time to do it.

OCCUPATIONAL CHANGES

PROMOTION, SUCCESS, AND ECONOMIC SECURITY

Promotion and success do not seem to be hazardous events or occasions of crisis, and for many they are not. Yet suicide studies reveal that promotion can be the "last straw" that leads some people to the decision to commit suicide. The person who is promoted to a prestigious position may feel incapable of performing as expected in the new role. An anticipated promotion can also be a crisis point. The new position in a company brings increased responsibility as well as higher rank and status. It also requires a change in role relationships among peers. If the move is from ordinary staff worker to management position, the person may fear loss of acceptance by the peer group he or she leaves (Kanter 1977).

The combination of loss of familiar supportive relationships at work and the challenge of unfamiliar work becomes too much to handle. A person's vulnerability to crisis in these circumstances is affected by several factors:

1. The general openness of communication channels within the company or human service agency.
2. The person's ability to openly discuss questions and fears with a trusted confidante. If the person's work performance evaluation and outside evidence indicate his or her ability to do the job, the problem is probably one of self-confidence, which can often be boosted by a friend or counselor. Confiding a lack of self-confidence to one's supervisor at this stage might cost one the promotion.
3. The person's perception of self and how one should perform in a given role. People who experience promotion as a crisis are often perfectionists; they become impatient with themselves when they make a small mistake.

The "Success Neurosis" and Sex Roles

A crisis stemming from promotion has also been called the "success neurosis." Success neurosis is frequently seen in women who view themselves in what they perceive as second-rate or second-best positions. If they have worked primarily in the role of housewife and mother, they may become suddenly immobilized when other opportunities arise. This can happen even when they have openly expressed a desire for new horizons.

CASE EXAMPLE: ANGIE

Angie, age 37, had been doing volunteer work with the mental health association in her local community. One of her special projects was helping handicapped people run a confection stand for local Parks and Recreation Department events. Because of the high quality of her work—which she could only acknowlegde self-consciously—her friends urged her to open and manage her own coffee house. She finally did so, and the project was a glowing success. Angie suddenly found herself in the limelight, a situation she had not anticipated. She couldn't believe it would last. After a few months, she began feeling tense and depressed and thought vaguely about suicide. She talked with her physician about her problem and was referred to a psychiatrist for help.

Crises associated with promotion and success are usually "quiet crises." People in this kind of crisis are not acutely upset, but feel generally anxious and depressed and express bewilderment about being depressed. They feel disappointed that they can't measure up to their own expectations because, in light of their anticipated or actual promotion or success, that have every reason to be happy. They are unable to sort out and relate their feelings of depression to their lack of self-confidence and rigid expectations of themselves. A deep fear of failure may lead to the idea of suicide in the event that the person really does fail.

Anxiety, depression, and suicidal thoughts may move a person in this kind of crisis to seek help. Usually he or she will go to a local crisis clinic or private therapist. Several crisis counseling sessions are often sufficient for the person to:

- Express underlying fears, insecurity, and disappointment with self.
- Gain a realistic perspective concerning actual abilities.
- Grow in self-confidence and self-acceptance.
- Use family and friends to discuss feelings and concerns openly rather than viewing such expression as another failure.

Short-term crisis counseling may reveal deeper problems of low self-esteem, rigid role expectations, inflexible behavior patterns, and habitual reluctance to communicate feelings of distress to significant people. Psychotherapy should be offered and encouraged, for these people are high risks for suicide if other crisis situations arise (Greenspan 1983). But in addition to offering individual assistance, as crisis workers and as a society we need to examine the structures and differential expectations and rewards that place women at greater risk of failing in their career aspirations. For example, executive women (unlike executive men) who want to avoid being "derailed" on the career ladder typically must jump through two hoops—traditional masculine behavior and traditional feminine behavior (Morrison, White, and Van Velsor 1987). This is a new version of the old adage: women must be twice as good to get half as far. One consequence of such stress might be an obsession with work, to the detriment of a healthy balance between work and other activities (Schaef and Fassel 1988).

Promotion and success can result in another kind of crisis: one between spouses when a woman earns more than her husband. Traditionally, girls and women have been socialized to play inferior, and boys and men are taught to think of themselves as failures if they do not earn more than women (Roberts 1976, Rubenstein 1982, p. 37). The price for maintaining these stereotypes is very high for both men and women. For some men married to successful women the risk of early death from heart disease is 11 times more frequent than in other marriages (Rubenstein 1982, p. 37). In a study of egalitarian marriages (versus those in which a woman held a stereotypical female job) the chance of divorce was twice as high, while psychological and physical abuse was also higher (Rubenstein 1982, p. 38). These findings are supported by other studies of violence (such as Dobash and Dobash 1979, Yllo and Straus 1981).

The origins of such crises can be traced to cultural values and the tradition of men doing public work and being paid well for it, and women doing private work in the home and not being paid for it (Etheridge 1978, Reiter 1975). When women do work outside the home they are often expected to do so in traditional female nurturant or supportive jobs such as nursing, teaching, and clerical work (Reverby 1987)). Since the majority of women work outside the home for economic, psychological, and social survival, the points of stress and potential crises are numerous as long as traditional values prevail (Yllo and Straus 1981). For many of these women the cost of caring is very high (Sommers and Shields 1987) and will get higher as the number of elderly and people with AIDS increases, unless men begin to assume equal responsibility for the caring work of society (see also Kessler and McLeod 1984 and Turner and Avison 1987). Crisis counseling or therapy is indicated for individual men and women struggling with these issues. The long-term results, however, will be limited if there is not simultaneous attention directed to the social change strategies relevant to these crises of sociocultural origin (see Chapter 2; also, Greenleaf 1982, and Kanter 1977).

Institutional Barriers to Promotion and Economic Security

Aside from regressive cultural values about men, women, and work, there are institutional barriers to promotion for millions of workers: ethnic minorities and poor women (Sidel 1986). Disregard for minorities and women is expressed concretely in persistent and alarming job bias despite civil rights legislation. Thus, values and the profit motive support race, class, and sex discrimination, which in turn reinforce traditional values (Boserup 1970, Seager and Olson 1986, WFPHA 1986). Such social problems can lead to homelessness, child neglect, marital discord, bitterness, withdrawal from the mainstream of social life, drug abuse, suicide, and violence (see Chapters 6, 7, and 8).

Numerous studies (see Chapter 2) underscore the work of Caplan (1964), Hansell (1976), and others documenting the need for intactness of one's social, cultural, and material supplies in order to avoid personal crisis. Pearce and McAdoo (1982), writing for the National Advisory Council on Economic opportunity regarding the "feminization of poverty," state:

> *The typical outcome of a marital breakup in a family with children is that the man becomes* single, *while the woman becomes a* single parent. . . . *Men generally do not become poor because of divorce, sex-role socialization, sexism or, of course, pregnancy. Indeed, some may lift themselves out of poverty by the same means that plunge women into it: the same divorce that frees a man from the financial burdens of a family may result in poverty for his ex-wife and children.*

This situation is dramatized by the fact that within a year of divorce the standard of living for women decreases by 73% and for men increases by 42%. The largest percentage of poor women and children are members of racial minorities, which underscores the combination of race, sex, and class bias. As a group, women still earn only $.70 to every dollar earned by men. To offer psychotherapy or only crisis counseling alone instead of job training, daycare, and advocacy for adequate housing represents a misunderstanding of the problem, its origins, and solutions. Rather than recycling these old problems, a fresh look "upstream" to their source holds the most promise for reducing crisis proneness and long-term negative outcomes for victims of discrimination (see Crisis Paradigm, third box, right circle). Kircheimer (1980), quoting day care economist Dr. Mary Rowe, states:

> *Child care is the most basic division or labor in any society. At the point where men take equal responsibility for nurturing, women will be able to participate equally in building, creating. . . . Women will never have equality in the arena of paid work until men have equal opportunities in terms of unpaid work.*

WORK DISRUPTION

Just as promotion and success can be a source of crisis, so can work disruption or change in one's work role. In Chapter 2, involvement in meaningful work was cited as one of the basic attachments necessary for physical and social well-being (Verbrugge 1982). Western society's attitude concerning work, especially in the United States, is highlighted by a tendency to value people and to offer them respect in proportion to how much money they earn and the socioeconomic status they derive from such earning. In a very real sense, Americans have absorbed the deeply embedded cultural value: "You're worth what you earn."

Conversely, the unemployed or those receiving public assistance are generally devalued. A deeply ingrained value system regarding work tends to evoke a suspicion on the part of the "haves" that the "have-nots" are ultimately responsible for their own misfortune and could remedy that misfortune if they tried harder. Yet social problems such as unemployment are very complex and not readily solved by simplistic solutions such as "trying harder." For example, unemployment can often be related to discrimination because of race, sex, age, or ill health. Usually, the unemployed are deeply regretful of their position. While general unemployment rates are down, the standard of living is also down for many, and the unemployment rate for ethnic minorities is double the general rate. Unemployment, whether by firing, layoff, or because of a personal problem like illness, is frequently an occasion of crisis. Breed's (1972) study of completed suicides revealed that, especially for men, suicides were frequently associated with work failure.

Regardless of the reasons, the person in crisis because of unemployment is usually in need of a great deal of support. If unemployment originated from personal sources, individual crisis intervention is indicated. People unemployed because of economic recession or discrimination should receive individual support. However, they are less likely to feel hopeless and powerless if they are also put into contact with groups devoted to removing the underlying sources of their stress through social change strategies. This includes policy changes that would prevent corporations from simply closing US plants, laying off hundereds of employees, and moving to a developing country where labor is cheaper without any collaboration with or consideration of the workers who have built their lives and life savings around loyalty to the company. The primary origin of crisis for a worker thus laid off is the profit motive. The appropriate response, therefore, should include linking such a person to groups advocating labor-management policy change (see Crisis Paradigm, third box, right circle).

Standards of personal success for most of us hinge on involvement in work that is personally satisfying and of value to the external community. For example, a middle-aged woman who finds that her wife and mother roles are not enough to meet her work needs may experience crisis with repeated failure in her job-hunting efforts. Or, a 55-year-old man in a middle management position who is prematurely retired may begin to drink or may attempt suicide as a way of dealing with the crisis of job disruption. These and other work-related crises are within the common province of personnel directors, occupational physicians and nurses, or anyone the would-be worker turns to in his or her distress.

CASE EXAMPLE: RUSSELL AND JENNY OWENS

Russel Owens, age 52, was a civil engineer employed for 20 years as a research consultant in a large industrial corporation. When he lost his job because of a surplus of engineers with his qualifications, he tried without success to find other employment, even at less pay. Family financial needs forced his wife Jenny, age 47, to seek full-time employment as a biology instructor. She worked only part time before. Jenny was grateful for this opportunity to advance herself professionally. She always resented the fact that she had made little effort previously to excel at a job, partly because Russell did not want her to work full time. Gradually, however, Jenny became resentful of having to support herself, her husband, and their 16-year-old daughter, Gwen, in addition to assuming all responsibility for household tasks. She therefore urged Russell to do at least some of the housework. Since Russell never before helped in this way, except for occasional errands and emergencies, Jenny's expectations struck a blow to his masculine self-image beyond the sense of failure and inadequacy he already felt from his job loss.

Russell also found it difficult to follow Jenny's advice that he seek help about his problems of depression and increasing dependence on alcohol. The strain in their marital relationship increased. Jenny eventually divorced Russell, and Russell committed suicide.

Russell's drinking problem and eventual suicide might have been avoided if immediate help had been available to him at the crisis points of job loss and threat of divorce. Such help might also have resulted in a constructive resolution of Jenny's resentment of Russell concerning the housework.

THE FARM CRISIS

Similar dynamics are visible in the national farm crisis. Farmers not only face a threat to their source of livelihood, but also to their way of life. One study revealed that 33.7% of family-size farms were in serious or extreme financial trouble (Olson and Schellenberg 1986). While it is possible that some farm foreclosures can be traced to individual mismanagement, in general the problem originates in policies that favor unbridled corporate accumulations of agricultural resources and profits at the expense of individual farm families. For example, federal price supports for farm products are cut back because of a "surplus." Yet in New England, where 500 Vermont dairy families have been driven off their farms, there is no milk surplus. Rather, the large amounts of milk at issue are from huge corporate farms in California (Wilhelm 1988). It is ironic that, in a country of immigrants who fled Europe and prized the opportunity to earn an honest living on the land, people are now in crisis because public policy favors corporate monopoly over the nation's breadbasket. No doubt the suicides, alcoholism, violence, and family conflicts arising from the farm crisis will continue unless grassroots efforts and public policy (as proposed by the Vermont legislature) reverse the conditions causing so much pain and despair among the nation's rural citizens. One such grassroots organization is Farm Aid Rural Management (FARM) in Bismarck, North Dakota. The goals of this self-help group are:

1. To establish that it is in the best interest of this nation, country, and people, that "generational" farms be allowed to remain in the hands of present owners until such time as they work their way out from their difficulties.
2. To relay to the people who come to us for assistance any and all options open to them, a better understanding or finances, and an explanation of what laws and attorneys are available to assist them.
3. To stabilize and comfort, to assist and uplift the families that come here for guidance, to let them know that they still represent something good that they helped create (homes and farms), and that this place is a haven where they always are welcome.

RETIREMENT

Some people look forward to retirement. Others dread it. For many people, retirement signifies loss of status, a reduced standard of living, and a feeling of being discarded by society. The experience is more pronounced when one is forced to retire at an early age due to illness or other disability. It is a time of stress not only for the retired person, but for family members, especially wives who do not work outside the home. Suddenly a homemaker has to adjust to having at home all day a husband who often feels worthless and who may have developed few outside interests or hobbies apart from work.

The attitude people hold toward retirement depends on the situation one retires *to*. The pleasure or pain of retirement is also influenced by the person's life-style as a whole. Key areas of concern in evaluating a person's retirement situation include:

1. Does the person have any satisfying interests or hobbies outside of work? For many, work has been the main focus all

of their adult life, and most of their pleasures are essentially work related

2. Does the person have a specifically planned retirement project? For example, some people plan to study literature, carpentry, or cooking when they retire.
3. Does the person have a comfortable place to live?
4. Does he or she have enough retirement income to manage without excessive dependence?
5. Is the person in reasonably good health and free to manage without hardship?
6. Has the person been well adjusted socially and emotionally before retirement?

Even if the retired person's circumstances are favorable in all or most of these areas, retirement is still an occasion of stress. We live in a youth-oriented society. Retirement signals that one is nearing or has already reached old age, and after that, death. The relationship between retirement and transition into old age is discussed more fully in the next chapter.

For some people, retirement is not an issue or occasion for crisis. They may be self-employed and simply keep working at a pace compatible with their needs and inclinations. Such people usually prepare for a reduced pace and have a healthy attitude toward life in each development phase, including old age.*

Those, however, who are in crisis as a result of retirement should have the assistance accorded anyone experiencing a loss. They need the opportunity to grieve their former status, explore new ways of feeling useful, and eventually accept their changed roles.

RESIDENTIAL CHANGES

Moves across country or to a different continent require leaving familiar surroundings and friends for a place with many unknowns. Even though the would-be mover may have many problems in the place called home, at least he or she knows what the problems are. Pulling up stakes and starting over can be an exciting venture, an occasion of joy, of gaining a new lease on life, a challenge, a source of deep distress, or an occasion of crisis.

*A new view of the life cycle suggests three phases: learning, earning, and returning. Thus, instead of "retirement," people have an opportunity to return wisdom and other values to society, and to have something returned *to* them after their years of learning, earning, and caring for others (Schoonover 1987).

Consider the young woman who grew up in the country or a small town moving to the city for the first time. She asks herself: Will I find a job? Will I be able to make friends? Will I be unbearably lonely? Will I be safe? Or, the career person looking for opportunities asks: Will things be any better there? I wonder how I'll manage not seeing my family and friends very often? Lastly, consider the immigrant: How will those foreigners accept me? Will I be able to learn the language so I can get along? Who will there be to help me if things go wrong? What if I want to come back and don't have the money?

ANTICIPATED MOVES

These are a few of the many questions and potential problems faced by people who consciously plan a move with the hope that the move will improve their situation. Even in these instances, moving is a source of considerable stress. It takes courage to leave familiar territory, even when the move would free one from many negative situations. No matter what the motive for the move, and despite the anticipation of better things to come, people in this transition state experience a sense of loss.

To prevent a crisis at this time, the person planning and looking forward to a move should avoid denying feelings of loss. Even when a person is moving to much better circumstances, there is usually the loss of close associations with friends or relatives. As in the case of promotion or success, the would-be mover often does not understand her or his depression, which is probably related to denial of feelings and guilt about leaving friends and relatives. Understanding and expressing these failures helps the person keep an open relationship with friends left behind, and frees the person to use and enjoy new opportunities more fully, unburdened of misplaced guilt or depression.

People who plan and look forward to a move are vulnerable to other crises. Once they reach their destination, the situation may not work out as anticipated: the job may be less enjoyable than the one left. The person may lack the gregariousness to seek out and find new friends. Envisioned job opportunities may not exist.

Social isolation and the inability to establish and maintain satisfying social attachments make one vulnerable to crises and even suicide. People who have satisfying supports can help prevent crises among those who have recently moved and who have not established a reliable social support system.

UNANTICIPATED MOVES

The potential for crisis is even greater for those who do not want to move but are forced to. Consider the family uprooted to an unknown place because of a job transfer, the inner city dweller—especially an older person—dislocated because of urban renewal (Fried 1962, Gans 1962), the victims of disaster moving from a destroyed community, people evicted because of unpaid rent, mental patients who have been discharged to communities without adequate shelter and social support, battered women and their children forced to leave their home to avoid beating or death, political or war refugees who must leave their homeland, or migrant farm workers who move each year in the hope of earning a marginal substance. There are also thousands of teenagers and young people who are either running away from home or simply "on the move." Often they lack housing, food, and money. Finally, there is the ordinary traveler enroute from one place to another, who loses money or belongings.

In spite of the crisis potential of moves for many, recent research suggests that moving can also be an occasion for growth (Singular 1983). While highly mobile families may have fewer deep individual friendships, the family unit many feel closer to one another and have a strong self-concept as a result of successful coping in diverse circumstances. Psychologists counseling people with emotional problems related to relocation identify four phases one can anticipate in trying to cope with a move: (1) decision making—the less input one has in the decision, the more potential there is for trouble; (2) preparation, involving mastering the many details preceding a move; (3) separation from the old community, including acceptance of the sadness and loss involved; and (4) reinvestment through involvement in one's new community (Singular 1983, p. 46). These phases are akin to grief work and the rites of passage discussed in Chapters 4 and 11.

HELPING THE MIGRANT

Where is help available for the numerous people in crisis related to migration? Crisis centers and mental health agencies are appropriate for people who are under great stress before a move as well as those who are anxious and upset after the move. Social service agencies and services for aging persons should also provide anticipatory guidance and crisis counseling to all groups forced to move because of a planned project such as urban renewal. Unfortunately, such support and counseling is not available or is not given in many instances.

Case Example: Noreen Anderson

Noreen Anderson, age 61, was confined to her apartment with a serious muscle disease. She was forced to retire at age 58 and had felt lonely and isolated since then. She did not have family in the area but did have many friends. However, they gradually stopped visiting her after she had been confined for a year. Now

her apartment building was being converted to condominiums that she could not afford. The heat had been turned off in March (in a cold northern US city). Everyone in the building had moved out except Noreen, who was unable to move without help. Fortunately, Noreen's phone was not disconnected. She called various social service agencies for help, including the government-funded Welfare Department. Finally, she was referred to a local crisis center.

An outreach crisis counselor went to Noreen's apartment. She expedited an application through a federal housing agency for a place for Noreen in a senior citizen's housing project. The counselor also engaged an interfaith volunteer agency to help Noreen pack, and processed a request for immediate physical supplies through Catholic Charities. Noreen was grateful for the help received after her several desperate telephone calls, but by this time she was depressed and suicidal. The crisis counselor saw her in her new apartment in the senior citizen's housing project for several counseling sessions. She helped Noreen get in touch with old friends again. The counselor encouraged Noreen's friends to visit her on a regular basis. Retired Senior Citizen Volunteers (R.S.V.P.) also visited Noreen, which helped relieve her isolation and loneliness. Noreen was no longer suicidal at termination of the counseling sessions.

Traveler's Aid Society

The Traveler's Aid Society has been doing crisis intervention work with people in transit for years. Caseworkers of this agency see travelers at the peak of their distress. The traveler who calls the Society is often without money, without resources, or fearful in a strange city. In extreme cases, the person may be beaten, robbed, or raped. The Traveler's Aid Society caseworker gets in touch with identified relatives; assures emergency medical services, food, and emergency housing; provides travel money; and assures the traveler a safe trip home. Unfortunately, the Traveler's Aid Society is poorly linked to other crisis services in most communities. It has low visibility as a social service agency, is often poorly funded, and does not operate on a 24-hour basis in most places. A close working relationship with a 24-hour crisis service could remedy this situation. The relative isolation of this agency often results in the Travelers' Aid staff handling suicidal or emotionally upset travelers by themselves, without the support of crisis specialists who should be available.

International Institute and Other Support

The International Institute also helps people in crisis related to immigration. The Institute's unique contribution is crisis work with refugees and immigrants who do not know the local language. Inability to speak a country's language can be the source of acute crises related to housing, employment, health, welfare, and legal matters. Institute workers, all of whom speak several languages, assist refugees and immigrants in these essential life areas.

There is an International Institute in nearly all major metropolitan areas, where most refugees and immigrants first settle. Health and Social Service personnel can refer immigrants who are unaware of this service on arrival. The langauge crisis is so acute for some immigrants that they may be mistaken for insane and taken to a mental hospital. Intervention by a multilingual person is a critical part of care in such cases.

As is the case with the Traveler's Aid Society, this important social service agency has low visibility in the community and is not linked adequately with 24-hour crisis services. Needed linkages may become routine as crisis services become more comprehensive and cosmopolitan (Hoff and Miller 1987).

The actual and potential crises of immigrants and refugees have become more visible as international tensions gave grown. People persecuted or sought out for protest refuge and political asylum in friendly countries with greater frequency. Cooperation between private and public agencies on behalf of these people is paramount to avoid unnecessary distress and crisis. In addition to legal, housing, language, and immediate survival issues, refugees experience the psychological pain of losing their homeland. No matter how we may have been treated, most of us have a strong attachment to our country birth. Whether this bond is broken voluntarily or by threat to life, we need an opportunity to mourn the loss and find ways to substitute for what was left behind. One way that refugees and immigrants cope with their loss is to preserve their customs, art, language, ritual celebrations, and food habits. These practices provide immigrants with the security that comes from association with their familiar cultural heritage. Sensitivity of neighbors and agency personnel to immigrants' cultural values, along with control of our own ethnocentrism, can go a long way in helping refugees feel "at home away from home."

HOMELESSNESS

Some people live in cardboard boxes, ride the subway all night long, or stay in doorways of public buildings until they are asked by the police to move. Some sleep on steel grates to catch steam heat from below. Some battered women and their children move from shelter to shelter, staying the limit at each because battering does not fit the city's criteria of eligibility for emergency housing; one mother of three finally bought a tent and camped in a city park.

There are an estimated 3,000,000 homeless people in the United States, while three or four times that many double up with family and friends.* Unless drastic action is taken, this figure will increase to 19,000,000 by the end of the century. The majority of these people are women and children. Besides having no secure place to stay, homeless people are frequent victims of rape or robbery of their few possessions; homeless youth are often victims of child prostitution; among elderly homeless, some are disabled, some are deaf or blind, and some have symptoms of Alzheimer's disease. Contrary to popular perception, a good percentage of the homeless hold low-paying jobs that do not provide enough to pay inflated rental prices. Many are victims of eviction because of condominium conversions intended for upwardly mobile, mostly white professionals. At no time since the Great Depression have homeless people represented such a cross-section of American society.

Homelessness strips people of their self-respect, denies people of their most elementary rights as citizens, and blights the future of the nation's greatest resource—children. The crisis of homelessness is dramatized in the following poem written by Andy Kane, a homeless man in Boston who is resisting a "fall into the void" (Adams 1988).

When you're homeless in Boston

To be homeless is to be left out
To be left out in the cold.
To be alone and sad
To be kicked like a dog.

Spinning around like a top that's lost its head
To the tunes of a lone midnight
When the cold winds hit to the bone
The bitter reality "To be or not to be?"

All that I know now is to keep moving,
To know the warm stop spots
Bus station, library, airport, train station
A master of transportation depots am I.

When you are homeless in Boston
You play mega-beds every night at the shelter.
Maybe your number will be drawn
So you can get a flop for the night.

When you are homeless in Boston
You become accustomed to writing fiction

---

*In December 1982 the US Congress held its first hearing since the 1930s on homelessness as a national problem.

On your job applications
When address and phone numbers are asked.

When you are homeless in Boston
And staying at one of the shelters
You are told
When to sleep, wake up, eat, shower.

When you are homeless in Boston
You stop believing in yourself,
In God, in your country.
You become ultra-cynical and bitter.

Then you start saying stuff out loud
In public places or on the streets.
People laugh at you.
You become their entertainment.

Soon the mind becomes a jumble
Of mass fragments that seem unpieceable
For when you are homeless in Boston,
You stand in a phone booth
Calling agencies and rental companies.

When you get to the agency, they are polite,
Tell you to come to their office,
Talk, leave—so much for the agencies.

When you are homeless in Boston
You go to the labor pools,
Work for the minimum wage
Which is slavery when we consider
The dollar's purchasing power.

Troubled and distressed by what I see
And experience as you, condo developer,
Rush off to your next deal, and you,
Real estate man, rubbing your hands
At the profits after, of course,
You've disposed of the last tenants.

The New Boston, Quiche Lorraine Tyranny.
The arrogant wealth of the nouveau riche
Expresso bars and slick-talking fools,
Sucking the life blood from the land.

Through this horror
Of real estate speculation,
We can clearly see the life blood,
The Juice, the very soul
Being taken out of Boston.

But, remember, my friends,
Not long ago you started something:
The tea—you threw it overboard.

Come on now, have you forgotten?

Standing in phone booths
Talking to the wind,
Smoking a cigarette,

Standing in phone booths
Calling for help
Calling to God!

The crisis of homelessness is due primarily to the severe cuts in federal funds to build or rehabilitate low-income housing and to the over-priced real estate market that is generally free of obligation to include low and moderate-income housing in their speculative ventures. Haphazard policies and bureaucratic ineptness are also responsible. As Jonathan Kozol (1988) relates from his months with the homeless in one of New York's welfare hotels, the city spends $1900 per month for a family of four, thus supporting enormous profits for a modernized poorhouse. But as Holly, one of Kozol's informants said:

> *All this time I had been looking for apartments I was lots of places that I didn't have the money for. . . . $270 a month was my budget limit (for rent). . . . I used to tell them (the New York City officials): "All the money you will pay for me to stay in a hotel? You can't give me half that money* once *to pay the rent and rent deposit? I could get me an apartment. You won't ever see me any more."*

These problems are all exacerbated in the case of the homeless mentally ill, who are victims of a failed deinstitutionalization program and inadequate community planning (Hoff et al. *in press*).

What do we do for people who have no place to sleep, or who are at risk of dying from exposure to the elements in spite of affluence all around them in the richest country in the world? People often react to the homeless, who appear on a doorstep or beg for a quarter, with embarrassement and discomfort. But regardless of how charitably people respond to individual appeals for help, the crisis of homelessness in a humane, democratic society entails more than personal goodwill or charity. Although there is still a tendency to blame the victim (Ryan 1971), people do not choose to be poor or homeless. As Kip Tiernan (1987) of the Elderly Homeless Coalition in Boston says: "I'm tired of conservatives saying piously, 'Ah yes, the poor—they're always with us.' I'm tired of liberals who wave a cot or a sandwich at me when I shout for justice, not charity." As emphasized throughout this book, a crisis of social origin demands a social response. Thus, the interrelated social, cultural, and economic factors—along with discrimination based on race, sex, and age—that precipitate crises of homelessness must be addressed in a comprehensive proactive manner (Hoff 1983, Rapp and Chamberlain 1985). While we should support individual efforts like Andrew Kane's to market his poem for the Cambridge Homeless Fund, such efforts will never be sufficient to avoid further crises of homelessness without a change in public policies affecting housing (see Crisis Paradigm, third box, social change agentry).

SUMMARY

For happiness we need physical health, a good self-image, meaningful work to support ourselves, and a secure place to live. Many people are threatened with the loss of these basic necessities. For some, such a threat or loss is an occasion of crisis. People in crisis because of these threats to health, self-image, and social security most often come to the attention of the front line workers: nurses, physicians, social workers, employers, clergy, housing authorities, and others close to people's daily struggles. Helping people at these initial crisis points can make enormous differences in the final outcomes of these transition states, while removing the socioeconomic roots of crises like homelessness commands urgent public attention.

REFERENCES

Adams JM: From the streets, a cry of pain. *Boston Globe.* February 1, 1988.

Anders RL: When a patient becomes violent. *Am J Nurs* 1977; 77:1144–1148.

Bartolucci G, Drayer C: An overview of crisis intervention in emergency rooms of general hospitals. *Am J Psych* 1973; 130:953–960.

Boserup E: *Women's Role in Economic Development.* St. Martin's Press, 1970.

Breed W: Five components of a basic suicide syndrome. *Suicide Life-Threat Behavior* 1972; 2:67–97.

Brink P (editor): *Transcultural Nursing.* Prentice-Hall, 1976.

Brody H: *Stories of Sickness.* Yale University Press, 1988.

BWHBC (Boston Women's Health Book Collective): *Our Bodies, Ourselves,* 3rd ed. Simon and Schuster, 1984.

Caplan G: *Principles of Preventive Psychiatry.* Basic Books, 1964.

Childs RE: Maternal psychological conflicts associated with the birth of a retarded child. *Mat Child Health Nurs* 1985; 14(3):175–182.

Chernin K: *The Hungry Self: Women, Eating and Identity.* Harper and Row, 1985.

Conrad P, Kern R (editors): *The Sociology of Health and Illness: Critical Perspectives.* St. Martin's Press, 1981.

Dobash RP, Dobash RE: *Violence against Wives: A Case against the Patriarchy.* Free Press, 1979.

Ehrenreich J (editor): *The Cultural Crisis of Modern Medicine.* Monthly Review Press, 1978.

Ehrenreich B and English D: *For Her Own Good: 150 years of the Experts' Advice to Women.* Anchor Books, 1979.

Etheridge CF: Equality in the family: Comparative analysis and theoretical models. *Int J Wom Stud* 1978; 1:50–62.

Farberow NL: Suicide prevention in the hospital. *Hosp Comm Psych* 1981; 32:99–104.

Farm Aid Rural Management. *Statement of Purpose.* Bismarck, ND, 1987.

Fiumara NJ: Sexual behavior and primary and recurrent herpes genitalis. *Med Asp Hum Sex* (May) 1980; 151–152.

Foster G, Anderson BG: *Medical Anthropology.* Wiley, 1978.

Frankfort E: *Vaginal Politics.* Quadrangle Press, 1972.

Fried M: Grieving for a lost home. In: *The Environment of the Metropolis.* Duhl LJ (editor). Basic Books, 1962.

Fuller B, Foster GM: The effects of family/friend visits vs. staff ineraction on stress/arousal of surgical intensive care patients. *Heart Lung* 1982; 11(5):457–463.

Gans HJ: *The Urban Villagers.* Free Press, 1962.

Garrison J: Network techniques: Case studies in the screening-linking-planning conference method. *Fam Proc* 1974; 13:337–353.

Goldberg H: *The Hazards of Being Male.* New American Library, 1976.

Greenleaf N: *Labor Force Participation by Age of Registered Nurses and Women in Comparable Occupations.* (DN Sci dissertation.) Boston University School of Nursing, 1982.

Greenspan M: *A New Approach to Women and Therapy.* McGraw-Hill, 1983.

Hamilton R: *The Herpes Book.* Houghton-Mifflin, 1980.

Hansell N: *The Person in Distress.* Human Sciences Press, 1976.

Hoff LA: Interagency coordination for people in crisis. *Inform Referral* 1983; 5(1):79–89.

Hoff LA, Miller N: *Programs for People in Crisis: A Guide for Educators, Administrators and Clinical Trainers.* Boston: Northeastern University Custom Book Program, 1987.

Hoff MD et al.: Double jeopardy: Serving the homeless mentally ill *(in press)*.

Hutt ML, Gibby RG: *The Mentally Retarded Child: Development Education and Treatment,* 3rd ed. Allyn and Bacon, 1976.

James CR, Stall R, Gifford SM (editors): *Anthropology and Epidemiology.* Reidel, 1986.

Jamison KR, Wellisch DK, Pasnaw RO: Psychosocial aspects of mastectomy. 1. The women's perspective. *Am J Psych* 1978; 135:432–435.

Kanter RM: *Men and Women of the Corporation.* Basic Books, 1977.

Kavanagh KH: The cost of caring: Nursing on a psychiatric intensive care unit. *Hum Org* 1988; 47(3):242–251.

Kessler RC, McLeod JD: Sex differences in vulnerability to life events. *Am Sociol Rev* 1984; 49:620–631.

Kirchheimer A: Of women and men and tasks. *Boston Globe.*

Knox RA: Study finds much surgery is needless. *Boston Globe,* 1981.

Kozol J: *Rachel and Her Children: Homeless Families in America.* Crown, 1988.

Kuenzi SH, Fenton MV: Crisis intervention in acute care areas. *Am J Nurs* 1975; 75:830–834.

Landy D (editor): *Culture, Disease and Healing.* Macmillan, 1977.

Lindemann E: *Beyond Grief.* Jason Aronson, 1979.

Maxwell MB; The use of social networks to help cancer patients maximize support. *Cancer Nurs* 1982; 5:275–281.

McCloskey JC: How to make the most of body image theory in nursing practice. *Nurs 76* 1976; 6:68–72.

McElroy A, Townsend PK: *Medical Anthropology in Ecological Perspective.*

Millman M: Medical mortality review: A cordial affair. In: *Dominant Issues in Medical Sociology.* Schwartz HD, Kart CS (editors). Addison-Wesley, 1978.

Moore LG et al.: *The Biocultural Basis of Health.* Mosby, 1980.

Morrison AM, White RP, Van Velsor E: Executive women; substance plus style. *Psychology Today,* 21(8): 18–27, 1987.

Murray R (editor): The concept of body image. In: *Nursing Clinics of North America.* Saunders, 1972.

Olson KR, Schellenberg RP: Farm stressors. *Am J Comm Psychol* 1986; 14(5):555–569.

Parkes CM: *Bereavement: Studies in Grief in Adult Life.* Penguin Books, 1975.

Pearce D, McAdoo H: *Women and Children: Alone and in Poverty.* Washington, DC: National Advisory Councol on Economic Opportunity, 1982.

Penman DT et al.: The impact of mastectomy on self-concept and social function: A combined cross-sectional and longitudinal study with comparison groups. *Wom Health;* 1987 11(3/4):101–130.

Polak P: The Crisis of Admission. *Soc Psych* 1967; 2:150–157.

Polak P: Social systems intervention. *Arch Gen Psych* 1971; 25:110–117.

Polak P: A model to replace psychiatric hospitalization. *J Nerv Ment Dis* 1976; 162:13–22

Ptacek LJ et al.: Respite care for families of children with severe handicaps: An evaluation study of parent satisfaction. *J Comm Psychol* 1982; 10:222–227.

Rapp CA, Chamberlain R: Case management for chronically mentally ill. *Soc Work* 1985; 30(5):417–422.

Reiter RR (editor): *Toward an Anthropology of Women.* Monthly Review Press, 1975.

Reverby S: *Ordered to Care: The Dilemma of American Nursing, 1850–1945.* Cambridge University Press, 1987.

Richardson BK: Psychiatric inpatients' perception of seclusion room experience. *Nurs Res* (July/August) 1987; 36:234–238.

Roberts JI: *Beyond Intellectual Sexism: A New Woman, a New Reality.* New York: David McKay Company, 1976.

Rubenstein C: Real men don't earn less than their wives. *Psychol Today* 1982; 16:36–41.

Ryan W: *Blaming the Victim.* Vintage Books, 1971.

Schaef A, Fassel D: Hooked on work. *New Age J* (Jan–Feb) 1988; 42–48, 57–63.

Schain W: Patients' rights in decision making: The case for personalism versus paternalism in health care. *Cancer* 1980; 46:1035–1041.

Schoonover P: Personal communication, 1987.

Shannon J: Politics of heroin and alcohol. Workshop: Role of the suicide prevention center in substance abuse treatment. Ninth Annual Meeting, American Association of Suicidology, Los Angeles, CA, 1976.

Seager J, Olson A: *Women in The World: An International Altas.* Simon & Schuster, 1986.

Shipes E, Lehr S: Sexuality and the male cancer patient. *Cancer Nurs* 1982; 5:375–381.

Sidel R: *Women and Children Last. The Plight of Poor Women in Affluent America.* Penguin Books, 1986.

Singular S: Moving on. *Psychol Today* 1983; 17:40–47.

Skorupka P, Bohnet N: Primary caregivers' perceptions of nursing behaviors that best meet their needs in a home care hospice setting. *Cancer Nurs* 1982; 5:371–374.

Sommers, T & Shields, L. 1987. *Women take care.* Gainsville, Fl: TRIAD, 1987.

Sontag S: *Illness as Metaphor.* Farrar, Straus and Giroux, 1978.

Surgeon Generals' Workshop on Violence and Public Health *Report.* Washington, DC: Health Resources and Services Administration (HRSA), 1986.

Tiernan K: They're elderly and homeless and falling through the cracks. *Boston Globe.* November 1, 1987.

Turner RJ, Avison WR: Gender and depression: Assessing exposure and vulnerability to life events in a chronically strained population. Paper presented at APHA meeting. New Orleans, October 1987.

Verbrugge LM: Work satisfaction and physical health. *J Commun Health* 1982; 7(4):262–283.

Weisel J: Helping kids face the hospital. *Parade,* 1979.

Werner-Beland JA (editor): *Grief Responses to Long-term Illness and Disability.* Reston, 1980.

Wilhelm D: Dairymen plead for farms' survival. *Boston Globe.* February 7, 1988.

World Federation of Public Health Associations. *Women and Health: Information for Action Issue Paper.* Washington, DC: American Public Health Association, 1986.

Yankelovich D: How students control their drug crisis. *Psychol Today* 1975; 9:39–42.

Yllo K, Straus MA: Patriarchy and violence against wives: The impact of structural and normative factors. Presented at the National Conference for Family Violence Researchers, Durham, New Hampshire, 1981.

Zborowski M: Cultural components in responses to pain. *J Soc Iss* 1952; 8:16–30. Also reprinted in: *The Sociology of Health and Illness: Critical Perspectives.* Conrad P, Kern R (editors). St. Martin's Press, 1981.

CHAPTER 11

STRESS AND CHANGE DURING LIFE PASSAGES

RITES OF PASSAGE: TRADITIONAL AND CONTEMPORARY

Transitions, passages, and status and role change: How are these terms related? What do they mean for people in crisis? Webster defines transition as "passage from one place, state, stage of development to another; change; the period in which such a change is effected." The *Dictionary of the Social Sciences* defines status as "the place of individuals and groups with respect to the distribution of prestige, rights, obligations, power and authority within a society." People are evaluated socially by their contribution to the common good and by other criteria such as birth, marital alliance, sex, race, age, sexual preference, wealth, and power (Mousnier 1969, p. 15). One's status is related to but different from one's role: status refers to *who* a person is, while role is *what* a person is expected to do within a given social-cultural milieu (Zelditch 1968, p. 251).

What do these social concepts have to do with people in crisis in the clinical sense? It is, after all, a normal part of human life to grow and develop through childhood, adolescence, middle age, old age, to death. It is also common to marry, give birth, and lose one's spouse. Anthropologists and psychoanalysts for years have referred to these transition states as "life crises" (for example, Chapple and Coon 1942, Erikson 1963, Freud 1950, Giovannini 1983, Kimball 1960). There is a difference, however, in the anthropologic concept of life crisis and its common usage by crisis intervention clinicians, even though, as Golan (1981, p. 7) states, there is something in common between the two conceptions of high stress situations. In anthropology, "life crisis" refers to a highly significant, expectable event or phase in the life cycle, marking one's passage to a new social status, with accompanying changes in rights and duties. Traditionally, such status changes are accompanied by ritual (such as puberty and marriage rites) designed to assist the individual in fulfilling new role expectations, and to buffer the stress associated with these critical—though normal-life—events. In traditional societies, families and the entire community, led by "ritual experts," are intensely involved in the life passages of individual community members. This anthropological concept of life crisis corresponds roughly to the "anticipated" crises discussed in the clinical literature on crisis (see "The Origins of Crisis" in Chapter 2). "Crisis" in its clinical meaning flows from the tradition of Caplan (1964) and others (such as Golan 1969), who emphasize the sudden onset and brief duration of acute emotional upsets in response to identifiable traumatic events. In this sense, adolescence, marriage, giving birth, and middle age are not crises except in extraordinary circumstances, such as when the bridegroom fails to show up, or the expected infant is stillborn—unanticipated traumatic events that accompany the transition. Transition states are "critical" life phases, not necessarily traumatic, but with the *potential* for activating an "acute emotional upset" in the clinical sense. They are turning points, social-psychological processes involving the challenge of successfully completing social, developmental, and instrumental tasks such as:

- Changing social role, such as single to married.
- Changing image of self, such as young to middle-aged, healthy to sick.
- Gathering material resources to support a new family member.

As "turning points" in the developmental process, these "life crises" fit the classic definition of crisis as a period of both danger and opportunity. They also highlight the importance of social, cultural, and material supplies (Caplan 1964) necessary for individuals to avoid acute emotional upset. Another connection between the anthropological and clinical definitions of crisis is the fact that individuals in acute emotional upset do not exist in a social vacuum; they are members of particular cultural communities. People in crisis are therefore influenced by social expectations of how to behave and by values guiding their interpretation of expected and unexpected life events—factors that figure strongly in the way one resolves a particular emotional crisis.

Thus, if it is unclear *who* a person is, *what* he or she is expected to do, or *how* the person fits into familiar social arrangements based on cultural values, status or role ambiguity is activated. Status and role ambiguity can create so much stress that a person with conflicting or changed roles may withdraw from social interaction or may try to change the social structure to redefine the anxiety-provoking statuses (Douglas 1966, Weiss 1976, Zelditch 1968). For example:

- If pregnant teenage girls sense that they are expected to drop out of high school, they are more likely to be poorly educated, unemployed, dependent on welfare, and marry early, which enhances their future crisis proneness.

- If widowed people sense that they are a threat to social groups of married people, they may feel cut off from social support and thereby increase their risk of emotional crisis around traumatic events.
- If men interpret their wives' higher earnings as a threat to their image as primary providers of material support, the risk of violence against wives, divorce, and heart disease for husbands increases (Rubenstein 1982).

An important means of reducing the stress and minimizing the chaos associated with such role ambiguity is the constructive use of ritual. One of the most dramatic differences between traditional and urban or industrialized societies is the relative importance of ritual and the separation between the sacred and profane. With an increase in industrialization comes a corresponding increase in secularization and decrease in sacred ceremonialism. In his classic work *Rites of Passage*, van Gennep (1909, p. 11) distinguished three phases in the ceremonies associated with an individual's "life crises": rites of separation (prominent in funeral ceremonies); transition rites (important in initiation and pregnancy); and rites of incorporation (prominent in marriage). A complete schema of rites of passage theoretically includes all three phases. For example, a widow is *separated* from her husband by death; occupies a *liminal* (transitional) status for a time, and finally is *reincorporated* into a new marriage relationship (Goody 1962).

These rites protect the individual during the hazardous process of life passages, times considered potentially dangerous to the person if not supported by the community. Ritual thus makes public what is private and social what is personal, and gives the individual new knowledge and strength (LaFontaine 1977, Leach 1954, p. 15–16, Turner 1967, p. 50). For example:

- A person who loses a loved one needs a public occasion to mourn.
- A couple who are intimate and cohabiting desire social approval (often through marriage).
- A dying person who is anointed has new knowledge of the imminence of death and greater strength to accept death.
- A divorced person needs community support following a failed marriage—in short, a ritual for public recognition and acceptance of a new role.

Rites of passage are not developed to the same extent by all societies (Fried and Fried 1980). Until recently, it was generally assumed that rites of passage are relatively unimportant in modern societies: public and private spheres of activity and various social roles (such as worker, parent, or political leader) are more clearly separated than in traditional societies and hence in less need of ritual specification. However, there is no evidence that people in a secular urban world have less need for ritualized expression during transition states (Kimball 1960, pp. xvi–xvii). The modern discarding of ritual can be understood in part as a move toward greater freedom of the individual. Ritual can be a powerful mechanism for maintaining the status quo in traditional and contemporary societies (Durkheim 1915), less ritual implies more personal freedom. Thus, while some rituals protect the individual during stressful transitions, they have a communal purpose as well. The social function of ritual is illustrated in the following examples of traditional and contemporary rites of passage at adolescence and marriage.

Case Example: Adolescence among the Samburu

Among the traditional Samburu of Kenya, a polygynous gerontocracy [society ruled by elders] as described by anthropologist Spencer, young men are kept in a marginal position vis-a-vis the total society and are forbidden to marry until around age 30, an institution known as "moranhood." The stated reasons for the extension of moranhood and delay in marriage age of young men is that they are not worthy because of their "delinquency" and that there are not enough marriageable women available. The real reason, however, is more probably to preserve the concentration of power and wives among the older men (Hoff 1978, Spencer 1965, 1973, 1978). Similarly, the controversial practice of female "circumcision" in some traditional societies impresses on women the norm of conformity to traditional gender roles (Hosken 1981, Ngugi 1965).

Case Example: American College Campuses

Thirty miles from Reno, under a star-filled desert sky, a lone pickup truck grinds to a halt alongside the Pyramid Lake Highway. Three men slide out of the cab and stagger to the back of the truck. All wear black felt hats adorned with a yellow patch that depicts the setting sun. The three grin at the sight that greets them: five youths, their clothing flecked with vomit, are sprawled across the truckbed like bags of cement.

The five are ordered to get up, and four struggle to comply by easing their way down from the tailgate to the road. One remains on the truck bed, a dark-haired giant wearing a thick Fu Manchu mustache. The three youths with hats are amused and clamber aboard to wake him. They laugh drunkenly as they shake him.

Suddenly, one youth tears open the limp young man's coat and puts an ear to his chest. All laughter ceases. The only sound is the whistling wind that bends back the sagebrush as it passes.

The dead youth was a 23-year-old University of Nevada football player. His death concluded a three-day drinking spree required for admission into a suspended, but still active, campus club called the Sundowners. . . . A second Sundowner pledge was hospitalized the same night. His blood alcohol count registered .456 (a person is legally drunk with a .10 reading).

A grand jury investigating the case determined that the five pledges had been pummeled, ridiculed, cursed, and intimidated by approximately 10 of the 30 Sundowner members . . . with the apparent encouragement of the membership (Nuwer 1978).

Conservatively, about one million youths on American college campuses pledge annually to perpetuate the established beliefs, ideals, and values of fraternal societies. Not unlike their Samburu brothers who are considered "unworthy" of marriage, or a Somalian sister who undergoes circumcision so as not to be a disgrace to her family (Ngugi 1965) American college youth during admission to fraternities undergo the ritual purification of "hazing." There is a public outcry against hazing rituals in the United States by parents who have lost children—a total of 60 since 1971—to this destructive practice. As a result, many states now have anti-hazing legislation. In Massachusetts, for example, the law forbids any dangerous initiation activities, requires pledges to be informed of the law, and specifies punishment of violators or those who fail to report hazing.

Case Example: Marriage among the Samburu

The social value imbuing everything in Samburu society is *nkanyit*. This keystone of Samburu morality includes notions of respect, honor, shame, duty, politeness, avoidance, and decency, with the overriding emphasis on respect. A woman is taught to respect, fear, and avoid the elders from an early age. Her training induces her to accept the difficulties of marriage to an elder two to three times older than herself, a situation that makes the marital strains more understandable. As in most societies, girls and women are valued less than boys and men; all girls are brought up with the idea of being good wives, an investment for their kin and husbands.

After marriage a woman rarely goes home again, as this would endanger the tenuous stability of the marriage even more. Samburu women learn very early their inevitable lot of complete subordination and that the reputation of the clan hinges on their good behavior, not unlike the sexual double standard elsewhere. These notions are reinforced through the marriage ritual. Spencer characterizes the marriage ritual as a form of "brainwashing" and marriage for the average woman as *the* crisis of her life (Spencer 1965, 1973, 1978, Hoff 1978).

Case Example: Marriage for American Women in the 1980s

Unlike their Samburu sisters, marriage and especially the ritual of the wedding day itself are high points in the lives of many American women. Like their Samburu sisters, however, most American girls and women are socialized to view themselves as failures if they cannot marry and retain a husband. Caught up in the emotinal "high" of the wedding ritual with dreams of "living happily ever after," the average bride is unconscious of the social significance of the ritual of being "given away" by her father and relinquishing her own name to assume that of her husband (Chapman and Gates 1977). Many women willingly interrupt or delay careers to support their families through unpaid and devalued household work. Many are happy and secure in their role and testify that their dreams have come true. Millions, however, are battered, as the marriage licence seems to have been transformed for some into a "hitting licence" (Straus, Gelles, and Steinmetz 1980); they feel trapped and become convenient objects of violence (Browne 1987, Dobash and Dobash 1979, Hoff 1984; see also Woman Battering in Chapter 8). Or they become "displaced homemakers" through widowhood (Jacobs 1979, Lopata 1973). Many women are left behind for younger women, especially after the age of 40, when women are considered "over the hill" while men become more "distinguished." Often this occurs after women have sacrificed education and career opportunities in order to fulfill the social expectation of building a stable home. Among women heading households alone, 55% are poor (Newberger, Melnicoe, Newberger 1986, p. 708).

These examples suggest that ritual serves to maintain society or various subgroups in a state of traditional equilibrium—each person behaving according to accepted roles. As discussed in earlier chapters, however, maintaining traditional social roles, often reinforced through the negative use of ritual, can exact a considerable price from certain individuals, for example, more heart disease and suicides for men, social isolation or death for adolescents by suicide or manslaughter, and battering or poverty for women. The case examples also illustrate a continuum between traditional and contemporary rites of passage and suggest that people in all times and places need ritual. The questions are: what kind of rituals are needed, and under what circumstances should they take place? How can ritual be helpful for the individual in transition as well as for society?

Ritual holds a paradoxic place in a secularized society. On the one hand, it is viewed as a sign of an earlier stage of social evolution. On the other hand, certain rituals are retained, but without critical examination of their expression in contemporary life. In modern life, three general approaches to ritual are observed: (1) Ritual is often denied any relevance. (2) Some of its most oppressive and destructive aspects for individuals remain from ancient tradition or are recycled to include the abuse of alcohol, guns, or cars, and medical technology to prolong life. (3) When ritual is observed it is highly individualized, as in the rite of psychotherapy, in which the 50-minute session and other practices are observed. Such rituals are complemented by "medicalization" and its focus on individuals rather than groups in modern urban societies.

These interpretations of ritual, however, are in the process of change. Meaningless and destructive rituals are being dropped entirely or are being questioned. For example, many American women today retain their last names after marriage, and *both* parents of the bride *and* groom (rather than only the father of the bride) participate in the marriage ceremony. Similarly, cultural awareness is replacing the condemnation of "savage" customs of "primitive" peoples (Fanon 1978, Paul 1978). Barbaric rituals, oppression, and violence are no longer seen as the province of any one society, traditional or modern.

Our task as crisis workers is to consider the place of ritual during critical turning points of life, particularly as it relates to crisis prevention. Whether or not critical life passages also become occasions of emotional crisis will depend on:

1. What the individual does to prepare for anticipated transitions.
2. The nature and extent of social support available to the individual during turning points.
3. The occurrence of unanticipated hazardous events (such as fire, accident, illness, or loss of job) during critical phases of life.
4. Our creativity as crisis workers in helping individuals and

families develop positive contemporary rites of passage where there are few or none.

Traditional and contemporary rites of passage are compared and the continuity between them illustrated in Table 11-1. The successful passage of individuals through critical turning points in the developmental process depends on a combination of personal and social factors (O'Neill and O'Neill 1974, Sheehy 1976). Transition states highlight the dynamic relationship between the individual, family, and society (see Privacy, Intimacy, Community in Chapter 5). For example, adolescents who choose marriage and/or parenthood although they are personally unfit for them may become liabilities to society, and may face more complex problems during later stages of development. On the other hand, the reason they are personally unfit might be traced to inadequate support from adults and to the complex social, economic, and cultural factors that affect adolescents and their families (Newberger, Melnicoe, and Newberger 1986).

The role of individuals and families during transition states demands the successful completion of several tasks. For instance, among the traditional LoDagaa in Ghana (Goody 1962), widows are metaphorically buried by being dressed in premarital "fibres" to signify that they are again adolescents without husbands. They are also fed, as a symbolic last supper of husband and wife and as a test of the widow's possible complicity in her husband's death. The widow's acceptance of food is equivalent to an oath to the ancestors of her innocence. The widow cooks porridge and flicks some on her husband's shrine to show that she has not committed adultery. These rituals are dramatic in that they involve not only the individual and the family, but the entire community.

In contrast, in contemporary society there is the stereotype of the widow who sets the table every night for her dead husband. A possible reason for this behavior may be that the widow had no social, public occasion to cook her "last supper." She lacks the necessary community support to separate from her previous role, abandon her private illusion that her husband is still alive, and proceed to a new role without her husband. This example illustrates the tremendous importance of moving beyond the individual and the family to such social creations as widow-to-widow clubs—a contemporary substitute for the elaborate death rituals of traditional societies (See Loss, Change, and Grief Work in Chapter 4).

Golan (1981, pp. 21–22) outlines the specific tasks to be accomplished by individuals and families during transition states. Her division of "material-arrangemental" tasks (such as exploring resources and choices in the new role) and psychosocial or affective tasks (such as dealing with feelings of loss and longing for the past) corresponds to the emotional, cognitive, and behavioral steps in effective crisis coping (see Chapter 4). However, the effectiveness of these individual and family coping strategies greatly depends on the social and cultural setting. If a society is poor in constructive ritual, if familiar, secure routines and supports in an old role are not

Table 11-1

Rites of Passage in Comparative Perspective

		Contemporary American Rites	
Life Passage	**Traditional Rites***	**Unexamined or Questionable**	**Newly Emerging or Suggested**
Birth	Attended by family and/or midwife; birth occurs in natural squatting position Death risk is high if there are complications	Medicalized birth: pubic shaving, ultrasound, drugs, episiotomy or forceps, horizontal position Absence of family and friends unless specially arranged Death risk in the US is the highest among 15 developed countries	Natural childbirth aided by husband's or friends' coaching in home or birthing center, attended by midwife with backup medical care for complications Death risk is low when attended by properly trained midwife and medical backup is available for special cases
Adolescence	Puberty rites	Hazing on college campuses Religious rites of confirmation and Bar Mitzvah† Obtaining driver's licenses†	Supervised college initiation Support and education groups in high schools, churches, and colleges, such as those concerning menstruation, sexuality, driving responsibly without drinking, and parenthood Relating traditional religious rites to modern life
Intimate relationships: beginnings and endings	Betrothal and marriage rites; required remarriage of widow; or, remarriage may be forbidden	Bridal showers; stag parties† Traditional marriage rites	Egalitarian marriage ceremony and contract Consciousness-raising groups for men and women regarding traditional versus egalitarian male and female roles Divorce ceremonies Support groups for the divorced or for parents without partners
Middle age	Not generally ritualized; general increase in social value and respect by community; postmenopausal women may be regarded as asexual	Labelling of menopause as "illness"; individual psychotherapy and drugs for depression; estrogen replacement therapy for women Men past youth become more "distinguished"; women are often devalued further	Education and peer support groups for menopausal women Support groups for couples to redefine marriage relationship to avoid "empty nest" and other midlife crises

Table 11-1

Rites of Passage in Comparative Perspective (*continued*)

Life Passage	Traditional Rites*	Contemporary American Rites: Unexamined or Questionable	Contemporary American Rites: Newly Emerging or Suggested
Old age	Not generally ritualized; general increase in social value and respect by family and community Infirm elderly are cared for by family	Forced retirement Institutional placement for care	Economic and social policies to support care of elderly at home; respite services for caretakers Senior citizen programs such as part-time or shared jobs
Death	Usually elaborate, extended rituals involving family and entire community	Eighty percent die in institutions with restricted family involvement Mortician has become the main "ritual expert" Children often barred from death and burial rituals Prescription of tranquilizers to survivors after death of a loved one	Social support to aid in "grief work" Hospice care for the dying; support for family to care for dying member at home Support groups for cancer patients Inclusion of children in death and burial rituals Enhancement of funeral director's role to assist with grief work Widow-to-Widow and other self-help groups for survivors

*These rites vary widely among societies. No attempt is made to summarize them here; they are cited to illustrate continuity with modern practice. For an introduction to traditional transition rituals and further references, see Fried and Fried (1980).

†These rites are not always used to their greatest positive potential.

replaced, and if there is little awareness of the need for social support, even the strongest individuals may be unnecessarily scarred during passage through life's developmental stages. The challenge of moving on to a new stage of development or role becomes a threat: "Will I succeed or fail?" "What will people think if I fail?" "No . . . I don't think I can face having this baby—not without the help of its father." "Life just isn't worth living if I can't keep on working. . . . I'm worth more dead than alive."

Keeping in mind the traditional and contemporary rites of passage and their relationship to stress and crisis in modern society, we can discuss the hazards and opportunities of these normal passages from birth to death.

During these passages, crisis counselors and health and mental health professionals can be thought of as contemporary "ritual experts" (see Crisis Paradigm, third box, lower circle.)

BIRTH AND PARENTHOOD

STRESS AND CRISIS POINTS OF PARENTHOOD

The state of parenthood places continous demands on a person from the time of conception until at least the child's eighteenth birthday. Parents must adjust to include an additional member in their family group. Such adjustment is especially difficult for first-time parents. Many people assume the role of parenthood willingly. Such parents regard their children as a welcome burden. The unique pleasure and challenge of bearing and nurturing a child through childhood into adult life outweighs the ordinary problems of parenthood.

Some parents fall into their role unwillingly or use it to escape from less tolerable roles. Consider, for example, the adolescent who seeks relief from a disturbed family home and uses pregnancy to force an early marriage, or the woman who may have more chlidren than she can properly care for emotionally and physically. Some women have been socialized to view themselves as having no other significant role than mother and wife. Others do not limit their pregnancies because of religious beliefs forbidding artificial contraception. Still others lack the knowledge and means to limit their pregnancies. Unwanted children and their parents are more crisis-prone than others. Emotional, social, and material poverty are imporatant contributors to their crisis vulnerability (Donner 1972, Le Masters 1965).*

All parents, whether or not their children were wanted, are under stress and strain in their parental role. Parenthood requires a constant giving of self. Except for the joy of self-fulfillment and watching a child grow and develop, the parent-child relationship is essentially nonreciprocal. Infants, toddlers, and young children need continuous care and supervision. In their natural state of dependency they give, in return for their parents' caring, the needy love of a child that says, in effect, "I am helpless without you, take care of me, protect me."

Some children, in fact, are not only dependent and needy but for various reasons are a source of grief to their parents. Their difficult behaviors, for example, trouble at school or drug abuse, often signal trouble in the parents' marriage or in the entire family system.

*See Newberger, Melnicoe, and Newberger (1986) for a review of the complex factors contributing to crises in the American family

Sometimes parents try to deal with these troubles by themselves, struggling for a long time with whatever resources they have. Often they are ashamed to acknowledge that there is a problem with the child. They view any problem as a reflection of self-failure. Still other parents may not have access to child and family resources for help, either because the resources do not exist or because they cannot afford them.

Chronic problems of parenthood often persist until a crisis occurs and finally forces parents to seek outside help. Common examples of ongoing problems are a child's getting into trouble with the law, running away from home, becoming pregnant during adolescence, being expelled from school, or making a suicide attempt (see Chapters 5, 6 and 8).

Parents usually seem surprised when these problems occur, but evaluation of the whole family often reveals signs of trouble that were formerly unobserved or ignored. Teachers, recreation directors, pastors, and guidance counselors who are sensitive to the needs of children and adolescents can help prevent some of these crises. They should urge parents to participate in a family counseling program *early,* at the first sign of a problem. It is important for counselors and parents to keep in mind that even if preventive programs are lacking, it is never too late to act. An acute crisis situation provides, once again, the opportunity for parents and child to move in the direction of growth and development, and for the parents to fulfill their needs for generativity.

COMMON CRISIS POINTS FOR PARENTS

Common points of crisis for parents include the following:

Death of a Child

Crisis often occurs after the death of a child not only because of the parents' acute loss, but because the death requires parents to reorder their expectations about the normal progression of life to death (that is, parents usually precede their children in death). Thus, the loss of a child is like no other death experience. Some claim it is felt more acutely than loss of a spouse. It is also keenly painful to accept the fact that death has cut off the child's passage through life. Besides being a profound loss, death of a child threatens the parents' perception of parenthood and the normal life cycle (Knapp 1987).

The sudden death of infants is known as crib death. The exact cause of these deaths is still unknown, hence the medical designation: sudden infant death syndrome (SIDS). With no warning signs, the parents or babysitter finds the infant dead in its crib. They bring the infant to the hospital emergency room in the desperate but futile hope of reviving it. The parents or caregiver have fears and guilt that they may somehow have caused the death. The fact that emergency room staff may look suspicious or blaming of the parents complicates this crisis. Indeed, the emergency staff must rule out the possbility of child battering, which they cannot do without examination.

Whether or not the child was battered, emergency personnel should withhold judgment. Parents in either case are in crisis and need understanding and support. Those in crisis over sudden infant deaths should be offered the opportunity to express their grief in private and with the support of a nurse. Hospital chaplains can often assist during this time and should be called in accordance with the parents' wishes. Parents should also be given information about self-help groups of other parents whose infants died suddenly in their cribs.

The most widely known and used group for parents whose infants have died is the Sudden Infant Death Syndrome Foundation. This is a national organization with chapters in all states and major cities. The program includes support from other parents, counseling from maternal-child nurse specialists, education through films, and a speakers bureau with medical and lay experts on the topic.*

The following case example illustrates the crisis of SIDS for parents and how negative outcomes of this crisis might have been avoided through crisis intervention by the pediatrician and others.

Case Example: Lorraine

I can't begin to tell you what my life was like before Doris at our local counseling center helped me. Six months ago my second child died from what they call "crib death." She was two months old. When Deborah stopped breathing at home I called the rescue squad. They resuscitated her and took her to the hospital. Deborah was kept in the intensive care unit for two months. Finally, the hospital and doctor insisted that we take her home. When we did, she died the very same day. I was completely grief stricken, especially since I am 41 years old and had waited so long to have a second child. Our other child, David, is seven. I just couldn't accept the fact that Deborah was dead. My husband and the doctors kept telling me to face reality, but I kept insisting on an answer from the pediatrician as to why Deborah had died. I began having chest pains and problems breathing. Several times my husband called the ambulance and had me taken to the hospital for elaborate heart tests. My doctor told me there was nothing physically wrong with me.

I went home and things got worse. My husband became im-

*Further information about SIDS is available from: National SIDS Foundation, Inc., 310 South Michigan Avenue, Chicago, IL 60604; telephone: 312-663-0650.

patient and annoyed. I worried day and night about doing something wrong with David and eventually causing his death. The school principal finally called me to say that David was having problems at school. I realized I was being overprotective, but I couldn't help myself. The school recommended that we go to a child guidance clinic with David. I resisted and went back, instead, to my pediatrician and insisted once again on knowing the cause of Deborah's death. The pediatrician was apparently tired of my demands and recommended that I see a psychiatrist. I felt he was probably right, but also felt we couldn't afford a psychiatrist; we had spent so much money on medical and hospital bills during the past year. I became so depressed that suicide began to seem like my only way out. One night after an attack of chest pain and a crying spell, I was so desperate that I called the suicide prevention center. The counselor referred me to the local counseling center where I saw Doris.

At first I was terrified at the thought of going to a public place to get help. Our family had always seen only private doctors. Except for our money problems, I would never have accepted the center's recommendation. But they assured me that the crisis and counseling center was for *anyone* who had a problem. I can't begin to tell you how my life changed after a few weeks of help from Doris. We discovered together that I was suffering from a delayed grief reaction. Through several counseling sessions I was able to truly mourn the loss of my child, which I had not really done through all those months of trying to keep a "stiff upper lip" and be "brave" as my doctor and husband wanted me to be. I also discovered that I was feeling regret and some guilt for becoming pregnant in the first place. My doctor had warned me of the dangers. Doris and I included my husband in some of the counseling sessions. On her recommendation I finally joined a group of other parents whose infants had died of crib death. I began to understand my fear of causing David's probable death and could finally let go of my overprotectiveness of him.

I didn't know that places like this crisis and counseling center existed. I only wish I hadn't waited so long before I finally got help.

While crib death has special features, the death of other children is also traumatic and requires similar support and opportunities for grief work. "The Compassionate Friends" is a self-help group offering friendship and understanding to bereaved parents after the death of a child—by illness, accident, or suicide. This international organization was founded by a pastor in England and now has over 200 chapters around the United States.*

*Information about its purpose and how to begin a chapter can be obtained from: The Compassionate Friends, National Headquarters, P.O. Box 1347, Oakbrook, IL 60522; telephone: 312-990-0010.

Birth of a Stillborn Child

The response of a mother at this crisis point is similar to that of mothers giving birth to a handicapped child: anger, loss, guilt, and questioning (see Chapter 10). Mothers ask: "Why did this have to happen to me? What did I do wrong? What did I do to deserve this? Parents' need for grief work and the critical role of medical and hospital personnel is highlighted in the case of Gerry.

Case Example: Gerry Henderson

Gerry Henderson, age 29, gave birth to a stillborn child. Immediately after delivery the child was taken out of the delivery room. Gerry never saw the baby; she was asleep from the anesthetic given her. The obstetrician told Gerry's husband Tom that the child was stillborn and convinced him not to see the baby though he asked to do so. Together with hospital authorities, Tom, who was numb and frightened, made immediate arrangements to cremate the baby without consulting Gerry. The baby was not given a name. No one from the family attended the burial service; it was handled completely by hospital authorities. Tom was convinced that this was the best way to spare his wife any unnecessary grief.

When Gerry woke up, these facts were announced to her by her husband and the nurse. She was beside herself with shock and grief, but Tom thought it best not to talk about the matter. Gerry was essentially alone in the hospital with her grief. The nurses had a hard time handling their own grief, and so were unable to offer Gerry support.

When Gerry returned home from the hospital, her cousin invited her to come for a visit. Gerry's cousin had just had a new baby herself. Gerry felt she could not possibly face seeing another woman's live and healthy baby without breaking down. She was urged, however, to make the visit by her mother-in-law and husband who said, "After all, you have to face reality sometime." Gerry refused to go to her cousin's house, though this caused further strain between her and her husband. Gerry's grief and tension reached a point that she began hearing the sound of a baby crying at various times during the day and during her sleepless nights. Since she knew there was no baby, Gerry was afraid she was going crazy. She was barely able to complete simple household chores.

After one week of lonely agony, Gerry walked into a nearby crisis clinic, where she cried inconsolably and poured out the above story to a counselor. Gerry's husband Tom was asked to come in as well. Through several crisis counseling sessions, it became apparent that Tom was as shocked and grief stricken as his wife, but believed that the only way to handle the infant's death was to "act like a man," not talk about his grief, and try to keep going as though nothing had happened. The cremation and not naming the baby were Tom's symbolic way of trying to wash away the problem. Gerry's mother-in-law and cousin joined in one of the counseling sessions. They were helped to understand the importance of not forcing Gerry to relate to another child while she was actively grieving over the loss of her own.* Their support was enlisted in ways that Gerry decided would be helpful to her at that time.

After Gerry and Tom did their "grief work" with the help of the counselor, Gerry was able to resume a normal life without the child she had anticipated. Eventually she was also able to relate to her cousin and her cousin's child without hostility.

The lack of contemporary rites of passage for mourning and dealing with death in hospitals is highlighted by another recent example:

Case Example: Infant Death

A woman gave birth to twins who both died about 10 minutes after birth. The parents were not religious and struggled alone with their decision about how to mark the short life and death of their children. Their grief work was not helped by the fact that people kept referring to the infants as "stillborn." To the mother especially, it was very important for people to realize and acknowledge that she had given birth to live, not dead, infants.

Miscarriage is another common source of misunderstanding. Because many women miscarry without knowing it, some regard all miscarriages as the simple passing of body fluids. An insensitive "You can always try again" fails to take into account the mother's bonding with the unborn life or that she may not want to try again. A mother needs to mourn this loss within the

*Note, in contrast, that Mona Anderson (Chapter 10) was encouraged to see her sister's child after grieving and accepting the reality of her own child's condition; Gerry's loss was denied and, unlike Mona, she was unsupported in her grief and pressured by a reality she was unready to accept.

framework of the meaning the pregnancy had for her and her family, in spite of others' possible dismissals of the event as relatively unimportant (see Borg and Lasker 1981).

The Medicalization of Birth

The potential crises surrounding birth and parenthood are colored further by controversy about Caesarean births. Traditionally, Caesarean birth was selected when there was risk of life for the child or mother (approximately 4% of births; see Arms 1975, p. 114). Rates of Caesarean births in some American hospitals are now well over 25%. There is perhaps no event arising from birth and parenthood that shows more sharply the difference between traditional societies and Western societies. Birth in the US has come to be identified as an elaborate medical event in which mothers turn over the unique birthing process to physicians, drugs, and surgery. The hazards of medicalizing the natural event of birth are described by Arms (1975). The development of birthing centers and increasing use of midwives is an outgrowth of public debate over birth as a natural event (BWHBC 1984, Inch 1984). Ideally, the management of birth should be in natural settings with trained midwives with obstetrical consultation available for medical complications during birth to avoid the possible crisis of unnecessary death. Such medical intervention is required in only a small percentage of total births. For most births, medicalization is itself a hazard to be avoided (Arms 1975).

Illness of a Child

Similar intervention is indicated for parents whose children are seriously ill, have had a serious accident, or are dying. The modern, relaxed visiting regulations in most hospital wards for children have reduced the crisis possibility at this time for both parents and child. Parents are encouraged to participate in their child's care so that the child feels less isolated and anxious about separation from parents, and the parents feel less threatened about their child's welfare (see Illness, Accidents, Surgery, and Hospitalization in Chapter 10).

SINGLE PARENTHOOD

Divorce and Single Adoption

There were an estimated 1,182,000 divorces reported in the United States for 1980, a record high (NCHS 1981, p. 8). Since then the rate has stabilized. The parent who gains custody of the children has the responsibility of rearing them alone, at least until remarriage; the other parent experiences a loss of his or her children. The loss is more acute if the divorced parents live in different cities or different parts of the country. If the loss is accompanied by a sense of relief, guilt usually follows. To assuage guilt, the relieved parent may shower the children inappropriately with material gifts or accuse the other parent of being too strict, inattentive, or uncaring. This crisis point of parenthood can be anticipated whenever the divorce itself is a crisis for either parent. Divorce counseling can help avoid future crisis.

The increase of "no-fault" divorce laws and attention to the needs of children in divorce settlements will also help prevent crises for parents and children. While divorce affects children of all ages, preschoolers are at greatest risk following divorce. However, as already discussed, it is not so much the divorce itself, but the manner in which parents conduct themselves, as well as poverty, (especially for women) that cause the greatest stress on children of divorced parents (Newberger, Melnicoe and Newberger 1986, p. 689–691; Sidel 1986). Existing laws do not adequately address the crisis of divorce, as attested by the incidence of "child snatching" by the parent denied custody. Another problem faced by many mothers is the awarding of custody to fathers on the basis of their greater financial security, even when these fathers have not been the primary caretakers of the children (Chesler 1986). While the increasing interest of fathers in parenting their children is applauded, to award them custody primarily on a class basis is a cruel punishment of mothers, who have assumed the major burden of child care throughout history. This growing practice also highlights the need for social change to address women's economic inequality. As Newberger, Melnicoe, and Newberger (1986, p. 709) write: "If working wives and female heads of household were paid the wages of similarly qualified men about half the families living in poverty would not be poor." This economic disparity is exacerbated by the fact that many fathers abandon parenting altogether after divorce (Side 1986, p. 104) and the majority of divorced women receive no alimony or child support (Newberger, Melnicoe, and Newberger 1986, p. 693).

Teenage Parenthood

The problems and hazards of single parenthood are increased for a teenager with no job and an unfinished education. The infants of teen mothers are also at increased risk of death, battering, and other problems exacerbated by the poverty of most adolescent parents (Newberger, Melnicoe, and Newberger, pp. 681-685). Increasingly, teenage mothers do not automatically drop out of high school because of pregnancy, do not marry only because they are pregnant, and do not give up their babies. Hospitals and social service agencies are now establishing collaborative programs with high schools that include an emphasis on health, sex education, parenthood, and career planning. There is also growing recognition that the prevalence, problems, and hazards of teenage pregnancy will not subside until values and opportunities for women in society change. Counselors and others working with young mothers—many of whom are from low-income or troubled homes—repeatediy note that these girls see mothering as their only chance for fulfillment. Life to them seems hopeless in terms of happiness through career or education. Indeed, there is still widespread social, cultural, and economic reinforcement of the notion that a woman's major value to society is her capacity for motherhood.* A young woman may sense that she has little chance to contribute anything else to society, and says in effect, "But I *can* produce a baby." Thus, a girl may not plan to conceive, but once pregnant she finally finds meaning in her life; she now will be important and necessary—at least to a helpless infant.

Gay Parenthood

The contemporary stresses of parenthood include those of gay parents. There is probably no group of parents more misunderstood than gay parents. The myth and fear is that gay parents will bring up their children to be gay. Another myth is that gay men are much more likely than straight men to abuse children. As a result, lesbian and gay parents may lose custody of their children for no other reason than their sexual preference. Gay people of both sexes may be denied adoption if their sexual preference is known. For example, community protest in Massachusetts resulted in the removal of a foster child from the home of two gay foster parents, only to have the child abused six months later in a "normal" foster home. Crises around gay parenthood might decline with reflection on the following facts: The vast majority of parents are heterosexual; yet these straight parents have reared millions of gay people. The necessary role models of either sex and sexual preference exist for *all* children in many social contexts besides the home. Also, the majority of child sexual abusers are heterosexual male relatives.

SURROGATE PARENTHOOD

In a landmark decision, the New Jersey high court declared that paying a woman to have a baby constitutes illegal babyselling, and perhaps is criminal and potentially degrading to women. Nevertheless, controversy over this technological response to the desire of childless couples for children will probably continue, with proponents citing the Bible in support of their position, and opponents noting that the last time human beings were bred for transfer of ownership was during slavery (Harrison 1987). The parenting issues of infertility and the right of procreation are cited as rationales justifying surrogacy. However, infertility rates are highest among low-income racial minority groups, due in part to greater exposure to various hazards, while lower rates among affluent women are traced largely to later age at attempting pregancy. Surrogate babies, therefore, are born to poor women and paid for by affluent white couples. In the US the price of a surrogate arrangement is usually $10,000 for the mother, with another

*In theoretical circles this is known as biological determinism, a view that has been bolstered for many years by Freudian psychoanalytic theory (see Chodorow 1978).

$15,000 going to the sponsoring agency; women in Third World countries are paid much less or nothing at all. Also, while procreation is a right, this right cannot be exercised at the expense of the primordial right of another woman to the child she has nurtured and birthed. The preventive approach to the infertility that has spawned surrogacy includes removal of environmental and workplace hazards (see Chavkin 1984 and Chapters 9 and 10), and child care provisions that would allow career women to have children at earlier ages without compromising their jobs.*

FATHERHOOD IN TRANSITION

A discussion of parenthood in the 1980s would be incomplete without considering the changing notion of fatherhood, especially in regard to prevention of parent-child crises. The changing role of fathers is related to several factors: (1) the growing number of mothers who work outside the home; (2) increasing realization of the benefits to children of being reared by two parents rather than one, and (3) a new awareness by fathers of what they miss emotionally through marginal involvement in parenting (Merton 1986). However, there are strains in this transitional process (Gregg 1986, Shapiro 1987). Levine (1980), consultant and researcher on child care and social policy, cites three factors that work against the American father taking a more active role in childrearing: (1) the lack of role models for male participation in child care, (2) differentiation of male and female pay scales in the labor market, and (3) many women's ambivalent feelings about men's active participation. Since child care is the only area where women routinely exercise certain control, it is unlikely that they will readily give it up so long as they have limited access to other arenas of power.

The poor record of child-care policy in the United States is related to the traditional role of fathers. In an in-depth examination of child care in the United States compared with culturally similar Western European countries, Foreman (1980) found that the United States, for all its technological skills and economic power, is far behind other industrialized nations in adapting to the needs of working parents in policy and practice. There is also increasing evidence that poverty and inadequate child-care services, not maternal employment, have the most adverse effect on young children (Gerson 1986, Newberger, Melnicoe, and Newberger 1986). Both individuals and the general public are becoming aware of the importance of this issue for children and parents. For example, popular author Salk (1982), in *My Father, My Son: Intimate Relationships*, talks to fathers about expressing their feelings, showering love on others, and learning to be a

*For further discussion of the complex emotional, legal, and ethical ramifications of this issue, readers are referred to: Arditti, Klein, and Minden 1984, BWHBC 1987, Corea 1985.

"real person." Corporation executives are also realizing greater business returns, more employee satisfaction, and reduced absenteeism as a result of provoding child-care benefits.

ADOLESCENCE AND YOUNG ADULTHOOD

Opinion regarding the age span of adolescence varies in different cultures and according to different theorists. The Joint Commission on Mental Health of Children in the United States considered youth up to age 25 in the program it recommended for youth in the 1970s. The extent of adolescence is influenced by such factors as: (a) length of time spent in school, (b) age at first marriage, (c) parenthood or the lack of it, (d) age at first self-supporting job, and (e) residence (with or apart from parents). In general, adolescence can be considered in two stages—early and late. Late adolescence overlaps with young adulthood, particularly for those who prolong vocational and educational preparation into their early and mid-twenties.

DEVELOPMENTAL CHALLENGES AND STRESS

During early adolescence the major developmental task is achievement of "ego identity" (Erikson 1963). Adolescents and young adults must give up the security of dependence on parents and accept new roles in society, including responsibility in the work world and achieving a capacity for intimacy. The adolescent struggles with the issue of independence and freedom from family. On the one hand, the young person is very much in need of the family's material and emotional support. On the other hand, he or she may resent the continued necessity of dependence on parents. Interdependence–a balance between excessive dependence and independence—is a mark of growth during this stage.

Developmental tasks during late adolescence include finding and adjusting to a place in the world apart from immediate family, and devloping a capacity for intimacy in one's chosen sex role. These tasks may involve finding and holding a satisfying job; succeeding in college, technical training, or graduate school; and choosing and adjusting to a life-style such as marriage or communal living.

Success with the developmental tasks of adolescence depends on what happened during one's infancy and childhood. An unhappy childhood is the usual precursor to unhappiness for an adolescent or young adult. Successful completion of the tasks of adolescence or young adulthood can be accomplished only if parents know when to "let go," and do not prevent the young person from making decisions she or he is capable of making independently. Young people today simultaneously face new opportunities and terrifying threats, often with insufficient support in either instance.

Our society has been described as youth oriented. This does not mean that we particularly value younger people; instead, it shows that we devalue older people. In fact, the necessary services for both normal and troubled young people are grossly lacking in many communities. For example, many schools do not have guidance counselors or school social workers. The youthful population in every community should have access to emergency hostels where young people abused by their parents or seeking refuge from conflict can go. There should be housing for youthful offenders in special facilities with a strong community focus (*not* with hardened criminals). And all schools should provide suicide prevention programs (see Chapters 6 and 7).

HELPING YOUNG PEOPLE

Parents, teachers, pastors, youth directors, guidance and residence counselors, and school nurses are in powerful positions to help or hinder young people in their quest for identity and a meaningful place in society (see Van Ornum and Mordock 1987). Help may mean simply being available and attentive when a young person is upset and wants to talk; offering information the young person needs in order to make decisions about career, education, or marriage; guiding young people in the use of counseling and other resources when they find themselves in a crisis; or acting as a youth advocate in instances of neglect, abuse, or other injustice.

The crisis intervention principle of doing things *with* rather than *to* and *for* troubled people is particularly important when trying to help the young (see Chapter 4). Since a major developmental task of adolescence is finding a unique place and achieving healthy interdependence, a counselor's inattention to this principle can defeat the purpose of the helping relationship. Certainly a young person in trouble may be in need of a caring adult to make certain decisions for him or her. But the same principle applies here as in work with troubled adults: The troubled person should participate in any decision affecting him or her unless it is evident that he or she absolutely cannot make certain decisions. Then the counselor should be ready and available to act on his or her behalf. Some adults assume that young people are incapable of making any decisions or of accepting any responsibility. In contrast, others force the adolescent to make decisions and assume responsibilites he or she may not be ready for. Either attitude brings trouble for the adolescent or young adult. Crises and ongoing problems such as drug abuse and delinquency can often be avoided when young people have the support they need to meet the demands of this phase of development.

CASE EXAMPLE: NORA STAPLES

Nora Staples, age 17, and her sister Jennifer, age 16, moved to a large city 300 miles from their home in order to get away from their abusive father. Their grandparents, the elderly Staples, in-

vited Nora and Jennifer to stay with them, although their living quarters were cramped and they were not well-off financially. Nora and Jennifer's parents divorced when the children were eleven and ten, respectively. Their mother left the area after the divorce, and the girls had not seen her since. For four years Nora and Jennifer stayed with an aunt and uncle who lived near their father's home.

When Nora was 15 and Jennifer 14, their father insisted that they live with him. He expected them to cook and keep house, which they did without complaint; they were afraid of what he would do if they rebelled. On weekends their father went on drinking binges. Every month or two when he came home late at might he would put both girls out of the house and lock the door. At these times they would go back to their aunt and uncle's house for a couple of days until their father insisted they come home again. The aunt and uncle were finally threatened by the father if they ever took the girls in again. When they heard this, Nora and Jennifer hitchhiked to their grandparents' home.

Two weeks after arrival at her grandparents' home, Nora began talking about shooting herself. The grandmother called a local crisis clinic. The counselor and Nora's grandmother talked for about fifteen minutes, after which the grandmother was able to persuade Nora to talk with the counselor. Indeed, Nora had obtained a gun and was seriously considering suicide. She felt angry with her father, though she had never let him know. She also felt guilty about leaving him, although she couldn't bear being with him any longer. Now she felt she was a burden to her grandparents and saw no point in going on. Nora agreed, however, to come in to the crisis clinic for counseling to deal with her problem. She also agreed to a plan to dispose of the gun with the help of her grandparents and the police. The counselor learned that Nora's grandparents were also angry and disgusted with their son for the way he had treated Nora and Jennifer, but that they also had felt helpless until now.

In spite of her problems, Nora managed to graduate from high school with honors at age 17 and was offered a scholarship by a nearby private college. She was undecided about whether to accept the scholarship or get a job to help support herself while living with her grandparents.

The service plan for Nora and the grandparental family included the following:

1. Individual counseling sessions for Nora to deal with her anger and misplaced guilt regarding her father, to help her make a decision about college or work, and to explore alternatives other than suicide as a way out of her despair.

2. Family counseling sessions for Nora, her grandparents, and her sister Jennifer to help them deal together with their feelings about the situation, to find ways of supporting one another, and to find a solution to the problem of crowded living quarters.
3. Collateral conferences with the Child Welfare Department to obtain financial support for Nora and Jennifer and to enable the grandparents to find a larger residence.

Nora, Jennifer, and their grandparents were also advised of their rights and the resources available to them to press charges of neglect against the father if he came to take the young women away with him, as they suspected he would do within weeks.

By the end of eight individual counseling sessions and six family sessions Nora was no longer suicidal. She had learned that the scholarship would be available to her the following year if she chose to delay going to college. She therefore decided to stay with her grandparents for a year and get a job to help support herself. One factor in this decision was Nora's realization, through counseling, that she was very resentful of having had to assume so much responsibility for her father and his needs. She said she wanted the chance to live in peace and quiet with a family for a while. Also, she felt deprived, as a result of her disturbed home situation, of the opportunity to live the way most teenagers do.

She also gained the strength and courage to follow through on charges filed against her father when he came to demand that she and Jennifer return to his home. A restraining order was obtained against their father, and he was directed by a family court to make regular support payments to Nora and Jennifer while they continued to live in their grandparents' home. Custody of Nora and Jennifer was vested with their grandparents.

A six month follow-up contact revealed that Nora was much happier and had decided to go ahead with college plans. She was advised of college counseling services available to her should she become upset and suidical again.

Young women like Nora and Jennifer, like all youth, need special support to avoid crisis during their passage through adolescence. If adolescents come from troubled families we need to pay particular attention to the social and family approaches discussed in Chapter 5. But even if family disturbance and deprivation are not apparent, many young people complain that they do not feel *listened* to. Parent effectiveness training should begin in high school and include a focus on listening, loving, and giving, as well as discipline and nonviolent positive control approaches. Adult guidance from schools, churches, and recreation directors should supplement family support with creative approaches. Hazing tragedies, teenage gangs, and similar negative group associations attest to the tremendous need of young people for peer belonging and acceptance along with adult guidance. Extreme hazing activities are remarkable not only in their destructiveness, but in their lack of mature adult input. Rites of passage for adolescents are necessary. The challenge, though, is to develop contemporary alternatives that reflect sensitivity to adolescents' simultaneous needs for support, guidance, independence, and group belonging. For example, when considering the current threat of AIDS and adolescents continuing abuse of alcohol, groups such as Students Against Drunk Driving or discussion sessions on AIDS and responsible sexual behavior can function as such "contemporary rites of passage" during this critical developmental phase (see Crisis Paradigm, third box, lower circle).

HELPING A FAMILY IN CRISIS

More consistent efforts are also needed within social service and mental health agencies for family approaches to the problems of adolescents. The interrelated stresses and crises of parents and their children, along with several intervention strategies, are illustrated in the following example of a family in crisis.

CASE EXAMPLE: THE PAGE FAMILY

Donald Page, 44, and Ann Page, 39, had been married for 20 years and had four children: Alice, age 20; Michael, 18; Betsy, 14; and Gary, 9. Donald worked in a local automobile factory and was drafted into military service at age 26. Two years later he returned home as a disabled war veteran. Ann worked as a secretary prior to their marriage and returned to work when her husband was drafted into the service. When her husband returned, Ann continued to work in spite of her husband's objections. The Pages moved to a small farm on the outskirts of a large city. They leased the farmland and Donald stayed at home most of every day doing odd jobs around the farm. He did few routine household chores, even though Ann worked full time outside the home. The Pages had a bleak social life and, in general, their marriage and family life was strained.

The Page children felt isolated because it was difficult to see their friends except during school hours. Alice had a baby at 17 and dropped out of her junior year in high school. She and her mother quarreled constantly over responsibility for the baby, who lived in the family home. After two years of this fighting, Alice's parents asked her to find a place of her own, which she did. Meanwhile, Ann threatened to report Alice to child welfare authorities if she didn't start assuming more responsibility for her child. Ann really wanted to keep Alice's baby herself, for she had wanted another child. Alice also talked about giving her baby away to her mother.

Meanwhile, Betsy was reported to be having problems in school, and teachers suspected her of taking drugs. Betsy had been belligerent at home, refusing to do chores and staying out late. Finally, Betsy ran away from home and was returned by police after three days. Donald and Ann were advised by police and school authorities to seek help for Betsy. They did not follow through and continued alone in their struggle to control her behavior. Michael tried to help both Betsy and his parents, but he felt pulled between the two parties. Gary was the "spoiled" child, and occasionally asked why everyone was fighting all the time.

When Betsy's school problems heightened, she was threatened with expulsion and a week later ran away again. This time when police found her, she threatened suicide if she was taken home. Police therefore took her to a community mental health emergency service. Betsy was seen by a crisis counselor; she begged to be placed in a detention center rather than go back home.

After several hours with Betsy, the counselor was able to persuade her that she could help her and her family make things more tolerable at home and that a detention center was no place for a girl her age—at least not until other alternatives had been tried.

Meanwhile, Betsy's parents were called and asked to come to the crisis clinic. Betsy felt hopeless about anything changing at home, though she expressed the wish that somehow things could get better. Two situations she particularly hated were: (a) her father and mother fighting about what she could and couldn't do and who she could and couldn't see, and (b) her mother's and Alice's constant fighting about Alice's baby. If these situations at home didn't change, she said she just wanted to die.

The Pages agreed to a contract for eight crisis counseling sessions that were to involve the entire family, including Alice. One of the sessions was with the parents, Alice, and Betsy only. Another session was with the parents, Betsy, the school guidance counselor, principal, and home room teacher. Goals of the counseling sessions included:

1. Improving communication among all members of the family and cutting out the contradictory messages Betsy was receiving.
2. Helping family members detect signs of distress among themselves and learning to listen and support one another when troubled.
3. Working out a mutually agreeable program of social outlets for Betsy.

4. Working out a plan to divide the chores in a reasonable and consistent way among all family members.
5. Arriving at an agreeable system of discipline that included rewards and punishments appropriate to various behaviors.
6. Helping Alice make satisfying decisions regarding herself and her baby.
7. Developing a plan to work cooperatively with Betsy's teachers and the guidance counselor to resolve Betsy's problems in school.

Family members agreed on various tasks to achieve the above goals. For example, Donald and Ann would set aside some private time each day to discuss their problems and disagreements about discipline—out of the children's range of hearing. Betsy agreed to follow through on certain chores around the house. If she failed to do so, Ann agreed *not* to pick up after her and to discuss disciplinary measures with Donald. Alice would seek individual counseling to assist her in making a decision about herself and her child.

Two of the counseling sessions were held in the home, which was observed to be quite crowded. One result of this meeting was helping the family work out ways of assuring individual privacy in spite of cramped quarters.

The threats of Betsy's suicide attempt and school expulsion were crisis points that moved Donald and Ann to work on underlying problems in their marriage. These problems made parenthood more difficult than it might otherwise have been. After eight crisis counseling sessions, the Page family existence was much less disturbed but by no means tranquil. However, Betsy was no longer in danger of being expelled from school, and she at least preferred her home to a detention house. Donald and Ann Page agreed to marriage counseling for themselves after termination of the crisis counseling contract, to help make their future years as parents less burdensome. The attention directed to dealing with marriage and total family problems may decrease the chance of Betsy following in her sister's footsteps and becoming pregnant out of wedlock.

INTIMATE RELATIONSHIPS: BEGINNINGS AND ENDINGS

Intimate relationships are important; a break in intimate attachments can lead to crisis. In this section, the beginnings and endings of intimate relationships are discussed briefly as one of the major transition states.

INTIMACY AS A BASIC NEED

An intimate relationship refers to any close bond between two people in which there is affection, reciprocity, mutual trust, and a willingness to stand by each other in distress without expectation of reward. The emphasis in this definition is on psychological and social intimacy, though a sexual relationship may also exist. Whether one is married, single, or living with someone of the same or opposite sex, intimate relationships are essential to a happy productive life. Sexual relationships alone do not necessarily imply intimacy as her defined (see Assessment Forms in Chapter 3).

Intimate relationships comprise part of society with the formation of social and emotional bonds between people. Some of the more common relationships and intimacies are: (a) courtship, (b) marriage, and (c) deeply committed friendships outside marriage. Entering into such a relationship is a major event with important social-psychological ramifications. Common endings of intimate relationships include divorce or widowhood. While these endings of intimate relationships are highly visible, other less official disruptions of close bonds can be equally traumatic and crisis producing.

At the beginning and ending of an intimate relationship the people involved undergo a change in role and status; from single state to married, from spouse to divorcee, from associate to friend, or from friend to forgotten one. When beginning a new intimate relationship, old secure roles must be abandoned and replaced by a new unfamiliar roles. If the person changing roles is lacking in personal and social resources, taking on a new role may be the source of crisis. Often a role change results in feelings of loss and the mourning of what one has given up. When the familiar role of lover, spouse, or trusted friend ends, a person may lose a sense of security. He or she may experience crisis because a basic needed attachment is severed, and may again face the challenge of role and status change. Thus, transitions into and out of supportive intimate relationships are among the more common occasions of crisis for many people.

Besides couples who begin and end intimate relationships, couples who choose to remain childless also experience strain. Reasons for remaining childless include support for zero population growth, inability to cope with the responsibility of parenthood, and difficulty in finding adequate day-care facilities for children. Couples often meet with social disapproval from others who assume that the basic purpose of marriage is procreation. In effect, the message is: You can have intimacy if you assume the social responsibility of producing and rearing children. The National Alliance for Optional Parenthood is working on gradually changing the public's attitude toward childless marriage.

Gay and lesbian couples face similar disapproval, despite the movement to assure equal rights to gay people. Supervisors in the city of San Francisco, for example, have recently guaranteed gay couples the same employment insurance benefits as other couples. Gay men often face additional threats to intimate attachments related to the AIDS crisis.

EXCESSIVE DEPENDENCE ON INTIMATE ATTACHMENTS

Since intimacy with others is an integral part of our lives, deep emotion and importance are attached to intimate relationships. Our feelings about these attachments affect our thoughts and behavior in regard to the people concerned. For example, some people have unrealistic expectations of those they love, and may behave in unusual ways when the bond between loved ones is threatened or severed (Vaugh 1987). In contrast, some people have such deep fear of possible rejection that they repeatedly resist offers of friendship, love and, intimacy. Crisis can occur at the beginning of attachments or when the intimate relationship is disrupted, as in divorce, death of a spouse, or betrayal by a friend.

Halpern (1982) discusses "addictions" to people—excessive need to be attached to someone special—as well as the dynamics of "person" addiction: how to break away, and the beauty and positive aspects of solitude. Remembering Halpern's maxims and those described in other self-help books can help buffer the crisis potential when breaking out of addictive or destructive relationships. For example:

1. You can live—and possibly, live better—without the person to whom you are attached.
2. A mutual love relationship should help one to feel *better*, not worse about oneself.
3. Guilt is not reason enough to stay in a relationship.
4. Some people die of destructive relationships. Do you want to be one of them?
5. If someone says: "I'm not ready for a relationship," "I'm not going to leave my spouse," or "I don't want to be tied down," believe him or her.
6. The pain of ending a relationship, like other crises, won't last forever. In fact, it won't last as long as the pain of not ending it.
7. We are whole and valuable as individuals apart from particular relationships.
8. When we end a destructive relationship we open our lives to new possibilities.

SINGLES, ISOLATION, AND DIVORCE

Considered within the privacy, intimacy, and community dynamic (see Chapter 5), an excessive dependency on intimacy usually results in a neglect of basic needs for privacy and community. On the other hand, attachments to people who are not good for us can be fostered by the threat of social isolation.

Social opportunities, especially for the single person who has moved recently to a new community, are often lacking. In many communities social events are organized around couple relationships. Consequently, a single person may find it extremely difficult or impossible to feel comfortable in a tightly knit society that demands that people participate as couples. Many communities now have "singles" organizations where single people of any age can make friends and enjoy a wide range of social activities. However, despite the existence of these clubs, it is still difficult for a single person to establish satisfying social relationships after changing location. Fortunately, the single state is now being accepted by many as a fulfilling life-style. This should make it easier for the single person to establish social contacts in a new community.

If a person is *not* single by choice and is also *not* able to make friends easily, he or she is likely to be crisis prone. Psychotherapy may be indicated for such persons if they are chronically unhappy or depressed because of their single status. People like this who are living alone and are depressed are also a greater risk for suicide. In general, the risks of isolation and crisis responses like suicide are greater when the person is single because of divorce, separation, or widowhood.

Divorce is particularly hazardous in the following circumstances: (1) when the burden of care and support of young children falls entirely on one parent (see Stress and Crisis Points of Parenthood earlier in this chapter), and (2) among older people whose value systems have no place for divorce. Until very recently, divorce in the latter category was rare. It is now increasing rapidly and is overwhelmingly initiated by men (Cain 1982). The crisis potential of these non-mutual divorce actions is high because of:

- Lack of expectation.
- Contradiction of deeply held values.
- Widespread absence of social support structures for these special groups.
- Consider the following example of what divorce can mean to an older person.

Case Example: Helen

Helen, age 64, was not allowed to continue working in the same government agency as her husband Tom when they married 35 years ago. It was understood and accepted that a husband should have the advantage of career development and the wife should

tend the home and children. Giving up her fledgling career as a civil servant was not a problem for Barbara, as it was also understood and expected that marriage was for a lifetime and that her future economic support was secure. When Barbara was 60, Tom, then age 64, left her for a woman 25 years his junior. Barbara felt devastated and suicidal, going over and over with her friends and two adult children that somehow it must have been her fault. Repeatedly she said that Tom's death would have been preferable to a divorce.

Barbara had a hard time acknowledging to anyone but her family and closest friends that she was divorced. She felt ashamed and frequently referred to herself as a widow. Barbara could not understand how her daughter Caroline, also divorced, could be so apparently unruffled by the event (Caroline had no children, worked as a writer, and preferred her single life). At age 60 Barbara's only marketable job skill was baby-sitting. She was also a good gardener and cook, but had no paid work experience in these fields. Besides being mateless at age 60, Barbara barely escaped homelessness. By a stroke of luck she obtained the marital home and was able to rent one room so she could pay taxes and utilities. There were no legal provisions, however, for her to receive benefits from her husband's pension.

In spite of these hardships, Barbara scraped by, came out of her depression after two years, and now takes advantage of senior citizen travel packages, and attends adult education classes. She is attractive, charming, and dearly loved by her friends and family, and acknowledges at times that she may be better off without Tom in spite of occasional loneliness. Two years ago Barbara turned down the marriage proposal of a courtly but sickly man, age 80. While she was fond of this man, she resisted tying herself down to what she anticipated would eventually turn into a nursing role, especially after adjusting to her new freedom.

The harsh realities of the single life are contradicted by stereotypes of swinging singles with a carefree existence. The single state without children does provide greater freedom to pursue one's career or engage in other activities, but the hazards of single parenthood speak for themselves. Every life-style has its advantages and trade-offs; for example, greater freedom and less responsiblity may be balanced against greater insecurity in old age. Pollner (1982), through an analysis of film, exposes the popular belief that men are much better off single than married. Social research in the last century, beginning with Durkheim (1915), consistently reveals that marriage in fact is more advantageous and ego-protective for men than it is for women (see also Kessler and McLeod 1984, and Oakley 1981). On the other hand, men and women who have never married are better adjusted and are less at risk for suicide than those who have lost a spouse by any means. The hazards to individuals in these transition states would be modified by contemporary rites of passage such as divorce ceremonies and acceptance into widows' clubs. Lacking such social supports can leave single people in a permanent liminal (transitional) state (van Gennep 1909), as they are never quite reincorporated into the community in their new role.

MIDDLE AGE

The term "middlescence" has been applied to those past adolescence but not yet senescent. Stevenson (1977, p. 1) identifies two stages in this period of adult life: middlescence I, the core of the middle years between 30 and 50; middlescence II, the new middle years extending from 50 to 70 or 75. This division contrasts with the US Census Bureau and popular opinion, which define middle age as the time between the ages of 45 and 64. Until very recently little attention has been paid to the middle years except in the negative sense of stereotypes about being "over the hill," sexually unattractive, unhappy, and depressed.* People in midlife are literally caught in the middle: They have major responsibilities for the young and the old. They are the primary figures in society's major institutions: family, business, education, health and social service, religion, and politics. Besides doing most of the regular work of society, they are also its major researchers, with the understandable result that they have focused their research primarily on groups other than themselves.

Because of the relative lack of attention given to the midlife period, it is not surprising that many popular notions about midlife are the result of myth and folklore. Considering also the influence of medicalization, this major life passage is often recast into a "disease" to be treated. The reality is that most people in midlife:

- Are happier than they were when younger.
- Lead highly productive and satisfying lives.
- Have stable jobs.
- Have met the major challenges of education and parenthood.
- Are securely settled in a community in purchased rather than rented housing.
- Enjoy a network of satisfying social relationships.
- Have more disposable income and financial security than either the young or old.

*See Golan (1981, p. 283) for recent works on midlife passage and crises; also, Levinson et al. (1978).

- In many cases, enjoy good health and feel physically and mentally vigorous.

In general, middle-agers today have more options than in earlier times because they are healthier than before. Census bureau data reveal that women age 45 can expect to live 35 more years, and men 29 more years. Popular beliefs about middle age lag behind these statistical predictions.

Many, however, experience midlife as a threat. If a person at midlife is married and has children, familiar parenting roles may no longer fill one's day; husband-wife roles also need redefining. If not single by choice, a middle-ager may see the chances for marriage as decreasing. Men may be threatened by a diminished sex drive and leveling off of career advancement opportunities. Women in careers face the same threat; women without careers must meet the challenge of returning to school or resuming an interrupted career. The onset of menopause may threaten a woman's sense of feminine identity and attractiveness. Both men and women may perceive their lives at middle age as quickly slipping away before they achieve what they want for themselves and others.

The success of men and women in dealing with these midlife changes depends on:

- Their psychological health and general outlook on life.
- Lifelong preparation for this stage of human development.
- Social support and economic security.

Some people are trapped into the false security of living as though life were an unending fountain of youth. Such people may avoid health preparation for the developmental tasks of midlife. Or, if they are socially isolated and lack the financial assets necessary to pursue education and leisure activities, midlife can increase their crisis proneness. In spite of the advantages middle-aged people have, this developmental passage is as hazardous as other transitions, though it is not as hazardous as popular stereotypes would have us believe.

Among all the myths associated with middle age, none is more widespread than that of female menopause as a disease. Significant efforts to undo this stereotype include publications such as *Our Bodies, Our Selves* by the Boston Women's Health Book Collective (1984), which is now in its third edition and has been translated into many foreign languages. It is now widely accepted that menopause is a natural transition state, *not* a disease, in spite of bodily and mental changes such as hot flashes and a changing view of self past child-bearing age. Not only does menopause not require medical intervention for distress in the majority of cases, but estrogen replacement therapy, so popular in the past, is now linked with cancer of the uterus in postmenopausal women (Ehrenreich and English 1979, p. 315). Menopause support groups now take the place of estrogen replacement "therapy" during this important transition state. In such groups, women receive factual information (which is often rare and imprecise from the mainstream gynecology profession) and support in coping with the physical and social-psychological changes accompanying the cessation of menstruation (MacPherson 1985).

Men undergoing the climacteric could benefit from similar support groups. Coming to terms with middle age could influence the behavior of men who cope with changes in themselves by establishing liaisons with younger women.

OLD AGE

It has been said that we are as old as we feel. Many of the issues discussed regarding middle age apply to old age: psychological outlook, social support, and economic security are critical factors affecting the crisis proneness of old people. The issues concerning retirement, noted in Chapter 10, also apply to many elderly people. Many old people are at special risk for crisis. For example, minority elders have lower money incomes than white elders; three-fourths of the elderly below poverty level are female; older women earn one-third of wages/salaries of older men; low-income elderly are 3.4 times more likely to have limiting chronic conditions than high-income elderly (Estes 1986). Also, with the federal cutbacks in domestic programs since 1981, greater burdens of caring for increasing numbers of elders fall on women (Doress and Siegal 1987, Sommers and Shields 1987). The needs of elders are being addressed through the work of advocates for the elderly such as Senator Claude Pepper of Florida, Maggie Kuhn of the Gray Panthers, the Older Women's League, the American Association of Retired Persons, and increasing numbers of elderly at large. A recent emphasis on gerontologic research and graduate training programs in universities also can contribute to the long-range welfare of the elderly. Many of the myths about old age are an extension of those about middle age; for example, old age is a disease, and old people are uniformly needy, dependent, and asexual.

ATTITUDES TOWARD THE ELDERLY

Cultural values and the policies and practices flowing from them do not change rapidly. Old people are not as highly valued in mainstream American society as they are, for example, in some Native American communities and most non-Western societies. Recent social emphasis on the small nuclear family has virtually displaced the extended family arrangement in most Western societies. Grandparents, aunts, and uncles are no longer integrated into a family home. Children, therefore, routinely have only two adults (their parents) as role models and supporters. In cases of death, desertion, or divorce, children are even more deprived of adult models.

Fortunately, this is changing with attempts to expose children and old people to each other, for example, in nursing homes.

Older people experience even greater hardship than do children by their exclusion from the nuclear family. They feel—and often are—unwanted. Often they are treated as guests, and have no significant role in matters of consequence in their children's families. When older people, because of health or other problems, do live with their grown children, additional tensions arise. The older person may become impatient and irritable with the normal behavior of the grandchildren. Space is sometimes insufficient to give everyone some privacy, or the old person may seem demanding and unreasonable (Gubrium 1976).

SERVICES FOR THE ELDERLY

Stress can be relieved and crisis situations prevented when special public health and social services are available to families caring for an older person. In some US areas, outreach workers from the public office for aging make regular contacts with older people in their homes. Names of needy people are obtained from pastors, welfare, and mental health workers.

Outreach service such as this is very helpful in preventing crises and avoiding institutionalization. Contrary to public perception, only 5% of old people live in nursing homes. Where public services are lacking, the lives of many older people can take on a truly desperate character (see Abuse of Elders in Chapter 8). The situation is particularly acute for the older person living alone who is unable for physical or psychological reasons to get out. Senior citizen centers now exist in nearly every community. Every effort should be made to encourage older people to use the services of these centers. This may be the only real source for keeping active physically and for establishing and maintaining social contacts. Such physical and social involvement is essential to prevent emotional, mental, and physical deterioration. Some people will need help in order to use these services: money and transportation to get there, or counseling to convince them to use the service.

Other services for the elderly in the US include:

- Retired Senior Citizen Volunteers (R.S.V.P.)—available for various kinds of volunteer tasks.
- Phone Line (or similar services), which maintains a roster of names of shut-in people (elderly or disabled) and calls to assure the person's safety and contact with a helping agency.
- Meals on Wheels, an organization making and delivering hot meals to the incapacitated.
- Help Your Neighbor and similar public and private organizations available to the isolated and distressed.

Visiting nurses are another key resource. Often a nurse can detect stress or suicidal tendencies. In addition to the above services for older people, all agencies for the aging should maintain active contact with the local crisis center. Workers from the center should assist in acute crisis situations.

CASE EXAMPLE: ANTONE CARLTON

Antone Carlton, age 77, lived with his wife, Martha, in a run-down section of a city. Antone was nearly blind and had had both legs amputated, a medical necessity due to complications of diabetes. Antone and Martha survived on a poverty-level income. Martha, age 68, was able to take care of Antone. Then she was hospitalized and died of complications following abdominal surgery. Antone was grief stricken; he and Martha were very close and, of course, he was dependent on her. After Martha's death a visiting nurse came regularly to give Antone his insulin injection. The nurse arranged for Antone to get help with meals through the food and nutrition service of the welfare department. However, this service did not meet the many needs Antone had. Within weeks the apartment became infested with roaches.

One day Antone's house was broken into, and he was beaten and robbed of the few dollars he had. This happened a few hours before the nurse's visit. She found Antone with minor physical injuries, but he was also depressed and suicidal. The local crisis center was called and an outreach visit made. The crisis outreach team assessed Antone as a very high risk for suicide. Antone, however, insisted on remaining in his own home. The services of Help Your Neighbor were enlisted for Antone, especially to provide for an occasional visitor. Homemaker services from the Welfare Department were also arranged. A week later, Antone was beaten and robbed again, but he still refused to move out of his home. The nurse inquired about a senior citizen housing project for Antone. They refused to accept anyone as handicapped as Antone, although he did consider leaving if he could move to such a place. After a third robbery and beating a few weeks later, Antone agreed to move to a nursing home.

INSTITUTIONAL PLACEMENT OF THE ELDERLY

In Antone's case a nursing home placement was a means of resolving a crisis with housing, health care, and physical safety. However, admission to a nursing home is an occasion for crisis for nearly every resident. Also, while some people do well in a nursing home, for many institutionalization marks the beginning of a rapid decline in physical and emotional health status. A new nursing home resident will invariably mourn the loss of his or her own home or apartment and whatever privacy it afforded, no matter how difficult the prior circumstances were. New residents resent their dependence on others, regardless of how serious their physical condition may be. These problems are less acute for those who need intermediate-level care; their health status does not require such complete dependence. In domiciliary-level care, residents remain independent and are much less subject to crisis.

If a person has been placed in a nursing home by family members, he or she may feel unloved and abandoned. Some families do abandon the old parent, often not by choice, but because they cannot handle their own guilt feelings about placing the parent in a nursing home, no matter how necessary that placement might be.

The most stressful time for a nursing home resident is the first few weeks after admission. The new resident's problems are similar to those of people admitted to other institutions: hospitals, detention facilities, or group homes for adolescents. Crisis intervention at this time will prevent many later, more serious problems such as depression, suicidal tendencies, withdrawal, refusal to participate in activities, and an increase in physical complaints. Studies reveal that a significant number of elderly people simply give up after retirement or admission to a nursing home and die very soon thereafter (Seligman 1974). Hopelessness in these cases is the forerunner to death. Elderly people admitted to nursing homes should be routinely assessed for suicide risk.

Besides having to deal with feelings of loss, resentment, and rejection, some people placed in nursing homes do not get a clear, honest statement from their family about the need for and nature of the placement. This contributes further to the person's denial of his or her need to be in the nursing home.

Nursing staff who are sensitive to this crisis of admission to a nursing care facility are in a key position to prevent the negative outcomes noted above. The newly admitted resident—*and* his or her family—should be provided ample opportunity to express their feelings associated with the event. Family members should be persuaded to be honest with the resident about the *reality* of the situation. Family members will feel less guilty and more able to maintain the social contact needed by the resident if they do not deny the situation. Staff should actively reach out to family members, inviting them to participate in planning for their parent's or relative's needs in the nursing care facility. This will greatly relieve the stress experienced by an older person during the crisis of admission and adjustment. It will also reduce staff crises. When families are not included in the planning and have no opportunity to express their own feelings about the placement, they often handle their stress by blaming the nursing staff for poor care. This is a desperate means of managing their own guilt as well as the older person's complaints about the placement.

Besides the crisis of admission, other crises can be prevented when nursing care facilities have: (a) activity programs in keeping with the age and sociocultural values of the residents, (b) programs involving the residents in outside community events, and (c) special family programs. Unfortunately, the quality of nursing care facilities frequently reflects our society's devaluation of older people. Funding is often inadequate, which prevents employment of sufficient professional staff.

Retirement and the realization of old age are times of stress but need not lead to crisis. Societal attitudes toward old age can change so that this stage of life can be anticipated by more and more people as another opportunity for human growth. In some societies retired people are called on regularly to work several weeks a year when full-time workers go on vacation. There are many other opportunities in progressive societies for older people to remain active and involved. Many crises in the lives of elderly citizens can be avoided if they are accorded more honor and some post retirement responsibilities.

How we treat our elderly citizens can account for the marked difference in death rituals in traditional and modern urban societies: in modern societies many people are dead *socially* (by forced retirement or familial rejection) long before physical death occurs; therefore, society needs only to dispose of the body—no need for ritual to transfer social functions (Goody 1962). This cross-cultural observation leads to this chapter's closing section on death, our final passage through life.

DEATH

Death is the final stage of growth (Kubler-Ross 1975). It marks the end of life and is the most powerful reminder we have that we have only one life to live. The beauty, rather than the horror, of this message is that it moves us not to waste our one and only life.

Death has been a favorite topic of writers, poets, psychologists, physicians, and anthropologists for centuries. Volumes have been written by authors such as Feifel (1959, 1977), Mitford (1963), Glaser and Strauss (1965), Sudnow (1967), Kubler-Ross (1969, 1975), Kastenbaum and Aisenberg (1972), Aries (1974), Fulton et al. (1978), and others. There is even a science of thanatology (study of death and dying). Yet death is still a taboo topic for most people. This attitude is unfortunate. It means the loss of death as a "friendly companion" to remind us that our lives are finite. Such denial is the root of the crisis situation that death becomes for many. Vast and important as the subject of death is, consideration of it here is limited to its crisis aspect for health and human service workers.

ATTITUDES TOWARD DEATH

Death is not a crisis in itself, but becomes one for the dying person and survivors because of the widespread denial of death as the final stage of growth. As Tolstoy wrote so eloquently in *The Death of Ivan Ilych,* the real agony of death is the final realization that we have not really lived our life, the regret that we did not do what we wanted to do, that we did not realize in and for ourselves what we most dearly desired. This face was borne out in research by Goodman (1981), who compared top performing artists' and scientists' attitudes toward death with a group who were not performing artists or sceintists but were similar in other respects. She found significant evidence that the performing artists and scientists were less fearful of death, more accepting of death, and much less inclined to want to return to earth after their death if they had a chance. Having led full and satisfying lives, they were able to anticipate their deaths with peace and acceptance. They had "won the race with death."

The denial of death, so common in our society, is a far greater enemy than death itself. It allows us to live our lives less fully than we might with an awareness and acceptance of death's inevitability. Through the works of Elisabeth Kubler-Ross (1969, 1975) and many others, we have made progress in dealing with death openly. However, ours is still a death-denying society. Thousands of health professionals and families still refuse to discuss the subject openly with a dying person. The AIDS crisis makes the need to come to terms with death more urgent than ever (see Chapter 12).

Many problems and crises associated with death, dying people, their families, and those who attend them in their last days might be avoided if death were not denied. As noted by Kubler-Ross (1969, 1975), Fagerhaugh and Strauss (1977), and others, nurses, physicians, ministers, and family need to become open, communicative companions to dying people. However, nurses and physicians often avoid talking openly with dying people about their condition. Dying patients pay a high emotional price when this happens. The numerous examples of avoidance cited in Kubler-Ross's classic book, *On Death and Dying* (1969), still apply in many situations unless the staff has had extensive sensitization to the practices recommended by Kubler-Ross, Epstein (1975), and others.

Such denial of death, and the inability or refusal to come to terms with death is a critical issue for crisis workers on general, not just on behalf of the dying. Why? Because death, as suggested in earlier chapters, is a prototype of sorts for *all* crisis experiences. That is, many crises arise directly from the death of a loved one. But all crises and life passages comprise a "mini-death" in the *loss* experience common to them all. The successful resolution of crisis, then, is crucially connected to the process of coming to terms with various losses: loved one, job, health, home, physical intactness, or former role. Helping people through these losses—finding a new role, substitute relationships, or emotional healing, for example—depends heavily on whether we are comfortable with the topic of death and our own inevitable mortality. A healthy attitude toward our own death is our most powerful asset in assisting the dying through this final life passage and comforting their survivors.

In a culture without strong ritual and social support around dying, the major burden of positively dealing with death falls on individuals. Crisis workers and health professionals associated with death professionally can make their work easier by attending courses on death and dying, which are widely offered on college campuses. Sensitization to death and its denial in modern society is also aided by reading anthropologic and other works on the topic; see especially: Bloch, 1971, Cutter 1974, Fried and Fried 1980, Goodman 1981, Goody 1962, Rosenthal 1973, and Tolstoy 1960. Intensive workshops focusing on our own denial of death through sensitizing exercises are another means of forming death awareness. Such workshops have provided the stimulus for some to become aware of the preciousness of every moment. Coming to terms with our own death not only can change our life and eventual death, but it also lays the foundation for assisting others through death.

HELPING A DYING PERSON

In our society most people whose deaths are anticipated die in institutions such as hospitals or nursing homes, not in their own homes. Proportionately more people with AIDS, however, die at home. Rosenthal (1973), a young poet dying of leukemia, struck out against the coldness and technology that awaited him along with death in a hospital. He tells his remarkable story of facing his death and living fully until that time in *How Could I Not be Among You?* (1973). On learning of his imminent death from leukemia, Rosenthal checked out of the hospital, moved to the country, and did the things he wanted to do before dying.

Many others are not able to die in self-chosen circumstances. Most people will continue to spend the last phase of their lives in hospitals or nursing homes. These dying people deserve to have the shock of their terminal illness tempered by those who attend them. Nurses and physicians are, of course, technically efficient and generally compassionate. However, their own denial of death often blocks them from dealing with dying patients in an honest, open manner. As a result, they may not be helpful in their interaction with dying patients and their families.

Crisis intervention for a person who has learned of a diagnosis of fatal illness begins with awareness of one's own feelings about death. This is essential if one expects to be a source of support to a dying person. Next in the helping process is understanding what the dying person is going through. Wright (1985) refers to the acute, chronic-living, and terminal phases of a person's response to a life-threatening illness. Family members and everyone working with the dying should also be aware of dying as described by Kubler-Ross (1969) in *On Death and Dying* (her findings are based on interviews with over 200 dying patients).

Kubler-Ross identifies five stages of dying: denial, anger, bargaining, depression, and acceptance. All people do not necessarily experience all the stages, nor do these stages occur in a fixed, orderly sequence. Kubler-Ross's work is most useful for sensitizing health and hospice workers to some of the major issues and problems faced by the dying.

1. *Denial:* Typically, denial is expressed with, "No, not me," on becoming aware of a terminal illness. People deny even when they are told the facts explicitly. Denial is expressed by disbelief in X-ray or other reports, insistence on repeat examinations, or getting additional opinions from other doctors. It is the basis for the persistence of various "quack" remedies. Denial is necessary as a delaying mechanism so the person can absorb the reality of his or her terminal illness. During this phase, the person is withdrawn and often refuses to talk. Nurses, physicians, ministers, and social workers must wait through this phase and let the person know that they will still be available when he or she is finally ready to talk. Pressing a person to acknowledge and accept a bitter reality before he or she is psychologically ready may reinforce the need for defensive denial. Self-help groups (such as those sponsored by Omega and the AIDS Action Committee in the Boston area) are a contemporary substitute for traditional rites of passage through this important transition state.*

2. *Anger:* When denial finally gives way, it is often replaced by anger: "Why me?" This is more difficult for hospital staff and family to deal with than denial, as the person often expresses the anger by accusations against the people who are trying to help. The person becomes very demanding. No one can do anything right. He or she is angry at those who can go on living. Nurses are frequently the targets of anger. It is important for them to understand that the anger is really at the person's unchosen fate, not at themselves. They must stick with the patient and not retaliate or withdraw—recognizing that the anger must be expressed and will eventually pass.

3. *Bargaining:* With the evidence that the illness is still there in spite of angry protests, the person in effect, says, "Maybe if I ask nicely, I'll be heard." This is the stage of bargaining. The bargaining goes on mostly with God, even among those who don't believe in God. Bargaining usually consists of private promises: "I'll live a good life," or "I'll donate my life, my money to a great cause." During this phase it is important to note any underlying feelings of guilt the person may have, or regrets at a life not lived

*For more information about the Omega Hospice and Bereavement Program, a nonsectarian service program, write: Omega Report, Cambridge/Somerville Catholic Charities, 270 Washington Street, Somerville, MA 02143; telephone: 617-776-6369.

as idealized for him- or herself. The dying person needs someone who can listen to those expresions of regret.

4. *Depression:* During this stage of dying, people mourn the losses they have borne: body image, financial, people they love, joy, role of wife, husband, lover, or parent. Finally, they begin the grief of separation from life itself. This is the time when simple presence or touch of the hand means much more than words. Again, acceptance of one's own eventual death and the ability to be with a person in silence is the chief source of helpfulness at this time.

5. *Acceptance:* This follows when anger and depression have been worked through. The dying person becomes weaker and may want to be left alone more. It is the final acceptance of the end, awaited quietly with a certain expectation. Again, quiet presence and communication of caring by a touch or a look are important at this time. The person needs to have the assurance that he or she will not be alone when dying. Messages of caring will give such assurance.

Awareness and understanding of our own and of the dying person's feelings are the foundation of care during the crisis of terminal illness and death. Crisis intervention with families of dying people will also be aided by such awareness and understanding. Since dying alone is one of the fears of the dying person, communication with families is essential. Families should not be excluded from this final phase of life by machines and procedures that unnecessarily prolong physical life beyond conscious life. Family members who help the dying person by their presence will very likely become more accepting of their own future deaths. Denial of death and death in isolation do nothing to foster growth.

THE HOSPICE MOVEMENT

One of the most significant recent developments aiding the dying person is the hospice movement founded by Dr. Cecily Saunders (1978) in London in 1967. Dr. Sylvia Lack (1978) extended the hospice concept to the United States (McCabe 1982). The hospice movement grew out of awareness of the needs of the dying and concern that these needs could not be adequately met in hospitals focused primarily with curing and acute-care procedures. A main focus of the hospice concept is the control of pain and provision of surroundings that will enhance the possibility of dying as naturally as possible.

Lack has identified ten components of hospice care (McCabe 1982, p. 104):

1. Coordinated home care with inpatient beds under a central autonomous hospice administration.
2. Control of symptoms (physical, sociologic, psychological, and spiritual).

3. Physician-directed services (due to the medical nature of symptoms).
4. Provision of care by an interdisciplinary team.
5. Services available 24 hours a day, 7 days a week, with emphasis on availability of medical and nursing skills.
6. Patient and family regarded as the unit of care.
7. Provision for berreavement follow-up.
8. Use of volunteers as an integral part of the interdisciplinary team.
9. Structured personnel support and communication systems.
10. Patients accepted into the program on basis of health care needs rather than ability to pay.

The hospice movement is a promising example of a new awareness of death in modern society and the importance of supporting the rights of the dying. The pivotal place of this service for the dying is underscored by the AIDS crisis and by increasing numbers of other people who may prefer to die at home. As more people opt for hospice care, however, the need for respite for families and more hospital-based hospices will also increase (Wegman 1987). Assistance for the dying person is supported by the "Dying person's Bill of Rights," adopted by the General Assembly of the United Nations (1975, p. 99).

I have the right to be treated as a living human being until I die.

I have the right to maintain a sense of hopefulness however changing its focus may be.

I have the right to be cared for by those who can maintain a sense of hopefulness, however changing this might be.

I have the right to express my feelings and emotions about my approaching death in my own way.

I have the right to participate in decisions concerning my care.

I have the right to expect continuing medical and nursing attention even though "cure" goals must be changed to "comfort" goals.

I have the right not to die alone.

I have the right to be free from pain.

I have the right to have my questions answered honestly.

I have the right not to be deceived.

I have the right to have help from and for my family in accepting my death.

I have the right to die in peace and dignity.

I have the right to retain my individuality and not be judged for my decisions which may be contrary to beliefs of others.

I have the right to discuss and enlarge my religious and/or spiritual experiences, whatever these may mean to others.

I have the right to expect that the sanctity of the human body will be respected after death.

I have the right to be cared for by caring, sensitive, knowledgeable people who will attempt to understand my needs and will be able to gain some satisfaction in helping me face my death.

Throughout our lives, hazardous events and transitions can be occasions of crisis, growth, or deterioration. So in death, our last passage, we may experience our most acute agony or the final stage of growth. Whether or not we "win the race with death" depends on:

- How we have lived.
- What we believe about life and death.
- The support of those close to us during our final life crisis.

SUMMARY

Life passages are mini-deaths. In each of these transition states we leave something cherished and familiar for something unknown and threatening. We must mourn what is lost in order to move without terror to whatever awaits us. Preparation for transitions—whether from one role to another, one life-cycle stage to another, or from life to death—is helpful in averting acute emotional crisis during passage. To assist us in this all-important life task, we need contemporary "ritual experts", mature, caring people willing to support and protect us from tumultuous waves that might block our successful passage though life. These modern-day ritual experts are crisis counselors, members of self-help groups, pastors, health professionals, family, neighbors, and friends—people who care about people in crisis.

REFERENCES

Arditti R, Klein RD, Minden S (editors): *Test-tube Women.* Pandora Press, 1984.

Aries P: *Western Attitudes toward Death from the Middle Ages to the Present.* Johns Hopkins University Press, 1974.

Arms S: *Immaculate Deception.* Bantam Books, 1975.

Bloch M: *Placing the Dead.* London: Seminar Press, 1971.

Borg S, Lasker J: *When Pregnancy Fails.* Beacon Press, 1981.

Browne A: *When Battered Women Kill.* Free Press, 1987.

BWHBC (Boston Women's Health Book Collective): 4 *Our Bodies, Our Selves,* 3rd ed. Simon and Schuster, 1984.

BWHBC- Boston Women's Health Book Collection. Commercial Surrogacy Information Packet. (Available for $15.00 from BWHBC, 47 Nichols Ave., Watertown, MA 02172)

Cain BS: Plight of the gray divorce. *New York Times Magazine.*

Caplan G: *Principles of Preventive Psychiatry.* Basic Books, 1964.

Chapman JR, Gates M: *Women into Wives: The Legal and Economic Impact of Marriage.* Sage, 1977.

Chapple ED, Coon CS: *Principles of Anthropology.* Henry Holt, 1942.

Chavkin W (editor): *Double Exposure: Womens' Health Hazards on the Job and at Home.* Monthly Review Press, 1984.

Chesler P: *Mothers on Trial: The Battle for Children and Custody.* Seattle: Seal Press, 1986.

Chodorow N: *The Reproduction of Mothering.* Berkeley: University of California Press, 1978.

Corea G: *The Mother Machine.* Harper and Row, 1985.

Cutter F: *Coming to Terms with Death.* Chicago: Nelson-Hall, 1974.

Dobash RP, Dobash RE: *Violence against Wives: A Case against the Patriarchy.* Free Press, 1979.

Donner GJ: Parenthood as a crisis: A role for the psychiatric nurse. *Persp Psych Care* 1972; 10:84–87.

Doress, PB & Siegal, 1987. *Ourselves, Growing Older.* New York: Simon & Schuster 1987.

Douglas M: *Purity and Danger.* Routledge and Kegan Paul, 1966.

Durkheim E: *Elementary Forms of the Religious Life.* London: Hollen St. Press, 1915.

Ehrenreich B, English D: *For Her Own Good: 150 Years of the Experts' Advice to Women.* Anchor Books, 1979.

Erikson E: *Childhood and Society,* 2nd ed. W. W. Norton, 1963.

Estes CL: Older Women and Health Policy. Paper presented at Women, Health and Healing Summer Institute. University of California, Berkeley, June 30, 1986.

Fagerhaugh SY, Strauss A: *Politics of Pain Management.* Addison-Wesley, 1977.

Fanon F: Medicine and colonialism. In: *The Cultural Crisis of Modern Medicine.* Ehrenreich J (editor). Monthly Review Press, 1978.

Feifel H (editor): *The Meaning of Death.* McGraw-Hill, 1959.

Feifel H (editor): *The Meanings of Death.* McGraw-Hill, 1977.

Foreman J: U.S. far behind in child care policy for working parents. A 5-part series. Boston Globe.

Freud S: *Totem and Taboo.* Routledge and Kegan Paul, 1950 (German ed. 1914?).

Fried NN, Fried MH: *Transitions: Four Rituals in Eight Cultures.* W. W. Norton, 1980.

Fulton R et al. (editors): *Death and Dying.* Addison-Wesley, 1978.

General Assembly of the United Nations: Quoted in *Am J Nurs* 1975; XX:99.

Gerson K: Briefcase, baby or both? *Psychol Today* 1986; 20(11):30–36.

Giovannini M: Personal Communication, 1983.

Glaser BG, Strauss A: *Awareness of Dying.* Aldine, 1965.

Golan N: When is a client in crisis? *Soc Case Work* 1969; 50:389–394.

Golan N: *Passing through Transitions.* Free Press, 1981.

Goodman LM: *Death and the Creative LIfe.* Springer, 1981.

Goody J: *Death, Property and the Ancestors.* Tavistock, 1962.

Gregg G: Putting kids first. *The New*

York Times Magazine. April 13, 1986.
Gubrium JF (editor): *Time, Roles and Self in Old Age.* Human Sciences Press, 1976.
Halpern H: *How to Break your Addiction to a Person.* McGraw-Hill, 1982.
Harrison M: BWHBC. Commercial surrogacy information packet.
Hoff LA: *The Status of Widows: Analysis of Selected Examples from Africa and India.* (Masters dissertation.) London School of Economics, 1978.
Hoff LA: *Violence against Women: A Social-Cultural Network Analysis.* (PhD dissertation.) Boston University, 1984. University Microfilms International number 8422380.
Hosken F: Female genital mutilation and human rights. *Fem Iss* 1981; 1(3):3–23.
Inch S: *Birth Rights.* Pantheon Books, 1984.
Jacobs RH: *Life after Youth.* Beacon Press, 1979.
Kastenbaum R, Aisenberg R: *The Psychology of Death.* Springer, 1972.
Kessler RC, McLeod JD: Sex differences in vulnerability to life events. *Am Sociol Rev* 1984; 49:620–631.
Kimball ST: Introduction to *Rites of passage,* by van Gennep A. University of Chicago Press, 1960 (French ed. 1909).
Knapp RJ: When a child dies. *Psychol Today* 1987; 21(7):60–67.
Kubler-Ross E: *On Death and Dying.* Macmillan, 1969.
Kubler-Ross E: *Death, the Final Stage of Growth.* Prentice-Hall, 1975.
Lack S, Buckingham RW: *First American Hospice.* New Haven, CT: Hospice, Inc., 1978.
LaFontaine J: The power of rights. *Man* 1977; 12:421–437.
Leach E: *The Political Systems of Highland Burma.* Norwich, England: Fletcher and Son, 1954.
LeMasters EE: Parenthood as crisis. In: *Crisis Intervention: Selected Readings.* Parad HJ (editor). New York: Family Service Association of America, 1965.
Levine J: Quoted by Kirchheimer A in: The Family in the '80s: Fatherhood in transition. Boston Globe.
Levinson DJ et al.: *The Seasons of Man's Life.* Knopf, 1978.
Lopata H: *Widowhood in an American City.* Cambridge, MA: Schenkman, 1973.
McCabe SV: An overview of hospice care. *Cancer Nurs* 1982; 5:103–108.
Merton A: Father hunger. *New Age J* (Sept/Oct) 1986; 22–28, 72.
Mitford J: *The American Way of Death.* Simon and Schuster, 1963.
Mousnier R: *Social Hierarchies.* London: Croom Helm (translation), 1969.
National Center for Health Statistics—Monthly Vital Statistics Report. Vol 29. Annual summary of births, deaths, marriages, divorces: United States, 1980. Hyattsville, MD: US Department of Health and Human Services, Public Health Service, 1980.
Newberger CM, Melnicoe LH, Newberger E: *The American Family in Crisis: Implications for Children.* Special Issue: *Current Problems in Pediatrics* 1986; XVI(12):670–739.
Ngugi W: *The River Between.* London: Heinemann, 1965.
Nuwer H: Dead souls of hell week. *Hum Behav* (Oct) 1978; 53–56.
Oakley A: *Subject Women.* Pantheon Books, 1981.
O'Neill N, O'Neill G: *Shifting Gears.* New York: Evans, 1974.
Paul JA: Medicine and imperialism. In: *The Cultural Crisis of Modern Medicine.* Ehrenreich J (editor). Monthly Review Press, 1978.
Pollner M: Better dead than wed. *Soc Pol* 1982; 13(1):28–31.
Rosenthal T: *How Could I Not Be among You?* Braziller, 1973.
Rubenstein C: Real men don't earn less than their wives. *Psychol Today* 1982; 16:36–41.
Saunders C: Hospice care. *Am J Med* 1978; 65:726–728.
Seligman MEP: Giving up on life. *Psychol Today* 1974; 7:80–85.
Shapiro JL: The expectant father. *Psychol Today* 1987; 21(1):36–42.
Sheehy G: *Passages.* Dutton, 1976.
Sommers T, Shields L: *Women Take Care.* Gainsville, FL: Triad. 1987.
Spencer P: *The Samburu.* Routledge and Kegan Paul, 1965.
Spencer P: *Nomads in Alliance.* Oxford University Press, 1973.
Spencer P: Personal interview, 1978.
Stevenson JS: *Issues and Crises during*

Middlesence. Appleton-Century-Crofts, 1977.

Straus MA, Gelles RJ, Steinmetz S: *Behind Closed Doors: Violence in the American Family*. Anchor Books, 1980.

Sudnow D: *Passing on: The Social Organization of Dying*. Prentice-Hall, 1967.

Tolstoy L: *The Death of Ivan Illyich*. New York: New American Library, 1960.

Turner V: *The Forest of Symbols*. Ithaca, NY: Cornell University Press, 1967.

van Gennep A: *Rites of Passage*. Chicago: University of Chicago Press (French ed. 1909), 1960.

Van Ornum W, Mordock JB: *Crisis Counseling with Children and Adolescents*. New York: Continuum, 1987.

Vaugh D: The long goodbye. *Psychol Today* 1987; 21(7):37–42.

Wegman JA: Hospice home death, hospital death, and coping abilities of widows. *Cancer Nurs* 1987; 10(3):148–155.

Weiss RS: Transition states and other stressful situations: Their nature and programs for their management. In *Support Systems and Mutual Help: A Multi-discipinary Exploration*. Eds., G Caplan and M Killilea. New York: Grune & Stratton, 1976.

Wright LK: Life-threatening illness. *J Psychosoc Nurs* 1985; 23(9):7–11.

Zelditch M: Status, social. In *International Encyclopedia of the Social Sciences*. Ed., DL Sills. New York: Macmillan Co. & The Free Press, 1968.

CHAPTER 12

People with AIDS: A Crisis Update

"Working with Ted changed my life. . . . I'll never be the same" (hospice volunteer).

"Having AIDS is a blessing in a way. . . . It opened my spiritual being" (42-year-old man with AIDS).

"It's so humiliating [to be so dependent on people]. . . . I think I'll kill myself" (23-year-old man with Kaposi's sarcoma, dying of AIDS).

"The nurses really want to be here [a hospital AIDS unit in Boston]. . . . Lance [who had no appetite] forced himself to eat one of the chocolate chip cookies I made because 'You made it just for me.' . . . I almost cried, there was such a bond there" (psychiatric liaison nurse).

"Through this experience [working with people with AIDS] I have found me" (volunteer with AIDS Action Committee).

"I can't move my legs at night, but if I touch even one person, then maybe it will help them be good to my boy who lost his mother to this horrible disease" (woman dying of AIDS).

These statements from people with acquired immunodeficiency syndrome (AIDS) and those who help them dramatize the *opportunity* and the *danger* of *the* crisis of the modern world. This final chapter elaborates on the meaning of these vignettes and related experiences in social-psychological and cultural perspective. The chapter also reveals that, when judgment and avoidance replace understanding and assistance, the resulting fear, prejudice, and ignorance can cause insult to be added to injury for individuals and families in crisis because of AIDS. Finally, the AIDS crisis and its demand for a humane and effective response dramatize the need to address related societal crises that affect people with AIDS and their families: lack of a national health plan, homelessness, and the nursing shortage.

This chapter is based on interviews and other interaction with the following persons: Robert Cabaj, Don Cooper, Dave Dumas, Lee Ellenberg, Rosa Matara, Michael Gross, Rhonda Linde, Betty Morgan, Lori Novick, Lucy Sewall, and ongoing work with the Boston AIDS Action Committee, and Worcester Area AIDS Project.

AIDS: ILLUSTRATION OF THE CRISIS PARADIGM

The Crisis Paradigm informing this book describes the experience of people in crisis and the process of using the *opportunities* a crisis provides and avoiding its *dangers*. Earlier chapters have shown that success in crisis work requires understanding the origins of a particular crisis experience and tailoring intervention strategies to these distinct yet interrelated sources. AIDS is not only an epidemic of global proportions—a pandemic—but it typifies life crisis as a whole and cuts across the ramifications of life crises already discussed: loss, grief, and mourning; suicide by despairing people with AIDS; anti-gay violence; social network support; family and community crises; status changes in health, residence, and occupation; and finally, life cycle transitions and death.*

The traumatic event of being diagnosed with a fatal disease reverses the natural progression of life span development, forcing the person with AIDS to face death at a life phase when energy, independence, sexuality, and community involvement are at their peak rather than in decline. A person who tests positive for the AIDS virus (HIV) may feel similarly overwhelmed (see later section on testing). Add to this the prevalence of AIDS among groups already despised or disadvantaged (gay and bisexual men, blacks and Hispanics, intravenous drug users) because of sex-role prejudice and the effects of racism and poverty, and AIDS can be viewed as not only the most tragic epidemic of this century, but as the paradigmatic or typical life crisis—for those suffering from AIDS, for those caring for them, and for the global community. Not only for the individuals confronting AIDS, but for all of us, perhaps no other crisis will present greater danger or opportunity for the human community. In addition to the 150,000 cases of AIDS reported in 128 countries since the epidemic began, another 150,000 new cases are predicted for 1988 (The Nation's Health 1988).† Let us examine this crisis in detail from the perspective of people with AIDS and those who help them.

*Readers are referred to other standard texts for historical overview (Shilts 1987), medical/nursing facets (Centers for Disease Control, Durham and Cohen 1987, Kurland 1987, NLN 1988), and routine home care (Hughes, Martin, and Franks 1987) of people with AIDS.

†While figures quoted are from the most recently available public health sources, global research findings may render them inaccurate very quickly. However, caring for persons in crisis because of AIDS or AIDS-related anxiety will remain stable within the framework of crisis management for very sick and dying people, with the added burden of societal rejection for some. For current statistical information readers are referred to: *AIDS Weekly Surveillance Report*, Center for Disease Control, US Public Health Service, Atlanta, Georgia 30333. The national AIDS Hotline number is 1-800-342-AIDS.

Case Example: Daniel

Daniel is a 38-year-old bisexual man who has been diagnosed with AIDS for 18 months and is now living in a hospice managed by the local AIDS Action Committee (AAC). Pneumocystis pneumonia was the occasion for Daniel's several hospitalizations in the past 18 months. He is down from his usual 185 pounds to 130, has periodic bouts of nausea and diarrhea, and some beginning neurological involvement that affects his gait. Once a successful health care worker and artist, Daniel lost his human service job because of federal cuts in domestic programs and could not find another job. Getting AIDS further reduced his employability. He is now without a paid job and receives $409 in Social Security disability payments per month. He is also eligible for $10 worth of food stamps per month, but for that amount "I couldn't be bothered," he said.

Daniel says that he was "cancelled by Medicaid three times for no reason. . . . When I left the hospital I had no money, no job, no apartment. . . . I'm still struggling with the VA for the benefits coming to me. If it weren't for AAC I would have been out on the street. I was lying in bed with tubes and PCP [pneumocystis carinii pneumonia] and the social worker said, 'Well, if worse comes to worse, we'll have to put you in the Pine Street Inn' [a shelter for homeless men]. I jumped out of bed, tore my tubes out, and chased her down the hall, Someone on the staff forced her to apologize. . . . After working in the system for as long as I have I know that she should have done more for me than that. As if it's not bad enough to have AIDS, but I'm slapped in the face. . . . I got a dose of what the elderly and the homeless go through. You know, I say 'forget your cure.' What would I ever want to come back [from death] for? Homelessness? Poverty? I have no regrets. . . . I used to be seen as a pillar of strength, then people saw me as sick and no longer there for them, but slowly they're coming back. So, I don't have a regular job anymore, but now I'm a teacher and counselor [helping other people with AIDS], and I work three hours volunteering at a local men's shelter. I also do liaison work at the hospital where I was a patient. Yes, I get weak, but now I do what I can when I can and as much as I can. There's not the same pressure as before. . . . As long as I don't set expectations, there's no disappointment."

Case Example: Sophia

Sophia, age 30, has a 4-year-old son whom she placed with relatives as an infant because she could not care for him properly as long as she was an IV drug addict. Though she had symptoms for about four years, Sophia was only diagnosed with AIDS two years ago. [Initially she was diagnosed with AIDS related complex (ARC), used by the Center for Disease Control (CDC).] She suffers from night sweats, thrush, shingles, chronic fatigue, abscesses, a platelet disorder, and central nervous system involvement, including seizures and memory loss. Through her 12 years as an addict, Sophia worked as a waitress and a prostitute to support her drug habit. "It's hard to realize that all the things I dreamed about if I was drug free can't be now because of AIDS. . . . I thought having a baby would help me get my act together. I was wrong, but I would never hurt my son. . . . I don't take pride in too many things I've done, but I spared Michael by putting him in a stable environment. I'm not sorry I had Michael because he's what keeps me going now. . . . If it weren't for him I probably would have killed myself already. I'm not through doing what has to be done—helping other drug users, and letting my son know me better. And I do a lot of talks for doctors and nurses about AIDS.

Michael and I spend every weekend together. . . . I'm making some videos for him so he will remember who I was and how much I love him. He knows to say "no" to drugs. . . . Behind every addict, you know, there is a child, a lover. It's people's responsibility to set aside their biases, to take care. . . . I have my problems, but at least I can care for someone else's pain, maybe because I've been close to pain. Some say they should lock up prostitutes, but don't tell me it's my fault that a man rides around in his Mercedes-Benz looking for sex instead of being faithful to his wife. I have wonderful friends. . . . When the memory problems get worse I'll give one of them power of attorney because my family judges me very harshly—for my addiction, prostitution, and now AIDS. . . . plus I'm a lesbian—and if I left it to them they would put out all the people who care about me when I'm dying. None of my family come to see me when I'm in the hospital. It's sad—I've spent half my life finding myself and now I'm going to die, but I have an opportunity to plan my time and get closure, and that's good.

Daniel and Sophia are at peace; indeed, talking and being with them is an inspiration. Both are doing meaningful work. At his young age Daniel feels he has accomplished much of his life's work, though he still wants to write his memoirs. Dan does not seem to be afraid of death. When asked if he would commit suicide if his symptoms included a new crisis point, dementia, he said "No . . . it could be tough, though, because I've always been very independent and self-sufficient. . . . I had to fight like hell to get what I have now, but if it came to the point where I needed more care and they don't respond, well, I'm going anyway." As Daniel's neurological symptoms progressed, his struggle to remain at peace intensified. He also was stressed by the fact that some of his friends could not face the reality of his approaching death, but instead of expressing their pain and impending loss, they either avoided him or made fleeting visits stating they "didn't have time" to talk. Daniel's occasional angry outbursts toward his friends may also be displacements of the anger he feels about dying but which is difficult to express because it implies a contradiction to his "caretaker" and "nice guy" image of self. Sophia readily expresses her sadness and pain, but says her work is not done yet, so she keeps going, and no longer feels like killing herself.

How did Daniel and Sophia arrive at the peace and acceptance they experience in spite of constant physical pain and knowledge that they are dying? By what process did Daniel win his "fight like hell" to get where he is? How did Sophia come to manage her ultimate life crisis in a constructive manner and finally give up her addiction to drugs? The Crisis Paradigm illustrates the process of dealing with the crisis of AIDS and how people with AIDS can capitalize on the "opportunity" of this tragic unanticipated event to arrive at "positive resolution" and avoid the "danger" inherent in crisis. The following discussion elaborates on the paradigm using the AIDS crisis experience and illustrations from the lives of Sophia and Daniel.

CRISIS ORIGINS

Although AIDS was initially viewed as a "gay" disease, people now generally recognize that the HIV makes no distinction based on race, class, sex, age, religion, or sexual preference. For those it strikes, a diagnosis of AIDS is an unanticipated, traumatic event of overwhelming proportions (see Crisis Paradigm, top circle, first box). With the growing belief that over half of HIV carriers will eventually come down with AIDS or ARC unless new treatments are found (Petit 1988, p. 4), we may only have seen the tip of the iceberg. Present medical knowledge and the lack of a cure also amounts to an almost certain prediction of death for most AIDS patients within months or a few years. However, as Haney (1988, p. 251), a person with AIDS, notes, prediction about how long the person has to live "is simply a game of statistics and fortune-telling. Doesn't it make more sense to help the person with AIDS to focus on the possibilities of living with AIDS rather than on a

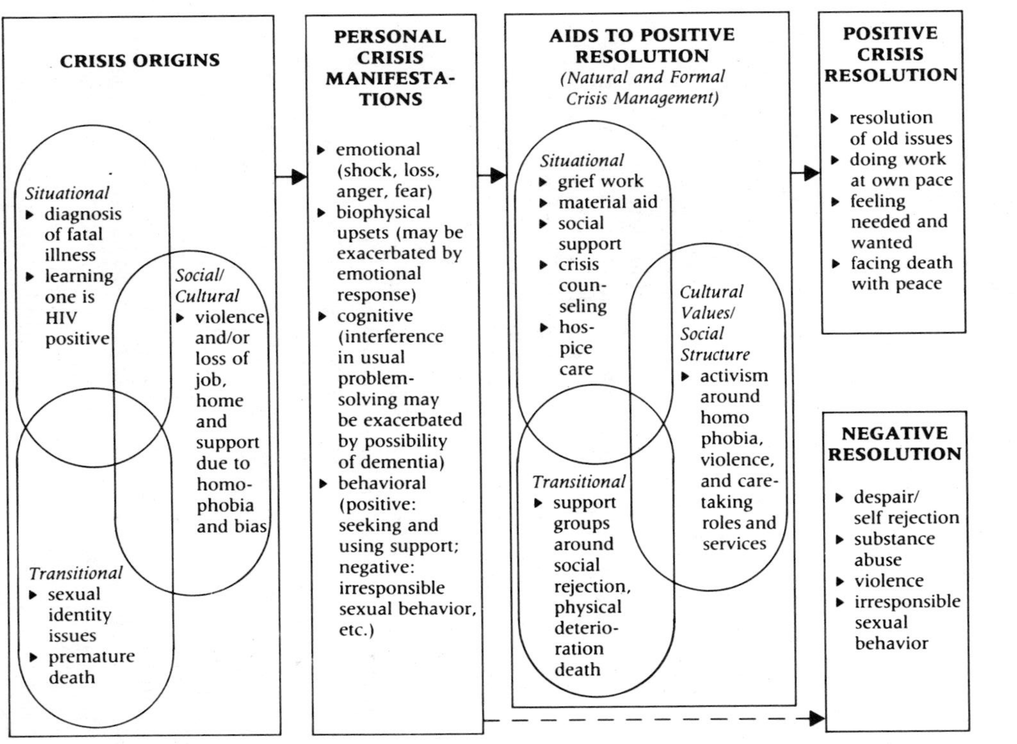

CRISIS PARADIGM

Crisis origins, manifestations, and outcomes, and the respective functions of crisis management in interactional relationship applied to a person with AIDS or testing HIV positive. The solid line from "origins" to positive resolution illustrates the *opportunity* for positive outcomes of the AIDS crisis; the broken line depicts the potential *danger* of the AIDS crisis in the absence of appropriate aids to individuals and responses by society.

negative self-fulfilling prophecy?" As with any statistical predictors, then, we must remember that—without instilling false hope—there are always individual exceptions to the pattern, as revealed by the fact that a few people have lived well beyond the predicted time of death. As noted in Chapter 2, the timing of a life event influences its effect on people. In the case of AIDS, facing the final transition, death (one's own and that of many friends), during youth or early middle age—at the height of involvement with life—reverses the natural order of things and demands extraordinary support. And families of persons dying with AIDS must come to terms with the reversal of their natural expectation to precede rather than follow their children in death.

Another developmental challenge and reversal concerns the issue of "coming out" for gay men. Having resolved gay identity and life-style issues, in some cases deciding not to "come out" to family, and now faced with a terminal illness, a gay man with AIDS sees old issues resurface as he informs his family of his illness, which implies his homosexual preference if he does not overtly reveal it. This revelation constitutes either a new developmental challenge for him and his family centering on sexual identity, or instigates further loss through rejection by family who cannot accept having a homosexual son (see Crisis Paradigm, lower circle, first box). In the cases of both Daniel and Sophia, their families have still not come to terms with the life-styles and sexual preferences of their children. This means that the potential support of family during the crisis of AIDS is not realized by either of them. Sad as this is, however, we see that Daniel and Sophia did not allow family rejection to exacerbate their problems; rather, they availed themselves of alternative sources of support—loyal and trusted friends.

Once a person is affected and diagnosed with AIDS, other events often follow: loss of job, home, friends, and sometimes family. But these losses are closely tied to social-structural and cultural factors, unlike temporary homelessness due to a fire, or the unexpected death of a loved one from an illness that is not stigmatized (Sontag 1979) (see Crisis Paradigm, right circle, first box). Complicating this facet of the AIDS crisis is the lack of a comprehensive plan for health and housing for the poor, sick, and disadvantaged (especially in the United States). This general social problem is exacerbated for people with AIDS (currently most prominent among gay and bisexual men and IV drug users) because of homophobia and anti-gay prejudice (see Stress, Crisis and Illness in Chapter 2, Krieger 1988 and Rounds 1988). In some cases, prejudice is carried as far as anti-gay violence against anyone known or suspected of being gay. As Rhonda Linde (1988) notes, AIDS becomes an excuse for society to heap more abuse onto groups that prejudiced people would like to get rid of anyway. Analysis of several dozen opinion polls reveals that despite public education about AIDS 20–30% of respondents favor primitive measures such as quarantining or even tattoing persons who are HIV infected (Blendon and Donelan 1988). Thus, for people with AIDS, or at high risk for AIDS, the origin of crisis is not as straightforward as in sudden infant death syndrome (SIDS), for example (see Chapter 2). Rather, as Daniel's and Sophia's cases illustrate, the origins are intertwined and produce personal crisis responses clearly related to the triple origins in the Crisis Paradigm, responses that sensitive crisis workers must be attuned to if the dangers of crisis are to be avoided.

PERSONAL CRISIS MANIFESTATIONS

The person afflicted with AIDS will experience most of the common emotional responses to a traumatic life event (see Chapter 3 and second box of Crisis Paradigm). Anger springs not simply from being striken by the ultimate misfortune of facing an untimely death, but also from unfair or violent treatment by a society with limited tolerance for anyone who is different or is perceived as "receiving deserved punishment for a deviant life-style." Besides feeling angry, persons who get AIDS through a blood transfusion may feel self-righteous as they compare their misfortune to those they perceive are afflicted because of their own behavior. Anxiety is felt not only for one's own health and welfare, but also for one's lover or previous partners whom one may have infected. "Survivor guilt," as noted for Holocaust survivors in Chapter 9, may also surface for those who have lost partners and loved ones to AIDS. Some may also feel guilt or shame over their gay life-style, having incorporated societal homophobia (fear of homsexuality and homosexuals) (Dunkel and Hatfield 1986). Sophia says, for example, "I can't take pride in too many things I've done," but she does not wallow in guilt, nor is she ashamed of being lesbian even though her family condemns her for it.

Denial of the medical facts and the need for behavioral change, especially if accompanied by free-floating anger at being infected, may result in irresponsible sexual behavior and the risk of infecting others. On the other hand, when Sophia was told she had AIDS (after being tested without her consent), no one told her about cleaning her "works" (needles, etc.) with bleach or practicing safe sex. She regrets that she may have infected others, but if she did, it was out of ignorance, not malice. In general, the most ethical approach is to inform a sex partner of one's infection status. Crisis counseling and support are clearly indicated for infected persons who act out their anger by placing others at risk. Sexual decision making is a complex process often not amenable to a simplistic "just say 'No' " approach (Bochros 1988, p. 255)

Sadness over loss of health and impending death is compounded by fear of losing friends and/or lover and the necessary support to face early death. These fears have not materialized in either Dan's or Sophia's cases, but occasionally Dan has an anxiety attack when people who promise to do things for him either forget or are late.

Anxiety's usual interference in cognitive functioning during crisis may be exacerbated with AIDS because of the fear of dementia. For example, normal forgetting may be interpreted as a first sign. AIDS Dementia Complex (ADC) may sometimes be the only sign of AIDS (Joyce 1988). Sophia is clearly planning for this possibility by arranging for a friend to act with power of attorney on her behalf. In the case of another dying person with AIDS, Charlie, flashes of awareness and clarity pierced his general comatose state, so that he was able to make known his wishes not to employ heroic measures to keep him alive.

In general, the emotional and biophysical stress responses common during any life crisis are exaggerated here because of sociocultural facets of the crisis that are usually beyond the control of an individual to manage alone. Additionally, the physical toll that the disease exacts usually includes drastic energy reduction, which in turn increases stress because of inability to engage in physical stress reduction activities.

While these general crisis responses to the trauma of AIDS are illustrated in the lives of people like Daniel, Sophia, and their families, we must remember that AIDS is different for each person. This fact underscores the importance of careful individual assessment to ascertain effective and ineffective coping with the crisis and lays the groundwork for assistance tailored to the interrelated origins of this crisis. Table 12-1 summarizes effective and ineffective coping with AIDS and forms the foundation for planning crisis management strategies with the affected person and his or her family, lover, and other network members.

AIDS TO POSITIVE CRISIS RESOLUTION

Soon after Daniel was diagnosed with AIDS in 1986, a psychiatrist walked into his hospital room. Dan asked, "Why are you here?" The psychiatrist responded, "Your doctor thought you . . ." Dan said, "Tell him to talk to me." In the traditional psychiatric model, this response would have been interpreted as "resistance." However, in the crisis model, not only is Daniel's response not considered abnormal, but the engagement of a psychiatric consultant without Dan's consent ignores one of the most fundamental principles of successful crisis intervention: planning *with* the person in crisis (see Chapter 4).

But if Dan rejected the help of a psychiatrist and was on bad terms with the hospital social worker, what else was available to help him cope as effectively as he did with the crisis of AIDS? Let's listen to Daniel's explanation: "Sure, I was angry, sure I was scared . . . but they don't understand that throughout my life I've had to turn to myself. Once I can face it, I have to help my family and friends to understand." But does this mean that Dan didn't need any outside help? Not at all. Rather, it underscores the often repeated position of this book: people have been managing crises since the beginning of time (natural crisis management). Also, in spite of his spirit of independence and self-sufficiency, Dan recognized his need for support and accepted it. He said that the hospital nurses were wonderful and that friends on the outside and his previous attitude helped the most. Also, Dan said that he was greatly strengthened by helping his friends go through death. Many

Table 12-1

Effective and Ineffective Crisis Coping with AIDS by Person with AIDS and Family Member(s)

Person in Crisis	Personal Crisis Manifestations	Crisis Coping: Ineffective	Crisis Coping: Effective
Person with AIDS	Emotional	Denial of medical facts and probability of death Repression Depression Hatred of self	Grief work Communication of feelings with caring persons
	Biophysical	Additional stress symptoms of emotional origin	Physical symptoms limited to opportunistic infections Resistance to additional stress symptoms
	Cognitive	Conviction of being punished for life-style or sexual preference Failure to accept reality of illness	Recognition and acceptance of the reality and horror of the disease and all it implies
	Behavioral	Irresponsible sexual behavior placing others at risk Violence Substance abuse	Safe sex practices Preventive health practices: diet, rest, exercise, relaxation Acceptance of love and necessary assistance Preparation for death
Family member of person with AIDS	Emotional	Denial of medical facts Inappropriate self-blame for child's sexual preference	Grief work Unconditional acceptance regardless of sexual preference or life-style
	Biophysical	Additional stress symptoms of emotional origin Burnout from failure to care for self	Resistance to additional stress symptoms and burnout through self-care and acceptance of support and respite
	Cognitive	Perception of AIDS as a "gay" disease Clinging to myths about contagion, etc.	Recognition and acceptance of medical facts about AIDS
	Behavioral	Judgment and blaming of person with AIDS Avoidance and withholding of support and love	Expression of caring through communication, hugging, etc. Material support and assistance with activities of daily living

volunteers cite a similar growth process in their support work with people with AIDS (Stulberg and Smith 1988). One "buddy" with Boston's AIDS Action Committee said: "Sometimes I feel guilty because it seems like I get more than I give." He also said of standing by a man dying of AIDS: "I've never been so compelled by anything in my whole life. . . . What a gift it was to be able to be with him. . . . Nothing I've done since has been as honest."

What about Sophia? Precisely what did she have or receive that assisted her along the path of constructive coping with AIDS? Sophia tells of being hospitalized for abscesses, violating hospital rules by "shooting up" on the ward, and leaving the hospital only to collapse shortly afterward. She knew that without treatment she would probably die, but having a drug fix at the time seemed more important. Later she checked back into the hospital and was confronted by the head nurse who said: "You ruined my day. . . . I can help you, but here are the rules. . . . Are you willing to keep them?" "You know," Sophia said, "that nurse did me a real favor. She was furious with me and I don't blame her, but instead of burying her anger she confronted me and I could tell that she did it because she cared." Sophia contrasted the nurse's response to that of a dentist who refused to treat her but also refused to wear gloves: "I sent the dentist an AIDS information packet and a note: 'I'm sad for you that your ignorance is putting you at risk.' "

These responses highlight the repeated point made by people with AIDS: they are not victims and do not want to be treated as victims; they are people in crisis. Dan's case illustrates that those with poorer psychological health than his prior to a traumatic life event are more vulnerable to possible negative outcomes of crisis (see Chapter 3). Thus, Dan's healthy self-concept was a buffer against absorbing society's prejudice in guilt and self-blame. Rather than blaming himself, Dan says that "AIDS made me aware of the strength and courage I have." When someone in the hospital suggested "You're being punished," Dan said: "Excuse me, I've received a blessing you'll never understand." For those of us less ready for death than Dan is, it is important to remember that emotional healing from life's traumatic events requires the individual in crisis to make sense out of the experience, to process it in his or her personal meaning system (see Chapter 2 and Antonovsky 1980 on "coherence"). In Dan's case, his relationship to God is a definite aid to his continuous coping with the disease and its old and new demands, and his success in finding meaning in life despite his suffering. For example, when Dan's immune system became weaker and weaker, he was advised to discontinue volunteer work at the men's shelter to protect himself from further infections. He then substituted his on-site volunteering with a monthly monetary donation out of his meager welfare funds. (See Haney 1988.)

Similarly, Sophia finds meaning in her suffering and a reason to keep going for the sake of her child and whatever influence she can have on the drug problem and helping health professionals to learn about AIDS. Her lifelong proximity to suffering and pain has apparently heightened her sensitivity to the needs and pain of others. Assistance to Dan, Sophia, and many like them during crisis is available primarily through groups like the AIDS Action Committee in Boston, which provides housing and hospice care, and neighborhood people who help as needed with mowing the lawn, keeping the sidewalks clear, and tilling the garden when physical strength fails. With this kind of assistance Dan and others in his hospice house are able to live a normal life in the community and face their impending deaths with greater comfort than institutional care would provide. Dan has great fear of being put in an institution, saying he would rather be dead. His residence in a hospice house allows him to use his remaining strengths to the greatest possible capacity. For him this includes activism on behalf of other people with AIDS (especially speaking engagements and interviews), and liaison work at a hospital. The gradual return of his old friends has also helped, and Dan has made new friends as well. Relationships with some of his family members remain strained, but Dan is not consumed with guilt, anxiety, or pain about this. While he loves his family dearly and regrets his emotional distance from some of them, he does what he can to help them understand, and simply hopes that for their own sake they will come to greater understanding of him and his life-style before he dies. Dan's family has rejected offers of support groups to help them through the crisis of Dan's illness. Sophia's family also rejects such support. While Sophia also mourns her family's emotional distance from her, she is grateful that they pay her rent and provide her with a car to get around.

POSITIVE CRISIS RESOLUTION

The crisis management strategies that aided Daniel correspond to the interrelated origins of his crisis: situational, transitional, and social-cultural (see third box of Crisis Paradigm). Together, they led to growth and development for Dan (see upper right box of Crisis Paradigm); for example, he says that getting AIDS has been the occasion for him to resolve with his ex-wife old issues around his bisexuality. He is no longer rushed and overworked. He feels needed and wanted by the homeless men and others with AIDS and has a healthy circle of friends, including a cadre of mental health professionals who enjoy rapping with him. His adjustment to a healthy interdependence allows him to maintain as much independence as he can, while he does not hesitate to ask for the help he needs now and may need as he gets closer to death. Dan says that AIDS has forced him to take a "closer, more intense look at life, so now I'm more ready to leave it." In fact, Dan is not unlike the top performing artists Goodman studied (1981), who had "won the race with death." Like them, Dan feels fulfilled, feels ready to die, and has no desire to return.

For Sophia, in addition to her educational work with health professionals and the importance of being there for her son as long as possible, she says: "There's a reason for this. . . . I went on the radio and made

$53,000 for the AIDS Action Committee. It makes it meaningful. I feel robbed by this disease, but it's an opportunity to plan my time and get closure, and that's good."

AVOIDING NEGATIVE CRISIS OUTCOMES

But for one of Dan's friends with AIDS, Jesse, things did not go as well—at least temporarily. Jesse had Kaposi's sarcoma. His skin was dying; he was being eaten away. Jesse also had neurological involvement and some beginning symptoms of dementia. He found it humiliating to have people do things for him that he was used to doing for himself. Dan helped out by putting reminders up around the house to compensate for Jesse's growing mental impairment. One day Jesse declared to Dan that he just couldn't go on any more: "I want to kill myself" (see lower right box of Crisis Paradigm). Here is Dan's response to Jesse: "Jes, no matter how bad this hits us, let's face it together. . . . I'm in pain too. You know where I'm at. . . . Let's share it. You're strong . . . look at what you've done for others." Jesse did not commit suicide, but died in the hospital a couple of weeks later. Jesse's death is not unlike the one described earlier, which was such an inspiration to a "buddy" with the AIDS Action Committee. The fortitude and acceptance with which Charlie faced death was experienced as a gift by all those who stood by him to the end, even though it was a strain—an agony that even the buddy wanted to be over.

As we examine the interchange between Dan and Jesse, it is clear that Dan did not simply talk Jesse out of suicide. First of all, the issue of suicide for people dying of AIDS raises all the ethical issues discussed in Chapter 6. In the case of AIDS, it might be easier for people to favor "rational suicide" than in other crisis situations. Thus, many would argue for the right of people dying with AIDS to commit suicide rather than suffer the horrors of physical and mental deterioration. However, as tragic as AIDS is, Daniel, Sophia, and thousands like them tell us that life can be meaningful and worthwhile in spite of great suffering. Also, in relation to the social and cultural dimensions of the AIDS crisis, if those afflicted with AIDS experience insult added to injury through anti-gay scorn and violence and then decide to commit suicide, those of us left can well ask whether such suicides, even those considered "rational," have been "manipulated" by us (Battin 1980) through our failure to respond to those in crisis with the care needed and without judgment. If a caretaker or friend of a person dying of AIDS requests assistance to commit suicide, the caretaker must not only be familiar with ethical and legal issues regarding suicide, but should consider hidden messages as well. For example, a person in severe pain may not consider suicide the only option if provided with appropriate pain relief measures. Clear communication and understanding of the real message are crucial here. Dealing with such a request requires peer support and possibly consultation with a mental health professional experienced in work with suicidal people.

While the topic of suicide and AIDS is not yet thoroughly researched,* it appears that people with AIDS, like most people dying of cancer, do not wish to kill themselves even though some individual and couple suicides have been reported (Marzuk et al 1988). Perhaps the greatest challenge for supporters of people with AIDS is to help create a milieu that will make it unnecessary for them to choose suicide. Such an environment would underscore the love and caring that helps the dying put their material affairs in order, say goodbye to lovers and family after reconciliation (hopefully) and healing, be recognized and valued for their place on this earth, and thus be ready for life's final stage (see Chapter 11, Death).

WOMEN AND CHILDREN WITH AIDS

Sophia and Daniel illustrate commonalities among people with AIDS: shock, anger, loss, and mourning a shortened life. But because women constitute a smaller percentage of people with AIDS, about 7% in Western industrialized societies and 50% in Africa, we may tend to overlook them and some of the special issues they face. For example, women with AIDS may experience greater stress around appearance as they deteriorate physically. This is because of judgments of women based on cultural definitions of female acceptability. Women have the additional stress of worrying about becoming pregnant and possibly transmitting the virus to offspring. Fortunately, having her child infected with the AIDS virus was not one of Sophia's many stressors.

While the efficiency of male-female versus female-male transmission of HIV is still unknown, researchers generally believe that the virus is less easily transmitted from woman to man than the other way around (Richardson 1987). Thus, female prostitutes have more to fear from their clients than their clients do from them (Knox 1988), despite the publicly expressed concern about prostitutes as a major source of spreading the virus. Similar risk factors operate for the female sex partners of IV drug users with AIDS. Since only about 5% of the men with AIDS do not fall into known risk groups (gay, bisexual, IV drug users, hemophiliacs, or receptors of a blood transfusion), it is difficult to interpret whether the source of their infection is from visiting an infected prostitute, since many men would rather admit to visiting a prostitute than desiring a man for sex (Richardson 1987, p. 37).

Female prostitutes, perhaps more so than gay men, are scorned by most in society (as Sophia's case amply illustrates), and thus it is easy to scapegoat them for spreading AIDS. In Africa, where AIDS is distributed

*For example, Stulberg and Smith (1988) found in a survey that 20.6% of 301 gay men *not* diagnosed with AIDS or ARC had thought about suicide because of AIDS, though no suicide risk assessment data were included (see Chapter 6).

equally between women and men in the heterosexual population,* female prostitutes in particular have been blamed for its transmission. Prostitutes who have AIDS or are HIV positive already receive discriminatory treatment; blaming these women for AIDS also reveals the general double standard regarding prostitution (eg, arresting the women, but rarely if ever their patrons) and the economic disadvantages of women that drive many of them into prostitution in the first place. Similar dynamics operate in regard to the traffic in sex, for example, women who are kidnapped, raped, and sent to places like Japan or Europe and forced into prostitution to service tourists (Barry 1979). Women like this who get AIDS are in crisis not only because of a fatal illness, but primarily because of the worldwide sexual and economic exploitation of women (Seager and Olson 1986). In other words, their crises around AIDS are primarily of social and cultural origin.

A problem faced by those prostitutes (and many other women) who attempt to have safe sex by using condoms is that many men refuse to cooperate, and in some instances physically abuse the prostitute—a contemporary version of making the traditional responsibility for contraception be borne exclusively by women. This issue highlights the additional danger presented by AIDS if people ignore the imperative to change stereotypical male/female sexual behavior and accept equal responsibility for safer sex.

An additional hazard for women with AIDS is linked to the pregnancy risk. That is, if they are also IV drug users (the largest group of women with AIDS) and fail to prevent pregnancy, their ability to take care of a child will be even more limited because the problems connected with drug use are added to the debilitating effects of AIDS. Sophia's foresight in this area moved her to place her child with a stable family when she was unable to overcome her addiction. Additionally, a woman whose child has AIDS will probably feel guilty and angry whether she does or does not have AIDS herself.

Lesbian women, while in the lowest risk group for AIDS, nevertheless are also affected by the crisis. Sophia traces her infection to dirty needles to support her drug habit, not her lesbian status. As significant others for gay men, some lesbians will suffer the loss of friendships through the deaths of these men. They are similarly affected by greater anti-gay discrimination and violence, primarily because of inaccurate portrayals by the media and public ignorance about how AIDS is spread. Lesbians are also concerned if they are considering artificial or self-insemination. Finally, lesbians as

---

*The marked difference between African and Western rates of AIDS among heterosexuals has been attributed to infected blood transfusions; increased incidence of vaginal bleeding during intercourse among women with scar tissue from clitoridectomy and infibulation (Hosken 1981); greater vulnerability to HIV infection due to poverty and generally poorer health status; lack of sterile technique in traditional circumcision rites and possibly in poor hospitals. Research has yet to confirm these possible explanations.

women are among the majority of AIDS caretakers (see Caring for People with AIDS in this chapter).

The tragedy of AIDS is even more poignant in respect to children. While the adult with AIDS can come to terms with the inevitability of death and work through the crisis, including its implications for his or her previous and future sexual behavior, children with AIDS obviously cannot. This implies that there is an additional challenge for parents with AIDS to prevent pregnancy, and for caretakers to treat and care for children with AIDS with extraordinary compassion and attention to the disenfranchised states of the parents who brought them into the world—blacks, Hispanics, IV drug users, and the poor in general (*AIDS: Report of the Surgeon General 1987*).

Similarly poignant and tragic is AIDS or fear of HIV infection following rape. While this double crisis affects male victims of rape, the majority of rape victims are women. The emotional trauma for such victims is overwhelming, particularly in the face of continuing public attitudes of blaming the crime of rape on its victims and prosecuting very few assailants (see Chapter 8). If these attitudes prevail, rape victims may continue to blame themselves not only for the rape, but for AIDS as well, and in addition, they must face all that any other person with AIDS confronts in an untimely death.

THE WORRIED WELL, AIDS ANXIETY SYNDROME, AND TESTING

Anxiety about AIDS is not restricted to those in known high-risk groups, such as gay men. Men who have visited a prostitute once may fear HIV infection and consider suicide a more desireable option than revealing marital infidelity. Or a suburban housewife may feel guilt about an affair, which is expressed in unrealistic concern about AIDS infection. AIDS thus becomes the "coatrack" on which to hang all kinds of issues that have been unresolved (Linde 1988, Krieger 1988, p. 264). Of the 301 undiagnosed gay men surveyed by Stulberg and Smith (1988), those in monogamous relationships experienced less psychological stress than those without a stable intimate relationship. In this same group, older gays (between ages 26 and 50) were twice as likely as younger gays to have thought about suicide because of AIDS. In another version of the stress/illness cycle, some of the "worried well" feel compulsively driven to preventive health practices like jogging in the hope of warding off either acquiring or activating the HIV infection. The challenge in this area is to unbundle realistic concern about AIDS from anxiety about various other issues such as sexual practice, sexual preference, or traumatic events like the Vietnam war. (See Post-Traumatic Stress in Chapter 8.) Krieger (1988, pp. 263–264) suggests five steps in a counseling approach to persons with heighened anxiety about AIDS and fears about sexual transmission of AIDS: (1) obtain accurate information;

(2) assess fear of prior exposure; (3) learn to protect oneself and others; (4) gather strong peer support; and (5) address related issues such as homophobia, addictive attachments to dangerous sex, or guilt over sexual or drug use behavior. Everyone working with the "worried well" and people in high risk groups for AIDS should be thoroughly familiar with the clues to suicide, risk assessment techniques, and strategies of suicide prevention discussed in Chapters 6 and 7.

This leads to consideration of the controversial issue of testing for infection with HIV. If testing were more definitive than it is, opinion might be less divided. Testing reveals if one is infected with the virus, but not whether he or she has AIDS. Since it takes a while for antibodies to form, even if a person were exposed yesterday, he or she could test negative today, thus potentially conveying false reassurance. In general, opinion is equally divided between the advantages and disadvantages of testing. Since a positive test can send psychologically unstable people into panic and possible suicide, testing should be carefully considered in each case. Also, people who may have absorbed society's homophobia and feel self-loathing may request testing to "prove" that they are "sinful or immoral." Thus, counseling and ongoing support services for those who either are considering testing or have been tested are essential. Such services are available through groups like the AIDS Action Committee and health centers that are sensitive to the AIDS crisis.

While the issue of testing will probably remain controversial as long as much remains unknown about the disease and drugs to treat it, testing is definitely indicated when pregnancy is being considered for one who has symptoms and a differential diagnosis is needed (Linde 1988). In all cases, however, individuals should have a choice about being tested (Galea, Lewis, and Baker 1988). Those who are psychologically healthy enough to deal with the unknown and who have greater tolerance for ambiguity may choose not to be tested. The situation is similar to that faced by people at risk for various genetically transmitted diseases. For example, Marzuk et al. (1988, p. 1336) suggest that suicide risk among persons with AIDS may be greater than among persons with Huntington's disease.

CARING FOR PEOPLE WITH AIDS

As of this writing, US Surgeon General C. Everett Koop predicted that there will be no cure for AIDS, and that a vaccine will not be discovered before the end of this century. Let us hope that this prediction is eventually proved false. But since the present moment finds us in precisely this position, the challenge for caretakers to face this crisis with knowledge, skill, compassion, and caring could hardly be greater. We have seen from our opening case examples that Daniel and Sophia have come through the first crises of AIDS to the point of peace and acceptance of eventual death. They managed to do so with a combination of natural and formal crisis management strategies.

We have also seen that their personal coping abilities compensated in part for the extra stress they endured because of less than ideal approaches by some health care providers, and that they understand and accept those around them who cannot understand.

Others with fewer resources, however, may not come through life's final passage to death with peace, fulfillment, and the comfort of family and friends without extraordinary assistance from various caretakers. Families and/or lovers in crisis over the impending loss of loved ones and the emotional cost of caring need similar help. In short, providing for others whose needs are very great also demands caring and understanding for the caretakers. The general stress on those who care for others has been documented in Chapters 2, 5, and 6.

While women outside of Africa are less at risk for AIDS, large numbers of women have joined the gay men's community in mobilizing care for people with AIDS. And in the family network it is not uncommon for mothers of gay or bisexual men to know about their sons' sexual identitiy while fathers remain unaware. This results in a large emotional burden for these women that they have not been able to share with their husbands. Similarly, in the case of infants and children with AIDS, the major burden of care falls on mothers because of continued inequality in society over caretaking roles in the family (see Chapters 5 and 11). In hospitals as well, women constitute the majority providing care for the acutely ill and dying; in addition, they face the stress of overwork because of the acute nursing shortage. As so often in the past, so now with AIDS, the cost of caring is born disproportionately by women (Sommers and Shields 1987). Significantly, as the gay men's community mobilized to support their sick and dying members, they were joined chiefly by lesbian and heterosexual women. This fact reveals that much work lies ahead in assuming equal responsibility for meeting society's need for caretaking roles, regardless of gender or sexual preference.

In caring for people with AIDS, extraordinary stressors must be dealt with: fear of contagion (though this is decreasing with increased education); stigmatization stemming from association with devalued members of society (Goffman 1963); confrontation with issues of sexual identity, one's own risk of AIDS, and death; assuming power of attorney roles; dealing with suicide issues; and finally, simple overload from association with the depths of pain and tragedy surrounding people with AIDS, their families, and lovers. The enthusiasm of thousands of volunteers and others who have mobilized around the AIDS crisis certainly acts as a buffer to some of the stress because, as many caretakers attest, new meaning has entered their lives through their work with people with AIDS. This is no small accomplishment in a death-denying society.

The principle of providing ongoing support for all AIDS crisis workers and family members must be applied in order to prevent burnout and the eventual loss of needed staff (Hoff and Miller 1987). Also, among families, knowledge and ability to care for a dying loved one varies, requiring that professionals provide what families may not be able to. This lack of knowledge implies the need for a comprehensive system of respite service for families offering care at home, plus skilled home nursing assistance wherever needed. This is particularly important in view of the CDC and the World Health Organization (WHO) projections of future AIDS cases: out of a pool of one to two million HIV-infected people in the US, it is estimated that 70,000 cases will have developed with a cumulative death toll of 179,000 people by 1991 (AIDS 1987, Kneisl 1988). The challenge of facing great numbers of new cases will probably not be met if the general caretaking issue and nursing shortage are not addressed at a societal level by providing appropriate work conditions and monetary incentives to attract people to caretaking professions such as nursing. This challenge is even more dramatic in rural and other communities where "difference" is less tolerated and resources often scarcer (Rounds 1988).

Groups in the forefront of the AIDS crisis (SHANTI in San Francisco, Gay Men's Health Crisis in NYC, AIDS Action Committee in Boston) have recognized the stressors on caretakers and have provided support groups and staffing arrangement that offer respite from the stress of caring for dying people. People working with persons with AIDS cite the following factors as most significant for self-care and the prevention of burnout from the constant giving and confrontation with loss and death:

- Support groups.
- Being connected to a community of caring people.
- Reading, taking time to smell the roses, watch the sunset.
- Calling people—when I need them, when they need me.
- Unconditional accepting of love on both sides.
- Realizing there is more to life than material riches.

These support and coping strategies apply to both formal and informal caretakers: volunteers, nurses, physicians, family members, friends, lovers, and anyone caring for people with AIDS. As one volunteer says, however, "[Caretaking] is very painful. . . . Don't go into it if you don't want to grow. By seeing other people's pain you grow yourself." Betty Clare Moffatt (1986) writes poignantly about this growth process for herself, her family, and friends after learning about her son's diagnosis of AIDS and after standing by him to the end. The current QUILT and NAMES project stands as a national symbol of caring, grieving, and growth through AIDS (Ruskin, Herron, and Zemke 1988). (See Loss, Change, and Grief Work in Chapter 4.)

Some families, however, are too afraid, lack information, or for other reasons seem unable to respond compassionately to people with AIDS. For example, the parents of one young man, Bob, dying of AIDS at home, planned a birthday party for him, expecting it would be his last. They invited 100 relatives, but not a single one came. When Bob died, however, everyone came to the funeral. The parents felt bitter for a time against their relatives and their church for not being there when Bob and they needed them most. They explained their relatives' behavior on the basis of Bob's gay identity. But they have finally worked through the worst part of their grief and are grateful for the opportunity to have had Bob with them, to care for him, to support him while dying. This experience has given new meaning to their life and now they give public talks about it, hoping to influence other parents not to reject a dying child and to set aside their fears and biases about sexual preference. Fortunately, with public education the attitudes of church representatives and others are changing to greater compassion. For example, ecumenical healing services in various churches are becoming common. People who might otherwise despair under the weight of the AIDS crisis are finding new meaning and community support in these ritual gatherings (see Crisis Paradigm, third box, lower circle).

While some have the choice of volunteering to work directly with people with AIDS, most families and those in the health and social service professions do not. The pandemic nature of the AIDS crisis means that practically everyone is affected, at least indirectly, and the enormity of caretaking needs demands that the burden be shared within the human community. This will probably not happen, however, without learning all we can about AIDS, without attention to caring for ourselves to prevent burnout, and without acceptance of the challenge to grow from humane involvement with the AIDS crisis. Concern about these needs of the caretakers of people with AIDS is expressed in the AIDS Action Committee requirement that volunteers attend support group meetings at least twice a month. Similar support sessions are available for family members and nurses routinely caring for AIDS patients in homes, hospitals, and hospice houses (Robinson, Skeen, and Walters 1987). As the numbers of people with AIDS increase, necessary care must increasingly be absorbed by mainstream health and social services and not be left primarily to alternative agencies such as the AIDS Action Committee. Similarly, support services for caretakers should become a routine part of the total service program if we are to meet the challenge of providing all the care demanded by this crisis.

OPPORTUNITIES AND DANGERS FOR SOCIETY

Clearly, judgmental attitudes and moralistic diatribes against the gay community compound the pain and crisis of individuals, their families, lovers, and others most closely affected by AIDS. Not only do such responses harm various suffering individuals, but they damage the detractors as well, since one mark of a humane and civilized society is its ability to care for the sick, the "different," and the suffering and dying in a compassionate manner. Partly because much is still unknown about AIDS, and partly because of punitive attitudes, there is continuing risk that society will respond to this crisis harshly and in a manner unwarranted by facts already known, especially the fact that *AIDS is not transmitted by casual contact.* For example, a recent proposition in California would have required public health officials to establish camps where people with AIDS as well as anyone infected with HIV could be quarantined, whether healthy or unhealthy (Kneisl 1988). Fortunately, the proposition failed because of opposition by various activist groups. Blendon and Donelan (1988) believe that the persistence of hostility toward infected persons should be addressed through federal legislation that would prevent people from acting out their feelings against individuals with AIDS or HIV infection. As Sweden's Prime Minister Carlsson noted during the Fourth International Conference on AIDS, science alone is not enough. The struggle against AIDS is a struggle against intolerance and fear, and "therefore a struggle against the darker side in ourselves" (McLaughlin 1988, p. 17).

There is also the danger that anti-gay discrimination and violence will continue to increase as a response to AIDS. Another danger is the continuation of attitudes, especially among men, that see sexual fulfillment primarily in terms of sexual intercourse. AIDS presents an extraordinary opportunity to address these social and behavioral issues and bring about needed change.

Only the threat of nuclear holocaust (see Chapter 9) provides the global community a more urgent opportunity than the paradigmatic crisis of AIDS to mobilize together, combine efforts, and reconsider policies and the distribution of national resources. Aside from the terrible disease that it is, AIDS can be viewed as a catalyst to address issues that we might otherwise continue to ignore, such as the need for a national health plan, the caretaking crisis, and advocating equal rights for all. As the AIDS crisis unfolds for the individuals and families affected around the world, our attempts to understand people with AIDS and communicate compassionately with them and their families can increase the opportunities for personal and community growth and forestall such dangers as suicide, violence, bigotry, and the creation of scapegoats for societal problems.

REFERENCES

AIDS: Report of the Surgeon General's Workshop on Children with HIV Infection and Their Families. Washington, DC: US Department of Health and Human Services in conjunction with The Children's Hospital of Philadelphia, 1987.

Antonovsky A: *Health, Stress and Coping.* San Francisco: Jossey-Bass, 1980.

Barry K. *Female Sexual Slavery.* Avon Brooks, 1979.

Battin MP: Manipulated suicide. In: *Suicide: The Philosophical Issues.* Battin MP, Mayo DJ (editors). St. Martin's Press, 1980.

Blendon RJ, Donelan K: Discrimination against people with AIDS: The public's perspective. *N Engl J Med,* 1988; 319(15):1022–1026.

Centers for Disease Control: *AIDS Weekly Surveillance Report.* Atlanta: Department of Health and Human Services.

Dunkel J, Hatfield S: Countertransference issues in working with persons with AIDS. *Soc Work* (March/Apr) 1986; 31(2).

Durham JD, Cohen FL: *The Person with AIDS: Nursing Perspectives.* Springer, 1987.

Galea RP, Lewis BF, Baker LA: Voluntary testing for HIV antibodies among clients in long-term substance-abuse treatment. *Social Work,* 1988; 33(3):265–268.

Gochros HL: Risks of abstinence: Sexual decision making in the AIDS era. UX. *Social Work,* 1988; 33(3):254–265.

Goodman LM: *Death and the Creative Life.* New York: Springer, 1981.

Goffman I: *Stigma.* Prentice-Hall, 1963.

Haney, P. Providing empowerment to the person with AIDS. *Social Work,* 1988; 33(3):251–253.

Hoff LA, Miller N: *Programs for People in Crisis: A Guide for Educators, Administrators, and Clinical Trainers.* Boston: Northeastern University Custom Book Program, 1987.

Hosken F: Female genital mutilation and human rights. *Feminist Issues,* 1981; 1(3):3–23.

Hughes A, Martin JP, Franks P: *AIDS Home Care and Hospice Manual.* AIDS Home Care and Hospice Program, VNA of San Francisco, 1987.

Joyce C: Assault on the brain. *Psychol Today* 1988; 22(3):38–44.

Kneisl CR: The role of the psychiatric nurse in the AIDS epidemic. In: *Psychiatric Nursing,* 3rd ed. Wilson HS, Neisl CR (editors). Addison-Wesley, 1988.

Knox RA: Study: Vaginal sex is poor conduit for AIDS. *Boston Globe.* Feb. 15, 1988.

Krieger I: An approach to coping with anxiety about AIDS. *Social Work,* 1988; 33(3):263–264.

Linde R: Keynote address at workshop: AIDS and Mental Health Professionals. Boston, MA, 1988.

Marzuk PM et al.: Increased risk of suicide in persons with AIDS. *AMA,* 1988; 259(9):1333–1337.

McLaughlin L: A nation's war on AIDS. *Boston Globe.* June 17, 1988, p. 17.

Moffat BC: *When Someone You Love Has AIDS: A Book of Hope for Family and Friends.* Santa Monica, CA: IBS Press in association with Love Heals, 1986.

National League for Nursing: *AIDS Guidelines for Schools of Nursing.* August 1988.

Petit C: 11-Year incubation found for AIDS. *San Francisco Chronicle.* June 15, 1988, p. A4.

Report of the Surgeon General 1987. 150,000 new AIDS cases worldwide this year: WHO. *The Nation's Health.* Feb. 1988

Richardson D: *Women and the AIDS Crisis.* Pandora Press, 1987.

Robinson B, Skeen P, Walters L: The AIDS epidemic hits home. *Psychol Today* 1987; 21(4):48–52

Rounds KA: AIDS in Rural Areas: Challenges to Providing Care. *Social Work,* 1988; 33(3):257–261.

Ruskin C, Herron M, Zemke D: *The QUILT: Stories from the NAMES Project.* New York: Pocket Books, 1988.

Seager J, Olson A: *Women in the world: An international atlas.* New York: Simon & Schuster, 1986.

Shilts R: *And the Band Played On.* St. Martin's Press, 1987.

Sommers T, Shields L: *Women Take Care: The Consequences of Caregiving in Today's Society.* Gainsville, FL: Triad, 1987.

Sontag S: *Illness as Metaphor.* New York: Farrar, Straus & Giroux, 1978.

Stulberg I, Smith M: Psychosocial impact of the AIDS epidemic on the lives of gay men. *Social Work,* 1988; 33(3):277–281.

SELECTED BIBLIOGRAPHY

Antonovsky A: *Health, Stress and Coping*. Jossey-Bass, 1980.

Arms S: *Immaculate Deception*. Bantam Books, 1975.

Attorney General's Task Force on Family Violence: *Final Report*. US Department of Justice, 1984.

Bateson MC, Goldsby R: *Thinking AIDS: The Social Response to the Biological Threat*. Addison-Wesley, 1988.

Battin MP, Mayo DJ (editors): *Suicide: The Philosophical Issues*. St. Martin's Press, 1980.

Bellak L, Siegel H: *Handbook of Brief and Intensive Emergency Psychotherapy*. Larchmont, NY: CPS, 1983.

Bennis WG, Benne KD, Chin R (editors): *The Planning of Change*, 4th ed. Holt, Rinehart and Winston, 1985.

Borg S, Lasker J: *When Pregnancy Fails*. Beacon Press, 1981.

Bott E: *Family and Social Networks*. Tavistock, 1957.

Brody H: *Stories of Sickness*. Yale University Press, 1988.

Brown GW, Harris T: *The Social Origins of Depression*. Tavistock, 1978.

Browne A: *When Battered Women Kill*. Free Press, 1987.

Brownmiller S: *Against Our Will*. Simon and Schuster, 1975.

Burgess AW, Holmstrom LL: *Rape: Crisis and Recovery*. Prentice-Hall, 1979.

BWHBC (Boston Women's Health Book Collective): *The New Our Bodies, Ourselves*. Simon and Schuster, 1984.

Cain AC (editor): *Survivors of Suicide*. Charles C. Thomas, 1972.

Campbell JD, Humphreys JH: *Nursing Care of Victims of Violence*. Reston/Appleton-Century-Crofts, 1984.

Caplan G: *Principles of Preventive Psychiatry*. Basic Books, 1964.

Caplan G: *Support Systems and Community Mental Health*. Behavioral Publications, 1974.

Chavkin W (editor): *Double Exposure: Women's Health Hazards on the Job and at Home*. Monthly Review Press, 1984.

Chernin K: *The Hungry Self: Women, Eating and Identity*. Harper and Row, 1985.

Chesler P: *Mothers on Trial: The Battle for Children and Custody*. Seattle: Seal Press, 1986.

Conrad P, Kern R (editors): *The Sociology of Health and Illness: Critical Perspectives*. St. Martin's Press, 1981.

Corea G: *The Mother Machine*. Harper and Row, 1985.

Dobash RP, Dobash RE: *Violence against Wives: A Case against the Patriarchy*. Free Press, 1979.

Doress PB, Siegal DL, and the Midlife and Older Women Book Project: *Ourselves, Growing Older*. Simon and Schuster, 1987.

Ehrenreich J (editor): *The Cultural Crisis of Modern Medicine*. Monthly Review Press, 1978.

Erikson E: *Childhood and Society*, 2nd ed. W. W. Norton, 1963.

Fagerhaugh SY, Strauss A: *Politics of Pain Management*. Addison-Wesley, 1977.

Farberow NL (editor): *Suicide in Different Cultures*. University Park Press, 1975.

Farberow NL: *The Many Faces of Death*. McGraw-Hill, 1980.

Farberow NL, Shneidman ES (editors): *The Cry for Help*. McGraw-Hill, 1961.

Feifel H (editor): *New Meanings of Death*. McGraw-Hill, 1977.

Finkelhor D: *Child Sexual Abuse: New Theory and Research*. Free Press, 1984.

Fried NN, Fried MH: *Transitions: Four*

Rituals in Eight Cultures. W. W. Norton, 1980.

Gelles RJ, Cornell CP: *Intimate Violence in Families.* Sage, 1985.

Getty C, Humphreys W (editors): *Understanding the Family: Stress and Change in American Family Life.* Appleton-Century-Crofts, 1981.

Gibbs L: *Love Canal—My Story.* Albany: State University of New York Press, 1982.

Goffman E: *Stigma.* Prentice-Hall, 1963.

Golan N: *Passing through Transitions.* Free Press, 1981.

Gondolf EW: *Men Who Batter: An Integrated Approach to Stopping Wife Abuse.* Holmes Beach, FL: Learning Publications, 1985.

Goodman L: *Death and the Creative Life.* Springer, 1981.

Goodrich TJ, Rampage C, Ellman B, and Halstead K: *Feminist Family Therapy.* W. W. Norton, 1988.

Greenspan M: *A New Approach to Women and Therapy.* McGraw-Hill, 1983.

Grollman E: *Living—When a Loved One Has Died.* Beacon Press, 1977.

Halleck S: *The Mentally Disordered Offender.* Washington, DC: American Psychiatric Press, 1987.

Hansell N: *The Person in Distress.* Human Sciences Press, 1976.

Hatton C, Valente S, Rink A: *Suicide: Assessment and Intervention,* 2nd ed. Appleton-Century-Crofts, 1984.

Hendin H: *Suicide in America.* W. W. Norton, 1982.

Herman JL: *Father-Daughter Incest.* Harvard University Press, 1981.

Hoff LA: *Violence against Women: A social-cultural Network Analysis.* (PhD dissertation.) Boston University, 1984. University Microfilms International, Number 8422380.

Hoff LA, Miller N: *Programs for People in Crisis: A Guide for Educators, Administrators, and Clinical Trainers.* Boston: Northeastern University Custom Book Program, 1987.

Holmstrom LL, Burgess AW: *The Victim of Rape: Institutional Reactions.* Wiley, 1978.

Illich I: *Limits to Medicine.* Penguin Books, 1976.

Jacobs RH: *Life after Youth.* Beacon Press, 1979.

Joan P: *Preventing Teenage Suicide: The Living Alternative Handbook.* Human Sciences Press, 1986.

Judson S (editor): *A Manual on Nonviolence and Children.* Philadelphia: New Society Publishers, 1984.

Kastenbaum R, Aisenberg R: *The Psychology of Death.* Springer, 1972.

Kempe H, Helfer RE (editors): *The Battered Child,* 3rd ed. University of Chicago Press, 1980.

Klerman GL (editor): *Suicide and Depression in Young Adults.* Washington, DC: American Psychiatric Press, 1986.

Kozel J: *Rachel and Her Children: Homeless Families in America.* Crown Publishers, 1988.

Kubler-Ross E: *On Death and Dying.* Macmillan, 1969.

Kurland ML: *Coping with AIDS.* Rosen, 1987.

Landy D: *Culture, Disease and Healing.* Macmillan, 1977.

Levine S, Scotch N: *Social Stress.* Aldine, 1970.

Levinson DJ et al.: *The Seasons of a Man's Life.* Knopf, 1978.

Lukas C, Seiden HM: *Silent Grief: Living in the Wake of Suicide.* Macmillan, 1988.

Maltsberger JT: *Suicide Risk: The Formulation of Clinical Judgement.* New York University Press, 1986.

Marris P: *Loss and Change.* Routledge and Kegan Paul, 1974.

Martelli L, with Peltz FD, Messina W: *When Someone You Know Has Aids.* Crown, 1987.

Maslow A: *Motivation and Personality,* 2nd ed. Harper and Row, 1970.

McGee RK: *Crisis Intervention in the Community.* University Park Press, 1974.

Miller JB: *Toward a New Psychology of Women.* Beacon Press, 1976.

Mills CW: *The Sociological Imagination.* Oxford University Press, 19XX. 1959.

Moffat B: *When Someone You Love Has AIDS: A Book for Family and Friends.* Santa Monica: IBS Press in association with Love Heals, 1986.

Monahan J: *The Clinical Prediction of Violent Behavior.* Rockville, MD: National Institute of Mental Health, 1981.

Newberger CM, Melnicoe LH, Newberger E: *The American Family in Crisis: Implications for Children.* Special issue:

Current Problems in Pediatrics. XVI(12): 670–739.

NiCarthy G: *Getting Free: A Handbook for Women in Abusive Relationships,* 2nd ed. Seattle: Seal Press, 1982.

Parad HJ (editor): *Crisis Intervention: Selected Readings.* New York: Family Service Association of America, 1965.

Parkes CM: *Bereavement: Studies of Grief in Adult Life.* Penguin Books, 1975.

Perlin S: *A Handbook for the Study of Suicide.* Oxford University Press, 1975.

Pfeffer CR: *The Suicidal Child.* Guilford, 1986.

Pillemer KA, Wolf RS (editors): *Elder Abuse: Conflict in the Family.* Auburn House, 1986.

President's Task Force on Victims of Crime: *Final Report.* US Government Printing Office, 1982.

Richardson D: *Women and the AIDS Crisis.* Pandora, 1987.

Richman J: *Family Therapy of Suicidal Individuals.* Springfield, 1986.

Rieker PP, Carmen EH (editors): *The Gender Gap in Psychotherapy: Social Relations and Psychological Processes.* Plenum, 1984.

Rofes EE: *I Thought People Like That Killed Themselves.* San Francisco: Grey Fox Press, 1983.

Rosenthal T: *How Could I Not Be among You?* Braziller, 1973.

Russell DEH: *Rape in Marriage.* Collier Books, 1982.

Russell DEH: *The Secret Trauma: Incest in the Lives of Girls and Women.* Basic Books, 1986.

Ryan W: *Blaming the Victim.* Vintage Press, 1971.

Schechter S: *Women and Male Violence.* South End Press, 1982.

Schell J: *The Fate of the Earth.* Knopf, 1982.

Selye H: *The Stress of Life,* rev. ed. McGraw-Hill, 1976.

Sheehy G: *Passages.* Dutton, 1976.

Shneidman ES: *Suicide: Contemporary Developments.* Grune and Stratton, 1976.

Shneidman ES: *Definition of Suicide.* Wiley, 1985.

Shneidman ES, Farberow NL (editors): *Clues to Suicide.* McGraw-Hill, 1957.

Sidel R: *Women and Children Last: The Plight of Poor Women in Affluent America.* New York: Penguin, 1986.

Sommers T, Shields L: *Women Take Care: The Consequences of Caregiving in Today's Society.* Gainsville, FL: Triad, 1987.

Sontag S: *Illness as Metaphor.* Farrar, Straus and Giroux, 1978.

Sourkes BM: *The Deepening Shade: Psychological Aspects of Life-threatening Illness.* University of Pittsburgh Press, 1982.

Speck R, Attneave C: *Family Networks.* Pantheon, 1973.

Stevenson JS: *Issues and Crises during Middlescence.* Appleton-Century-Crofts, 1977.

Straus MA, Gelles RJ, Steinmetz SK: *Behind Closed Doors: Violence in the American Family.* Anchor Books, 1980.

Surgeon General's Workshop on Violence and Public Health: *Report.* Washington, DC: Health Resources and Services Administration (HRSA), 1986.

Tavris C: *Anatomy of Anger.* Simon and Schuster, 1983.

Tolstoy L: *The Death of Ivan Illyich.* New American Library, 1960.

van der Kilk BA: *Psychological Trauma.* Washington, DC: American Psychiatric Press, 1987.

van Gennep A: *Rites of Passage.* University of Chicago Press, 1960 (French ed. 1909).

Van Ornum W, Mordock JB: *Crisis Counseling with Children and Adolescents.* New York: Continuum, 1987.

Warshaw R: *I Never Called It Rape.* Harper & Row, 1988.

Wells JO, Hoff LA (editors): *Certification Standards Manual,* 3rd ed. Denver: American Association of Suicidology, 1984.

INDEX

(*continues*)

(*continues*)

(*continues*)